# The Diaries of
# Samuel Bamford

EDITED BY
MARTIN HEWITT
&
ROBERT POOLE

ST. MARTIN'S PRESS/NEW YORK

THE DIARIES OF SAMUEL BAMFORD

Copyright © 2000 by Martin Hewitt and Robert Poole

First published in 2000 in Great Britain by Sutton Publishing Limited

St. Martin's Press, Scholarly and Reference Division,
175 Fifth Avenue, New York, N.Y. 10010

First published in the United States of America in 2000

Library of Congress Cataloging-in-Publication Data
A catalog record for this book is available from the Library of Congress

ISBN 0-312-21598-3

Typeset in 10/12pt Baskerville MT.
Typesetting and origination by
Sutton Publishing Limited.
Printed in Great Britain by
Bookcraft, Midsomer Norton, Somerset.

# CONTENTS

LIST OF PLATES                                                    v

ACKNOWLEDGEMENTS                                                 vii

INTRODUCTION                                                      ix


PROLOGUE: IN THE BELLY OF THE BEAST                               1

1.   LOOKING AROUND                                              11
2.   THE OLD RADICAL                                            34
3.   HAWKING AND RECITING                                       73
4.   GOD HELP THE POOR                                          93
5.   BREAD OR A STONE?                                         112
6.   SIR JAMES KAY-SHUTTLEWORTH                                132
7.   PRIDE AND CHARITY                                         158
8.   POVERTY AND PRIDE                                         193
9.   ROYAL BOUNTY                                              216
10.  JUST COMPENSATION?                                        247
11.  ILLNESS AND INSURANCE                                     268
12.  PALMERSTON AND THE PENSIONS                               290
13.  SUBSCRIPTION                                              319
14.  HIS LAST CAMPAIGN                                         337
APPENDIX 1:  SAMUEL BAMFORD: RIGHT AGAINST WRONG               358
APPENDIX 2:  PARLIAMENTARY REFORM, BY AN OLD RADICAL          367


SELECT BIBLIOGRAPHY                                            371

INDEX                                                         373

*The publication of this book has been assisted by a grant from The Scouloudi Foundation in association with the Institute of Historical Research.*

# LIST OF PLATES

1. Manchester Literary Club, *c.* 1864.
2. Middleton's Agricultural Show, 1864.
3. Samuel Bamford, 1856.
4. Jemima Bamford, 1858.
5. The "stereoscopic likeness" of Samuel Bamford, 1859.
6. Thomas Mills, of the *Middleton Albion*.
7. Samuel Mellalieu.
8. The Old Boar's Head, Middleton.
9. Poster for Bamford's Middleton reading, July 1859.
10. A page from the diaries, February 1861.
11. The opening page of the diaries.
12. A ticket for the dinner in Bury that marked Bamford's return to the Reform platform.
13. Moston Bottoms, *c.* 1867.
14. A programme for one of Bamford's readings, 1859.

# ACKNOWLEDGEMENTS

A project such as this, which has taken five years from conception to publication, is bound to incur many debts of gratitude, and we are now pleased to be able to acknowledge these. David Vincent and Dorothy Thompson gave important early support to the project, and we are also grateful for the comments of many other scholars over the years, particularly on those occasions in Leeds, Manchester, Preston, York and Middleton where Bamford and his diaries have enjoyed an outing.

Gill Parsons transcribed the diaries with great skill and patience, and offered other valuable assistance. Morris Garratt was generous with help over local sources, and he, with Middleton Civic Association and the Lancashire & Cheshire Antiquarian Society, put on an excellent Sam Bamford day in Middleton in March 1999. We have relied constantly on the staff of Manchester Local Studies Unit, who have been expert and friendly throughout. The staff of the Local Studies Libraries at Middleton, Oldham and Rochdale have also been very helpful. Permission to transcribe and publish the diaries was kindly granted by the Manchester Library Services, and the photographs are reproduced by permission of the Metropolitan Borough of Rochdale Recreation and Community Services Department (plates 1, 2, 3, 4, 5, 6, 7, 8), and the Manchester Libraries Committee (plates 9, 10, 11, 12, 13, 14).

Our two institutions, Trinity and All Saints College and St Martin's College, gave indispensable academic and financial support for the project over several years. The final publication of the diaries has been assisted by a grant from the Scouloudi Foundation.

We would also like to thank Sutton Publishing, for having the faith and (we trust) foresight to take on the project in the belief that so detailed a work can indeed find a wider public readership. We hope Samuel Bamford's diaries have less trouble than did Samuel Bamford himself in appealing to several audiences at once.

Otley and Lancaster
January 2000

# INTRODUCTION

At the end of February 1858, Samuel Bamford celebrated – if that is the right word – his 70th birthday. He was, as he wrote in the first entry of the diary reprinted in this volume, "in tolerably good health", although "suffering occasionally from rheumatism and weakness of the lungs" (28 February 1858). For a man of his humble background, without children to support him in his old age, he was in the fortunate position of having physically undemanding employment as a minor civil servant at Somerset House in London. He was not, however, contented. Confined all day in a dusty book repository where his duties were routine and insignificant, surrounded by functionaries who treated him condescendingly, and in the service of a system whose history repelled and disgusted him, he "wish[ed] heartily [he] were well quit of the place" (21 March 1858). Indeed, he was on the verge of throwing up his comfortable position, and exchanging it for the uncertainties of a return to Middleton, Moston and Harpurhey, those satellite villages on the north-eastern outskirts of Manchester which were his "home", where he hoped to be able to eke out a living by giving readings and recitations, supplemented by the proceeds of reprints of his published writings.

Although by the time he eventually took the plunge and tendered his resignation Bamford had spent seven years at Somerset House, it would scarcely have been possible to find employment more alien to his whole character and life history. For he was one of the foremost northern radicals of the post-Waterloo era, and for all his life had been driven by an overwhelming sense of the injustice of a political system which denied political rights to the majority, while bearing hard on the poor so as to line the pockets of the rich. "Hart spent most of the day ordering the arrangement of papers", he noted on 16 April 1858, "and Foster looking after the books and papers of what they call 'the fine room', – the place in which documents belonging to the Department of 'Fines and Seizures', are to be kept. What a term! indicative of a system at once *horrible* and *mean*. The very words repel and disgust me, *Spies* and *informers* are the vermin that live [and] prosper on this system."

In starting a diary in the weeks before he finally resigned his position, and in continuing it once he had returned home to Lancashire, Bamford bequeathed to history one of the most remarkable sets of documents of any nineteenth-century working man. They reveal not only the Janus-like situation of an old radical in mid-Victorian England, but also the acute difficulties faced by any Victorian working man seeking independence and dignity in a society marked by economic dependence and social division. In this introduction we hope to place the diary and its diarist in context, by providing a brief outline of his life, introducing significant developments of the later 1850s, especially in respect of the movement for parliamentary reform, and by identifying those areas for which it seems to us that the diary is especially illuminating. We also explain how we have prepared Bamford's complicated manuscript for publication.

## SAMUEL BAMFORD: A BRIEF LIFE

It is difficult to summarise so rich and eventful a life as that of Samuel Bamford in a short space, but fortunately there is no need to. Bamford's own autobiographical circular, dealing with his radical period and its aftermath, is reproduced as Appendix 1. The diary itself also contains several substantial additions to Bamford's autobiography: a nostalgic speech at Middleton on 3 January 1859, a self-justifying letter to James Kay-Shuttleworth on 9 October 1860, and a spirited riposte to a critic in the *Manchester Examiner and Times* on 4 May 1861. The late W.L. Chaloner's introduction to the 1967 edition of the autobiography provides a valuable short biography, as does Morris Garratt's more recent *Samuel Bamford: Portrait of a Radical*, which also includes pictures and extracts from sources.[1]

Bamford was born in Middleton, one of the small weaving villages clustered to the north-east of Manchester, in 1788. His father was an artisan weaver and a Methodist, and sometime Governor of the poorhouse in Salford, where half the family, including Samuel's mother, and nearly young Samuel himself, died of fever. He received a good smattering of education, including spells at the grammar schools in Middleton and Manchester. Quitting full-time education when still a boy, he held in quick succession a series of jobs ranging from east coast sailor to Manchester warehouseman, marrying his childhood sweetheart Jemima in 1810, soon after the birth of their only child Ann. He was in Manchester at the time of the Luddite disturbances in Middleton in April 1812.

By 1816, however, Bamford had returned to Middleton, where he was employed as a handloom weaver and was heavily involved in the upsurge of working-class radicalism which greeted the final defeat of Napoleon in 1815 and the passage of the Corn Laws. He became secretary of the local Hampden Club and its delegate to the famous Crown and Anchor meeting of January 1817, where he played a key role in persuading William Cobbett of the need to press for manhood, rather than household, suffrage, arguing that military conscription provided a practical foundation for political citizenship. Subsequently, he was one of the principal organisers of the reform meeting in 1819 on St Peter's Field in Manchester. This became the occasion of the infamous "Peterloo massacre" when the Manchester yeomanry attacked a peaceful crowd of over 60,000 people, killing eleven and wounding over 500, many of them women. During this period Bamford was arrested five times, and after Peterloo he was convicted at York of unlawful assembly and attempting to alter the laws of the country by force; he was sentenced to 12 months imprisonment, served in Lincoln jail.[2]

After his release Bamford returned to Middleton, but he did not long remain a

---

1. W.L. Chaloner, ed., *The Autobiography of Samuel Bamford. Volume 1: Early Days* (with introduction), *Volume 2: Passages in the Life of a Radical* (1967); Morris Garratt, *Samuel Bamford: Portrait of a Radical* (1992). See also M. Hewitt, "Radicalism and the Victorian Working Class: the case of Samuel Bamford", *Historical Journal*, 34.4 (1991), 873–92, and Joe Pimlott's *Life and Times of Sam Bamford* (1991) which is strong on visual material. Robert Poole is currently working on a biography of Bamford.

2. See *The Trial of Henry Hunt and Others* (1820); Bamford, *Homely Rhymes, Poems and Reminiscences* (1864), 7–9; *Wheeler's Manchester Chronicle*, 24 August 1833; *Manchester and Salford Advertiser*, 30 January 1836; entries for 8 April 1859, 11 August 1859, 15 September 1859.

handloom weaver.[3] In common with many political prisoners, he found that the experience of imprisonment had created resentments and put distance between himself and his former comrades, and he turned from political activism to writing. His first slim volume of poetry, *The Weaver Boy*, had appeared in the spring of 1819, and while he was imprisoned his "Lancashire Hymn" was sung to impressive effect by crowds gathered all over the Manchester region to mark the anniversary of Peterloo. A much larger volume of his *Miscellaneous Poetry* was published in 1821, a mix of romantic and pastoral poems, verses celebrating local scenes and incidents, and heroic odes to fellow reformers. In 1826 he dissuaded powerloom breakers from visiting Middleton and nearby towns. By this time he had become the Manchester correspondent of a London daily newspaper, the *Morning Herald*, and for many years he contributed Middleton material to the *Manchester Guardian*, with whose chief reporter, John Harland, he shared antiquarian interests. Bamford's accounts of the meetings he reported, revealing as they did his increasing impatience with the more violent forms of platform rhetoric becoming prevalent in radical circles at this time, strained his relations with some elements of working-class radicalism.[4] His reputation suffered further in the early 1830s when he was "compelled to undertake the office of constable" at Middleton, and became in consequence embroiled in a long-running dispute with some of his former radical colleagues.[5]

The 1830s were difficult years for Bamford in many respects. In 1834 he suffered the greatest blow of his life, the death of his only daughter Ann, twenty-five years old and unmarried. His earnings from journalism were not enough to allow him to live comfortably, and they had to be supplemented by various short-lived enterprises, including spells as a newsagent and a seller of porter by commission. By 1839 he had given up journalism and was attempting to make a living as a literary figure. Over the next eleven years he produced the works of autobiography and commentary which made his name: the autobiographical *Passages in the Life of a Radical* (1839–41) and *Early Days* (1848–9); an expanded volume of poetry, *Poems* (1843); a collection of sketches, articles and letters, *Walks in South Lancashire* (1844); and a revised edition of the pioneer dialect writer Tim Bobbin's *Dialect of South Lancashire* (1850), with an historical introduction that hinted at other work to come. He became a central figure in the extraordinary flowering of working-class literary life which marked Manchester in the 1830s and 1840s, centred on the convivial circle of Manchester poets who met at the Sun Inn, and which included writers and poets such as Charles Swain, John Bolton Rogerson, John Critchley Prince, Robert Rose, John Teer and Benjamin Stott.[6]

---

3. Chaloner, introduction to *Early Days*, and sources cited therein; diary entries for 3 January 1859, 9 October 1860, 4 May 1861; James Dronsfield, *Incidents and Anecdotes of the Late Samuel Bamford* (1872).

4. See *Manchester and Salford Advertiser*, 30 January 1836; and a later account by William Marcroft of one confrontation with Richard Oastler, *Oldham Standard*, 2 May 1925.

5. See the various exchanges in the *Manchester and Salford Advertiser*, 1831–3, especially 13 April 1833.

6. See Martha Vicinus, "The Literary Voices of an Industrial Town: Manchester, 1810–1870", in H.J. Dyos and M. Wolff, eds, *The Victorian City* (1973); B.E. Maidment, "Class and Cultural Production in the Industrial City: Poetry in Victorian Manchester", in A.J. Kidd and K.W. Roberts, *City, Class and Culture. Studies of Cultural Production and Social Policy in Victorian Manchester* (1985); and the series of articles "Songs of the Working Classes" and "Manchester poets and rhymesters", which appeared in the *Manchester Guardian* 1839–40, and 1841.

The "hungry forties" were Bamford's harvest time. *Passages* gained him national recognition. He was read approvingly by Gladstone, written admiring letters by Thomas Carlyle, and visited by Jane Welsh Carlyle. His poem "God Help the Poor" featured in Elizabeth Gaskell's Manchester novel *Mary Barton* (1848), its author characterised as "fine-spirited" and noble.[7] His publications brought him a modest income which he was able to supplement by occasional appearances as a lecturer, and by other forms of literary activity.[8] He also received occasional donations from wealthy patrons, and became a frequent speaker at meetings designed to promote self-education and mutual improvement among the working-classes.[9]

In the twentieth century Bamford's considerable reputation (his autobiography was described by E.P. Thompson as "essential reading for any Englishman")[10] has rested on his vivid portrayal of the radical movement before and after Peterloo. But his writings in this period, and especially *Passages*, had a very clear contemporary purpose. They were aimed quite explicitly at opposing Chartism as it developed from 1839 onwards under the leadership of Feargus O'Connor. *Passages* was studded with barbed asides about the Chartist movement which was prospering as Bamford wrote; he disliked what he saw as its self-indulgent demagoguery, its easy rhetoric of violence, its hostility to other reforming campaigns, and its refusal to learn anything, so Bamford felt, from the lessons of the past. And of course, Bamford's popularity with his middle-class readers rested as much on this rejection of Chartism as on his passionate account of the earlier reform movements.[11] Not surprisingly, suspicions of Bamford's political loyalties, and resentments at the patronage he was receiving, grew apace.

In reality, Bamford's income from writing, even when supplemented by occasional donations from wealthy readers, was always precarious, and in 1846, as he neared the age of sixty, a subscription was begun to provide for him in his declining years. Ultimately, however, despite the disapproval of many of the leaders of the subscription movement, Bamford insisted on taking the money it raised in a lump sum, rather than in the form of an annuity, and much of it was used to finance the publication of *Early Days*. As a result by 1850 Bamford was again in straitened circumstances, and – in a move which seemed to many of his Middleton neighbours to confirm their suspicions that he had long been a kind of spy in the pay of government – he accepted the employment acquired for him by the patronage of John Wood, chairman of the Board of the Inland Revenue, which he was about to relinquish with great relief as the diary commences.

During his seven-year stint in London, Bamford managed a limited correspondence with figures such as John Harland and the young dialect writer Edwin Waugh. He was

---

7. Elizabeth Gaskell, *Mary Barton* (1848), ch. 9.
8. For example, in 1846 he was offered 10 guineas by the Manchester Mechanics' Institution for three lectures, see Manchester Mechanics' Institute, "Minutes", 25 August 1846, University of Manchester Institute of Science and Technology. In 1843 he also served as one of the judges for a literary competition run by the *Oddfellows Magazine*, at that time edited by John Bolton Rogerson.
9. *Manchester Courier*, 6 May 1848; *Manchester Guardian*, 24 May 1848, 18 January 1851.
10. E.P. Thompson, *The Making of the English Working Class* (1963), 836.
11. Hewitt, "Radicalism and the Victorian Working Class", 873–5.

the occasional guest of Thomas Carlyle at his home in Chelsea and the drinking companion of the Northumberland poet Robert Story, a fellow clerk at Somerset House, but he never felt at home in London and his emotional ties with south-east Lancashire remained strong. He had plans for writing a history of Lancashire, although these unfortunately came to nothing. He published an account of his role in the Middleton Mechanics' Institute affair of the 1820s, and contributed three fictional sketches about the 1853–4 Preston cotton lockout to *Cassells Illustrated Family Paper*.[12] He also kept up a steady stream of interventions in the local press, which often aimed at setting the record straight. His return to Middleton offered an opportunity to finish the job.

The Middleton to which Bamford returned in 1858 – for his native town was always the focus of his activities, despite his residence in Moston – was just beginning its somewhat overdue Victorian urban renaissance. It was an ancient parish and as late as 1770 the village appeared small, ramshackle and rustic. At the time of Bamford's youth, however, Middleton was sharing in the golden age of handloom weaving. Even as the rise of the powerloom exerted increasing downward pressure on wages in the 1820s and 1830s, the local handloom weavers were able by and large to protect their incomes by moving upmarket into finer cottons and silk. As late as 1849, the *Morning Chronicle*'s visiting reporter, Angus Reach, was struck by "the scattered streets of an old-fashioned village", and "heard on all sides the rattle of the shuttle. Still the aspect of the place was half-rural."[13] This latter comment was something of an exaggeration for by 1850 the area had developed a considerable factory sector. In 1845 the Middleton Old Hall had been demolished to make way for two cotton mills and a gasworks, and soon afterwards the long-established dyeworks of Silas Schwabe at nearby Rhodes had erected a 300-foot chimney. When Bamford returned in 1858 Middleton, along with the contiguous out-township of Tonge, had become a manufacturing centre with a population of some 14,000 people, and was just beginning the process of acquiring a Victorian urban and cultural infrastructure to match its economic status. Not the least of the ironies surrounding Bamford's ambiguous status between the middle and the working classes was that at the same time as he became involved in the efforts to promote the status of his home town, he himself could afford to live only in the unimproved working-class out-township of Moston. (See Plate 14.)

## BAMFORD AS A RADICAL

It is easy to read Bamford's history up to 1858 as being entirely typical of many nineteenth-century working-class radicals, whose early reforming zeal was dimmed by first-hand experience of the coercive powers of the state and the fickleness of popular

12. C.W. Sutton, *Lancashire Authors I* (MCL), at entry for Ben Brierley; Bamford correspondence with Waugh and Harland (MCL); *Manchester Examiner and Times*, 7 April 1858; Middleton Local Studies Library cuttings, LCB.BAM and G3.BAM; Bamford, *Some Account of the Late Amos Ogden of Middleton* (Manchester, 1853). *Cassells Illustrated Family Paper*, 28 January, 11 February and 25 March 1854.
13. Angus B. Reach, *Manchester and the Textile Districts in 1849* (1972), 98–109.

support, and who came to seek in literary activity the sense of self-fulfilment and social approbation which they had failed to find in political activism. There is no doubt that many of his neighbours and many of the leaders of radicalism in Manchester and district saw him as a turncoat, and it was not so long ago that even historians without a strong ideological axe to grind were describing him as a "renegade" and an apostate.[14] Yet although Bamford has been treated harshly by history, his story is more complicated than such one-dimensional dismissals allow.

In the first place, it has become increasingly apparent in recent years that there is no simple opposition between radical activism and the kind of literary career which Bamford attempted to carve out for himself. For a long time the kind of working-class autodidacticism which Bamford seemed to represent was dismissed as being inextricably bound up in the absorption and imposition of middle-class values. The limitations of the poetic form, channels of publication and structures of patronage were all seen to subvert potentially radical impulses and encourage dependence and deference. More recently, however, historians and literary scholars have begun to recognise the vital role which song, ballad and poetry had in the first half of the nineteenth century in expressing radical ideas and binding radical identities.[15] Whatever the pressures under which they wrote, there is no doubt that the Manchester working-class poets, of whom Bamford was one, did make an important contribution to local radicalism right through the Chartist period. Poets like Teer, Stott, Prince and Rogerson appeared frequently in the chartist paper, the *Northern Star*, and even Bamford, despite his known hostility to the Chartist leadership, was not entirely neglected.[16] This literary activity provided an important conduit for ideas and images, both within working-class radicalism at any one time, and also between successive phases of the movement.

Moreover, recent reinterpretations of the history of nineteenth-century radicalism enable us to take a more balanced view of Bamford's political career, in that they have involved greater emphasis on the continuities of working-class political beliefs in the nineteenth century; historians have become reluctant to use support for Chartism as a benchmark of radical identity. In the process, the version of non-Chartist radicalism which Bamford espoused has been restored, at least in part, to a place as a vital part of the radical tradition. It is now becoming possible to see that Chartism, although undoubtedly for a few years the most vociferous and widely supported working-class radical movement, was in reality only one of many strands of radicalism in this period, and that its rigid refusal of any forms of cooperation with other radical groups progressively eroded its support during the 1840s and 1850s.[17] Gradually over these decades, the bulk of working-class radicals came to adopt the kinds of pragmatic reformism which Bamford was championing from the 1820s onwards. From this perspective, far from being a renegade, Bamford was merely in the vanguard of a

---

14. J. Belchem, '*Orator Hunt*'. *Henry Hunt and English Working Class Radicalism* (1985), 1.
15. Anne Janowitz, *Lyric and labour in the romantic tradition* (1998).
16. Hence, for example, his "God Help the Poor" was published in the *Northern Star*, 25 November 1843.
17. For the Manchester case see M. Hewitt, *The Emergence of Stability in the Industrial City. Manchester, 1832–67* (1996), especially ch. 8.

movement which ultimately created the broadly based alliance on which the Victorian Liberal party came to be centred.

This is not to deny that to some extent the reforms of the 1830s did moderate his stance, encouraging him in the belief that the political system was amenable to rational pressure. For many working-class radicals the provisions of the 1832 Reform Bill – the vote in urban constituencies to all those occupying houses of an annual rental value of £10, in the counties of copyholders and leaseholders of land of an annual rental of £10, and tenants-at-will paying an annual rental of at least £50 – were even worse than the previous situation. They feared, with some justification, that the newly enfranchised middle classes would prove most reluctant to share their new rights with the rest of the people. Bamford was more optimistic: he thought the Reform Bill a "beginning" towards the "noble end" of the triumph of freedom. "It struck at, and cut off the root, of the borough-mongering system," he wrote in 1843; "the Whigs, supported by the people, made a great step", establishing "the charter of a fresh principle".[18] He was confident that further extensions of the franchise could now be achieved.

Bamford's difficulties with Chartism did not lie in the "six points" which made up the Chartist programme. His commitment to universal manhood suffrage, the ballot, abolition of the property qualification for MPs and equal electoral districts did not waver. As his speech at Bury in November 1858 (reproduced in Appendix 2) shows, he believed that these were in the process of being achieved, and wanted to see the reform movement put its weight where it was most needed. He did come to have doubts about the importance of annual parliaments, but only because he felt that the underlying aim, the continued accountability of MPs to their constituents, could be obtained in other ways which would avoid the need for the disruptive and potentially damaging excitement of a general election every year. Similarly he came to downplay the importance of payment of MPs by suggesting that those for whom a wage was a necessity could be remunerated out of a voluntary subscription. It may be true, therefore, that by the 1840s and 1850s Bamford's radicalism had lost something of the ferocity of his early adulthood, but the charge that he had ceased to be a radical can in no way be sustained.

Some of Bamford's later moderation can be traced to a certain disillusion with his youthful belief that the hardships of the country derived entirely from the exclusion of the working classes from politics. As he aged, he came increasingly to believe that changes in political structures would need to be accompanied by what at times he described as a "moral reform", by which he meant changes in the values and cultures of the country, so that greater emphasis was placed on the education and rational development of the individual. "Th[e] Chartist reform is, however, only a husk – a shell", as he wrote in 1858, "it is an *outside reform* only; we must have an *inner* one ... and so, I hope, proceed to a state of freedom as complete as human imperfection can accomplish."[19] At the same time, his more immediate problems with Chartism derived

---

18. Bamford, *Poems* (1843 edition), 149.
19. Letter of Bamford to *Manchester Examiner and Times*, 3 November 1858 (referred to in the diary, but the cutting is missing).

from tactics and personalities. He drew a powerful lesson from his Peterloo experiences
that platform agitation would never prevail if it attempted to achieve its aims by
intimidation and violence. His dispute with the Chartists was largely derived from the
no-compromise policy which O'Connor championed: when this prompted the Chartists
to attempt to thwart the Anti-Corn Law League campaign for a repeal of the Corn
Laws, Bamford was particularly scathing in his indignation, likening it to a slave who
refused to eat anything unless he was freed. As he explained to one of his friends in the
1850s, "The Chartists insist upon having everything or nothing, but I would take part,
and think well of it, and get the rest when I could."[20] Suspicious of middle-class
leadership and patronage, he nevertheless recognised the need to build reforming
alliances, and came to feel that O'Connor's repeated appeals to class hostility were
designed to serve his own interests in retaining the absolute loyalty and control of the
movement, rather than the real interests of the people as a whole.[21] Under the
leadership of O'Connor's successor, Ernest Jones, however, "official" Chartism had
clung obstinately to its O'Connorite stance, and in the process had perpetuated the
division of the parliamentary reform movement, and condemned working-class
radicalism to isolation and impotence.

Significantly, however, by the end of 1857 and the early months of 1858, this
Chartist fundamentalism was finally giving way to a more flexible approach. The
radical movement suffered a series of setbacks in the 1857 general election, with the
defeat of several of its leading figures including in Manchester the galling defeat of the
radical-Liberal MPs Thomas Milner Gibson and John Bright, by the conservative-
Liberals Sir John Potter and John Aspinall Turner. In February 1858 a general Chartist
conference formally committed the movement to working with middle-class
parliamentary reformers, and in the same month Edward Hooson, the leading
Chartist figure in Manchester, announced his support for the new stance: "one step
with the middle-classes, and then the Charter".[22] This rapprochement saw a
considerable escalation of reform activity in England. In Manchester by the end of
1858 two rival camps had emerged: the more moderate and mainstream Lancashire
Reformers' Union, led by wealthy calico printer Edmund Potter and closely aligned to
the rump of the Anti-Corn Law League, and the more radical Manhood Suffrage
Association, with the ex-Owenite newsagent and publisher Abel Heywood as
president. For the next few years these associations, and the rival reform aspirations
they represented, struggled both to impose themselves as the approved model, and to
broaden the base of active support for reform. Meanwhile, throughout the region new
associations or branches of bodies such as the LRU were organised, and a widespread
revival of reform activity occurred.

Although there is no mention of these developments in Bamford's entries for the
early months of 1858, it cannot be entirely a coincidence that he was finally coming to
a resolution to quit his government post in London and return to Lancashire at

---

20. James Dronsfield, *Incidents and Anecdotes*, 6.
21. See Hewitt, *Emergence of Stability*, esp. 246–60.
22. *Manchester Guardian*, 14 February 1858.

precisely the time when events both locally and nationally were promising an end to his uncomfortable position on the political sidelines. Virtually at a stroke, the new alliance vindicated Bamford and restored him to the mainstream of working-class radicalism, promising a renewed market for his radical writings, especially *Passages in the Life of a Radical*, and an augmented demand for his services as reciter, lecturer and platform speaker. On the surface, therefore, Bamford returned at an especially favourable juncture, at a time when, as the reform meetings he attended at Middleton in January 1859 nicely exemplify, the renewed impetus towards parliamentary reform coalesced with local initiatives designed to enhance the town's civic status. Unfortunately, as it turned out, the next few years were not at all easy ones for working-class radicalism, or for those who sought, like Bamford, to carve out a modest niche for themselves as footsoldiers in the parliamentary reform movement, or to use it as a springboard for local improvement.

The new reform alliance was born out of failure rather than optimism and parliamentary politics in this period remained in the confused state it had been in since the 1840s, when the split of the Tories and the emergence of the "Manchester School" radicals had muddled party identities and made government the art of holding together loose coalitions of opinion.[23] The reformers faced two problems. On the one hand, the alterations that the national leaders of the reform movement, headed by John Bright, felt required to limit themselves to were so cautious that they failed to ignite any popular enthusiasm in the country. On the other hand, the very moderates whom this retreat was supposed to placate then seized upon the lack of popular enthusiasm as a justification for continuing to withhold their support for reform. In part, the debate over reform resolved itself into the contest of different histories of the radical movement in the nineteenth century and in particular whether the 1832 Reform Act had demonstrated that a moderate extension of the franchise would make further reform more or less likely. Moreover, as each abortive reform "agitation" came and went it became increasingly difficult to mobilise the people to fill out mass meetings and monster demonstrations. Reformers were therefore confronted with the need to balance the episodic and potentially dispiriting process of manifesting reform opinion with efforts to encourage an ongoing and sustainable reforming culture, based around a renewal of institutions for political education and rational recreation.

As a result, the activity recorded in the pages of the diary took place against the backdrop of a confused and fluid political situation. For most of the period the country was being governed by a whig-Liberal government led by Lord Palmerston, although briefly between 1858 and 1859 this was replaced by a minority Conservative administration led by the Earl of Derby and Benjamin Disraeli. Palmerston was himself extremely unenthusiastic about further parliamentary reform, and in this he

---

23. There are many studies which give detailed insight into the confused politics of this period, and the interactions between the key politicians, including John Prest, *Politics in the Age of Cobden* (1977), Miles Taylor, *The Decline of English Radicalism, 1848–58* (1995), E.D. Steele, *Palmerston and Liberalism* (1991). For a broader study which puts the reform struggles of these years in context, see M. Bentley, *Politics without Democracy, 1815–1914* (1984).

reflected the dominant feeling in both houses of Parliament throughout this period. The result was a succession of reform bills, each of which tried and failed to strike an effective balance between the desires of reformers and the fears of their opponents. Hence in early 1859 John Bright, the acknowledged leader of the reformers, introduced a bill which called for the vote for all poor-rate payers in the cities, and those paying £10 rental in the counties, but which largely sidestepped the issue of the franchise to concentrate on the redistribution of seats. The Tory government responded with an even weaker proposal. "We cannot suppose", commented Edward Stanley to Disraeli, "that a ... bill such as we shall pass shall satisfy Manchester." Although a public meeting in Manchester under the chairmanship of the mayor voted by a large majority in favour of Bright's scheme, in ward meetings throughout the city in the early months of the year it was met with often successful amendments in favour of manhood suffrage.

Nevertheless, in the winter of 1859/60, with Palmerston back in power, Bright retreated and endorsed Lord John Russell's bill for a £6 borough franchise, which would, on Bright's own admission, have enfranchised scarcely more than 100,000 of the working classes in the whole country. Reaction in Manchester ran the traditional gamut: moderates welcomed it as much as could be expected given the general apathy, ex-Chartists rejected it as insulting, and pragmatic democrats such as John Watts lamented it as "Neither worth blessing nor cursing."[24] Through the first six months of 1860 Bright did work hard to try to drum up support for a new measure, even attempting at speeches such as his one in the Free Trade Hall in April 1860 to conjure up trade union assistance. Once again, however, the bill failed to arouse popular enthusiasm, and was quietly shelved in June.[25]

Although a further bill was introduced in the autumn of 1860 by Lord John Russell, there appeared to be little stomach in the country at large for a renewed agitation. Writing to John Bright at the end of January 1861, Thomas Milner Gibson commented that his "own private opinion" was that Parliament and the public would not allow the government to carry "anything worth having".[26] Barely a ripple of reform activity was apparent in Manchester, and when the Lancashire Reformers' Union met for its annual meeting in February, exchanges between the two wings of the reformers were especially tense.[27] Before the end of the month Russell's bill had once again been abandoned, protest in Manchester being confined largely to one not very well attended meeting in the Town Hall at the end of March. To all intents the reform agitation had collapsed entirely. Just at the period that Bamford's diaries come to an end, a further effort was being made to inject some life into the campaign, but in reality the movement remained exactly where it had been at the beginning of 1858, at the commencement of Bamford's diaries.

---

24. See account of Manchester Reform Association meeting, *Manchester Weekly Advertiser*, 10 March 1860.
25. For details of the agitation and the Manchester Constitutional Defence Association, see *Manchester Guardian*, 16 May 1860.
26. Milner Gibson to Bright, 31 January 1861, quoted in Steele, *Palmerston and Liberalism*, 130.
27. See *Manchester Guardian*, 6 February 1861.

## THE DIARIES

The diaries, stuffed with letters and cuttings documenting Bamford's daily life and reflecting on the past (see plate 10), are a remarkable survival. There is nothing like them for any other nineteenth-century working man, and indeed, despite Bamford's clear desire to leave a record for posterity, it is only by chance that they have survived. They were preserved in a chest of old books and papers which were eventually passed down to Walter Law Worthington, a Manchester solicitor, from his aunt Simms; how she came to have them is unclear, although she may have been related to Bamford. One evening Richard Knowles, a Macclesfield antiquarian, himself distantly related to Bamford through the marriage of Bamford's sister Mary, was a guest at the Worthington house. Knowles related what happened in a letter to the librarian at Manchester.[28]

> We were sitting round the billiard-room fire smoking at [the] time, and Walter's wife said to him "I wonder if Dick knows anything about those old papers in the chest" and fetched from a chest in the room, an old parcel done up in newspaper of ancient date and placed it on Walter's knee. After opening it, he asked me "Did you ever hear of a fellow named Bamford? I don't know why my great aunt kept this, and it is waste paper to us, and my wife wants to destroy the litter." I replied that if it was Sam, I knew very well who he was, as we had his "Life" at home, and he was connected by marriage of his sister.
>
> So I borrowed it and when I returned it, saw nobody at [the] house, but received a letter later, saying that I should not have done so, [and] if it was any use to me, too keep it. So some months after they had promised to bring [the] parcel round in [the] care, I cycled over and fetched it here. Aunt Simms may have been related to B. I never asked John, and today Walter would not know.

Knowles donated the manuscripts to Manchester Central Library in June 1940. It appears that in a subsequent process of conservation they were gathered together into four board-bound volumes, divided roughly equally, but otherwise arbitrarily.[29] Originally the diaries were made up of octavo-sized booklets of plain paper, usually of 16, 24 or 32 sheets. They may have been made up by Bamford himself from larger sheets for economy. Normally he wrote only on one side of the paper, leaving the verso clear for occasional additions and increasingly for insertions. As he went on, he collected a large number of cuttings from the local newspapers which dealt either with his own activities or those of people and events with whom he had some connection. In all, the diaries contain copies of nearly 200 letters (both to and from Bamford); a large number of newspaper cuttings (over 500 column inches, or about 100,000 words in total), covering both Bamford's own public activities and also other people or events on which Bamford felt drawn to comment; and about twenty items of printed ephemera,

---

28. Knowles to the Librarian, Manchester Central Library, 18 July 1940; Biographical Cuttings Collection, Manchester Central Library.
29. There are no surviving conservation records for the library for this period, and so it is impossible to ascertain the precise form the diaries were in on acquisition.

including the various revisions of the "Memorial" which Bamford had printed expounding his claims to support, and later to compensation, for the wrongs he had endured during the Peterloo era. These were generally pinned into the diaries, the smaller cuttings usually in gaps left in the entries themselves, the larger cuttings, copies of letters he had sent, and letters and envelopes he had received usually on the blank facing pages. It is possible that some of the larger printed items, such as the posters of his recitations which Bamford preserved, were simply inserted loosely in the leaves. During the process of conservation, the pins appear to have been removed. Where Bamford left sufficient space, the cuttings have been pasted directly into the diary entries; otherwise they have been pasted on facing pages, the longer ones often cut into several overlapping leaves. At the same time, copy letters and letters received were either tipped into the volumes, or attached to new leaves which had been inserted.

As a result, the original structure of the diary is difficult to reconstruct; sometimes spaces and pin marks give clear indications of where Bamford placed material, while in other instances it is necessary to rely on context and references in the diary entries. It is not clear if the surviving diaries are virtually complete, or part of a longer series of which the rest are not extant. There is evidence in the diaries themselves for the view that they were once part of a larger collection of autobiographical material. Bamford referred in correspondence in February 1859 to "my letters of 1858, and ... the fragment of a diary for a previous year which I don't at present recollect". Two years later he was "burning old and useless letters and papers", although some months later he could still refer imagined readers of his diary to "my continued memoires". Nevertheless, despite the gaps and loose ends, the diary possesses a certain self-sufficiency. It begins at a natural landmark in Bamford's life, on the eve of his 70th birthday, and its opening sentence ("This day I compleat the 70th year of my age") has strong echoes in the openings of contemporary journals and autobiographies.[30] He must already have all but made up his mind that he would give up his position at Somerset House once he had discharged the symbolic obligation of a seven years "apprenticeship", and known therefore that he was recording his last days in London. The London section of the diary has a kind of completeness: 72 neat blue pages, the folios numbered from 1 to 36 in Bamford's hand, concluded with a cutting about the railway disaster he survived on the way home pinned on the back. Likewise, the date of the resumption of the diaries, 1 August 1858, was the occasion of Blackley wakes, for Bamford the first local wakes holiday after his return. The annual wakes holidays were, over most of Lancashire, the social hub of the year, and Bamford's account of Middleton wakes is one of the great set pieces of *Early Days*. It is an apt starting point for the diary of a homecoming.[31]

---

30. See, for example, the example chosen by David Vincent to open his book on working-class autobiography, "I, James Bowd of Swavesey in Cambridgeshire have now Reached to my 66th Anivarsary day and beign unable to go out to Labour I was sitting at hom My Mind was taken back to the Early stages of my Life...", *Bread, Knowledge and Freedom. A Study of Nineteenth Century Working Class Autobiography* (1981), 1.

31. R. Poole, "Samuel Bamford and Middleton Rushbearing", *Manchester Region History Review* VIII (1994), 14–20.

Similarly, it would not be surprising if Bamford's diary-keeping had fizzled out at the end of 1861, even though there is no indication of imminent cessation in the final entries of the diary. The entries in the final month had become shorter and more perfunctory; we know that Bamford's eyesight was becoming more and more impaired, and that Mima, his wife, was beginning the final decline which eventually resulted in her death in October 1862, and that in his wife's previous periods of illness Bamford had found it difficult to find time or inclination to write up the diary.[32] It seems quite likely that his own failing eyesight, the onset of Mima's slow final decline, and the removal of his immediate want by the establishment of a regular income from a few wealthy well-wishers, caused the diary to lapse around this time, even though Bamford himself lived for another ten years.[33]

This impression is confirmed by a close inspection of the diaries themselves. The London section originally seems to have been a single notebook of 72 pages, the folios numbered 1 to 36 by Bamford. The second notebook, which begins on 1 August 1858 after a three-month gap, is numbered continuously by Bamford from 37, showing that there is nothing missing in between. Here Bamford numbers each side he has written on, and the numbering is irregular from 37 to 49. The third notebook, beginning on 28 August, is numbered 50 in Bamford's hand, and thereafter each notebook is numbered, reaching 83 on 11 October 1861. The diary ends in mid-sentence on 26 December 1861 and the back of the last page is badly faded, indicating that it was left out unbound for a long time. A reference at the beginning of the diary – "Mr Page 13 July 1862" – suggests that it may have been continued at least until then; equally, however, he may just have been using the outside of the first notebook as a notepad. An apparent attempt by an early archivist to continue Bamford's numbering from 51 causes some confusion, but this is soon given up, and the whole of the papers are now numbered in archival pencil, covering used and unused pages, diary text and insertions, in sequence from 1 to 1,368.[34]

Whatever the exact nature of the surviving material, the result of Bamford's own writing and compilation, overlain by later conservation, is a complex text, carefully constructed, rather than merely the sum total of a sequence of individual entries.[35] There is plenty to indicate that Bamford made little effort to maintain a discipline or rhythm of daily writing. On occasion he records days in which he stayed in writing up the diary. At other times it is clear that the entry casts a retrospective glance at a particular event. The entry for 22 April 1861, for example, includes a copy of a letter he wrote to the press complaining about "exaction by railway officials" on his journey

---

32. See entry for 10 June 1860.
33. For an account of Mima's final months, see *Homely Rhymes*, 16.
34. The evidence for this attribution is, first, the different hands, and second, the different methods used. Bamford's notebook numbers have a distinctive half-circle underlining, similar to his earlier folio numbers. Bamford numbers erratically, omitting unused pages. The putative archivist numbers consistently, including pages which were clearly inserted later to carry items previously pinned by Bamford within the text.
35. We are not, indeed, the first to try. In the 1960s Mr W.J. Smith, under the supervision of W.H. Chaloner, editor of the Frank Cass edition of *Early Days*, transcribed the greater part of volume 1; the transcript is now with Chaloner's papers in the University of Manchester, John Rylands Library.

home that evening. The letter and entry must have been written later, for a weary Bamford only arrived home late in the evening. A note immediately following shows that the entry was indeed only completed on 2 May, when he received the letter back from the newspaper, and inserted it with a further comment in the diary. The evidence of the layout suggests that Bamford quite frequently returned to existing entries to add supplementary material initially forgotten, or to provide a later gloss on his original opinions.

The diaries as a whole include more than a quarter of a million words of text and insertions. In the confines of a single volume there has been space for barely half of this. The editorial process has reflected a desire to make the diary available to a variety of potential readings, without over-burdening the reader. This edition presents the full text of Bamford's diary entries, virtually all of the correspondence, and the most significant of the cuttings. A few short formal letters have been briefly summarised, and a more systematic process of selection and summary has been applied to the bulk of the cuttings. This was a difficult exercise, because of the extent to which the diary entries and the cuttings exist in a form of dialogue with each other. We have included all material which relates directly to Bamford, except where several essentially identical reports of the same event were retained in the diary, or where the cuttings contain somewhat repetitive accounts of his public career. We have, however, noted every cutting or insertion, however minor, and offered a brief description, focusing on those aspects which seem to have attracted Bamford's attention, or which provoked his comments. Wherever possible we have identified the source of newspaper cuttings, so that recourse can be had, if necessary, to the original paper.

In preparing the text for publication we have endeavoured to retain it as far as possible in its original form, while at the same time making it as easy as possible to read. In doing so, we have largely followed Bamford's own principles, as evinced in his letter to his publisher John Heywood on 8 March 1859, in which he commented that: "the copy which the author furnishes must be adhered to; ... Punctuation and intervals are under the discretion of the reader and corrector for the press, but the verbal matter cannot be displaced except by the authors consent, to do that might cause a change in the whole character of the book."

We have retained Bamford's sometimes idiosyncratic spelling and rendering of place names (a matter on which he held very firm views).[36] Bamford's handwriting was clear and regular and there are few genuine illegibilities, except occasionally in the letters of Bamford's correspondents, and in those copy letters which are damaged. Where significant parts of the text are illegible or lost, we have marked the gap with an ellipsis; where readings are conjectural, we have warned the reader in a footnote. For the letters, we have omitted the formal apparatus of date, address, etc., at the top in favour of a brief editorial summary, but (apart from a slight physical rearrangement on the page) we have left the valedictions as they are; they reflect those subtle niceties of

---

36. The correctness of his version of some place names (such as Mosston for Moston) was one of Bamford's little sensitivities, and he was severe on anyone who sought to revise them into the conventional form; see Bamford to George Tweddell, entry for 25 December 1859.

formality and familiarity which were so important to the Victorians. In all other respects we have indicated where we have made good obvious slips of the pen, or the accidental omission of words, by the use of square brackets. Where Bamford has revised his original entry by the addition of a few extra words, we have indicated this by the use of slashes thus: /added word(s)\. Where the additions have involved more than a few words (usually by the addition of material on the vacant facing page), we have presented this material as part of the text, indicating in a footnote its status as supplementary material.

In the interests of legibility, and because Bamford displayed no consistency in the matter, we have silently expanded all ampersands into "and". Because Bamford's punctuation makes little distinction between comma and period, or colon and semi-colon, we have where there was any doubt as to Bamford's intention followed modern usage. We have endeavoured to keep the use of lower and upper case as Bamford rendered it; but for some letters (such as "a" or "o") there is little to distinguish the two, and in cases of uncertainty we have reproduced them as per modern conventions. We have standardised (and in the few cases where Bamford went temporarily awry silently corrected) the dating of each entry. The character of Bamford's own dating style remains apparent from those sub-entries where the date is repeated; here we have left his original usage.

The diary contains references to a large number of Bamford's acquaintances, as well as to prominent figures in the social, political and literary life of the district. In many cases Bamford's entries provide sufficient context for placing the individuals mentioned, and for this reason, and in order to avoid cluttering the text with essentially superfluous background information, we have provided brief notes only for those figures for whom we judged that further biographical contextualisation would be helpful. We have drawn primarily on four sources of biographical information: the *Dictionary of National Biography* (identified as *DNB* in the notes); Frederick Boase's *Modern Biography* (identified as Boase); the extensive biographical references catalogue at the Manchester Central Library, from which it has been possible to identify a full obituary (referenced), or simply a reference (MCL) to the various sources of information indicated there; and the files of Middleton Public Library, which have also yielded references to obituaries or other material in the local press. No attempt has been made to provide comprehensive biographical coverage for figures featuring in the various newspaper cuttings. The finished product is very much a joint effort. The result, we trust, is a faithful rendition of the diaries, with minimal corrections of a kind which Bamford himself would have expected, and which makes a complex document clear and accessible to the later generations of readers whose attention the author always had in mind.

## BAMFORD THE DIARIST

The diary is open to different types of readings, and indeed the two editors tend towards different positions on this. Robert Poole believes that Bamford clearly intended the diary as a coherent whole, as a piece of literature; he regards Bamford's later insertions as deliberate attempts at revision of a single, essentially linear text, his careful placement and labelling of the additional material as deliberately designed to guide later readers to the precise sequence of the material. He is fairly confident that the surviving evidence enables a reconstruction to be made of the original form of the diaries and their contents, and that the care of their arrangement is evidence of Bamford's aspiration to use them as the basis for further instalments of his memoirs.

At the same time it is difficult to see how a purely recording function could have of itself been sufficient to bring Bamford to diary writing. We must not forget, despite the almost obsessive appearance of Bamford's activity (and his considerable published output), that writing, and especially letter-writing, did not come easily to Bamford. At the end of the 1840s he had confessed to Elizabeth Gaskell that he would "rather walk 20 miles than write a letter any day", and he confessed to one of his correspondents in 1859 that "it is always the last thing with me to commence writing a letter".[37] It would seem, therefore, that the purpose of the diary was not merely to record, but to be an active element in, the process of managing his public position, providing him with the accumulated information to ensure that, as he put it in discussing a speech in Bury in November 1859, that his activities "had a circulation *wide enough*".[38] In this regard, Martin Hewitt is particularly intrigued by the degree to which the diary can be approached as a complicated, multi-faceted text, whose significances lie not only in what the diaries formally record, but in the textual practices and the patterns which make the diary less a laboratory of the self (Patrick Joyce's description of the diary of Edwin Waugh)[39] than a workshop of the public persona, of the autobiographical presence. From this perspective the diary can be read as a detailed account of the struggles of one working-class radical to negotiate the complex political and socio-economic cross-currents of the years around 1860, carefully arranged, and with at least some aspiration to formal publication.

From whatever perspective the diary is approached, the themes of nostalgia and reform remain crucial. At the outset, Bamford's involvement in an attempt by the local Mechanics' Institution to reinvigorate and reform Blackley wakes gave him a cultural rather than an overtly political platform on which to mark his return to public life. He followed it up by other speeches and letters to the press setting out his own views on popularising Mechanics' Institutes, and with readings in December at both the Manchester and Salford institutions. Mechanics' Institutes were an uncontroversial liberal cause by this time, but in Bamford's outspoken insistence on the need for them to be run by working men themselves without the patronising interference of middle-class patrons we can detect the spirit of the old radical. In his insistence that this should also involve social events and readings, we can also detect a note of enlightened self-interest.

Bamford's pre-occupation with his own past runs through the diaries like a silver thread. In the first few months back in his old stamping grounds, he walked out and about, visiting the people and places of the past. The encounters were often

---

37. Chapple and Pollard, *The Letters of Mrs Gaskell* (1966), Letter 59; Bamford to Mrs Shiel, entry for 5 April 1859.
38. Entry for 7 November 1859 (emphasis ours).
39. P. Joyce, *Democratic Subjects. The Self and the Social in Nineteenth Century England* (1994).

disappointing, the memories at times bitter (as on 15 September 1858); later visits to his daughter's grave (6 April 1860) and to the Manchester workhouse where half his family had died of fever when he was a child (23 September 1860) were particularly poignant.[40] Other encounters recalled old resentments, feuds and betrayals. He had returned because he preferred his Lancashire past to the routines of mid-Victorian London, but the past was now fragmented, distant and painful. At the same time as readjusting to his home territory, Bamford had to adjust to the present, not least because he still had to earn a living. Having left Somerset House at the age of seventy without a pension, he arrived back in Lancashire with only £2 in the world, all debts cleared. Even though in 1858 he was able to obtain £20 for the copyright of a new edition of his *Passages*, it was not long before the spectre of poverty loomed, and throughout the diary period penury was a constant danger.

He had hoped to establish himself as the returning grand old man of Lancashire reform, giving public readings, republishing and perhaps continuing his books, and supporting progressive causes, in a virtuous cycle of self-advertisement. It soon became clear that this would not earn him a living. Although he was able to sell an edition of his *Early Days* to John Heywood in February 1859 for £20, he could not interest any of the local publishers in the reissue of his *Walks in South Lancashire*, and his hopes for a continuation of his autobiography came to nothing. His only other success was a final edition of his poems published in 1864. Nor did his various public performances ever provide a reliable income. He enjoyed a respectable dinner in his honour at the Albion Hotel, Bury, at the end of October, and popular success at the start of 1859 with an appearance at a reform meeting in Middleton. The old reformer was cheered and lionised, the wrongs of the past were acknowledged and condemned, and he was invited to move the resolution to establish a new Middleton Reform Association. A dinner was held in his honour at Middleton Literary Institute the following day. Over the next three years he gave readings all over the area from Manchester to the north and east, with encouraging results but never with the kind of popular success for which he had hoped. Ticket sales did little more than cover costs, and significant profits always depended upon donations from well-to-do sympathisers, whom he always risked alienating with his pride and touchiness over the details of the arrangements.

Was Bamford an effective public performer? Ben Brierley recalled that "His antiquated style of delivery often provoked merriment when it was not intended; and a peculiar stammer which he could not overcome was another source of fun."[41] Against this must be set some of the more sympathetic press reports he preserved; at a reading in Oldham in August 1859 it was claimed that "The pieces in the programme were read with great clearness, discrimination, and judgement, and frequently elicited bursts of applause." He explained to one critic that allowance had to be made for infirmity and shortness of sight, and showed himself open to constructive criticism over the content of his readings.[42] Nor should we underestimate, as did some of his more comfortably equipped patrons, the sheer physical ordeal for a seventy-year-old man of

---

40. Entries for 15 September 1858, 6 April 1860, 23 September 1860.
41. Ben Brierley, *Home Memories and Recollections of a Life* (1886), 63–4.
42. Entry for 3 August 1859; and see Plates 9 and 14.

braving wild or foggy Lancashire winter nights to travel by foot, bus and train to perform at chilly halls many miles from home.

The increasingly frailty of Bamford and of his wife, Mima, cast a growing shadow over the diaries. Always frailer than her vigorous husband, Brierley recalled that by the time of their return to Lancashire "the shocks of fortune had nearly shaken [Mima] to pieces". She suffered a long illness in May and June 1860, through which Bamford nursed her. Her exclusion from his social life will not endear him to modern readers, and like virtually all working men of his generation he assumed his wife existed in the domestic sphere.[43] His affection for her was no less profound for that, and the prospect of losing the soulmate, housekeeper and "cherry bud" of his life was dark indeed. During her increasingly alarming illnesses the diary almost ceases, along with his public life. Bamford himself was constantly struggling to keep healthy and active, and seems to have suffered a slight stroke in March 1861. Mima's first stroke followed in September. She died a year later.

The irony was that Bamford's success as a public figure, and thus his means of earning a living in his old age, depended less on his own vitality than on the health of the movement for parliamentary reform which found in him a useful figurehead. Bamford remained in principle a manhood suffrage radical, but the legacy of his hostility to Chartist lobby continued to strain relations with the more radical wing of the reform movement and meant that it was from more moderate Liberal circles that he gained most encouragement. In both literary and political terms, therefore, Bamford was a dependent guest of the middle classes. He was always going to be a difficult guest. The sturdy pride and manly independence which Bamford placed at the centre of his own character revolted continually at this subservient position, but without any alternative source of income he was forced into the uncomfortable accommodations and deferences required to secure the patronage of middle-class men whose social prejudices and hypocrisies he had come to despise. He complained of being excluded from respectable gatherings, but when sent invitations he often refused them. "Why should I dance at their feasts?" he enquired after declining an invitation to the testimonial dinner of the retiring secretary of the Mechanics' Institute; "I should be taken there to be merely a witness of the triumph of one who has made friends by being the pliant servitor of a clique, a party, which I have not been, [and] never would be!"[44]

Refusing this invitation, Bamford went on instead to accept one to a hearty dinner for the aged working men of Blackley at a local pub, where he clearly felt far more at home. In truth, he appreciated simple, unpretentious people and pleasures: the visits of old friends at wakes time; gifts of apples or simnel cake; time spent with friends such as James Dronsfield on Sunday afternoons. He took up, at least in print, the cause of working-class writers thrown on hard times, and in particular threw himself into the campaign to commemorate the sadly neglected Edwin Butterworth, although his

43. Catherine Hall, "The Tale of Samuel and Jemima: Gender and Working-class Culture in Nineteenth-century England", in H.J. Kaye and Keith McClelland, eds, *E.P. Thompson: Critical Perspectives* (1990).
44. Entry for 17 February 1861.

personal campaign in favour of bread for the living rather than stone monuments to the dead contained more than a streak of self-interest.

The pressures on working-class writers in this period were severe in a way which is difficult to appreciate today. Martha Vicinus has described the "Burns syndrome" common to many: education attained with great difficulty, gradual recognition on the pub circuit, sudden success based on middle-class patronage, but then "easy access to drink, a breakdown of steady working habits, a subsequent lowering of poetic effort and death in poverty". Bamford himself felt these pressures, as his diaries vividly show, enjoying a drink with friends but also aware of the loss of independence that came from accepting treats, not to mention the other consequences. One Sunday after such a session he had to be "nursed all day, by frequent swigs from my bottles of ale, behind the kitchen door; a rather more comfortable and enticing way of coming round after whisky punch; but, no more".[45] He scorned his fellow poets for their weaknesses – Elijah Ridings for sponging, John Critchley Prince for plagiarism, Robert Story for toadying to patrons and Waugh for adultery – and watched sadly as first John Bolton Rogerson and then Story died in poverty and alcoholism, but inwardly he must have recognised his own potential for similar failings. He supported the young Joseph Ramsbottom's early poetic efforts, and even found some fellow feeling with the preposterous "Kirkby Stephen poet" John Close in his exposure to public ridicule. Above all, however, and like so many other working-class writers, he identified with Robert Burns, at first scorned by his own community but in the end triumphant.[46]

Bamford experienced some demoralising slights in these years. His failure to be invited to a reform meeting where Bright himself paid tribute to the heroes of Peterloo was one, while his contempt at his exclusion from a Middleton reform meeting because he was not already an elector still smokes off the page.[47] Above all, however, there is the scar left by the "Rupertino" affair. Writing as "Rupertino", James Dronsfield's friend R.S. Gowenlock warned that the Bamfords would "wither away in obscurity under the blighting hand of want" and live "in dread of the workhouse" if they did not receive help.[48] Gowenlock and his friends were delighted with the published result; Bamford and his wife were mortified at this undisguised appeal to charity, and Bamford said so: compensation, yes; charity, never. Gowenlock, mortified in turn, submitted a long and injured reply but Bamford had to have the last word:

> We have never been ashamed of honest poverty, and hope we never shall be; but we have always maintained that self-respect which has exacted the respect of others. Whatever may have been our exigencies and our difficulties, we have never made a talk of them. We have kept them to ourselves, scarcely a friend so much as distantly alluding to them. In the humblest condition of honest life there is such a thing as

---

45. Entries for 23–4 September 1859.
46. Martha Vicinus, *The Industrial Muse* (1974), 141–2 and chs 4–5; David Vincent, *Bread, Knowledge and Freedom* (1981), ch. 8; *Early Days*, ch. 26; entries for 19 February 1859, 2 January 1861.
47. Entries for 11 December 1858, 14–20 May 1859.
48. Entry for 22 February 1860.

becoming pride, and that pride we have constantly endeavoured to be worthy of, and to maintain. "Rupertino's" letter has, however, torn the veil of decent privacy away.

It is impossible to decide who was the more injured party, Bamford or his would-be relieving officer, but the sharpness of the stigma of Victorian charity can still be felt across the centuries.

It took a man of the tact, generosity and insight of Sir James Kay-Shuttleworth to win Bamford's trust, and even here silence made him suspicious. The developing friendship between the two men, with their shared likes and dislikes, their shared secrets over the genesis of Kay-Shuttleworth's historical novel *Scarsdale*, and their shared pleasure at partly overcoming the class barrier between them, is one of the more interesting features of the diaries. The stiffness of Bamford's apparently chance encounter with John Bright, mutual admirers wary of each other's motives, is evocative in a different way.[49]

Such sensitivities also bring into sharp focus the particular watchfulness with which Bamford sought to mould his public image in this period, and hint at the way in which the diary can be read as part of a sustained process of what could be described as autobiographical management. Bamford had returned to Lancashire hoping in effect to make a living by trading on his reputation as radical and poet. The diary records an intensification of Bamford's letter-writing to the press, involving subtle negotiations of voice and authority. He writes under his own signature to advance suggestions about the nature of the reform campaign and platform, and under various *noms de plume* as he intervenes in debates about his own status as the longest surviving radical prisoner of 1817 and 1819. On one occasion he even feels obliged to intervene in another anonymous correspondence to insist that he was not a party to it (29 August 1858). He was also vigilant over the nature and extent of the press coverage of his platform performances, maintaining regular personal contacts with newspapers in Manchester and the surrounding towns, revising copy concerning his speeches, urging the publication of a letter, offering a poem. In the diary he annotated cuttings reporting his own interventions and others whose contents touched on matters in which he took an interest. The diary also records his most direct activity of self-writing in the preparation, printing and circulation of a succession of drafts of a circular "Right Against Wrong", in which he made a steadily expanding case for compensation (see Appendix 1). At times his observations seem little more than fits of pique that adverts for his readings have been placed in unfashionable portions of the papers, self-congratulating observations at the way his ideas have been taken up by the great and good, or egotistical sensitivities to any slight or challenge to his self-importance. But the thrust of the broader pattern is a sustained and systematic concern with the management of his public face, and especially of his autobiographical narrative, with a clear eye on the verdict of history.

---

49. Entry for 15 November 1859.

As has already been noted, Bamford had always intended to continue the autobiography provided in *Early Days* and *Passages in the Life of a Radical*, which had together only taken the story down to 1821. He occasionally hinted darkly in the diary at plans to expose his antagonists in print; when a local Mutual Improvement Society failed to read a speech he sent, he warned them: "I shall notice the affair again at my own time and in my own way" (3 November 1859). Cross-references to his published autobiography suggest that he saw the diaries as part of a wider project. He had also harboured ambitions while at Somerset House to write a history of Lancashire in his own lifetime. The restricted opening hours of the British Museum had thwarted his plans for a county history. He confessed to James Kay-Shuttleworth in August 1860, after his return to Lancashire, that his "thoughts and wishes are nearly absorbed in a desire to establish a kind of chronicle of the events ... of the chief incidents of my own course of life ... such a document is due, both to my own name ... and to those who live to inhabit the land after we are gone". Alas, his energies were "so fully absorbed in devising the means for an honest and decently organised subsistence" for himself and his wife, that he knew such a volume was increasingly unlikely. In consequence, his diary became his insurance policy with posterity, a place where he could record his experiences and opinions, illustrate the limits to liberal thought and freedom which he felt still beset society, dispense just verdicts on opponents from the past, and record the deeds of those few who did render the old radical his due.

Bamford lived in an age which blurred the lines between history and memory, in which change was often measured genealogically through biography and autobiography, and in which collective memory and popular history shaped social identities.[50] In particular, nineteenth-century radicalism was, as James Epstein and others have noted, predicated on popular history of this sort, in which a powerful myth of the subversion of Saxon democracy was inextricably intertwined with the life histories of the movement's leaders, Hunt, Cobbett, O'Connor, Jones, *et al.*[51] Although in some respects by the end of the 1850s radicalism was losing its reliance on an heroic past, competing versions of the history of the first half of the century remained absolutely central to debates over parliamentary reform. While moderate radicals sought to impose a version of history in which the 1832 Reform Act marked the triumph of gradual class collaborationist liberalism, ex-Chartists sought to present it as a desperate holding measure, and a betrayal of the struggle of the working class for political rights. It was John Bright's willingness to invoke the spirit of Peterloo while speaking the language of limited franchise extension which enabled him to bridge the gap between these two wings. Similarly, Bamford recognised that his sufferings at the

---

50. R. Samuel, *Theatres of Memory. Volume I* (Verso, 1994), especially 6–17; Pierre Nora, "Between Memory and History: Les Lieux de Memoire", *Representations* 26 (Spring 1989), 7–25 (a translation of the "Introduction" to his three-volume work, *Les Lieux de Memoire* (1984–9)).

51. James Epstein, *Radical Expression. Political Language, Ritual and Symbol in England, 1790–1850* (1994); for other explorations of the centrality of popular historical narratives to radicalism, see W. Stafford, *Socialism, Radicalism and Nostalgia. Social Criticism in Britain, 1775–1830* (1987), John Belchem, *Orator Hunt*. See also the comments of David Vincent in *Testaments of Radicalism*, and John Saville's introduction to R.G. Gammage's *History of the Chartist Movement* (1969 edition).

time of Peterloo, his unswerving commitment to universal suffrage, and his aloofness from Chartism, could make him a potent symbol both of the progress which had been achieved, and the distance which still needed to be travelled.

In this sense, Bamford was not attempting merely to propagate a particular life story self-interestedly, in the search for pension or patronage. Throughout the diary he makes it clear that he does not want a pension if this can only be obtained on the grounds of his literary activities; what he seeks is "just compensation only", a pension which recognises past wrongs, affirming the particular autobiographical thread which emphasises his political sufferings and vindication.[52] His pension-seeking was enmeshed in his broader radical activities in which he attempted to regenerate working-class radicalism and other movements of working-class self-help by mobilising his own life history. There were limits to which this kind of politics of memory could be taken, and a danger that memory could slide into reminiscence. Nevertheless, we should not doubt the degree to which Bamford's autobiography did provide a narrative through which contemporaries were able to define their politics. Hence the letter Bamford received in March 1859 from a Barnsley radical, who, commenting on his own experiences as a disillusioned Huntite and Chartist, noted that "your ideas as express'd in you[r] Book just realise my own thoughts, and I shall ... hand the "Passages" down to my children as an invaluable legacy in the hopes that they will be enabled to avoid the rock whereon I was wrecked".[53]

At times the modern reader might find Bamford an uncomfortable acquaintance. He had an unshakeable belief in himself, and a prodigious capacity for discerning slights and insults, and in his diary he elevated the vituperative aside to an art form. His self-centredness could be all-consuming, and, not surprisingly, he made enemies much more easily than he made friends. One day he could complain about the respectable "snobs" who cold-shouldered him on the bus to Manchester, the next he could record with pride how he himself had ignored some old enemy. At times his suspicions turned to paranoia. In the autumn of 1860 he became convinced that he was being followed by spies, and later he decided that he had been systematically followed by spies "since I first went to Somerset House".[54] We should remember, however, that Bamford had real grounds, albeit distant ones, for at least some of his feuds. He had, in the oppressive years of 1817–21, been spied upon, entrapped, betrayed and imprisoned; he had nearly lost his life at Peterloo, and he traced the later death of his only daughter to an illness – consumption? – contracted while he was imprisoned and unable to support his family. But he could also be sensitive to his own paranoid tendencies: "I have experienced so much hypocrisy [and] double-dealing that

---

52. Entry for 11 October 1860; it might be that this determination was partly a question of pride and desire to dissociate with what he saw as the placemen and time-servers on the Pension List, see entry for 11 September 1859. There is also some sign of a change in stance by the end of the diary period; in June 1861, for example, he remarks that he would be prepared to accept "remunerations for services rendered", entry for 4 June 1861.
53. John Widdup to Bamford, entry for 2 February 1859; cf "John Ward" (Wakefield), *Manchester Examiner and Times*, 24 April 1872, and comments in the *Middleton Albion*, 27 April 1872.
54. Entries for 5 and 20 September 1860, 4 April and 16 June 1861.

I have become almost distrustful of everyone, and every transaction. God help me! Am I losing my senses?" he exclaimed in his diary on 9 March 1860. At the same time, from those close to him he inspired a devotion which rose above his pettiness, and from a wider circle of fellow-reformers and acquaintances he obtained respect and regard. During the ten further years which he lived after the diary peters out, cushioned by a pension subscribed to by the Chadwick circle and looked after by a cousin, Mrs Hilton, he grew his hair and beard to patriarchal effect, and became both a well-loved local character and the revered elder statesman of Manchester's continuing literary renaissance. When he died on 13 April 1872, at the age of eighty-four, his interment saw the whole of Middleton halted as the cortège passed: forty-three carriages and several hundred foot followers, all in the best Peterloo formation of fifty-three years before. No Lancashire working man had ever had such a funeral.

The tribute over his grave, the monument subsequently erected at Middleton, and the continuing fascination that he has exercised since his death should serve as final reminders, if reminders are needed, that Samuel Bamford was not a man who can be encompassed by a single phrase or a single image. Above all, from the pages of his diary emerges a compelling portrait of a nineteenth-century working man in all his contradictions: poor and proud, principled and pragmatic, self-reliant and dependent, steeped in the past and driven by visions of the world as it might be. This edition, we hope, remains true to Bamford's intent to accumulate a record of his struggles to provide for himself and his wife as they entered old age, of his campaigns for a recognition of, and compensation for, the wrongs he had suffered in the cause of reform, and of his unquenchable commitment to the bettering of the lot of the ordinary people with whom he had always lived by a steady union of political agitation and individual self-improvement. We hope its wider circulation will help to rescue the man and the working classes with whom he identified from the slanders of contemporaries and the unthinking of historians, and to restore to Bamford what he craved above all in these years: some control over the life story and significance of Samuel Bamford, weaver, poet, patriot and radical.

# IN THE BELLY OF THE BEAST

*As the diary opens, Bamford was approaching the end of his seventh year of employment under the Commissioners of the Inland Revenue at Somerset House in London. Although many would have envied the relatively undemanding work and regular income, Bamford was straining hard against a yoke he had never really reconciled himself to. He did not feel at home in London, his employment brought him constantly into contact with elements of the power of the state which he despised, and he was subject to the endless episodes of social tension inevitable on the employment of a proud working-class northerner amongst London clerks and government functionaries. Disputes over the process of reorganising and weeding out the books under his control which were commencing as the diary opens, were clearly the final straw, and this short section of diary records Bamford's resentments and the firming up of his resolve to resign his employment once he had completed his seventh year.*

**Sunday 28th February.** I this day compleat the 70th year of my age. Mima is in her 69th year, and we are both in tolerably good health. I however suffering occasionally from rheumatism, and weakness of the lungs, and she from cramp in the limbs.

**Monday 1st March.** Hart, one of the accountants of M[r] Synes department having been appointed to take an account of the books under my care, on a new plan set forth by M[r] Syne, he has also, by M[r] Synes permission and with his cognizance interfered in the arrangements proposed by me for the sorting and placing of the papers, now in the course of being removed and transferred to new presses fitted up in rooms appointed for their future deposit. M[r] Syne has also sent down, his son, M[r] Louis Syne, a M[r] Foster, and a M[r] Brown to superintend the sorting and sending off, of such papers and books as may be deemed fitting for removal to the Stationery Office as waste, these gentlemen have also engaged from half a dozen to half a score of labourers and carpenters, as assistants to remove the papers and books. I have become greatly withdrawn from taking any part in the removal. I see every thing is done in a reckless and ignorant manner without method, or due consideration, and I am therefore determined not to be mixed up with these proceedings. The rooms, by directions of Messrs Hart and Hawthorne, – neither of whom know anything whatever about the business – [have] been fitted up most preposterously with shelves and presses, not at all adapted to the books and documents they are to contain. Such a mess with books and papers lying about, joiners working by candlelight, and ancle deep in shavings and other combustibles: labourers hurrying to and from with bundles of writings, papers filed in the lobbies where the carpenters are at work, placing and displacing; moving, and removing, ordering, and recalling of orders, doing and undoing. Since the days of Balaclava, in any affair not connected with war, such a mess of confusion has surely not been seen. I however am clear of it; and will remain so.

**Tuesday 9th.** They, that is the four Superintendents and six men, are sending off papers from the room where they have been stowed. Every bundle they inspect, or pretend to do so, for, in consequence of the remarkably <u>clever</u> arrangements agreed upon by these <u>gentlemen</u>? it is found that a number of papers have been thrown to the waste which should not have been so assorted: Some Bank returns also, which were ordered to be sent away are now to be retained, and these blunders and mistakes can only be rectified by examining the papers as they are thrown out to be loaded in the van. The books also which were set apart to be disposed of are to be again examined, and some of them retained. The <u>gentlemen</u> superintendents arrive at half past ten to eleven. At twelve the[y] go to dinner. When the men go at half past one to two, they return to their <u>arduous</u> <u>work</u>? and leave off at half past three to four. What they are to receive <u>extra</u> for their attendance I do not know, probably, never must know; but I have heard their extra allowance was to be six shilling a day.

**Wednesday 10th.** The superintendents have been busy sorting and sending off waste papers. Many are found intermixed which should not have been there: a consequence of the bad arrangements, and confusions attending the removal.

**Thursday 11th.** Foster, Hart and Brown began sorting books in my room.

I thought they had probably heard of some of the strong expressions of opinion which I had perhaps too unreservedly expressed respecting their very clumsy, and disorderly manner of proceeding, in the removal of the papers, for they now seemed disposed to carry on their work without my intervention or assistance in any respect. So I merely stood by and watched them, merely ordering Morris to mount the ladder and hand down the books as the numbers of the lots were called over from my "new rough list". It was about half past eleven when they began, and before they left off, they had already cleared one range and a half of shelving, the books having been ticketed, and handed off to another room, where they were to be viewed by M$^r$ Syne, who would then determine whether or not they should be sent off to the Stationery Office. The business was thus carried on. Foster or Hart called over the number from my list; Morris handed the lot to Kingsbury, who handed it to Mickleston, who placed it on the top of the other books, with which Hart having some weeks before numbered the table left them there, instead of deciding whether they should be replaced on the shelves or sent away: Brown having prepared a ticket with the number of the lot, it was attached to the books, and they were carried to a room at the top of the lobby and there arranged on the floor. Three men were in attendance carrying these books, so I soon found there was not any occasion for my attendance; but I remained watching with interested amusement the helplessly bungling, and floundering endeavours of these <u>clever</u> <u>men</u> to carry out M$^r$ Synes great jumble of getting rid of his rubbishy papers and books. I had frequently declared, to whoever might give occasion for the expression, that one great mistake in the Accountant Generals department, was the retention, and storing up of a huge mass of old foisty, rotting, stinking books and papers, the frequent removal, necessarily imperfect arrangement, and care of which had and would have, probably in weekly wages and other expenses, swallowed up more than the money value of the entire mass. Papers 150 years old, mildewed, rotten and stinking like muck; and mouldy foisty old books dating from 1638. I therefore told these gentlemen, when they were clearing the shelves, it was the best move I had seen since I came to Somerset Place, though I also expressed my disapproval of the manner in which the movement was carried into effect. The whole thing, in fact, was badly arranged.

First I ordered the lowest room in the lobby to be fitted up with shelving of dimensions suitable to the books which were to be deposited on them, and this was done, but when the shelving of the next room came to be arranged, M$^r$ Hawthornes judgement was deemed requisite and he ordered the compartments to be made without reference to the size of the books they were to contain. Why should he be suffered to interfere at all? What could he know about the books? and who so fit to determine what was requisite as myself, or, if I was not there, Morris, my assistant but M$^r$ Hawthorne had the ordering of this room, and most of the fittings were preposterously disproportioned to the vol[ume]s placed upon them. M$^r$ Hart next appeared and commenced his task of new arrangement, by disarranging the books of [the] Compartment of Taxes, which by his direction were taken from their shelves, and laid on the floor, and on the great table in the next room (my room, as it may be called). Next he interfered about the fittings of the two rooms at the head of the lobby, which by his orders were made of most absurd dimensions as may be seen. I saw how things were going, and that a mess would be made of the whole affair, so I determined to let M$^r$ Hart have his own way, and see what he would do. Next M$^r$ Syne, urged I think, rather premptorily, by the chairman, and perhaps not quite satisfied with Harts management ordered three additional superintendents, and as many labourers as might be requisite, to remove all the papers to the rooms which had been fitted up with shelving. This was done with a degree of precipitancy and confusion the consequences of which it will take a long time to correct. Great lots were ordered to be sent away, others to be detained, and the next day perhaps those to be retained were also ordered to be disposed of; it also happened that in the confusion arising from the variety of orders, papers which should have been retained and placed on the shelves were thrown into the waste room, whilst other lots which had been distinctly ordered to be sent away, were recalled. Thus with confusion worse confounded, they went on until all the condemned papers, and many books were carted off to the Stationery Office in Westminster. No note taken; nor any account kept of what was thus disposed of. And now three out of the four of these very expert gentlemen are at work on the books in my room. I tell them I hope they will give the shelves a thorough cleansing of all rubbish, indeed I should not much regret if they cleared the place, locked the door, and did not leave a book or a paper to be taken care of: I am heartily tired and disgusted with the flunky snobbery, and double dealing of nearly all I meet with, in, and about this place.

**Saturday 13th.** They have nearly cleared the excise books from one side of my room, and I wish them "God Speed", but I say to them, what better are you for pulling the books from the shelves and placing them in yonder room? Hart says that M$^r$ Syne may see them. And what wiser will he be for having seen them in yonder place? Will his seeing them yonder afford him any especial information. Wont you when he sees them, have to refer to my rough list, and tell him what they are? And could not you have done the same had they remained on the shelves here. Such lots as you thought might be sent off, being ticketed as they appear in the list? Why carry them to yonder room unless their being <u>there</u> will afford M^r Syne some especial information. There was a slight pause, and then Hart replied. Their being yonder will tend to their being sent away. Well, if you think so, I replied send them by all means, but I am afraid it wont have that effect, This was just before dinner (12 o'clock).

Foster selected a curious old book, small /no 149\ size – "Boards orders" 1713, and said he would take that for himself: he crossed it out of the rough list, marking it as "waste". When at one o'clock I was going upstairs Foster passed me and had, apparently, that book and one or two others in his hands.

When I returned after dinner Brown and Foster only were in attendance on the book business: they went away early, and I found they had ceased to remove the books to the waste room, and had commenced ticketting them as they were in their places on the shelves.

Hart had complained of being ill and coughing all night, and after dinner he only stepped down during a few minutes to confer with Foster as to which of the men should be sent away. I said two should be retained for Monday morning, but they determined that one only should; and that, not the one whom Morris suggested. So they direct in every thing.

**Sunday 14th.** Much consideration as to whether I should attend any more at Somerset Place or not, but, at last, I think I had perhaps best go in the morning, were it only to observe how they will proceed with their very clever operations, perhaps to give Syne a hint, should I see him, and a fair occasion offer – that I neither care for him, nor his trumpery, paltry, employment.

14 Sunday. At home, ill enough at ease in my mind: strongly desirous to quit the place at once, but cautiously pondering and scheming how I was to earn an honest subsistence if I did so. Torture is what I daily and nightly endure. Would not any course of life or even death, be preferable to this?

**Monday 15th.** The books which they had caused to be carried up the lobby, to the "waste room," they are now having brought back, reexamined, some retained, and others finally condemned as waste: things are more and more in disorder amongst the books, and I impatient at seeing such goings on asked M^r Syne if he would sanction my application for leave of absence during four days? to which he readily assented. Hart complains of being unwell, and expresses a wish to get rid of the job.

**Tuesday 16th.** Foster and Brown only are in attendance this morning. I write my letter for leave of absence, and present it to M^r Syne who would have entered into conversation about the "muddle" we had below, but I kept my distance, saying I did not know what the gentlemens plans were, and consequently could not give an opinion respecting them: they might turn out better than present appearances seemed to warrant and I should be glad if they did. He said he hoped they would finish the business soon, and I said, he had better not expect it would be done <u>soon</u>, for, from what I had observed if he entertained that expectation, he would be disappointed.

Went down below, regulated my things on the desk, and to lunch at one o'clock, after which I did not return, but took the half day as is usual on such occasions.

**17. 18. 19th. 20th.** At home and about home.

**Sunday 21st.** Mima's birth-day. She now enters on her 70th year.

Saw Morris who tells me things are in greater confusion at Somerset Place, than when I left on Tuesday. I know not what course to take: great difficulties appear however I may act. I wish heartily I were well quit of the place.

**Monday 22nd.** Found things much confused at Somerset Place. Foster still going through the books and Hart and Brown rearranging them in the next room, which means in fact, they were disarranging them: they seem not to have any idea of beginning at the beginning of a thing. For instance, the beginning of a room is the entrance, and properly acting they ought to begin and follow the order of rotation from the beginning, instead of which they walk across the room to a nook near the window, and make their beginning there.

**Wednesday 24th.** Going on as usual, doing and undoing. Moving a little forward and then backward. Foster acknowledges himself "in a fix". Young Watts, who does not once in twenty times that I meet him, condescend – as he thinks – to speak, had the assurance to accost me in the park, and to thrust his company on me all the way to Somerset House. He is in the Secretarys department at the old tax factory, and believing that what I said, or the substance of it, w[oul]d go again, perhaps to higher quarters. I spoke freely, on being questioned, respect[in]g my present position, and the sad confusion we were in at our place. Speaking of the books that were in my care, he supposed I must have fallen in with some of Burns's correspondence, but I reminded him, Burns was only a gauger, and consequently did not correspond with the Board. Watts said he would have been nothing more than gross animal had it not been for the vein, which served to raise him above the mere animal instincts. I mentioned having seen a cast of his skull, the owner of which, remarked, that the only peculiarity about it was its inordinate animal development. We passed on to Parliamentary reform, and I said it was not understood either by the people, or their Parliamentary and political friends, the real condition of the people was not understood by those above them who only sought a knowledge of them by information derived from Magistrates, parsons, ladies, ladies maids, poor law officers and such like: and thus we arrived at our place of attendance, the great "lubber-slum", of England.

**Friday 26th.** One of the clerks came down and spoke in an undertone to Hart and Foster, and from what the latter said I understood the question to be relative to the time they reckoned as having been employed down stairs. Foster said "I came on the 25th," which must mean the 25th Feb. Hart commenced on the books, or rather pretended to commence, a week or two previously. We shall perhaps learn what this reckoning of time means, since it must mean over time, with a view to extra payment: and if that be it, extra payment will be reckoned for the four superintendents during the removal of the papers, besides payment of the many extra assistants, as many on one or two occasions, I should think, as 12 or 14. A pretty penny this removal of papers and examination of books will have cost ere it is finished.

Muckleston, an assistant had placed a ladder so that I could not get to my desk. I desired him to remove it; he was attending upon Hart; Hart said he must not go then: I insisted that he should. Hart said I had no right to go there (into the next room to mine) to interfere. I replied that it was he who interfered, and again ordered the man to remove the ladder, which he then did. I see I shall have a regular blow up with this fellow Hart. In the course of the day he produced a paper and handed it to Foster, who gave it to Morris with an intimation which I did not hear. It was a requisition from M$^r$ Gripper for a book showing the return of population and amount of assessed taxes in 1832. Morris referred to the Catalogue and produced two books, neither of which contained the required information.

Hart then said he should refer the matter to me, and gave me the paper, which ought, in fact to have been handed to me in the first instance. He directed Morris to take one of the books upstairs to M$^r$ Gripper, whereas Morris ought to have been ordered by me, and no one else: the paper also ought to have been signed, which it was not. I must hold tight rein, with a snaffle bit on these pretensious fellows: and if I do, a hundred to one, Syne will not back me, though acting according to his orders.

**Saturday 27th.** Nothing unusual: Foster is removing books from shelves fitted for them to others which dont hold them.

Brown writes labels, which ought to have been in <u>printed Capitals</u>: he will write perhaps a score or two in a day, whereas by types and a press, thousands might have been produced in the same time.

These clever gentleman seem to be progressing towards inextricable confusion. Let them "go ahead", and when they are at the further end, I may perhaps speak, that is, if I remain at the place until then.

**Thursday 1st April.** The week has passed as usual, pulling down account books, labelling them: putting them up, then shifting them. Next finding they were wrong[ly] placed, and again removing them. I have been entirely neuter, not interfering or offering any suggestion, but looking on, and considerably amused by their continued blunders and embarrassments. Both Hart and Foster seem rather more cool on the job they have undertaken, perhaps they are not to have the amount of remuneration they expected. Hart did [not] this day, make his appearance at all, and Foster was only down about a couple of hours. I have not, during all the time tendered the least advice, nor shall I do: they shall e'en work out the thing in their own way, if they work it out at all. I did however, on Wednesday say to Brown, that if Foster and Hart had undertaken to examine the books and throw out such as were useless, they would have been found qualified for the task, but when in addition to that they undertook to <u>arrange</u> the books they engaged a business for which they were not competent, and that if I had undertaken the arrangement I should have done it in one tenth of the time they would occupy according to their present rate of progress. This, no doubt, Brown would report to them again, and I rather think it has had some affect on their views: Both are apparently beginning to have enough of the job. I have helped them by writing labels: but in other respects it has been an amusement to me. Hart asks where a book of such a number is? I reply I dont know, the books have all been disarranged, and any reference to my old catalogue has been rendered useless: the book indeed may have been sent away. M^r Sargeant sends for a certain paper of income tax returns, and the reply is, the papers are all in confusion, we dont know where it is, nor where to look for it, but will endeavour to find it; we accordingly guess its whereabouts, but the paper is not to be seen, perhaps it has been thrown amongst the waste, in the confusion, and been sent away. We report therefore, that we cant find it, and believe we have not got it. Today, I receive my salary, £11.8.0. and treat myself to a lunch of bread and cheese, and and a draught of Scotch ale.

**Good Friday.** At home all day. Wrote a note of excuse to Ord.

**Tuesday 13th.** The books of my department are in a better state of arrangement than hitherto. And Foster and Hart seem to think the worst is nearly over, but they are mistaken. Hart was here during the forenoon, and absent afterwards; he complains of being unwell. After dinner Foster commenced sorting the papers; the books not yet half finished. Morris says there has been a rumpus upstairs. M^r Syne is not satisfied about the progress his three Superintendents have made: and there is a demur about the heavy charge they have sent in for <u>overtime</u>. I suppose, from this, they reckon their services as extra, or over time, though they are performed during office hours, and when they are supposed to be at their desks.

**Thursday 15th.** M^r Syne has been down looking over to-day, and from what I have heard he was not satisfied with the state in which he found things. A great portion of the books will have to be shifted again, some of them for the 5th or 6th time: the shelving will have to be altered, some portions must be pulled down and put up in another form, so there will be a mess of confusion again. Hart is superintending the arrangements of the papers, that is, in his way, which is doing, and undoing, putting up, and pulling down, the floor and passages all the time littered with bundles of accounts, of all sorts in mixed bewilderment. It is really amusing to observe their embarrassment. Syne poor fellow, comes and looks at all this; and goes away again without appearing to have the least notion of either beginning, middle, or end of the thing. He seems just as helpless as his very clever superintendents are.

**Friday 16th.** Hart [spent] part of the day ordering the arrangement of papers, and Foster looking after the books and papers of what they call "the fine room", – the place in which documents belonging to the Department of "Fines and Seizures", are to be kept. What a term! indicative of a system at once <u>horrible</u> and <u>mean</u>. the very words repel and disgust me. <u>Spies</u> and <u>informers</u> are the vermin that live [and] prosper on this system.

**Saturday 24th.** This morning I wrote out and sent to M^r Syne a letter of which the following is a copy.

Depository of Books and Papers
24th Ap. 1858.

Dear Sir

On the 21st of this month was compleated the seventh year since my honoured
friend, the late M^r Wood[1] first gave me employment at Somerset House. I have
wished for the accomplishment of this date, as an approach to the term of my
servitude here, and I beg to inform you that I wish to retire from my present
situation on the 1st of May – Saturday next.

I shall perhaps be pardoned for mentioning that, according to usual wont and
custom, several days are due to me as <u>holidays</u>, and if you would sanction my
letter to the Board for six days leave of absence – which I understand are due –
I should perhaps not be required to attend on business, after this day.

I remain, Dear Sir
Your Obedient Servant
Sam^l. Bamford

L.T. Syne Esq^r.

Morris, my assistant, took up the note, and did not return during what seemed a
considerable time: and when he did come, as I did not put any questions, he went
about his usual avocations, and did not speak: at length, after about an hour had
elapsed, one of the men in M^r Garlands room came, and delivered a note which was as
follows.

Sir, – M^r Syne has desired me to inform you that he has no objection to your
taking the few days absence you wish to have now. It will however be right that
you should make application to him in the usual official manner.

I am Sir,
Your ob^t. serv^t.
Rich^d Gripper

I had already prepared a letter of application in the usual form, to the Board, for leave
of absence during six days, and that letter I immediately took up to M^r Syne who said it
was no longer necessary to apply to the board, as the head of each Department had
now authority to grant leave of absence. I apologized, and said I would withdraw that
application, and write another in proper form: he said that would do; he could alter the
address, but I preferred withdrawing it, and writing another. He was writing a letter
when I entered the room; he asked me if I had received a note from M^r Gripper? I said
I had: the one before him, he said was intended for me, and I replied that I should be
happy to receive any communication he might think proper to make. He expressed a
wish for my welfare; said he thought my late occupation amongst old books and papers
had not been entirely suitable to my taste. I said it certainly had not; but I was prepared

---

1. John Wood (1790–1856), MP for Preston, 1826–32; Chairman of the Board of Inland Revenue,
    1849–56; Boase.

to expect that in every phase of life there would be something more or less disagreeable: he said, as he had begun his letter he would write it out, and send it down, and so I withdrew to make an application to him, in the <u>now</u> proper form. This I did forthwith, and was about sending it up by Morris when one of the Board messengers entered and said Sir Alexander Duff Gordon[2] wanted to see me. I did not first recollect at the moment, and asked who Sir Alexander was? the reply being that he was one of the Commissioners, and was over at the Board room.[3] I therefore gave Morris my application to M$^r$ Syne, and told him he might mention to M$^r$ Syne that Sir Alexander had sent for me. I went with the messenger, and being shown into a room, a tall and good-looking gentleman presently entered and asked if I was the author of the life of a Radical? I said I was: my name was Bamford: he took a seat, and desired me to do the same, saying that both himself and his lady had been greatly pleased by the perusal of my books. I said I was happy in having contributed to the pleasure of himself and lady Duff Gordon and that from very many of my leaders I had received similar testimonials of approbation. He asked if I was engaged in literary productions now? and I replied that I was not <u>so</u> much engaged as I could wish to be; that when I came to London at first I hoped a probation of some years would have ended in an arrangement of some kind, whereby I might be enabled to devote the remainder of my days to the collecting and arranging of materials for Lancashire history which were at the British Museum. Materials which I alone could properly select and arrange inasmuch as they embraced incidents and transactions, of many of which I was personally cognizant, and should be able to illustrate by my own notes and recollections, such as no other person could furnish. He asked if that could not be done whilst I retained my situation at present? I said I had no hopes of that as the library would be closed in the evening: not until eight o'clock, he thought in summer time. I acquiesced in that but said I felt I was not so young as formerly, and now, after being absent from home during eight hours, I wanted refreshments, and after that repose: he assented to that, and mentioned how he and lady Gordon had been interested by my writings particularly by my description of an old hall some where near Manchester. I said that would probably be the old hall at Middleton, which according to my recollection approached nearest to the discription of the hall of Cedric the Saxon in the novel of Ivanhoe,[4] of anything I had seen or heard of elsewhere: there was once also a fine old hall at Radcliffe, the property of the Earl of Wilton; it was framed on massive beams of black oak, which seemed to have hewn and shaped by the axe, but it had been many years ago pulled down in order to furnish a site for labourers cottages.[5] Sir Alexander said he had only just learned that I was employed at Somerset House, and he felt a desire to see me; adding, as he took my hand, and moved towards the door, that he was happy in having made my acquaintance. I said I felt honoured by his attention, and so we parted.

On my return to my room, I found a letter on my desk, which was as follows.

---

2 Sir Alexander Duff Gordon (1811–72), Commissioner of the Inland Revenue 1856–72; minor figure in London literary circles; Boase.

3. Sentence inserted on facing page.

4. The great hall of Cedric the Saxon is described in chapter 3 of Sir Walter Scott's *Ivanhoe* (1819).

5. See *Walks*, 172–3.

Inland Revenue, 24 Ap 58.

Dear Sir,

I regret to learn by your note of this morning that you are about to leave us, and trust that you will find the means of passing the remainder of life in some pursuits more congenial to your philosophical mind, than, I am afraid your occupation here has been.

Allow me to assure you of my sincere respect for your character, and that it will be at all times gratifying to me, to hear of your welfare.

I remain, Dear Sir,

Always Sincerely yours

L.T. Syne.

Sam^l Bamford Esq^r.

The books and papers are yet in great confusion, and wearying to contemplate, though certainly, slowly approximating to something like order. I came away at four o'clock. and thus ended my servitude under Her Majestys Honourable Commissioners of Inland Revenue.

***Newspaper cutting***, *unattributed, but dated by Bamford 10 May 1858.*

---

### THE NUNEATON RAILWAY ACCIDENT

Amongst the passengers in the ill-fated train was Mr Samuel Bamford, the well-known author of "Passages in the Life of a Radical" who was coming on a visit to this district where he formerly resided. He was in a second class carriage, – the third from the engine. On feeling the collision, Mr Bamford threw himself upon the seat of the carriage and escaped uninjured. The carriage immediately preceding the one in which he was seated, and the one behind it, were both crushed. Mr Bamford speaks in the warmest terms of the great kindness and hospitality shown by the farmers and others residing near the scene of the catastrophe. He states that they hastened to the spot in great numbers, bringing water, and in one case a large stone bottle of brandy – remedial agencies which proved to be extremely valuable.[6]

---

Mr Page 13 July 1862.[7]

---

6. This was a considerable smash. On 9 May 1858 the 9 a.m. London Euston to Manchester train was derailed south of Northampton when it hit a cow which had wandered on to the line through a gap in a hedge. The train ran down an embankment and six of the eight carriages were "more or less shattered", including the Manchester carriage; one was torn clean off its chassis. A train came from Nuneaton to pick up the survivors and take them to Nuneaton, where the Manchester passengers got the next connection, arriving in Manchester at 6 p.m. Only after the clearing up began was it found that, as well as the six seriously injured, there were three bodies in the wreckage. It was thought remarkable that more of the 100 passengers were not injured: *Manchester Examiner and Times*, 11–13 May 1858.
7. This entry seems to have been added later; the significance of this is not clear, except that it shows Bamford writing in the diary six months after the last extant entry.

# 1

# LOOKING AROUND

*The Bamfords initially settled in a cottage in Moston, Harpurhey, a mundane working-class township three miles from Middleton, down the lane (and down market) from his former rustic retreat in Blackley. After a gap in the diaries occasioned probably by a combination of the disruptions of their relocation and the trauma of their narrow escape from the Nuneaton railway disaster, significantly, Bamford resumed his diary on the occasion of the Blackley wakes. These annual parish festivities had been the great feast of the year in the Middleton of Bamford's youth, and concern with questions of improving recreation both through traditional festivities such as the wakes and harvest homes, and in newer institutions such as the mechanics' institutes, was one of the motifs of these early months back in Manchester. Otherwise, Bamford was active in overseeing the final stages of the reprint of his* Passages in the Life of a Radical, *an edition of which he had sold to the Manchester publisher Abel Heywood soon after his return, and in renewing old acquaintances and revisiting old haunts.*

**Sunday 1st August.** Blakeley Wakes.

Bethel, wife and daughter came uninvited, as they always do: had tea, and to avoid their calling a second time, we went to Grimshaws. Grimshaw and Mary Ann called after tea, and we went with them over the clough to Charlestown.

Dronsfield[1] and some friends called as they were going home; made them welcome to a jug of my ale, and after some pleasant conversation they departed.

**Monday 2nd.** The Fete of the Blakeley Mechanics Institution took place. Recorded in the annexed report which I wrote, and which the honorary secretary could not have done if it would have saved him.

**Report**, *from the* Manchester Guardian, *9 August 1858.*

---

## BLACKLEY WAKES AND MECHANICS' INSTITUTION

The Directors of the Blackley Mechanics' Institution, deeming it advisable to endeavour to give a better direction to the amusements of the annual wakes, which commenced on Sunday (week), caused the following address to be distributed in the village and neighbourhood.

That the old English customs of our forefathers in the celebration of their feasts, wakes, and other annual modes of rejoicing, have in these manufacturing districts been long perverted from their original designs, and their modes of celebration are facts which are both undeniable, and to be regretted. Ancient simplicity of enjoyment,

---

1. James Dronsfield (1826–96), of Hollinwood, blacksmith and later superintendent of the Oldham gas and water supply, and also a local historian under the *nom de plume* "Jerry Lichenmoss"; see Oldham Local Studies Library, newspaper cuttings.

truthful and honest sincerity in friendship, and kindly and neighbourly feeling, are much less prevalent than they were within the memory of persons now living. A few observant inhabitants of Blackley have noted these changes with regret, and wishful to aid in restoring, and, if possible, in improving upon the customs of our forefathers, they have formed a Committee, who, after various meetings, and much consideration, have deemed it best to solicit the aid of the respectable inhabitants of Blackley in endeavouring, by every dissuasive and better example, to restrain at the ensuing wakes, if not entirely to prevent, drunkenness, gambling, quarrelling, and fighting; to encourage exhibitions of running, leaping, and climbing, with other peaceful feats of agility and strength; to arrange processions, with dancing, music, and choral singing, after which tea parties may succeed, when readings and recitations of prose and poetry may be introduced; whilst hospitality to invited guests, courtesy towards strangers, oblivion of past offences and grievances, and a renewal of kindly feeling amongst neighbours, will be strongly recommended. Should the proposals, which are respectfully tendered, meet with the desired response, they may, perhaps, in the same amicable spirit in which they are put forth, be adopted at other places; and may prepare the way for improved regulations on successive recurrences of the Blackley annual wakes. The active assistance and co-operation of the well-disposed of every class and denomination will be thankfully accepted by the Committee.

C.L. DELAUNAY,[2] Hon. Sec.
Blackley Mechanics' Institution, 21st July 1858.

---

*This is followed by an account of the proceedings, describing the various traditional sports and games which were organised, and the concluding tea party, at which Bamford gave a brief speech in which he expressed "regret that such institutions generally appeared to be existing in a kind of torpor, hoped they would commence a more active life, and intimated means that would tend to such a result. He knew not any reason why free readings should not be given once a week at least; and when rooms were too small, during these fine evenings, open-air readings should not take place. As an example he gave an affecting little piece, called "Dora," from one of Tennyson's poems."*

**Thursday 5th.** Attended the inauguration of the Brotherton testimonial.[3] Mr Binney[4] got into the omnibus in Market Street; he had a newspaper, and our eyes meeting, he nodded and said, "how are you"? "how do you do", was the reply, and so began and ended our recognition, I never afterwards bestowing a look. Thus terminates, I suppose, my acquaintance with Mr E.W. Binney, – now a F.R.S. and consequently not to be mated with one who has not some sort of a ridiculous handle to his name.

---

2. Charles Delaunay (dates not known), secretary to the Blackley Mechanics' Institution, of the Roman Catholic Delaunay family of Blackley, dyers.

3. For Joseph Brotherton (1783–1857), MP for Salford, millowner, advanced Liberal, in Peel Park, Salford; *DNB*, see obituary, *Manchester Examiner and Times*, 8 January 1857.

4. Edward W. Binney, FRS (1812–81), Manchester worthy, leading force in the geological society, and patron of working-class botanists. He contributed substantially to the support of Bamford in his final year. MCL.

Saw Mr and Mrs Shuttleworth[5] in Peel Park. I would have escaped their notice, but could not: they both gave me their hands: he wanted to know why I had not written to him? and I reminded him that he had never answered my last letter, nor called to see me since I sent him the tract about Amos Ogden,[6] now about five years ago. I said I was the last man in the world to obtrude either my correspondence or my presence on any person, and that was the reason I had not called on him, or written to him. He regretted there should have been a misunderstanding; expressed his wish to be of service to me at any time, and thus I lost one friend to-day and regained another; of the sort.

5th. Went to Manchester; took the report to the newspapers.[7]

5th.[8] Mr Hutchings, secretary to the Manchester Mechanics Institution, introduced himself to me at Peel Park. I had been pointed out to him by some one, and he was quite delighted to have met with me: spoke highly of my works, would take an opportunity for calling upon me: hoped I would call on him at the Institution, should be happy to see me, etc., etc., etc.

Met him again in Market Street. He had been thinking it would be a good thing if I would give them a lecture or something of the kind: it could be easily arranged and would be profitable to me. I assented, and said I must indeed do something of the kind since I had not any other means in view whereby to earn a living. He should like me to spend and evening with himself and a few friends, young men of the Institution, when the subject of lecturing could be talked over. I said I was at his service any time, gave him my postal address and we parted.

*Report, from the* Manchester Weekly Times, *7 August 1858 of a meeting of the liberal electors of Chorlton at the Clarendon Inn, Oxford Street, to select the parliamentary representative for Manchester. The proposed candidature of Thomas Fairbairn[9] was rejected in favour of Thomas Bazley,[10] because of Fairbairn's opposition to the ballot. During the proceedings it was announced that Richard Cobden had written intimating he would not stand for Manchester because "he could not trust such a constituency, for 'they had stoned the prophets'",[11] and would stand for Rochdale instead.*

---

5. Probably John Shuttleworth (1786–1864), Manchester cotton merchant and longstanding radical; see Michael J. Turner, *Reform and Respectability. The Making of a Middle-Class Liberalism in early 19th century Manchester* (1996), 18–20 and *passim*; MCL.

6. Samuel Bamford, *Some Account of the late Amos Ogden of Middleton* (1853). Amos Ogden (1764–1850) was a Middleton silk handloom weaver, Methodist, Jacobin and Peterloo veteran, who had been an associate of Bamford's in the Middleton Hampden Club and the Middleton Mechanics' Institute, with whom Bamford had split acrimoniously around 1827 when Ogden became a client of the earl of Suffield; see note for entry of 26 November 1859.

7. That is, the report on the wakes.

8. The rest of the entry for this date inserted on facing page.

9. Thomas Fairbairn (1823–74), had been the leading promoter of the magnificent "Art Treasures Exhibition" in Manchester in 1857, but after his failure to secure the Liberal nomination in 1859, and the rejection of a grandiose Art Gallery scheme he proposed in 1860, he quickly withdrew from Manchester life; MCL.

10. Thomas Bazley (1797–1885), cotton manufacturer, president of the Manchester Chamber of Commerce 1845–59, and MP for Manchester, 1858–80; *DNB*.

11. Bamford's emphasis.

**7th.**  The report appears in the Weekly News and the Courier.[12]

Called in the evening at Brierleys[13] in Whitley Street who went with me to have a peep at Rogerson.[14] Called at Abel Heywoods[15] about a proof, and at bottom of Oldham Street stumbled on Robert Story[16] the Northumberland poet whom I had supposed to be in London at his work as usual. He was about "three sheets in the wind", as I could see; as was also, his nephew, "doctor Story", as he calls himself. They were going to a carousal of a party of Scotchmen, or North Countrymen at least, at the Blue Bell in Mill Street, and would have had us with them but we excused ourselves, and got away from them as quickly as we decently could.

Rogersons I found to be a dull affair, the company were few in number, and the conversation was not interesting. Scholes, the drinking, spunging rhymester came in, and obtruded some of his specious platitudes in conversation; two glasses of Rogersons hard ale were quite enough for me, and so we left, and went to the Moulders Arms near Portland Street where the company was all up stairs in the music saloon and so we had a quiet glass of grog and a cigar each below. I have not any taste for modern music. Ingham, the landlord came just before we came away, and took the liberty to introduce a Mr Somebody, whose name I forget, secretary to some "Society of Foreigners" or "Society for Foreigners" one of those schemes I have no doubt, which are vamped up to make a living for the original schemers. We took a cab at New Cross, and had a glass each at Harperhey, parting at the toll bar.

**Sunday 8th.**  In the afternoon a daughter of one of our old neighbours at Middleton called to see us, and brought with her one whose grandfather and father had always been enemies of mine, and of my cause, that of Parliamentary Reform. Old Jonny Turner however never had many ideas of his own, and he acted more from the promptings of others than from any principle of opposition. He was a great bully, and as usual, a coward, when his match came up. Soon after my return from Lincoln Castle, he tried to fasten a quarrel on me, but was reminded by the company that I could not fight, being under bond to keep the peace. His son Bob, the father of this girl, when a boy about the age of my daughter Ann, used to ill treat her when going to the well for water: he upbraided her with her father being a Radical, and in prison – as at that time I was – and he even went [to] the length of beating the child, who amongst all my Middleton friends, found not one to protect her. I always disliked the fellow, and

---

12.  That is, the report on the Blackley Wakes.

13.  Ben Brierley (1825–96), popular dialect writer of Radical sympathies and later editor of *Ben Brierley's Journal*. See Owen Ashton and Stephen Roberts, *The Victorian Working-Class Writer* (1999), 97–121. (See Plate 1.)

14.  John Bolton Rogerson (1809–59), Manchester poet and former cemetery keeper, among the founders in 1842 (with Bamford) of the Sun Inn literary circle. His volume *Musings in Many Moods* was published in 1859. See entry for 24 May 1859; *Ben Brierley's Journal*, March 1872.

15.  Abel Heywood (1810–93), ex-Owenite, newsagent, bookseller, printer, eventually publisher (including of the reprint of Bamford's *Passages*); ultra-radical candidate for Manchester 1859 and 1865, Mayor of Manchester, 1862–3; *Manchester Guardian*, 21 August 1893.

16.  Robert Story (1795–1860), artisan poet, admirer of Scott and Burns and a client of the Duke of Northumberland. He had been a fellow clerk at Somerset House, see entries for 6 June 1859 and 23 August 1860; "Introduction" to J. James, ed., *Lyrical and Other Minor Poems of Robert Story* (1861), and *DNB*.

probably always shall do, but I did not, on account of the sins of the father entreat this daughter of his with less civility. I would rather however that neither her, nor any other of that family or kin were introduced to my house in future.

**Monday 9th.** Went to Heywoods again about a proof. Corrected it, and found Story, his nephew and another person apparently waiting for me opposite Heywoods shop. We must have a glass, and I went with them to the next tavern where I was informed they were about setting out to Wilmslow, to see Mr R.H. Gregs[17] gardens. I was invited to join the party, but made excuse of other engagements, and the party went into Martins, the leather cutter, preparatory to their setting out. Story, it seemed, had been wishful to leave Somerset House, but his patron the Duke of Northumberland had advised him to remain, intimating that when he (Story) could not remain in his present situation any longer, something would be devised for his future subsistence. His wife, it seems was with him in Manchester but I neither invited him nor his wife, to come and see us. I had not forgotten the shamefully shabby return her and her daughters made for our plentiful hospitality when [we] were in lodgings at Portland town.

The report of Blakely Wakes appeared in the Manchester Guardian of this day.

Monday 9th.[18] Met Stores Smith[19] in the street, and after a handsome apology, or rather fair explanation of his reason for not writing, we shook hands, Smith saying he would come up and see me at Moston.

Story, saw him in Oldham St. He, his nephew the doctor, Martin; and another were going to Wilmslow to see R.H. Gregs gardens: going, in fact, a tuft hunting.[20] I made an excuse and got away, so I have done with Story, for this year, I suppose.

**Tuesday 10th.** At home writing up this diary and sending off to John Bright M.P.[21]

**Thursday 12th.** Mills[22] of Middleton writes wanting something for the paper.

Sent him a copy of "Early Days" to make extracts from.

**Sunday 15th.** Brierley called.

**Monday 16th.** 39 years since our great Peterloo meeting at Manchester: what changes in the time.

Called at New Inn, and stopped too long.

---

17. Robert Hyde Greg (1795–1865), of the Styal Gregs, Unitarian cotton master, who adopted increasingly conservative attitudes after the repeal of the Corn Laws; *DNB*.

18. The rest of this entry is on the facing page.

19. John Stores Smith (1829–92), active supporter of Cobden and Bright, literary figure after publishing a study of Mirabeau in 1848, and briefly in partnership with Leigh Hunt; *Manchester Guardian*, 2 February 1892.

20. "Tuft hunting": hob-nobbing with social superiors.

21. John Bright (1811–89), millowner, a leading figure in the Anti-Corn Law League, and the pre-eminent national spokesman for parliamentary reform in the 1850s and 1860s. MP for Manchester 1847–57, and for Birmingham 1859–89; *DNB*.

22. Thomas Mills (1826–92), founding editor of the *Middleton Albion* (1857), active local improver and leading figure in the formation in 1860 of the Middleton and Tonge Cotton Mill Company; *Middleton Albion*, 29 August 1892. (See Plate 6.)

**Tuesday 17th.** Saw Whyatt the son of my old friend at Openshaw. Called at Rogersons, who showed me, in the Examiner of yesterday, a letter signed "Cranberry" in derision of one of "the Bards" who had called on him to sell a book.

Saw Sam Wolstoncroft who tried one of his shabby tricks in the omnibus; a half penny short: at home to dinner, five o'clock.

**Wednesday 18th.** Went to Jacksons at Station town (Jumbo)[23] to see about photographs. They have several of my portraits, but they are not yet tinted: will be next week: showed me some good bits taken in Boggart-ho. cloof.[24] Baited at John Harrisons: saw Mills of "the Middleton Albion". Geo Cambells son, from Manchest[r] was at the Asshetons Arms: and old Ashton the chimney builder,[25] would here have had me sit and talk with him in the bar, but I would not: was very glad to meet with James Hall from Liddall Moor: had a glass with him at Harrisons and came away by omnibus.

**Saturday 21st.** Middleton Wakes.

**Monday 23rd.** As I had not seen or heard from Hutching since the 5th, as I expected to have done, I called upon him at the Mechanics Institution, David Street. He did not say anything about my spending an evening at his house, in company with a few young men, his friends, as he had proposed that I should, when I saw him in Market St. but talked about having seen Mr Charles Delaunay, and my going to meet him (Hutchins) at Delaunays. If he thinks that I am to be shifted, and stuck like a peg, in any place he or Charles Delaunay choose, he will find himself mistaken. He said I should see or hear further respecting the appointment in the course of a fortnight: so I will wait and see what will turn up out of this improvised acquaintance. I never yet found such good for anything. He showed me through the place; several classes of youth, of both sexes were under instruction. The reading room was – at the time – but thinly attended. A full length portrait of Sir Benjamin Heywood,[26] brought the unpleasant reflection, that he had not been a friend of mine; and on second thoughts I am inclined to commence my career of reading and reciting, in any room rather than in one under his patronage.

In going to Newton Heath, by the omnibus, got seated next to McD – the school keeper at Flixton, but I affected not to see him, and so made return for his "coolness" at London. Came back through Middleton, stopped a while at the wakes, and thence home by omnibus.

**Wednesday 25th.** The following appeared in the Examiner and Times.

---

23. Jacksons were a prominent local family of photographers and artists, based at Middleton Junction, also known as Stationtown or Jumbo (the site of one of the late Owenite communities, see Percy Redfern, *The Story of the CWS* (1913), 19–24).
24. Boggart Hole Clough, a local beauty spot, and later public park.
25. John Ashton (dates not known) of Blackley, builder in 1846 of the 321 ft chimney at the Schwabes' dyeworks, Rhodes – "the colossus of Rhodes".
26. Sir Benjamin Heywood, FRS (1793–1865), prominent Manchester Unitarian Liberal of the 1820s and 1830s, and leading light in the founding of the Manchester Mechanics' Institute; *DNB*.

***Letter***, *from the* Manchester Examiner and Times, *25 August 1858, from "Cranberry" continuing a controversy with "Gooseberry", "Fairplay", and "Unpensioned" over the poetic accomplishment of several local "bards", whom he had earlier criticised as "windbag" poets.*

"Cranberry", I understand, is a person who has corresponded with the paper under the signature of "Pryngle Lane", or some such affected name: who he is, or what he is I know not further than that he is a writer for newspapers: nor do I know anything of the correspondents whom <u>he</u> quotes. <u>Gooseberry</u>, <u>Fairplay</u>? <u>Unpensioned</u>: the latter might almost seem to point at <u>me</u>, but I know not anything either of <u>him</u> or <u>them</u> never having felt interested in the matter.

**Friday 27th.** Dyson called at my house, he said he had been to Oldham, thence to Middleton, where hearing I was in Mosston, he came forward. He complained sadly of his neighbours at Astley, whom he described as a worthless ignorant set; he invited myself and wife to go visit him and wife, but I am not very desirous to do that. I am much inclined to doubt his having been a true friend and neighbour to me; and I am not at present inclined to recommence a familiar acquaintance with him.

**Saturday 28th.** At home all day.

**Sunday 29th.** Mills of "the Middleton Albion" came over and we had some talk about the paper. He seems wishful to sell it, or to get a company of share holders to join him, or to be enabled to get more advertisements. He discribed the people of Middleton as singularly diffused and incoherent on all public matters, whether in <u>politics</u>, <u>religion</u> or <u>towns affairs</u>; there was not any party that could be depended upon. Three Tory Magistrates had lately been appointed by a Tory underhand manoeuvre. He was invited to attend a meeting in the township of Tonge to deliberate and determine on the Magisterial selection, or rather to agree upon and prepare a memorial for such recommendation, and when he arrived at the place of meeting, he found the recommendation already agreed upon, and the memorial signed. He understood the document had been drawn up by Mr Rutter[27] at Manchester; it recommended that [James] Lees Esqr. of Alkrington Hall, The Revd. [Matthew] Lawler incumbent of Tonge,[28] and Mr Thomas Dickins,[29] silk dyer of Tonge should be appointed Magistrates, and they were; they are all Tories in principal, and      Stubbs the Guardian for Alkrington, and Stavacre,[30] the overseer are both of the like kidney.[31]

---

27. Probably W.S. Rutter (*c.* 1794–1869), Tory solicitor, and coroner of Salford Hundred 1832–69, notable for his legal challenge to the incorporation of Manchester in the early 1840s.
28. Revd Matthew Lawler (1809–60), incumbent of St Michael's Church, Tonge, JP; *Middleton Albion*, 28 April 1860.
29. Thomas Dickins (1817–95), Middleton cotton and velvet dyer (Dickins and Heywood); active JP, Chair of Salford Board of Guardians; *Manchester Guardian*, 19 January 1895. (See Plate 2.)
30. Joseph Staveacre (*c.* 1801–84), of Hall Brook, Tonge, assistant overseer, and from May 1862 improvement commissioner for Tonge, "a staunch Conservative, and a thorough Churchman"; *Middleton Albion*, 4 October 1884.
31. Three first names were left unsupplied in the original.

So much for Tory underhand contrivances; the old serpent is not dead yet. The whole of this thing appears to have been got up by Stubbs, the Guardian, Stavacre, the Overseer, and Joe Dyson, the relieving officer, acting probably under the direction of Rutter at Manchester, who again would be the puppet of some more influential person who "touched the wire, and pulled the string". The old Tories are evidently at work in covert manner.[32]

I advised Mills to canvass the town thoroughly for advertisements; to get some downright good, startling leading articles for his paper; to distribute handbills urging persons in business to advertise, and to take out his quack advertisements, and fill the space with interesting news articles.

**Letter**, *from the* Manchester Examiner and Times, *31 August 1858.*

---

### "CRANBERRY" AND OTHERS

*To the Editor of the Manchester Examiner and Times.*
Sir, – Although you have pronounced the correspondence between "Cranberry and the Bards" to be closed, I think you should in fairness permit me to state, that I have not written or dictated, or caused to be written or dictated, a single line of the correspondence; and, with the exception of "Cranberry's" two splenetic effusions, I have not seen one word of it.

An expression in "Cranberry's" last communication leads me to offer this disclaimer as an act of justice to your obedient servant,
SAMUEL BAMFORD
Moston, Harpurhey, August 30th, 1858

(We insert with pleasure Mr. Bamford's disclaimer, though we are not aware that he was suspected of having any hand in the "bardic" controversy, and the allusion in "Cranberry's" last letter had reference to another person – ED.)

---

**Wednesday 1st September.** At Middleton. Called at Mills's; Anns Grave; John Harrisons. Alice Walker will come over and see us.

Came to Grimshaws, Charles-town, where Mima was having her tea. Part of John Fords apples stolen: this is the second or third year of his apples being taken and still he leaves the remainder on the trees. Met C Delaunay, and promised to go with him and Hutchins to tea on Friday.

During conversation at Middleton, it came out that at the Horticultural Exhibition on Wakes Tuesday, a number of prizes were awarded to persons who had fraudulently exhibited articles not of their own growing; but which they had procured by purchase from other people. This, I should suppose, will put a stop to their trumpery horticultural shams. The same thing, no doubt, has been extensively practised at many of the like exhibitions in various parts of the country.

---

32. Last two sentences inserted on facing page.

**Thursday 2nd.** Received a letter from Miss Hargraves at London; and another from Mr. E.W. Binney, who has not before written to me since Augt 1857. He writes now about the dismissal of Mr Edwards[33] the Librarian at the Free Library. The details I now find in the proceedings of the Manchester City Council.

**Friday 3rd.** C. Delaunay called and I went with him to tea. Mr. and two young Delaunays. Hutchings from Manchester, Saml. Wolstencroft and self: talked about various things in old times, with Mr D, and on going away Hutchings said they (the directors of the Mechanics Institution), would give me the use of their lecture room, and the playing of the organ in! Very handsome, I thought. Wet and dark night coming home.

**Saturday 4th.** Manchester. Called on Mr Lloyd who read to me a copy of the reply he intends sending to my letter of the 20th Augt. which was satisfactory.

Mrs Hopwood, who had called on me several times in London, wanting my aid in procuring a situation for her son, entered the omnibus before it started to return. I know not what to make of her: she seems to be moving about in a very questionable manner: she last called on me at Somerset House, and was then residing in some street (lodging, as she said) in the neighbourhood of Tower hill: Now she says she is living down here, (neighbourhood of Blakeley) "until she has compleated a little business". She got out at the New Inn, and seemed to be making her way to some house in or near Barns Green, but I did not further notice her. She is living separated from her husband: and has, so she stated, a competency.

*Editorial, from the* Middleton Albion, *4 September 1858, on "Harvest Homes", praising the harvest home organised by Archdeacon Dennison at East Brent, and concluding:*

An occasional meeting of classes, upon a common footing, enables a man, by observing the conduct of those whom he is taught to look up to and respect, to elevate himself; so let us teach our agricultural servants and their families, however uneducated, by association, example and kindness, what is expected of them, and what their real duties are, and their natural perception will, we are sure, quickly point out to them the superiority in every point of view of a rationally spent harvest-home, when compared to the guzzling and demoralisation too frequently attendant on such festivals.[34]

**Monday 6th.** Met near Harperhey, Tom Barlow, a secret agent of the Police, as I believe, and also a manufacturer of and dealer in illicit spirits: he is brother to the late Jonny Barlow of Middleton; the profound villain who was once my most particular and trusted friend, and who rewarded my kindness and confidence with viperous

---

33. Edward Edwards (1812–86), library promoter and first librarian of the Manchester Free Public Library; *DNB*.

34. The sentiments here clearly parallel Bamford's own attitudes towards the reform of wakes and other traditional holidays, and especially his wish to see greater social interaction between rich and poor.

calumny. I had the curiosity to watch this Tom, and saw him go down a passage into a yard adjoining the shop of Leech the taxman and Beer seller at Barns Green; after stopping a short-time down the entry, he came out and pursued his road towards Blakeley, and at the gates leading to the farm house near the top of Valentine Brow, he disappeared, but whether he entered the farm yard, or went on the way I could not ascertain. Pretty certain however, that he was either after some secret police business, or something connected with his whiskey trade. (Coals) 2/3

**Wednesday 8th.** Went to Heywoods and found he had not sent the conditions of our agreement to be stamped. He seemed not to think the stamping necessary: said he had never been required to stamp any agreement he had made with an author. On which I offered to destroy both the agreement and copy if he would give the former to me. He s[ai]d it had best be kept and he would enquire about the stamping today. This last was in consequence of my having expressed an opinion that a fine would have been incurred if the stamping was omitted. I went to stamp office and learned that 14 days were allowed for stamping agreements, instead of three months, as I had supposed – and that to have one stamped after the expiration of 14 days would cost ten pounds: but there was not any fine for omitting to have a document stamped. Called again at Heywoods and left a note for him to the above effect. This omission to get the agreement stamped is a breach of the understanding there was betwixt us, and I don't like it: I trusted to Heywood in confidence that he would rigidly adhere to what was agreed upon and understood by both of us.[35]
    Walked back to Barns Green with Mills of the Middleton Albion.

**Thursday 9th.** There is something wrong going on betwixt Mary – our neighbour, and old Folds. She is young and inexperienced, and I must get Mrs M. to caution and advise her.
    Walked through Crumpsall and saw Old Dame Crapper in Smedley Lane.
    Stopped at Cheetham Hill, and looked at the Cottage in which Catherine[36] died: what scenes since then.[37]
    Cemetery Inn, Ashmore and two gents named Derbyshire fire-brick manufacturers. Called at New Inn and stopped too long.

**Friday 10th.** To Manchester: bought a peck and ½ of malt, and Mima brewed it.

**Saturday 11th.** Sent copy of 2nd vol to Heywood by post: also proof received this morning.
    Mr Ashmore gave me a good acc[oun]t of Mrs Hopwood. He s[ai]d her husband was in business and doing well, when took to drinking and all went to confusion. She had property derived from her own relatives on which she subsisted, and took care of her sons: he said she was a decent respectable woman, and I was glad to hear it.

---

35. Final sentence inserted by Bamford on facing page.
36. One of Bamford's early loves: see entry for 6 January 1860, and *Early Days*, 205–22, 281–7.
37. Inserted on opposite page.

**Sunday 12th.** B. Brierley called, and in afternoon we went to his house to tea.

**Monday 13th.** A long walk for health up Middleton road and past Litchford Hall: down Mwll Lane, Crab Lane head past Charters residence, but did not call. Called at John Holts to ask about his health: found he had returned home from the Infirmary – his eye cured, but sight nearly gone. Catherine: <u>my</u> <u>Cathy</u> was it seems, the aunt of Holts mother, who on one occasion would have drawn me into conversation about her, but I declined. Very hot day, but my long walk did me good, I found.

**Wednesday 15th.** To Middleton by Bus, thence walked to Bowlee through the coppice wood. The young plantations there, planted by <u>friend</u> Lord Suffield,[38] not looking so well as I expected though some fine oaks may be left standing when the other timber is cleared out: Find the little hut which used to be a hush shop shut up, desolate and in ruin. Alas the jolly bouts we used to have there – this not the hush shop where the doctor pulled Doggys neck in when it got broken in the fight with [the] poacher. Talked with several persons on Bowlee, who almost seemed to know me. Jonny Briggs dead it seemed: they knew him, "he was wildish a bit"; Jim, also, the Poacher, they knew. Children squandered. Not any allusion to Jims sad end. Did I know Jim and Jonny then? Oh aye. I knew them both very well. Then, "I'd been opoth Bowlee afore", queried a fine looking old dame smoking her pipe? "Aye mony a time. When I and Comrades used to come for shuttles to Jonty Jacksons on a Sunday morning, it was too often noon ere we returned home and more than once we had to go through the Coppy wood "i neet dark". I thought they would have called me to recollection, but none of them did, and I passed on. At "The Blue Ball" where we mostly stopped to smoke and tipple, all old things had passed away and —— Fenton who had been at the house during my sojourn at London, and who consequently, had at <u>third</u> <u>hand</u>, or should have had, all the newspapers I sent to Chartres – after the Blakeley neighbours had done with them – was gone to live at Radcliffe Bridge, and these people knew not anything about the newspapers, though they had been at the house nearly a year and a half. Chartres must therefore have been making some other hand of them during that time, at least: and I should not wonder, – considering that he has never called on me, never had, as it were the heart to "face up" – if he has been acting some underhand game towards me, in other respects besides the misuse of the papers. They were to be sent to Fentons on Bowlee for general use of the neighbours. At the Royal Oak where the doctor[39] was feasted after his capture in Simister lane, all was quiet, so I did not step in being in some haste to return to Middleton. Saw people in Boardman Lane who knew me: nearly all the old

---

38. Edward Harbord (1781–1835), 3rd Earl of Suffield, whose family were the largely absentee lords of the manor of Middleton from 1765 to 1845. Bamford loathed the tory Suffields, and had fallen out with them over various issues; see the entry for 2 October 1858, and *Some Account of Amos Ogden*.
39. Dr Joseph Healey of Middleton, one of Bamford's closest comrades in the post-Waterloo reform movement; see *An Account of the Arrest and Imprisonment of Samuel Bamford* (1817), reprinted in Chaloner, ed., *Early Days*, 330–63, and *Passages*, 31–5, 41–3, 80 (which gives an account of his capture in 1817).

one[s] gone. Stopped to speak with Wm Jones at Rhodes, and whilst doing so Bill Summerskill Lees came past on a small shabby poney gig, or car, looking much less in bulk than when last I saw him. He has been dangerously ill I understand, and let him die when he will, a bad one will leave this world. Jones wondered "what that fellow could be doing now"? I said "perhaps he was going a collecting rents" or words to that effect.

Doctor Dicken[40] was not at home, so I went on, and got to Middleton in good time for the omnibus.

Went with Mima, in the afternoon to Ann Fords at Charlestown, to tea, homely and kindest hospitality, always awaits at the humble board of these honest people. John made us accept a handkerchief full of fine apples from his own trees.

Got home at eight o'clock, rather tired with my two walks.

**Thursday 16th.** Walked with Mima to Tonge; thence through what used to be Tonge Springs to Jumbo, and to Jacksons at Station Town, or what I so name. Her likeness was taken by Photograph; a very good one and I am to go for it on friday next. Walked back to Middleton (Mima would walk) and returned by 4 o'clock omnibus. Met with Dr Dickin in the market place, who came with us in the Bus. Mima quite overcome with the heat of the day, and sickly. Coming down the brow to Blakeley an old woman who had just been knocked down by a cab and run over lay on the side of the road. Dickin examined her and found a wound on the front of one leg, but not any bones broken. She was lifted into the Bus, and conveyed to the Infirmary, where, as I find by the papers, she died the following day. Blame did not it seemed apply to the driver of the cab, who however, ought certainly not to have left her. Both Mima and myself unwell from the long walk, the heat, and not having customary refreshment at noon.

**Friday 17th.**[41] My neighbour Kenyon had placed a bundle of slabs, waste bits, which he is allowed to bring from the workplace in my coal heap, but I took them back, and declined having them, not being quite certified of his authority to bring such things away. I suppose he took this much amiss, and on Saturday, Sund. and Monday he was very unwell, and never spoke to me.

**Saturday 18th.** Finlan,[42] Clark Cropper,[43] and Bethel came as a deputation to invite me to consent to take the chair at a Chartist meeting at the Corn Exchange on the

---

40. Oswald Dickin (1805–64), long-established Middleton doctor and surgeon; *Middleton Albion*, 26 November 1864. (See Plate 2.)
41. On facing page.
42. James Finlen (or Finlan), active chartist during the 1850s; in 1856 he fell out with Ernest Jones, the leading figure in the late Chartist movement, over Finlen's attempts to revise the old Chartist newspaper, the *Northern Star*.
43. Edward Clark[e] Cropper, Manchester chartist, active from the mid-1840s, delegate to the 1852 national Chartist convention, and by this date living in Oldham; see entry for 4 September 1859.

n[igh]t of Monday week. I would not consent to take the chair, but said I would attend: they might expect my attendance life and health permitting. They had tea: and after that we went up the lane to the New Inn. Where I was so weak as to sit and take <u>three</u> glasses of whisky punch. Bethel had a printed list of contributions tow[ar]ds their meeting, as I supposed from Ivie Mackie,[44] Sir John Potter,[45] Sir Elkanah Armitage[46] and other notables of Manchester. Finlan paid for <u>two</u> glasses for me, and <u>would</u> do though I objected, and had a dislike to the treating. They stopped till nine o'clock, and then I had a difficulty in getting rid of them: they were for "seeing me home," but I insisted they should not; at last told them I would not have them: that my old woman would be gone to bed; and that we did not, and would not "keep London hours." A last I would accompany them to the toll bar on the Harperhey road, and doing so I got clear at last. Finlan I perceived was touched with the liquor he had taken. I don't like these deputations and begging of subscriptions. Expenses must come out of them, and my <u>two</u> glasses which Finlan paid for, will, I suppose, be lumped in the disbursements. This is a beggarly [way] of reviving and supporting a great Cause, like that of Parliamentary Reform.

**Sunday 19th.** Dronsfield, and a friend of his came over before I was out of bed. Talked about sad end of Princes wife at Ashton,[47] and the very inconclusive evidence which appears to have been given at the Inquest: of Waugh,[48] and his song "Come Whoam to thy Childer an Me" whilst his wife and children were at the very time in Marland Workhouse, and he was living with another woman in Strangeways: this was rank hypocrisy and astounding impudence. Dronsfield said if B. Brierley put confidence in Waugh, he would betray him, as soon as it suited his convenience to do so.

   Dronsfield wants a party to meet, and we are to make a preliminary arrangement of the matter. John and Robert Pearson from Middleton came over, and I wrote for them a note to the Editor of the Guardian for advice.

**Saturday 25th.** Received a letter from Brierley requesting me to go down and spend the evening. Attended, and went with him to Cloggers Arms. One of the Barns's singing a sleepy humdrum song. Argument on supply and demand followed, heard more real, thoughtful expression in the course of half an hour, than I had done amongst working men at London during seven years. Brierley sung, "The gloomy

---

44. Ivie Mackie (1805–73), self-made wine merchant, Scot, living in Manchester from 1842, city councillor 1847–68, mayor 1857–60; MCL.

45. Sir John Potter (1815–58), cotton spinner, Liberal, Unitarian, eldest son of Sir Thomas Potter, mayor, 1848–51, MP for Manchester, 1857–8; MCL.

46. Sir Elkanah Armitage (1794–1876), Pendleton cotton master, Liberal, mayor of Manchester 1846–8; MCL.

47. That is, the wife of John Critchley Prince (1808–66), reedmaker and Lancashire poet; *DNB*.

48. Edwin Waugh (1817–90), dialect writer and leading figure of the Manchester literary scene. His dialect poem, "Come Whoam to thi Childer an me", a wife's appeal to her drunken husband, published in 1856, established his reputation; *DNB* and M. Vicinus, *Edwin Waugh* (1984). (See Plate 1.)

night" of Burns:[49] a gloomy affair indeed. El[ijah] Ridings,[50] the spunging old humbug, made his appearance, uttered some frothy tautological rubbish, and we came away. Mima had followed to Brierleys, so about eleven o'clock we returned home,[51] B accompanying us to Harperhey.

**Monday 27th.** Mr Livsey[52] from Bury came to see me: on what account I dont know, as he did not say why, only because "I was an old acquaintance", and a staunch reformer. I could not but suspect however, that something else was in view. Went with him to Barns Green thence to Crab lane head and down to three arrows from whence I walked to Middleton, and so home by Omnibus.

**Wednesday 29th.** At home writing. B. Brierley came in evening, and whilst we sat talking Mr H. Gibson[53] and C.L. Delaunay came in. They talked about my books: how well they would do if published with illustrations. Gibson mentioned several objects at Middleton which would be quite suitable for wood cuts; talked about Mechanics Institutions: my lecturing, and various other matters. Mr Delauney wished me to attend at the Institution, Blakeley, on Friday night, and I promised. They two went away, and Brierley soon after followed.

I see by placards there is to be a grand inauguration of the Mechanics Institution at Harperhey on Saturday evening: Thos Bazley Esqr in the chair; and "several influential gentlemen are expected to attend."

**Friday 1st October.** Went to Middleton to see a proof of my letter to the Middleton Albion, on Mechanics Institutions. Saw a proof and corrected it. At night attended at the Blakeley institution where I offered several suggestions for its improvement: well received, and a vote of thanks passed.

**Saturday 2nd.** Attended by invitation at the opening of the new Mechanics Institution at Harperhey, very well received by the chairman and directors: repeated my suggestions made at Blakeley, and afterwards read "A Stranger in Lancashire," from my Walks, which caused much amusement.

---

49. A poem of landscape and loss; see Burns' *Collected Works*, ed J. Cairney (1995), 372:

> Farewell, old Coila' hills and dales
> Her healthy moors and winding dales
> The scenes where wretched fancy roves
> Pursuing past unhappy loves!
> Farewell my friends! Farewell my foes!
> My peace with these, my love with those –
> The bursting tears my heart declare
> Farewell, my bonnie banks of Ayr.

50. Elijah Ridings (1802–72), Manchester working-class poet, weaver and bookseller, Peterloo veteran, anti-corn law campaigner and Chartist; *Manchester Guardian*, 19 October 1872.
51. Bamford originally wrote "we came away".
52. James Livesey, see circular, entry for 16 October 1858.
53. Henry Gibson, attorney, see entry for 7 October 1858.

Being hot when I came out of the room went and sat down in Ashworths parlour with C. Delaunay and B. Brierley: and came home after twelve o'clock.

Sat 2d. The following letter appears in the Middleton Albion of this day.[54]

**Letter**, *from the* Middleton Albion, *2 October 1858*.

---

*To the Editor of the Middleton Albion*

Sir, – Agreeing with the general tenor of your excellent leading article of last week, I fully coincide with your conclusion, that "Mechanics' Institutes are failures," and, "are not supported by mechanics." The first and greatest error commences with their very foundation; they are, with but few exceptions, originated and promoted by individuals who, with the best intentions, are sadly ignorant of the business they take in hand. 'The consequence' is as you state, that, 'they fall into the most pernicious error. They load the shelves of their reading rooms with books admirable in *their way*, but totally miscalculated for exciting a taste for reading in those for whom they are intended.' A case illustrative of this I have recently found among my papers; it is an extract from an article furnished by me to the *Manchester Guardian* of December 1st, 1849, wherein, under the head, "A glance at some Mechanics' Institutions," it states that 'about the year 1825 a few working men resolved to endeavour to found a mechanics institution at Middleton; that they collected what books they could amongst themselves, and shortly after received a considerable present of books from friends in London; that they took a room, and *opened it gratis to the public once a week*, when *select passages were read from useful* and *interesting works*, and discussions thereupon ensued.' The article then goes on to the state that the third Lord Suffield, having contributed £25 to the funds of the institution, and many books having been purchased with his money, a *veto* was given him on the books which were to be admitted, that his lordship might know that his donation had not been misapplied; that '*the great difficulty of the committee was to find out and promote a taste for reading at all*; and the first batch of books were selected chiefly with a view to that end; that the weekly readings, which had been well attended, were by his lordship's desire discontinued; and the institution became a more close, quiet, and orderly concern than heretofore, but its vitality seemed to be tamed also." Here you are, the institution went on very well, it prospered and gained strength whilst the room was thrown open once a week, whilst useful and interesting extracts were read to the public and discussions thereupon were allowed; but when this mentally animating and rational exercise of thought was put a stop to, the concern languished; and I may add, for I was one of the founders, and am the only one surviving, that the ownership of the books was afterwards, at the instance of two of the original trustees, thrown open to anyone paying a penny a week; that the chartists then got possession of the library, and they afterwards quarrelling among themselves, the books were at length divided and appropriated by a few of the members, and have not, so far as my knowledge extends, ever been heard of since. and thus disappeared the first mechanics' institution founded at Middleton.

---

54. This sentence and cutting inserted opposite.

Had the few working men who commenced this undertaking been kept to themselves they would, in all probability, have given it a long continued existence, they tried to excite *a taste for book amusement* in the first place, by publicly reading, according to their several abilities, extracts from interesting publications; and these readings, whilst they excited the attentions and awakened the feelings of the auditors, tended to improve their own capacity for such exercises. Apt remarks frequently ensued, which led to replies; nor were homely wit, smart repartee of good tempered and enjoyable mirth, though sometimes a little boisterous, discountenanced. These readings, in fact were occasions for *entertainment* as well as *instruction*; and their recurrence was becoming a matter of weekly pleasurable anticipation. True, we sometimes took passages for reading which tended *not* to the *honour* of tyrants and oppressors, but which disrobed them of tinsel and ermine; which combated *wrong* in every direction, and which supported *right*, however humbly it was impersonated. Such was the course we had marked out, which was not altogether approved of by our well meaning superiors, which mechanics' institutions are not allowed now to pursue, which institutions do *not* afford the requisite mental inducement to mechanics; which institutions also do *not* embrace very many of the opportunities and means which lie within their reach, and which are, although mechanics institutions in name, not in reality, supported by mechanics – I am, sir, your obedient servant,
SAMUEL BAMFORD.
Mosston Dale, Harperhey, 20th September, 1858.

---

**Sunday 3rd.** Dronsfield and three of his friends called in the evening: read them some passages from Tennysons[55] poems: after which they went forward to Brierleys.

Brierley had been up in the morning talking about last nights performances, for <u>he</u> also had recited a piece.

**Monday 4th.** The following article appears in the Examiner and Times (Manch[r]) The following notice only, appears with reference to me, in the report of the Harperhey inauguration. It is scarcely just, as I was received with marked applause, both whilst speaking and reading: <u>Exam[r] and Times</u> Oct 4th.[56]

***Report****, from the* Manchester Examiner and Times, *4 November 1858: a very brief account of the meeting, noting that it was "addressed by Mr. Samuel Bamford, the veteran author of "Passages from the Life of a Radical" (who offered some practical suggestions for the improvement and popularising of mechanics' institutions)".*

The "practical suggestions," certainly the few things I uttered, are either by the indolent reporters or the sagacious Editor consigned to limbo: the reason perhaps is that they appear in another part of the paper, see "<u>Blackley</u> <u>Mechanics</u> <u>Institution</u>".

---

55. Alfred, Lord Tennyson (1809–92), the poet laureate from 1850, and author of much of the era's most important poetry, including *In Memoriam* (1850), and *Idylls of the King* (1859); he was perhaps second to Burns in Bamford's favour as a poet; *DNB*.

56. Final two sentences, the cutting and the following sentence inserted on facing page.

*Report*, *from the* Manchester Examiner and Times, *4 October 1858.*

---

## BLACKLEY MECHANICS' INSTITUTION

At a general meeting of the members of the above institution, on Friday night, a paper was read on "The failures of mechanics' institutions, and the causes of such failures," which the paper imputed to the injudicious selection of publications by the directors, and the consequent indifference and non-attendance of the working classes. Mr. Samuel Bamford said the cause of failure lay either with the working classes or the institutions, or with both; if with the former, much might be said in excuse of them; but, believing, as he did, that the institutions themselves were not made so available for usefulness as they might be, and as they ought to be, he would offer a few suggestions for their improvement. He had thought often and long on the subject, and could not help being struck by the inefficiency and incompleteness which the management of such undertakings generally exhibited. It was not the providing of a room, nor the placing on its tables books and newspapers, that would set up and establish in prosperity a mechanics' institution. These things were good in their own way, but the working classes required inducements more in accordance with their material capacities and acquirements. He was convinced that a wide sphere of attraction was at the command of such institutions if they would only avail themselves of it. Under such persuasion, he would submit for their consideration some suggestions, which he believed, if adopted and carried into effect by the members of this institution, or of any other, would cause a great and beneficial change in its condition and future prospects. In the first place, he would propose that public readings, free of any charge, should once a week be given. He would throw open the doors and invite the neighbours and inhabitants generally to attend and partake of the amusement. This might in many instances create a taste for book amusement where it never before existed. Seeing what good things books contained persons hitherto indifferent to them might be led to read for themselves, whilst, at the same time, it would be a means for improving the person who read. The reading should be done by members, some of the most apt readers being selected; and if they were not faultless in their first efforts, successive exercises, and hearing others more correctly read, would tend greatly to their improvement; thus, such readings would benefit both the readers and the listeners; and drawing attention from without the institution, they would increase the number of members and enlarge the amount of their funds. Secondly, he would propose that frequent readings and recitations should take place amongst the members themselves. Romance, history, biography, poetry, might be successively quoted, and this exercise would give the readers ease and facility of expression, whilst it would prepare them for exhibitions before the public. Thirdly, he would propose that appointed discussion should frequently take place. Night schools for reading, writing, arithmetic, grammar, and geography, he would also propose. The establishment of vocal and instrumental music classes he thought would also be beneficial. Frequent excursions on foot by the members to neighbouring localities he would also suggest; and in these excursions knowledge of botany and geology might be cultivated. At wakes and times of general holiday mechanics' institutions should promote athletic exercises, also music, dancing parties, and processions, and general renewals of friendly customs and observances. On all occasions the members of Mechanics' Institutions should cultivate most kindly feelings amongst each other; they should seek to gain respect for themselves by respectful demeanour to all with whom they associated or communicated; they should be to each other as brothers and true Christian friends, sympathising with, and assisting the unfortunate and afflicted; rejoicing with brother members in their prosperity and happiness. And throughout life cultivating truthful, honourable, and respectful intercourse with all their acquaintance of the human race. The address was received with applause; warm commendations by the chairman and several members followed, and a unanimous vote of thanks was passed. Some discussion ensued, and ultimately it was agreed as a beginning that a public reading should shortly take place, Mr. Bamford consenting to be the reader for the first night.

---

The Comet very visible, with a star (Venus) seen through the light, near the head of it: the Comet looks like a world on fire: tail an immense length.

**Thursday 7th.** Took in my acc[oun]t with Heywood, who paid, and was seemingly in a sullen and distant mood: which mood, if he knew how exceedingly indifferent I felt about either himself or his airs, he would scarcely take the trouble to exhibit.

Fell in with Mr Gibson Att[orne]y, and after buying two New Testaments, one the Roman Catholic version, and the other the Protestant one, we went to a tavern and had a glass of toddy each, then came home in the 'bus.

**Saturday 9th.** Went to Manchester and saw Hutchings at the Mechanics Institution, who lent me a copy of Tennysons Poems, his own copy, and "The Princess," and "In Memoriam," out of the Institutional library. He also invited me to frequent the news and reading room whenever it suited my convenience. He also desired me to write my name on the title page: it was his wifes book, he said, and she would be pleased. I gave my anagram which will surely do.

**Sunday 10th.** At home, a very wet stormy day: as Milton says,
                      "Wet Octobers torrent flood"[57]
He took correct note of times and seasons.

**Monday 11th.** A rather damp morning but well enough for a walk, so I started for Jacksons at Jumbo, or rather at "Station town," to look after my wifes picture. Stopping on the top of Tonge Springs to examine a heap of gravel where I had before picked up a curious stone or two, someone tapped me on the shoulder. It was Mr Livsey from Bury who had been at my house and had followed and found me thus occupied. I returned with him down to Middleton and we sat down at the Asshtons Arms, where over a glass of whisky toddy, (I cant drink ale, house ale, my wifes brewing has spoiled me for that) we talked over the business he was come about, which was to deliver a formal invitation to dine with a party of friends at Bury, the time was to be on the 28th inst. and the place, the Albion

---

57. From Milton's "A Maske Performed before the President of Wales at Ludlow" (1634).

Hotel. Mr Wrigley of Bridge Hall Mills,[58] and the Grundys, sons of /late\ Edmund of Park Hills, whom I once reckoned amongst my friends, but whom, during some eight or ten years I had lost both sight and hearing of, were to be of the party: so putting aside all retaliation of their late coldness, I promised to attend and meet them. Livsey said something also about some one of the party having an idea of asking Charles Swain[59] "to meet me," a thing which I did not encourage at all: though I did not intimate that it would be distasteful to me. I rather considered it to be a matter to be settled amongst themselves though I did not suppose that Charles Swain would accord with the political feelings which would be exchanged: he would in fact be entirely out of place, and I did not think he would attend.

Livsey took his way up Middleton towards Heywood, and I went to Jumbo. Sat for a stereoscopic likeness of myself.

Made an agreement with Jacksons to furnish me with photographic portraits of myself, for the forthcoming edition of my "Life of a Radical", should Heywood decline to publish an engraved portrait about which I have not heard anything yet; and very likely therefore he wont. Single portraits to be charged to me at 6d each, and stereoscopic ones at 1/- the couple.[60]

Brought away my wifes likeness, a rather good one, and, when I asked how the acc[oun]t stood betwixt them and myself was informed they had not any account against me.

I think they must have done well with my portrait, or they would not have been thus satisfied.

Came to Middleton, and after hobnobbing with Rev Clarke, Dr. Liddle (whose manner as usual, much amused me) I returned by the omnibus.

Called the New Inn, Mrs Wilkinsons where, there being a rather full bar, I proposed a memorial to the Post Master General for a letter box, or pillar, which being instantly adopted, I undertook to write the memorial.

**Thursday 14th.** Took back to the Mechanics Institution, David Street, Tennysons Poems, (Mr Hutchings copy) and "The Princess." Bought a New Testament. Called at Peats, and after getting two quarts of mussles came home.

**Friday 15th.** Went down to the Institution at Blakeley expecting to find a meeting of members and to pay my money, but except three or four reading no one was there: the meeting had been put off; no books, no one to render an account, and so almost disgusted I came away.

**Saturday 16th.** Fell in with a man at Harperhey who gave me a sad account of the way in which accounts are kept, and money matters settled at the Blakeley Institution. I must enquire further.

---

58. Thomas Wrigley (1808–80), reputedly the largest paper manufacturer in England, see entry for 29 October 1858; Boase.
59. Charles Swain (1801–74), Manchester Poet; significantly awarded a civil list pension of £50 in December 1856; *DNB*. (See Plate 1.)
60. See Plate 5.

**Cutting**, *from the* Manchester Weekly Times, *16 October 1858.*

---

### A REAL AND ORIGINAL "COME WHOAM TO THI CHILDER AN' ME"

The following is a literal and verbal copy of a letter which, was sent by "Jonny," a silk weaver, then residing on Bowlee, to his wife, who, in consequence of a disagreement, during one of his "fuddling bouts," wherein she received "a tup or two," packed up her "duds," and went to her relatives in Alkrington, leaving "Jonny" to take care of himself and three children: – "Mi Hever Deer Betty, I send yu theese fu lines hoppin the wil find yu in good elth has the leave mie hat pressint, exceptin won hor too pints of hale, which I av ad whith Hedmun; un won hor too moor this hafternuon, hat Jacks an Billy Meddocroft has rites this. Mi Hever Deer an deerist whife, I shanno hav mitch drink, for to tel the thruth, I conno drink we theaw hart from wom, for ov no stummick for nothin, an I conno hate nothin has I shud like to doo, an I conno sleep at neet my feet har so kowd, mi yed his so wot, and mi hart warches has iv it wud braste. Mi deer Betty the chilther har shrikin for thur mam, an iv theawl kom wom, theaw shal liv I futhur, as weel as to kud wish; theaw shal go to bed wen theaws a mind, and get hop wen theaws a mind; theaw shal have a glas o rum hevery moring o the life, or a glas o' gin other; an Ile wurtch like a slave to keep thee an the chilther kumfurthobble; an theaw shal hav a nu bonnit bowt hat Fieldins, an a new geawn, an a nu kirtle an nu shoon, o agen the klub dey. So prithee deer whife kom whom, an dunno make no moor nonsense obeawt hit; an iv hever I sthrike thee ogen, or have a finger at the, Ile sine a stampt papper at Ile be willin to goo to prissun for hit. Mi deer tak theese things into konsitherashun; an pak hop thi klooas, an lyev yore foke, for theawl find nobbodde attle doo has weel for thee has thi hone haffectionhate usban, JOHN ———" –

The letter was sealed and dispatched by a trusty messenger, and the result was, that Betty packed up her "klooas" and shortly afterwards arrived at home, when the poor "skrikin chilther" were comforted, their tearful eyes were wiped with motherly tenderness, whilst mother herself was in tears. "Jonny," half maudlin with "another pint," cried also; but ere long the fire was new kindled, the hearth was swept, the house put in comfortable trim; the young ones were suppered and sent to bed; and though "Jonny" had now and then his "bouts" and would have, he was ever afterwards an amended husband.

---

The above appeared in the Manchester Weekly Times of Sat. Oct. 16 1858, taken from my original and written about twenty years before by my self, the man being Jonny Briggs. B

**Sunday 17th.** Robert Fitton,[61] with his wife and girl called to see us at dark: also C.L. Delaunay and Mr H. Gibson stepped in the latter showing me a book with a wood cut frontspiece of Bewick the Artist[62] and wanting me to have my forthcoming Radical embellished in a similar manner, but I declined: he asked would I consent to his calling

---

61. Possibly Robert ("old Bob") Fitton, master cotton spinner of Shaw; see George Richardson, *Biographical Sketch of the life of the late Robert Fitton, Cotton Spinner, etc, of Shaw Lodge, near Oldham* (1878).
62. Thomas Bewick (1753–1828), Newcastle wood engraver and radical; *DNB*.

on Heywood, the publisher to induce him to the same course, but I said he had better not, but leave it to be arranged by me. I thought this interference scarcely proper.

**Monday 18th.** Received a circular and a card for the "Bamford dinner" at Bury, on the 28th inst. I scarcely know how I can go: I shall want a new coat, and I can very ill afford one.

*Letter, J. Livesey, Bury, to Bamford, 18 October 1858, on a circular invitation from Joseph Chattwood[63] to a dinner for Samuel Bamford, the "Veteran Lancashire Worthy", at the Albion Hotel, Bury, on 28 October (price 3s 6d), together with a ticket for the event.*[64]

Dear Sir,
I only send you this to show you the way the business has been conducted.
I am Dear Sir yours truly.
James Livesey.

**Tuesday 19th.** The Manchester Guardian has the following, which is an extract from the speech of the Earl of Carlisle at the Distribution of "The Mechanics Institute and the Society of Arts Certificates" on Monday 18th Oct – 58 = Guard. Oct 19th.

*Cutting, from the Manchester Guardian, 19 October 1858, giving an extract from the Earl of Carlisle's speech on mechanics' institutes, urging that they be made "more attractive and amusing ... and cosy" in order to encourage "social intercourse".*

Had his lordship seen my address to the "Blakeley Mechanics Institution" in the Examiner and Times of Oct 4th. does any one think? The Editor says

*Extract from an editorial,* Manchester Guardian, *19 October 1858, noting that "Following up a suggestion, made by one of the directors of the institution, the Earl hinted that in order to make Mechanics' Institutes more popular, we must first make them more attractive."*[65]

How very enlightened these Earls and Editors have become. The Editor also says in his leading article,

*Extract, from the same editorial, commenting: "these Institutes have been exteriorly and interiorly too imposing to suit the humble circumstances of those for whom they were intended ... Nothing can be better than the proposal to hold numerous social meetings during the year, and encourage the members to enjoy themselves and form friendships with one another."*[66]

---

63. Joseph Chattwood (d. 1875), Bury and later Manchester solicitor, active member of the Manchester Literary Club; MCL. (See Plate 1.)
64. See Plate 12.
65. Bamford's emphasis.
66. Bamford's emphasis.

Whilst the Earl of Carlisle was distributing certificates of merit, might he not have given one to the humble "Lancashire weaver" who furnished him with some good ideas for his speech?

**Wednesday 20th.** Took back Tennysons "Maude" and "In Memoriam" to the Institute. Had half a glass of ale with Hutchins, who annoyed me, by an introduction to a gentleman who came in. I hate these impromptu introductions. Higginson of Blakeley, did the same, the impudent little monkey, whilst waiting for the omnibus in High Street.

**Friday 22nd.** The Guardian of this day in leading article on the Athenaeum <u>Soiree</u> of yesternight, concludes with the following passage.

***Extract*** *from an Editorial,* Manchester Guardian, *22 October 1858, suggesting that the Manchester Athenaeum should organise social gatherings, and capitalise on the talents of the members themselves, rather than being "entirely dependent for social and literary culture on indifferent strangers".*

The very advice I gave the members of the Blakeley Institute: <u>See</u> <u>article</u> <u>in</u> <u>this</u> <u>Diary,</u> <u>Monday</u> 4th Oct.
   Mark Smith from Heywood called.

**Sunday 24th.** B. Brierley called in the morning.
   Afternoon. Mills of Middleton, Ridings, Allan Mellor,[67] called. Also C.L. Delaunay.[68]

**Tuesday 26th.** Ordered a new coat at Peacocks in St Anns Square, though I could very ill afford the outlay, but I thought my friends at Bury should not be ashamed of my outward appearance.

**Thursday 28th.** My coat came home, and it is not to my satisfaction: spoiled in the laps: cost £3.6.6. net money: a jogger to my purse.
   Took the Bus at Hydes Cross; Livesey, Chatwood, and Crompton[69] met me at Whitefield, conducted me to the Albion when I learned for the first time that Waugh from Manchester was to be one of the party, an arrangement of which, had I been consulted – as I ought to have been, I never should have assented. My reception was most kind, the table well set out, the company very respectable, and more numerous than I had anticipated. The evening was spent very agreeably, and on my health being given, I spoke, and read from notes as follows. (See other side)[70]

---

67. Allen Mellor (1834–88), of Middleton Junction. Senior manager at Firwood Mills, Mill Hill, for James Cheetham, prominent local Liberal and patron of the arts and literature; *Middleton Guardian,* 24 November 1888.
68. Bamford has deleted "and at night Dronsfield and".
69. Tom Crompton of Bury; see entry for 8 December 1859.
70. There are pin marks in the diary here, but the item is missing.

**Friday 29th.** Went with Mr Chatwood[,] Waugh and Hardwick[71] to view the works of Mr Wrigley at Bridge Hall Mills, the largest paper Manufactory in England so we were informed. Most excellent arrangement: Everything in exact working order, and I came away greatly pleased by what I had seen, excepting a number of young women who were engaged in cleaning rags and waste previous to their being thrown into the vat, the employment appeared to be deteriorative of health from the dirt, and the dust flying about: the females however did not appear sickly, but smutty and soiled and I thought the tainted air they breathed must eventually affect their constitutions.

Mr Edwin Wrigley conducted us through the works, and after signing the book in the lodge, we, by Mr Chatwoods persuasion took a ramble to the hills of Birkle – a very silly ramble as I thought at the time; yet I suffered myself to be persuaded, a weakness – that of being persuaded against my own commonsense – of which I will endeavour to be less frequently guilty than I have hitherto been. We certainly got a good lunch of fried ham and eggs at a public house, at Carr, and then went over the hills to Bury, but what a traunce, to come all this way to eat ham, to see stone quarries, and Birkle chapel – a pretty little building certainly – and so return to Bury, a little jaded, and not much wiser than [when] we went.

A reporter from the "Bury Times" came to the hotel, and from Mr Chatwoods dictation took down a report of last nights proceeding, but so brief – and to me unsatisfactory, that I afterwards sent word desiring him not to forward it to the Manchester papers, which however, it would seem he did.

Came back with Waugh and Hardwick by Omnibus, and arrived at home a little after nine o'clock.

**Saturday 30th.** Not a word about the dinner in the Manchester papers: so I am satisfied the reporter has obeyed my instructions, not to send any notice.

**Sunday 31st.** Dronsfield and        [72] from Hollinwood at my house, came to arrange about their forthcoming social gathering, and I promised to attend.

Went at night to Manchester, and left copies of my address at Bury with Peacock[73] of the Examiner, and with a clerk at the Guardian Offices.

---

71. Charles Hardwick (1817–89), man of letters, editor, lecturer; in 1857 elected Grand Master of the Manchester Order of Oddfellowship, editing the *Oddfellows Magazine*, 1862-8, one of founders and stalwarts of the Manchester Literary Club; *DNB*, *Manchester City News*, 13 July 1889.

72. Gap in the original.

73. Henry B. Peacock (dates not known), journalist with *Manchester Examiner and Times*, later editor of the *Manchester Weekly Times*.

## 2

# THE OLD RADICAL

*On 28 October Bamford had spoken at the reform banquet at Bury, an event which heralded an attempt to re-establish himself as a public advocate for parliamentary reform as well as a literary figure. Bamford's concern about the newspaper coverage of his contribution, and his energetic efforts to secure the publication of the full text of his speech, were typical of his attempts to actively manage his public profile from this point onwards. As 1858 drew to a close the question of reform had again become a live political issue, with the fall of the Palmerston government and its replacement with a minority Conservative government headed by the Earl of Derby and Benjamin Disraeli. John Bright led radical liberals in a campaign for a substantial measure of reform short of manhood suffrage, while the government introduced its own, extremely limited, reform bill. Bamford was quickly drawn into the renewed campaigns, advocating manhood suffrage in principle but willing in practice to support any step towards it. This might have provided a firm foundation for his attempt to develop a remunerative career as a reader and reciter, and he gambled on holding his first major public reading in Manchester itself – a city whose public he both feared and needed. It was a near-disaster, attracting only a sparse attendance and raising for Bamford the spectres of poverty and want. After this, the heart-warming success of a dinner in his honour in Middleton at the start of January provided a tremendous boost, especially when followed by a meeting in Oldham at which he was heartily cheered. Even so, there was no great surge of interest in his readings, and by the end of February his correspondence was again hinting at anxiety as to the future.*

**Monday 1st November.** The following verbatim copy of the reporters notes at Bury, appears at the foot of the <u>last</u> column of <u>news</u> in the Manchester Guardian: <u>At</u> the <u>foot</u> of the column!! that is one of the many shabby ways in which "gentlemen of the press" know how to cold shoulder any one who is too independent to succumb to their influence. <u>Friend Harland,</u>[1] I thank for this piece of shabby spite.

***Report**, from the* Manchester Guardian, *1 November 1858, giving a brief account of the dinner to Bamford at the Albion Hotel, Bury, attended by "nearly 40 of the friends and admirers of Mr Samuel Bamford ... Mr Bamford gave a sketch of the progress and present position of Parliamentary reform", and there were contributions from Edwin Waugh, Charles Hardwick and Thomas Wrigley.*

Saw Mr Garnett about the insertion of my address, who will give answer tomorrow.

**Tuesday 2nd.** Mr Garnett declines to insert my address, combatting as strongly as unreason can, against my inference that because the property qualification is removed, manhood suffrage is conceded in principle. Peacock tells me it will appear in the Examiner.

---

1. John Harland (1806–68), long-time head reporter on the *Manchester Guardian* (retiring December 1860), antiquarian, literary figure, and acquaintance and correspondent of Bamford's; *DNB*. (See Plate 1.)

**Wednesday 3rd.** The Examiner gives my address at length; an adoption which I certainly did not expect so readily. Went to Middleton and saw Mills, who will give it in his Albion. Paid Smethurst for coals.

Called to see C. Delaunay: and the reading at the Institute was put off. Gin and water, which I don't like.

**Thursday 4th.** Went to Manchester: called and paid Peacock the balance of his note, 6/6.

**Friday 5th.** The Manchester Examiner of this day, in giving an account of Mr Bazleys address to the electors of the Collegiate Church Ward, has the following passage.

*Cutting, from the* Manchester Examiner and Times, *5 November 1858, reporting Bazley's pledge to, if requested, make an annual account of his activities as MP to his constituents, and resign if his general conduct was found unsatisfactory.*

It is, no doubt a response to my enquiry at Bury, and has been caused thus promptly by the appearance of my address in the Examiner and Times. Both Manchester and Oldham, have now, so far as Mr Bazley is concerned, annual Parliaments, or their equivalent.

It would appear as if my address, which appeared in the Manchester paper on Wednesday, and would be read in London the same night had startled the Roebuck party of reformers,[2] for on Thursday a meeting was held, the proceedings of which are reported as follows, in the Guardian of this day.

*Report, from the* Manchester Guardian, *5 November 1858, of a meeting of supporters of Parliamentary Reform at the Guildhall Coffee House, London. John Bright was nominated to bring in a reform bill which would include both an extension of the franchise and a substantial redistribution of seats. An amendment in favour of manhood suffrage was defeated leaving the extent of the suffrage to be determined by the framers of the bill. Thomas Bazley sent his apologies.*

The same day. – the day after the appearance of my address the Oldham Reform Association also met and are reported as follows in the Saturdays Guardian.[3]

*Report, from the* Manchester Guardian, *6 November 1858, of a reform meeting at Oldham, with a number of short speeches on the question of reform. Many speakers favoured waiving the question for the next Parliamentary session rather than have an unsatisfactory measure passed, "and the necessity of all classes of reformers uniting was dwelt upon forcibly".*

---

2. John Arthur Roebuck (1801–79), radical MP for Bath, and then Sheffield, 1849–79, increasingly seen as a renegade to radicalism; *DNB*.
3. Entry and cutting inserted opposite.

**Saturday 6th.** My address as it appears under the date, Wed 3d.[4] was given in the Middleton Albion. I had been over and corrected the proof.[5]

Our Social Meeting at Hollinwood went off very well. Self, Rogerson B. Brierley, Jas Greaves, Allan Mellor, Dronsfield, Collin,[6] Fletcher attended, about 100 in company all very cheerful and agreeable. Other meetings will probably follow, they all seemed so well pleased with this.

Waugh, Peacock, Prince and E. Ridings absent, for which I was not sorry.

Collin sung an excellent song. I must get a copy of it. Arrived at home at 2 a.m.

**Sunday 7th.** At home all day unwell: My Bury address in Weekly Times, Middleton Albion, and Oldham Advertiser, so that has had a circulation wide enough.

**Monday 8th.** Still not well: Went to Manchester, and on my return, Mrs N. my sisters daughter here. Who <u>not</u> having heard of my dining at Bury, or seen my address in the papers, as she pretended, I let go away as wise as she came in that respect. Mima had blabbed the thing before I came and Mrs. N. wanted to see a paper: no doubt she knew all about it, but wanted to mistify us, so I let her go as aforesaid.

**Tuesday 9th.** Received an invitation to attend a lecture at the Literary Institute, Middleton: the letter had been posted at Middleton on Saturday. but being directed Moston Lane, only had been delivered at Newton Heath, and did not come to hand until a day too late.

The following appears in the Examiner and Times of this day.

**Letter**, *from the* Manchester Examiner and Times, *9 November 1858.*

---

### REFORM MARTYRS

*To the Editor of the Examiner and Times*
Sir, – Is not Mr. Bamford wrong in his statement that he is the only surviving radical who suffered imprisonment for the reform doctrines, written on the banners of Peterloo? I know of four now living in Manchester and its neighbourhood who were incarcerated, – I am yours, a friend of one, called
TOMMY THE BAKER

---

I reply as follows.

**Copy letter**, *Bamford to Editor,* Manchester Examiner and Times, *9 November 1858.*

---

4. That is, the report referred to in the entry for the 3rd.
5. This address is not pasted into the diary; for the text, see Appendix 2.
6. Probably Samuel Collins (1802–78), the Lancashire poet; see entry for 2 March 1859.

## Reform Martyrs

*To the Editor, Manchester Examiner and Times*

Sir, <u>Tommy</u> the <u>Baker</u>, cannot have understood what he was writing about. Mr Bamford never has said that "he was the only surviving Radical who suffered imprisonment for the reform doctrines inscribed on the banners at Peterloo". What he did say, was that "he was the last of the prisoners of 1817, and 1819 consecutively", or, on both occasions.

One of the prisoners of 1817 is living at Rochdale: and in Manchester and other places there may be several of the latter date, but Mr Bamford is the only person living who was imprisoned at both dates, in 1817, when the *habeus corpus* Act was suspended, and in 1819 for attending the Meeting on Saint Peters field. I may as well state, that for peacefully and constitutionally promoting parliamentary reform, and Free Trade, he has been confined in a greater number of prisons than any other Englishman living.

Yours respectfully,<br>Corrector.

9th Nov. 1858.

**Wednesday 10th.** The following appears in the Examiner and Times.

**Letter**, *from the* Manchester Examiner and Times, *10 November 1858.*

---

### PARLIAMENTARY REFORM.

*To the Editor of the Examiner and Times.*

Sir, – I see by your paper of this day that a meeting of the electors and non-electors of Manchester is to be held in the Free-trade Hall, on the night of Friday next, to consider the important question of parliamentary reform.

I sincerely wish the citizens may come together prepared to debate calmly and temperately, when debate is required, and to decide justly and wisely, on such questions as they may have to determine. At the present eventful period, not less than at Trafalgar, England has a right to expect that "every man will do his duty;" and as one effort towards the common endeavour, I will, with your permission, offer a few ideas for the consideration of all whom they may concern.

1. Would not all the good of annual parliaments be obtained, if representatives stood pledged to render an account of their parliamentary stewardship at the end of every session, and to retire, should their conduct not have been satisfactory to their constituents? Mr. Bazley gave these pledges at the meeting of electors for the Collegiate Church ward; so far as he is concerned, therefore, when he is returned – and that is all but accomplished – Manchester will have decided its own duration of membership, by annual accountability and annual liability. Might not similar pledges be obtained from the present honourable member? And then the contract would be complete. The voters of Salford might probably exercise similar influence with their representative; those of Bolton, Stockport, Ashton, Rochdale, and Bury might perhaps do the same. We should then have, in South Lancashire, a compact lot of constituencies, deriving all the benefits of annual elections, without their disadvantages; and that would be a good beginning for a national change.

2. The property qualification having been annulled during the last session of parliament, the poorest honest man of the community is eligible to sit as member; and can so monstrous an absurdity be persisted in; as that he shall be qualified to make laws, and not qualified to vote at the election of those who make them? The poorest man must have the franchise given him; it cannot long be otherwise; the thing will be so palpably, so uselessly unjust, that it cannot be persisted in, and manhood suffrage must take its place.

3. Previous to this, or indeed to any considerable addition of voters, would it not be well to provide for them the security of the ballot?

4. Adjustment of representation to population is requisite; it would, however, involve a large amount of detail and arrangement, and would probably not be completed in one or even two sessions. Meantime the ballot should be brought into operation. Manhood suffrage cannot be long denied; it is inevitable; and all the benefits which annual parliaments would confer may be had when the voters require them. Payment of members is optional with constituencies, any day or any hour.

Such is the view I take of parliamentary reform, as it at present stands: Mr. Bright, and the gentlemen of the reform committee at London seem to have adopted a different theory. With them I would not dispute about matters of mere detail. If they can't, or won't, act on opinions other than their own, let Reformers accept theirs as far as possible. Dissension and opposition in the ranks of reform are now to be especially avoided; he is a traitor who foments and encourages them; and I would say to the party above-mentioned, if you cannot come over to my annual parliaments and manhood suffrage, I will join you in triennial parliaments and household suffrage. – Waiting meantime in the expectancy that the justice and expediency of all I desire will ere long be acknowledged and acted upon, I am, sir, your obedient servant, SAMUEL BAMFORD.

Moston Dale, Harpurhey, 8th November, 1858.

---

Went to Hollinwood and saw Dronsfield, Travis and others. Mr Haugh will draw up a report of the "Social Gathering" and send it to me by post.

**Thursday 11th.** Haugh sends a note by post saying he will forward the report by a messenger this afternoon.

The following appears in the Examiner.

*Cutting*, *from the* Manchester Examiner and Times, *11 November 1858: Bamford's letter of 9 November, without the underlining.*

It would appear, from what is stated in the paragraph on the other leaf, that the admirers of Mr Bright, have deemed it necessary to take active measures against the untrammelled freedom of my speech at Bury, as the following paragraph in the days Examiner, seems to indicate.

*Cutting*, *from the* Manchester Examiner and Times, *11 November 1858, reporting that "a meeting of Reformers" at Bury had passed a resolution expressing confidence in Bright's leadership of the Reform movement.*

Dronsfields little girl arrived just before dark, bringing Haughs report of the Social Gathering which I corrected, and sent by Omnibus to Mills at Middleton.

The little girl, I sent, as directed by a note from her father, by Omnibus to Manchester paying the guard for her carriage, and desiring him, also a female passenger[,] to set her down at the end of Swan Street.

Mr. —— of Woodside, whom I saw in the bar at new Inn, very pressing in his invitations for me to call and see him.

**Friday 12th.** The following appears in the Examiner and Times of this day.

*Report, from the* Manchester Examiner and Times, *12 November 1858 of a meeting in St Michael's ward, Manchester, at which Thomas Bazley stated that "he was personally favourable to manhood suffrage" but thought it would be rejected by the present House of Commons, and "it would be the wise plan to ask for rating suffrage [as well as triennial parliaments and the ballot], in the first instance, and manhood suffrage would no doubt soon follow".*

*Report, from the* Manchester Examiner and Times, *12 November 1858, of a grand public luncheon, involving the presentation of a testimonial, a gift of £5000 and a silver writing casket, to the Town Clerk of Manchester, Joseph Heron, with several laudatory speeches by prominent Manchester figures.*

The adjoining shows the difference between the estimation in which the services of a humble sufferer in a national cause are held, and those of a well paid town clerk. The radical of 40 years, gets slight, insult and calumny, the town clerk, a silver casket and 5000 pounds.[7]

At the meeting in the Free trade hall on Friday night, Dr. John Watts[8] said

*Report, from the* Manchester Examiner and Times, *13 November 1858, of a Reform meeting at the Free Trade Hall. Watts argued that working men with the vote would be more law abiding, before continuing:*

---

... There was another argument, and a very capital one, in favour of manhood suffrage, which one of the oldest and best of the Manchester radicals had put forward during the last few day. There was not a man in that room, however low is position in life might be, who was not eligible to be made a member of parliament. But on what principle should a man be held eligible to make the laws and yet not eligible to choose the law-makers? (Cheers and laughter.) He said Samuel Bamford had hit the right nail on the head on that matter, and this monstrous inconsistency could not be allowed much longer.

Mr. S. POPE, hon. Secretary of the United Kingdom Alliance said he could accept the resolution which had been submitted to them, for he never was able to

---

7. Written in landscape down the side of the page on which the cuttings are pasted.
8. John Watts (1818–87), Owenite lecturer, insurance agent and educational reformer; *DNB*.

understand the philosophy of a property qualification. He was sure that the argument of Bamford, before alluded to, must be regarded as final.

---

It would seem the question of Manhood Suffrage is under consideration by the Bury Reformers.

**Report**, *from the* Manchester Weekly Times, *13 November 1858, of the Bury reform meeting noticed in the* Examiner *of the 11th, but noting additionally that it was a meeting of non-electors, attended by some 130 people, and that after the resolution was passed "<u>considerable</u> <u>discussion</u> on the subject of <u>manhood</u> <u>suffrage</u> took place. The meeting was finally adjourned until <u>next</u> <u>week</u>." (Bamford's emphasis).*

The adjoining from the Middleton Albion Nov 13th. /58

**Report**, *from the* Middleton Albion, *13 November 1858, of "AN EVENING WITH THE POETS", at the Filho Inn, Hollinwood, including songs speeches and readings from a number of local poets, including John Bolton Rogerson, Ben Brierley, Sam Collins, and of other literary figures, including Allen Mellor, James Dronsfield and W.C. Ridings. Responding to the toast "The Lancashire Authors",*

---

[Bamford] was received with repeated cheering. He gave the meeting an account of his early trials and struggles and very aptly quoted passages from his own poetry illustrative of the condition of the country at various times. He recited his poem describing the watch and ward system about the year 1816, entitled "Gonnerheads oth' nation;" also his poem on the Death of Canning, and several others, including some extracts from Burns, and concluded by some pleasing and satisfactory remarks upon the present prospects of a reform in parliament, and sat down amidst prolonged applause.

---

**Sunday 14th.** Dawson, his wife and child here.

**Monday 15th.** Went to Manchester, bought gloves. The Times (London) of this morning, I see has suppressed Dr. Watts's allusion to my Bury address about the monstrous absurdity of the same man being "allowed to make laws and not allowed to vote at the election of those who make them". That, in fact, is a stunner, and they dont like it.

Charles Delaunay calls at night, and tells me about a room at Barns Green, suitable for public meeting. I have often thought about having a recitation there, but did not know there was a room.

**Wednesday 17th.** Read at the Institution Blakeley, a better muster than I had expected, and reading seemingly gave much satisfaction.

**Thursday 18th.** Saw James Graves's foolish report of the Hollinwood affair in the Oldham Advertiser, and wrote to deny it. Gave the following to the Editor of the Middleton Albion.

*Report*, *from the* Middleton Albion, *20 November 1858.*

---

### BLAKELEY MECHANICS' INSTITUTION

On Wednesday evening, Mr. Samuel Bamford gave a reading and recitation of prose and poetry, at the above institution. He commenced with an extract from the Ancient Triads of Britain, showing the manner in which our native land was first peopled. He next read an extract from that remarkable production, "The Saxon Chronicle," and stating that he had recently heard an inhabitant of Blakely assert in public company that, William the Conqueror, by introducing the feudal system, and the law of primogeniture, laid the foundation for the present greatness and prosperity of our nation, he read the account of William, as given in the above publication, and written by the compilers of the said Chronicle, which completely negatived the assertion that he was a benefactor to this country, whose greatness and prosperity is founded on the genius[,] industry, and perseverance of its labouring population alone. A passage from a beautiful poem from Rogerson's "voice from the town," was next given, the house of commons scene from "Passages in the Life of a Radical" followed, Tennyson's "Morte D'Arthur," "Sleeping Palace," and part of "Locksley Hall," were next given; one or two of Mr. Bamford's own poems came next, and the reading was closed by two extracts from Mr B. Brierley's "A Day Out," which produced continued mirth and enjoyment. The performance was repeatedly applauded, and an unanimous vote of thanks was awarded. Some conversation ensued as to the meaning and intent of the Triadical form amongst the Ancient Druids; and, after arranging for a reading next week, the meeting separated.

---

*Letter*, *from the* Oldham Advertiser, *18 November 1858.*

---

### HOLLINGWOOD LITERARY GATHERING.

*To the Editor of the Oldham Advertiser.*

Sir, – Your informant respecting the above social meeting has misunderstood my meaning. How could I be guilty of so preposterous an utterance as that of saying, "I contemplated visiting Oldham, Waterhead Mill, &C, for the purpose of meeting similar parties," when I had not the least idea that such parties were intended, or would ever assemble. Mr. Greaves expressed a wish to meet me again at some of the places mentioned, and I stated the pleasure I should feel in meeting old friends, if any were left, whenever I might be in the neighbourhood, or whenever such meeting might be arranges. Further than this I could not be expected to say, and certainly never intended. – Yours obediently,

        SAMUEL BAMFORD.

           Moston Dale, Harpurhey,

November 18th, 1858.

---

**Saturday 20th.** Went to Manchester, Brierley with me. Looked at Union Chambers in Dickinson St, wont do – Some disorderly fellows at Rogersons, so came away. Called at Belfields, who said he would interfere and get me a ticket, as a guest to the approaching feast to Bright and Gibson.[9] I desired he would not interfere at all but leave the matter to its due course. Came home.

**Sunday 21st.** Mills and Kent from Middleton came over and I went with them to Allan Mellors, whence to Royton. Looked at two of the working mens seminaries, took notes, and back to Middleton whence took coach and home,

**Monday 22nd.** At Oldham with Mills and Travis saw the Colliers ox roast and procession. Met Hayes of the Advertiser and John Schofield, and back through Hollinwood, and Manchester, very foggy and I coughed a great deal.

**Wednesday 24th.** Wrote and dispatched the following.

***Letter***, *Bamford to Editor of the* Manchester Guardian, *24 November 1858.*[10]

### REFORM MEETING

*To the Editor of the Manchester Guardian*

Sir, will you allow me a few words with "An Old Reformer," whose communication appears in your paper of Monday?

How stands the argument for "manhood suffrage," the claim for which appears to have caused much alarm in your correspondent? By the law, any man is eligible to become a member of Parliament. We, the advocates for manhood suffrage, say that any man who is fitting to be a member of Parliament, is fitting to be a voter and that consequently any man is fitting to be a voter. Is he wise enough and worthy enough to make laws? and shall he not be deemed wise enough, and worthy enough to vote at an election? Such is our argument, and such the "authority" on which it is based; and I should observe with much interest any reasoning process by which "an Old Reformer," or any one else, would upset that.

Insinuations about manhood suffrage "leading to communism"; about men "of Doctor Watts's calibre," "keeping poverty to get the property of others," are beneath reason and I regret that any one claiming to be a reformer should have resorted to such expressions. Are we to have the old rabid terror again? are we to fall back on the foul savagery of 1817 and 1819? to the bitter feuds of class against class, of rich against poor, of employers against employed? Cannot the expediency or nonexpediency, the right or the wrong of a serious question be argued without the introduction of abusive and untruthful imputations from either party? Your

---

9. Thomas Milner Gibson (1806–84), Cobdenite MP for Manchester 1841–57, and leader of the campaign for the repeal of taxes on knowledge; *DNB*.

10. The final two paragraphs, which were not printed, have a line through them, and the editor's comment as published has been written on the reverse.

"Old Reformer," and those of his "calibre," may, if they choose, adopt such a line of discussion, but I trust they will not meet with any replication on that style: I trust the working men, the "non electors," of this city and district, will show their opponents an example of a more manly and rational bearing; and that, however others may conduct themselves they will maintain a demeanour worthy of their great and truthful cause.

This cry of "property in danger," is only an attempt to revive the persecution with which reform and reformers were assailed forty years ago. You Sir cannot have forgotten that the columns of Harrops vile press,[11] and those of the "Church and King" newspapers throughout the County teemed weekly with unfounded aspersion of those who sought that great change which has since been concede[d], and found to be a ~~great~~ benefit to the nation at large. "Chapped hands and greasy night-caps" was one of Harrops derisive phrases, "Dividers of property, and destroyers of social order," was another of the choice accusations made against us. Well, the abuse went for what it was worth: it was endured and had its day: forty years have passed; very few either of the wronged or the wrongers remain; a new generation stands in their place. A nation much improved, of greater intelligence, of more refined habits ~~stands~~ is before and around us, and if in these days either "Old Reformers," Young Reformers", or "No Reformers," cannot argue a question, the principle of which the law has already decided, without descending to abusive and unfounded ~~expectation~~ insinuation ~~they had better remain silent~~.[12]

I am Sir, Probably an Older Reformer than your correspondent;
and am certainly,
A Real One.
Nov 24th. 1858.

**Friday 26th.** The scrap attached only appears.

*Letter, from the* Manchester Guardian, *26 November 1858: the first paragraph of Bamford's letter of the 24th, with the Editorial observation that: "We have been compelled to curtail the preceding letter. It seems to us that there is no analogy between the cases of the electors and the elector. Both are called upon to exercise important public functions, for which the one is qualified by the choice of his fellow citizens, whose discretion it is unnecessary to fetter by restrictions. What analogous qualification would the other have if "manhood suffrage" were established? – Ed.* Guard"

Robertson[13] at Suffrage office gave me a copy of Mr Potters[14] pamphlet on reform, which I had not seen before.

---

11. The reference is to James Harrop (1763–1823), and his papers, *Harrop's Manchester Mercury* and the *British Volunteer*, both active tory papers in the post-Waterloo era; MCL.
12. The deletion of the final few words seems merely to be Bamford emphasising the deletion of the whole paragraph by the editor.
13. James Robertson: secretary of the Manchester Manhood Suffrage Association.
14. Edmund Potter (1802–83), calico printer of Dinting Dale, Derbyshire, active Manchester Liberal, MP for Carlisle; *DNB*.

**Saturday 27th.** Belfield asked me if I had got a ticket for the soiree. Shook my head, and said I could not afford to give five shill[ing]s.

A man named Grimshaw from Blakeley village, called and spent an hour.

**Letter**, *from the* Middleton Albion, *27 November 1858, from "OBSERVER", endorsing the comments made in the previous Saturday's paper by Yebby Truscales, the leading character in Bamford's dialect sketch, "A Rural Drama", on the benefits of advertising in the local press.*[15]

The above is from the Midd[leton] Albion of today.

27 Sat. Wrote again as follows. Which did not however appear until the 1 Dec.[r]

**Letter**, *from the* Manchester Guardian, *1 December 1858.*[16]

---

## THE REFORM MEETING

*To the Editor of the Manchester Guardian*
Sir, – Although I decidedly disapprove of your suppression of the better part of my letter of the 24th, I withhold further allusion to that subject, and address myself to your argument. You say, "there is no analogy between the cases of the electors and the elected; both are called upon to exercise important functions, for which one is <u>qualified</u> by the choice of his fellow-citizens, whose discretion it is unnecessary to fetter by restrictions." Here it seems to me you err, by a misapplication of the word qualified. Both are qualified, eligible, fitting, to be elected; any man is; but those elected only are authorised to take their seats in Parliament. Any man who is elected is <u>authorised</u>, and any man may be elected. You ask, "What analogous qualification would the other have, if manhood suffrage were established?" Exactly the same, I reply; both are <u>qualified</u>, as the law stands: one is elected and <u>authorised</u> to take his seat to-day, and the other may by the same process follow him tomorrow. But though non-voter A my be sent to Parliament, being deemed wise enough and worthy enough to make laws, he cannot vote at the election on non-voter B. He may become a leader in the House, a high functionary, a minister of state, but unless he have a property qualification, he cannot vote at an election; and herein consists the anomaly which we, of the "manhood suffrage" school, say ought to be, and must be, eventually abrogated.
– I am sir, probably an older Reformer than your correspondent, and am certainly,
    27th November 1858                                    A REAL ONE.

---

Called at Dr. Watts's, and at the manhood suffrage office, paid my shilling and got a card of membership. Robertson said he would have sent me a circular the week following. Went to Rogersons, who was making up his new vols – very handsome books. Called at Belfields and at Grants, who was very chatty; bought a rabbit and came home by bus.

---

15. The text of this sketch by Bamford is inserted in the entry for 15 December 1858.
16. Bamford's emphasis throughout.

**Sunday 28th.** Received by post, one of Rogersons vols of poetry, too much for him to give, but must I make it up in something else.

Henry Grimshaw and wife called at night.

**Monday 29th.** Read "Reform in 1859" a pamphlet by Mr Edm[un]d Potter of Dinting, it is dated Oct 12th and one passage is as follows. "What stranger reason could be urged against the continuance of a franchise based merely on a property qualification, than the recent repeal of the Members qualification? Surely if a member need not be rated to the poor, an equal privilege should be given to the elector." The same idea which I, having long thought about it, enunciated at Bury on the 28th of the same month. This pamphlet of Mr Potters is not well written. He has some good points, but they are not well arranged, nor distinctly expressed. The facile, slip-shod, non important way in which the above extract is given, serves as an example.

**Tuesday 30th.** Received 1500 cards from Mills and the accompanying note.

***Letter***, *Thomas Mills to Bamford, 30 November 1858.*

Dear Mr Bamford,
I send you herewith 500 each Blue, Orange & White Cards for your reading, & hope you will be successful. Let me know when & where you intend giving your first essay.

I have the pleasure to inform you that we have finally determined to give a dinner in honour of yourself in consideration of the important services you have rendered the cause of Reform, & I trust you will accept the same though humbly offered.

The present arrangement stands thus
1st. The dinner to take place at the Asheton Arms on Monday Jany 3rd 1859.
2nd. The tickets to be 1s/6d each, for which sum Mrs Walker will get a plain substantial dinner.
3rd. Mr Allen Mellor is appointed Chairman of the Committee and myself the Secretary to the whole proceedings.
We shall meet again next Sunday Evening at 6 o'clock and should you have any suggestion or wish for any particular form or scheme to render the matter more agreeable to yourself I should be most happy to hear from you at your earliest opportunity.

I am, My dear Sir,<br>Yours faithfully,<br>Tho<sup>s</sup>. Mills

P.S. Did you get an Oldham Chronicle of last Saturday's. It contains a paragraph of our visit to Royton[;] have not got a copy or would have enclosed it herewith. TM

**Wednesday 1st December.** Sent the following reply.

**Copy letter**, *Bamford to Thomas Mills, 1 December 1858.*

Dear Mills,

I thank you for sending the cards: they will do very well; but you have not inclosed a bill.

The other matter which you mention, is certainly very pleasing to my feelings; and if carried out, it will in reality confer greater credit on my entertainers than on myself: it will be a just and an honourable acknowledgement for past services on behalf of my fellow subjects of the present generation, and of their fathers before them. I must own, I had but faint hopes of any tangible recognition of my endeavours. I had suffered obloquy and neglect so long that I had ceased to expect any thing else during my life: and had settled down in the determination that however <u>others</u> might feel in their duty to me, I would not fail in my duty to my country: but would be content with the reward which I knew would one day be mine, that of an honest fame, for a life honestly devoted to the good of my Country, and that without ostentation or pretence to extraordinary merit.

There are several reasons why, I think, I had best have a knowledge of the details before they are carried into effect. You will act as secretary, and I should wish to have some conversation with you; but I had rather <u>not</u> appear too often in Middleton pending the preparations, lest people should say it was <u>I</u> who was making the arrangements: I would rather not come this week, at any rate, and if you could take the Bus some evening before your Committee meet we could perhaps decide on some matters necessary for consideration on Sunday night. On Friday night you cant come: I will expect you tomorrow. Come to tea. Have you seen my letter in todays Guardian. "A Real One"? Get me an Oldham Chronicle if you can.

Yours truly<br>Saml. Bamford.

Rochdale folks are going to dine Bright: have they taken the hint from you?

**Copy letter**, *Bamford to Mrs Shiel,[17] London, 1 December 1858.*

My Dear Mrs Shiel,

Thus you see, after a long delay, a far too long silence, I take up my pen to inscribe a few lines. The truth is I am at all times a very dilatory correspondent, and I have not had anything to communicate which I thought would interest you: anything of a public nature which has appeared in the papers, you will of course have seen. Even now I have not matter worth your notice to fill up this letter, only I have been so long, so very rudely silent that I feel I must for very shame write something. You know all about our Cottage: I have told you before how we are situated: well, we are just as we were when I last wrote. Mima, however I may say has better health here than she had in London: she is more active; more vigorous

---

17. Mrs Shiel was Bamford's landlady in St John's Wood, London.

in the performance of her household duties than when lodging in New Street. She bakes her own bread: she brews for me a bottle or two of good brown ale – far better than your bitter public house stuff, or your nondiscript porter, and I find her good malt beverage is far preferable, in point of health, for me, than anything I could obtain in your great City. On one subject however I have to say – for I can express in confidence to you – and that is, that the cause of anxiety which used to haunt you – happy should I be to hear that you no longer felt its pressure – is uncertainty as to the means of procuring a honest, and respectable subsistence. I am too far advanced in years to engage in heavy labour, and for light work, young active men are generally preferred. One course remains open to me and that is lecturing, or readings and recitations of my own productions in prose and verse: there's a business which I think I could manage, and if something better does not turn up I shall be compelled to try it. Many of our former friends here appear very cold towards us. Very few of them have come to visit us, or have sent invitations to see them: so I have just paid them back in their own coin, and have neither approached them, unless by accident, or have looked the way they were. I have a heart as proud, and as disdainful, as the proudest of them (the miserables! they are afraid we should become troublesome!)[18] for I know not why a poor honest man may not walk the earth with the dignity of a King for,

> "The honest man, though e'er so poor
> Is King of men for a that."[19]

Fortunately I have been enabled to exist without asking one of them, or a single human being, for so much as a crumb of bread. I have sold an edition of my Life of a Radical to a bookseller, and on the proceeds of that sale I have been enabled to get on tolerably well, so far: but this cannot last long: and then for my experiment in public.

And now how are dear Maurice and Pauline? poor dear ones, had I the means, my regard for them and you should not be expressed in words alone: we would go out again, when spring returns, to get nettles for the pot of broth, and flowers for sweet bouquets: we would ramble in the deep dark woods and cloughs which abound here, and we would find the nests of the Throstle, and the lark, and other wild birds; tell them this: and we both send them, all we can communicate, our tenderest blessing for them and their dear and kind mother. I am delighted to hear so good an account of your son Bernard. I hope he will persevere in his studies, and will eventually become a[n] honour, and a consolation to his widowed mother: the successful course he is pursuing must already have been a great relief to your heart. May it continue until his triumph is accomplished. Richard I hope will follow in his brothers noble footsteps, and become to you an additional blessing. I hope your niece <u>Missy</u> has not been discouraged but is about making another effort. Write at your earliest convenience and believe us both yours truly, S & J Bamford.

---

18. Material in brackets added landscape down the side of the letter.
19. From Burns' famous poem, "Is there for honest poverty" ("For a' that"), frequently quoted by Bamford.

**Thursday 2nd.** Mills from Middleton has been over, and from what he says it appears that W.C. Ridings of Middleton saw his brother Elijah at Manchester on Sunday, and informed him of what was taking place at Middleton with respect to myself. W.C. added also that he had invited his brother to the dinner, but he would not come, nor would Edwin Waugh either. (Waugh and Elijah are a couple that hunt together.) It would next seem that Elijah fell in with, or hunted out my neighbour Wilmot, – of whom I know not anything except that he is a cigar dealer, and apparently, a very good natured man. On Wednesday evening he comes to me and asks me to join in a scheme to render Elijah a service by putting a little money in his way. It was to have a kind of literary gathering of Lancashire poets at the Cemetery Inn, Harperhey: a dinner at 1/6 each. He Wilmot to act as chairman, Elijah as Secretary and the remainder of any Moneys left to be given to Elijah for his services as Secretary. I promised to consider the matter over, and to call upon him with my answer this day – if I came to Manchester, but I have not been. It afterwards came out, that Wilmot would call on certain gentlemen in Manchester to ask for subscriptions: this rather awakened my suspicions, and I determined not to be mixed up with any money begging: as it would all be reported as being done with my approbation and if there was any rascality which I strongly suspect there would be, I should bear the blame. I have therefore thrown the whole thing overboard.

**Friday 3rd.** Found Wilmott and Elijah at the writing room over the newspaper office in Brown St. They were drawing up an advertisement for a preliminary meeting. I told them I would not have anything to do with the business until I had seen the advertisement and the result of the meeting they were preparing to call.

**Saturday 4th.** Went to Rogersons, and told him all about this concern.
Received the adjoining note Marked A.

*Letter*, *James Robertson to Bamford, 3 December 1858 (on circular headed paper of the Manhood Suffrage Association) (marked A by Bamford).*

Dear Sir,
We are to hold a public meeting of the Manhood Suffrage Association on Tuesday evening next in the <u>People's</u> <u>Institute,</u> <u>Heyrod</u> <u>St</u>.
   Mr Heywood will preside and the committee would hold it as a favour if you could attend and take part in the proceedings on that occasion.
   As the placards have to be published tonight we will take the liberty of announcing your name and hope to have you with us on <u>Tuesday</u> <u>Evening</u>. The Chair will be taken at 8 o'clock precisely.
   Dr. J. Watts and Mr Roberts[20] are to be present.

---

20. William Prowting Roberts (1806–71), the "miners' attorney", and ally of Ernest Jones, the Chartist leader; *DNB*.

Should it prove impossible for you to be present pray let me have a note from you as early as you can.

I am Sir,

Yours respectfully,

J. Robertson,

59 Princess St.

The Advertisement appears as follows.

*The advertisement is missing.*

The following is in the Middleton Albion. (B)

**Letter**, *from the* Middleton Albion, *4 December 1858 (marked B by Bamford).*

---

ADVERTISING

*To the Editor of the Middleton Albion*
SIR, – With reference to the letter of OBSERVER in your last week's paper, I beg to say that many persons, such as shop keepers, and others in business, are deterred from advertising by the inability to write out, cleverly, and in proper form, what they would wish to express in an advertisement. They require the assistance of one who is acquainted with such things and would gladly make known the quality of their goods, and of their prices, if they had some one at hand to put it down properly in black and white. Such a person, however, is not always to be had, and I am strongly of opinion that if you, Mr. Editor, were to make it known in your columns (and I think you might, making a small charge for your trouble) that you would undertake to put all advertisements sent to you into proper form, you would speedily have a considerable addition of matter in your columns. Excuse the liberty I take in throwing out the hint, and believe me to be
YOUR WELL WISHER
Faraway, December 2nd, 1858

[We feel grateful to our correspondent for this kind hint, and assure him we should at all times be ready to assist, free of charge, any person who might commission us to give publicity to anything he may have to sell, or any other matter of business. – ED.]

---

**Sunday 5th.** Mills from Middleton comes and we arrange several matters ab[ou]t the proposed dinner.

Afternoon. Brierley tells me that Martin of Oldham street says the proposed Literary gathering is for the purpose of putting Waugh forward. I doubt not that something very curious and amusing will turn up on Monday night.

Evening, three young men from the Middleton Literary Institute came and invited me to their soiree on the 4th Jan next.

**Monday 6th.** About half a dozen met at the Commercial, and after much round about talk, Wilmot confessed that the proposed establishment of a Literary Institute was for the purpose of giving Ridings the situation of secretary with a salary. I repudiated this idea, said we would not have any sailing under false colours: and offered, if a dinner was got up for Ridings benefit to attend, and contribute my best efforts towards making it effectual. After much discussion, and some disagreement, during which Ridings made his appearance, – seemingly just recovering from drink, it was agreed to have a dinner, and the meeting was adjourned to the Cemetery Inn, Harperhey, on Thursday night.

**Wednesday 8th.** The following is from the Examiner and Times of this day.

*Report, from the* Manchester Examiner and Times, *8 December 1858, of a meeting of the Manhood Suffrage Association on 7 December, chaired by Abel Heywood. The meeting discussed a letter from John Bright MP justifying his stand in favour of ratepayer suffrage. Bamford moved the resolution in favour of manhood suffrage, but argued that "Mr Bright ought not to be tethered" and proposed rephrasing the resolution as an opinion rather than an instruction, adding that "he was as much in favour of manhood suffrage as anyone present, but if could not get the whole 'hog' he would get what he could". He later proposed another amendment, "That this meeting does not intend or propose to adopt or sanction any course of action which may have the effect of neutralising or embarrassing the efforts of Mr. Bright and his friends in their endeavours to obtain a widely-extended suffrage." The chair refused to accept any amendments, and the original resolution for manhood suffrage was passed unanimously.*

**Thursday 9th.** Wilmott, Silas Wood, Brierley and myself met: neither Tawns the treasurer and landlord, nor Ridings were in attendance, so Wood moved to adjourn to another day, and it was agreed to, thus putting an end to the Ridings scheme.

**Friday 10th.** The great Soiree to Gibson and Bright at which I was not invited to attend. Many people, and long speaking, Bright making the following allusion to the great meeting of 1819.

*Newspaper report, unattributed, of the soirée for John Bright MP on the 10th. Bright's speech celebrated the contrast between the present time, with the government drawing up a new reform bill, and the time of the Peterloo meeting, when:*

on the spot on which we are now assembled, thousands of the population of Manchester and of this neighbourhood met here, not in this magnificent building, but under the wide canopy of heaven, they met only to plead with the government and parliament of that day, that they might be permitted some share in the government of the country, and that they might be permitted further to possess that representative right which one would think no man would ever deny another – the right of disposing their labour in the open market of the world. That meeting was disrupted by the rude arm of the military. You remember the tragedy of that day, proving at once the tyranny and brutality of the government and the helplessness and humiliation of the people.

How could he have the conscience to make such an allusion before a meeting from which the only remaining leader of that day was shut out, studiously neglected and ignored. They cannot understand the supreme contempt which their petty, their would be annoyance awakens in my head.[21]

**Saturday 11th.** Several persons have this day, at Manchester, expressed their disgust at my being overlooked, and not appearing at last nights Meeting. The band it seems struck up, "Should auld acquaintance be forgot" and the meeting took up the words, but whilst they remembered old acquaintance, they forgot the <u>oldest</u> acquaintance of all.

Stoning of prophets is, it seems, still to be the practice of the day.[22] May God forgive them.

*Advertisement, from the* Manchester Guardian, *11 December 1858, for Bamford's Readings at the Mechanics' Institute, Wednesday 23rd.*

The above is cut from the middle of the 2d col of the 1st page Manchester Guardian, where I suppose my very good friend Harland had placed it that it might not be too obtrusively prominent.

This will develope something. I shall probably see more of both my real friends and my enemies.

Ch. Delaunay comes at near four o'clock this afternoon and presents me with a circular to attend a meeting of the "Council of the Institutional Association."[23] I had only just arrived from Manchester, and could not return on the instant: This was, no doubt what Delaunay wished, he having kept the circular from the 8th and now presented it during the last half hour which remained before the meeting.

*Letter, J.W. Hudson*[24] *to Bamford (care of Mr C. Delaunay, Blackley), 8 December 1858, on headed notepaper of the Institutional Association of Lancashire and Cheshire.*

Dear Sir,
You were elected a Member of the Council of the above Association on 3rd December. I have great pleasure in requesting the favour of your attendance at the next Council meeteing to be held in the Athenaeum on Saturday next the 11th inst at 1/2 past 4 o'clock prompt no 10 room.
Your obed[t] serv[t]
J.W. Hudson
for D. Morris
Hon. Sec.

---

21. Inserted (probably later) on facing page.

22. A reference to Cobden's strictures on the result of the 1857 election in Manchester, see entry for 7 August 1858.

23. That is, the Institutional Association of Lancashire and Cheshire, a union of Mechanics' Institutes.

24. James William Hudson, secretary of the Manchester Athenaeum 1849–58, and Lancashire and Cheshire Union of Mechanics' Institutes, (until dismisal, *c.* 1865), see B.R. Villy, "James William Hudson", *Manchester Review* (1962–3), 352–61.

Betty Collinge and her daughter came from Rochdale twixt 9 and 10 at night, and I had to get out of bed to go out and find them lodgings. I dont like such unforeseen interruptions of relatives.

**Sunday 12th.** William Collinge, my Godson came to dinner, and after tea, they took their departure; not being pressed to stay.

Mills from Middleton and Kent came and we made some further matters relative to the forthcoming dinner.

Will Ridings seems cold about it, they tell me, and I explained the reason by narrating the part I had taken with respect to his unworthy brothers affair. Will knows Elijah is a scrawl and nothing better, and yet he seems to suppose that he should be treated with respectful consideration.

Oswald Dicken is, it seems, to be chairman of the dinner party. I dont much like the nomination.

**Monday 13th.** At Belfields, at Manchester several gentlemen expressed their disappointment at my absence from the soiree on Friday night. Belfield had written to George Wilson[25] to know the reason of my not being invited, but had not received any answer. I hope some one will force a reply. It ought to be taken up by the newspapers: but Harland, of the Guardian is no longer a friend of mine; to that quarter I cannot therefore appeal; whilst the Examiner is directly under the influence of George Wilson and the party with whom, I am not, nor probably ever shall be associated.

**Tuesday 14th.** Mills sent me a proof, the cards for [the] dinner, and of the circular. I corrected the letter and returned it by omnibus.

**Wednesday 15th.** Received the annexed invitation from an old friend and sent an acceptance of same.

*Envelope and letter*, *Thos Clowes, Steam Brewery, York Street, Chorlton on Medlock, to Bamford, 14 December 1858.*

> Dear Sir,
> I have a few friends in reform coming to take tea with me on Friday evening next at 7 oclock at my house 109 York St C on M to start a Reform Association in this division of our City. I should be most happy of your company, and shall be glad to accomadate you for the night.
> > Yours sincerely,
> > Thos Clowes

Went to Middleton in afternoon, and had some talk with Mills about the dinner: a reform association is, it seems to be started same day. Very proper I think.

---

25. George Wilson (1808-70), leading figure of the Anti-Corn Law League, and thereafter of the "League" or "Newall's Buildings" party of advanced Liberals in Manchester; *DNB*.

The following I sent to the Middleton Albion, but of what date I have not taken any account.

**Newspaper cutting**, Middleton Albion, *20 November 1858*.[26]

---

### RURAL DRAMA

*SCENE. A street in Rochdale: enter a Middleton shopkeeper, looks around, stops at bottom oth Blackweatar, and seems in deep thought.*

Heigho! I welly wish I'd not comn toth markit today; things lookn darkish wi me. Theres yon flower felly, I paid him th' part ov his acceawnt, an a decent part too I thought, but he seemt reyther shy o' dooin ony moor bizniz, and sed he munt ha a shillin a sack moor iv I took ony; th'chees felly I ha paid, an sharp Sam at th' bridge end I mun see this afternoon. I mun get through I sum teaw, but I lippn o havin a tight job on it afore I get whom agen.

*Enter another shopkeeper coming down Yorshur-street.*
   *Approaches the first and accosts him.*

   Well Yebby, heaw arto today.
   YEBBY. – Pratty weel o' misel, but reyther maundurt a bit; heaw art theaw Dusty?
   DUSTY. – Oh I'm bravely imi bizniz matters, but two oth childer or ill oth cryes; theres olis sum mack ov o' drawback i this ward.
   YEBBY. – There is lad, but wheer duste liv neaw, I hanno seen the uz twain o'years.
   DUSTY. – I liv op i Wardleworth heer, an Ive just hawve an heawr to watch ov a chap at owes meh for sum fents; lets just slip intoth Amen Corner, an hav a glass, an a pipe, and tawk things oer a bit.
   YEBBY. – Wi O meh heart, for I want summut to live'n meh this doage day.

*SCENE. The kitchen at the Amen, a good fire burning, a table, with pots of ale, drinking tots, pipes, and Tobacco; company talking by twos and threes. Enter the two shopkeepers, who take seats and call for ale.*

   YEBBY. – An so theaw ses at theaw art dooin bravely as far as bizniz is consarnt; theaw ust to be summut like misel, reyther hobblet a bit; heaw hasto skeamt it?
   *Dusty drinks, fills the tot, and hands to Yebby, and replies.* Why theaw sees when furst I began a shoppin, things wurn very awkurt indeed. I wurcht hard at meh flannel loom, th wife slubb'd and span, and weern as careful an tentin as we cudn be, but still we cudno get forrud. I bowt the very best o shop stuff at I cud lay meh hands on, an we sowdn at nowt but a decent profit, but nobody coom. We cudno part with stuff unless weedn ha gan it, an that theaw knows wud never doo.
   YEBBY. – Never ith ward, I'm sure.

---

26. See entry for 27 November 1858.

DUSTY. – Well, I wundurt wot the firrups cud be th' matter; meh fleawr wur fusst rate, meh meal wur as good as ony at ever coom o'er Blackstonedge, meh butter I bowt at sharp Sam's, meh cheese an bacon at Benny Yeb's, I gan good prices for em O, an still nobody coom to buoy. I wur very deawn, an the wife wur very deawn; we began o thinkin it wud never onser. At last sharp Sam sed to meh, I think yeaw dusno sell mitch stuff Dusty; and I sed nawe I dunno, I wish I did. Whey, he sed, theaw shud doo as other foke dun. Heaws that, I sed. Theaw shud avertise, he onsert, givin meh a cunnin wink wi his ee. Look ith newspapper o Setturday, an see heaw mony o tradesmen on shopkeeprs like thisell advertis'n; mon theres nowt dun neaw a days beawt advertisin; an iv theawl tak that plan theawl sell plenty o stuff. I'll uphowd the, an theaw may have a decent profit too. So th' next Setturday I advertist; it wur a good bowd advertisement, an no lies noather. That weekend we sowds moor stuff; a matter ov a duzzen fresh customers coom toth shop; th' week after I advertist agen, an th' bizniz mended, an I kept advertisn for mony a week, till weern welly pood eawt oth place for stuff, an sin then ween had quite enoof to do wi buyin in an sellin eawt; an so theaw sees I'm wot they co'n reggilur istablisht in ith shoppin line.

YEBBY SOLUS. – As soon as I yerd this fro meh friend Dusty, I seed wheer I'd misst it. That arternoon I fac'd op sharp Sam, an th' tothers very bondly. I laid in also a fresh lot o saleables; an neaw, Mester Edittur, iv yo'n hav the goodniss to put a line or two i yore papper I'll try wot a good truthful advertisement or two will doo. I dunno want puffin, but gradely honnist truth, and nowt elz. Yo may say at I've fleawr an meal, an butter, an cheese, and bread, an bacon, mawt, hops, tay coffey, swop, treycle, an O'th reggilur shop stuff, oth very best quallotty, an at as lowe prices as con be afforded. Yo con write this deawn in a proper form, an print it in yore next papper, an I'll coe an pay yo.

YEBBY TRUSCALES.

---

**Friday 17th.** Mr Hutchings, at the Mechanics Institution undertakes to find me what assistance will be necessary on the night of my readings and recitations; very good, very few tickets have been sold either at the Institution, or the booksellers. Belfield has sold most, about a dozen perhaps.

Went to the party a[t] friend Clowes's, in Chorlton on Medlock, a respectable and select party, Alderman Clarke[27] one of them: a good set out of tea, beef tawe[,] tongue and other things to correspond, after which whisky. A chairman and speeches, my health being drunk, and I being called on first. Afterwards a proposal to form "A Chorlton on Medlock Parliamentary Reform Association." All agreed in the main thing, and at ten o'clock I left the[m to] discuss the details, and arrived at home 1/2 past eleven, tired and flat to rest, with a mouthful to eat and a tot of my home brewed ale.

**Saturday 18th.** A very wet morning: at home all day. Got the annexed from Mills of Middleton.[28]

---

27. Possibly Walter Clark (d. 1867), Manchester Commission Agent, active municipal Liberal, pro-Bright.
28. No annexe.

**Sunday 19th.** Mills and Ogden came from Middleton: they are of the Committee of the proposed dinner, and we discussed about some of the toasts for the evening. The toasts stood on their list, as at present prepared, "The Queen": "the town and trade of Middleton", "the Guests" etc. I proposed that "the Prince Consort and the Royal family" should follow "the Queen," but Ogden objected, saying we had nothing to do with them. I urged that it would be only a poor compliment to the Queen, to drink her health, and not that of her husband and children, and that Ogdens wife, or that of any other man would view it in the same light. The matter was left undecided, and I must try again when I meet the Committee. I rather think it is a point on which I shall be, and ought to be decided. We should not allow Chartist republicans to have it all their own way, they will spoil the character, and the harmony of the meeting.

Mr Whitehead, silk manufacturer, had sent for 20 tickets, and got them on Saturday night.

The Middleton Albion, in its leading article says,

***Editorial***, *from the* Middleton Albion, *18 December 1858.*

---

A nice opportunity is about to be afforded us, when actions for reform might very properly be commenced. A banquet is about to be given to an old townsman, Samuel Bamford; a veteran reformer, and, very properly styled the Lancashire bard. After felicitations proper to such occasions, and especially to this, it would be as *easy* to talk over the reform prospects of Middleton, as we think it is the *duty* of every townsman to do, upon such an unusual occasion, under such an unusually favourable aspect of public affairs.

---

Before this appeared it had been determined to commence a reform association at the dinner on the 3rd Jan 1859.

**Monday 20th.** Belfield has sold a good many tickets. Cant say how the others are getting on: did not call on them.

Sent three tickets for readings to Dronsfield.

**Tuesday 21st.** The Examiner has the following paragraph [about] tomorrow, this day.

***Cutting***, *from the* Manchester Examiner and Times, *21 December 1858, drawing attention to an advert for Bamford's forthcoming reading and briefly rehearsing his claim as a "veteran reformer" to public recognition.*

**Wednesday 22nd.** Found a too small attendance at the Mechanics Institution awaiting my readings and recitations. A few introductory observations led me to an extract on Burns, from a publication by Chapman and Hall, written by Thomas

Carlyle[;][29] a very foolish and incoherent production as I think, but in which is one striking passage which I gave, and commented upon pp.67 to 69. Then followed my account of how I became a versifier, and I repeated my "Snow Drop," my "Farewell to my Cottage," "Lines on the Death of a Late worthy and respected M.P." "The lost Ones," etc. which were repeatedly applauded. Then Charles "The Ships, the Ships," with some observations, and animadversions on his pension, which I deemed shabby, like all the rest of Palmerstons pensions.[30] Rogersons "Nothing More," with like observations on the shabbyness of his pension, followed. Who are the Free from Princes poems, and a passage from Waughs Sketches of Lancashire Life were given in succession, with commendatory remarks. My "Song of Heroes," followed, and as a contrast to it,[31] an extract from Count Segurs Campaign in Russia, a terrible discription of the sufferings of the French Army during its retreat.[32] "A Dream of Fair Women," from Tennyson, with passages from "Locksley Hall," and "the Sleeping Palace," came next, and then Jimmy the Jobber from Brierleys "A Day Out," led to the beautiful stanzas from Tennyson, commencing, "Ring out wild bells to the wild sky." Which concluded the performance, at 10 minutes to ten o'clock, I having been an hour and 50 minutes on my feet.

The performance seemed to have given quite as much satisfaction as I had expected. At the conclusion Edm[un]d. Buckley Esq[r].,[33] who is probably the richest man in Manchester, and more than that, who has long been a friendly patron of my books came forward and shook hands cordially, desiring me also to be sure and let him have all the publications I might put forth.

Dronsfield and two friends from Hollinwood, Martin of Oldham Street, and Josh Taylor, Auctioneer – an old Middleton neighbour [–] accompanies me to Oldham Street, where after a glass of warm whisky, I took a cab to Harperhey, and so came home, rather tired, and not much the richer.

During the night terrible apprehension of exigency want and destitution haunted me. The citizens of Manchester, notwithstanding the friendly intimation in the

---

29. The passage read by Bamford is from pages 67–9 of a shilling softcover edition of Thomas Carlyle's *Burns* in the series "Reading for travellers: a new library of railway literature." "Amid the vapours of unwise enjoyment, of bootless remorse, and angry discontent with Fate, his true loadstar, a life of Poetry, with Poverty, nay with Famine if it must be so, was hidden from his eyes." In Carlyle's narrative, Burns turns away from French politics, "comes into collision with certain official Supervisors; is wounded by them; cruelly lacerated, we should say ... His life has now lost its unity: it is a life of fragments, led with little aim ..." He finally suffers calumny and misfortune, and is snubbed by "the Dumfries aristocracy ... Burns now sleeps 'where bitter indignation can no longer lacerate his heart'". (The last phrase comes from Jonathan Swift's self-penned epitaph, which concludes: "Go, traveller, and imitate if you can one who with all his might championed liberty.")

30. Henry John Temple, 3rd Viscount Palmerston (1784–1865), Prime Minister 1855–8, 1859–65, the dominant political figure of the diary period, not least for his lack of enthusiasm for parliamentary reform. For his treatment of Bamford's attempts to obtain a pension see especially Chapter 12; *DNB*. The reference here is to Charles Swain, see entry for 11 October 1858.

31. This part of the sentence added opposite, and the word "next" deleted.

32. "My 'Song of the Heroes' served as a contrast" deleted.

33. Edmund Buckley (1780–1867), of E. Buckley and Co., carriers; one of the largest merchant houses in Manchester; Conservative MP for Newcastle under Lyne, 1841–7; MCL.

Examiner and Times of the day previous had "ignored their obligations for benefits received 40 years ago," and the victim of wrongs and injuries which had never been righted or redressed, was left almost a loser by this his first endeavour to "earn a subsistence by useful and talented exertion." How different the reception these people gave to Charles Dickens, whose audience amounted to nearly as many thousands, as mine did dozens. Dickens's pen had been on many occasions imbued with gall towards the employing class of Manchester. Much disparaging misrepresentation had he repeatedly given currency to, yet when he came amongst these people, they followed, and fawned upon him like whipped spaniels. When he came, begging for the widow of Douglas Jerrold,[34] it was the same. His pen had always a viperous taint towards the Lancashire manufacturing employers, yet, on behalf of this lady, who was already well provided for Dickens walked away with hundreds in his pocket. Such is the humour of our Manchester friends at present, and I may thank my stars I suppose, that, after paying all expenses I shall probably have as much as 10/- left in my pocket.

**Thursday 23rd.** This is a bad go: something must be done: it wont do to sit cogitating and brooding at home. Coals are mainly done and absolute want and starvation will soon be in the house.

Went to Salford and saw Mr Chadwick the borough treasurer,[35] who very kindly and readily gave me a note to Mr. [Urquhart],[36] secretary to the Mechanics Institution, and he and he very kindly and readily, gave me the use of the large room for Thursday evening next. I am to have the room free of charge, admitting the members of the Institution also free.

My friend Belfield has sold for me more tickets than any one else.

I forgot to leave tickets for the reporters at the offices of the Guardian and Examiner. A complimentary notice however appeared in the latter paper, of the 23rd. This was all [they] could do to serve the old Radical.

**Friday 24th.** Left a letter of acknowledgement for Mr Hutchings, at the Institution: Called on Rogerson, who paid me 3/- for tickets he had sold: same from Clowes of York Street, Chorlton, Medlock, who also kept me to dinner and ordered a copy of my forthcoming Radical with Autograph and Photograph. His brother did the same, Clowes is very kind: Mrs C was at my reading, and says she liked my first piece "The Snowdrop" best of any.

Came home unwell; Christmas eve; not a happy one, low spirited and gloomy: tried to keep up: could not eat at tea. Mima chopped up some pork, veal, and a rabbit for a pie and that will be our Xmas fare, with a bottle and a piece of ale. 10/6 left to keep Xmas with, dark look out!

24. Sent the following to Mr. Hutchings.

---

34. Douglas Jerrold (1803–57), the editor of *Douglas Jerrold's Weekly Paper* and then *Punch*; *DNB*.
35. David Chadwick (1821–95), borough treasurer of Salford and a great company promoter; Liberal MP for Macclesfield, *c.* 1868–80; see *Manchester Guardian*, 20 September 1895.
36. See entry for 26 December 1858.

**Copy letter**, *Bamford to E. Hutchings, 24 December 1858.*

Dear Sir,
If after experiencing the kind and considerate indulgence of the Directors of your
Mechanics Institution, I omitted to express my sincere thanks to them for the
same, I should feel self accused of ingratitude, [a] sin to which, I trust I am not
much given. Will you therefore do me the favour to make known to them my
thankful sentiments for their having placed a room at my disposal when on
Wednesday night I gave a reading and recitation.
    To yourself I owe many obligations: your uniform kindness to me, until recently
a stranger, has left impressions which, in any time I can expect to live, will never
be effaced, may your goodness of heart be speedily and plenteously rewarded,
and, should you live to my age, may you every where meet with that helpful
attention, which you have shown to, yours very truly, and gratefully,
Samuel Bamford.
    E. Hutchings Esquire.

P.S. I have engaged the room at the Salford Mechanics Institution, for Thursday
evening next; I am to have it free, admitting, on the same terms, the members of
the Institution: an arrangement I should gladly have made with you, had the idea
been suggested. S.B.

**Account slip**, *in Bamford's hand, for sales of tickets by Mr Taylor at Manchester Mechanics'
Institution, who has sold 3 out of 53 two-shilling tickets for reserved seats, and 32 out of 46 one-
shilling tickets, yielding £1 in all. Bamford's comment: "Very encouraging (?)"*

**Saturday 25th, Xmas day.** Not well: wanted a breathing walk so went to
Middleton to get my "Early Days" from Mills and to hear any news that was stirring.
Mills showed me a number of letters received, some from persons declining to attend
at my dinner, and others from persons who would come. Oswald Dickens declines
being chairman. A thing I had expected. Mills said the Committee proposed inviting
him to continue at his post, but I advised that he should not again be asked. Sold
about 70 tickets, Mills said, a number which I think quite enough, or rather more than
enough. Very wet, and so returned inside the omnibus.
    Mima had an excellent pie for dinner which I relished after my mornings trip.
    The Middleton Albion has the following extract from my "Early Days".

**Cutting**, *from the* Middleton Albion, *25 December 1858: a synopsis of a segment of Bamford's*
Early Days, *dealing with Christmas.*[37]

**Sunday 26th.** Receive the following.

---

37. See *Early Days*, 134–6.

*Letter*, *John Urquhart to Bamford, 24 December 1858, on headed notepaper from Salford Mechanics' Institution, Great George Street, Salford.*

Dear Sir,

I understand from Mr Chadwick that you only propose to let our members in to your Lecture "free" and that you will charge the Public for admission. I misunderstood the matter. I thought the proposition was to give a lecture to the members only, and therefore said – "we will pay for printing posters" – but as such is not the case you will permit me to withdraw the offer to <u>print</u>.

    We are obliged for your kind offer to deliver a lecture and you may have the room with gas etc. for Thursday evg next, <u>free of charge</u>, provided the members of the Inst. have free admission.

Apologising for the mistake

I am Dear Sir,

Yours truly

Jno Urquhart

Hon. Sec.

**Thursday 30th.** Gave a reading and recitation at the Mechanics Institution Salford. Pretty well attended, and I saved some money by sale of tickets before the reading took place. Mr Morris of Potters & Morris took twenty shillings worth. Mr Brooks (John Brooks and Co) took twenty five shillings worth, Sir Elkanah Armitage and Sons, five shillings worth, at Messrs Shorrocks Sons & Co ten shillings worth. Mr David Chadwick, Borough Treasurer, Salford, five shillings, and Alderman Goadsby,[38] and the Mayor, both ultra Radicals. one shill[ing] each. Whilst Mr Bazley, the newly elected member for Manchester, received me very courteously, conversed with me a considerable time, and took ten shilling tickets. By these means I was enabled to attend in comfort the feast and meeting, next mentioned.

**Monday 3rd January.** The accompanying reports give a very condensed and imperfect report of what took place.

*Resolution slip, carefully written in Bamford's hand.*

3rd Jan 1859.

3rd Resolution.

That in Consequence of the present state of the political world it behoves the inhabitants of Middleton and surrounding townships to bestir themselves and form an association for the effectual accomplishment of the objects specified in the foregoing resolution.

Moved by Mr Samuel Bamford

Seconded by Mr John Lancashire Jnr

---

38. Thomas Goadsby (1805–66), chemist and druggist, Mayor of Manchester 1861–2; MCL.

Supported by Mr Samuel Barlow

And I move, that in pursuance of this resolution that an association to be called the Middleton Reform Association be now established.[39]

**Report**, *from the* Oldham Advertiser, *8 January 1859: a briefer account of the dinner which is reported in the next extract, noting that 75 sat down to dinner.*

**Report**, *from the* Middleton Albion, *8 January 1859, of the dinner on Monday 3rd January to establish a Middleton Reform Association, at the Assheton Arms, Middleton (where Bamford had been taken in 1819 following his arrest at Peterloo). A succession of speakers recalled Bamford's endeavours and imprisonment in the cause of reform and his shabby treatment after Peterloo by some of his neighbours, recited some of his poems, and finally called for three cheers for him. Bamford responded with an address. "He explained the meaning of the terms veteran and bard and his claim on the title of parliamentary Reform leader. His father had composed verses and 'the Germs of Genius,' had probably been transferred to him, and he repeated one of his father's poems. He then went on to explain the happenings of the morning of 16th August, 1819, and his peaceable demonstration strategy." After Bamford's speech, various resolutions on parliamentary reform were proposed and enthusiastically endorsed, including the final resolution, proposed by Bamford, that a Middleton Reform Association be established.[40]*

**Editorial**, *from the* Middleton Albion, *8 January 1859, emphasising the importance of the reform movement in Middleton and urging reformers to renounce perfectionism and unite around a common programme.*

**Tuesday 4th.**   A Soiree of the Literary Institution is reported as follows.

**Report**, *from the* Oldham Chronicle, *8 January 1859, of the first tea party and soirée of the Middleton Literary Institution, held in the Middleton Temperance Hall, with 350 sitting to tea, including Thomas Dickins, Peter Seville, Edwin Waugh, Bamford and, in the chair, John Cheetham, MP.[41] Cheetham gave a conventional speech in favour of educational progress and then spoke of Bamford.*

---

He had little occasion to speak of how knowledge elevated a man in Middleton, and especially when he had only to turn his head and see their friend and his friend

---

39. Last sentence written on the back of the resolution slip.
40. The *Middleton Albion* on 15 January 1859 reported a second reform dinner attended by some 100 persons, "principally working men", at another local inn. The Albion explained "being considered by a few that it [the meeting of 3rd January] was a middle class gathering, the present occasion was determined upon for the purpose of giving the working classes an opportunity of speaking out on this question." A motion in favour of manhood suffrage, the secret ballot, equal electoral districts and shorter parliaments was passed, and a more radical amendment referring to the "glaring evil" of government and the "right" to vote gained little support. The meeting then voted to amalgamate with the 3 January meeting "based on the resolutions passed".
41. John Cheetham (1802–86), Liberal, cotton manufacturer (George Cheetham and Sons), MP for South Lancashire, 1852–9, and for Salford 1864–8; president of the Cotton Supply Association; close associate of Benjamin Heywood and Revd William Gaskell; Boase.

Samuel Bamford. (Applause.) It had been said that Tim Bobbin was the Lancashire Burns, and he believed that it was not less just to say that the mantle of Tim Bobbin had fallen on Samuel Bamford. (Hear, hear.) He had no doubt that Mr Bamford would be the first to admit that to the cultivation of his mind he owed the position which he maintained in this country, as well as to that honest, manly, English independence which he had evinced through life, that urgent desire which he had manifested to promote the welfare of his fellow-countrymen. (Hear, hear.).

*After some further formal business, Bamford himself spoke:*

He explained that the card stated he was to give a reading, and the programme stated he was to give an address – (laughter) – so he would give a short address, and conclude with a reading. (Hear, hear.) He was very glad to see his old neighbours and friends, and the sons and daughters of his neighbours and friends, form so respectable a meeting – he might have said handsome, becoming, comely, but they knew what he meant. (Hear, hear and laughter.) He had many happy reminiscences connected with Middleton, and he hoped when they came to be his age, they would have the same. (Hear, hear.) He did not know how that he could do better, as he was addressing an audience at a literary institution, than explain how he came to have the literary knowledge he possessed. It would amuse, and might instruct them. His parents were poor folk, "at th' Back o'th Brow, Middleton." He was the youngest of six or seven children. His father was a muslin weaver, and trade was very bad. It was in the dreadful times of '94, when the French revolution had occurred, and democracy was said to be about to visit England. In that year his father fainted for want of food, when he was coming from Ashton, and he (Mr. Bamford) had often gone through the fields and wondered which was the exact spot. (Hear, hear.) He was a tall lad, and wore petticoats, as all lads did in those days, until they became kilts – (laughter) – waded in the brook, catching roach, or wandered on the banks, gathering primroses, or other flowers, until one morning his mother gave him 6d., and sent him to school. That was his first advance in life – he was a scholar – (laughter) – but he had to take a book, and the only book his mother could find being a psalter (or book of psalms and hymns), he had to sit by himself, as there was no psalter class in the school. (Laughter.) He afterwards got a "Reading-made-easy," but he did not progress much under that master (old John Kenyon), and his next remove was to a school near Hanging Ditch, Manchester. He did not go backwards there, but he did not go forward, though his master tried to cultivate his intellect by raising knobs on his head. (Laughter.) He was wishful to learn but the faculty of retention was not there. He went to another old gentleman, who tried an improvement on the former master's system, by nearly pulling his hair up by the roots – (laughter) – and afterwards tried what effect slapping the ball of his hand with a flat ruler would have (laughter). Those things did not do, and he did not get on well. Next he went to the Manchester Grammar School, where he had to be by seven o'clock in the morning, or receive a flogging with a cane. He sometimes got thrashed, but not often, and he made such progress there (which he attributed to having to rise early) that in twelve months he was the best English reader in the school, and was ready for promotion to Latin. His father, however, said "What do you want with Latin? You will never be a doctor or a parson," and time showed that his father was correct for he had not been either a doctor or a parson. (Laughter.) He read all the books he could find. He read in Revelations about death on a white horse, the angel with one foot in the sea, and the other on land, and other wonderful things; and he read about George and the Dragon, Jack the Giant Killer, Tom Hickathrift, and Robin Hood. He delighted in the Robin Hood ballads. Once his father locked him in the chamber, and in an old chest of drawers he found some sugar, which he immediately knew what to do with – (laughter) – and a volume of Milton's Miscellaneous Poems. He read "Il Penseroso" and the other poems, and afterwards got a copy of Pope's Homer, and read all about gods and goddesses. He became quite imbued with poetry. When he became a young man he worked at Wilkinson's warehouse in Peel[42]-street, and having a deal of leisure there read Burn's Poems and Cobbett's Register – the latter making him a politician. He thought if a Scottish ploughboy could write poetry he could also, and he wrote a piece which he though very fine, but would not recite it to the meeting. (Laughter.) His first published poem was "The Snowdrop." Mr Bamford recited the poem. When he had written it down he said, "if this is not poetry, poetry never was written." (Laughter.) It appeared in one of the Manchester papers. He occasionally wrote rhymes on various subjects, some rather offensive to his neighbours, for he had become a politician, a Radical, though that term was not in existence then, and was first employed by *The Times* as a stigma on parliamentary reformers. He was fascinated as much by Cobbett's prose as Burns' verse, though he was often completely wrapped in the latter's poems, especially in "The Braes of Ballochmyle." Mr Bamford recited that poem. As he became older he fell under the irresistable fascination of love, and very much in love he was, for he seldom did things by halves. (Hear, hear.) He had briefly shown them how he came to be designated "the Lancashire poet and Parliamentary Reformer." He would not go into politics, but he would say he was for every man having a vote, at all events every married man, for those who were too lither and worthless to take a woman by the hand for better or worse ought never to have a vote for a member of Parliament. (Laughter and applause.) Mr Bamford concluded by reading one of his prose sketches.

---

*The proceedings concluded with a discussion about the opening of literary institutions on a Sunday, in which Bamford stated that his suggestion for Sunday opening had been made "in conversation, and the matter was never seriously entertained"; a speech from Edwin Waugh, who at Bamford's request recited "Come whoam to thi childer an' me"; and dancing.*

**Thursday 6th.**   Received the following circular.

**Circular**, *David Morris to Bamford, 5 January 1859.*[43]

Institutional Association, Lancashire and Cheshire, 1 Market Place, Manchester.
5th January 1859.

---

42. Bamford's correction of the paper's "Peter".
43. David Morris (dates not known), millowner, leading Manchester Liberal, prominent supporter of temperance associations and working-class self-help, secretary of the Institutional Association of Lancashire and Cheshire, lecturing widely in 1859–60 on Manchester poets. (See Plate 1.)

Dear Sir,
Will you please attend a council meeting in the Manchester Athenaeum next
Saturday @ 5pm prompt, & oblige
                                    Dr Sir
                                          Yours Truly
                                              David Morris

**Saturday 8th.**  Attended the Council Meeting, a formal dull affair and afterwards a
soiree at the Harperhey Mechanics Institution, where I gave a short address & read
"Jimmy the Jobber," from B Brierleys "A Day Out." Much amusement.

**Tuesday 11th.**  Chas Field of Oldham with whom I had corresponded before on the subject, appoints a reading for the Literary Analytical Institution, to take place on the 24th Inst.
     Rogerson writes requesting my attendance at a celebration of the centenary of birth
of Robert Burns. I know not what reply to make as I know it will be, if kept as such
affairs generally are, an exceedingly drunken orgie.

**Wednesday 12th.**[44] John Heywood,[45] Bookseller Manchester writes for a compleat
set of my publications. I call upon him and explain that they are not to be had. All out
of the trade. He is inclined to negociate for 1000 copies of my "Early Days," a copy of
which I leave for him to examine.

***Letter and envelope***, *Andrew Stewart,*[46] *Rochdale, to Bamford, 15 January 1859.*

Mr Bamford
Dear Sir,
I am in receipt of yours of the 11th Inst. and in reply beg to assure you of my best
wishes for your success on your intended visit to Rochdale. I may say however
that my determination is not to take any prominent part in political matters
during the period of my Mayoralty.
     We are all busy preparing for a grand soiree to Mr Bright which will come off
on the 28th Inst, and I would recommend you to postpone your visit until that is
over as I know many Gentleman who would be likely to patronise you will be
busily engaged every evening until after that period.
     I shall be glad if you will call upon me when you come over when if I can
render you any assistance I shall be glad to do so,
                                    Meantime
                              I am Dr Sir
                                          Yours Most Respecty
                                              A. Stewart.

---

44. Entry inserted on the opposite page.
45. John Heywood (d. 1864), printer and publisher, brother of Abel Heywood; MCL.
46. Andrew Stewart (*c.* 1797–1870), of Rochdale, woollen manufacturer, Liberal, mayor 1858–9; *Rochdale
     Observer,* 24 September 1870.

The following explains itself, I had not the requisite funds to go.

***Letter***, *John Cheetham, Eastwood, Stalybridge, to Bamford, 14 January 1859.*

> Dear Sir,
> I beg to acknowledge receipt of your note, intimating your intention to visit this locality for the purpose of giving an evening's reading and recitation from your own works.
>     If you think my patronage of any service to you I shall be happy to give it. My evenings next week are all occupied, but the week after I might be at liberty.
>                                   Yours truly,
>                                   John Cheetham

**Monday 24th.** My reading as follows. Well pleased; got a guinea and all expenses.

***Newspaper report***, *unattributed, giving an account of Bamford's readings on Monday 24 January at the Temperance Hall, Oldham, for the Oldham Analytic Literary Society, to a moderately numerous audience.*

***Report***, *from the* Middleton Albion, *29 January 1859, of Bamford's Oldham reading. Bamford gave a brief resumé of the circumstances of the post-Waterloo reform agitation, including his account of how he converted Cobbett to manhood suffrage and various extracts from his* Passages in the Life of a Radical.

---

> During these readings he was repeatedly greeted with hearty cheers. He next recited an old reform song of his composing, celebrating a contest for the reformer's banner and cap of liberty, at Stockport, about the year 1817, when the constables and yeomanry were glad to retreat. He also gave some other verses composed during his imprisonment at Lincoln, and concluded by reciting in broad dialect, "a piece from 'A Day Out,' by Mr. Benjamin Brierley, during the reading of which the audience were in almost continued laughter".

---

**Tuesday 25th.** Tuesday. Could not attend the Burns Centenary. Took severe cold last night, and now laid up with rrheum.

***Copy letter***, *Bamford to S.P. Robinson,*[47] *1 February 1859.*

> Sir,
> Yesterday I sent to your office at Newalls Buildings, for a card of Membership of

---

47. Smith Phillips Robinson (*c.* 1809–85), Unitarian and Liberal; active Anti-Corn Law Leaguer, mostly behind the scenes; secretary of the Free Trade Hall Committee, and secretary of the Lancashire Reformers Union (see *Manchester Guardian*, 11 April 1885). Prominent in the dispute with Bamford at the time of his first testimonial subscription in the late 1840s.

"The Lancashire Reformers Union," when you were so kind as to send me also for which I thank you, a card of admission to the Conference which is to be held this day. It is however a blue card, not for the hustings – and heat and pressure of a crowd are to me positive inflictions. I must decline the pleasure I might have otherwise experienced.

I Remain Sir

Your obliged Servant

Samuel Bamford.[48]

**Letter**, *from the* Middleton Albion, *5 February 1859.*

---

### REFORM LEADERS.

*To the Editor of the Middleton Albion.*

Sir, – In looking over the names of the parties delegated to represent the great body of Lancashire reformers at the recent conference held at our Free-trade Hall, I felt exceedingly disappointed at the omission of a name, which, from its association with reform movements for a long period past, ought to have found a conspicuous place in the list of reformers of the present day. I allude to Mr. Samuel Bamford. Whether inadvertence, or wilful neglect on the part of those who assume to be Mr. Bamford's supporters, or whether indisposition on the part of Mr. Bamford himself, I know not; but it certainly looked like a grave omission on the part of some one, when on looking round at the assembly of reformers who met together on Tuesday last, we missed the venerable countenance of one of Lancashire's foremost men of 1817 and '19.

I am sure it would have moved the hearts of all present to see the great leader of parliamentary reform of the present time side by side with one who braved the dungeon and the scaffold on behalf of similar principles when it was dangerous to assert them. Perhaps some of your correspondents can explain the cause of this omission, for if I am informed aright, Mr. Bamford is in some manner connected with the Middleton Reform Association, and I for one among many other expected to meet the old gentleman at the Free Trade Hall as one of the representatives of that association. Now that the cause of reform hath a roof over its head, it is but fair that those who stood upon the naked field when sabres flashed around them, should be recognised in the time of peaceful agitation, or when it is not dangerous to have their names associated with reform movements. – Yours, etc.,

Middleton February, 3, 1859            DEFERENCE.

(The omission was purely accidental. – ED. M.A.)

---

**Tuesday February 8th.** Sold 1000 copies of Early Days to John Heywood for £20.00.

**Report**, *from the* Oldham Chronicle, *12 February 1859, of a meeting held at the Temperance Hall, Middleton, chaired by Thomas Dickins JP, to consider petitioning the government for Middleton*

---

48. Text altered from "the pleasure of attending, remaining, Sir".

*to be incorporated as a parliamentary borough. The attendance was disappointing and little interest was shown. Bamford was among the speakers.*

Mr. Samuel Bamford stood forth from a sense of duty and that only. He thought he should not be discharging the obligation he owed to them and the country at large, if he did not express his sentiments on that measure. With regard to the evidence of the deservingness of Middleton and the adjoining townships being represented in parliament, there could not be one word of dispute with any right-minded and right-hearted man. What had been said by the previous speakers had been to him perfectly conclusive. A person could enlarge very much on the property and industry of Middleton, but with regard to their intelligence he did not want to praise them too much. But there was no doubt the people of Middleton and the adjoining townships were as intelligent as many districts that could be mentioned. With respect to property, it could be truly said that more working men sat under their own roof tree in Middleton than in any district which embraced a similar population in England, he might say in Europe. (Hear, hear.) They might also fairly conclude that there was more money subscribed to benefit societies than in any place of equal property and more money and house clubs. It also might be asserted that there was more property entrusted to the working classes to take to their own homes and work in that district than in any district in England – (hear, hear) – and that spoke well, not only for the industry, but for the integrity and trustworthiness of the people. (Hear, hear.) Then there were a large number of Sunday Schools in the town. He had written ten or twelve volumes of works; and he first learned to write in the Methodist Sunday school. No child in Middleton could do that now, for writing was not taught in the Sunday school. It was taught when he went, and that was taught in the days of religious fervent of Methodism under John Wesley and the old original Methodists. He thought it would be better if more latitude was given to the instruction in Sunday schools, and the children were taught something substantial on Sunday which would tend to their welfare on a Monday. (Hear, hear.) He thought they were perfectly right in seeking better representation in parliament, but he doubted if they would succeed the way they were going to work. He had given his adhesion to Mr Bright's bill, and felt restrained to wait until he saw the result of that before he took another step. (Hear, hear.) When that was disposed of, if it was favourable, all would be well, if it was not favourable, fresh ground must be broken, and they must try for something better. They were right in applying to the Earl of Derby, but he doubted whether that nobleman would accede to their request, because of the party with whom he was connected. But if he offered them a representative, they would have to consider on what terms they would have one, for they had, as yet, said nothing about the suffrage. He could not but consider that they were taking a proper course, and he wished them all success. (Applause.)

**Report**, *from the* Middleton Albion, *12 February 1859, of the above meeting, adding that "Mr Bamford [said he] was very happy to see the worthy magistrate, Mr Dickins, in the chair; a better choice for a chairman could not have been made; he had known him long as a kind and upright employer, whilst he was well assured that in his private capacity he was a most respected gentleman.*

*It would be well if we could see others of his class and station more frequently taking part with working people on occasions like the present."*

**Saturday 12th.** Mills the Secretary of the Middleton Reform Association having received the accompanying circular, the committee met and replied by saying they deemed it best not to take any further step in advance until they saw the intended Government measure for reform before the House. That they tendered many thanks for the offers of co-operation and would not fail to claim it when requisite.

***Circular*** *from the Lancashire Reformers' Union, Manchester, dated 8 February 1859, proposing the prompt formation of a reform organisation in the recipient's locality.*

**Thursday 17th.** Received the first proof from John Heywood, to page 32. Sent it back by next post.

Laid up with old pain in hip and groin.

***Letter****, Thomas Clowes to Bamford, 14 February 1859.*

My Dear Sir,
I took the liberty to propose you as one of the general council of the Lancashire Reformers Union and you were duly elected. A few of our Chorlton Friends are having a Tea and Coffee party, it is a social affair at Hoopers the Medlock Inn, Brook St at 7 tomorrow night. I and they are wishful for you to be there. If you will come it shall cost you nothing and I will find you a dormitory if you wish to stay all night.
> I am most Resp.
> Thos. Clowes.

***Copy letter****, Bamford to Thomas Clowes, 15 February 1859.*

My Dear Sir,
I regret very much having to inform you that I cannot attend at your social party this evening. I am laid up with rheumatism, or something of the sort; and must, at any rate, remain indoors until I am better.
   I thank you for your friendly remembrance of me at the Reformers Union, the directors of which are welcome to any credit which the omission of my name until this late period, may have conferred. To me, their notice or inattention have been, and still are, matters of perfect indifference: one duty only has been ever present, that of a true and consistent Parliamentary Reformer.
> Yours truly
> Saml Bamford.

***Letter****, John Smith (Blackley Mechanics' Institution) to Bamford (n.d. but post-marked 16 February).*

Sir,
I have to inform you that at the annual meeting held in the Institution you were unanimously elected as one of the vice Presidents for the year 1859.

And I may inform you that the committee meet on the last Friday in each month* at which your attendance would most truly oblige.

Yours obediently

John Smith,

Hon<sup>y</sup>. Sec<sup>y</sup>,

* Meeting commences at 8 o'clock in the Library.

**Friday 18th.** Took a hot bath for rheumatism: very agreeable, and I think [it] did me good.

**Saturday 19th.** The first really kind enquiry respecting my worldly prospects and means of living which (my friend John Wood of London excepted) had been put to me during the last eight years, appears in the following letter from one almost a stranger. Binney and Harland, never seemed to think of such a thing as asking "how I was getting on," or "Whether I was happy". Whether "anything could be done to improve my situation." John Stores Smith did at one time write me a letter or two on the subject, but he had soon enough of that, and like the others has now given me "the cold shoulder," entirely. Neither George Nelson,[49] his wife, nor any of the family have ever exhibited the least curiosity on the subject of my weal or woe. Mrs Schunck, Miss Jewsbury,[50] Wm Mort, Hepworth Dixon[51] (whose patronage, when I first went to London I could not endure, any more than that of the little contemptible grub, of a Douglas Gerald)[52] Thomas Carlyle, not a jot better than the rest. All their friendship evaporated like wreaths of steam. Now comes a stranger kindly enquiring, and he, I suppose will, shortly disappear as the other have done, and I remain in ignorance of the cause. What a world! and what its friendship.

**Letter**, *Charles Potter[53] (Oldham) to Bamford, 16 February 1859.*

Eleven O'clock Wednesday Night

Dear Sir,

Since the short visit I paid you on Sunday morning last something has lain very heavy at my heart with respect to you, and when I inform you the cause of the same, you will perhaps forgive me for thus writing you.

---

49. Husband of his sister's daughter, see ibid, 24 September 1861.
50. Geraldine Jewsbury (1812–80), Manchester novelist; it was apparently at her house that Bamford met Thomas Carlyle (see E. Mercer, "Geraldine Ensor Jewsbury", *Manchester Quarterly* XVII (1898), 300–21); *DNB*.
51. William Hepworth Dixon (1821–79), Manchester-born historian and man of letters, editor of *The Athenaeum*, 1853–69; *DNB*.
52. That is, Douglas Jerrold.
53. Charles Potter (1832–1907), Oldham artist, former weaver, and liberal, whose portrait of Bamford subsequently hung in the Manchester Reform Club (*Manchester City News*, 30 March 1929); see *Oldham Express*, 1 April 1882, *Manchester Literary Club Papers* xxxiv (1908), 517–23. (See Plate 1.)

Amongst other topics during our conversation at the breakfast table was a few touching remarks introduced by you, with respect to your Brother Poet Robert Burns, and you read me an extract from Carlyles life of the same which touched me very much, but the Bard must have been possess'd of a prophetic soul, for I find in looking over his correspondence a letter introduced and addressed to Mrs Dunlop, dated Edinburgh 30th April 1787 where he writes these words. I know what I may expect from the world, by and by – illiberal abuse and perhaps contemptuous neglect, but he wisely says in another epistle to Cunningham. Let wealth shelter and cherish unprotected merit, and the gratitude and celebrity of that merit will richly repay it.

Now with respect to your circumstances Mr Bamford is the reason of me writing you at the present, for the question has haunted me like a dream all this week, and I cannot rest another night without inquiring. Therefore I must humbly beg of you to answer me candidly, and if I find you indifferently circumstanced, I will with Gods help endeavour to commence a movement in Oldham, which I have no doubt will put some money in your purse, and whatever you write me shall be held sacred betwixt us, for no eyes shall see it except mine own on no account. I most solemnly promise you.

Believe me

to Remain Sir

Most Truly Yours

Charles Potter.

Mr Samuel Bamford
Bard-of-M.

P.S. I have much pleasure to inform you that I have got the Pilgrimage – to Robin Hoods Grave – written by Sam<sup>l</sup> Collin admitted in the Oldham Advertiser, which will be published on Saturday next.

Yours truly

C. Potter

Sent a reply of which the following, if legible, is a copy.

**Copy letter**, *Bamford to Charles Potter, Oldham, 20 February 1859.*[54]

My Dear Potter,
I must tell you that your very kind letter of enquiry rather astonished me; not from any idea of impropriety which it awakened, but from its being expressed in a tone of sympathy and friendly solicitude to which I have been so little accustomed. Would you believe that the kind enquiries you have thus made are such as have not been addressed to me either verbally or in writing by any one, or more, of my numerous professed friends; or very kind seeming relations during the last eight years,

---

54. The copy is not good, and some elements of the transcription given here are conjectural.

excepting my friend the late John Wood of London. Such a query as to where I was living, whether I was happy or miserable, or whether anything might be done to improve my circumstances, has never during that time come to my ears or my eyes, from any friend or agitant during the time I have mentioned. Your enquiry therefore came upon me quite unexpectedly. I read it, myself not unmoved, whilst my wife was in tears; tears of thankfulness to you, and of deep regret for the loss of those who have shamefully withdrawn their kindness in our old age and our days of trouble. Shame to them; for I have not knowingly given any cause for disruption of friendship, yet they disappear like wreaths of mist; no longer seen, no longer heard of. Such has been the friendship which we have experienced in the world, and in Manchester particularly. Letters, which for my own vindication, I have taken care of will explain all this when I am no longer capable of action or utterance. And if my letters and miscellaneous papers only get into right hands, when I am no more, the world will learn how I have been dealt with. Poor Burns, you quote him aptly. I, as much as he, have been prophetic, have been compelled by the depth of my own feelings, to be so. On p.439 of the new edition of my Radical I say, speaking of humble men of great talent, "they are not tainted with the irredeemable sin of political leadership. I am, and am also prepared for the consequences", etc, and the consequences have been pretty evident of late.

Just the tragedy of Burns over again; his whole career was a tragedy, sometimes sad, sometimes mournful, but always with dramatic tendency to the last leave. Yes, I as well as Burns know what "I may expect," perhaps, ere the ground closes over me. "Illiberal abuse, and contemptuous neglect". And this brings me to the latter part of your letter, your enquiry respecting my circumstances.

You must know that I abandoned the employment in Somerset House in almost as poor a condition as when I occupied it. I owed [not] anything, for I would not be in debt to anyone, and after I had paid the fare of myself and wife to Manchester, and the carriage of our goods to our domicile at Mosston, I found myself wondering how long we could make a couple of pounds last, which I still, lucky fellow, found in my pocket. I need not tell you it was soon cleaned out and I was forced to ask a friends advice as to how a certain stamp for 2-10-0 which I happened to recollect having, could be negotiated. He at once, in the most handsome manner offered me cash for it, and so removed the cause of present exigencies. About this same stamp I will tell you more another time, and if I should forget, a full explanation of it will be found amongst my letters of 1858, and in the fragment of a diary for a previous year which I don't at present recollect. This was a very seasonable relief, and just as that was expended, I had the good fortune, so it appeared to me, to sell the copyright in a thousand copies of my Life of a Radical to Mr Abel Heywood, for thirty-eight pounds ten shillings. This gave me time to look around me and to compleat my calculations, and when at the end of nine months from my first coming down, pressure was again bearing hard upon me, I sold the copyright of my 'Early Days' to John Heywood, brother of Abel, for twenty pounds, and on this I am at present subsisting. I have not a farthing of a pension; I have a soul above asking for it, or indeed accepting such a thing, save as <u>compensation</u> for obloquy, injury and imprisonment forty years ago, for advocating the very changes which the government, and the great statesmen of the realm have since carried into effect. You therefore see that I have not any permanent or reliable source of income whereon to depend, & my only expectations are founded on the countenance I may receive in my readings and recitations, which, as yet, have proved very limited; the profit allowed me from the sale of a few copies of my books may also add a little to my table.

Samuel Bamford[55]

**Sunday 20th.** Still very unwell from rheumatism, got a good wash in cold water this morning, and now (afternoon) I am much better.

**Monday 21st.** Went to Man^r. and left the agreement at the Stamp office to get stamped.

Deliv'd Mr Wilkinson, Major St. his copy of Radical.

Took out four copies from Abel Heywoods, making 12 I have had.

At P. Grants for a glass of ale and Bread and Cheese.

Saw Josh Taylor in Corporation Street, Ald Boomhead, John Middleton and others. Came home by bus at 1/2 p 12.

Found Potter from Oldham had called.

**Tuesday 22nd.** Mills from Middleton and Potter of Oldham. Decided on a course of action in conjunction with the latter.

Wrote to Clowes of Chorlton on Medlock respecting my attendance at their next meeting.

**Wednesday 23rd.** Went to see brother William, who, having first compleated his 74th year is dying of a dropsy.

David Morris sends me a circular.

**Thursday 24th.** Removed to one of Mr Halls houses, just above, in Hall Street, rent 2/6 weekly.

**Saturday 26th.** Compleated removal. Gave up the key to Luke and paid the rent.

**Sunday 27th.** Mima went to see William. Messrs Potter and Gowenlock[56] from Oldham called and something was done towards an arrangement for reading and

---

55. The letter has a postscript which is partially lost to cropping of the letter, but which includes the phrases, "NB I suppose you have my .......... must see. ..... I have been very unwell this week, or I should probably have come to Oldham".

56. R. Scott Gowenlock (dates not known), of the *Oldham Advertiser*, poet and minor literary figure. A staunch supporter of Bamford during these years – occasionally too staunch, see his letter of 22 February 1860 and the ensuing exchanges.

recitation. Messrs Gibson and C.L. Delaunay also called. Gibson purchasing one of my radicals, as did also Gowenlock.

**Monday 28th.** Went to Middleton, intending to go to Jacksons, the artists at Junction town (Jumbo) but gave that up. So stopped at Middleton, and went to look at our Anns grave thinking to bring away with me a small pot of snowdrops for our window at Moston, they were all however too far blown, and going back, for removal this season, which I was surprised at. The sextons wife (Benj. Heywoods) tells me the snowdrops on that grave are earlier than any others in the Country. Brought my shoes from the mending, 3/8 cost, and came back by 2 o'clock Omnibus.

On examining the stone on my fathers grave I found that his first Samuel died on the 12th Feb 1789. I had hitherto understood that I was born on the 28th Feb 1788, but this inscription tells me I am wrong in that supposition. As he died on the 12th Feb 1789, it is very likely that I was born 16 days after his death, which would be the 28th Feb 1789, and that my parents chose to replace their lost Samuel by a second, and so continued the name in me. If this was the case I am only 70 years of age this day, instead of being 71 as I had supposed.

I will get the register of christenings examined.[57]

---

57. Bamford was actually born on 28 February 1788, and baptised on 11 April. His infant brother, also Samuel, was buried on 14 January 1788, see Garratt, *Samuel Bamford*, 6.

# 3
# HAWKING AND RECITING

*The beginning of March saw the publication of Bamford's own "edition" of* Passages, *with the addition of a photographic portrait. This enabled Bamford to add to his continuing efforts to make a living via public recitations and sales of his book. This was important because the new edition of his* Early Days *was still only being printed in March. The Conservative government's reform bill was defeated in March, and a general election in the Spring interrupted the reform movement, and spoiled the market for further public readings, but Bamford was still able to take an active role in attempts to establish a Middleton Reform Association. Part of the problem was that a great deal of the energies of Manchester radicals were being devoted to further the parliamentary candidacy of Abel Heywood, whom Bamford loathed. Instead Bamford found himself drawn more closely into the circle of the more moderate Manchester Liberals, serving (with mounting frustration) on the Council of the Lancashire and Cheshire Union of Mechanics' Institutes, and attending the reform conference organised by the Lancashire Reformers' Union in April. Bamford issued the first version of his autobiographical circular in March, but even so, as the end of the winter platform season loomed, and as funds dwindled, his anxieties as to the future were increasing.*

**Tuesday 1st March.** Received the following letters. Went to Manchester and saw Mills of Middleton by appointment. Looked round by Victoria Market, bottom of Deansgate, Market place, and Corporation Street, but did not find any suitable situation for the publishing line. Went to John Heywoods in Deansgate and mentioned about proofs of my Early Days coming in very slowly: he promised to speak to the printer. Took out four copies of Radical for A Heywood; introduced Mills to Doherty the quill dealer in Sugar Lane, and returned weary by the 4 o'clock 'bus.

***Printed circular***, *Lancashire Reformers Union to Bamford, informing Bamford that his name has been added to the General Council of this Society.*

**Wednesday 2nd.** Went through Charles town to Jacksons at Junction. Got 9 photographs of self, making my total 10, and total of stereoscopic cards 12. A very good likeness of Sam Collins the poet of Hale Moss.[1] Walked back to Middleton, and home by 4 o'clock bus.

Called at James Kents Tong Lane, and had a long chat with him. James is all right, but the Middleton people are I think getting slack about their reform association. Is sinister influence at work here again?

**Thursday 3rd.** At home all day, preparing the photographs, putting up blinds etc.

---

1. Samuel Collins (1802–78), local handloom weaver, poet and radical, "the bard of Hale Moss", near Chadderton. His collected poetry was published in 1859; *DNB*.

**Friday 4th.** Went with Mima to see William whom we found better taking a happy oblivious nap. Left him a jill of whisky as a change from his long continued gin. Called and left an advertisement at the Exam<sup>r</sup> office and came home by 'bus.

**Saturday 5th.** The following appears in the Exam<sup>r</sup> and Times.

"Bamford's Life of a Radical, a new Edition, 1 vol, with photographic portrait, 6/. Also Steroscopic likeness of the author, views of Moston Hall, Booth Hall, Middleton Church, Wood-end Farm, Boggart Ho Cloof, 1/- each; Address. Samuel Bamford, Moston, Harperhey, Manchester."

Attended Council of the Institutional Association. David Morris, full of self appreciation, after a long ramble moved to withdraw a motion he had once before made. A long twaddling discussion, and after all it was found there was not any motion to withdraw. So came home, not very well.

**Sunday 6th.** At home all day, very quiet.

**Monday 7th.** Went to see William and found him much better.

Note from John Widdup, Barnsley as follows.

***Letter***,[2] *John Widdup, Barnsley, to Bamford, 28 February 1859.*

Sir,

I know not how you may receive a note from one wholly unknown to you but I have determined to risk your displeasure and write to you, the reason of which is to thank you sincerely for the Pleasure I have received in peruseing your "Passages in the Life of a Radical" haveing got the second edition about three weeks ago and so interested have I been in it that I have read it twice through. I endeavour'd to get the first edition at the time of its publication but could not succeed. I read some of the extracts given in the "Manchester Guardian" of that time and from them I formed a very unfavourable opinion of you for like yourself at the fore end of your Political life I was a devoted admirer of Henry Hunt and for any one to speak in disparagement of him was in my opinion worse than High Treason but of this Idolatory I got cured for one day at an auction sale I bought his Memoirs written while at Ilchester and they convinced me that my devoted Patriot was an overbearing Tyrant one who would rather "Rule in Hell than serve in Heaven".[3]

I am a working man and took a leading Part in the chartist movement of 1839 an[d] one fine morning in the month of August in that year I found myself snugly locked in York Castel charged with having incited her Majestys subjects to rebel against her crown and dignity but twenty years have considerably altered my ideas on Political matters. In fact I cannot tell you better than to say that your ideas as express'd in you[r] Book just realise my own thoughts and I shall feel proud to

2. With envelope addressed to 'Samuel Bamford, Author and Poet, Blakeley, Near Manchester'.
3. The reference is to Satan in Milton's *Paradise Lost.*

hand the "Passages" down to my children as an invaluable legacy in the hopes that they will be enabled to avoid the rock whereon I was wrecked for like yourself I have learn'd the proper value of popular applause. I know what the cheers of an unthinking crowd are worth for when I went to Prison I left the Barnsley Northern Union near a thousand members strong and when I returned in six weeks after on Bail they had all vanished and all the consolation I got was that I was a <u>damned fool</u> for going as far as I had at that time. Like thousands of others I bought a <u>Pike</u> to use as a sound politica[l] argument and I have it yet and would not take its weight in gold for it as it serves two very good purposes first it is always before me as a standing monument of my former <u>folly</u> and secondly it affords me many a hearty laugh at the wild notions that we poor mortals fall into. There is one thing that I oft say respecting it, that at that time I was prepared to use it in carrying the Charter I am now as fully prepared to use it in opposition to the enactment of the Charter for of all the evils that could fall on us there can be nothing worse than the Despotism of a mob[.] I have not forgot the Tyranny of the O'Connorites with those who would not join in their wild Land scheme[.] I lost the friendship of many for my opposition to it, some of which friendships have never yet been renewed – Hopeing that you will pardon me for thus trespassing on your time and wishing you long life and good health I remain your humble servant

John Widdup

P.S. It may interest you to know that one of your old co Defendants at York George Swift is liveing a few miles from this town he is one of my most intimate acquaintances he is a hale hearty old man and still a shoe maker.[4]

**Tuesday 8th.** The following.

***Letter***, *Gilbert French,*[5] *Newport Square, Bolton, to Bamford, 12 March 1859.*[6]

My Dear Sir,
I found the advertisement in the Manchester Examiner of Saturday and avail myself of the information.
    I shall beg you to send me by railway when you are next in Manchester a copy of the life, and also of each of the stereoscopic photographs – and <u>I beg the favour of your autograph in the volume, and on the back of the stereoscope of "the author."</u>[7]
    I enclose a post office order in your favour for 12/-, this may not exactly balance the charge but I shall be glad to set it right when we next meet at the

4. George Swift (dates not known), Lancashire radical and Peterloo defendant, acquitted at York. His account of Peterloo is in MCL.
5. Gilbert James French (1804–66), Bolton draper, president of the Bolton Mechanics' Institute 1857–8, published biography of Samuel Crompton, inventor of the spinning jenny, in 1859; MCL.
6. Seems to have been misdated by French.
7. French's emphasis.

Athenaeum where I trust we may meet for more profitable purpose than we did on Saturday night last.

I have the honor to be

my dear sir

Your very obed<sup>t</sup> friend

Gilbert J. French.

***Copy letter**, Bamford to Gilbert French, 9 March 1859.*

My Dear Sir,
I have this morning forwarded to your address, a copy of the Radical, with photographic portrait and Autograph: also a stereoscopic likeness, with autograph and anagram at the back. The charge for the whole, carriage included is 7/4; and 4/8 therefore remains to your credit in my hands, for which I shall have pleasure in settling with you when I see you; and that cannot be longer delayed than when business, really requiring the attention of mature and rational beings, calls us to the Athenaeum.

With many thanks for your kind requirements,

I remain My Dear Sir,

Your obliged Humble

Servant.

Samuel Bamford

**Tuesday 8th.** Also a sheet of proof from John Heywood, in which finding some rather presuming alteration, I wrote as follows.

***Copy letter**, Bamford to unnamed reader, 8 March 1859.*

The Gentleman who reads for the press, has my thanks for several very proper alterations which in this sheet and the preceding ones he has suggested: those I have approved of have remained, those I have declined have been rubbed out. But several alterations appear in the present sheet, which, I think, are scarcely required, and which I would rather not sanction. Such as that for instance in p63 where <u>tomb</u> is put for <u>grave</u>: as that at p60, which is out of all character; that at p86 which is not required, that at 82 where the expression is not at all improved. Alterations should in the first instance appear in <u>pencil</u>, and those I admit will remain, but <u>the</u> <u>copy</u> which the <u>author</u> <u>furnishes</u> <u>must</u> be <u>adhered</u> to; Mr Heywood has undertaken that: Punctuation and intervals are under the direction of the reader and corrector for the press, but the verbal matter cannot be displaced except by the authors consent, to do that might cause a change in the whole character of the book.

**Wednesday 9th.** Took a parcel for Mr French to the railway office, and left corrected proof at John Heywoods. Rogerson was not yet downstairs, but I left a copy for him. Got pay for the P.O order 12/-: left a copy at Josh Taylors, Tib Lane 6/- and came home by omnibus.

**Thursday 10th.** Set off to go to Oldham but met Potter on the road who was coming to my house. We called on the Jacksons and I left them a copy of Radical. Potter and I came on to Middleton, but finding there w[oul]d not be any 'bus before 1 o'clock, we strolled round the back oth brow, I pointing out to Potter the house in which I was born, and various other old associations, The Church Yard: my daughters grave with crocus & primrose springing. A graceful and majestic beech tree in the brow behind the Suffields Arms public house. Mason Arms, Albion Offices, and by Omnibus home, where Potter took a short lunch and went on to Manchester.

**Friday 11th.** Went to the general meeting at the Mechanics Institute, and chosen chairman. The Balance Sheet should have been examined & sanctioned or disallowed, but there was not any balance sheet forthcoming: The auditors could not get the original accounts from Mr C L Delaunay, & he did not appear at the meeting. The accounts, it apppears, are in a very irregular condition, and he refuses to produce them. Auditors and myself invite Mr D to meet up at Sam^l Wolstoncrofts at 8 next Friday night.

New rules read, discussed & with a few alterations passed.

**12th, 13th Sat & Sund.** Very wet days; at home. Mary Ann Sund. afternoon.
Returned proof to p128 to John Heywood.

**Monday 14th.**[8] Received a letter from Field of Oldham[9] inviting me to a tea party and soiree in aid of a memorial to the memory of late Edwin Butterworth[10] of Bury.

**14 & 15 Mond & Tuesd.** At home writing out my case.

**Wednesday 16th.** Went to Middleton and thence by rail to Oldham. Called on Potter and dined at his house. My portrait rather too young and too good looking for my years: there is a certain expression of the eyes which I am pretty certain does not belong to me: he has not very successfully copied the photograph by Jackson, however on the whole it is a very clever picture on the whole.

After dinner we called on W.H. Fletcher and saw a very Silenus, by Reubens[11] as they say. I rather think it is a copy from Reubens: one hand is badly drawn. Called at Heyes's of the Advertiser but he was not at home. Looked through the Lyceum; a very handsome and well finished and well furnished new building, with spacious news room and well stocked library: in one of the upper rooms, or rather closets, apparently seldom used found an old box without lid, but covered by part of an old torn banner beneath which were a quantity of old newspapers (Manchester Observers) pamphlets and sheets of writing which Potter said were relics of the library of the late Edwin Butterworth, and

---

8.  This entry on facing page.
9.  Charles Field, Secretary of the Union Club, Oldham, see ibid, 1 December 1859.
10. Edwin Butterworth (1812–47), Oldham journalist, local historian, diarist, educator, improver and Liberal.
11. Sir Peter Paul Rubens (1577–1640), Flemish painter; possibly referring to his "Drunken Silenus" (1618).

regretted they should lie in so neglected a condition. The writing appeared to be something relative to history and was I believe, so far as my recollection enabled me to judge, in the hand of of James Butterworth,[12] Edwins father: it was a better hand than Edwin ever wrote. The newspapers were chiefly Manchester Observers of 1817, 18 & 19 and amongst other contributions were two pieces of mine "The Fray of Stockport," 1818, and "Harrisons Hope," of, I think, 1821.

These papers should be examined carefully, assorted, and those worth preserving should be covered and deposited in a place of security.

Went to the Red Lion public house where I met Field, and told him I accepted his invitation. Some conversation. Mr Roy the landlord who takes much interest in literary matters, a Mr —— Secretary to some literary body, and it was concluded that a kind of literary gathering should take place of which I should have due notice. Came up to the Angel where I saw Kay Clegg and some of the Guardians, and from thence to the junction by rail and walked to Middleton. Missed the 7 o'clock omnibus and came to Blakeley by cab. 2/- Went to Mechanics Institution and gave a reading, after which home.

**Thursday 17th.** At home all day. Mima went to Manchester. Came back very much wet.

**Friday 18th.** Went to Middleton and found the Reform Committee had met the night previous and sent off Jos[h] Wolstoncroft to Newalls Buildings to ask on what terms the Middleton folks could amalgamate with them and now have a deputation to attend a public meeting. This I felt to have been a very improper proceeding and as the committee were to meet again at 9 o'clock p.m. I went over a second time and represented that they had acted precipitately in not calling the Middleton Reform Association together and taking their instructions before entering into an amalgamation and requiring a deputation. I reminded them that they had not yet put their own association into a proper form; that payments had not been agreed upon nor times of meeting, nor place of meeting; that a room aught to be taken, that Mr Mills was desirous to resign the duties of Secretary, and another with proper salary should be appointed: that they had as yet not done anything towards putting the association in operation, neither opposed the government reform bill nor supported Mr Brights, & that they should properly constitute themselves before they talked of amalgamation with [an]other body.

Mr Lawton moved and H Whalley[13] seconded "that the resolution of last night be rescinded". Mr Wolstoncroft at this time entered the room & gave an account of his interview with Mr S.P. Robinson at Newall's Buildings. He said it would be necessary that we should properly constitute ourselves into an association; payments not less than a

---

12. James Butterworth (1771–1837), father of Edwin, Oldham poet, author, radical, school teacher, postmaster and local historian. He wrote a poem in Bamford's honour while Bamford was imprisoned in Lincoln jail (*Homely Rhymes*, 62–3).

13. Henry Whalley (1826–77), of Middleton, manager at the Schwabe cotton mill, a Liberal, Wesleyan, and supporter of the Mechanics' Institute and Free Library; *Middleton Albion*, 29 December 1877. (See Plate 2.)

shilling a year, one third of which to be retained for our own expenses & the remainder to go to the fund at Manchester in support of the general fund: When this was done, on proper application being made, we could amalgamate, & a deputation would be appointed to attend our meeting. Mr Wolstoncroft added many observations of his own, and seemed desirous that these proposals should be acted upon forthwith, but the motion previously made being put to the meeting was carried: and the amalgamation & deputation were for the present shelved: to the chagrin, as I believed, of Mr Wolstoncroft, who seems rather pleased with his recent missions as "go between". I then moved that all those who gave in their names as members of the association on the night of Jan 3ᵈ should be waited upon, and requested to attend a meeting at 8 o'clock on the night of Thursd next or that they should be written to by circular. The former was preferred. Contributions to 1/- a year, and about 8/- were paid down. Wolstencroft remarking that now only had the association been commenced. He was taken up by several who referred to the enrolment of names on the night of the 3d Jan. the appointment of a Committee, treasurer, secretary, etc, as well as to subsequent meetings of the committee. – Turner was appointed to go round and visit the members, and it was ordered, that he at the same time collect as many yearly payments as he can. Wolstoncroft again remarked that this was the commencement of the association; an assertion which was scanted by the others present. 1/2 past ten, a fine moonlight night, and I walked home.

**Saturday 19th.** Went to see William and found him nearly same as last time. Weak, but not with much apparent pain. He rests better, gets very weak, and seems to be spitting his liver away.

Attended Council of the Institutional Association; a council of an Institution which in my opinion is of very questionable utility; the business seems to be got through in a loose desultory and non efficient manner, carried on chiefly in a low conversational tone, and without any system of business performance. I am wearied and disgusted with sitting in useless attendance. I cant hear one half of what is said, and I am in a mind not to go any more. Charles Delaunay was there, and took care to inform me that he had settled on Friday night with the Auditors of the Blakeley Mechanics Institution. He did not mention the two copies of Radical he had written for. He is a very uncertain character to deal with.

**Sunday 20th.** Potter from Oldham, and Jackson from Junction came, and we talked about indifferent matters until they went at 8 o'clock, to get back by rail from Newton Heath Station.

**Monday 21st.** This day Mima is 70 years of age.[14] Went to Manchester to see Peacock by invitation, found him in his room at last, and his suggestion was that I should get some one, or join with some one to make all proper arrangements about my readings and that auxiliary scenic attractions should be made use of. A young person of talent, and an artist especially wou[l]d be useful. I said if either he or any

---

14. Written in landscape down inside margin.

other friend could open a way whereby the thing might be rendered successful, I should be very grateful. I said more about my una[d]justed, unrequited claims to public compensation; remarking that not one friend, literary or otherwise, had said one word or written on line on the subject. (I thought he seemed to wince at that) finally he offered to give me a letter of introduction to Mr Hammersly, principal of the school of art[15] and I left him with an understanding that he would see Mr Hammersley, and other parties on the subject.

**Tuesday 22nd.** A note informs us that William died at a little past ten on Sunday night; I went up and saw Mrs Nelson, and it was arranged that the funeral should take place on Thursday afternoon, at the New Cemetery Eccles Road. Nelsons bearing all the expense, have consequently the whole of the arrangements.

***Report***, *from the* Bolton Chronicle, *of the second of two lectures at the Bolton Mechanics' Institute on Samuel Crompton, by the President, Gilbert French, which concluded with an appeal for funds to establish a Crompton Literary and Scientific Institution in the town.*

**Wednesday 23rd.** Wrote to Mr French as follows, with reference to his lecture on Samuel Crompton.

***Copy letter***, *Bamford to Gilbert French, 23 March 1859.*[16]

My Dear Sir,
I beg to thank you for the Bolton Chronicle which you gave me on Saturday evening. I have been deeply interested by the account of that great, worthy and shamefully ill used man, Samuel Crompton which you gave in your lecture at the Mechanics Institution. John Kay of Bury, the inventor of spinning by the fly-shuttle and lathe, like that persecuted worthy was harried out of the country and died in poverty in a foreign land. . . .

I regret having to say that I was not, on Saturday evening, much better gratified than on the previous occasion. The fact is, I am verging towards deafness; and the business being chiefly conducted in a conversational tone, and that, not a very distinct one, I derive but small interest from what is going on; and am very sensible of my inability to render any efficient aid.

I think the attempt to exclude boys under a certain age from reading rooms is founded on a wrong estimate of human nature; and if only half a dozen youths – out of as many hundreds, are thrown back to <u>dunce-hood</u> who can estimate the injury done to that generation?
                    SB

---

15. J.A. Hammersley (d. 1893), principal of the Manchester School of Design (later the School of Art) *c.* 1849–62; MCL.

16. The central portion of this letter has been severely damaged and is illegible.

**Friday 1st April.** Sent copies my circular. (Samuel Bamford) to And<sup>w</sup> Stewart Esq<sup>r</sup>, the May[or]. Jack Mellor Esq<sup>r</sup>, Town Clerk, and Ald. Livesey of Rochdale:[17] we shall see with what effect.

**Saturday 2nd.** Attended meeting at the Union Club Room tea party and Soiree, to raise a fund for memorial to Edwin Butterworth. Mr P. Seville in the Chair. Very good meeting, though a miserably wet night. Self and B Brierely spoke and read. Much applauded, both of us. Came away at about 1/2 past 8 after promising to go again and take 6 copies of Radical on Wed. next. Lost my favourite stick and landed at Miles Platting Station. The following notice of my Radical appears in the Oldham Advertiser of this day. Very kind of Gowenlock.

*Review*, *from the* Oldham Advertiser, *2 April 1859, of* Passages in the Life of a Radical, *probably by R.S. Gowenlock, praising it at length.*

---

We hail Mr. Bamford's book, because it contains the independent outspeakings of an earnest mind upon subjects deeply affecting the interests of the masses of society, and is, altogether, such an one as the world is only now and again favoured with.

Mr. Bamford has recorded the events in a way that few could equal – none could excel ... in a style that none but a self-educated poet-historian can write... . Mr Bamford is not only a narrator but a philosopher. His reflections are as profound as his picturings are brilliant. He deals not merely with facts, but with the causes from which they spring and the consequences to which they tend... . Earnest in the cause of human progress, Mr. Bamford has at the same time the philosophy to discover, and the manliness to point out, the difficulties and dangers that stand in its way. Reformers – young reformers especially – should not fail to possess themselves of Mr. Bamford's book.

---

**Monday 4th.** At Middleton. Chairman of Reform Meeting.

*Report*, *from the* Middleton Albion, *9 April 1859, of "a very enthusiastic meeting" of the Middleton Reform Association on 4 April. Bamford was voted into the chair, having assured the meeting that he would allow amendments to be proposed, remarking that "He did not like the modern way of appointing a chairman previous to the time of holding the meeting, but would rather recur to the old-fashioned mode of electing him instanter on the spot." He urged the speakers "to bear in mind that the longest speeches were not always the best". Representatives from the Lancashire Reformers' Union attended, and a lengthy debate ensued. A motion that the 1832 Reform Act was inadequate was passed unanimously. A motion by delegates from the Lancashire Reformers Union for a male ratepayer franchise, the ballot, "fairer" electoral districts and shorter parliaments was passed by majority vote, with a minority supporting a Chartist amendment for manhood suffrage, the ballot, equal electoral districts, annual parliament and payment for MPs.*

**Tuesday 5th.** Wrote as follows to Mrs Shiel at Brompton.

---

17. Thomas Livesey (d. 1864), Rochdale radical and one-time mayor; see J.A. Garrard, *Leadership and Power in Victorian Industrial Towns, 1830–1880* (1983), 127–9.

**Copy letter**, *Bamford to Mrs Shiel, 5 April 1859.*

My Dear Madam,

Your kind letter of the 25th ult was very welcome indeed. It is true, I had been long – too long, without writing to you, or sending you a newspaper, and had often reproached myself for the omissions; but something, some engagement of present urgency always intervened to prevent me from taking up my pen. An effect, I think I have intimated to you already, that it is always the last thing with me to commence writing a letter. Not but I am always glad to hear from an old friend, especially to hear of their welfare and happiness, but when I should reply I encounter a task, which the busy incidents of life too often furnish an excuse for evading. Thus, you see, I frankly make known to you my weakness in this matter, and as I am faded and also self-condemned, I hope you will be forgiving.

So yourself, Morris, (should it not be Maurice?) and Pauline, are all well. I am glad to hear that, and Bernard when he comes home will a source of joy and compleat satisfaction to you. I hope he has not ommitted to cultivate his remarkable talent for ..... has been abroad. I trust ... instructors would appreciate his capacity in this line, and would accordingly encourage him, by all means to cultivate it. If he gets nicely settled when he returns, and there are in London, very many liberal patrons of the arts, he will be a comfort to himself, and a great help to his little brother and sister as they advance in years. Richard, will I hope eventually equally repay your kind motherly anxiety and care on his account, and if only you can get your children well up and settled in the world, you will have a good reason for hoping to enjoy a serene and contented advance in years, and that is as much as we can hope for in life.

Of ourselves, I have the satisfaction to say we are both in as good health as two old folks of our years can expect. We are living within a few yards of the house we occupied when last I wrote to you. We have a very good cottage, of four rooms, at 2/6 per week, coals at 7$^d$ the hundred, laid down at the door, milk, better than you get at London at 2/4 the quart, and water for nothing. All would be well enough, were it not for the state of exigency in which we feel ourselves, and to which I am beginning to be almost reconciled. Indeed, I am nearly persuaded, people of our condition have not any right to expect stability, or certainty of subsistence. When I came down here, God knows, I knew not, any more than the man in the moon, how we should subsist from day to day. But some way or other, something has always turned up just when we were on the verge of extremity, and we have not during the eleven months that I have been without actual salary experienced one days deprivations of happiness, so I am well nigh persuaded it will always be so, and that by fits and starts, as the saying is, we shall be enabled to scramble on to the end of our days. At any rate, whatever comes of it I shall never stoop to any discreditable humiliation. I have sold 1000 copies – the copyright of them – of two of my books, and I expect to sell the copyright of another shortly; this money has given us breathing time and has helped us wonderfully through the winter. You will see from the inclosed circular, what are my hopes and prospects for the future; you will see that my case is such an one as no other man in England could present. I think the statement must secure me plenty of engagements, and as I am yet able and willing to work in that way I and my little woman shall bid adieu to anxiety respecting the means of subsistence. And if Morris and Pauline were here, would we all have some pleasant rambles in these woods and hollow dells. I would have them out on a ... ready to go getting nettles for broth and wild ... for afternoon tea. We have not any ... as yours, but we have plenty of ...[18]

Both your kindest respects<br>Sam<sup>l</sup> Bamford

**Wednesday 6th.** To Oldham. Called on Potter, and went with him [to] Buckleys Kings Arms. I had many years ago known Buckley, but had forgotten him, and found him now grey haired and a kind of sedate and formal snob, rather distant and consequential. We went to Ryes at Red Lion. Rye not within, nor a single soul in the bar parlour. Potter went to look for Field the Analytical Secretary, who should have helped me off with the seven copies of Rad which I had, at his invitation, brought. Field was not at home; he was gone to Manchester, so left books in care of Potter, handed them to Mrs Rye until he had an opportunity for seeing Field. Could not hear of my stick, so came away by the 6.15 train, and got down at Newton Heath.

**Thursday 7th.** to Rochd. The Mayor was not at home. Called at Reed Inn, only one Scotchman in the bar, for a wonder, and he was reading the newspaper. Mrs Robertson not at home: off at Blackpool: her niece who knew me officiating during her absence. Did not see one person, in going down Yorkshire Street, whom I knew, but several stared hard at me. Went to Smiths X Keys, Cloth Hall Street. A plate of nice potato pie and glass of ale: then into parlour, where I got a hot whiskey. Smith and I talking things over. He will see Livesey and sev[era]l others, and will try to get up a reading for me. Went again to the Mayor a little after two o'clock. He was gone out to take a ride and phaeton and not be at home before 5 o'clock, so came away, and gave him up for this time. Smith went with me to Millway and came off 3.10 train. Mrs Williamson in same carriage. Went to the Inn at Junction, waiting for trains, and treated her to 2d of peppermints: A very decent and respectable little old woman. Doctor Dicken, John Johnson of Stakehill, Ald Stickup and son, others in the bar parlour of Asshetons Arms. Got sev[eral] glasses of whisky hot and two cigars. Dickin, who had had two of my circulars, said I ought to have a national recompense provided. Came away by seven o'cl[oc]k train and found Mima waiting at Ben Walkers, Little Park. She came with me and lost Greaves's dog, which had stolen out after her when she went in the morning. I hope it will not be found again. I told old Greaves I did not want to be bothered with any ones dog.

The annexed appeared in the Middleton Albion of Sat 2d Apr.

***Cutting***, *from the* Middleton Albion, *2 April 1859, giving the text of Bamford's circular* (see Appendix 1).

**Friday 8th.** Manchester, took proof back. Saw one of the young Heywoods. Belfield, saw Life at Rogersons. Home rather late.

---

18. Sections of this letter, especially the last few sentences, are illegible.

**Saturday 9th.** Was accosted in Market Street by S.P. Robinson, whom I did not know, until he told me. I said I had just been at his office in Newalls Buildings. What was it for? and was it anything he could do for me? Yes I wished to attend the Conference on Tuesday, and, as I could not endure the stifle and pressure of a crowd I wanted him to give [me] a platform ticket. That he would do with pleasure; I was one of the General Council, and had only to come and present myself, but he would give me a ticket also; and be sure and visit the rooms at Newalls Building: they /(the Reformers Union)\ would be very glad to see me at anytime: he repeatedly pressed me to be sure and come, and I promised I would. So am to call on him for a ticket. Saw Waugh with whom I had a long confab at the Clarence and at The King in Oldham Street. Peacock had been saying something about the copyright of my books, that a Committee might be formed to permit a subscription for the purchase of the Copyright of the whole of my works, and the purchasing of an annuity, for myself and wife, or the making of some other suitable provision for us. I said it was a business that certainly might be done but it was a thing I could not start myself: if Peacock, or some other friend once set it agoing, no doubt it would proceed. We talked long about this matter and Waugh said he would speak to Peacock again about the matter.

Bought two pounds of steak in the new market house; this is for a good potato pie for Sundays dinner. Came in Bus – called at New Inn, and walked down the lane with Jos<sup>h</sup> Hall.

The annexed articles are from the Oldham papers of this day.

**Report**, *from the* Oldham Chronicle, *9 April 1859, of the meeting at the Oldham Analytic and Literary Club on the 2nd April, to consider the best way to memorialise Edwin Butterworth. The speakers included Peter Seville (chairman), James Schofield, Bamford, Brierley and Ambrose Hurst. Bamford was called on to speak to "the memory of the late Mr. Edwin Butterworth", and was heartily cheered on rising, saying:*

… it was customary to address such assemblies as ladies and gentlemen, but he would rather call them his honest fellow countrymen and women. (Cheers.) He thought nothing could be more attaching and respectable than woman, and what bound their affection more closely than that sacred name of woman – the name given to the real mother of us all. No one could desire more than to be an honest man and woman, and as regarded this town Burns might have said –

Oldham, which ne'er a town surpasses,

For honest men and bonny lasses.

With regard to Mr. Butterworth he was well acquainted with him as well as his father, who during the time of his (Mr. Bamford's) captivity for advocating the cause of political freedom, sent scraps of poetry to him whilst in prison to cheer him in his solitude. (Hear, hear.) He (the speaker) after acquiring the rudiments of education – and he might mention that he had learned writing at a Methodist Sunday-school – became a correspondent of one of the London papers in the year 1826. Although the post was not very remunerative, still it was more than he obtained at the loom, and he gave the latter up. (Laughter.) In that situation he did what he could to expose the deplorable condition of the hand-loom weavers and of the manufacturing districts generally. Whilst attending the petty sessions at Hollinwood and Oldham he used to meet Mr. Samuel Butterworth who came to take reports of the proceedings, and after he had left off, he was succeeded by his son, Edwin Butterworth. Edwin used to come to the court in his humble, meek unobtrusive manner, and stand at the bar with his little book, and put down the proceedings in small writing in a little crank hand. Nobody seeming to notice him, he (Mr. Bamford) asked him to come inside, out of respect to himself and his father. He gave Edwin a great deal of advice and instruction in his new occupation, (as on the death of his father he continued correspondent for the Manchester papers,) and also to seek more remuneration as he was but inadequately paid. He also advised Mr. Fielding, Middleton, to do the same, but he knew not whether they ever acted on his suggestion or not. He (Mr. Bamford) lived at Blakeley at the time, and Edwin used to go to his house frequently and to converse on various subjects. The last time he went there he seemed depressed and low spirited, and he tried to cheer him; but he continued in the same state. He accompanied him over the moss towards his own house, which was not far distant, but something struck him then that he was not as he should be. The next information he obtained was that he was very ill. He (Mr. Bamford) and Mr. Fielding went to see him, and they then saw him in his little chamber lying in a state of insensibility and his recollection nearly gone. He was labouring under low typhus fever of a very bad type. He died the following day. With regard to the object of the present meeting he had rather heretical opinions. He thought that it was a very poor reward for a person, after having been neglected through life, and his talents unappreciated and left in penury and want, to erect a monument over his remains. (Hear, hear.) It was, however, the way of the world. He thought if anything were to be done that the grave ought to be surounded with a modest paling, enclosing a little garden with green moss and evergreens, as emblems of his everlasting purity, with a tablet on which it should be stated that he was a local historian, and then his books would tell all the rest. (Hear, hear.) He thought that whatever the testimonial should be it should correspond with the habits and mind of the man. (Hear, hear.) He thought the simpler the better. Let them try to do something sublime, and simplicity was an element of sublimity. (Hear, hear.)

---

*Bamford was followed by Ben Brierley, who praised Butterworth's works and read his own sketch "A Day Out"; then by Joseph Fielding,[19] who agreed with Bamford on the need to support living authors rather than memorialise the dead. He also recalled Bamford's role as "schoolmaster" to himself and Butterworth:*

---

He used to get them to recite "Brutus and Cassius". (Mr. Bamford: But I could never drive it into you.) (Great laughter.) They were full of play when young, but Mr. Bamford gave them a good beginning and put them in a proper way to go on

---

19. Joseph Fielding (1800–61), of Middleton, born into a local weaving family and successively a weaver, night school teacher and journalist. A Wesleyan, hostile to Chartism. Fielding's laudatory obituary of the Peterloo veteran Amos Ogden, whom Bamford regarded as a turncoat, provoked Bamford's riposte, *Some account of the late Amos Ogden of Middleton* (1853). The similarity of his career to Bamford's may account for some of Bamford's persistent hostility towards him: see entry for 20 October 1859.

to further acquirement. (Mr. Bamford: They were good as far as learning went. But that Brutus and Cassius they could never get through). (Great laughter).

---

**Report**, *from the* Oldham Advertiser, *9 April 1859: another account of the Butterworth memorial meeting.*

**Sunday 10th.** At home, not very well.

**Monday 11th.** Sent the annexed to the Oldham Advertiser.

**Copy letter**, *Bamford to R.S. Gowenlock, 11 April 1859.*

My Dear Sir,
I have to crave your forgiveness for not thanking you, which I aught to have done before this, for your very kind and favourable notice of the recent reissue of my Life of a Radical. The opinions you express are very gratifying indeed, which the terms in which they are presented, confer not less honour on their writer than they do on the writer of the book reviewed. I shall always feel very much your debtor for the obligation, which you have thus so handsomely bestowed. The full and discriminative exercise of your pen, will, most probably aid in the disposal of the present edition of the book; and though most prominently, the publisher will be the largest and most immediate gainer by the sale, it will tend to facilitate the demand for another edition, and will consequently promote my interests. For many reasons I am therefore your debtor, and shall feel it /a\ duty which I owe to you, to endeavour to repay the obligation in a way more tangible and effective than by mere thanks. I hope Brierley is doing something which will be really useful for your paper, and whether he does or not I shall feel a pleasure in dropping you a trifle as opportunity occurs.
                    I remain, Dear Sir,
                         Yours most truly and respectfully,
                              Samuel Bamford.

**Copy letter**, *Bamford to the Editor of the* Oldham Advertiser, *11 April 1859.*

*The Late Edwin Butterworth.*
Sir,
On reading your report of the tea party and soiree in memory of the late Edwin Butterworth, I found I had omitted in addressing the meeting, a circumstance which has frequently, since Mr Butterworths decease, made a strong impression of regret on my mind. I mentioned about his coming to my house at Blakeley, and appearing depressed and low spirited, and about my going with him over the moss, and trying to cheer him. I did not know at the time that he was embarrassed by money obligations, so I did not touch upon anything of that kind, but tried to draw him away from his thoughtful mood by cheerful conversation.

Had I obtained the least idea of the real cause of his depression I might probably have devised means for obviating his embarrassment, and I am quite certain that I should have felt it both a pleasure and a duty to have used those means promptly, and with my whole heart. He parted from me however, and I did not see him again until he was prostrate, and almost unconscious. In speaking of this visit afterwards to a friend he regretted not having made his situation freely and unreservedly known to me, saying, at the same time, he was of opinion that I should have struck out some plan for having his affairs regulated and settled. I also, when I heard of the real cause of his unhappiness, was much grieved at my not having had an opportunity to serve him. Which I felt might have been done without difficulty, by the aid of one or two kind and zealous friends, and I believed he had many such, who only required to have his case made known to them.

His mortal remains will now, I presume, have due respect paid to them, and his literary remains, might, I think be applied to an useful purpose. On one of my recent visits to your borough, I was shown a box in one of the upper rooms of your very excellent Institution, the Lyceum; the box was without a lid, and an old banner only part concealed a number of papers, some printed, others in manuscript which it contained. The writings seemed to be in the hand of Old Mr Butterworth, Edwin's father; at least, on seeing them the recollection of the old mans penmanship was clearly presented to my mind. There might be other writings in the box, some of Edwins perhaps, but I did not move them for examination. Something like writings stitched into books, I think I also saw, together, all in a jumble, with a number of old newspapers (Manchester Observers) of 1818 and 1819. In one of these old papers was a song which I wrote. I think in the early part of 1819 called "The Fray of Stockport".[20] I should be glad to hear that Edwin Butterworths literary remains should be examined, carefully adjusted so far as that can be done (his old fathers also) and secured in a manner which shall render them available for reference, or other use, whenever such may be required.

I am Sir

Yours respectfully,

Samuel Bamford.

Went to 12 Newalls Buildings to get a platform ticket from Mr S.P. Robinson. He said a ticket was not necessary, that no one would prevent me from entering, and I might choose my own seat, only go in good time: or at the very worst I had only to show my blue ticket, and all would be right. A tall elderly gentleman came to speak to Mr Robinson, and the latter took the liberty to inform me that the gentleman was Mr

---

20. There are five lines of deleted matter: "and which I inscribed to Joseph Harrison, at that time a better reformer, undergoing a long imprisonment in Chester Castle. So having attended a Parliamentary reform meeting, and proposing that Sir Charles Wolseley should act as "legislaterial attorney," for the above borough, which has since been so far reformed, as to send two members to Parliament." Revd Joseph Harrison (1780–1848), a Stockport reformer, was imprisoned for a seditious sermon delivered in July 1819, and the subject of Bamford's poem, "Harrison's Hope"; see entry for 5 June 1859.

Richard Ashworth[21] of Turton and introducing me as Mr Sam. Bamford author of "Life of a Radical." Mr Ashworth, seeming surprised, looked [at] me earnestly, and taking my hand expressed pleasure at meeting me, he had not known me before, except by name. My book was an excellent production, and sign of a healthful thoughtful mind, a honour to the working class of Lancashire. He was coming out, as a candidate for Salford at the ensuing election; we talked a few minutes about indifferent things and then he left us.

I detest these impromptu introductions.[22]

**Tuesday 12th.** Went to Newalls Buildings, and not being able to find my blue ticket of membership I got another. Mr Senior, the Hall keeper, invited me to walk up without my showing my ticket; it seemed he remembered me. The meeting was very well attended, and I, being in good time, got a comfortable seat in the front row, which I preferred to one on the platform. Mr Barns spoke well, and Mr Bright made a clear, understandable speech, but, as he is much given to, of late, it was too long; he spoke with difficulty towards the latter end of his address, coughing at every three or four words. I could not but think he was doing too much in the way of speaking, and there were those who afterwards said "they (his friends) would kill him by calling him out to speak too often". "That he had a <u>heart</u> <u>disease</u> and should be careful not to get excited." The conference was not a conference at all, which it aught to have been; it was merely a meeting got together to hear a few speeches from selected speakers, the only apparent result being an immensity of shouting and clapping, which detracted from the dignity and gravity of a thoughtful English assembly. Came home by Bus and foolishly stopped a[t] Tom Kays, writing for him a couplet.

**Wednesday 13th.** Went to Rochdale; very stormy forenoon, found the Mayor at the Court on the Bench. A number of Magistrates were sitting and some one of them ordered the police to find me a seat, which was done accordingly. The magistrates recognized me; the police did not; they were an entirely new set of men to me. The large room was well filled with very decent looking people chiefly of the working class. They were all seated, and very good order was preserved. I went out, to Smiths at the Cross Keys, where I met Edwin Greenwood, the artist.[23] Went with him to the Golden Ball to enquire of Thomas Livesey, who had shortly before left the place; went again to the court room and waited until the business was closed when I had an opportunity for speaking to the Mayor, who, I thought, received me somewhat coolly, but directed me to come to his house at about two o'clock. Went b[ac]k to the Golden Ball, and got a glass of ale and a

---

21. There was no Richard Ashworth in the Turton Ashworths, and this is likely to be Henry Ashworth (1794–1880), cotton spinner, founder and leading light of the Anti-Corn Law League, close confidant of Cobden, and parliamentary candidate for Salford in 1859; see Rhodes Boyson, *The Ashworth Cotton Enterprise: the Rise and Fall of a Family Firm* (1970).
22. Located beneath the cuttings; but seems to relate to the introduction to "Richard Ashworth".
23. Edwin Greenwood (*c.* 1809–), jobbing portrait painter and balladeer, apparently active in Rochdale until the early 1870s; see A.G. Parke, "Rochdale Artists", tps, Rochdale Local Studies Library.

very poor Welch rabbit for lunch, and then attended on the Mayor. The house was all in disorder, painting and upholstering, and I was shown into a room where everything was in confusion. The Mayor came and took a small chair, making me occupy his large one. So I mentioned about his having probably received a circular of mine, which he said he had. I said the plan proposed in that appeared to me the most eligable and becoming way in which a person of my years and past course of         24 could seek to obtain a livelihood. He did not disapprove of my idea, but said it w[oul]d be quite futile to attempt to get up anything of the sort until the election was over; until then people would be incessantly engaged: Committee and ward meetings would be taking place every night, and the men who would probably act in my behalf would be deeply engaged in election business. He would however, advise me to see Mr Livesey, put my affair into his hands, (he had spoken to the Mayor about it) and be guided by his advice. This plan entirely agreed with what I had heard before, and with my own previous opinion, and so after some chat on various subjects of by gone days I bade his worship a good morning. Going towards Drake Street, for the rail-way, I found Livesey watching a funeral in Church Lane. We went into a tavern opposite and there he expressed the same opinion respecting my business which the Mayor had done. He said the best plan he thought, would be for himself to introduce the subject at some of their large Committee Meetings, I to be in attendance to give any required explanation. He would ask the Mayor to take five pounds worth of tickets, he was rich, and could well afford to do that; he himself would take one pounds worth, and passing the list round, he would obtain as many names as possible for as high a number of tickets as possible: the thing would be done at once, and I should be secured a fair remuneration for a lecture, or a course of three lectures. I said I should prefer the latter as one lecture would not afford sufficient opportunity for the exercise of his abilities. So we parted with the understanding that he would let me know when to come over to Rochdale. Came by rail to Middleton; stopped at Walkers, and at T Mills's and so home by omnibus.

**Thursday 14th.** Went across the clough to Ann Fords where a tot of her ale did me good. Called at Grimshaws, and so home where I corrected my circular.

**Friday 15th.** Took corrected circular to Ireland and Cos,[25] got it put in type and saw a copy. Went with Waugh to see his portrait, drawn by Percy[26] in chalk, very like Waugh, but rather too smart, and dandyish, I thought. It is to be lithographed. Waugh told me Tom Cooper,[27] the Chartist was coming to Manchester, to lecture. This I suppose is to keep me in the back ground.

---

24. Blank left in diary.
25. Publishing company of Alexander Ireland (1810–94), Manchester literary figure, editor of the radical-liberal *Manchester Examiner and Times*, and publisher of Bamford's final volume of poetry in 1864; *DNB*.
26. William Percy (1819–1903), Manchester artist and prominent member of the Literary Club; painted portrait of Bamford which subsequently hung in the Manchester Reform Club; see *Manchester City News*, 30 March 1929.
27. Thomas Cooper (1805–92), Leicester Chartist and then lecturer and writer of Christian apologetics, editor of *Cooper's Journal*, author of *Purgatory of Suicides* etc; see *DLB*, IX, 51–7.

**Saturday 16th.** At a meeting at the Free Trade Hall last night, to promote the election of Abel Anything, Ald Goadsby in the chair, Elijah Dixon said that "42 years ago he suffered eight months imprisonment for the cause of Parliamentary Reforms. He had laboured in the cause ever since" (he has only laboured for himself to accumulate money) "and he believed that the attainment of the object they had in view was merely a matter of time." This I suppose was a set off against my circular, stating that I was "the earliest English political sufferer now living." I certainly had forgotten that Dixon was, like myself, arrested under the <u>Habeus</u> <u>Corpus</u> Suspension Act, and was liberated when the suspension expired.

Got my corrected circular from Ireland and Co and brought it home and dispatched a number by post.

**Sunday 17th.** Potter came and brought the Oldham Advertiser containing my letter of the previous week on Edwin Butterworth.

Both the Advertiser and the Chronicle write in severe terms (not too severe) on the conduct of J.M. Cobbett.[28] Gowenlock, after the election is over, intends giving my circular, as a matter of news, with some observations of his own. A new Paper, the <u>Protector</u> published at Ashton, gives it this week in full: the old version.

**Monday 18th.** Went to Ashton thinking it possible I might get up a reading this week, for funds are getting very low, and something must be done. Called on John Grundy,[29] who advised me to see the Mayor, Mr Hugh Mason,[30] the two Messrs Buckley, and the two Messrs Higginbottom, and if I could only get them to take an interest in the business, the thing would be done. Went to Hugh Masons Mill, the young woman at the gate asked for my address and I gave her my card, returning she said Mr Mason was engaged, and then added "he wished to know my business." I hesitated feeling hurt that any evasion should be attempted towards me; would I call again she asked. I demurred to that, saying it was a long way to come on a fruitless errand. Tell Mr Mason, I said that my business will be very brief, and I shall not detain him many minutes. She went, and returning showed me up the steps to a kind of hall or ante room, the door of another handsome and spacious apartment was open; it was carpeted, and appeared to be furnished with every convenience in fashionable style. Two gentlemen were seated and conversing in the place, and during about a quarter of an hour I looked at some handsome plates and large map of India which were appended from the wall. At length feeling tired I took a seat on one of the two

---

28. John Morgan Cobbett (1800–77), son of William, solicitor, MP for Oldham 1852–65, 1875–7; Boase. Oldham politics had been complicated since the 1840s by a Cobbettite faction which continued to support the nominal radical J.M. Cobbett, even as he moved ever more obviously in a conservative direction. In 1859 Cobbett was opposed by two progressive radicals, W.J. Fox and J.T. Hibbert, but refused to stand down, attracting enough Liberal support to defeat Hibbert by eleven votes.

29. John Clowes Grundy (1806–67), print seller and one of the leading patrons of the arts in Manchester; Boase.

30. Hugh Mason (c. 1817–86), Ashton cotton manufacturer and paternalist, leading Liberal, temperance campaigner, and mayor of Ashton 1858–60; *Manchester Guardian*, 3 February 1886.

benches, which were the only sitting furniture in this room. After a few minutes the two gentlemen, still talking entered the room where I was, and one of them departing, left me in company with the other whom I did not know, but supposing him to[31] be the Mayor, I addressed him as such, and found I was right. I stated to him that being desirous to earn a honest and respectable livelihood, I wished to have an engagement for a reading and recitation at Ashton, and that [if] I could obtain his patronage, and that of his neighbours, the Messrs. Buckley and Higginbottom I thought a remunerative audience would be brought together. He at once said that nothing whatever could [be] done in that way until the expiration of four or five weeks. (A damper to my hopes, for while in the grass was growing, the horse would be starving.) The elections must all be settled before there would be the least chance of my engaging any gentleman in my business. I remarked, there would not be any contest in that borough: he replied certainly not, but the County elections must be attended to befor[e] any other matter, and that would engage nearly every influential gentleman in the place. When the County election was over, and all that was settled, he would do all he could to meet my wishes, but until then it would be utterly vain to attempt anything in the way I proposed. I could not but acquiesce in what he said, and so thanking him for his promised aid at the proper time I came away with a sadly depressed heart, and in consequence of the view Mr Mason held, which I deemed a correct one, I did not call on the Messrs. Buckley nor Hegginbottom, but went to my friend Grundys and from thence took the omnibus to Manchester.

I afterwards heard that T. Milner Gibson, was in Ashton that day, and I surmised that the gentleman whom I found with Mr Mason was him.[32]

I could not but remark that I was not asked to take a seat in the better room: such is the difference which the pride of wealth prescribes betwixt a person in humble life, however meritorious, and one of higher pretension, though perhaps of vastly inferior worth and talent.

I expected seeing old Mr Thomas Mason;[33] this was the young one, Hugh, which I met, and when he came I did not know him.

Something must be done, so I made an excuse to call on John Heywood, with the printed leaf of various commendatory notices of my former edition of Early Days. John had sent me the last proof sheet of the present edition which he had in the press, and I thought this a favourable opportunity for sounding him as to any further speculation with my works. So I saw him, and after giving him the article I had brought, I asked him what he proposed doing next in the way of publication? he mentioned my poems, and Walks in South Lancashire, and said he would buy an edition of the latter from me: he wished to see the copy, but I said it was in a state of disorder, part printed, part in MS. He thought there would be a difficulty in judging as to its extent, and

---

31. This marks the end of the first volume, as currently bound.
32. This and following two paragraphs inserted on facing page.
33. Thomas Mason (c. 1782–1868), father of Hugh, founder of Thomas Mason and Sons (Oxford Mills), director of the Midland Railway and other commercial undertakings; one of the largest cotton spinners of his day.

consequently as to the price, and I suggested that he could pay by the sheet, as the printing went on; he seemed to approve of that idea. I proposed calling again the day following, but he said I had best let it lie over for a fortnight, and he would then be more at liberty to proceed with the business. So I promised to see him again at the fortnights end. Called at Belfields. Some animated conversation about Bazley, Turner, and Heywood, the latter huffed, and spoken of slightingly. I did my best to render him justice, without placing him on a par with the other gentlemen, which indeed I could not do with truth.

Called at Tom Ks, smoked a cigar, and came home with neighbours Heath and Phillips.

# 4
# GOD HELP THE POOR

*By the second half of April the Bamfords' financial circumstances were becoming desperate. John Heywood had still not published the new edition of* Early Days, *and the stinging insult of being excluded from the Middleton reform meeting as a non-elector reignited Bamford's old fears of being surrounded by a "clique of enemies". He was soon reduced, despite the damage to his pride, to borrowing from friends, and picking up the odd profits from selling on copies of* Passages *which he obtained from Abel Heywood at a discount. Immediate crisis was staved off by the sale of tickets for readings at Rochdale and Stalybridge; but the cautious stance of the new Liberal government led by Lord Palmerston was a setback to the reform movement to which Bamford's public fortunes were linked; he had to work hard making personal application to the leading figures in the two towns to take tickets, and he found the inevitable slights and disappointments increasingly difficult to stomach.*

**Tuesday 19th.** A dolorous awakening this morning. A fortnight to wait before I can do any business with John Heywood; five weeks before anything can be effected at Ashton. A score on, of a matter of 15/- at the shop – as my wife says – a stack of coal that will not last two days, and only 19/6 in money in the world, whilst silver spoons and my wife's dress are already at kind uncles:[1] How is this to be ordered? The Lord only knows. I certainly cannot see my way out of this difficulty except by one thing. Stopped at home all day, pondering on my present situation, and writing up this diary.
God help the poor.[2]

**Wednesday 20th.** Went to Middleton, thinking to get up a reading for Monday night, but Mills did not give me the least encouragement. Said all the folks would be off to Manchester and other places on Monday, and Tuesday, and on Wednesday a tea party or other thing was to come off, so gave up the idea of a reading until a better opportunity. Money however, must be obtained by some means, and God knows I don't see how or whence, except by actual beggary, or something equivalent to it.

Mr Oswald Dickin happening to come into the parlour of the Masons Arms, whilst I rested, with a glass of ale, alluding to position, and wrongs of former days he said the Country ought to provide myself and wife, a maintenance during our lives. Oh who is to do it? said I. "Those up there," said he, nodding at a plate of the Anti Corn Law League, which hung over the chimney piece. Mills, of the Middleton Albion, had just before expressed a similar opinion as to the Country taking the matter up; so I perceive there is a growing tendency to that effect in the Country, for the same sentiments I have repeatedly heard at Manchester. Walked there and back, and got in coal at night.

---

1. That is, the pawnshop.
2. A reference to Bamford's poem, which was reproduced in chapter 9 of Elizabeth Gaskell's *Mary Barton* (1848), and also appears in his own *Homely Rhymes*. His father had written a poem of the same title in the hard year of 1793, set to the tune of "God Save the King" (*Early Days*, chapter 1). Bamford's own was also a song, set to "Christians Awake" by the Manchester Jacobite John Byrom, a hymn adopted by Middleton's Methodists; see entry for 16 May 1859.

**Thursday 21st.** Walked to Chorlton on Medlock, to see my friend Clowes. Mrs Clowes made me take some very good roast beef and a glass of excellent ale, and after chatting with her and her aged mother, in the 84th year of her age, Mr Clowes returned from an election committee meeting he had been at. We talked about a variety of matters, and amongst other things he said he had shown my circulars to several friends, and he and others had agreed to get up a reading for me, and he wished to know what sum I should require in such a case. I said, if the reading did not produce any any thing I would not require anything, and if they guaranteed me from loss, I w[oul]d be satisfied with whatever sum remained after deducting the expenses. So it was understood that I should have a reading in Chorlton at any rate, after the elections were over.

Amongst others he had shown a circular to Geo. Wilson who would assist in promoting the reading, and wished I would frequently come amongst the reformers at Newalls buildings.

**Friday 22nd.** In the afternoon (Good Frid.) was annoyed by the undesired visit of a very presuming body from Manchester, who stopped [to] tea, and remained until we were obliged to invite her off. Chas Delaunay and Saml Wolstencroft called, they had been out canvassing electors of Blakeley, in the interest of Cheetham and Heywood, and I thought from what they said, and their rather dispirited manner, they had not met with much success. Very many, they said, of the /liberal\ voters, were not registered, and consequently were thrown out for this year. Such will I believe, be found to be the case throughout the Country, and if so, the Derbyites knew the game they were playing when they dissolved Parliament.

Chas Delaunay has been a great promoter of readings by Walter Montgomery,[3] who got three guineas and all expenses for a performance at Blakeley, when 4/2 were left in the pockets of the Directors. Another reading is to come off at Harperhey, and in the face of these facts Delaunay had the conscience to ask me to <u>read</u> with <u>him</u>, at Harperhey, on one of the ensuing nights. Montgomery to get his <u>three</u> <u>guineas</u>, and I to receive <u>thanks</u>. And yet Delaunay seems to consider himself a friend.

**Saturday 23rd.** Spent the evening at "the Review Society", in Newalls Buildings. Thomas Cooper there: formerly was very skinny and scraggy looking, so they tell me, now he is quite plump, and full faced, much pitted with smallpox, smooth and anxious is the more proper term. Such is the improvement effected by his turning from atheist to Christian Gospel minister. He seemed glad to see me, and told me that my description of Hunts intense egotism was confirmed to him, by both Hetherington[4] and Cleave.[5] He only stopped a short time: he was going to lecture that night; he is quite a lion amongst the parsons, and at his performance, has generally a lot of them about him.

3. Walter Montgomery (1827–71) (real name Richard Tomlinson), actor and reciter; *DNB*.
4. Henry Hetherington (1792–1849), leading radical of the 1820s and 1830s, editor of the *Poor Man's Guardian*; *DNB*.
5. John Cleave (*c.* 1795–1850), radical journalist, editor of *Cleave's Weekly Register*; *DLB*, VI, 59–63.

The societys proceedings were rather a dull affair. Some good readings from Shakespeare, (it being his birth day) but greatly too long. Some singing, recitations, and punch, also and extempore speech or two. On the whole the evening passed agreeably, and I came home in a cab which they paid for, at one in the morning. Percy, the artist and several others, wished me to sit for a portrait to match with the one Percy has taken, of Waugh, which is to be lithographed.

**Monday 25th.** Went with James Dyson to New Inn, to take Omnibus for Middleton. After that rode to Manchester, to 12 Newalls Buildings, but there not being any meeting of the General Council, I did not remain many minutes. Mr Robinson, one Warburton[6] and another person were the only ones in the committee room, and in a short conversation with the former, he said the only meetings held at present were those of election committees with which the Council of the Union had not anything to do.

**Thusday 28th.** War has commenced. The Austrian troops have crossed the Ticino. Where, or how, or when, will this end?

**Saturday 30th.** Bazley and Turner returned for Manchester. Abel Heywood (anything) 2022 behind Turner.
   The Manchester Examiner and Times, has the following

*Cutting*, *from the* Manchester Examiner and Times, *30 April 1859, announcing the Austrian invasion of Italy.*

**Sunday 1st May.** At home. Fine air, but cold.

**Monday 2nd.** Paid rent this morning, and I have just 11d left.
   The war in Italy is proceeding as will be seen.

*Cutting*, *from the* Manchester Examiner and Times, *2 May 1859, reporting on the progress of war from Vienna, Turin and Weimar, giving details of Austrian advances.*

Went to Manchester; called on John Heywood who was waiting to have an hydraulic press at work before he could finish and bring out Early Days. Saw Waugh at Slaters,[7] and went with him to the Clarence. Mr Whitworth was there, Mr Waller, son of the preacher who was confined,[8] Mr Crockford, silk manufacturer and lastly Mr —— brother in law to Jacob Bright.[9] Sat hobnobbing over whisky punch too long, borrowed 2/6 from Slater and came to Barnes Green. Quarrelled with John Brundrick. Very foolish.

---

6. Possibly William Warburton, Salford cotton master and advanced Liberal, leading figure in the Salford Ballot and Reform Association, 1859–64.
7. Probably the bookshop of Edwin Slater, of Slater and Heelis, bookseller in Manchester from 1852, see entry for 10 May 1859.
8. The preacher is Sam Weller, Methodist preacher, tried for unauthorised preaching in Ashton.
9. Jacob Bright (1821–99), younger brother of John Bright, advanced Liberal, parliamentary candidate for Manchester in 1865, MP 1867–74, 1876–85, 1892–5.

**Tuesday 3rd.**  At home, very low, and dissatisfied with self and every thing about me.

**Wednesday 4th.**  Something must be done, so start for Middleton with 6d in pocket. I am thinking about Rochdale. Must try and sell some tickets, no other way except borrowing, and that must be the last thing done: alas, the first thing.

Borrowed a sovereign from Mills at Middleton, and went on to Rochdale by train. Saw Livsey at the Election Committee room in Bailey Street, but they were balancing their electioneering accounts, and he had not time to stay with me. Saw Abm Moore also, once a good friend, but now older and <u>colder</u> also, methought. Learned that John Bright had just been at the Committee, with his son. Livsey will see Smith towards Sunday, and with him, make out a list of names to which may be addressed circulars, after which I may wait on the parties for the sale of tickets.

Found Smith at home, the X Keys in Cloth Hall Street. He agreed with what Livsey had assented to, and on my asking his opinion as to whether or not I had best go up to Cromkey Shaw and see some of the Brights he strongly advised that I should go. So I went up and saw Mr Jacob Bright who approved of my plan of sending circulars and afterwards waiting on the parties for the sale of tickets. He said he would render me all the service he could, and did not doubt that his brother John would do the same: He advised me to see the Mayor, after proper delay, as his sister lay dead in the house at present: and also to call on the late Mayor, Mr Heap,[10] which I promised to do: He also undertook to speak to his brother on my behalf, who he was of opinion would be glad to patronize my undertaking. And I said, if I secured his patronage and that of his brother Johns, I should have a success. Hastened down to Smiths, and informed him of my good beginning, which pleased him very much: hurried up to the RW station, took a ticket for Oldham, and just got on the platform as the train came in, so after a short delay at the Middleton Junction landed at the station. Called first on friend Charles Potter who afterwards joined me at the Angel Inn, where I was taking refreshment on a welch rabbit and a glass of ale. Potter would have had me stop and take tea at his residence, but I had not dined, and I wanted something substantial. I was not "tea hungry" at all, and had I been at home I should have declined that beverage. He had not sent me, as usual, my Oldham newspapers, and on reminding him of the omission he was, I thought, somewhat embarrassed and imputed the neglect to the great excitement of the election, so I thought no more of the subject. We went down to Buckleys, the Kings Arms, where I, after some delay, got to see Wrigley the secretary to the County election Committee. I delivered to him a message from Mills at Middleton, respecting the sending down of an Omnibus to be ready for the following morning, to take voters to Rochdale. Afterwards fell into company with Mr Councillor Taylor.[11] Mr Taylor gave me an order for six copies of my Radical, and paid me for them, two copies to have photograph and autograph, and 4 without: Mr

---

10. Here and in the entry for 13 May Bamford is referring to Robert Taylor Heape (1813–88), flannel manufacturer and mayor 1857–8, 1876–7; see Charles and Richard Heape, *Records of the Family of Heape* (1905), 183–211.

11. John Taylor (1819–81), weaver, book-keeper and eventually millowner, Unitarian, Liberal, mayor of Rochdale, 1866–7.

W. Buckley ordered two copies and paid for them: to have photograph and autograph. So I did not entirely lose by [my] visit to Oldham. I distributed some of my circulars, and besides my gain in money, I believe I made some advances towards having a reading and recitation at this place. Mr Councillor Dronsfield accompanied Potter and myself down the street, towards the station, and I got off comfortably by the 9.30 train, landing at Miles Platting station, whence I hastened home on foot.

**Thursday 5th.** Potter, who had business at Manchester, called according to agreement and walked with me to Manchester. I called at Abel Heywoods for the books, 8 copies, and paid £1. 7. 0 for them, the shab-rag not allowing me full trade discount of 25 copies for 24, because I do not, I cannot indeed afford, to take and <u>pay</u> for, the whole 24 at once. And I am determined never to take a book out of his shop on credit. He is a shab-rag, a Jew, and has latterly become quite a snob. I dispise such characters. I gave the books and photographs, with autographs written on them, to Potter, who will deliver them at Oldham.

*Cutting* (*apparently from a book*), *of George Smith's*[12] *poem "The Neglected Bard"; Bamford has asterisked the title and written underneath, "Written as Mr T. said some time since, with an eye to Critchley Prince".*

*Cutting, from the* Middleton Albion, *25 May 1859, of George Smith's poem, "A Mountain Home".*

**Friday 6th.** Went by train to Staley Bridge where nearly the first person I saw was Mr Sadler, who is now, he informed me superintendent of police at this place. I enquired for the Commercial Inn, at which Sadler was quite pleased, the landlord being a friend and acquaintance of his, and one of the right sort, a well informed man, a very respectable character. I had not previously known Mr Smith, but he knew all about me, having read my books: he was a poet, I found, and he showed me several pleasing pieces of his composition. A tall, elderly, grey haired, venerable looking man. A gentleman came into the bar parlour who was introduced to me as Lieutenant Buckley, one of the three survivors who blew open the gates with powder bags, and for his daring on that occasion he was made a Lieutenant and received the Cross of Valour. He was a fine soldier looking person and was to have a banquet in his honour before his return to India. He discribed some of the horrors which appeared on the British troops entering the city, and sadly narrated how his own wife and three children had been massacred inside the city, before it was taken. I distributed several circulars, Mr Buckley, after reading one attentively, asking for several others for himself to distribute.

Mr Smith undertook to send me over a list of names to which circulars should be sent, and seemingly taking a hearty interest in my cause, promised to have a reading got up.

---

12. George Smith (1793–1860), Stalybridge mill-manager, publican (of the Commercial Inn) and poet ("the Moorland Minstrel"); MCL.

**Saturday 7th.** Attended a meeting of the Institutional Council. Nothing worth attending for. Mills did not send my Middleton newspaper to day.

**Sunday 8th.** Middleton Albion has not come to house: this is what I get for having borrowed a sovereign. Truly, what ills arise from poverty. "God help the poor."

**Monday 9th.** At Manchester, seeking And. Wallace in Hulme. A long walk up Moss Lane brought me to 119 Mulberry Street. And not at home. Back again, down Deansgate, John Heywood [would] not be in until one o'clock. So went to Belfields and got a glass of ale and bread and cheese, was very hungry, or should not have eaten the cheese: Heywood was in /at one o'clock,\ but not to be found in his large up and down stairs place, so was referred by his son to Mr Clegg who does the literary part of the business. My book, Early Days, was out at last: got a copy, and had some talk with Clegg about the price for 1000 copies of my poems: mentioned thirty pounds and left him to consult with Heywood about it.

Left a circular, with Mr Simpson, to be sent to Mr Lloyd at Foxhill Bank: Saw Robt Peat near the exchange, who reminded me that tomorrow will be the anniversary of the rail way smash at Nuneaton.

Sold a copy of Early Days at Belfields, 2/6 and gained 8d by it: odd gains worth picking up.

**Tuesday 10th.** Surely this is an auspicious day to me. Last year escaped almost miraculously at the rail way smash, and this morning whilst at breakfast received a list of names, for circulars, from friend Smith, of Staley Bridge: better still, another letter from that generous and kind hearted gentleman, Mr Sam[l] T. Hobson of Liverpool, inclosing a p.o. order for five pounds.

*Letter*, S.T. Hobson, 43 Catherine Street, Liverpool, to Bamford, 9 May 1859.

Dear Sir,
I am obliged by the interesting sketch you have sent me of your past experiences
& future objects.
   It is owing to the efforts and endurances of such sturdy, able, & independent
men as you, that the governed have wrested from haughty irresponsible
dominion, what share they have in the government of the country.
   I fear it will be out of way to be of much personal assistance in the promotion
of the objects you have in view, but by way of doing something towards them, and
to mark my respect for you and your patriotism, may I beg your acceptance of the
enclosed P.O. order?
                         Yours very truly
                         Sam[l] T Hobson

Went to Manchester and drew the money, in a five pound note, which got changed at Love and Bartons, buying postage stamps, and envelopes. Paid Slater, the bookseller the 2/1 which Waugh borrowed of him for me, on Mond. last week (the 2d) took another copy of Early Days & left it with Belfields waiter for the gentleman who ordered it yesterday. John behaves more liberally with respect to the books than his brother Abel does, who is a shab-rag, and a snob: 1/10 each, or 12 1/2 copies for 1.2.11. I intimated to Clegg that, as I had a number of additional pieces to insert in next publication of poetry, it might perhaps be as well if I were paid at so much per sheet, furnishing matter as the printing advanced. Something was also said about a continuation of My Life of a Radical, which Heywood might publish in monthly parts, I supplying copy as required. all these things to be considered and determined on in a short time.

**Wednesday 11th.** Received three newspapers, and a list of names, from friend Potter of Oldham. Wrote to Mr Hobson, as follows.

***Copy letter***, *Bamford to Samuel Hobson, 11 May 1859.*

Dear Sir,
Accept the only return which I at present can make in acknowledgement of your very kind and generous communication the 9th instant. Encouraged by your benign consideration, I feel authorized so far to obtrude my confidence as to say that your token of approval was much enhanced in value by the opportune time of its arrival, as well as by the kind sentiments by which it was accompanied. I shall make very sparing use of the money, and shall often recur to your note with pleasure. I had not any idea whatever, nor any expectation of claiming pecuniary aid from my friend[s], by the few circulars which I have forwarded. Nor, with your exception have I conspired in instances as your case. My only hope has been that a sense of justice would induce my fellow countrymen to patronise my honest endeavours, as may enable me to realize the few requirements of life, so long as myself and my aged partner remain in this state of existence. I am quite willing, or desirous, to endeavour for our bread, so long as I am able to work. I think it is every poor man's duty cheerfully and earnestly to labour as long as capacity to do so remains, and I look upon a person so engaged, as being far higher in character and position, than one who rather than exert himself seeks an ignoble dependence on government sustention or Literary Fund aid.
    I hope you are of opinion, that my views and wishes for the remainder of life are just and commendable. I have not passed my long and varied life, so far, without laying up a store of observation which, if I have opportunities for imparting to my fellow subjects, must be useful to them as well as interesting: hitherto, however, I have met with but small encouragement, and I am almost of opinion there is a clique of enemies about me, who would fain render me desolate and helpless in my old age. I remain dear Sir
                    Your obliged servant,
                    Sam¹ Bamford

11th May Wednesday. Went to Middleton paid Mills the sovereign I had borrowed and got a circular for a reform dinner on Monday. He said his wife had forgotten to send the newspaper.

**Thursday 12th.** Manchester. Saw Clegg at John Heywoods, he said Mr Heywood would purchase editions of all my writings if I would mention terms to which he could agree.

Made up 29 circulars for Stayley Bridge, to be posted tomorrow.

*Dinner invitation circular from "Messrs Cheetham and Heywood's Committee", to a free dinner at the Roe Buck Inn, Middleton, on Monday 16 May, with a formal discussion on the reform question to follow.*

**Friday 13th.** At Rochdale. Went to Livseys house at Wellfield. An old mean looking stone building in the yard of a factory in ruins. Livsey not at home and wife could not say whether he would come to dinner or not. Roads very dusty and unpleasant: went right up to Cromkey Shaw[13] at once and saw Mr Jacob Bright, who received me very affably; advised me about the room, the advertising, the price of tickets, etc, and concluded by handing me half a sovereign for tickets for himself, and his brother John: said also he would /try to interest\ "these other folks," meaning, as I supposed, the members of the reading society connected with the mill, and he should expect seeing me, or hearing from me again. Went again into the town to make search for Livsey: he had only just left the Brunswick Hotel. One Doctor Nuttall, half drunk, detained me in the street. Livsey not to be found. Went to Smiths at Cross Keys, he had not been there, nor had Smith seen him, as Livsey promised when last I was at Rochdale. I begin to doubt Livseys integrity in this matter: went back to Brunswick, and waited until Mr Joseph Heape Taylor came from the Bench of Magistrates to his warehouse, when I followed him, and he took five shilling tickets, hoping my speculation would succeed. Went again to /the\ Brunswick where the Superintendent of Police, and another person were taking pale ale. Got a welch rabbit and glass of ale, and then went to Smiths, and took a glass of whisky. George Ashworth was at dinner, the man said, and when I went again his youngest son said he would not be at the warehouse that afternoon, so appointed to call again next Wednesday. Called on the Mayor, Andw Stewart, who received me cordially in his parlour, and after some unimportant conversation said he should take one pounds worth of tickets. This though a decent order, seemed rather small after Livseys presuming intimation that the Mayors order aught to be for "five pounds worth."

Took the Public Hall in Baillie St. for which am to pay 1/-5/0. To be used on Friday the 27th inst.[14]

Smith came with me to Rail Station: I am to go again to Rochdale next Wednesday, and meantime Smith will see Livsey and try to make something out of him. Left 10/- worth of tickets with Smith, so if I may reckon 10/- Brights 10/- the Mayor 20/- and Livsey 20/- I shall have as good as sold three pounds worth of tickets; not a bad beginning. Came to Middleton, and from thence by Bus home.

**Saturday 14th.** At home all say being tired after my yesterdays fagging about. In the afternoon received a precious document from Mills at Middleton.

---

13. Cronkeyshaw.
14. Inserted opposite.

**Letter**, *Thomas Mills to Bamford, 14 May 1859.*

My dear Mr Bamford,

I am exceedingly sorry at having to retract the invitation I took upon myself to give you to attend our dinner on Monday night.

My impression at the time was that an Elector could invite a friend whether such friend was or was not a voter, but at a meet$^g$ held last night it was finally resolved that none but those persons who are now on the register or that are likely to be induced to be be placed on, in the liberal behalf, should be <u>eligible</u> to attend the dinner.

You will no doubt understand my attachment to you has not waned in the least, the only regret I have /is\ that I have fallen into error in the matter & for which you may blame but I hope will pardon me.

I hope you will not be /grievously\ offended. I shall be better able to explain further when I next see you.

I had purposed coming over tomorrow Sunday but find a pressing engagement will prevent me the very agreeable pleasure.

I rem$^n$ very truly yours,

Tho$^s$ Mills

Will you please return me the circular. T.M.

Sent the following reply.

**Copy letter**, *Bamford to Thomas Mills, 14 May 1859.*

Dear Mills,

Your letter of this afternoon has some what surprised me; and I should /feel\ indignant were it not that I pity, rather than condemn, the cast of mind which could dictate an open and studied insult to an old veteran, who had carried chains in the cause of reform, before the young /men\ of your committee were born: as if the insults and injuries which I suffered 40 years ago, were not sufficient, the persecution of <u>mean hatred</u> must be revived in the present day; and by parties calling themselves "Parliamentary Reformers", against the oldest representative of the wronged and suffering classes during the worst days of the 19th century. Were I alone concerned I might suffer this outrage to pass with the contempt which it deserves; but as duty to my character, and to the cause with which my name must ever be associated, requires that such notice shall be taken of it, as will fix the blame, the stigma of their base transaction, on the right persons, I shall as they will, speedily find, adopt full and effective means for that purpose.

Remaining, Dear Mills

Yours truly

Samuel Bamford

Mr Thomas Mills

**Sunday 15th.** Posted 29 circulars for Stayley Bridge and 11 for Rochdale.

James Kent of Tonge Lane, Allan Mellor of Junction Town and Tho[s] Mills of Middleton came in the evening and explained the subject of the above letters as follows. Mills had been quite distressed in his mind, thinking, from my letter that I intended taking some very strong measure, as public newspaper exposure, in retaliation for the insult; the affair however, now stands thus. On Wednesday, I met Mills and Fallows, the overseer, in the street at Middleton, when they informed me of the intended dinner on Monday next, and Fallows suggested that I should be invited. Mill assented, and so it was agreed upon. Afterwards I saw Mill and Fallows at Millss residence, when Mills gave me a circular inviting me to be of the dinner party. On Friday night, there was a meeting of the dinner committee, when, at the instance of Sam[l] Mellalieu,[15] a nephew of the old Mellalieus, great persecutors of radicals in the days of persecution, it was resolved, that no person should be eligable to join the dinner party, who was not a voter on the liberal side, or likely to become such: Whether or not, it had oozed out that I was already invited, there is not, as yet any evidence to determine: the resolution however was passed, and Mills, the secretary was so awe-struck, his mother being the natural daughter of the uncle of this Sam[l] Mellalieu /and\ from her father she has great expectations – that he durst not, avow the invitation given to me, and so the point was finally settled: then, of course he had to write to me, recalling the invitation, and I, indignant, at the supposed intended insult, wrote to him as above. The resolution however, sign of a base and niggardly mind, quite natural to the person from whom it emanated, was passed in ignorance, as is supposed, by the committee of my having been already invited, and not with the intention of recalling any invitation to me. That certainly does away with the most offensive view of the affair, though I cannot entirely divest myself of suspicion that Mellalieu intended it to prevent my being invited, his uncle, and indeed the whole family of those Mellalieus being indicated by that passage in My Life as a Radical, which will be found at p     though the foot note does not apply exactly to them, but rather to another party.[16]

Mills said, he was the more impressed to be silent at the committee meeting by the fear lest he should injure his mothers interests with her father, knowing, as he did, that S Mellalieu was a private enemy of hers, and jealous of her fathers final intentions with respect to her. So the passage in my books shows why Sam. should have a motive for

---

15. Samuel Mellalieu (*c.* 1807–84), magistrate and associate of the family weaving and cloth retailing business in Middleton; *Middleton Albion*, 21 June 1884. According to one account, the sister of Bamford's wife had married into the Mellalieu family; see *Heywood Advertiser*, 22 August 1919 (cutting in Middleton Library). (See Plate 7.)

16. As is confirmed by the comment in the entry for 20 May, Bamford is here referring to *Passages* (1858 ed.), 36–7, which refers to parties in Middleton in 1817 who were not averse to repeating malicious rumours about radicals to the authorities in Manchester: "This sort of information was always being brought to Middleton by parties who, being in the manufacturing line, visited Manchester twice or thrice a week for the purposes of disposing of their goods." This edition has a supplementary footnote which comments that "If this brood of reptiles is even now extinct, it is because the 'secret service money' of the Manchester Corporation is applied to better purposes than nurturing the worst of all characters – bad neighbours! Having, from loss of occupation, ceased to be paid spies these fellows undertake other engagements; and now act as slanderers of private character."

wishing [to] exclude me from the dinner, and the consideration about his mother accounts for Mills remaining silent with respect to the invitation he had given to me.

The Mellalieus have only very recently – within these few weeks; certainly since the /last\ publication of my Radical – begun to take part in this reform business. They have doubtless got to see the passage in my book, and hence have begun to act in the reform movement, in order that they have a means for annoying and contravening me. But they, and the whole lot of Middleton reformers, as they at present stand are not worthy of my attention.

The old persecution of this mean and sordid family, is thus being revived under a new guise.

**Monday 16th.** Stayley Bridge, Smith at Commercial said he was taking tea on Sunday with a Manchester gentleman who knew me; the Rev^d W. Gaskell:[17] He had informed Mr G. of my having been over at Stayley Bridge, and of my intention to give a reading, when Mr G. said he hoped I should be successful, from which I gathered that Mr. G. was still friendly, that is, as a friend who takes care to be too far off to be troubled with ones troubles, though near enough to be one of the "we ers." when good luck turns up. Smith said he had read "Mary Barton", and noticed the passage about myself and my poem.[18] I said Mrs Gaskell[19] had totally forgotten her humble friend, since she went to London and became located in the house of a Lord. Smith asked what Lord? and I said Lord Atherton, that was the title I thought. Smith asked me if I had ever seen the grand bridge in Atherton park at Leigh? I said I had, and he informed me it was built by his grandfather, who also built the acqueduct at Barton, under Brindleys[20] directions. Called on Mr Robert Platt,[21] at the mill with whom I had some conversation: he questioned me about my present pecuniary resources, and my prospects for the future, and I frankly told him I had no resources, except incidental ones, and that my future prospects were such as I was now about to exercise in Staley Bridge: he gave me a sovereign to begin with, promised to attend my reading, and I left him 50 shilling tickets, on speculation, as I suppose.

Went with Smith and took the Town Hall for my performance on Wednesday the 25th and paid 15/-. Called at the residence of W. Bayley Esq^r,[22] the Mayor, but he was at the farm "in Yorkshire," the maid said.

Went by rail to Greenfield and thence to Oldham where I arrived somewhat tired: took place in 6-15 train to Newton Heath, saw Potter in the train, and arrived at home weary with my days travel.

Left 50/ shilling tickets with Smith.

---

17. Revd William Gaskell (1805–84), Unitarian minister at Cross Street Chapel, Manchester, husband of Elizabeth Gaskell; MCL.

18. Bamford's poem "God Help the Poor" is recited in chapter 9 of Elizabeth Gaskell's *Mary Barton* (1848).

19. Elizabeth Cleghorn Gaskell (1810–65), Manchester novelist, wife of William; *DNB*.

20. James Brindley (1716–72), engineer and canal builder; *DNB*.

21. Robert Platt (1802–82), Stalybridge yarn manufacturer and JP: see Hill, *Bygone Stalybridge*, 228–35.

22. William Bayley (1803–91), Stalybridge cotton manufacturer and railway promoter; first mayor of Stalybridge in 1857, see Hill, *Bygone Stalybridge*, 258–9.

**Tuesday 17th.** At home all day. Mima went to Fern Hill.

**Wednesday 18th.**[23] Rochdale. Called on Mr Lord, Sal., Drake Street, who took 4 3$^d$ tickets. Oliver Ormrod[24] took 4 shilling ones. Mr Hamilton opposite 2/- Called at Reed Hotel and left tickets to sell. And at H. Kelsall Esq$^r$ who took 1/- worth.

Gave Smith 1-5 0 for the room, and 3/- for the advertisement: left tickets at the newspaper office, and shall have a good paragraph for the money.

Tom Livsey has never made his appearance: he has been found wanting in the day of trial.

Smith had occasion to see Mr Bright, the M.P. respecting a Mr James who had been speaking disparagingly of him, and having finished that business he introduced the subject of my intended lecture at the Public Hall. Mr Bright said he had heard of it, and Smith said he aught to take me by the hand, and give me a lift, at which Bright laughed. Smith repeated again and again that he aught to give Bamford a lift, he was an old friend to reform, and a sufferer, and Mr Bright had the power to render him great service. When coming away, he turned round, and said be sure now you dont forget Bamford. When Mr B replied, "he would consider on it". They were in the front of Mr Brights residence, where he and his lady were walking when Smith joined them, and during the conversation, the latter pointing to a part of the moor, beyond the mill, showed them the very spot of ground where in 1817, Bamford held the first public meeting ever held in Rochdale to petition for reform. The soldiers were drawn up, the rain came down in torrents, but Bamford arranged and carried on the meeting successfully. He told Mr B. also about my leading them up to the great meeting at Manchester; about my trial, and imprisonment, and after all Mr Bright would only promise to "consider upon it"?. Most benign undertaking, to "consider" whether or not, a young Parliamentary sprawl like this, should patronize, lend a helping hand to an old veteran, in the decline of his days. Came round by Middleton, took a glass with W.C. Ridings, and first called on Mills, in whom I thought I could see a change of manner. Going the way of all the rest, I suppose.

**Thursday 19th.** Stayley Bridge, Went to the clerks office at the Town Hall, and got the date of performance altered to Wednesday the 1st June. Met a Mr Williams at Smiths: a clerk at the railway who was of opinion the stones at Pots and Tons are not Druidicial, and gave various reasons for his opinion: he thought they were merely moor stones furrowed and marked by time and the elements. There was not any thing in connection with them or the place they occupied, which indicated that the antient Druidicial symbol at any time existed on the spot, which symbol he explained as having reference to a triangle, the emblem of the triune Deity. I recited to him my poem of Penarfon, which seemed to please him, he being a Welchman. Went to seek the Mayor, and after visiting two of his vast manufacturing establishments, found him at his residence, on the Ashton

---

23. Bamford has 17th in error, and his dating is one day behind until Sunday 22nd.

24. Oliver Ormrod (1811–79), of Rochdale, tanner and currier, dialect writer and active newspaper writer and editor, used the *nom de plume* "The Felley fro Rachde"; see Henry Colley March, ed., *The Writings of Oliver Ormrod* (1901).

Road. He came out to me, and at once took twenty shilling tickets; he also very frankly said he would do anything he could to serve me; he would patronize my undertaking in any way which [would] be the most effective. I thanked him, and ventured to hint at his being the Chairman: he said he could not foresee how he should be engaged on the day of the performance, but if he could not preside he would engage a respectable party, who would. He also said I must communicate with him again; he should be in Manchester, his warehouse was 40 Moseley St. and I might call there; on any Tuesday he was always there. Went back to Smiths, and afterwards called on Doctor Hopwood,[25] who took 5/- worth of tickets. Got a glass or two of ale and a welch rabbit at Smiths, and drew up an advertisement for the papers on Saturday. Called at the mill of Mr John Marsland, who took ten shillings worth of tickets. So came on to Ashton. Mr Fielding of the Protector, would insert my advertisem[en]t twice for nothing – very kind – and would send slips to the other two papers. Came off by rail at 5 o'clock, and got home much tired with tramping the pavement and the dusty hard road. This is indeed old age, and twere better one were at rest, and out of the way in the eternal silence.

**Friday Morning 20th.**[26] Got the following from Smith at Rochdale.

*Letter*, *James Smith, Rochdale, to Bamford, 18 May 1859.*

> Dear Sir,
> In a very few minutes after you left me Mr Thos Livsey came to my house on your Business, and he is very anxious for every thing to be done that can be to get a good house. I suggested to him about a chairman. I said it should be either Jacob Bright, the Mayor or him T. Livsey. He said he would take the Chair if Mr Bright or the Mayor refused – I gave him 5 tickets at 1/- and 10 at 3/- and he will see me again in a day or 2 and everything he can do he will as far as his power lays. he wished me to drop a line to you this night. I conclude with my best respects and remain yours truly – James Smith

Frid.  Rochdale. Left tickets with Mills in Drake Street. Called at the Bank and got sale for one shill ticket from W. Fenton Esq$^r$. and magistrate. Left a copy of Early Days with Mr Howard, wool stapler, Blackwater Street, he not being within, to call some other time for payment 2/6. George Ashworth, J.P. was not at the warehouse, so sent a ticket to one of the sons who was down at the mill. Lad returned saying the son was engaged, and would be so for some time. In coming away down the street saw a pheaton standing at the bottom, and a gentleman alighting from it. Met him, he was Mr Ashworth Senr, so thought, now I was sure of a good demand for my paper wares. I moved, and he recognised me. Asking if "ladies would attend", I said "I hoped they would, so he took one shilling ticket saying I must see him again, and he ultimately agreed to leave any order he might have at the warehouse where I might call for it.

---

25. Robert Hopwood (1814–97), of Stalybridge; surgeon, town councillor from 1857 and mayor 1861–4: see Hill, *Bygone Stalybridge*, 285–7.
26. Entry inserted on facing page.

Met Smith in the street, and as he wa/n\ted tickets I turned back with him and gave him what he desired. He had seen Livsey who called the other day just after I had left. He took a number of tickets to dispose of and promised to aid in my undertaking with all his means, and if neither Mr Jacob Bright nor the Mayor would preside, he would, if it were agreeable to me. So now if he takes the matter well in hand I shall have a prospect of doing well at Rochdale, notwithstanding the shabby patronage of some of the would be thought "great ones", and the general tendency to very retentive money habits, of the people. Called on Mr Holgate, solicitor, who said he should not attend my readings, they were too secular a character for him: this from a person whose daily business from morn till eve is of a purely secular character. How men do blind and hood-wink themselves: he has, it would seem become very religious. Reads his bible and family and must now set an exact example to his children. Mr W. Roberts, the Poor Law Auditor was present, and an elderly gentleman, named Heap I think. Mr Roberts asked why I left employment a[t] London? and I told him: the others also hearing me, that I thought the situation beneath me, Mr Holgate said pride was a bad thing. I said, honest, manly pride, arising from conscious integrity, was one of the best feelings we could cultivate, and I was conscious of being worthy of something better than my Somerset House situation. Why asked Roberts, what was my situation? and I said I was superintendent of Books and Papers in the Accountant Generals department. A very easy post no doubt, he said. Easy enough, I replied, I had not any complaint on that score, but it was beneath me and so I gave it up. We all came out of the office together, it being dinner time, and then Roberts said he would have one ticket, so giving me a shilling. I gave him a ticket and going directly to the station, for I had enough of these sordid people for that day, I came to Blue pits and walking thence to Middleton – for I wanted to see the old country. I came to Barns Green by Omnibus.

**Saturday 21st.**  Manchester. Got the remaining 8 copies of my Early Days from John Heywoods. Clegg had not anything further to say about the copyright of my poems, or of the continuation of my Life, so came away without anything being done, of that sort. Belfield shy as he has been on several occasions lately, I must have him explaining some of these days: Bought some beef and three pints of gooseberries, and came home by 1/2 p 12 'bus.

Got Mills's newspaper, the Middleton Albion, from which I learn that several persons attended the dinner of the County Electors on Monday last who were <u>not</u> voters, and consequently I must have been just as <u>eligable</u> to attend as they were. The first person who spoke to the toast, Samuel <u>Barlow</u>, was a non voter. After him came Henry Whalley, another non voter, as I believe. Allan Mellor, another, followed. Joseph Wolstencroft, another and John Dewhurst another. The whole affair, taken from beginning to end seems inexplicable to me, except that the Committee passed a Resolution that <u>I</u> above all others, was to be excluded. It seems to have been a scheme against me personally: a kind of counteraction to please some parties who were mortified by the compliment paid to me on the 3d Jan\. Some of the money was collected, part was a gift, and I should like to know who the parties were that found the money. I must get to know the names of the Committee, and who the parties were that moved the excluding Clause. I shall then have an idea who have been my secret enemies, and who has been moveing the unseen pegs and wires. The dinner in the Albion is styled "Demonstration of Liberal Electors": it was a demonstration of private spite and malice quite as much as anything else. I preserve the report of it on the other leaf. Did the Demonstration proceed from the party at Newalls Buildings, with a view to damage my appearance at Rochdale, or was it an emanation of the "reptile brood" at Middleton? However it was I will come square with them some of these days.

*Report, from the* Middleton Albion, *21 May 1859, of the dinner for about 100 of the Liberal electors of South Lancashire belonging to the Middleton district, Roe Buck Inn, Middleton. The meeting passed, without controversy, a motion in favour of parliamentary reform, and another resolving to look after the electoral registration of the locality.*

*Editorial, from the* Oldham Advertiser, *21 May 1859, on the subscription fund for the Edwin Butterworth memorial, supporting the claims of all worthy individuals who serve "the good of mankind" to public recognition, rather than only military and political figures.*

**Sunday 22nd.** Brierley, and his little girl came in the afternoon, and a little later Potter stepped in, so we all took tea. Potter had been talking with Gowenlock who will give an article in next Saturdays paper, something about me. He also said a reading was being got up for me at Oldham. A pretty piece of poetry, on May, by Brierley, appears in the Oldham Advertiser.

King buttercup.
In his dreamy flowerdom

tiny bells on nodding stems
Ringing elfin minstrelsy

Here are dainties to allure.
From his feast the epicure
For the simple honeybee
Hath a sweeter feast than he.

True poetry are all these passages.

We talked about a general gathering on some day, of men of genius and literary taste. Gowenlock had been speaking of something of the sort, and the idea is to be further considered. Gowenlock has an article on departed men of worth and talent, and especially referring to the late Edwin Butterworth. Thirty pounds have it seems been already promised towards a memorial to be placed at or about his grave. This, if well laid out would be quite sufficient to mark the resting place of any man. As for grand monuments they are all insulting fudge to the dead who were neglected during life.

**Monday 23rd.** Rochdale. Saw Mr Jacob Bright at the Mill who undertook to be chairman if the Mayor was not. Said one half of the 10 tickets which he had taken were for his brother John. Said he did not know where his brother John was: he was about somewhere, and he durst say, he would be glad to attend the reading.

Sold Geo. Ashworth and sons ten shillings worth of tickets, they will attend.

Deliv'd the Mayor, his twenty shillings worth of tickets, and he will be chairman unless something occurs to prevent his attendance, but at all events I may announce that he will preside.

Went to printers and ordered 50 posting bills to be up tomorrow. Smith will order and look after the posting of them.

Came away at 4 o'clock, and walked to Middleton, very dusty and hot, took 6 o'clock Omnibus and came home, tired, /old age again\.

The following are from the Sentinel and Observer of Saturday.

**Cutting**, *from the* Rochdale Sentinel and Observer, *21 May 1859, directing readers to the advertisement for Bamford's forthcoming readings, and quoting from his circular.*

---

### SAMUEL BAMFORD'S READING AND RECITATIONS.

At half-past seven, on the Evening of Friday, the 27TH inst., in the Public Hall, Baillie-street, Samuel Bamford will read and recite select passages from his own writings, and those of other authors. – Tickets to Front Seats and Platform, 1s. to Body of the Hall, 6d.; Gallery, 3d.; may be had at the office of this paper; the Reed Hotel; at the Cross Keys, in Cloth Hall street, and at Mr. W. Mills, Bookseller, Drake-street.

---

**Tuesday 24th.** Called on Mr Bayley at 4a Moseley Street: and he said Doctor Hopwood would be the most fitting gentleman to act as chairman at my reading at Stayley Bridge: for himself he could not undertake to act, as probably he should be absent from the neighbourhood. Doctor Hopwood, he repeated, was by far the most eligible person to preside and if I agreed, he would call on the Doctor and speak to him about it, so I agreed. Mr John Cheetham, after considering some time, gave me an order for 20 shillings worth of tickets, half of them to be 3d ones, to be left at the Counting House, at the Mill.

McWhinnie, the bookseller, was in the Omnibus, and he told me, the new reform association under T.B. Potter,[27] was arranged for the purpose of uniting all parties of reformers, under a new management: in fact to sink the old Newalls Buildings clique, and to get rid of George Wilson and S.P. Robinson: the split amongst the reform party, in consequence of their direction, having, in fact, lost the return of the liberal candidates; to which opinion I partly agreed.

With sorrow I read the adjoining advertisement in this mornings paper: when I showed it to Brierley, he lifted up his eyes. Money, we poets cannot be expected to give, but I suggested that a few of us might give him the profits of a reading, if his friends would prepare a room, and advertise, to which Brierley assented.

---

27. Thomas Bayley Potter (1817–98), son of Sir Thomas Potter, cotton spinner and active Liberal, increasingly radical after the death of his brother Sir John Potter in October 1858; *Manchester Guardian*, 8 November 1898.

***Newspaper cutting***

---

The Public are appealed to on behalf of Mr. JOHN BOLTON ROGERSON, the Poet, who is in the greatest difficulties. His furniture has been seized for debt; he is, and has been for some years, incapable of locomotion; his eldest son, the victim of consumption, lies at the point of death; and his family are in extreme destitution. A few of his friends are anxious to do something to aid him, and have commenced a subscription on his behalf; and any sums that parties are inclined to contribute will be received at the office of this paper.

---

Wrote to Rogerson see next leaf.

***Copy letter***, *Bamford to J.B. Rogerson, 24 May 1859.*

Dear Rogerson,

I am much grieved at seeing your advertisement in the paper this morning. Those who would gladly hasten to the rescue have not money at command, but I think "The Bards" aught to offer you the proceedings of a general reading, your friends providing a room, and paying for advertising. I have suggested this to Brierley, and he agrees with it, if however the suggestion is acted upon let me know before the matter goes further, or the readers are selected.

    If the idea be taken up, and the thing managed judiciously, I think something handsome might be raised.

Yours truly

Sam<sup>l</sup> Bamford.[28]

**Wednesday 25th.** Called on David Harrison,[29] the richest man – so reputed [–] in Stayley Bridge, found him in a darkish, mean looking room, his counting house, or parlour, at his Mill. Told him I was about to give a literary entertainment, and "had a few tickets to dispose of," with a huff of scorn, "Oh we dont attend to such things here," was his reply; he turned to his writing, and I turned and came out, determined not to offer another ticket for sale on this occasion. My friend Smith of the Commercial, will see Doctor Hopwood, about being chairman, and if the doctor demurs he will take the chair himself, which is quite satisfactory to me. I would rather he were in the chair than the doctor, who I met and scarcely recognised in the street, I not distinctly knowing him: he returned only a very slight salute, but he is a great man in the place, and a magistrate it seems. The great men here, as I have had it repeatedly intimated, like to have much deference shown: they like to be waited upon, and be solicited, deferentially, for their favours. I dont relish that mode of proceeding, I said; nor I neither said my friend, but it is the way here.

---

28. Rogerson died on the Isle of Man on 19 July 1859; see *Ben Brierley's Journal*, March 1872.

29. David Harrison (1791–1872), of Stalybridge, prominent cotton spinner, High Constable of Stalybridge and Deputy Lieutenant of Lancashire, and staunch supporter of mechanics' institutes; see Hill, *Bygone Stalybridge*, 254-6.

Came with Smith to Ashton and called at the Standard, the Reporter and the Protector offices, and ordered the advertisements for Saturday. Came by rail to Miles Platting, and took tickets for Rochdale, but storm threatening I got out at Middleton Junction. Called at Jacksons, got another photographic likeness for Doctor Pegg, and then by train to Middleton. Mills gave me the names of the Committee who voted the exclusion resolution for the late dinner; they were Edm^d Fallows, who was present when Mills invited me, and I believe suggested it. John Hughs, Lawton, Sam^l Mellalieu, H. Whally, and T. Mills. Mellalieu was the chief promoter of the thing, and for reasons, no doubt, which I have already alluded to.

The Ashton Reporter gave a handsome notice of my public claims, and the Protector gave one more kind (see other leaf) of May 21.

***Editorial***, *from the* Ashton Protector, *21 May 1859.*

> Our friends will find in our advertising columns an announcement that SAMUEL BAMFORD, justly called the Lancashire Bard, purposes to give one of his interesting recitations at Stalybridge. All who value honesty and consistency in public men, and who are sensible of the obligations under which this generation lies to those whose labours and sufferings secured the enlarged freedom now enjoyed, will certainly attend and give public and substantial proof of their respect for the earliest English political sufferer now living. When patriotism is so much lauded, and patriots so scarce, SAMUEL BAMFORD will surely be sheltered and sustained in his old age by the generous people of this country. At any rate, the people of this district are not unmindful of his worth, nor indisposed, we trust, to reward it. We are sorry that our space this week is so fully occupied; but next week we shall give a lengthened notice of SAMUEL BAMFORD'S political life, and extracts from his published works.

***Copy letter***, *Bamford probably to the Editor,* Ashton Protector, *26 May 1859.*

My Dear Sir,
I have to thank you for the receipt, this morning, of four copies of your last publication; and especially for the very kind notice which you have given of me. I appreciate your kindness the more deeply, because I have, at present many detractors – secret ones – I know not why – and because, not one of the Manchester papers, one short allusion excepted has given me the least help in this my last battle of life – for if I fail in this, I dont see how I am to fight another. This however, must not be lost from want of exertion – one thing at once, and do it well, and let the future take care of itself. On Friday evening I read and recite at Rochdale, on Wednesday next, as you have announced, and these two demonstrations are the first movements of my campaign of 1859. If the press at Manchester were truly free, and if there were in it, or about it, one really good heart, I should be differently treated. Yours truly, Samuel Bamford.

Note: Accept the inclosed.

**Friday 27th.** Had a good, and very respectable attendance at my reading. The Mayor took the chair, and Mr Jacob Bright, several members of Mr G Ashworths family, Thomas Chadwick, and other leading characters were present, whilst a goodly array of operatives occupied the gallery. All were very attentive, and seemed much interested by what I read, which consisted of extracts from my Early Days, Radical, Walks, from Mr G Smiths scrap book, about poor Pickegree,[30] and Brierleys "Day Out." The company were however, too decorous, scarcely a cheer could be extracted, though the performance was evidently gratifying to them: they seemed as if afraid to "come out," as if awed by the reader, or by each other. Even the Mayor did not get a vote of thanks. I should have thought Jacob Bright, or Oliver Ormrod would have had the good taste to have proposed such a thing: it was evidently, not my place to do so, lest I should seem to be fishing for a like compliment to myself. The worthy Mayor however, had my most hearty thanks. A respectable company followed me down to Smiths in Cloth Hall Street, and we had a full room until about eleven o'clock. The morning following I balanced with Smith: paid the printers bill, bought a piece of nice beef, and came to Middleton, thence by omnibus, and so down the lane home.

Tom Livsey did not make his appearance at all. I thought how his great vaunts and swagger would turn out. /He has been fairly "weighed in the balance, and has been found wanting." Henceforth no reliance on Tom Livsey.\ I sent two tickets to the Editor of the Rochdale Sentinel and Observer, and the following is the notice which he gave of my affair.

***Cutting****, from the* Rochdale Observer, *28 May 1859.*

---

Mr BAMFORD'S readings last night at the Public Hall were respectably attended, his Worship the Mayor presiding.

---

The disgracefully brief notice opposite was all that the sham radical Editor of the Rochdale Observer could find in his heart to bestow on the appearance, and performance of an old veteran reformer. I blame others for this, as well as the Editor: there is a knot of sour rusty hearted beings in Rochdale, who never could forgive me, for becoming their superior, in action, real worth, and consequent popularity. Pity and contempt they have in return.[31]

---

30. For George Smith see entry for 5 May 1859.
31. Final sentence added opposite.

# 5

# BREAD OR A STONE?

*At the end of May Bamford's plight was brought to wider attention by a letter in the* Oldham Advertiser *which drew on the continuing Butterworth Memorial campaign to argue that due reward for living reformers such as Bamford was more important than erecting monuments to the dead. At the start of July the appeal was renewed in the pages of the* Middleton Albion. *Bamford responded to both letters, making more explicit than he had hitherto his hope that he could receive compensation for his "account" against the nation for past imprisonment and suffering. His circular was revised and reissued, and he continued to subsist largely on the proceedings of readings and occasional lectures.*

**Saturday 28th.** The annexed are from the Oldham Advertiser of this day.

***Letter***, *from the* Oldham Advertiser, *28 May 1859.*

---

### BREAD OR A STONE.

*To the Editor of the Oldham Advertiser.*
Sir,- I fully sympathise with the spirit of your last week's article, and also with that of the letter of one who signs himself "A Shilling." It is just that some enduring monument of the esteem of the people of Oldham for one who in his time laboured so much for the good of others without realising much benefit to himself, should be erected. There are, however, higher duties to be performed than paying compliments to dead bones, or bandying soft phraseology over a life we had permitted to pass away without a single attempt to gladden, or weeping over a grave we had perhaps assisted to dig. Whilst I therefore fully appreciate the character and unquestionable industry of the late Mr. Butterworth, and cannot object to any one putting a flower upon a grave which closed a life of thorns, I cannot at the same time but turn to the stern realities with which we are now surrounded and give a sympathy and a word for the worth that is living – living amid the struggles and anxieties of age and poverty and neglect, and to whom bread is as much a necessity as a stone to Mr. Butterworth is a justice.

Mr. Samuel Bamford has perhaps done more for his race than any other living man in the same sphere. In Lancashire literature he is unsurpassed, [in] truthfulness, pathos and interest; whilst he is the last of that race of Reform apostles who were honoured by the propagation of those great principles upon which our national greatness and social comforts have been built up, when to be a reformer it was necessary to be a man. Well sir, this Samuel Bamford having led reform on across fields of blood, through dark dungeons, over grim scaffolds, into the broad sunlight and flowery fields of the present times, when reform is not only the idol of the multitude, but the peace cry of every political class; – having done this, this Samuel Bamford is allowed to drag on a monotonous existence within the humble walls of a cottage at Harpurhey, unthought of and uncared for; – he is the warrior pining amid the blessings of his triumphs – the apostle starving in the millennium his genius, faithfulness, courage, and endurance have wrought out.

It is a humiliating fact, that it is very seldom that merit of the kind that Mr. Bamford is possessed of, is acknowledged and rewarded whilst the subject of it is amongst us; it is only when we discover the shadow of its departing wing, that we acknowledge that an angel has been with us, and then we forthwith build a monument to the worth we had slighted, and testify by it not only the departed's virtues, but our own blindness and stupidity. It is singular that this should be the case, but so it is. Is it I wonder, because we sink in morality as we progress in liberty? Is it because we are so innately vicious that we become indifferent to others, just in proportion to our receiving comfort to ourselves? I cannot suppose that such is really the case. I think the neglect of living merit may be traced to a cause, which though highly blameable, does not involve quite so much of absolute villainy. I believe that the origin of such neglect is really a sort of common weakness of humanity – that of being liable to be carried away with the excitements of the hour, rather than recognising those more solemn responsibilities which never yield without either discharge or penalty. I write this, therefore, with a hope that it will meet the eyes of some who will be able to do Mr. Bamford some good, and in a full faith that the reminder will be sufficient to induce them to do so.

A very wrong impression, I believe, has obtained as to Mr. Bamford's real position. It is commonly understood that he is in receipt of sufficient from government to support him. This is quite an error, as he does not receive, I believe, one shilling from that source. Indeed he has nothing, I believe, but what he earns by the exercise of his brain and pen; and so far as he is concerned, all that he wants are opportunities of gaining by these means – by giving readings, lectures, &c., – the means of supplying his own wants and those of her who has grown up beneath his shelter, like a primrose beneath an oak, and who has ever looked up to him with a smile, alike constant in the shade as in the sun, in the fierce storm of a November night as in the balmy calm of a morning in May. I have conversed with the old man, and I know that such is his highest ambition. I would however suggest something further. Mr. Bamford is now old, and cannot from his years be expected to go through much toil, even if he had the opportunity – and I trust that he will not be left without opportunity of giving to those who are only entering upon the path of active life, those counsels for which an extensive experience and a close observation have so eminently qualified him – he cannot go through much toil, I say, let therefore a subscription be entered into for the purpose of purchasing an annuity, for the joint benefit of himself and wife, sufficient to maintain them both in comfort for the few years they may have to continue amongst us. *One thousand pounds* would do this; and are there not in Lancashire one thousand men who would gladly co-operated in the undertaking? Surely there are. If so, let it be done – done quickly. Then, when the times comes – which Heaven defer – that we shall be called upon to erect a memorial over the resting-place of Samuel Bamford and his wife, we would be able to show upon the front of it – *appreciated living – regretted dead* – and we shall do so with the pleasant reflection that we do not erect a stone in mockery of an unheeded cry for bread.

I now leave the question of providing for the want of Bamford to those whom it may interest. I cannot suppose that they are few, and I can only say that I shall be most happy to form one of a thousand.

I know not how far this suggestion may meet approbation of Mr. Bamford himself. He may deem me impertinent when I only meant to be humane and Christian. To him I can only say that if I have erred I have done so from a good motive.

Of you sir, I can only beg that you will give my views upon this subject a place in your valuable paper, and that you will also do what you can towards furthering the object in view. – I am sir, yours, &c.,

ONE OF TO-DAY

May 26th, 1859.

---

***Editorial**, from the* Oldham Advertiser, *28 May 1859, using the occasion of a notice of the Butterworth memorial scheme to raise Bamford's claims, praising his political courage in ringing terms and quoting extensively from his circular.*

***Newspaper cutting**, unattributed, a brief history of Bamford's reform activities, arrest and imprisonment, taken from his circular.*

**Sunday 29th.** Brierley and his father here, and whilst they sat, Dronsfield, Travis, and another came: presently Gowenlock came, and then a troublesome intruder named Booth from Langley, who bothered about wills which he supposed were at Somerset House. I undeceived him, [and] at last got rid of him. Gowenlock went with Brierley and his father, after inviting us to his house for next Sunday. Dronsfield and his friends came again in the evening, bought 3 copies of Early Days, took some refreshment and went home.

**Monday 30th.** Called at J Cheethams Country house and drew a pound for tickets. Dined with Smith at Commercial, and came by train to Platting. The following from "The Protector" Ashton paper.

***Editorial**, from the* Ashton Protector, *28 May 1859, directing attention to Bamford's forthcoming reading. "We regret that some provision has not been made for his support in his old age. We rejoice, however, that he is still able to earn a respectable livelihood in a way so congenial to his tastes and so useful to the public." The paper urges support for "his last campaign in the war of life".*

***Poster** advertising Bamford's performance of "Literary Conversation" in the Town Hall, Stalybridge. The poster summarises Bamford's political career with a resumé of his arrests, imprisonment, and latter-day career, summarised from his petition.*

The annexed from the Ashton Reporter.

***Advertisement**, from the* Ashton Reporter, *for Bamford's readings at Stalybridge Town Hall; annotation "1/9 charged" crossed out.*

Here follows my Placard at Rochdale.

***Poster** similar to the one for Stalybridge, advertising Bamford's appearance at the Public Hall, Rochdale on Friday 27 May 1859.*

**Tuesday 31st.** Wrote to the Editor, Oldham Advertiser.

***Copy letter***, *Bamford to the Editor,* Oldham Advertiser, *31 May 1859.*

Sir,

My grateful thanks are due, and you have them from my inmost heart, for your very
kind and thoughtful pleading on my behalf, in your leading article of Saturday last,
and in the not less kind communication from some just and right minded
correspondent, which you admitted to your letter column. To that correspondent
I shall express my obligation through another medium, but both he and you have
enunciated sentiments which in days to come, will be quoted to your honour; for
though I occupy but a humble place in society, I have been, and am still, allied with
the great and high cause of my Countrys freedom and prosperity; and in the
promotion of that cause, I have without pretension of any sort, done and suffered
more, probably, than any other Englishman living, whilst, shame that it should be
possible, this very fact has, I have reasons for believing, created for me many enemies,
to unmask whom, and to gibbet them to infamy, is one part of the mission of these my
latter days. I have hitherto foughten the battle of life on my own resources, or mostly
so; and no man can say, and prove it, that under any trial of duty, I have been found
wanting. Crosses, losses, privations, exigency, contumely, outrage, unjust
condemnation, chains, imprisonments have each and all, been endured by me,
without an audible murmur, or complaint, and as inevitable conditions of the struggle
in which I had become engaged, and from which I shrank not, but let oppression have
enough, until it broke its own bonds. Certainly there have been moments of perhaps
too ardent hope, when I thought the time might possibly come during my stay in this
life, in which my countrymen might deem sacrifices such as I had undergone, worthy
of compensation, and that, as <u>compensation for the past,</u> I could, with self respectful
gratitude, accept, and becomingly assume, the enjoyment of my reward. Should such
a movement emanate from your suggestions, I shall have additional[1] cause to thank
you; and if it does not, my interests might /and, perhaps, will\ be very materially
served, and the comforts of myself and my aged partner, (a partner also in suffering for
the cause) be promoted by frequent engagements for readings and recitations.
I cannot conceive a more proper and fitting employment for the close of a long life,
than the communication of instructions, with some what of cheerful enjoyment also,
from the page of living experience: and in imparting such, I should not, like most
teachers of the class, have to borrow the bulk of my performances from the pages of
other authors, but, like the great genius of our time,[2] could produce interesting matter
with considerable variety, from my own writings.

A tragedy more deeply impressive, more practical, embracing higher character,
and more important results than any that Shakespear ever wrote; a tragedy of
actual life and death. A tragedy of the cottage, of the palace; of wolfish famine, of
voluptuous plenty, of freezing penury, of gorgeous extravagance, of cruel wrong, of
enduring right, of long sustained strife, and of glorious triumph, has been enacted

---

1. "Other" deleted and replaced with this.
2. I.e. Charles Dickens.

in this Kingdom since I can remember, and with such a page before him, /aided by his own reminiscences,\ why need an old man fail in interesting whatever company of Englishmen may come to listen.

I am Sir,

Your obliged Servant

Samuel Bamford.

**Wednesday 1st June.** Read and recited in the Town Hall, my friend Geo Smith in the Chair, J.R. Stephens,[3] and several of the Corporation on the platform, and a very fair attendance of respectable and intelligent looking people in the body of the room. I thought I performed pretty well and gave general satisfaction. The company at Smiths afterwards were rather too noisy, but very respectful to me, and I was kept out of bed till midnight. Of the tickets left with the booksellers only about three shillings were sold. Smith had sold a number, and Mr Platt out of 50 which I had left with him had sold six only, so my receipts were not so good as I had expected. Came away as soon as I could to Miles Platting, and so home weary in mind and tired in body.

**Friday 3rd.** Went to Oldham. Saw Gowenlock and renewed my engagement for Sunday. Went with him to his house and got some steak and very bad potatoes.

The above is what the Ashton Reporter, a Radical paper, of June 4th, says of my readings, he puts my notice, at the foot of the column and the <u>African Troupe</u> above it, though my reading took place the day before the other. A pretty beggarly radical he!

*Report, from the* Ashton Reporter, *4 June 1859, of Bamford's readings in Stalybridge, noting a moderate audience and summarising the pieces read.*

The following notice, though rather deprecatory, is far more honest, than that of the sneaking radical Hobson. It is from the Ashton Standard, edited by J.R. Stephens, and appears at the head of the column.

*Report, from the* Ashton Standard, *4 June 1859: a longer, more critical review of the above reading, commenting that the extracts from Passages "were read with an "earnestness and emphasis that showed he was an eye-witness", but suggesting that the poetry was less successful. In reading Prince's "The Mountain Minstrel", "We have no doubt the poet rightly understood the poet, but he failed to convey his own or his brother craftsman's feelings to the audience; his voice was monotonous, and his readings too hurried". Bamford's own poems were more "appropriately read and better received".*

---

He goes through his business much as if he were surrounded by his neighbours at Middleton; and it is in this spirit his audience must go to listen, if they [are to] come away satisfied. Young men or women going to hear Mr. Bamford, as they

---

3. Revd Joseph Rayner Stephens (1805–79), 'the Chartist Tory', fierce opponent of the New Poor Law, former editor of the *Champion* and at this date editor of the *Ashton Standard; DNB.*

would Montgomery or other professional readers, would leave the room grudging the time and money spent. He speaks and reads for full-grown men and women, who can discern and appreciate merit without the trappings of a finished elocution to quicken their mental perceptions... . His audience, though not numerous, was of the right sort, apparently disposed to meet him half way in his efforts to instruct and entertain.

---

**Sunday 5th.** Went to Oldham, with Brierley. Passed a dull forenoon. Caught in a shower at Busk and stepping into a Beer house got some indifferent ale. Back at last to Gowenlocks i.e. myself, Potter and Brierley as visitors. Roast beef and bad potatoes again to dinner. After noon dull: whisky did not affect me or the others: we were not in a right frame for drinking, so cut off before tea and down to Hollinwood, to the Filho and to Burns's Cottage, a beer house, where old Sam Collin and his friends were sitting to order measures about the publication of his book. Old Sam seems stupid, and dull, will not allow corrections of his spelling, which is frequently very imperfect. They are beginning to be dissatisfied with his obstinacy, and well they may: however I did not interfere. Came again, with Gowenlock, Brierley, Potter, Travis and Dronsfield to the Filho, where we stayed until shutting up time and then Brierley and myself had to walk home; served us right for stopping.

*Cuttings, from the* Oldham Advertiser, *4 June 1859: Bamford's letter of the 31st May, as reproduced above, with minor changes to punctuation, together with a copy of his poem "Harrison's Hope" and commentary.*[4]

---

### HARRISON'S HOPE.

#### A PRISON HYMN.
#### WRITTEN BY SAMUEL BAMFORD.

When confined in Lincoln Castle, for attending the Great Meeting on Saint Peter's Field, at Manchester, and addressed by him to JOSEPH HARRISON, a prisoner in Chester Castle, for attending a Meeting for Parliamentary Reforms at Stockport date about 1820.
  *Tune* – "The God of Abraham Praise;" a beautiful Hebrew melody, sung by the Old Methodists to one of their hymns commencing with those words.

> Not cloud of darkness there,
> But all was bright and fair,
> Hope smiled at the chains which hung in prison lair;
> Ah! Though the great combine,
> The lowly to confine,
> They cannot for one moment quench his hope divine.

---

4. For the full text of the poem see *Homely Rhymes* (1864), 113–14; verse three as printed here is a revised version.

> The prophecy of this hymn has been fulfilled: the millions *are free*, as compared with their condition at the time the lines were written: they have also arisen, and made their opinions understood, with a power which has vindicated humanity, and will yet do more.

My letter of 31 May, and my prison Hymn "Harrisons Hope", appear in the Oldham Advertiser of 4th June: the latter above.

Mills of Middleton and Allan Mellor came to my house on Sunday so sent Mills the newspapers he wanted by Bus on Monday.

**Tuesday 7th.** Page of the Market Office Department[5] has been snubbed for endeavouring to collect a little money for Rogerson: one of his superiors intimated that it was not becoming a servant of the Corporation to be seen taking part in such matters, so of course, Page has retired from the good work. He is surprised, he says, at the sneaking shabby spirit of some who have the power to do what is wanted. Abel Heywood is a shabby sneaking fellow, and behaved badly to him about the publication of his book. I said amen to this part of his declaration, he is a sneaking, shabby snob, "Abel Anything". Of about half a hundred Scotchmen who joined Rogerson in celebration of Burns's Centenary, only 4/- have been collected for the Manchester bard. 11/- were received, and 7/- of them were subscribed by Englishmen.

**Wednesday 8th.** Wrote as follows to the Editor, Ashton Standard.

***Copy letter***, *Bamford to the Editor of the* Ashton Standard, *8 June 1859.*

Bamford's Readings and Recitations

Sir,
Allow me to correct an error in your generally fair, and candid notice of my performance at the Town Hall Stayley Bridge on the evening of the 1st instant. You say "Prose was now succeeded by poetry, Mr Bamford selecting Prince's poem, "The Mountain Minstrel." We have no doubt the poet rightly understood the poet, but he failed to convey his own or his brother craftsman's feelings to the audience; his voice was monotonous, and his reading hurried." The poem, I must inform you, in justice to the author, was one, of many excellent productions by my friend, Mr Smith, the chairman: as was also the humorous piece which I read, narrating the triumphs and death of that noble game bird, "General Pickegree." I regret much, if in reading the poem, I failed to convey my own, or the authors feelings to the audience. I certainly wished to do so, but the fact was the type was, or appeared to me, different from that I had been conning over, and my sight not being so good as it once was, I experienced some difficulty in reading clearly and distinctly, as from the letter I had before used: So you see, it is with old people as

---

5. John Page (1819–99), local literary figure and prominent member of the Manchester Literary Club; wrote as "Felix Folio"; see *Proceedings of the Manchester Literary Club* (1899). (See Plate 1.)

it is with young ones, they require a little indulgence. All the remainder of your notice, though in some times rather depreciatory, I accept as being, on the whole complimentary. I have had other things to study, than the professional finish of "professional readers," their exact embellishment I have never aspired to; far other thoughts and wishes have occupied my head and heart; as I have generally understood my subject, so I have endeavoured to be understood, and your assurance that, "I go through my business in a homely style, as if reading to my neighbours at Middleton", convinces me at once, that my reading is just what it aught to be, the unaffected effort of a working man to instruct and amuse whoever may come to listen.

I am Sir,

Your Obedient Servant,

Samuel Bamford

**Report**, *from the* Manchester Examiner and Times, *8 June 1859, announcing a grand soirée at Peel Park, hosted by William Harvey, mayor of Salford, and of the consequent closure of the park to the public.*

The "local artists" see over, were not likely to respond to the invitation of such a patron as W. Harvey Esq$^r$. the Mayor of Salford,[6] who aims at having credit for being an encourager of the arts and of self improvement amongst the working classes; and who, when a self cultivated working man solicited his patronage of a literary performance he was about to give in the Mechanics Institution of Salford, munificently handed out a shilling, and took <u>two sixpenny tickets</u>. His pretensions to the character of a patron of the arts and artists, and to that of a promoter of self culture amongst the labouring population are all humbug! and appear to have /been\ appreciated as such, by the intelligent "local artists" who, I am glad to perceive, have treated his invitation with neglect. The pretentious snob aught to be snubbed. I preserve these slips as records of this famous transaction in the days of, "<u>Harvey Mayor</u>."

**Report**, *from the* Manchester Examiner and Times, *9 June 1859, of Harvey's grand soirée at the Peel Park Museum and Library, attended by 600–700 people, to inaugurate an exhibition of paintings and the iron gates presented by Lord Ducie. Local artists largely failed to respond to invitations to loan their works.*

**Friday 10th.** To Ashton and Stayley Bridge where Swallow, the reporter, and I, lunched on Welch rabbit. At the Old Boars Head, Ashton, met Mr Wood, son of the late Col. Wood of the Ashton Volunteers, whom I remembered having seen repeatedly with his regiment. A Mr Williams, who was described to me as a great radical, and also an admirer of "Tom Pain".[7] He quoted my argument at Bury that any man who was eligible to become a member of Parliament was good enough to become a voter,

---

6. William Harvey (1787–1870), Salford cotton spinner; prominent temperance advocate; Salford Alderman 1844–70, and mayor 1857–9; see *Manchester Courier*, 29 December 1870.

7. Thomas Paine (1737–1809), influential radical theorist, author of *The Rights of Man*, etc; *DNB*.

and said that he had never heard that propounded until [I] put it forth at Bury. I remarked that it was a proposition which the reformers generally, and the non-electors especially had not argued as they ought to have done; it was too conclusive for moderate reformers, who seemed to ignore it, and appeared beyond credibility and belief of the ultra manhood suffrage class, who never put it forward. Nothing had been done during the late election, by the reformers to advance the cause of reform: with the exception of Mr Bazley, at the Collegiate Ward, at Manchester not a single pledge, had, according to my recollection, been required or given. The reformers had neglected their opportunity, they had not been faithful to their cause.

From Staley Bridge to Greenfield, where I had to wait an hour; thence to Oldham, where I saw Amb[rose] Hurst[8] who intimated that my reading there would depend on Edwin Butterworth's concern. A thing I shall not submit to. I know not indeed why this person should be suffered to influence my proceedings at all.

At the Saddleworth station I was accosted by a poor, miserable looking being who seemed [to be] suffering from hunger and other privation: he was Hiram, Edwin Butterworths surviving brother, who had come to Saddleworth trying to sell a few clothes pegs. I gave him all the copper I had, and came away by train. I mentioned this incident to Hurst, and remonstrated with him on the cruelty of keeping forty pounds in the committees hands to erect a memorial to Edwin, whilst ten pounds would be enough for a gravestone, and the remainder might be applied to the relief of the living brother. So I left him; and know not how this affair will be carried on.

**Sunday 12th.** Brierley, his wife and little girl came up after tea, and remained until nearly dark.

**Monday 13th.** Oldham. Saw Potter and Gowenlock, the latter will speak to Mr John Platt and put forward a reading for me. Some one it seems is dissatisfied with something which has been stated on my behalf in the Oldham Advertiser, since the following appears under the head "Correspondence."

**Cutting**, *from the "Replies to Correspondents" section,* Oldham Advertiser, *11 June 1859.*

---

### One of Former Days.

In our opinion Samuel Bamford has done more for Reform, and to advance the interests of the working classes, than any other man living, in the same position in life. If "One of Former Days" does not think so, we cannot help it. We recommend to him a careful perusal of Mr. Bamford's published works. It may alter his opinion.

---

**Friday 17th.** Received and sent the following.

**Letter**, *G.B. Richardson, Hooley Hill, Audenshaw, to Bamford, 16 June 1859.*

---

8. Ambrose Hurst, a longstanding Oldham Radical, supporter of the Ten Hours movement, etc.

Dear Sir,

The members of the Lancashire Reformers Union of the Audenshaw Branch are
very anxious for you to deliver a lecture at Hooley Hill some time within a month
from this date and we have sent to your friend George Smith of Staley Bridge to
request you and you had just left his house when our note arrived and he says he
thinks you will be able to do so if you can. We think it will be of great service to
the Reform cause and we shall feel very thankfull if you will write and state the
conditions and time and we will let you know how far it will meet our own
convenience.

Yours Truly<br>G.B. Richardson, Hon. Sec.

**Copy letter**, *Bamford to G.B. Richardson, undated.*

Dear Sir,

If the members of the Audenshaw Branch of the Reformers Union think a lecture,
or a reading of mine, will be of service to the cause in their district, I shall deem it
my duty to attend their call. I am not, at present, engaged for any particular
night; your friends may therefore choose their own time, the sooner however, and
the more convenient for me, as I am in expectation of being wanted for several
places.

   The money conditions I leave to yourselves. You will provide a room, posting
bills etc., the copy of which bills I would draw up. I should also expect a dry
comfortable bed at a respectable private dwelling, and if one or two of your
committee could come over to see me, it would perhaps be as well, tomorrow,
Sunday. I am sure to be at home,

Yours truly,<br>Sam<sup>l</sup> Bamford

If you come across the country you should come through Droylesden and Newton
Heath. I reside better than a mile on this side of Dene brook.[9]

Went to see Mr Simpson at Manchester, but he like nearly everyone else was of[f]
holidaying. Called at one or two places, and then came home by Bus. The attendant
could not change a half sovereign as I went /in the morning,\ so I gave it (the fare)
to the guard of the one I returned by, the other not being in the way: saw him
however afterwards at Barnes Green, told him what I had done, and he said it was
right.

   The following is from Swallow, the reporter, at Ashton.

**Letter**, *S. Swallow, Old Cross Street, Ashton, to Bamford, 16 June 1859.*

---

9. Overwritten upside down at head.

My Dear Sir,
I drop this note to say that many of your friends, with whom I have conversed, wish you to let your reading stand over a <u>little</u> after this week.
Truly yours,<br>S. Swallow

I will send <u>list</u> etc on Monday the 20th.[10]

**Saturday 18th.** John Ford and Wm Collinge called and had a pot of ale. Also in the afternoon, Henry Grimshaw, Jane, and the three children. Talking about Christ's directions for Salvation I read to them that portion of Christ's Sermon on the Mount. Matt ch 6:v12 "And forgive us our debts, as we forgive our debtors": They argued that the sermon was meant for the Disciples only and not for the multitude, forgetting the 28th and 29 verses of chapter 7, "And it came to pass, when Jesus had ended these sayings, the people were astonished at his doctrine.

For he taught them as one having authority and not as the scribes." They were under the influence of their parson, and put a parsons interpretation on the passage.

My Middleton newspaper did not come. I suppose because the Oldham Advertiser has been giving me a lift, the Middleton man will drop my acquaintance.

**Tuesday 21st.** Went to Manchester thinking to draw a few shillings, but neither Belfield, nor Taylor the auctioneer mentioned the thing, and instead of improving my finances I returned about five shillings worse that I set out in the morning: this wont do.

***Advertisement**, from the* Manchester Examiner and Times, *23 June 1859.*[11]

---

SWIMMING ought to be part of a Youth's Education – Professor POULTON TEACHES the above useful art a[t] the Mayfield Baths Manchester and at the Greengate Baths, Salford.

---

**Thursday 23rd.** The above is from this mornings paper. Poulton is a kind of on and off clerk at Somerset House, an amphibious being, who can very conveniently serve his employers either on land or in water. Moving about hither and thither on various pretences, and for anything known to the contrary, sending up whatever information may be required. Every man in the place is expected to be willing to do the same. I dislike such characters, and consequently, avoid the whole lot. Poulton is at Mayfield Baths, "Hoyle & Sons", being not known friends of mine. This morning the following inane scrawl, in reply to mine of the 17th, comes by post. Hoyle & Sons, Mayfield, Poultons place of exercise, being on the envelope: a coincidence.

---

10. Added landscape on side.
11. The cutting is unattributed, but in all the Manchester papers for this date.

**Letter**, *G.B. Richardson to Bamford, 21 June 1859.*

Dear Sir,
We received your note will endeavour to carry out your request we could not make it all convenient to come over on Sunday we had a meeting last night put the thing in a shape agreed to look after a room etc., and we are thinking about having it in about 3 weeks before then soon as we can we will either send over a Deputation or write to you to complete the affair,

Yours truly,

James Crosby Chairman

G.B. Richardson Sec

**Friday 24th.** Clowes was away at Stockport, John Heywood seems to have had enough of buying copyrights for the present: no orders there. Belfield, though I spoke to him about it, did not pay the half crown, so I bought some tea and coffee, and came home minus several shillings: thus my very small means go, scarcely enough left for Sundays dinner and Mondays rent.

**Saturday 25th.** An invitation to attend the laying of foundation stone at Stock Brook Sunday School and Literary Institution on Saturday next.

**Sunday 26th.** Blakeley Mechanics Institution. Charles Delaunay has employed an attorney to recover a debt they owe him, so now, in extremity they write to me requesting my attendance on Tuesday evening. I shant go: they are a miserable set: unteachable, and the whole thing has been miserably conducted.

26 Sunday. Allan Mellor and two friends called, and we conversed chiefly on the expected laying of foundation stone next Saturday.

**Monday 27th.** Went to Oldham, met Potter in the street, and he returned with me up town. Met Gowenlock at Coronation Inn and he said a committee was formed to get up a reading for me: the committee to pay all expenses and I to take whatever the performance would make – very good – It did not appear however, that it could take place this week, or the next, the reason for which is probably, that a Company of the Theatricals are in the town, and occupying the public attention too much for my affair to have a good chance of being attended to: this I suppose is the reason. Meantime I must try to do something at Ashton for I am, on all sides, quite ashore. Gowenlock pressed me to accompany the Oldham tradesman's Association on their yearly trip, on Wednesday, and I partly consented first when I considered all matters, afterwards, I found I could not go. I had not a sixpence left, nor even respectable clothing. Gowenlock could have paid, or rather he did send me tickets for dinner and railway fare, but I had not as much as would have paid for a glass of punch – saying nothing of apparel, so gave it up.

**Wednesday 29th.** Got circular from Mills at Middleton, and sent same off to Ashton.
Mima found 18 pence in her pocket which she had thought was lost.

**Thursday 30th.** Mr Cobden[12] landed at Liverpool, and was waited upon by a deputation from Rochdale amongst whom was Thos Livsey: of course he made a speech to them. Also one to "The Liverpool Liberals," to "the Financial Reform Association," to "the Peace Society," to "the Liverpool Reform Club," and to "the American Chamber of Commerce." The newspapers are half filled with this kind of stuff, and whilst all this is going on I am circulating by post the address in my second circular, for which see the other leaf. But then Cobden and Bright are rich men: great men in the worlds passing estimation; whilst I am very poor: all however which they are praised, idolized for talking about I have <u>done, enacted</u>: they are the Officers, and must be gazetted. I am the Grenadier of the advanced guard: their fortune is to be praised and rewarded: mine to march, to fight and die unmentioned: but, "This cannot always be."

**Insertion,** *Bamford's revised circular (see Appendix 1).*

Thursday To Manchester, and coming home was I believe hocussed at Harperhey, and certainly had my pocket picked, by a party who pretends to respectability: he will be detected in some of his sharp practices, and then all will be flown abroad; he is a bad fellow, and behaves badly to his wife; beating and turning her out of doors, but this I have only recently heard of.

**Friday July 1st.** Borrowed a sovereign from Henry Grimshaw, and went to Middleton.

**Saturday 2nd.** The following leader, and correspondence appear in the Middleton Albion of this day.

**Letter,** *from the* Middleton Albion, *2 July 1859.*

---

### BREAD OR A STONE

*To the Editor of the Middleton Albion*
SIR, – A correspondence, with the above heading appeared about a fortnight ago in the *Oldham Advertiser*. I think the object a very desirable one, viz., an acknowledgement of the services of Samuel Bamford in the cause of the people, when it was not considered so respectable as it now is, to be an advocate for Reform in the Commons House of Parliament. Mr. Bamford has endured great and severe hardships in the cause, and well deserves a consideration. I think well of the proposition to do something during his lifetime, and shall be most happy to contribute £1 to the proposed fund for purchasing an annuity for him. I shall be glad to see the matter taken up with energy. – I am, sir, yours truly,          T.C.[13]
Rhodes, June 24th, 1859.

---

12. Richard Cobden (1804–65), free trader and leading light in the Anti-Corn Law League; *DNB*.
13. Almost certainly Thomas Coulborn: see entry for 24 July, etc.

*Editorial, from the* Middleton Albion, *2 July 1859, taking up the appeal of the preceding letter, and of a recent issue of the* Oldham Advertiser *(see entry for 28 May), which it quotes extensively, continuing:*

---

We believe an impression prevails that Samuel Bamford is in receipt of government pension, or endowment from the Royal or other literary institutions; but we can assure our readers that such is not the case, and that he has never received, never asked for, a single farthing from any of these sources. His only means of subsistence, and that of his aged partner and sharer of his political troubles, are derived from the sale of the copyright of his works, and from the uncertain result of readings and lectures. The first of these cannot hold out during any lengthened period, and the other is precarious; the least inclement weather may blight success; and his having passed the term allotted to human existence, of "threescore years and ten," the sands of life will become brief in their course. That erect and manly bearing will have to succumb to the decline of his physical powers, so that however willing he may be he cannot long sustain the labour and endure the turmoil of travelling in the night to and from the lecture room.

We hail with delight the offer of our correspondent who, we dare assert, is prompted by true feelings of philanthropy and generous kindness to pay a due acknowledgement to real worth before, as in the case of Robert Burns, it be too late, and a stone be given, after bread hath been withheld.

---

2 July Saturday. Attended the cornerstone laying of the new Sunday School at Stock Brook. Instead of Allan Mellor waiting for me as we had arranged, I met him and Whalley of Middleton already starting before my arrival. I thought they seemed strangely shy, and as their manner begat a correspondingly shyness in me, we went on without my joining much in the conversation. At Stock Brook, instead of being shown to Mr Smethursts residence, as I had been led to expect I should be, Mellor led us to a house occupied by one of the teachers, at the back of the row, whence, after sitting a short time, and not knowing what to make of this sort of thing, I called Mellor out and questioned him about the arrangement, when he said, the procession of scholars would set off from the school, a large room, upstairs, and proceed thence to the scite of the new building where the stone would be laid, after which I, and others specially invited would have tea at Mr Smethursts residence: and so it was. The scholars and teachers walked in procession to the place where the foundations were ready laid. A hymn or two were sung: prayer was made by one of the old teachers; the trowel /a silver one\ was presented to Mr Smethurst who went through the ceremony of laying the stone in the cavity of which was deposited a bottle containing an Oldham Chronicle, but not an Advertiser (Qʸ was this because the Advertiser had warmly advocated my cause? I have fears that an influence inimical to me, had been at work). After adjusting the stone, Mr Smethurst gave an appropriate address, and I followed with an account of Sunday schools as they were in my young days, 60 years ago; how we had writing as part of our instruction, and such writing was sanctioned, and supported by the old fathers of Methodism, the immediate associations and disciples of John Wesley. But as my address, or probably some portion of it will most likely appear in the Oldham papers, I shall not

state more at present. Another hymn was next sung: then prayer made, and the National Anthem concluded the proceedings. Many people were present, who seemed to be much interested by the proceedings, but I did not see or hear of any parson taking part, which was satisfactory to me. Mr Alderman Platt was mentioned as one who should have assisted, but, as was stated he was absent from home.

Six or eight, persons sat down to tea at Mr Smethursts. Mr S himself officiating at the head of the table, at which I was not greatly surprised at the time, Mr S being a bachelor. I made an excellent refreshment, being both hungry and thirsty, and decanters, cigars, etc., being introduced an animated discussion ensued respecting the right, or wrong, in a religious sense, of teaching writing on Sundays. I, and another elderly person were strongly in favour of writing. Mr Smethurst, & one or two others appeared to be less earnestly in its behalf, whilst the remainder were against it. The weather broke, and it appeared to be setting in for a wet evening; the discussion also had become tiresome, and I, begging to be excused on account of the weather, took my departure, and got to the railway just in time for a train to Newton Heath, whence I got home comfortably and in good time: Thus ended my Stock brook adventure.

**Monday 4th.** Went to Middleton and ordered a <u>third</u> set of circulars, 250.

The following from Dronsfield at Hollinwood.[14]

*Letter, James Dronsfield to Bamford, 4 July 1859.*

Dear Friend,
You must excuse me for not attending the stone laying. I did not know about it until the following day, as I certainly should have been there.
   You and Mima have not yet been over. I shall expect you both, on Sunday the 17 July when I intend to christen my little son, Bamford is the name we have given him, <u>fail not to attend</u>.
                    I am Yours
                    James Dronsfield

P.S. Please to send me 3 copies of your "Early Days" by Ophelia, she has the money for them in her pocket.
JD

**Tuesday 5th.** Oldham. Gowenlock s[ai]d he would order about my reading this week.

*Letter, G.B. Richardson to Bamford, undated, but postmarked 5 July 1859.*

Sir,
We have decided to have your lecture on Tuesday the 19th of July at 1/2 past seven o'clock in the evening in the Methodist New Connexion school room

---

14. On opposite page.

Hooley Hill and have secured the room and James Crosby Esq of Shepley Hall is appointed chairman on that occasion and he has also promised to accommodate you with Bed &c. We have also appointed a deputation to wait on you on Sunday next in the afternoon.

Please say if these arrangements do not suit you & if they do not we will try to alter them for your convenience.

Yours truly

GB Richardson, Sect

**Wednesday 6th.** To Ashton, the Mayor not in town, nor either of the Buckleys.[15] Geo Higginbottom "had not any answer," to my circular such is the vulgar insolence which these money stuffed puppies display when it suits their convenience.

Saw that harum scarum tory, Wood, at the "Old Dog," and cut his company as soon as possible. Finding it a bad day for my business, being the 1st Wed in the month, when all accounts are settled, I took train and came home.

**Thursday 7th.** Middleton. Borrowed a sov from Mills and ordered a room and posting bills for reading next Wednesday.

7th Thursday. Mills of the Albion advised me not to press for the insertion of the letter below. I had sent a copy however, to another paper, and a copy of "The Slanderer, Basest of Mankind," to the Oldham Advertiser, and the Man^r Exam^r & Times.

**Draft letter**, *Bamford to the Editor of the* Middleton Albion, *6 July 1859.*

Bamford's Compensation

Sir,

I have to thank you, also your correspondent T.C. for the kind sentiments you both expressed in my behalf, last week. And I beg to add, that I have not only, <u>never asked for</u> any /governmental\ endowment ~~governmental or otherwise~~, but I have never requested any friend, never commissioned any one to apply on my behalf, for any pecuniary consideration, from any prime minister, whig, tory, or Conservative, Lord, Earl, or Duke. I do not see however, why this should continue: The time has now, I think arrived, when I may fairly present my account to the nation, and to the government as the nations agents, and managers. I can tot up the debtors side, leaving the credits to be filled in, by those in power; and we shall then see what sort of balance will be struck: it has been owing long enough: forty years is a pretty long breathing time for a poor handloom weaver to allow a great, rich, and powerful nation. I shall have some curious items of damage, and claims of reparation. I have been spied upon, by "genial confidents," who in their blackest of heart, were "social traitors," "hooded vipers." I have been arrested on false information, chained and made an exhibition of through the country. I have been wrongfully imprisoned, falsely indicted, unfairly tried, unjustly condemned, and

---

15. I.e. the Buckleys of Mill Bottom, Waterhead, near Oldham, see entry for 25 July 1859.

imprisoned, and now I say, "here is my account." "I wish it to be paid. I am getting rather old, my old dame also, is not so active and blithe as she was fifty years ago, and we can do with a settlement now, very well." Thus shall I present my bill, if /it\ be duly honoured I shall be compensated. I wish not for anything more, – and what will otherwise remain a national reproach will be obliterated.

I am Sir<br>
Your Obd<sup>t</sup> Servant.<br>
Samuel Bamford.

**Friday 8th.** Paid Grimshaw his sov back, and most happy I was to discharge his obligation.

I was standing at the meetings of the two roads, waiting for Grimshaw, and had been marking the sov. with my teeth, for I like to mark them, when John Ford came up and asked several times what I had been looking at (at the sov. to see if it was marked) so I was obliged to show him, or to offend him by refusal; very much mortified: How offensive bad manners are, even when not so intended.

Very low again in money, so got a shoulder of lamb on credit from Mrs Needham 2/4. This is much against my ideas of rectitude: it seems shabby, shifty, and I feel humiliated.

**Saturday 9th.** The following are from the Middleton Albion of this day. The paragraph I do not entirely thank him for. Why did he not say something more than "the least", or nothing.

***Cutting***, *from the* Middleton Albion, *9 July 1859.*

> We beg to refer our readers' attention to an announcement on the top of the 2nd column of the first page of this impression. It is a notice of an earnest endeavour of an <u>old man</u>, to say the <u>least</u>, to earn a honest livelihood.[16]

***Advertisement***, *from the* Middleton Albion, *9 July 1859, for Bamford's forthcoming reading in Middleton, reproducing the text of the poster.*[17]

**Monday 11th.** The following very meagre report of my address at Stock brook is from the Oldham Advertiser of the 9th inst.

***Cutting***, *from the* Oldham Advertiser, *9 July 1859.*

> Mr. Samuel Bamford, author of the "Life of a Radical," &c., next spoke. He said that he was at any rate one of the oldest, if not the oldest Sunday school scholar,

---

16. Bamford's emphasis.
17. See below and Plate 9.

on that ground. He recollected the time when they were but slenderly attended, and when dissenting ministers in going to their places of worship, were hooted and reviled, but those things were now passed. The Sunday School at Middleton was originated by the oldest Methodist preachers, and those who had been in the habit of reading the 'Arminian Magazine,' or 'John Wesley's Journal,' would see the names of John Nelson and others. Those were the men who established the Sunday School; but those schools were in some respect different from the present ones, and children were not only taught to read but to write. It was not now considered proper to do so, but they had the example of those fervent and earnest men, who established Methodism, that they did not consider it objectionable. It was of the greatest importance in a manufacturing district that the youth should be instructed in writing. Mr Bamford related some of his early experiences, the difficulties he had to contend with, the pleasant sensations he felt when he discovered that he had at last acquired to read, and said that the Sunday schools were great blessings to the working classes, and the acquisition of reading opened to them a new world. (Hear, hear.) That institution, he understood, taught writing on Sundays, and he was glad that there was a knott of Christians who had the moral courage to do what they did on behalf of the poor man's child. He exhorted them to learn the children to write, and if they could not obtain copy books, slates and pencils might be obtained, and that would do a great deal of good. – (Hear, hear.) The children might be taught to write portions of Scripture, and they would by that means more easily commit the passages to memory. He also recommended them to introduce geography and if some religious friends might object to teaching the geography of Russia, Prussia, or any other country, they might get a map of the Holy Land, Egypt, and the other places mentioned in Scripture, and they could take the journeyings of the Israelites, and mountains, rivers, &c. If they had but a smattering of these things on Sunday they would be induced to go further and extend their knowledge of the various countries on the week days. – (Hear, hear.)[18]

---

The following is from the same paper.

**Cutting**, *from the* Oldham Advertiser, *9 July 1859.*

---

### BASEST OF MANKIND![19]

Who steals my purse, steals trash; 'tis something, nothing:
'Twas mine, 'tis his, and has been slave to thousands;
But he that filches from me my good name,
Robs me of that which not enriches him,
And makes me poor indeed.                                   *Shakespear.*[20]

Steal but a crust, and by the law thou punished art, of course;
But filch away a man's good name, and who shall deem thee worse?

---

18. Brief final paragraph omitted.
19. Bamford's poem is a slightly different version of "The Slanderer", published in *Homely Rhymes*, 228–9.
20. Iago, from *Othello*, Act III, scene iii.

Go, take a purse upon the road, and banish'd thou shalt be;
But rob a man of honest fame, and few will censure thee!
Nay, thou may'st *kill*, but *mind thou stab* with *private deadly* word;
And *poisoning* by *slander*, *is a murder not abhor'd*;
To robber, thief and murderer: with coward too, combin'd,
Is the *poison-breathing slanderer*, the *basest of mankind*.
And yet, 'tis not the slanderer, ye shun, like rabid hound,
It is the injur'd victim, sad and lonely with his wound:
Ah! Would not common sense, and barest justice, both demand,
The victim to restor? and take him kindly by the hand?
Whilst the *excrable slanderer* is *hooted through the land*;
Deep marked with *lasting* infamy's indelible brand.

BARDOFM

NOTE: The person who listens to the poisoned whisperings of a slanderer, whether glossed over by the term "privileged communication," or not, and is influenced by such communication, without having made known the fact to the injured party, becomes as guilty and degraded, as the slanderer himself. He denies the injured one an opportunity of self-defence, he acquiesces in, and indeed promotes, an act of moral assassination, often more cruel[21] and injustifiable, than murder by the knife. Still, he as well as the slanderer, may pass amongst "the respectables." – *Ibid*.

---

A copy of the same lines having been sent to the Manchester Exam[r] and Times the following is the way in which they were noticed.

---

BARDOFM – On such a text even a much better paraphrase might be considered "poor indeed."

---

If a shabbier act than common is to be performed, it will always be done by a <u>radical</u> Editor, against a <u>radical</u>; who asked this person for his opinion as to the merits of the composition. Not I certainly, see Exam[r] & Times, 12 July.

The annexed also is from the same Oldham paper.[22]

Received a funeral card of Ch. Smith Heywood

**Wednesday 13th.** With reference to the impertinent notice of my lines "The Basest of Mankind" sent the following to the Editor, Man[r] Examiner and Times.

"Sir, the lines headed as above, were offered for your insertion in the paper, or rejection. You neither do one, nor the other; but give an <u>opinion</u> which is just as requisite, as it is effective, and no more.
The writer,["]

---

21. Deleted in manuscript and replaced by "atrocious".
22. The item is missing.

**Poster**, *relating to Bamford's forthcoming readings in Middleton.*[23]

*Written on the folded front*:

Placard of my Reading

at Middleton

All these proposals were carried out and the letters between Mr Wood and myself, and Mr Syne and myself were read, Mr Howarth remarking, afterwards that this was a fair challenge, and he wished more Middletonians had been present.

---

23. See Plate 9.

# 6

# SIR JAMES KAY-SHUTTLEWORTH

*The news which Bamford received on 15th July that Sir James Kay-Shuttleworth, the educational reformer and one-time Manchester doctor, had been enquiring after him, ushered in a new episode in his life. He was at first suspicious, and it was another fortnight before the men met. In the interim he continued with his recitations, and launched a more direct campaign for "just compensation" by sending his circulars to several prominent radical MPs (whose responses intensified his frustration). When Bamford visited Kay-Shuttleworth at Gawthorpe Hall at the end of July (after Mima had pledged her best dress to get his only decent coat out of pawn) it became apparent that the intention was to employ Bamford in collecting material about the 1826 powerloom riots in south-east Lancashire for Kay-Shuttleworth's forthcoming historical novel* Scarsdale. *Payments for this work and the proceeds of three successful readings at Oldham enabled Bamford to live in considerably greater comfort through the summer and early autumn; these were times of contentment and even optimism.*

**Friday 15th.** John Heywood of Manchester tells me Sir James P. Kay Shuttleworth of Gauthorpe Hall, near Burnley,[1] called at his shop and purchased a copy of my Early Days. Sir James also desired him to inform me that he was going to London where he should remain a few days. After which he would return to Lancashire, when he would be glad to see me at Gauthorpe: on his return he would write to me, as he wished to see me, and make my acquaintance. I thanked Heywood, of course, for the trouble he had incurred in writing to me: and said I would communicate to Sir James, at London, which Heywood also advised.

What is the meaning of this? How does it happen that Sir James Kay Shuttleworth should only have found me out after this long delay, since my name first came before the public? Has one of my circulars accidentally go into his hand, or is there some hidden movement at work, either to benefit me – from very shame – or lead me astray to humiliation. I must be strictly on my guard. Heywood hand[ed] me the card over.

***Kay-Shuttleworth's card***
Sir James P. Kay-Shuttleworth, 38 Gloucester Square.

***Report**, from the* Middleton Albion, *16 July 1859.*

---

### LITERARY EXERCISES

On Wednesday evening Mr. Samuel Bamford, author of "Life of a Radical," etc. etc., gave a reading and recitation from his own and other works. The attendance, though

---

1. Sir James P. Kay-Shuttleworth (1804–77), of Gawthorpe Hall, near Burnley, educationalist and Liberal, author of *The Moral and Physical Condition of the Working Classes Employed in the Cotton Manufacture in Manchester* (1832), and secretary of the Privy Council Committee on Education 1839–49; *DNB.*

not numerous, was very respectable. Mr. Edmund Howarth was called to the chair, and after reading the programme of the evening, he introduced Mr. Bamford, who commenced his exercises by reading a chapter from his "Early Days," giving a short account of his father, also a germ of poetry, and a hymn composed by his father. He next described his first visit to the House of Commons in a tone not very flattering to the house, spoke of Canning's and Brougham's appearance there – of the uproarious confusion which prevailed when a speaker was declaiming against government, and how, when the working classes were assailed quietness prevailed, so that if a pin had fallen the noise could be heard. He next read and recited several of his poems, "The pass of death," "God help the poor," and by particular request, a piece in the Lancashire dialect called "Jemmy the Jobber."[2] Mr. Bamford next proceeded to inform the audience as to his ceasing to be a handloom weaver – how he came to be employed at Somerset House. It appeared that Mr. Bamford exchanged the shuttle for the reporter's pen, and was engaged on a London paper, at the time of dear bread, and when great discontent prevailed among the working classes, which resulted in breaking machinery at High Crompton and other places. His connection with the press as a reporter ceased in the year 1839. After this he commenced publishing his works. The first was his *Life of a Radical*, in parts, which paid him pretty well. Afterwards, an epistolary acquaintance sprung up with Mr. Wood, chairman of the inland revenue. Mr. Bamford began to think a settled employment would be better than that in which he was engaged, and he asked Mr. Wood if he could find him employment. Some time after he wrote Mr. Bamford informing him of a vacancy in the stamp department. Mr. Bamford went up to London as requested, got the appointment, and held the same till May 1858, having served a term of seven years. He stated that the nature of his occupation was not congenial to his tastes, and the part in which his duties were performed being lighted with gas, his health suffered. He also became daily more persuaded that neither the place, nor the employment, were either suitable or worthy of him, and he resolved not to spend the remaining few years of his existence in the trammels of a government harness. He therefore tendered his resignation, which was accepted with expressions of regret by the head of the department. With regard to his future prospects, he said he thought he could not better use the remaining term of his life than by giving the benefit of his experiences in instructing and advising those amongst whom he might dwell; and whether he succeeded or not, he was determined to merit success. Mr. Bamford sat down amid much applause.

Mr. Howarth said he was very much satisfied with the correspondence Mr. Bamford had read. He (Mr. H.) should have been glad to have seen more Middletonians present, as there was a deep impression in this town that Mr. Bamford had obtained the government situation by some improper means; but it seemed to him that things had been done in a strictly honourable way. His (Mr. B.'s) published works were better appreciated in distant parts than they were in his own town, and this was another fulfilment of the saying, that "a prophet hath but little honour in his own country," – By request Mr. Bamford recited his poem, "Tim Bobbin's Grave,"[3] after which the audience retired, highly pleased.

---

2. Bamford has crossed out a typographical error, "Jem-".
3. Bamford has crossed out the s after Bobbin. See *Homely Rhymes*, 80.

Realized about 1-10-0 by this exercise.

**Saturday 16th.** Wrote to Sir James Kay Shuttleworth as follows.

**Letter**, *Bamford to Sir James Kay-Shuttleworth, 16 July 1859.*

> Dear Sir,
> Mr John Heywood, of Manchester has delivered to me your card, and has also communicated your kind message. You are, as I understand, at present in London; and it may be some days, at least, before you return to Lancashire.
>     When you do return, I shall hope to see you; and my address, as above, will enable you to make known your wishes, as to the time and place, when and where, I may offer my respects. Until then I remain,
> Dear Sir, your obliged Humble serv<sup>t</sup>
> Samuel Bamford

I beg to inclose a couple of my circulars.

**Sunday 18th.** Went to Hollinwood, much against my inclination, which was to remain, the weather being very hot, however walked to Newton Heath, where I waited for the Omnibus, and rode to the bottom of Hollinwood, walking up to Dronsfields house. Dronsfield had pressingly invited me and Mima to go over and attend the christening of his young son, who was to be named "Bamford," after me. Well, Dronsfield was not washed when I got there and I did not perceive any signs of a christening: he soon however got himself shirted and dressed, and then we went and sat upstairs. Another friend came in, a woman, his wife's sister, who held the child, a fine little lad, on her knee. I found however, from expressions that dropped, that the christening had been given up for that day. The Godfather from Manchester could not come: Dronsfield said it could still be done, if I would join him as Godfather, but I said I had a strong objection to anything of the kind. I did not believe in all that was required, and I could not think of undertaking things which I could not, in conscience perform. Neither Dronsfield nor his wife seemed very desirous to have the ceremony performed that day: I said, if the child was mine, he should not be christened at all, I would take him to the registrar, and have his name there regularly entered, and that would do as well as christening. Dronsfield seemed doubtful whether the register would hold good in case of a claim to property. I said it would be just as good as a Church register, and so the matter dropped, and nothing further was said about the christening. Dronsfield, myself, his friend who had come in, his sister in law, his wife, and several of the children had a very good tea upstairs. After that we[,] Dronsfield, friend, and self, took a walk round by Chamber Hall, down the high road. Called at his mothers house, a beer house, where we had a quart of ale, from thence to Dronsfields again, then to Pollitts at the Filho where D and myself had each a glass of toddy. Thence D and friend accompanied me on the road past Sam<sup>l</sup> Collins at Hale Moss, past Nuthurst, and into Mosston where we parted and I came home in good time. Thus ended my christening adventure. I rather think Dronsfield was inclined to put off until next Sunday, on which will be "the Wakes" and he can keep both Wakes and christening on one day. Whether or not the child will bear my name, is I think, doubtful; nor do I greatly desire that it should, but rather one, more fortunate.

**18th Monday.** The annexed came to hand by Potter. Sent an apology on acc[oun]t of having to be at Audenshaw.

*Printed circular, from R.S. Gowenlock, Oldham, 15 July 1859.*

Sir,
An Adjourned Meeting of the Committee for arranging for TWO READINGS, by Mr Samuel Bamford, will be held at the Angel Inn, on Tuesday next, the 19th instant, at Eight o'clock in the Evening; and you are respectfully requested to attend, to aid in the promotion of the object, by your influence and advice.
    Mr Bamford will be present at the Meeting, to answer questions relating to points upon which information or explanation may be required, and to state the nature of the Readings he will be prepared to give.
                    I am, Sir,
                            Yours obediently
                                    R. SCOTT GOWENLOCK
                                            Secretary.

My wife's best shift, we find, had been stolen out of the drawer. The doors of our house, our landlords, and our next neighbour all open with one key. We cannot however suspect either of these persons: there are two others who seem queerish, but God forgive us if we suspect wrongfully. We must have a fresh key.

**Tuesday 19th.** At Audenshaw, where I read a lecture on Parliamentary reform, which I think was too radical for the promoters of the meeting who I found had drawn up a resolution approving of a ten pound qualification for counties and a five pound one for boroughs. I however, as bound in conscience, advocated manhood suffrage, and adduced arguments, strong ones, as I thought in its favour. All that I said appeared to be approved of, one individual excepted, the resolution of the committee was carried, and I was thanked for the lecture I had given.
    Mr James Crosby of Shepley Hall, and his lady, entertained me well. In the morning I went through his linen manufac[tur]y and then came by rail to Man^r.
    Two pounds for my lecture.

**Thursday 21st.** The annexed from Gowenlock.

*Letter, R.S. Gowenlock to Bamford, 20 June 1859.*

Dear Mr Bamford,
Your communication was sent to the Committee last night and was perfectly satisfactory to all present. I would have communicated with you previous to

getting the circulars printed had I had time to do so, but I was getting Mrs G. and two of the young G's off to Dublin and it broke considerably into my time.

The meeting passed a resolution that you are requested to give two readings in our Town Hall – One on the 3rd and the other on the 10th of Aug. next. If you will do us the favour of acceding to our request and if the times will suit you, will you please to draw up a programme of the reading, suitable for including in the papers as an advert, and for distribution in the form of small bills. I should like to have this in the papers on Saturday. Could you make it convenient to run up, as it could perhaps be done more readily in that way than by writing. The details of the arrangements I will give you when I see you. I trust you had a good attendance at your lecture at Audenshaw.

In great haste<br>Yours most truly<br>RS Gowenlock

S Bamford Esq.

Went to Oldham and arranged with him about printing & advertisement, but he persists in adding "Esq", to my name, which I don't like at all.

21. Thursday. The annexed from my late sisters grandchildren.

*Envelope containing a smaller envelope, with the name Elizabeth Frances Nelson on the flap, containing the cards of the Revd and Mrs James Milne Hamilton, Lightbounds, Halliwell.*

Miss Taylor sends us a boiling of nice fresh got garden peas.

What does this mean? I am at a loss to divine: something surely is moving unseen. Has she also read one of my circulars about "that class of friends who always ignore the unfortunate." She is however, a good lady, always was; and I desired the servant [to return,] and I expressed from my heart, my very best thanks.

**Friday 22nd.** Went to Middleton and paid Mills the sovereign I had borrowed from him: So now have 13/- left of the two pounds received at Audenshaw.

**Saturday 23rd.** Left my poems with John Heywood of Manchester, asking him £25 for copyright of 1000 cop[ie]s.

Sir James P. Kay Shuttleworth it seems, went to his shop, asking if Waugh and I were not preparing a history of Rochdale. Of course Heywood could not say anything about it, and Sir James handed his card expressing a wish to see me when next he visited Lancashire, which would be very shortly.

4/6 left of the 13/- after giving Mima 5/.

**Sunday 24th.** Page from the market office at Manchester, who has been a most kind and zealous friend to Rogerson, called and left a letter with me, to get if possible, an allowance of money from Rogersons late landlord, one Lamb, a Councillor of the Corporation.

Page told me of some scurvy trick played by Abel Heywood towards Page, by none of which however, was I surprised for I knew the fellow.

Wrote the two annexed notes, and shall forward them tomorrow.[4]

**Copy letter**, *Bamford to T. Coulborn Esq., Rhodes, Middleton, 23 July 1859.*

Sir,

Although considerable time has elapsed since the appearance of your kind notice of my case in the Middleton Albion,[5] I cannot forego the pleasure of expressing my thankful appreciation of your sentiments; and of your generous proposal to establish a fund for my benefit. The county however does not respond to your care; nor did I expect it would. If the thing is done at all, it should be undertaken by some powerful friend – if I had such – moving the government on behalf of the people: the latter, I consider – the nation – is justly my debtor; and the government, as the Nation's representative, ought to make amends for the injuries sustained. I am, Sir, with grateful respect,

your obliged servant,<br>Samuel Bamford

**Copy letter**, *Bamford to James Crosby Esq., 22 July 1859.*

Dear Sir,

I left my alpaca coat hanging in the lobby at Shepley Hall, and if you will have the goodness to bring it, or have it conveyed to your place of business in Manchester, I will, with many thanks, call for it.

With a grateful reminiscence of your kind hospitality, and most respectful compliments to Mrs and Miss Crosby, I am, Dear Sir,

Your obliged servant,<br>Samuel Bamford

Sent off also at the same time the programme of my readings at Oldham.

**Monday 25th.** Took train at Manchester and went to Werneth, whence I walked to Royton to the mill of Mr John Buckley, a son of my old friend George Buckley of Mill Bottom at Waterhead, near Oldham. Mr B had ordered a Life of a Radical, when once I met him at Middleton, and as I was getting rather short of that useful article money, I thought I would try and "raise the wind" somewhat by a speculation with the son of my old friend. He was not at the Mill, but one of his sons said he would be sure to be at home to dinner, which would be at one o'clock: it was then half past 12. So I left the book with the son saying I would wait his fathers coming at the public house close by. I went to the house, glad of a place to rest in, got a glass of ale, and almost fell asleep,

---

4. In fact, the two letters are dated one and two days prior to this date.
5. See 2 July.

when a youth came for me, his father had come to dinner, and I must go to the house: went and dined with the family. Mr B. Mrs B. five sons and two daughters, another son being absent. A very nice orderly family three of the sons being steady, attentive young lads, and the remainder of the offspring children. I had a glass of punch with Mr Buckley after dinner, and he paid me not only for the Radical, but also for a copy of Early Days, so I drew seven shillings, gave Mr B two copies each of Cartwrights and Hunts portraits, and walked to Middleton whence took the omnibus, and came home tired.

**Tuesday 26th.** I had 6/6 left, so the question was whether I should leave the rent unpaid, and go to Colne with the money, trusting to make more of it there, or remain, pay the rent, as usual and try my fortune once more at Manchester? Resolved on the latter paid Hall, and had four shillings left. Went to Manches^r & showed a copy, the only one left, of my Walks in South Lancashire to John Heywood, who said he would look it over, and give an answer next week. Met with one Cartledge, who gave me the useful information that Elijah Ridings associates with Willis,[6] Willis the scoundrel, who calumniated me to Tait of Edinburgh,[7] and Howitt, of London.[8] Knowing he thus associates Ridings can never be with me, on any but the most distant terms of acquaintanceship. I know the fellow, and shall keep him at arms length accordingly.

This morning the annexed letter came to hand.

*Letter*, *T. Clowes, Chorlton upon Medlock, to Bamford, 25 July 1859.*

My Dear Sir,
I was at a meeting last week at which I introduced your willingness to give us a reading from your own prose works. The thing met with general approbation, indeed it has done before, but we have had so many things to occupy attention here that there has been no fitting opportunity, but I am authorised to state that if it meets your approval we will be glad to hear you in Chorlton Town Hall as soon as the weather is a little cooler so that it will be bearable in the room. The plan is this, that three of us shall form a committee, and select from your own works such passages as they think proper, and report [to] you thereon for your approval, and we think and do not for a moment doubt, that we can get a pretty good audience one way or the other, and are willing to guarantee you at least three pounds and all, if any over and above that am[oun]t and the exp[ense]s. I hope you will not think I have neglected you. I can assure you that I have ever since I saw you felt a strong desire to promote your interest in this matter,
I am most respectfully
Tho^s Clowes

6. William Willis (*c.* 1808–61), Manchester bookseller, and one-time Chartist, who converted to Catholicism and became fiercely anti-democratic; MCL.
7. William Tait (1793–1864), publisher, of Edinburgh; *DNB*.
8. William Howitt (1792–1879), writer, journalist, editor of *Howitt's Journal*. A man of liberal and antiquarian leanings, he later produced a fictional account of Bamford; see entry for 5 November 1861; *DNB*.

Met Brierley in Rochdale Road, as I returned. He was only just come back from Oldham, where he had been last night, with Gowenlock, Potter, and Amb[rose] Hurst. Dronsfield he said, had not christened his son, nor did he intend doing so, he would have him registered instead, a course of which I approve. Gowenlock he said, was selling tickets for my Readings, so calling at Brierleys residence, I got the Oldham Advertiser, and find in it the annexed advertisement.

*Advertisement*, *from the* Oldham Advertiser, *23 July 1859, for Bamford's readings in the Town Hall, Oldham on the evenings of the 3rd and 10th August 1859, commencing at eight o'clock. Ticket prices from 2s. 6d. (platform) to 6d. (back) each.*

Came home tired enough, having walked all the way in the scorching sun.

**Tuesday 26th.** The annexed notice will show the difference which is made betwixt foreign political sufferers and one of our own nation, myself for instance.

*Cutting*, *from the* Manchester Examiner and Times, *26 July 1859, announcing publication of a report of the Committee of the Neapolitans Exiles Fund, which obtained subscriptions of £10,760, divided between 64 exiles, in handouts typically of several hundred pounds each. At the top of the cutting Bamford has written "Note this."*

**Wednesday 27th.** The annexed from the Ashton and Stayley Bridge Reporter of 23rd July, 1859. Received a programme of my proposed Readings and a letter from Gowenlock, so went to Oldham, and found G. out on business: Saw Potter, corrected the proof of programme and returned to Newton Heath, by 6.15 train. G. Nelson at the N.H. station.

*Report*, *from the* Ashton and Stalybridge Reporter, *23 July 1859, of Bamford's lecture on Parliamentary Reform to the Audenshaw branch of the Lancashire Reformers Union at the Methodist New Connexion Schoolroom, Hooley Hill.*

---

... Mr. Bamford on rising, was received with loud cheers. He defined parliamentary reform to mean simply an amendment, and not a reconstruction, of the constitution; and that view of the matter was held by Major Cartwright, William Cobbett, Henry Hunt, and other political celebrities of some 30 or 40 years back. They were in favour of annual parliaments, of manhood suffrage, and held that if a man were balloted for the militia he was entitled to a vote, on the ground that he paid in military servitude what others paid in taxes. Vote by ballot was not in the first instance on their programme, but was afterwards introduced. At Peterloo, they advocated the adoption of annual parliaments, no corns laws, enfranchisement of such large towns as Manchester, Birmingham and Leeds, and the abolition of the rotten boroughs, which had since in a great measure been adopted to the benefit of the country. The Chartists had added to this programme the abolition of property qualification for members of parliament, equal electoral districts, and payment of members. Mr. Bamford then entered into the merits and demerits of the five points of the charter; the sixth; that of property qualification, having been conceded. He considered that the people of Oldham had obtained an advantage almost equal in importance to annual parliaments, by having pledged their members to give an annual account of their stewardship, a system which might be carried out in other constituencies. As to universal or manhood suffrage, he thought that point disposed of when the property qualification was relinquished. It presented too great an anomaly to last. Thus at present a man, however humble, might become a member of the legislature, and at the same time not be able to exercise the franchise himself; or in other words, the law held him to be eligible to become a legislator, but not sufficiently qualified to give a vote. With respect to vote by ballot, he was strongly in favour of it, hoping committees and other organisations would be formed in every district so as to keep that important and most desirable measure before the public. Electoral districts should not be lost sight of, though he did not consider them as of so much importance as the ballot. *Rather than have an increased number of legislators, he would give additional votes to the electors according to the population of the borough.[9] As to payment of members, like that of annual parliaments, the electors had it in their own hands to decide, and he strongly condemned the apathy of the electors, as shown in their not demanding pledges from their representatives on these and other points he had mooted. He advocated the formation of a *witenagemot*, or house of delegates, where business on behalf of the working classes could be transacted, and their interests better attended to than at present; compared the present position of the English people with that of the last generation; and made an earnest appeal to the well-wishers of their country, to advocate a wide and sound measure of parliamentary reform, so that by their success England might still continue in that onward course of freedom which was her proudest boast and most glorious inheritance. – (Cheers.)

The usual vote of thanks were accorded, when the meeting separated.

---

* Error replied to.[10]

**Thursday 28th.** Entirely fast for money, only 4[d] left when I ret[urne][d] from Oldham, and this morning tis all gone. So Mima had no other resource – that I knew of – save taking my best coat to Uncles at Man[r]. She took it and getting 10/- bought a few necessaries and hastened back. How, or by what means I shall get my coat out for next Wednesdays reading, is a mystery to me.

Wrote a correction, to Ashton Reporter.

28 July Th. Wrote /somewhat\ as follows, and inclosed two of my circulars in each to the following M.P.s.

Sir

I learn from one of the Manchester newspapers of this week, that a donation of £5000 is awarded to Mr Barber the solicitor who was wrongfully convicted and transported.

I beg to say that I also am a sufferer from repeated outrages on my personal freedom, from unjust conviction by an ignorant and prejudiced jury, and from

---

9. Underlining by Bamford.
10. Manuscript note by Bamford.

wrongful condemnation, and imprisonment in consequence of that conviction. And I presume I have as rightful a claim to compensation in proportion to the injuries I suffered, as Mr Barber has.

The accompanying Circular contains a brief sketch only of my case, it is however respectfully tendered, in the hope that any claim for <u>just</u> compensation which I may submit to Parliament will have the powerful aid of your honourable support.

I am Sir,

Your Obedient Serv[an]ᵗ,

Samuel Bamford.

These notes and circulars have been sent to Thos. Bazley Esq. M.P., J.A. Turner Esq. M.P., to R.M. Milnes, Esq. M.P.,[11] and W.J. Fox Esq. M.P.[12]

**Friday 29th.** A letter from Sir James P. Kay Shuttleworth arrives inviting me to see him at Gauthorpe at 1/2 past 5 on Saturday afternoon, and remain till Monday at least. A fine mess, invited to pay a Sunday visit at a gentlemans Hall, and the only coat I have, which is fit for a Sunday just "put up the spout."[13] What is to be done now? Oh I must send an excuse. I cant go, thats decided. Mima says I <u>must</u> go; but how, is the question: she finds the keys, opens a drawer and pulls out a satin dress; that must be pledged to redeem my coat, and I must go. I did not know she has such a dress, in her <u>own</u> <u>keeping</u>; and wondered she did not pledge that at first instead of fastening my coat. Its no use, she says, talking <u>now</u>, the dress must go, and the coat be brought back. So she takes the dress, and comes back without the coat, having forgotten to take the <u>ticket</u> for the latter. She has brought a mutton chop with her, and a few peas, and we sit down to a late dinner. At four o'clock she sets off again to catch the 'Bus, but is too late, so walks to Manchester, a second time to-day, redeems the coat, and is again out of time for the coach, wearily therefore she comes home trailing at near seven o'clock, and we finish the day by rest and a refreshing cup of tea with

"Herbs and other county mosses".

***Letter****, James Kay-Shuttleworth, Gawthorpe, to Bamford, 28 July 1859.*

Dear Mr Bamford,
I so thoroughly <u>"knocked myself up."</u> as we say, by the work which I had before, at, and after the East Lancashire Examination that I never had neither strength nor courage to write to fix a day for your kindly promised visit.

Can you favour me with your company about 5 1/2 p m on Saturday afternoon next, and remain with me at least till Monday.

---

11. Richard Monckton Milnes (1809–85), London literary figure, active in getting a civil list pension for Tennyson; *DNB*.
12. William J. Fox (1786–1864), radical Unitarian, MP for Oldham, preacher and man of letters; *DNB*.
13. That is, pawned.

One line to say you are coming will suffice.

There is a Train by the East Lancashire Railway which arrives at Rose Grove Station at 5.17 p m

And another by the Lancashire and Yorkshire Line via Todmorden which arrives at Burnley at 5ʰ-6ᵐ and I believe goes on to Rose Grove.

We are about one mile and a half from Rose Grove Station.

I have several times read your Life of a Radical, and have just read a second time your "early days", & have much to say to you.

> Yours truly,
> J.P. Kay Shuttleworth

I have written to Sir James, as see other leaf.

**Copy letter**, *Bamford to James Kay-Shuttleworth, 29 July 1859.*

Dear Sir James,

Although not so well prepared as I could wish, for a Sunday-visit, at a gentlemans Hall, as you invite so kindly, and, 'have much to say,' I will come. Remaining,

> Dear Sir James,
> Your obliged Servᵗ
> Samuel Bamford.

My hat certainly is a little crushed on one side, and my trousers rather worn at bottom: my coat is good, my waistcoat barely decent, but Sir James has had poor Lancashire men, as his guest before now, /Old Buckston for instance,\ and he will I trust, excuse my barely passable appearance, Mima will sponge and trim up, as well as can.

**Saturday 30th.** A letter and parcel from Potter at Oldham puts me in good spirits for my trip to Burnley: see other leaf.

**Letter**, *Charles Potter, Lord Street, Oldham, to Bamford, 29 July 1859.*

*Mr Bamford.*

Dear Sir,

Herewith I send you a large Bill and Programme and am happy to inform you that everything is going on very well, and the tickets are leaving our hands very nicely, and we look forward to having a /good\ muster on Wednesday next. You will see that the <u>Mayor</u> and <u>John Platt</u> are going to preside, and no doubt will have a great deal of influence on <u>Oldham Exchequers</u>.

I must also inform you that I have placed your <u>portrait</u> in a prominent window in High Street for exhibition.

> Give my kind love to Mrs Bamford and
> Believe me
> Most Truly Yours
> Charles Potter.

A large green posting bill accompanies.

Arrived at Gauthorpe about 6 p.m., very cordially received by Sir James, who told me he wanted the information he had written about, in order to show, (in a publication, as I understood) the influence of education on the conduct of working men, as exhibited in their strikes, riots and other popular demonstrations. Stopped at Gauthorpe until Monday, when Sir James came with me to the gate at the village, on my way to the station at Rose Grove. Sir James giving me a sovereign for what he called "a retainer," that is, for more information. I rather think he is about writing some paper on strikes, turn outs, etc, for the next meeting of the British Association: at any rate if accounts of these disturbances by work men are to appear, it will be best for them that <u>truth</u> only should be made known.

Got the adjoining from W.J. Fox M.P. a piece of very lame logic.

**Letter**, *W.J. Fox Esq. MP to Bamford, 1 August 1859.*

My Dear Sir,
Your claim upon English Reformers is, I think, an undeniable one – but it differs from Mr Barber's case in this: he was erroneously convicted and the error acknowledged by Authority – In your case it was intended to convict you; you were condemned, not for crimes but for your merits – For Public compensation you have, I take it no chance until we have a Reformed Parliament, wh[ich] Heaven send soon.
                              Yours sincerely
                              W.J. Fox.

**Tuesday August 2nd.** Letter to Mr E. Hirst.

**Copy letter**, *Bamford to E. Hirst, Colne, 2 August 1859.*

Dear Friend Hirst,
In reply to your note which I received this day, I have to say that I really cannot just now inform you to within a few days, when I shall be able to pay you a visit. Tomorrow, and also on the 10th, I have to read and recite at the Town Hall, Oldham; as soon as those engagements are over, I shall, I expect, be at liberty for a week or two, and shortly after, of which I will give you notice, you may expect to see me in some cozy nook at our friends Mrs Earnshaws, for, as I have at present planned, I think I had best call in there, in the first instance, sit and rest me a short time and then request your company; of course we can hob nob a little, and afterwards for a couple of days, or so, I shall be at your service. So I have planned, at present & with kindest respects [of] self and Mrs B I remain truly yours,
                              Samuel Bamford

**Letter**, *David Morris, Manchester, to Bamford, 3 August 1859.*

Dear Sir,

Please attend a Council meeting of the Inst. Assn. next Saturday @ 5.30 p.m. in the Mechanics' Institution, David Street, and oblige.

> Dear Sir
> Yours truly
> David Morris.

**Letter**, *J.A. Turner*,[14] *London, to Bamford, 2 August 1859.*

Dear Sir,

I duly received your Letter of the 28th July and in reply I quite agree with you that you had great reason to complain of your treatment received in 1817 and 1819. I am old enough to remember that period well – I believe that men now speak out with impunity sentiments which caused you to be arrested and imprisoned – those were the days of arbitrary powers.

Still I apprehend that your case is so far different from Mr Barbers – that he has been pronounced <u>innocent</u> of the crime for which he suffered the utmost indignities of a penal settlement abroad – You it would be said, were condemned to imprisonment and underwent the punishment to which you were condemned by Law – <u>I</u> may say and <u>do</u> say that you suffered ignominy and chains very undeservedly but my opinions on this subject would not I fear prevail to such an extent as to induce the House of Commons to sanction a vote in your favour – the question would naturally be asked to what length must the principle be extended of making pecuniary compensation to persons who have been harshly and unjustly treated in times past? – and who is now to decide upon the propriety of verdicts and sentences given 40 years ago. –?

> With much respect and esteem,
> I remain
> Dear Sir,
> Yours faithfully,
> J. Aspinall Turner.

**Wednesday 3rd.** My 1st reading at Oldham Town Hall. Very well attended. G. Barlow Esqʳ., the mayor, in chair. Stopped at Gowenlock's all night, and in the morning, before I came away he gave me two sovs. on acc[oun]t, as he said, until the account of the tickets was got in.

The following are notices in the Oldham papers.

**Report**, *from the* Oldham Telegraph, *6 August 1859, of Bamford's reading in the Town Hall, Oldham. The audience was relatively small; the readings were "delivered in a praiseworthy style, and with a vigour and freshness somewhat surprising for a man of the advanced age of Mr. Bamford".*

---

14. J. Aspinall Turner (1797–1867), Manchester millowner and botanist, Whig MP for Manchester, 1857–65, having (with John Potter) ousted Thomas Milner Gibson and John Bright; MCL.

**Report**, *from the* Oldham Chronicle, *6 August 1859, of the same.*

**Report**, *from the* Oldham Advertiser, *6 August 1859, of the same, including details of Bamford's account of his employment at Somerset House, and his emphasis that he was not in receipt of any government salary or pension. "The pieces in the programme were read with great clearness, discrimination, and judgement, and frequently elicited bursts of applause."*

**Letter**, *James Kay-Shuttleworth, Gawthorpe, to Bamford, 3 August 1859.*

Dear Mr Bamford,
I am much obliged by your letter containing the results of your inquiries in Rochdale.

They revive my own recollections of various incidents – the strike against W Rostron – and W Kelsall – the loss of life at the Lockup – Kershaw's trial and transportation etc.[15]

I am however, sure that about 1820 – either a year or two before, or a year or two after – there were some other very strange rules of the Weavers' Trades' Union in Rochdale restricting labour in some form.

You would therefore much oblige me if without mentioning my name, you could continue your inquiries on this point, and all collateral questions, including among others

Any rules of any Trades Union at that time

The character of Kershaw and any anecdotes about him

The incidents of any attempts to "gather shuttles"

I remember well the incidents of the loss of life at the Lockup.

Bye and bye, I hope we may meet again.

Meanwhile oblige me by renewing and pursuing your inquiries on these & collateral subjects at Rochdale, and anywhere in the neighbourhood

Yours sincerely
J.P. Kay Shuttleworth

**Letter**, *Thomas Bazley Esq., MP, London, to Bamford, 5 August 1859.*

Dear Sir,
I am favoured with your letter requesting one to assist in seeking some form of compensation for the political wrongs which have been inflicted upon you. It would, I assure you, afford one sincere pleasure to be of service to you, but from all I can learn I seriously fear that your claim will not be listened to by either the Government or the Legislature, If however you wish to offer a petition I will most cheerfully present it next session.

M⁰ faithfully Yrs,
Thoˢ Bazley.

---

15. For a detailed account of the events of 1826 see William Turner, *Riot! The Story of the East Lancashire Loom Breakers in 1826* (1992).

The three letters from the great gentlemen M.P.s to whom I wrote on the subject of compensation (national) are above, and I leave them to the judgment of posterity, as replies to my circular (on the other side, and my note of the 28th July, aforesaid).

The following from Gowenlock. How should I spend nine hours in Oldham from one to eight – except at the public house? And that I neither can, nor will do; such associations tell to disadvantage.

**Letter**, *R.S. Gowenlock, Oldham, to Bamford, 9 August 1859.*

Dear Mr Bamford,
I shall expect you up at my house tomorrow in time for a bit of dinner. I have sent out a few circulars requesting one or two to be at the Kings Arms an hour or so previous to the commencement of the Readings, and I should like you to be present. You will give your dear wife to understand that you will stay all night again, as it is too far for you to think of returning after the fatigue of Reading. Present to her my kindest regards and assure her we will do our best to take care of you.
    I trust that we shall have better weather than we had last week.
                    Yours truly
                        R. Scott Gowenlock

**Bamford's circular**, *with a few minor amendments (see Appendix 1).*

**Letter**, *T. Clowes to Bamford, 10 August 1859.*

Dear Sir,
I am sorry that you have been so unfortunate in not finding me at Home, I met a few friends last night and on an early day a few of us shall meet to make some selections from your Books, and as soon as that is done I will write you to come over and meet us, when we will try to make definite arrangements as regards your readings.
            With kindest regards of self and friends,
                I am Most Resp[ectfully]
                        Yours
                            T. Clowes.

**Wednesday 10th.** My second reading. Got to the Kings Arms at 1/2 past 6 instead of at noon. Gowenlock, Potter and Yates not there, they came soon after, seemingly more cool than usual. Reading very well attended. John Platt Esq. in chair. Audience seemingly well pleased, and Yates gave out that a third reading would take place on Wednesday next. Stopped at Gowenlocks again, and again in the morning he gives me two sovs on account. I think this is not a very clear way of doing business, they ought, at any rate to have rendered an acc[oun]t of the receipts of the 1st reading.

**Letter**, *James Kay-Shuttleworth, The Victoria Hotel, New Brighton, Birkenhead, to Bamford, 10 August 1859.*

Dear Mr Bamford.

I came hither with my family on Monday to <u>rest</u> and to prepare for my work as Foreman of the Grand Jury at the Liverpool Assizes tomorrow.

I shall probably remain here until the 18th instant.

Your notes confirm my own impressions and reminiscences. I think that by a little labour you might collate a very interesting account of the

<u>Lancashire</u>

<u>Machine Breaking and Shuttle</u>

<u>Gathering</u>

<u>and</u>

<u>Strikes etc.</u>

Anything that I can do to promote your success in the preparation of such acc[oun]t, I would gladly attempt.

From you, such work must have a "<u>backbone</u>" of personal expression, or observation – much local color in the description of character, scenery, manners and incidents. In this woof, might be woven the weft of whatever other facts you could collect, a tissue with an alternative pattern <u>full of instruction and caution both to masters</u> and workmen might result.

I have an immediate object, and a more remote one in asking you to send me the documents, which in two packets have arrived by this morning's post & to make further inquiries.

Both objects require that I should <u>not be known</u> to be making these inquiries.

If I find that I can make any permanent use of your memoranda I will be careful to acknowledge the source whence I derive them.

Their use hitherto is to show me that my own memory has not deceived me as to the time, place, and other chief features of those machine breaking troubles.

You will much oblige me by continuing your enquiries and by coming to me at Gauthorpe again about the end of this month

Yours truly,

J.P. Kay Shuttleworth

Readings 10th Aug. Comments by Old<sup>m</sup> papers.

**Report**, *from the* Oldham Advertiser, *13 August 1859, giving a brief account of Bamford's second Oldham reading.*

**Report**, *from the* Oldham Standard, *13 August 1859, of the same.*

---

... At eight o'clock, the time announced for the commencement, there were very few present, but the hall became gradually more crowded, and eventually there was a good attendance... . The selections for the evening, which were mostly delivered with a pathos which showed that Mr Bamford sympathised deeply with the morals of the piece and the principles he was endeavouring to inculcate[,] were as follows, "Letter to an Editor," "Robert, the Waiter," "Locksley Hall," (Tennyson)

"Second Arrest," "Pass of Death," "View from the Tandle Hills," "The two Judgements," "Hymn to Hope," "The Woman of Musbury," "Oldham Local." ... The chairman [John Platt] – in responding to the vote of thanks ... said he thought his respected friend would better consult the feeling of his own hearers if on the occasion of another reading he confined himself more exclusively to a narration of his own experiences as exemplified in his own works.

---

*Report*, *from the* Oldham Chronicle, *13 August 1859, of the same, noting also: "'A Day Out', a very racy, humorous piece in the Lancashire dialect ... was by far the most effectually given of any of the pieces read in the course of the evening."*

**Sunday 14th.** Brierley and Potter, both called this forenoon. Potter went with Brierley to dinner.

Mills from Middleton called to tea. He had been to Droylsden, and seemed much fatigued.

Potter, I afterwards learned went with Brierley to Waughs residence in Strangeways, his business being to engage Waugh to attend my third reading, as an assistant, – this too, without consulting me. – Waugh was not at home; he was, as his housekeeper said, at Blackpool. With this news Potter returns to Oldham after calling at my house on his return, but still, never mentioning to me that his visit to Waughs was with a view to gain his attendance at Oldham on Wednesday. Well, but from Oldham a letter is dispatched to Waugh at Blackpool, requesting his attendance, and offering to defray his expenses, to Oldham and back to Blackpool, with (it could be scarcely be less) a handsome present besides; to this letter, Waugh made not any reply, and so Brierley and myself had to get through the task of amusing our friends of the working class. I did not – when I got to know of it – altogether like these concealed operations of my Oldham Committee. Had Waugh attended I should not have objected to act along with him, but I certainly felt a relief of mind, when I heard he was not coming. Even Brierleys attendance interfered with my plans, which aught not to have been disturbed at all, whilst his reading, the personal novelty excepted, lent not any additional attraction to the performance: He does not, at any time read well, and his pieces in the Lancashire Dialect would have been done better by myself. All however passed off very well, and at the conclusion Mr Yates made a long, and highly complimentary address in approval of my performances, and of my general character. I was really afraid Brierley would feel himself slighted, and I once or twice prompted Yates by mentioning Brierleys name, but all to no avail. Brierley, I am now of opinion did feel hurt, by something which occurred: he stopped at his fathers all night at Hollinwood, refusing either to come home in a cab, or to remain at Oldham all night. On Thursday forenoon he called at my house, on his way to his work at Manchester: On Friday Potter and myself called at his house, on our way to town, informing his wife of Mr Councillor Taylor having given an order for five pounds worth of the second edition of his "Day Out," this good news his wife would doubtless tell him of, but he has not, as yet (Monday afternoon) called to speak with me about it, as I expected he would.

I received for the three readings at Oldham £16.18.9: and allowing Potter for the trouble he had been at £2. 10.0 the net money was £14.8.9.

**Tuesday 16th.** Mr Thomas Coulborn, of Scarr, Petty, and Coulborn in the Square at Manchester called to see us: He had been reading my book in Wales, to his family, the week before: this day, he remarked, was the 40th anniversary of the great meeting, and he wished to see Mima, about whom he had been reading: he saw her, of course, and he put down a sovereign as his subscription towards my "compensation fund".

**Friday 19th.** Mrs Dawson[,] children, and two sisters were here to their tea. Glad to see Miss Hargreaves from London, but a lot at once. Three women and three children are rather too many for us.

Called this afternoon, with Potter at Scarr, Petty and Coulborns in the Square, and ordered new trousers and waistcoat. "One good turn deserves another."

**Saturday 20th.** Bought a new free and easy hat for 6/- never more to purchase a hat of the old chimney-pot sort.

The annexed are the comments of the Oldham press, on my third performance.

*Report, from the* Oldham Chronicle, *20 August 1859, of Bamford's third evening of readings at Oldham Town Hall.*

*Report, from the* Oldham Advertiser, *20 August 1859, of the same. Bamford was joined by Benjamin Brierley, who read extracts from his story "Our Day Out". The report notes that "the present readings were designed especially for the working classes, but we were sorry to observe that many more did not avail themselves of the opportunity, although there was a fair audience".*

*Report, from the* Oldham Standard, *20 August 1859, of the same.*

---

... Mr Bamford, who on rising was rapturously applauded, said the chairman had done him great honour for his past conduct. He was only a handloom weaver, but always honest, had ever experienced great pleasure in doing a good action, and would not do a bad one. In early life he had an engagement in a Manchester warehouse, and as his employer took in "Cobbett's Register," he (Mr. Bamford) used to take every opportunity of reading it. He thought the language so clear, so distinct, and the statements so humble, that it at once caught his attention, and he then became a reader of "Cobbett's Reasoner;" and naturally imbibed his opinions ... He consequently became a parliamentary reformer."

---

*After sketching his early career, Bamford read an account of his visit to a fortune teller, "Limping Billy",*[16] *and recounted how his taste for poetry had been fostered by reading the works of "that youthful genius" Chatterton and "The immortal Burns ... his idol, his poet par excellence", whose works had inspired him to write poetry. "As a specimen of the sublime in his idol poet, he then with great pathos recited the 'Braes of Ballochmoyle'." After further readings, Bamford recounted the tale of*

---

16. See *Early Days*, 203–5.

*his meeting with Joseph Coupe, the notable Lancashire ballad singer, and how Coupe and Joseph Lees had come to write the famous ballad 'Jone o'Grinfilt'.*[17]

My Middleton paper has again missed coming as usual.

**Sunday 21st.** John Coates and a party from Royton came over to see us, and then went to Middleton Wakes.

21 Sunday. The following curious kind of an invitation from Hooley Hill and another from my friend Clowes. I am at a loss to account for their motive in wishing to "select" the passages, unless it be to hear some of my Lancashire Dialect; but I shall be able to guess perhaps, when I have heard what they have to say and to propose.[18]

*Letter*, *G.B. Richardson, Mayfield Print Works, Manchester, to Bamford, 19 August 1859.*

Dear Sir,
Mr Crosby requested me to inform you that some of the Reformers of Audenshaw are intending to have a dinner on Saturday the 27th inst. at 5 oclock in the afternoon and to request you to come over and bring Mrs Bamford with you and spend the weekend with him at Shepley Hall and to come so that you can attend the dinner if it is convenient for you. With the best wishes of the Members,
                    I am yours truly
                        G.B. Richardson, Sec.

*Letter*, *James Kay-Shuttleworth, The Victoria Hotel, New Brighton, Birkenhead, to Bamford, 22 August 1859.*

My Dear Bamford,
I have been very hard-worked for ten days on the L'pool Grand Jury.
    Today I return to Gauthorpe to resume my usual pursuits.
    Your extracts from the Manchester Guardian are valuable to me, and I shall feel obliged if you can make them even more complete for the period of 1826 to which they relate. I should likewise be glad to have any extracts /or abstracts\ (brief) from the Editorial articles showing to what causes the depression of trade was at that time locally attributed. I of course am well aware of the historical view of the time, but I want to gather what were the local & transient feelings of the community.
    Your further researches in Rochdale will oblige me.
    I am much engaged at Gauthorpe this week, but I hope soon to persuade you to visit again.
                    Yours sincerely,
                        JP Kay Shuttleworth

---

17. See *Walks in South Lancashire*, 169–71. Bamford had been too credulous and (hinted Dronsfield later) had come to realise that Lees had been the sole author and Coupe the performer and populariser; Oldham Local Studies Unit, cuttings III, 28–54.
18. This comment must refer to the invitation from Clowes, see 27 August – the letter referred to here does not survive.

21 Sunday An invitation to Audenshaw on Saturday next, and another, for the same day, to Clowes's at Chorlton. I must take the latter, as there will be money at the end of it.

**Monday 22nd.** Wrote to Clowes, saying I shall come.

**Tuesday 23rd.** Went to Peels Park and found they had there a large file of the Man<sup>r</sup> Guardian: this will do very well, for matter for Sir James Kay Shuttleworth.

At the Manchester Free Library, not so good a file of old newspapers; their best being of the "Courier", and the London Times.

Found, when I came home, my trousers and waistcoat arrived from Scarr, Petty and Coulborns, – £2.0.0 net money.

**Thursday 25th.** Paid Scarr, Petty and Coulborn two pounds for trousers and waistcoat, but forgot to take the mans name to whom I paid it, the bill being already "settled same time."

Copying at Peel Park library until 1/2 past three, for Sir J. Kay Shuttleworth.

Met Brierley in Market street, "going to see Peacock," who I suppose will try to get something for a news paragraph out of him; home at 5 o'c[loc]k.

**Friday 26th.** Copying at Peel Park 14 slips. Bought 13 copies Early Day from John Heywood, /£1.2.0.\; bought also pair of scales for weighing letters, and weights: cost both together 3/3. Left my paper carrier at some place in the town, and rather mortified that I should have been so forgetful.

**Saturday 27th.** Found my paper case at John Heywoods. Went at three o'clock to Clowes's Steam Brewery, York St, Chorlton and saw Clowes; a Mr Royle whom I well remembered knowing many years ago; a Mr Priestley, of the Stock Exchange, as I was informed, and several others. They presented to me a programme of a reading which they proposed I should give at the Chorlton Town Hall, on the 20th ult. The terms £3.0.0 /positive\, and as much more as the receipts realized after defraying the expenses. I agreed, and brought with me a list of the passages they selected, from which I should make up a programme for the reading. Other readings to take place if the first was well received.

27. Saturday. An advertisement of which the following is a copy, appeared in all the Oldham papers (Chronicle, Advertiser, Standard, and Telegraph)

*Advertisement from the Oldham newspapers, 27 August 1859.*

---

### BAMFORD'S READINGS.

My series of Readings at the Oldham Town Hall, on the 3rd, the 10th, and the 17th inst; have been, in every sense, more successful than I had expected. To the ladies, therefore, who attended my conversations, to the gentlemen, and working men – to the reporters for, and conductors of the public press – to the two worshipful and

the one most worthy Councillors of the Borough, who presided as Chairmen – and
to the gentlemen who formed the committee of management, especially, my thanks
are due, and are hereby emphatically expressed, and respectfully tendered.
Mosston, Harpurhey,                      SAMUEL BAMFORD.
23rd August, 1859.

---

**Sunday 28th.** Brierley here at night. He is going to print and publish 2000 copies of
his "Day Out," Looney and Co. to print, and Kelly[19] to publish. He agrees with me,
that Waughs newest song "Owd Pinder," is rather smart as a composition, but wanting
in natural, and becoming sentiment, and in just moral. Not many either kind
husbands, or affectionate wives, (and all the rest are rubbish) will be found echoing it.

**Monday 29th.** Went to Manchester, bought Mima a pair of shoes; got wet, and
returned home instead of copying at Peel Park.

**Tuesday 30th.** At Peel Park copying; sent 20 slips to Sir James Kay Shuttleworth.

**Wednesday 31st.** At home; sent excuse to Hirst, and put off going to Colne till next week.
Wrote to Sir James Kay Shuttleworth, as see the annexed.

*Copy letter*, *Bamford to James Kay-Shuttleworth, 30 August 1859.*[20]

Dear Sir James,
Herewith you will receive 20 slips of copy, narrating events amongst the loom
breakers, and accounts of 1826 down to the termination of the shocking affair at
Chatterton. The paper from which I extract, goes on to narrate similar outrages
against machinery at several other places, and then occurs a long narrative of the
burning of Beaver's Mill,[21] of riots, robberies of shops, and breaking of machines at
various factories in Manchester. These narratives I propose copying and forwarding,
as soon as I have done with the country accounts should you deem them available
for your purpose. As I before intimated, after this, I could give a fair account of the
silk turnout at Middleton, and next in order would occur the turn out and shuttle
gathering, more in detail, at Rochdale. I have thought much about your suggestion
for my compilation of an account of the various turn outs, loom breakings &c: and
now I regret more than ever the throwing away, as it were, of seven years of the now
valuable period of my life, at Somerset House: had I been employed as I ought to
have been and as I wished to have been, instead of being set down to ... drudgery
I would have had.... of some ... m.s. on all those matters and things pertaining to
the records of our country; but it was not my desired good fortune to have the

---

19. David Kelly (*c.* 1821–91), Manchester bookseller and publisher. In the 1850s he took the lead in
    publishing several important Manchester writers, including Edwin Waugh and Ben Brierley; see
    *Manchester Guardian*, 5 November 1891.
20. This copy letter has faded considerably, and some sections are illegible; the version of the final three
    sentences presented here is rather conjectural.
21. See Turner, *Riot!*, 60–1.

opportunity for rendering that good service to future generations. A good book, as you suggest, set forth in a fair and candid spirit, with truthful discriptions allied to literary opinions, local feelings and idioms (occasionally) would be a valuable record for the lost ... . of food supply and suffrage. I have seen the times when I should have liked to undertake such a task [are now] over. In all truth, but sorrowfully, I must say, Sir James, that I don't feel as if I had a heart for it: the right opportunity was [not] to be had, and my thoughts and wishes are nearly all absorbed in the desire to establish a kind of chronicle of the events ... notices of the chief incidents of <u>my own course of life</u>. I think such a document is due, both to my own name, and ... humble fame, and to those who live to inhabit the land after we are gone. But situated as I am, I cannot now do that, as it should be fully done: my time is engaged, and my thoughts and ... are so fully absorbed in devising the means for a honest and decently organised subsistence for myself and my dear Mima; that is the first thing to be thought of, and when a little stability has been obtained, it may prove possible to take up the work again. I tell you all this because I think it only right that you should know why your suggestions are not acted upon. In transcribing these extracts for you, the past is before me: in undertaking the other work a greater amount of sustained exertion would be necessary than I could accomplish.

I am, dear Sir James, your obliged servant, Sam¹ Bamford

**Thursday September 1st.** At Peel Park copying. Packet to Sir James again.

**Friday 2nd.** At Peel Park.

**Saturday 3rd.** The annexed from Sir James with cheque for five pounds. Bought 1/2 peck apples 10d.

*Letter*, *James Kay-Shuttleworth, Gawthorpe, to Bamford, 2 September 1859.*

Dear Mr Bamford,
I would have written to you yesterday, but I was suffering from my plague of <u>Neuralgia</u>.
   <u>This</u> continues today – as it has done ever since Saturday evening – but I cannot delay sending you the enclosed cheque for Five Pounds (£5).
   You are not to regard yourself in any other light than as my personal friend, who has done me some service in collecting some materials for me, not for hire, but for goodwill; & who allows me the privilege of contributing slightly to the comfort of one whose genius I have long admired, & whose services to public freedom have been ill-requited but whose independent activity in a virtuous and ... age to not refuse to a friend the satisfaction of a slight tribute of regard and respect.
   Do not give yourself any further trouble, till I have had time to digest your mss. I will try to devote September to literary labour. August has been consumed by public duties.
   If I want you to help more I will not scruple to tell you. We understand one another. We are friends. We will help one another.

As to your literary schemes, we will discuss them all as soon as we can arrange another visit to this old Hall. A cheque on the Manc^r & Salford Bank is enclosed for £5.

God bless you

Yours truly

JP Kay Shuttleworth

**Sunday 4th.** Wrote to Sir James as follows, and sent of packet with accounts off disturbances, down to Macclesfield: also wrote as see annexed.

***Copy letter**, Bamford to James Kay-Shuttleworth, 4 September 1859.*

Dear Sir James,

Your very kind letter, with its inclosure, – a cheque for five pounds – came to hand yesterday, during my absence at Manchester. It would be affectation, unworthy of myself, humble though I am; and a very poor return for your beneficial testimonial of of approval, were I to pretend indifference, in a pecuniary sense, to the substantial demonstration which accompanied your note. I cannot, and I aught not, such are my present circumstances, affect to be insensible to the material service which your kind present will confer: I duly estimate it therefore; and tender all I can in return, – the fervent expression of my grateful sentiments. I will add however, that if there is any service which I can render you, such service you may freely command. I am gratified by being placed on the footing of, one of your humble "friends"; and you will, I trust, never find me unworthy of your good opinion.

I regret to hear that you have been suffering from a painful attack, the consequence, as I should suppose, of cold taken during the late stormy and changeful weather: I hope that by this time, the disorder will have ceased: and that you are again in the enjoyment of active health.

With respect to the continuation of correspondence on strikes, turnouts etc., I can only say that I am entirely at your service: The extracts which I have sent, and /now\ forward by this post, bring the sad history down to the Macclesfield outrages: a rather long article appears next /in the file\ relative to disturbances at Manchester, <u>subsequent</u> to those I have already forwarded: this Manchester article I purpose copying – or some parts of it – during the ensuing week: and that, I believe, will compleat the Guardians narrative of the series of turnouts, loom-breaking, and riots of the unfortunate early part of 1826. If, as I before intimated, an account of the silk turnout at Middleton in 1827–8, would be available, you will command it: the same also as to details of the shuttle gatherings at Rochdale in, or about 1829.

I remain, Dear Sir James,

Your obliged Humble Servant

Samuel Bamford.

**Monday 5th.** At Oldham: did not get home until late.

**Tuesday 6th.** At home, not well.

**Wednesday 7th.** To Colne. Friend Hirst, and his wife make much of me, but I was not in good condition: the weather also, cold, wet, and stormy: spent what would have been a very agreeable evening at "Packer Street", had I been in usual health, but I was not.

**Thursday 8th.** Another cold, showery, and gusty day. I was impatient to get it over though Mr and Mrs Hirst were very kind, and did all they could to amuse me: a very agreeable party again at "Packer Street" (the Hole in the wall) Mrs Earnshaw and her sister seem to live together in great kindness. On going home at night Hirst gave me 10/- which Mr Smith had given him for one of my "Early Days". Too much, and he must have books for it.

**Friday 9th.** Came away by 11.10 train. Hirst made [me] take 2/- which he said, a lady had sent for me, and I should give offence if I did not take it: so took it: she must have a book sent. I cant accept money in this way, except as payment for books. I didn't visit Colne to receive charitable contributions. These things are however well intended, and I must put up with them for sake of the kind motives which prompt them.

Arrived at home, tired, and not very well: had taken cold in consequence of my own carelessness: Bowels disordered.

9th Friday. and Saturday and Sunday at home. Jane Grimshaw and children came in afternoon, and then came Mr Varley a reporter for Oldham Standard, and a friend. Varley wanted my autograph put in his sisters book: A silly habit. I must give him the lines he desires beginning

Day hath departed, and here cometh night.

The annexed foolish advertisement in my account appears in Saturday Examr & Times.[22]

**Advertisement** *from the* Manchester Examiner and Times, *10 September 1859, for Bamford's forthcoming reading at Chorlton-upon-Medlock Town Hall.*

**Sunday 11th.** Brierley came during the forenoon: he had been conversing with Waugh, who said now was the time for my applying, or getting friends to apply to govt. for a "reward for past services," he thought my term "compensation for injuries received," was an injudicious one, and that my idea of applying to Parliament was futile. Hugh Mason, the Mayor of Ashton was the man to get it done at once, by engaging Milner Gibson to take it up. I said it was not for me to originate such a business, or indeed, to interfere in it: friends would be at liberty to see their own course, but I had not any great expectations from <u>friends</u>, from political friends at any rate; they (the reform party) had disgraced themselves by not having it done long ago. I was a poor man, but a very proud man: honestly, manfully proud, I trusted: and I would see the best of them in the furthest nook of hell sooner than go <u>begging</u> <u>them</u> to do it for me: if

---

22. Written in landscape down the margin.

done at all by them, it must be without my intervention. The only way in which I could act would be by petitioning the House of Commons /to\ grant me such "compensation for past injuries", as in its wisdom it might deem meet. This I could with propriety do on my own proper person and individual character, but I could not go and ask one of the great gentlemen, or any of the great parties, to take my cause in hand, and do for me, that which they ought to do without being asked, and ought to have done long ago.

**Monday 12th.** Went to Peel Park, and wrote out the remainder of the Guardians acc[oun]t of the disturbances at Manchester in May 1826; this for Sir James Kay Shuttleworth. This will probably finish my copyings at Peel Park, as the Librarian and curator have both kindly undertaken to apply, on my behalf, to have the files I may want, home with me. That would be a great obligation conferred. Bowels not well.

**Tuesday 13th.** At home; not well yet.

**Thursday 15th.** Went to Peel Park, and saw Mr Batsford the librarian, who, on my asking if anything had been done with respect to my having the files of newspapers with me home, said Mr Plant[23] had forgotten to mention my wish to the committee. I asked had I better make a written application; when he said, he would undertake to let me have a file. So I got the file for the year 1833 – the last year in which I corresponded with the Guardian – as one of it established reporters – and I was coming away with it, when I met Mr Plant in the Lobby, who congratulated me on my acquisition, but did not say anything about his having forgotten to bring my application before the Committee, neither did I. We talked about the blow up on the great Eastern,[24] and on the bad China news, and then I parted from him.

**Friday 16th.** Sent the original of the annexed to Sir James Kay Shuttleworth.

***Copy letter***, *Bamford to James Kay-Shuttleworth, 16 September 1859.*

Dear Sir James,
Herewith you will receive the conclusion of the Manchester Guardian's reports of the turnouts, and loom-breakings of operatives during the early part of the year 1826 and whatever further information may be desired by you, I will do my best to furnish as intimated in the letter which accompanied my last parcel which was forwarded on the 2d instant.

I have much pleasure in stating that, in future, I shall have greater convenience in acquiring information on matters of this sort, than I have hitherto had. The committee, or at least the superintendent of the Peel Park Library, at Salford, permit

---

23. John Plant (1820–94), Librarian at Peel Park, Salford, geologist and botanist, active in Manchester Literary Club; *Manchester City News*, 6 January 1894.
24. Isambard Kingdom Brunel's *Great Eastern* was the largest iron ship ever built at its launch in January 1858; already delayed by various technical problems, it was off Hastings, on its maiden voyage from the Thames to Holyhead on 7 September, when an explosion blew the forward funnel away. Brunel died on 11 September.

me to bring home any file of the Guardian I may wish to examine, and take extracts from: and I have now before me, the file for 1833, containing the reports which I furnished to that paper, during that year, which however, was the last year, in which I regularly corresponded with the publication, though during some years afterwards I occasionally transmitted articles of news. And now, if the profits resulting from my readings, only enables me to make things comfortable at home, – and I have reasonable hopes that they will – I shall embrace the opportunity I have long desired for collecting and arranging many useful and interesting, semi-historical records and notices, of transactions in South Lancashire, and on its borders, which I furnished to the Guardian; and shall be the better able to do that, from my own recollections of the events, somewhat connected and revised by the reading of the documents. My wife also having the files at home will be of service, by reading, whilst I write from her dictation; this will be a help, and a convenience I never could have had either at the British Museum, or at any public reading room: I, or rather <u>we</u>, may thus yet – late in life though it be, – rescue from oblivion, and accumulate in an available form, a good thick file of matter which, in somebody days may be wanted; and can never be so well prepared, as by one who was contemporary with the events, and on some occasions took part in them, or was an eye witness. This employment, easy and suitable enough for an old man, – I shall, I hope, be able to vary by rubbing up the reminiscences of my individual life, in continuation of those already published. After I have done with the Guardian I may – health remaining stedfast – possibly gain access to other files of newspapers with which I have corresponded; and if these things are accomplished, the great wish of my heart will be satisfied.

I have read with much interest your "Second Report of the East Lancashire Union of Institutions". You are engaged in a noble work; may your labours be crowned with good effect; and may you experience full pleasurable satisfaction.

You have expressed a wish that your name should not transpire in connection with this correspondence. I am not a babbler; and as you have cautioned me, I shall be as mute as death.

Remaining, Dear Sir James;

Your obliged humble servant, and friend[25]

Samuel Bamford

Still unwell in bowels. Sent for a bottle of physic: the greater part of which is laudanum: it makes me drowsy.

**Saturday 17th.** At home physicing – wrote to Gowenlock and Mrs to come tomorrow for early tea.

**Sunday 18th.** The Gowenlocks did not come. I had given – like a blockhead – the wrong time of the train; and consequently, I suppose, they missed it. Betty Jaques from Middleton, and her cousin kept us company for tea. Otherwise we were quite alone.

---

25. "and friend" added at side.

# 7

# PRIDE AND CHARITY

*Little came in the autumn of 1859 of the attempts of either the Lancashire Reformers' Union or the Manchester Reform Association to renew reform agitation in the district. At first all seemed well as the support of the Chorlton brewer Thomas Clowes ensured a good turn-out of leading Manchester liberals for a reading by Bamford at the start of the new winter season. Bamford was reminded of his ambivalent feelings towards such men, and despite (or perhaps because of) his need for the patronage of such figures, the diary entries of these months show Bamford preoccupied with the dangers of dependence and the virtues of self-reliance. Visits to middle-class friends, chance meetings in public (including a strange and perhaps contrived encounter with the Liberal statesman John Bright on 15 November), and encounters while out walking, all threatened Bamford's easily injured amour propre. At the same time, he was sharply reminded of the risks of patronage by the refusal of the Chadderton and Tonge Mutual Improvers to read out his address to them, and by the raking up in November of the unhappy affair of Lord Suffield and the original Middleton Mechanics' Institute in the 1820s. By the start of December, Bamford's winter platform campaign dominated his thoughts, and a well-supported appearance at Bury brought him a good purse (thanks, ironically, to one or two generous patrons), though its success was somewhat marred by his criticism of the press coverage.*

**Monday 19th.** Mima and I went to Manchester; bought a small lamp to write by, and brought away one or two articles, which had, some time ago, been left at our "Uncles".

Better of the bowel complaint.

Fanny Chorlton, our neighbour, has been informed, of a veritable truth, that I am employed in writing, and that I have two pounds a week from Government. Such is the news amongst these religious, and ignorant folk.

***Letter****, Joseph Priestley, Victoria Chambers, 9 Corporation Street, Manchester, to Bamford, 19 September 1859.*

> Dear Sir,
> Our friend Mr Clowes wrote to you on <u>Thursday Evening</u> asking you to send a list of subjects you had selected for your proposed "readings" at the Chorlton upon Medlock Town Hall, either to him, or to me, but as yet neither of us have heard from you. Will you have the goodness to send the selection you have made <u>without fail by the next post</u> after receipt of this, to Mr Clowes so that the programme can be got out without any more delay – Monday evening next is the time advertized for the readings, so that there is not any time to lose now.
> I remain, Dear Sir,<br>Yours respectfully,<br>Joseph Priestley.

– the following note and programme were posted to Mr Clowes.

***Copy letter****, Bamford to Thomas Clowes, 20 September 1859.*

Dear Sir,

I was surprised on receiving this morning, a note from Mr Priestley, requesting me to forward, by the next post, the programme of my purposed readings for Monday night. There must have been a loss, or a mistake, somewhere, as I posted the programme on Thursday last, at Harperhey, together with an explanatory note to yourself, and a copy of an advertisement, which I proposed ... including in ... that which had appeared.[1] I have not kept a copy of the programme; and I have not a certain recollection, either of the subjects proposed or the order in which they were arranged. I will however endeavour to produce you another synopsis, as nearly a copy of the one already provided, as my memory enables me to produce. I shall also, in order that, the possibility of further delay may be avoided, leave a copy of the enclosed with Mr Priestley at Victoria Chambers this afternoon.

I should mention that the programme was posted on Thursday by 3 & your note did not come to hand until Friday morning; and I, consequently, considered that my communication had been delivered by the time yours came to me, and all would be right, so I did not reply by return, as I otherwise should have done.

I made the programme a short one – as this is – because it tends to disatisfaction when more is proposed than time and other circumstances will allow the performance of. Neither is a programme of any great moment; Dickens, I believe, never issues them; and in many cases it must occur that they are inconvenient. In this instance, I shall either dilate, suppress, or vary: as in the progress of my task, I may find necessary.

I remain, Dear Sir,

Yours truly,

Samuel Bamford

Samuel Bamford's Readings

At the Town Hall, Chorlton upon Medlock on Monday 20th September 1859 at half past seven in the evening.

Synopsis

Social Conditions of Parliamentary Reformers sixty-five years ago.
The rural population; notices of some original characters
Condition of Parliamentary Reformers forty-two years ago
Sketches of Prominent Characters
Conflagration of Manchester
Home.
Arrests

**Tuesday 20th.** The annexed were left at the office of Mr Priestley, at Man^r.

*Copy letter*, *Bamford to Joseph Priestley, 20 September 1859.*

---

1. Parts of this sentence are obscured by a tear.

Dear Sir,

Herewith you will receive a copy of synopsis which, in accordance with your note of this morning, I have sent to Mr Clowes. I had written to him, forwarding a programme; and an advertisement of an improved form and when his note arrived on Friday morning I did not suppose that a reply to it was necessary, but expected to receive a <u>printed</u> programme before this, and was much surprised when your note came to hand this morning. Whether the accompany[ing] scheme please you or not, in ms, I am pretty certain it will in the reading as I can either add, diminish, or vary, as circumstances may require. I regret very much that you and Mr Clowes should have had so much trouble about this business. I hope to give you, and all friends satisfaction by the performance, I remaining /Dear Sir,\ Yours truly, Samuel Bamford.

Came back by the 1/2 past four Bus. Robert Consterdine was put inside, by a friend, a miserable, broken down, insane wreck of a mortal he was. I did not know him, until questioning the Conductor, he mention[ed] the name. This, the smart young fellow, who courted Miss Maria S. at Middleton, and, as old Amos Ogden told me, in his days of sycophancy and subserviency, used to meet, and sit with her in Old Amos's bedroom at the lodge. I wonder if his beloved would know him, or look upon him now.

Talking with Doherty, the quill dealer in Sugar Lane, about the late amateur performance, of which he told me he was the conductor; he asked me if their company could not <u>do something for me</u>? A thought which had never occurred to me. I replied that I thought they might, and the matter would probably have been further discussed, but at that moment a person came into the shop on business, so I withdrew until a more convenient opportunity.

**Letter**, *Joseph Priestley to Bamford, 20 September 1859.*

Dear Sir,

I beg to acknowledge the receipt of your favour of this date for which I am obliged.

The letter you refer to enclosing a programme and advertisement to Mr Clowes, has <u>not</u> reached that Gentleman.

If you have any preference for next advertisement, and will let me have a copy in time for insertion in Saturday papers – say early on Friday morning – I will attend to it.

I am, Dear Sir,<br>Yours respectfully<br>Joseph Priestley.

The letter was certainly posted: and I cant help believing it was delivered. SB.[2]

**Thursday 22nd.** Sent the annexed to Priestley. Wrote also to John Heywood about advertising.

---

2. Written on the reverse fold of the letter by Bamford.

**Copy letter**, *Bamford to Joseph Priestley, 22 September 1859.*

Dear Sir,

I should prefer the accompanying advertisement, as being more <u>directly</u> expressive, than the one which appeared on the 10th instant.

You might, I think, with propriety, speak to the people at the offices about giving it a good <u>prominent</u> position in the papers. The last was obscurely placed, and by many would probably be overlooked.

I could wish to have a printed programme or two, as soon as they are out.

Dear Sir,

Yours truly,

Samuel Bamford

<u>Bamfords Readings</u>

At the Town Hall, Chorlton-upon-Medlock, at half past seven P.M. on Monday the 26th instant, Mr Samuel Bamford will read select passages from his own works, "Early Days", "Life of a Radical" and "Walks in South Lancashire". Admission one shilling.[3]

**Friday 23rd.** At Manchester; Belfields, The Clarence, where I fell in with plenty who knew me, and several whom I knew. Tom Dewsbury (Jewsbury) a pompous old fool, who took me into a private room, in order, as he pretended to make known to me something of uncommon importance, and after all it was only to spout an extract from a speech by Henry Brougham,[4] in a law case (I think) for I paid very little attention, and left him abruptly; offended, I think. <u>Dick Lyon</u>, the son of my old schoolfellow, Dick Lyon, gave me an order for books: I have forgotten his address; so must find it out someway.

Too much toddy, but came off by the late Omnibus, and falling in with Ch. Delaunay called at New Inn, Barnes Green, where an agreeable set induced me again to stay. Singing was going on, and reciting, I giving "Farewell to my Cottage", and "Tim Bobbin'[s] Grave"; My health drunk with honours; a set speech made in my commendation: I replied, and last of all came home with a neighbour. All, "vanity of vanities."[5]

**Saturday 24th.** Should have been engaged in preparation for my reading on Monday, but head confused, and incapable of settling down to any regular train of thought, so nursed all day, by frequent swigs from my bottles of ale, behind the kitchen door; a rather comfortable and enticing way this of coming round after whisky punch: but, <u>no more</u>.

---

3. This draft advert was appended to the letter. Another copy, identically worded, appears separately.
4. Henry, Lord Brougham (1778–1868), Liberal politician, promoter of mechanics' institutes, and leading figure in the Society for the Diffusion of Useful Knowledge; *DNB*. See p. 253, n. 7.
5. Ecclesiastes, i.2.

**Sunday 25th.** This day I must have to myself in order to prepare for the morrow. Neither head however, nor stomach quite settled. What miserable work is this! Afternoon Mr and Mrs Gowenlock came, so I was struck off all work for the day, even had I been capable of any. Tea, and then went with Gowen[lock] to New Inn, just for a smoke; I could not refuse, so took a cigar and two toddies, which I would much rather have been without. After that, went with them to the coach, and so I was clear again, but the day was spent. I was dissatisfied in mind, and, on the whole, not well. The annexed from Clowes, was the only thing which gave me satisfaction.

**Letter**, *Thomas Clowes to Bamford, 24 September 1859.*

D[ea]r Sir,
I shall be glad if you come and take a cup of tea at my house on Monday and I will after that go with you over and assist you where necessary.
            Res^p Yours
                T. Clowes

**Flier** *advertising Bamford's readings at Chorlton upon Medlock with manuscript alterations and additions to the programme by Bamford.*

| | |
|---|---|
| Social Conditions of Parliamentary Reformers 65 years ago | Early Days p. 44 |
| Rural pop^n. characters | Early Days pp. 179:184, and Rad vol.1 p. 49:50 |
| Parliamentary Reformers 42 years ago | Rad vol.1 pp. 42–45 |
| Sketches of Leading Characters | Rad vol.1 pp. 16:18 |
| Conflagration of Manchester | Rad vol.1 pp. 39:41 |
| Healey in full practice.[6] | Rad vol.1 pp. 56 to 62 |
| Home, ~~Arrest Departure~~ | Rad vol.1 pp. 74:75 |
| Arrest | Rad vol.1 pp. 226 to 230 |
| Departure | Rad vol.1 pp. 232:33:34:35 |
| Robert the Waiter | Walks pp. 72 to 76 |
| Tom Woodford | Walks pp. 77 to 79 |
| A stranger in Lancashire | Walks pp. 267 to 272 |
| What should be done | Walks pp. 234 to 243 |

**Monday 26th.** Took tea at Clowes's, and he, his wife, his brother, and his brothers wife, walked with me to the Town Hall. Alderman Clarke, Geo Wilson, of Newall's buildings, and some four or five other gentlemen were in one of the rooms. I was

---

6. This, and the lines from 'Arrest', together with the page references, are Bamford's manuscript additions to the printed programme.

introduced, and after some talk, the purport of which I did not hear, we went upstairs into the large room which we found occupied by a very respectably dressed company: a good proportion of ladies being present. Mr Clarke took the chair, and briefly introduced me, which I felt to be perfectly non-requisite. I then made a few preparatory remarks, and commenced my nights exercise with the account of the Church & King mob at Royton, in 1794: the readings were very well received, being frequently applauded; the annexed programme will show the subjects treated upon; and they engaged me closely, near upon two hours.

Mr George Wilson afterwards delivered an address; which I could not hear well enough to clearly understand, only he spoke about myself and my readings in terms of approbation: one passage I did understand, though could not catch every word. He said he had recently been looking over some of Cobbetts works, and found that part wherein an account was given of the meeting at the Crown and Anchor Tavern in 1817, in which passage Cobbett stated that he was convinced of the practicability of universal suffrage, by what a weaver from Middleton had said, at the meeting. Mr Charles Sever, letter press printer followed Mr Wilson, and he also spoke, as I thought, strongly in my favour, suggesting also, as I understood, that other readings should be got up on my behalf. Dr Wheeler L.L.D.[7] sat on the other side of the chairman. I could scarcely believe my own eyes when I saw him, but he put out his hands, and took mine very cordially.

Near the commencement of the reading an elderly gentleman got up and said something, but what, I could not make out only, as it seemed to me, he found fault with something which I had put forth in print, (in my circulars, I suppose) and concluded by asserting, as I thought, that he was "the oldest Parliamentary reformer living," and then walked out, no one speaking, or taking further notice of him. His name, as I was /some days\ afterwards informed, was William Shuttleworth, a councillor of the borough of Manchester, and brother to Mr John Shuttleworth, late Stamp Distributor for the Manchester district.

Mr G. Wilson, Dr Wheeler, Mr Alderman Hardy, (as I understood) Mr Priestley, and several other gentlemen went with us to Mr Clowes's residence, where we had some, not very interesting or instructive conversation, Wilson taking the lead, chiefly about Mr Bright, Mr Cobden, and Parliamentary chit-chat, but most about the former gentleman. I took a glass of hot toddy, and shaking hands with them round, I came away at about eleven o'clock, Dr Wheeler coming out of the house with me. I wished to call a cab, and set off for home at once, but the Dr took hold of my arm, and, in a way forced me to walk with him down Oxford Street. I pondered in my mind, whatever he could want that he stuck so to me, and presently he asked how much I received for the nights exercise. I shut him off, with an evasive reply; he told me he was going to dine at six the day following, at Mr Dickens's the Magistrate, and silk dyer, at Spring Vale, Tonge. I said Mr Dickens was a very respectable gentleman, and a good employer. The Dr asked if I knew W.P. Roberts the attorney, of Manchester,

---

7. Possibly Thomas M. Wheeler (1809–62), attorney, long-time Chartist, Land Plan promoter and founder of the Friend in Need Assurance Society.

and some other character of the same party? (I forget whom) I said I did not know Roberts: and then the Dr asked again how much would I get for the reading that night, and angered by his pertinacity, and in order to get rid of it I said I might draw as much as ten pounds. I knew in fact, that I should have ten pounds for the money was put down for me at Mr Clowes's, but I declined taking it then, as I did not like to carry a <u>swag</u> of money through the town, at a late hour.[8] We now were close by St Peter church, and going across the street, I took a cab, bade my companion good night, and drove home, arriving about 12 o'clock.

He repeatedly assured me, – and I might, I must be convinced of the same; that he had come to hear me that night, entirely out of respect to myself, and not from any other motive. I, of course, thanked him; but I could not help surmising that he had other matters in view, remotely or directly. I recollected that he had lately been lecturing, at the Athenaeum, at Oldham, and I deemed it not improbable that his repeated enquiries were made with a view to some other engagement of the kind at some place. Time will perhaps open out these mysteries, but, I firmly believe, he intends making <u>a set</u>, at some place, perhaps Chorlton upon Medlock.

**Tuesday 27th.** Not well. Find I took cold from walking down Oxford Street, with Dr Wheeler, instead of getting a cab, as I wished to have done, and as I ought to have done. This comes of being over persuaded by persistent friends.

**Wednesday 28th.** Still not well by very much. I was over warm on leaving the town hall, and the same on leaving Mr Clowes's, and got chilly in walking in damp night air.

**Thursday 29th.** Wrote to Clowes, as annexed, which was returned on Sunday Morn[g] (Oct 2[d]) with note in reply.

***Copy letter***, *Bamford to Thomas Clowes, 29 September 1859.*

Dear Sir,
You are personally acquainted with the gentlemen, who acted with you as a committee in arranging preliminaries for my late Reading in your Town Hall; and I beg you will express to them individually or collectively, as may be most convenient, the deep sense of grateful obligation which their kind aid has impressed on my mind. I remain Dear Sir,
Your, and their obliged Servant,<br>Samuel Bamford.

*Response from T. Clowes undated, written on the reverse of Bamford's letter to him.*

---

8. This sentence added on facing page.

D[ea]r Sir,

I take the liberty of returning this for amendment. If agreeable to you, I wish you to say in addition to what you have said, that you shall be happy to have another reading at same place about the end of Nov<sup>r</sup> and then I will call our friends together and do both at once,

Yours truly,<br>T Clowes

**Monday October 3rd.**  Wrote the amended note as follows.

*Copy letter*, *Bamford to Thomas Clowes, 3 October 1859.*

Dear Sir,

You are personally acquainted with the gentlemen who acted with you as a committee in arranging the preliminaries for my late reading at your Town Hall, and I beg you will express to them individually, or collectively, as may be most convenient, the deep sense of grateful obligation which their kind aid, has impressed on my mind. My hearing was far from being distinct that night, /in the large room especially,\ and that prevented me from acknowledging as I otherwise should have done, what had been said by Mr George Wilson, and Mr Charles Sever: something also, I understood was mooted respecting my giving one, or more additional readings; and if such was the case, I may with propriety add, that my best endeavours, are, at any time, attendant on the requirement of yourself, and friends.

I remain Dear Sir,<br>Your obliged Servant,<br>Samuel Bamford.

3d. Monday. Dronsfield and a friend called. Miss Taylor sent two fine cauliflowers. Gave the messenger one of Brierleys "A Day Out," inscribed on the cover. Miss Taylor, "Bunk Ho," and a note with my "most respectful acknowledgements."

**Thursday 6th.**  Manchester. Called and left Rich<sup>d</sup> Lyon his books.

**Saturday 8th.**  A note from Mills, Middleton, with a card for the Agricultural dinner presented by "Mr Armitage". Who Mr Armitage is I don't know. What should I be doing at an Agricultural dinner?

**Sunday 9th.**  Went by appointment to dine and tea at Mr Greenwells, Pendleton. Mima should have gone with me, much ado of invitation having been expressed for both of us, but she had been unwell most of the week, from disordered bowels. So I, wishful not to put off my friends again, went alone. At one o'clock, not a single omnibus, or conveyance of any kind was visible in Market Street, and a saddening reflection occurred to my mind, of the vastly preponderating and deadly influence which priestcraft exercises in this great, rich, and, in many respects, intelligent City of

Manchester: small hope is there for real freedom, whilst the human mind continues in the meshes of clerical thrall which now confine it.

"Oh lord! how long shall this prevail?" I inwardly groaned: but all things are moving; are progressing; and this evidence of astounding stupidity, cannot always remain; the time is coming, when "the millions will be free;" free in <u>mind</u>, as well as in political institutions. In the square I took a cab, being desirous not to be much behind dinner time at my friends house.

Mr Greenwell, whom I found sitting in a small back room, with some books. He enquired why I did not come to dinner? and I said I <u>had</u> come to dinner, for anything I knew to the contrary: had I not dined then? Certainly not, I said. I came there to dine, according to appointment. I was a little late, having been disappointed in not meeting an omnibus. I took a cab however and after all was afraid I had caused them some inconvenience: Nothing whatever in the way of victual was to be seen or smelt in the place, or about. Would I have a stake fried? Oh no dont put yourselves to any trouble. A mouthful of anything will suit till tea-time. A small bottle of porter was produced, and there was rum: I did not like porter, I said; a cup of ale would be preferred: that with a little cheese and bread for a put off, would do very well. They had not any ale in the house, I was informed, so I sipped of the porter and waited until at last Mrs G brought in a tray with bread, salt and a couple[9] of what I suppose they called steaks, but which appeared to me like chops, cut from a leg of mutton previously cooked and now boiled in a pan. Coarse grained, tough stuff it was, and after my old stumps of masticators had mumbled one small piece, I had had quite enough. A spoonful or two of mashed up potatoes, dark looking, and not very tempting, with a little gravey, very little it was, from the chops; and some ketchup, all salt and water only, as it tasted, then a crumb of cheese, bread, and about half a glass of porter, and my dinner was finished.

Mr G. excused by saying they had dined early, because of the young people having to go to <u>the</u> <u>Sunday</u> <u>School</u>; oh I thought, "if that is the case I am glad I was not here; and I only wish I was away again." So it being a very pleasant afternoon I proposed a walk, and having taken a sup of rum and water, hot, we set out a[nd] strolled as far as G. Nelsons at Fern Hill, whom with his wife and his two daughters was just setting off, full sail for the Church at Pendleton. Mrs Nelson however on our arrival declined church going – the others went, – and we were herded into the dining room. I took some more rum, hot, and a biscuit and Mr G. a glass of port. We chatted during perhaps, half an hour, then strolled round the lawn, and so came away. I had a notion to get upon the high ground, and return by "Irlam oth Height" but my friend suggested going by Weaste-lane, to which I assented, he wishing me to see a remarkably fine pair of gates. These we found at the intrance to the mansion of Edward Tootal Esquire,[10] at "Weaste House," and whilst we stood looking at them, a decently attired elderly female came out of the lodge and explained to us, the meaning of the enigmatical cyphers which were worked into the ornaments of the gates. Very

9. The end of volume 2 as currently bound.
10. Edward Tootal (1799–1873), cotton spinner; see *Manchester City News*, 27 September 1873.

handsome the gates were; of beaten iron apparently: the letters were, E. & M. T. for "Edward and Margaret Tootal," and the gates, as the woman said, cost six hundred guineas, or pounds. But, with all their attractions, they led to just "no where"; and to the residence of a family who were "nobodies." "Weaste House," waste indeed; a narrow darkly looking avenue, or lane; and a large red brick house at the bottom. "You will be well off here," I observed, "you will want for nothing, with such people your close neighbours," "Ah!" she said "I once had a nice little cottage yonder," pointing towards a space beyond the wall; "but the next gentleman came and took the ground, and pulled down my cottage, and so, this lodge being at liberty, I came here, where I am cooped up between these walls from morning to night, all the year round." But you will have good neighbours, I observed; "Ah if you'll believe me, I have been here four years, and not one crumb of theirs, nor one drop of anything from that house, has passed my lips." I expressed astonishment. "Yes," she said, "but they have a very severe good-for-nothing housekeeper, who wont give anything, not a sup of broth, or a drop of milk; it must spoil and be thrown away before she will give it." I wondered they would keep such a servant: they surely must not know about her. "They know," the woman replied: "they know all about her ways and her management, both master and mistress know, and they like her the better for it." I had been ill, she said, and my doctor's bill came to upwards of two pounds. I showed the bill to Mrs Tootal, hoping she would do a little towards helping me to pay it, but she only looked at it, and said, I must pay it of course. I asked her how she contrived to live, having no allowance from the house; I have only the occupation of this dull little place, she said. My children keep [me]; they subscribe amongst themselves, and allow me five shillings a week. Well, here is a trifle to buy you a pinch of snuff, and I put a shilling into her hand; Mr G. gave her sixpence: she expressed many thanks, and we came away.

I was not at all surprised to hear this shabby account of these shabby Tootals. I had known the family "of old." Old Sally Tootal, his gran[d] mother was a lunatic in Salford Workhouse, and used to go moaning and crying round the yard all day over. Every thing was to her a source of grief; and her constant sorrow, and unceasing tears reminded one of that passage, "A wounded spirit who can hear." He[r] sons, she often told me were rich gentlemen, and kept a silk warehouse in Cannon Street, but they never came to see her, and she used to lament their neglect, which was always to her, a cause for a fresh effusion of tears. I knew them afterwards well; indeed they were too well known by silk weavers; they discharge[d] one, at least, of their putters out, because he refused to abate wages without a cause, or in other words, because he would not rob the working man, of the money he had fairly earned. It was currently stated as a fact, that a certain person was stationed at the warehouse door one Saturday morning and took down the amount of abatements as the weavers severally made their appearance, and he found that, before dinner, the abatements amounted to forty pounds. One of the brothers of this bad family is this man, this wastrel fellow, living at Weaste House. He is reputed to be immensely rich; he lives in splendid style, is a great railway director, a magistrate of the County, and of course, one of our most respectables of the City of Manchester.

From this place, my friend led me along what had formerly been a very pleasant field road betwixt Pendleton and Eccles, but now, it was walled on each side so high, – much higher than my hat, that it was more going along a deep gutter than anything else. The gentlemen occupying land on each side, have apparently been so fearful of their neighbours looking over the fence, that they have completely spoiled the walk. And one of these gentlemen is Mr Tom Bailey Potter, a son of the late Sir Thomas Potter, and one who will talk forever about the rights of the people: his side of the walk is more highly fenced, I believe, than is that of his very worthy neighbours: If the public should at any time come to their rights, these walls, the evidence of a spirit of miserably selfish arrogance, will be levelled, and the path be once more opened to the sun-light.

We returned to Greenwells, and after tea with himself, his wife, and two nieces, I was glad to get away and returned home at near ten o'clock. Mrs Greenwell had a word for everything; "the grey mare seemed to be the better horse."[11] They wished me to remain all night, but I had quite enough.

There is no place like home.

**Wednesday 12th.** Went to Ashton thinking to see Mr Hugh Mason about patronizing one of my readings before he went out of office. He was not at the mill, and his father Mr Thomas Mason, once a very good friend of mine, was "engaged," and could not see me. So I called at the banking house of Mr Coulthard in Stamford Street, and I saw him, and he promised to encourage me in what I proposed. The Country, he said, was under an Obligation to me for what I had done and suffered in the cause of reform. I next went to the mill of Rayner and Brothers, and saw Mr Rayner, who was putting on his better coat to go to dinner. "I have not time to attend to you," he said, "My conveyance will be here in a minute. I am off to dinner. I cant look after other folks business: I have enough with my own, and my work peoples." His conveyance, the footman sitting on the box, whip in hand, came up to the gate; he just touched his coat with a brush, put it on, I turned away in disgust and left him, to overtake me driving up the street, to his country house, and his plenteous dinner. I next walked across the market place, to the Town Hall, but Hugh Mason and the magistrates were gone, so I took a glass at a small public house, went to the station and took my place for Manchester; thence home.

**Friday 14th.** Oldham. Called on Gowenlock and took a glass with him at the Angel: did not call on Potter it is such a climb to his place. Afterwards stepped into Buckleys the Kings Arms, and there was annoyed by the impudence of a fellow named Fletcher, who attends on the billiard players up stairs. I shall snub this jack ass on the first opportunity: took a ticket at Mumps Station for Middleton Junction, and when I got there I found I should have to wait 40 minutes before a train for Middleton would arrive, so set off to walk, in company with Bob at Yebs,[12] whose reminiscences of old times, and old persons, – for he was in his 70th year – made the walk seem short, and very agreeable. Stopped at Mrs Walkers at Middleton, and came home by the 7 o'clock bus.

---

11. Sentence inserted opposite.
12. Hebers.

**Saturday 15th.** Twenty-five years this morning since my dear child died. Alas that day![13]

**Sunday 16th.** Potter and wife from Oldham should have been here to dinner and tea; but it turned out a very wet day, so they did not come.

**Tuesday 18th.** Went to Peel Park, and exchanged the file of Guardian 1833, for that of 1832. Got spectacles from Franks, had a glass with Stokes and came home.

**Thursday 20th.** At Peel Park examining Davis's account of the <u>Druids</u> and his Celtic Researches. 2 quarts of oil for lamp and walked home.

The Chadderton and Tonge Mutual Improvement Society are having a tea party on the 29th to which they have invited me; and now it seems, there is a <u>rival</u> <u>association</u>, which is having a tea party on the 22[d] – seven days before the other – which looks very much like spleen and malice. Joe Fieldings name also, is ominous of something unhandsome. See opposite advertisement.

*Two advertisements from the* Middleton Albion, *15 October 1859.*
*(i) First meeting of the Middleton Debating Society on 15 October, entrance 6[d].*
*(ii) "Education will stand your Friend when riches fail." First tea party of Lane End Literary Institute, Saturday 22 October, tickets 7[d]. Chairman: Joseph Fielding.*

**Friday 21st.** At Peel Park again. Mima went to Fern Hill: and Mrs N. coming accidentally to the library with two ladies, her visitors, she urged me to go up to dinner. So I went, but much against my inclination, dined. Came away about half past four, and got home at six. Very cold; downfall expected.

**Saturday 22nd.** The Examiner and Times people at Manchester should have given a notice of Brierleys new issue of "A Day Out," but instead of that they have inserted, in their <u>weekly</u> paper, a new article by him entitled "Rushbearings." A good thing enough, but, wanting the freshness, and originality of some passages in his "Day Out." The Examiner people, it seems wont notice his "Day Out"? Why, I cannot guess the reason of, unless it be that it has already been noticed, and handsomely commended in the Guardian. What pitiful disdain is this. A slight snow, very strange thunder today, not a crack, and loud report, as usual, but like the rolling discharge of vast artillery, at a great height above.

**Sunday 23rd.** Received this morning a posting bill of the soiree and tea party at Mills Hill, which it seems I am expected to attend on Saturday next. A whole lot of <u>great</u> <u>ones</u>, are to be present, McDougall <u>Esqr</u>, a manure manufacturer, in the chair. I am afraid these young fellows are going the wrong way to work with their Mutual Improvement: inviting a parcel of snobs to give them a start, instead of setting about it themselves; and acting on their own resources. I have been pleased with the idea that

---

13. Entry inserted opposite.

these "Mutual Improvers" would have sense and spirit enough to meet and improve on the Sunday, but, the array of names on the sheet opposite; these magistrates, parsons, and tories, will be the wrong people for encouraging <u>Sunday</u> <u>Improvement</u>.

**Poster** *advertising the first annual tea party and soirée of Chadderton and Tonge Mutual Improvement Society at the Baptist church, Chadderton, Saturday 29 October. Among the eight "gentlemen who have agreed to be present" is Bamford.*

During the night several reports of thunder like the roll of artillery, same as yesterday.

The advertisement of the Lancashire reformers union appears in Fridays Examiner and Times. In the notice we find a list of those who are to <u>manage</u> the affairs of the Union pending the meeting of Parliament.

A heavy snow this morning.

**Notice** *from the* Manchester Examiner and Times *of a meeting of the Lancashire Reformers' Union at Newall's Buildings, Thursday 27 October, 7.30.*

**Tuesday 25th.** Went to friend Clowes's at Chorlton upon Medlock: he paid me for some books which Mr Priestley and his (Clowes's) brother had: 9/6: from his statement it appeared that [what] both George Wilson, Mr Sever, and W. Shuttleworth said on the night of my reading at the Town Hall, was entirely in my favour. I was glad to learn that such was the fact, because the impression on my mind, caused by my imperfect hearing, was that Mr Wilson had spoken in a qualified tone respecting me, and that Mr Shuttleworth had decidedly objected to something which had been put forth in one of my circulars. Mr Clowes further said, that when the elections of Councillors for the various wards was finished, it was the custom for the retiring Councillors, the newly elected ones and their friends to have an amicable sitting down together, with a trifle of dinner, and so on: such would be the case this year, and on that occasion, he would take the opportunity to read my letter of thanks, and to propose, that another reading be arranged for. He seemed not to have any doubt whatever, that the idea would be adopted and acted upon, as, from all he could hear, my last performance had given eminent satisfaction to everyone who attended.

Whilst I was coming down Oxford Street, a gentleman came hastily out of his shop, took my hand, and expressed the pleasure he had derived from my performance at the Town Hall: he should be glad to hear me again, and if the opportunity occurred, he could sell a considerable number of tickets. I thanked him, and said another reading would probably be announced before long: these trifling instances of kind feeling show that people, strangers to me feel interested by my conversations.

Called at John Heywoods, but he was not within. Stepped up to the reform room at Newalls buildings and got some tickets for the meeting on Thursday night. S.P. Robinson complained much of the apathy of the people on the question of Parliamentary Reform. Cowan of Newcastle[14] had, he said, made the same complaint. I said that never since

---

14. Joseph Cowen (1831–1900), radical, active member of the Reform League, editor and proprietor of the *Newcastle Chronicle*, MP for Newcastle 1873–86; *DNB*.

I could remember were the great body of the working classes so well fed and clothed as they were at present: they had plenty of every thing such as I had never known before, and that made them indifferent to every consideration save that of their own enjoyment: the people I observed should be told of these things in very plain language: such language had not been addressed to them: the plain truth had been withheld, neither had the newspaper press done its duty. The neglectful indifference of the people had been smoothed over, and both press and people had been wanting to the good cause. Mr Robinson said I might have what number of tickets I wanted, so I went into the office and a boy gave me half a dozen, which I soon after disposed of to persons who I understood wished to attend the meeting. There was only one person, a boy, in the room at Newalls buildings, and I thought the place seemed indeed quite deserted. Came home by Omnibus; my <u>breathing</u> not being in the best order. Coughed considerably, with a difficulty of expectoration, and a tightness of the lungs.

**Wednesday 26th.** A stormy cold day. Kept quietly at home: and breathing easier.

**Thursday 27th.** Stormy and cold again: took a walk during an interval and then home to quiet.

**Friday 28th.** Account in the newspapers of the lamentable shipwreck of the "Royal Charter" on the rocks in Moelfra bay, Anglesey.

**Saturday 29th.** Wrote, as see the other page to the Chadderton and Tonge Mutual Improvement Society, forwarded by rail from Newton Station in a parcel containing books, – five vols.

*Copy letter, Bamford to Chadderton and Tonge Mutual Improvement Society, 28 October 1859.*

<u>Mr President and fellow workers in the cause of Mutual Improvement.</u> I regret that the state of my health, which has suffered from the sudden and severe change of the weather, will prevent me from joining your tea party and soiree tomorrow evening. I have been troubled from oppression of the chest, and difficulty of breath, all the past week; and I find it necessary to avoid changes of temperature, – as from a close room to out-door cold, and night air especially. – In attending your meeting, I should have to encounter these inconveniencies, without any pre-arranged means for returning home, or for being comfortably housed elsewhere; without also, any <u>strong</u> necessity for my coming, since I can transmit to you in writing, all that I should express were I in your company, and for these reasons I abandon the intention of attending.

Your work of <u>Improvement</u>, which I hope will be universally successful, should embrace <u>two</u> main branches; namely, improvement in knowledge which is to be derived from books; and improvement in knowledge resulting from reflection, and <u>self</u> examination. With respect to the former, I dont suppose I can do better than refer you to a striking example at once; an example which is to be found almost at your own doors, and certainly within less than one hours walk, of the place where, I expect you will be assembled when this letter is read to you. At Royton, you may or might have found, about twelve months ago a society of young men, occupying a very handsome building called "The Temperance Seminary"; they, like yourselves, are mutual improvers: at the time I have mentioned, they numbered about seventy members, all total abstainers from intoxicating drink: they had a library of 300 vols, their reading room was open from morning, to 10 in the evening of <u>every</u> <u>day</u>: their reading room was very comfortable and even handsome apartment, with a good fire, chairs, and benches, for seats, and framed plates, hung against the walls: gaming was not allowed in the place: classes met for mutual instruction on four nights each week, and reading, writing, grammar, and arithmetic were taught, with geography illustrated by maps and globes: the whole of the building where this society met was their own. Another mutual Improvement association occupied several upper rooms of a building in sandy lane: they called themselves "the Literary Institution", and numbered about 75 members, with a library of 220 volumes: they were all working men, and boys, ranging from perhaps ten to 25 years of age: their contributions were two pence a week, and their place was open from morning to night <u>every</u> <u>day</u> without distinction. They held a general meeting every three weeks for the exchange of books from the library, and special general meetings were held whenever special business required it: schools were open every night, when reading, writing, grammar, and geography were taught by, and amongst themselves: the most proficient instructing the others; they had a pair of handsome globes, and the rooms were hung round with excellent maps and charts. These were all working men and youths; they had commenced the undertaking themselves: had struggled with many difficulties at first, but had overcome all; they had fixed their way, had furnished their rooms (three if I recollect right) they had purchased maps, globes, books, and such requisites as made their place comfortable, all of which had been accomplished without the assistance of any person of wealth, or so called superior station and this, in my opinion is the way in which Mechanics Institutions, and "Mutual Improvement Societies", aught to be originated, and supported. Those of them who are necessitated to pecuniary aid of persons who are of a more wealthy class than workers, are like a ship sailing under false coulours: they are not sustained by mechanics or other working men, and ought not to claim the distinction of honest and honourable independence. Let working men therefore, in the conducting of all such institutions as those I am writing about, avoid the patronage of any who assume to be of a higher class than themselves: such connections though ever so well intended by the affluent, lead to embarrassment, dissatisfaction, and ultimate alienation of kindly feeling: the favoured party cannot help but forego first one small condition of self will, and then another, until, in the end he is completely enmeshed in the influence of his rich friend, his individual character is obliterated and his manly independence is gone. Those institutions at Royton, are entirely sustained by working men: they are honourably what they profess to be: they are, or seem at least, highly prosperous – the Literary Institute purposing to commence a suitable building, – the members are individually and collectively, a credit to the class to which they belong; these are the most prosperous

Institutions of the sort which I have heard of in England: and, what may seem strange, and perverse to some people, they are open for instruction the same on Sunday as on other days. Go to Royton therefore, I would say: mark the sort of book knowledge which is set forth there, and the rules and regulations under which it is obtainable: if you would prosper like them, use the means they do and be assured that though your beginning be "ever so humble" if you strive with clear heads, and good stout hearts, you will succeed and accomplish much good.

The other branch of Mutual Improvement, which is the moral one, depends more on individual character, than on rules and systems, laid down by books; we may therefore leave the book department, and betaking ourselves to reflection, and self examination, we shall find that we are entering on a higher course of improvement than the one hitherto receiving our attention. We have been appropriating the adornments of knowledge to our <u>own</u> benefit, and we have now to consider what is due to our fellow beings, not only of the human species, but of all others which come within the sphere of our creation, for all breathing beings are our fellows and brothers in the great mystery of life. First of all however: we should "love, honour, and succour," the venerable parents from whom we derived our human existence. Reprobate, and unhappy indeed must be he, who could look with indifference on the mother who bore, and tenderly nursed him during helpless childhood: ever let our hands wait upon her eye, our feet move in obedience to her exer[tio]n; let us beware of bringing sorrow to a mothers heart; the thought will be a sting in our minds during all our future life. To the affectionate father whose willing labour sustained our infancy let us pay tender regards and grateful obedience, reverencing his old age, and ministering to his failing wants. In our own persons and attire, let us scrupulously attend to cleanliness; we shall thereby secure comfort to ourselves, and be agreeable to others: cleanliness of mind, purity of heart should be still more sought after; guilelessness of thought, and innocence of low conversation, would follow: envy, the great bane of the working classes of England, would meet but with small encouragement in hearts so prepared against error and vice. Integrity, and strict honesty, would mark all our dealings with our fellow men; not that honesty, that which consists in paying <u>money</u> <u>debts</u> alone, but that which discharges, or endeavours to discharge all due obligations to others; that honesty which is thoroughly honest in word and in deed: which is the same, "yesterday, today, and on all other days": the same absent as when present, the same to a mans back, which it is to his face: cowards alone crouching under moral condemnation, find it necessary to vacillate and change, presenting a different aspect under every variable circumstance: an honest man needs not to change; he is one of the nobly self improved.
"These nobles, not by rank alone, mere title they ignore;
These writers sign, and ... seal, they must have something more;
... The honest mans, a king of men, and crowned by God alone."[15]

---

15. These lines, damaged, are an adaptation by Bamford of Burns's "A man's a man for a' that", which he often cited in one form or another.

... [16] That the Mutual Improvement Society of Middleton and Tonge may become imminently useful, and an example to all others, is the sincere wish of,
>                    Sir,
>                         Yours truly,
>                              Samuel Bamford.

**Sunday 30th.** Allen Mellor came over to see me, hearing I was unwell: he had attended at the Chadderton and Tonge Mutual Improvement tea party held at Mills Hill, and he said the Chairman – McDougall, (the Councillor McDougall of Manchester) did not read my letter at the tea party, or produce it, he only intimated that he had received a letter from me, "Such a letter as might be expected from a steadfast (or sturdy) old radical like him." The books were never mentioned: During the course of the evening Mr Cheetham Jun[r] was called upon to speak, but he excused himself, saying however, that he would, if it was agreeable, read Mr Bamford's letter: this the Chairman waived, and nothing more was said about it. Besides the Chairman, McDougall, two of his sons were present; his brother also, and his brothers wife were in attendance (his brother keeps a school at Flixton). Mr J.T. Hibbert,[17] the late candidate for Oldham, was present and spoke: he is at the head of a Mechanics Institution at or near Flixton, and is intimately acquainted with the Macs. Mr Peter Seville was also present and spoke at rather tedious length – he always does – Rev[d] J. Kightly spoke and Mr Jas Cheetham Jn[r]. offered to read my letter: towards the close, and when they were almost at a stand for speakers, Mr Allen Mellor was requested to say something, but he rose, put on his hat, and came out. The meeting was rather numerous: there was a good set of glee singers: the Mutual Improvers are a set of young working men, not known as being either readers or writer, or as being remarkably intelligent. They live chiefly at Jumbo and Lane end: I must go over and get their names, as I shall probably have something to say, both to them and their Chairman: the latter, I understand, is a strictly religious person, a preacher sometimes, very likely a Calvanist, – he is a Scotchman – He first came to this side of the country as a manure manufacturer: he was driven out of Salford by an action at law, in which he was fined £100 for the nuisance caused by his works: his place of operation was next at Chadderton, near Mills Hill, but the stench from his works there soon became so intolerable that the whole country set against it and another action would soon have compelled him to quit, had he not ceased to make manure; people from Royton, coming to the rail-way, were I understand particularly loud in their complaints of the muck manufacture; hence probably Mr McDougalls omission to read my letter, which contained statements to the credit of parties at Royton.

---

16. The text is damaged here. Two sentences argue that if people followed Bamford's precepts, the reputations of honest men would be restored and calumniators and confidential informers would be exposed and expelled from public life.
17. John Tomlinson Hibbert (1824–1908), barrister, MP for Oldham 1862–74, 1877–86. He became a considerable admirer of Bamford, and spoke at the dedication of the Bamford monument; *Manchester Examiner and Times*, 8 October 1877, *DNB*.

30 Sund. Allen Mellor came to see me, though what could have moved him to such a wish, I was at a loss to imagine, unless it was to communicate something reflecting the tea party last night. My letter it seems, was left by McDougall on the desk before him. Mr Cheetham Junr took the chair, when it had been vacated, and on coming away, he brought all the papers with him. Young Cheetham, so it seems most likely, would afterwards read my letter, probably copy it, and give Mellor a hint to come over and see with what sort of temper I learned that my document was put aside. A hint from Cheetham, would act as a <u>command</u> from Mellor, who is Manager at the mill, and is no doubt very willing to oblige Mr Cheetham, who is a good employer.

**Monday 31st.** Went to Lane End, and saw Mellor, telling him that as my letter had not been read at the meeting, nor my books acknowledged – or but very slightly so – I thought I ought to have them back again; the letter especially I wished to have returned. Mellor said Mr Jas Cheetham Jun$^r$. had it, but he would get it for me, so I arranged to go over again on Wednesday, when I would take the letter with me up to Oldham, and probably get it incorporated with the Chronicles report of the meeting. Mellor was very friendly, and came with me part of the way.

Called at James Kents Tonge Lane, and had a long chat with him. I read him the letter also, and he approved of the sentiments. A beautiful day.

31 Oct. Mond.[18] Called at Mills's Middleton, and left copy of my letter with his wife, for insertion in the Albion of Saturday.

**Tuesday 1st November.** Cold wet and stormy; at home all day.

**Wednesday 2nd.** Walked to Middleton and saw Mills who with many confused and inconclusive arguments and excuses declined giving my letter a place in the paper. I learned that he had been at Lane End, and had seen Mellor; had come home with him also from the meeting of the Institutional Association at Manchester, when something had been said betwixt the two about my letter: I could not think it possible that Mellor had been acting *fair* to my face, and falsely to my back. I should be sorry, to find him otherwise than truly honest, time will show.

2nd Wed. Walked from Middleton to Lane End, and met Mellor going from the mill to his dinner. On seeing me, he turned back saying the letter was in his desk, and he would fetch it. I went to his house and sat down, thinking him a long time in going that short distance. At length he came and gave me the letter and we sat down to a little dinner, during which nothing very material was said, I only intimating that I should take the letter with me to Oldham and should probably leave it with the people at the Chronicle Office for publication. I told him about Mills having declined it: at which he did not express any surprise. After dinner Mellor went with me to the station, and as we waited Mr Jas Cheetham Jun$^r$ came down the line from the Mill to the office <u>slightly</u> noticing me, as he went past: I gave him as <u>slight</u> a recognition in return, and

---

18. Bamford wrote "Nov." in error. Entry inserted opposite.

so paying him back in his own currency, I stood on the platform as good a man as he. These rich bearded and whiskered snobs: degenerate <u>Normans</u>! they deem it too great a condescension to show respect to a person in circumstances less affluent than their own. If they knew with what contempt I view them – and they might perceive it if they were not blind – they would pass along, and not annoy me by their pretentious recognition.

Called on Potter at Oldham and he went with me to the Standard office where I paid their account for advertising thanks after my last reading. Got a glass of toddy at the Angel, and then set off to walk to Middleton, Potter accompanying me to the canal at Mills Hill, whence he went to Lane End to call on Jacksons, for whom, I am glad to hear, he is likely to have permanent employment in touching up with colour some of their excellent photographs. Breathing rather difficult when coming from Oldham, and sorry I could not talk much with Potter, who was very kind. At Mrs Walkers, Middleton, was better after resting: took some hot toddy, and came off by the six o'clock 'bus.

**Thursday 3rd.** At home; received the annexed note from the secretary of the Mutual Improvement Society at Lane End, and sent in reply the letter marked B.

***Letter***, *J. Lees, Lane End, Chadderton, to Bamford, 2 November 1859.*

Dear Sir,
We received your parcel on the 29th and were very sorry that you did not come. Your address I am sorry to say through some cause or other did not get read. The chairman did just dwell upon it and that were all.
    We accept your present thankfully and are very much obliged to you for them.
                    Yours respectfully,
                    J. Lees.

***Copy letter***, *Bamford to J. Lees, 5 November 1859 (marked "B").*

Sir,
Your note of the 2$^d$ instant is before me; and I have to say, that the suppression of my address by the Chairman, and your Committee (for it was directed to both Chairman and Committee,) was, to myself, an act of great disrespect, and to the <u>Society</u>, a <u>direct</u> <u>insult</u>. Had you been an association of <u>gentlemen</u>, so called, Mr McDougall would have shrunk from the contemplation of such an act. I however happen to be only a <u>poor</u> <u>man</u>; your Committee and Society are of the same class, and hence the presumption which dared to treat us with disrespect. I shall notice the affair again at my own time and in my own way, and when your society has become sufficiently self "improved" to know what courtesy is due to them as sons of honest labour, such freaks as this, will not exhibited in your transactions. If proof were wanting of the propriety of working men acting with and <u>for</u> their <u>own</u> <u>class</u>, this transaction would supply such proof. Not that I would refuse the help or co-operation of a richer class: I would accept it when frankly tendered without

any presuming conditions, but I would not at any time <u>seek</u>, <u>solicit</u>, <u>crave</u>, the patronage of the rich; some act of assumption on one part, or of unworthy humiliation on the other is sure to follow: the rich, God help them, cannot understand the noble hearted pride of an honest poor man, and hence such liberties are taken with the poor, as this which I now justly denounce. I shall keep this address for reproduction at a proper time; its suppression is a disgrace to all those who were concerned in it. Things will not always – not long possibly – remain as they are at present, either with the workers or their employers: and a time will assuredly arrive, when every thought and expression of my letter will be reiterated with public approval; it was too good for the time and the occasion. And with that, content for the present, I remain,

Yours sincerely,<br>Samuel Bamford.

A very fine day: Claytons sale. Got 5/- by buying and selling again.

**Monday 7th.** The following extract from Lord Stanley's speech at the Peel Institution, Accrington taken from the Manchester Daily Examiner of this day.

*Cutting, from the* Manchester Examiner, *7 November 1859. Lord Stanley's speech praises small educational institutions run and supported by working men, such independence being "the best and surest guarantee of ... permanence and success ... (Cheers)".*

Confirmatory of my letters to the Lane End Mutual Improvement folk.

**Tuesday 8th.** Sent a newspaper containing the above to Allen Mellor at Lane End.

**Thursday 10th.** At Middleton. Stopped at Walkers with old friend Dicken, who says the Middleton people have behaved badly towards him (so they have) and he should like to leave the place – no wonder.

The following is the report from the Oldham Chronicle of 5th Nov. of the Mutual Improvement Society's meeting at Mills Hill, Saturday 29th Oct.

*Report, from the* Oldham Chronicle, *5 November 1859, on the first annual meeting of the Chadderton and Tonge Mutual Improvement Society, Saturday evening 29 October, in the Baptist Chapel, Mills Hill, Mr McDougall in the chair. The report concludes: "Thomas Dickins, Esq., of Middleton, and Mr Samuel Bamford, sent letters of apology for non-attendance, and the latter gentleman also sent an address in which he inculcated the advantages of self-reliance."*

*Report, from the* Oldham Chronicle, *5 November 1859, headed "GUARDIAN FIELDING: BEAUTIFUL – EXCEEDINGLY": a derisive attack on Joseph Fielding who, at a meeting of Oldham Poor Law Guardians, had called for an inquiry into the amount of beer consumed at the workhouse. Fielding is ridiculed as excitable and ostentatiously pious, and his speech dismissed as "nothing but idle talk".*

*Report*, *from the* Oldham Chronicle, *5 November 1859, of the final failure and winding up of the late Feargus O'Connor's Chartist land scheme.*[19]

*Editorial*, *from the* Oldham Chronicle, *12 November 1859, defending the Oldham Analytic Literary Institution against the "lecturing", "hectoring" and "truisms and educational platitudes" delivered by gentlemen speakers from Manchester at its recent annual meeting. Whilst "many so-called mechanics institutions ... are in effect nothing but middle class clubs", the Oldham Institution is an "eminently successful mechanics' institution, superintended and chiefly supported by working men for the benefit of themselves and their neighbours ..." and should not be criticised for its humble building.*

**Sunday 13th.** Dronsfield and another came in the afternoon. Nothing fresh.

**Tuesday 15th.** 25 years this day, since our dear Ann was buried. Gone like a dream, and we both here yet.[20]

Went to Mills's at Middleton and corrected proof of my 3rd circular, ordering 500 to be struck off.

Came back by the 1 o'clock omnibus and on getting up to it, a phaeton and pair stopped from which a gentleman whom I did not recognise stepped down and followed me into the 'bus. On looking at him I was surprised to find he was Mr. Bright M.P. He asked if I lived at Middleton, and I informed him I did not, I had only been at the printers. What Schwabes? he asked, and I said no, at the newspaper printers.[21] We were, I expected about to have some interesting conversation on the road, but my wishes were soon disposed of by a decent elderly man, and one younger, the former of whom accosted me as an old acquaintance, and whom I afterwards remembered as a Mr Clegg, I think that is his name, from Oldham. A strain of general conversation ensued, the old man alluding to "Burtonfeyght;" at which he intimated – so I understood him – that he was present.[22] "Aye," Mr Bright said, "Bamford was a general there was he not." I explained that I had not anything to do with that business, further than a strong sympathy with the rioters, and a great hatred of the machinery. That at that time I was employed in a print warehouse in Peel Street Manchester. "In Peel Street?" interrupted Mr Bright, apparently surprised; yes, in Peel Street I replied: I was employed at Manchester. My wife and child were at Middleton, and as soon as the warehouse was locked up I hastened home finding Middleton in a state of confusion and terror. Several persons had been shot dead, and the Scots Greys and Cumberland Militia were patrolling the streets. I felt rather surprised that Mr Bright

---

19. The Chartist Land Company had been started in 1845 by the Chartist leader Feargus O'Connor, whom Bamford regarded as a rabble-rouser. Intended to allow working men to purchase smallholdings, it fell into difficulties and had effectively ended years before.
20. First sentence inserted opposite.
21. Schwabe's was a large cotton print and dyeworks at Rhodes, near Middleton; see entry for 12 October 1861.
22. In April 1812, during the period of the Luddite riots, a crowd of several thousand people attacked Daniel Burton's powerloom mill in Middleton. Several were shot dead by the defenders and the military, and Burton's house was burned down.

did not know better than that I was a leader of the rioters that day. Something being said about Parliament, and the last Oldham election, the old gentleman said he intended going for Oldham the next time. Mr Bright said he did not see why he should not: the old gentleman evidently mentioning it as a qualification said there were more hands leaving his employ every night, than left the works of any master within twenty miles of Manchester. I asked where his mill was? – for I was not aware that he had more mills than one, he thereupon mentioned half a dozen such places: and I concluded that he meant, he had <u>shares</u> in the said works, and so might be said to be an employer – though not <u>the</u> employer of the whole of the hands. Mr Bright alluded to the general indifference of the people, the working classes especially, to questions of politics and said if the late strikes had been maintained on political grounds, instead of being directed against capital, the working men would have been enacting a far more sensible, becoming, and useful part.[23] I said it was not to be wondered at, seeing that such matters were tabooed in all our public schools, Mechanics Institutions, and places of gratuitous instruction. A stigma was attached to the pursuit of "the noblest study of mankind," that which led to the knowledge of a mans own rights and those of his neighbour. I also said, I remembered working mens turnouts which were diverted into political channels and became means in the hands of such as Feargus O'Connor, Oastler and others of that stamp, and the working mans cause suffered by the perversion. Mr Bright agreed that it was so, but <u>now</u> it would have been different. <u>Nem.</u> <u>Con</u>.[24] I asked Mr Bright what he thought of the San Juan affair?[25] and he expressed an opinion that the place belonged by treaty to the United States, but that it was not worth squabbling about, and that the difference would be settled amicably.

I left the 'bus at Barns Green, the two others having got out before me. Mr B shook hands and bid me a kind good day.

The following is a copy of my improved circular.

***Insertion****: Bamford's circular, now headed "Right against wrong", and dated 15 November 1859 (see Appendix 1).*

**Saturday 19th.** The following taken from the Middleton Albion, is a speech made by W Holden of Middleton at a public meeting, respecting the Free Library. My reply has been sent to the printer.

***Cutting****, from the* Middleton Albion, *19 November 1859, reporting William Holden's speech in favour of a free library in Middleton, which attributed public scepticism on the issue to the failure of previous attempts: "<u>There had been libraries in Middleton before. Lord Suffield got up a library here, but the radicals, Samuel Bamford and others, broke it up and divided the books</u>."*[26]

**Sunday 20th.** Jane and the children here to tea.

---

23. The part of this sentence after "politics" inserted opposite.
24. Sentence inserted opposite.
25. A recent naval confrontation between Britain and the United States over the ownership of the island of San Juan, between Vancouver Island and the state of Washington.
26. Bamford's emphasis.

**Monday 21st.** At Middleton. At O. Dickens: Mills intimates that Mellor and Whalley are intending something on my behalf.[27]

**Tuesday 22nd.** At Manchester, at Merchants Coffee House, meeting to arrange readings to assist Mrs Rogerson and children. Adjourned to Monday night next. Very foggy in Manchester and was much plagued with cough. Came by omnibus and coughed all night.

**Wednesday 23rd.** At home. Not at all well.

**Letter**, *Charles Field, Secretary of Union Club, Oldham, to Bamford, 19 November 1859 (received by Bamford on the 24th), inviting him to the inaugural ceremonies for the Butterworth memorial in Oldham on 26 November, and enclosing a "gentleman's ticket" for the tea party.*[28]

**Friday 25th.** The following from Mellor.[29]

My Dear Bamford,
I received your papers some days ago since which time I have been thinking how or by what means I could be of service to you, I have however determined upon a matter in the preliminary arrangements of which I have met with considerable success and support, and I am quite sanguine that the result will justify the attempt, and also enable me to be of practical service to you.
    I shall all [being] well be with you on Sunday morning next when final and full arrangements can be made in the matter in the meantime believe me
                    Yours truly
                    Allen Mellor.

**Saturday 26th.** The following letter appears in the Middleton Albion of this day.

**Letter**, *from the* Middleton Albion, *26 November 1859.*

---

### FALSEHOOD CORRECTED BY TRUTH

*To the Editor of the* Middleton Albion
Sir, – According to your impression of last week William Holden said, at the Free Library meeting "Lord Suffield got up a library here, but the radicals, Samuel Bamford and others, broke it up, and divided the books." Without stopping to expatiate on the baseness of this assertion, coming as it does from one with whom I have long been on friendly terms, the simple facts are, that Lord Suffield never did

---

27. The matter referred to is a reading at the Baptist schoolroom (see 13 December 1859), which netted Bamford nearly £4.
28. See cutting from *Oldham Advertiser*, 9 April 1859, above, for Bamford's contribution to the Butterworth memorial campaign.
29. Undated.

get up a library here: that Samuel Bamford and others never did appropriate a single volume of any library which existed in Middleton. On the contrary, it was Samuel Bamford and others who, in 1825, "got up" the first working man's library, commonly called a mechanics institution, which was established in that town. William Walker, and Robert Walker his father, both of Rhodes, Thomas Taylor, Amos Ogden, and myself, of Middleton, being the founders, I being, in fact, the originator.[30] We had already got a few books together to lend and exchange amongst ourselves, and were one evening pursuing plans for future and extended operations, when two gentlemen from London, whom I had known during our radical troubles in 1819, who had relieved the wounded at Peterloo, and had assisted those who had been persecuted and imprisoned, having business in the neighbourhood, paid a visit to my house. I was very glad to see them, made them acquainted with my neighbours who were present, and we informed the gentlemen what we had done in the library affair, and what we purposed doing. They cordially approved of our proceedings, and promised that on their return to London they would collect some books amongst their friends, and send them to us. This they did, and these books, with the few we had mustered amongst ourselves, formed the library of the first Middleton Mechanics Institution. We now took a room, drew up rules, and offered the use of the library to all who would come, on the same terms as ourselves. Our townsmen, however, did not show any strong preference for book amusement: the books were there, but the taste for reading was wanting, and we found that before much good could be effected by the library, a wish for the companionship of books must, by some means or other, be originated: we therefore adopted the plan of throwing open our doors once a week, and thus, not only offering books to the public, but even reading them for such as were either too ignorant or too indolent to read for themselves. This plan was successful: we read striking passages from history, biography, navigation or travels, explaining, in our humble way, such parts as required it; questions were asked, answers were given, discussions would sometimes take place, and whatever our conversations lacked in deep learning, was made up by our earnestness, sincerity, and an aspiration towards extended information. As our attendants at the readings increased, subscribers to our library did the same, and we were becoming a prosperous body, beginning to feel our young strength, when Lord Suffield, who had previously during my imprisonment at Lincoln Castle become acquainted with Amos Ogden, paid a visit to Middleton. He took much interest in our Mechanics Institution, made us a handsome present of money wherewith to purchase books, and consented to become our president; in return, however, for his money and his patronage, we gave him the power of removing any book to which he objected, and also, in deference to his wish, we ceased our public readings once a week. His lordship was one of the "Knowledge Diffusion" Society, of which the present Lord Brougham was a leading member.[31] They put forth various publications, very useful in their way, but not of the sort which would take in Middleton, being too learned and practical for the class to which they were offered. Lord Suffield's first instalment of money we spent in books, and in fitting up a room; but the charm of exertion, the vitality, had received a

---

30. See J. Fielding, *Rural Historical Gleanings of South Lancashire* (1852), 308–15; Bamford, *Amos Ogden*.
31. The Society for the Diffusion of Useful Knowledge, founded by Brougham and others in 1825, which promoted the Mechanics' Institution movement.

shock: our public readings no longer took place, and although we were more comfortably situated, we were also more dull, and, as we plainly perceived, less useful in the matter of book circulation. About this time my absence from the society's meetings was necessarily frequent. I had become connected with the London newspaper press, and my business almost daily called me from home, or if at home the writing out of my correspondence kept me there. The conducting of the institution consequently fell into other hands, Lord Suffield also gave up the presidency, and retired from the society, for reasons, as stated in his parting letter, which were creditable to his scrupulous conscientiousness. He had, in the exercise of his power as president, objected to a book, "Gibbon's Decline and Fall of the Roman Empire," and it was accordingly removed, but the act placed him in a position which he declined to maintain, and he accordingly withdrew. The institution now continued until the chartists became a numerous and urgent body, and with the view of rendering the books more useful, the place was thrown open to all who paid a penny a week: a larger room was taken (Turner's Garret) and a Sunday School, for reading, writing, and arithmetic, was commenced, and continued for some time. I had long before this ceased to attend the meetings at the institution, and the chief superintendence was exercised by Amos Ogden, Thomas Taylor, and some others of the new comers. Ultimately the chartists disagreed amongst themselves, the school, I believe, was given up, and the books (as I heard some time afterwards) were divided amongst four of the members, and conveyed to their separate dwellings, to be again produced whenever a future library should be established.

Such was the origin, progress, and the breaking up of the first Middleton Mechanics' Institution; and if this plain truthful statement does not suffice to put down such reckless aspersions as that of William Holden, public condemnation may perhaps have that effect. – I remain, Sir, yours respectfully,

SAMUEL BAMFORD.

Mosston, Harperhey,
    23rd. Nov., 1859.

---

**Sunday 27th.** Mellor, Mills, and the son of the latter, came over, and stopped till after noon. Mellor is in the course of preparing a reading for me at the Baptist Sunday School, Mills Hill, and we arranged that it should take place on Monday the 12th Dec$^r$ at half past seven in the evening. Mr Jas Cheetham Sen$^r$ to be in the chair, if possible. Gave Mellor 50 shilling ticket[s], 50 3$^d$ ticket[s] and 100 6$^d$ ones. A reading is also talked about at Middleton; to be held at the Suffields Arms; tickets 1/- each: and a dinner on the same evening. If these two proposals are carried out fully, I shall have a better Xmas that I expected.

**Tuesday 29th.** Went over to Mellor's who was in good spirits about the reading: he had sold 40 tickets in one day: Called at James Hunts: met Dicken at Middleton and came home by the 4 o'clock 'bus.

**Thursday December 1st.** Went to Middleton, but the posting bill was not in proof.
    Went to meeting of Rogersons friends at Merchant Hotel but nothing was done. Richardson not there.
    1 Dec. Thu. The following came to hand.

*Letter*, *Joseph Chattwood, Bury, to Bamford, 1 December 1859.*

My Dear Friend,
I duly received your circulars. I am glad you have concluded as per <u>circular</u> – now to come to business, I and Mr Livsey have been thinking that for <u>two Lectures or Readings</u> some six or eight pounds might be got – <u>perhaps more clear</u>. Now if this amount will be anything in your way for two nights please let me hear from [you] – and I will put the thing in form.

Yours very truly,<br>Jos. Chattwood.

**Friday 2nd.** Wrote to Chatwood accepting his offer, or three readings, if desirable; wished however to <u>see</u> the posting bill before it was worked off; and the advertisement before going to press: Would go over to see him on any morning after Sunday.

**Sunday 4th.** No reply to my letter in the last Albion.

**Thursday 8th.** Saw Mr Holden at Middleton who begged my pardon for the observation he made at the Free Library Meeting: said he had been misinformed, and had a sup of drink when he attended the meeting.
    8 Thu. Went to Bury and met Chattwood, Livsey, and another at Chattwoods. The latter showed a long list of subscribers to tickets for my readings which are to take place on the 21 and 22 instant at the Albion Hotel: ten pounds will be raised for me, and I am to choose the subjects for reading about.
    Came by the train through Heywood, to the Middleton Station; and thence to Middleton, where sure enough I found, at the Corner House Tom Crompton, from Bury who had come over to Middleton for <u>something</u>, what he did not explain, nor did I ask him, though I thought the circumstance <u>rather</u> <u>strange</u>: two friends of his I understood were also gone to some place, up Middleton, this also I thought <u>strange</u>, and I surmised their business was not of a friendly nature towards me, however, they were all apparently, very glad to see me, shook hands and compelled me, in a way to have toddy with them, after which, having a conveyance, they drove off, and directly appeared Mr Crossland, an attorney from Bury, who complained of their having left him after promising to wait for him: so it seemed they were all engaged in one business, whatever that might be. Mr Crossland made a great adoo about me; complimenting me on my patriotic career, and my constancy under suffering, alluding at the same time to my last circular, which it seemed he had perused: Several old Middleton residents and neighbours sat on the other side of the room, to whom his commendations might have been disagreeable, for they sat there and never spoke. Whereupon Mr Crossland remarked that a prophet "never received praise in his own Country." He also got [up] from his seat, came across the room to shake hands with me, and in doing so, he left a sovereign in my hand: This to me was all pleasing certainly, I was glad to see envious neighbours mortified, though with respect to the sovereign, I scarcely could consent to accept it, as Mr Crossland was rather touched in liquor. I shall however see him at Bury, and will make all right.

**Friday 9th.** Mr Clowes of Chorlton upon Medlock was not at home; he was gone to Macclesfield. I sat a short time with Mrs Clowes and her son, the latter telling me they intended getting up another reading in the beginning of the new year. Mrs C. had a sore throat and I got her some granulated nitre, and they were very friendly, and glad to see me.

**Saturday 10th.** The annexed appear in the Middleton Albion; the paragraph I scarcely thank the Editor for.

*Notice from the* Middleton Albion, *10 December 1859, advertising Bamford's forthcoming reading at Chadderton on 13 December, tickets 6d and 1s., quoting favourable reviews of his books from the* Athenaeum *and the* Manchester Guardian.

The 2nd annexed is from the Bury Times of this day. The Bury Times professes to be a radical paper, yet this Radical Editor puts my advertisement in the very worst part of his column, the direct centre, where the paper doubles up and the print escapes notice. Radical Editors always put their slights on radicals.

*Advertisement from the* Bury Times, *10 December 1859, supported by a short editorial notice, for Bamford's forthcoming readings at Bury.*

**Sunday 11th.** Mellor and his father in law came over; the latter suffering from a casual attack of Tic Dolouroux.

**Tuesday 13th.** A person named George Hulme came over from Prestwich, and expressed a wish that I should have a reading there. He had probably seen the advertisement in the Bury Times.

This evening my reading at Mills Hill took place, very well attended. A good sprinkling of the dear ones present, McDougall, Chairman who more than made amends for suppressing my letter at the Mutual Improvement Tea Party, so I did not recur to the subject. A good supper to about half a score at Mr Wilds after the reading was over. A very good, and comfortable bed for myself; a good and plentiful breakfast for Mr Wilde, Mellor, [and] myself the morning following, and three pounds, seven shilling in my pocket, with a probability that somewhat more may follow: No bad operation this, may all comfort and prosperity attend my friends Mellor and Wilde. Gave a very good reading and all seemed very much pleased.

**Thursday 15th.** Middleton, where I took rather more toddy than was requisite, smoked also a couple of cigars.

**Saturday 17th.** Still unwell from the cough, the ale is not yet out of me.

17th Sat. The following is from the Middleton Albion of this day.

*Notice, from the* Middleton Albion, *17 December 1859.*

### SAMUEL BAMFORD'S READINGS.

On Tuesday evening, at the Baptist School Mill Hill, Mr. Bamford, according to previous announcement, gave one of his literary entertainments. On the old bard's entrance into the room he was greeted with "Auld-Land Syne," from the organ, by Mr. Septimus Cheetham. Mr. McDoughall was called to the chair, and he feelingly alluded to Mr. Bamford's struggles and sufferings in the cause of parliamentary reform, when that cause was not so popular as at present. He (the chairman) thought that something substantial ought to be done for the old veteran and his aged partner to soothe their remaining years. There was a fair attendance, and Mr. Bamford acquitted himself in his usual respectable manner, and was frequently applauded. A vote of thanks was passed to the chairman, suitably acknowledged, and the proceedings terminated a little before ten o'clock. – (In our next issue we intend to give one of Mr. Bamford's pieces which was read on the above occasion.)

17th Sat. The following from the Bury Times of this day.

*Advertisement from the* Bury Times, *17 December 1859, for Bamford's forthcoming readings at Bury, supported by a warm editorial comment quoting from Bamford's circular and stating that: "his 'Passages in the Life of a Radical' gives a truer insight into the life and political conditions of the English people in recent times, than all the lives of political leaders that we know of put together".*

**Sunday 18th.** Brierley comes and tells me that himself, Potter, and one of the Jackson[s] have been talking about having a snug Christmas party, on New Years Eve. I gave my assent of course, so I suppose something will be ordered about it. Brierley says he cannot hear anything whatever of poor Mrs Rogersons affair; a strange proceeding this of Mr R.J. Richardson.[32]

Foggy, and a severe frost during the last three days.

Joseph Ramsbottom,[33] of Harperhey leaves me two poems "The Widow to her fatherless child," and "The Poachers Soliloquy," both very good pieces; A new Poet discovered.

**Wednesday 21st.** The annexed article about that wretch De Quincy is from the Examiner and Times of this day.

---

32. Reginald J. Richardson (1808–61), carpenter, radical journalist, surveyor; one of the leaders of Manchester Chartism and active in various radical causes in the 1840s and 1850s, including the Manchester Footpaths Preservation Society; see Paul Pickering, *Chartism and the Chartists in Manchester and Salford* (1995), 203–4.
33. Joseph Ramsbottom (1831–1901), a weaver who eventually became a partner in a textile firm, journalist and poet, and active member of the Manchester Literary Club. Best known for his volume *Phases of Distress* (1864); *Manchester Guardian*, 12 February 1901. See entries for 7 January 1860 and 31 October 1861.

**Extract** *from a critical obituary in the* Daily News *of the writer Thomas de Quincy, author of* "Confessions of an Opium Eater", *taken from the* Manchester Examiner, *21 December 1859. His undoubted intelligence and talent were reportedly wasted by his opium addiction, which caused him to turn on his own literary friends (including Wordsworth), robbed his attacks on others of credibility, and left his own life valuable mainly as a warning against the corruption wrought by opium.*

Arrived at Bury by the 6.30 train and found Chattwood and Tweddell in the travellers room at the Albion. Livsey came shortly after. Commenced Reading at 8. to a very fair attendance, and read till 9.30: very frequently cheered and company seeming much pleased. The commercial room pretty well occupied after the reading stopping with them till twelve o'clock.

**Thursday 22nd.** Should have gone with Chattwood and others to dine at Carr in Birkle, but day was foggy and I not very well, so excused, and the dinner was put off. At night, had again a rather good attendance at reading, though the weather was foggy and unfavourable. Read again till nearly ten o'clock, very much applauded. Kept company in the travellers room until twelve o'clock when slept, as before in a good warm bed. Chattwood handed over to me £9.11.3 and I gave Tweddell 15/- and would have given him more, for his trouble, but Chattwood said 10/- would be enough.

**Balance sheet** *for Bamford's two readings at Bury, 21 and 22 December.* [34]

|  | £ | s. | d. |
|---|---|---|---|
| 41 named subscribers, 1s. to £1 | 10 | 2 | 6 |
| On door, first night |  | 6 | 0 |
| On door, second night |  | 2 | 9 |
| Tickets sold |  | 4 | 0 |
| Total receipts | 10 | 15 | 3 |
| Expenses (room, printing) | 1 | 4 | 0 |
| Profit | 9 | 11 | 3 |

Tom Crompton, I am sorry to hear was a defaulter for monies which he had collected and his bondsmen had to make up the deficiency; he is not now in any office under the towns supervision and he appears rather low and downcast. I should have called on G. Booth pawnbroker, to take a cup of his excellent elderberry wine, but the fog was so dense, I and Tweddell could scarcely see our way. I coughed very much, so we returned to the Albion. John Kay called to see me, and I paid for a glass of rum, and gave him a shilling. Tweddell afterwards conducted me (I could not, by any possibility have found the way for the fogg) to the railway and I came off by the L&Y[35] line to Middleton Junction: train to Middleton just gone – as usual – so I walked it almost suffocated with fogg. At Middleton it was still worse, so I stepped into the Asshetons Arms and stopped there until the 'bus came at two o'clock when I returned home.

---

34. Editors' arrangement. The figures suggest audiences of 55–60 in all, or 25–30 a night.
35. Lancashire & Yorkshire Railway Company.

**Saturday 24th.** Received a dozen Bury Times and a letter (see annexed) the newspaper part of the business very badly done: several glaring errors, and misprints. I was very much chagrined and wrote to Tweddell about it.[36]

**Report**, *from the* Bury Times, *23 December 1859, of Bamford's recent readings, prefaced with the text of his circular, "Right against wrong".*

---

### MR. BAMFORD'S READINGS

Who has not heard of Samuel Bamford, the veteran Radical Reformer and political sufferer of the dark days of 1817–19, and one of the most gifted of our Lancashire bards and prose writers? To many of the inhabitants of the important district in which the *Bury Times* circulates, Mr Bamford is not only known as an author, but as a man "who dared be honest in the worst of times," and who forever maintained a high character in private life. He has not a few acquaintances who are proud to call him friend; accordingly it was with great pleasure that several[37] of the people of our town met Mr. Bamford, on the evenings of Wednesday and Thursday last, in the Albion Assembly Room, to listen to his readings from the Lancashire poets and prose-writers and to be amused and instructed by his illustrations of the Lancashire dialect. His stalwart form and massive head, crowned with the locks now whitened by 72 winters, would at once strike a stranger as belonging to no ordinary man; and when, in his plain and unpretending manner, he narrates incidents in his own life, or gives readings of his native dialect, one feels at once that Mr Bamford is himself thoroughly Lancashire, and possessed in no small degree of that Anglo-Saxon energy which has made this comparatively barren district one of the most important in the world. Mr Bamford is one of the few men living who are freely conversant with the Lancashire dialect so as to be able to interest an audience therewith, and the applause he met with on both evenings in Bury proved that he has not mistaken his vocation. As we pen this notice, we cannot help feeling, that it is to the labours and sufferings of men like Samuel Bamford that we owe the liberty of the press and the right of public meeting, which now makes England really "the envy of surrounding nations, and the admiration of the world." We trust that Mr. Bamford's announcement, which will be found in our advertising columns, will secure him many other audiences in this neighbourhood, assured as we are that they will go away delighted with the veteran's entertaining and instructive reading.

---

**Letter**, *George Tweddell, 21 Union Square, Bury, to Bamford, 24 December 1859.*

My Dear Mr Bamford,
I have posted you a dozen copies of the *Bury Times* containing your advertisement and my notice of your readings. The former is towards the bottom of the fifth

---

36. Bamford's letter to Tweddell is missing, but Tweddell's reply and Bamford's rejoinder give a good idea of its contents.
37. Bamford has written here: "hundreds".

column of the second page in what *I* should consider a good place. The notice, which Mr Heap had inserted without the least alteration, (for which I feel obliged to him) is in the second column of the third page. I thought it was best to write something that would be useful to quote, if necessary; and, though the paragraph was very hastily dashed off, and anything but laboured, I can assure you that it is perfectly honest, as it really expresses the truth as I feel it. God grant that every young man may feel as I do, and I can <u>then</u> assure you that <u>the liberties of England are safe</u>. But, alas! the Money Bag is the God of the many. I hope that you will have some good audiences during these long evenings in the various towns and villages of the Northern Counties, but you must not trust to mere advertising; a personal canvass for the sale of tickets in places where the Reformers are too apathetic to do it for you, alone will serve. I would also, if you will allow me, advise you to <u>stick</u> to the "Lancashire Dialect", and to a few of your own poems, and to selections from your "Life", as in these things you will stand without a rival; if you go more into general poems, even of Lancashire authors, but not in the dialect, every poor half-starved strolling player out of employment will if you begin to draw good companies, take up the calling. I know that no other man can come before the people with your claims; but few men have the kindness of heart of my poor old Grandfather, who allowed his old horse, "Tinker," to graze in the pasture for years after he was past service, simply because he had done his duty in former days. You resemble "Tinker" in having for many years "done the state some service," but I trust that you are not yet past service, – that there is years of good work in you yet, and I have no doubt that you will be able to do good by your readings. I know you will excuse the liberty I have taken in giving this advice, and only impute it to a sincere wish for your welfare. I write in great haste, but will be glad to hear from you at any time. I saw Mr Chattwood last night, and Mr Livsey this morning, and they both join me in kind love to you. I hear, from a dozen different people, that the poor old man who called upon you on Friday morning at the Albion (Kay) is held in very low estimation, and that he is quite a political renegade. The last vote he gave was in 1852, <u>against</u> the Reform candidate, and he has not had a vote since. I feel it an ungracious thing to write thus of a poor old infirm man whom I never saw before, but as he told you, in my hearing, that he was still a Radical, and talked of calling upon you, and as I (like others) noticed you give him something, I feel it a duty I owe to you, as your friend, to give you this information, though I trust I have too much charity in me to trample upon the fallen. Wishing you a Happy Xmas, I am Dear Mr Bamford,

> Yours very faithfully,
> George N. Tweddell.

**Sunday 25th.**  Wrote to Tweddell again as follows.

***Copy letter**, Bamford to George Tweddell, Bury, 25 December 1859.*

My Dear Tweddell,
I wrote to you this morning in haste, and now, resume my pen to write more at length, and first, in the due order of reply to your letter. I can readily believe that your paragraph was "dashed off in haste," since to me it *now* appears plain, that in your haste, after the word *several*, you forgot to insert, what no doubt you intended doing, the word "hundreds" making it read, as I am sure you meant it should, "several hundreds"; if it was not your mistake. it must have been that of the compositor, and the misfortune has been, after all, that you did not make sure and see a proof, before you resigned the matter to the office. I have long made it a rule, never to trust a compositor, when I can possibly see a proof myself. This however, as I said before, must be prominently corrected next Saturday. Meantime, I have amended with the pen, the dozen papers you sent me.

Some liberties also, have been taken with my copy at the office; and I must candidly confess, I don't like liberties, even the most trifling, to be presumed upon at any time. My circular is headed "Right against Wrong," and the compositor has made it "Right and Wrong" which is quite a different meaning, depriving the advertisement of its first strong and prompt appeal to attention: this interference ought not, by any means, to have been permitted. Then again, the proof cannot have been carefully read to copy. "Such a summary," it stands in the newspaper, the word is, being omitted, and so making nonsense of the expression. My "Mosston, Harperhey," is made into Moston, Harpurhey, which is entirely setting aside the copy, and following authorities which know not either the right orthography, or the derivation of the names: Compositors, it seems to me, aught to stick to their letters: and not to scan either the words or the sense of the matter they have in hand. The thing, as it stands in print, has certainly been a mistake; and I chiefly regret it because it may adversely influence engagements at other places. I thank you for your suggestions with respect to my course of future readings: I think your advice is very good; and if I don't wholly adopt it, I shall bear it often in mind. I may add, that, nearly the same advice has been more than once tendered to me; namely, to adhere to my own writings, and the story of my own life. George Wilson, the Newalls Buildings George, so advised me after my reading at Chorlton on Medlock. My thanks to you are not, however less on that account.

I inclose you a dozen postage stamps, and hope you will have the goodness to forward me papers to that amount, on Saturday next, in order that I may replace those of this week by a corrected impression; please forward them on Saturday, that I may receive them on Sunday morn. I send you 18 postage stamps for which let me have two or three papers and an Oddfellows Reciter by book parcel.[38]

I thank also you for your intimation respecting Old John Kay: you have just acted as a true friend, in all such cases ought, and would act, namely to warn me of unworthy associates. I had heard before, something about Johns being shabby in his political dealings: but he was an old friend, of 30 years ago; blind and

---

38. Sentence added in margin.

distressed, as I understood, and I could not pass his door without calling to see
him: he did not therefore obtrude his visit on me, and when I see him again
I shall rate him about his desertion of the old cause.

Dear Tweddell,

Yours truly,

Samuel Bamford.

**Saturday 26th.**  Received an invitation to the funeral of my old friend and neighbour
James Dyson, and in the afternoon attended it at Middleton.[39]

**Thursday 29th.**  Wrote to the Secretary of Blakeley Mechanics Institution.

***Copy letter***, *Bamford to C.L. Delaunay, Blackley, 29 December 1859.*

Mr Secretary

I will thank you to let me have an account of whatever money charges you have
against me on behalf of the Institution. You will also please to erase my name
from the list of members, as I do not wish longer to continue one.

Yrs Obedtly

Samuel Bamford.

**Friday 30th.**  Went to Manchester; took the file of the Manchester Guardian to the
Peel Park Library, and did not bring any other work out: sat 2 hours, reading a work
on the Druidical Temples of Wiltshire and then walked to John Heywoods in
Deansgate: paid him £1.2.0 for [the] Early Days I had had 21st Aug: took a glass with
R.J.Richardson, and talked about Rogersons affairs: Mr W. Fairbairn[40] had, he told
me, sent £25 to Mrs Rogerson, and she had not up to that time, acknowledged it – just
as usual – several other persons had also given Richardson money on her account and
Peacock had promised on half of one of his musical performances in the Free Trade
Hall. Sat with G. and others a couple of hours at Belfields, and then called at Kelleys
and so to the omnibus.

At Barns Green found a young man who gave his address as James Taylor 103,
Chester Road, Hulme. This person, I have some reasons for thinking, was a spy, sent to
learn my opinions and leanings on various questions. I did not like either the
appearance or the manner of the fellow, and he went away, not much wiser than he
came.[41] He had I understood, been waiting to see me during several hours; he
professed to feel greatly interested by my character, some account of which he had
found in the columns of the Bury Times. I did not altogether confide in him,

---

39. James Dyson (d. 1859), Middleton weaver and reformer, and a key defence witness (for Bamford in
    particular) at the Peterloo trial; see *The Trial of Henry Hunt and Others* (1820), 104–7, and entry for
    31 December 1859.
40. Sir William Fairbairn (1789–1874), self-made manufacturing engineer, prominent in mid-Victorian
    scientific circles; MCL.
41. These two sentences added opposite.

particularly as he was vouched for, by <u>two</u> persons residing in this neighbourhood, in whom I had very little faith: he however professed the strongest friendship, and as I did not know that his professions were not real I did not, indeed I could not, do less than act permissively, giving him implied credit for what he professed. I conversed with him in a manner as confidential as I thought the occasion warranted, promising also to forward to him a packet of my circulars; he undertaking to get me up a reading at Hulme. He went back by the nine o'clock Omnibus, and I came home.

**Saturday 31st.** At home all day, comforting my thirst with occasional tots of my wife's last brew. Very pleasant is a draught of good brown ale, under such circumstances: may I never want it.

Received the annexed letter from my friend Tweddell of Bury. I really don't know what to make of his construction of the word <u>several</u>: to me it appears the most perverse interpretation of a word which I ever knew. He may say what he will, and others may back him, but, beyond all dispute, or cavil, the word, as he employs it <u>damns</u> the whole of his paragraph about my reading at Bury.

*Letter*, George Tweddell, Bury, to Bamford, 31 December 1859.[42]

My Dear Mr Bamford,
I have to acknowledge the receipt of your two letters, the latter enclosing Postage Stamps to the amount of 1/6, for Oddfellows' Reciter and copies of Bury Times. The Reciter was posted by return: the copies of the Times will be sent off as soon as I can obtain them. I am sorry that any errors should have occurred in your Advertisement ... But I did not mean to describe the *whole* of your audience as "acquaintances who are proud to call you friend," and who accordingly met you with such great pleasure. You must be aware that that great part of your audience had no previous knowledge of you worth naming; and that even if I had reckoned the whole of them (as a careful reading of the notice will show I did not) in the passage which has given you offence, I could not have truthfully have written "several hundreds." Mr Chattwood – the most critical of my acquaintances – had pronounced the notice "a first rate one," before I heard your opinion of it; and I have heard numbers of people, who had no idea that I had written it, speak of it as one of the most favourable paragraphs that could be given. It is evident that they do not look upon the expression you complain of, as "damning the whole notice." Mr Chattwood has supplied Mr Heap with the number of tickets sold, and the amount of money received for them, to insert in his "notices to correspondents," as if in answer to an Inquirer. This will put the *number* in the most favourable point of view, as the greater number of tickets were not used on account of the weather, engagements, and other causes. Mr Wrigley, for instance, took £1 worth of tickets, and forgot all about them until next morning, (Friday) when it was too late to give them away ... on again looking over the notice, I must confess I can

---

42. This letter cut where indicated; Tweddell replies patiently to Bamford's criticisms of detail.

see no real cause for complaint, you will not consider me petted or conceited when I express my sorrow for having undertaken to furnish the paragraph ...

Wishing you a Merry Xmas, and that health and happiness may be yours for many years,

I remain, Dear Sir,

Yours very faithfully,

Geo. N. Tweddell.

**Cutting**, *from the "replies to correspondents" section*, Bury Times, *31 December 1859.*

---

INQUIRER.

In reply to your question as to the success of Mr Samuel Bamford's Readings at Bury, we are able to state that there were sold 123 tickets for the reserved seats, and 154 for the second seats. The total receipts (including money taken at the doors) were £10. 5s. 3d.

---

31 Sat. The above appears in the Bury Times. The following articles appear in the Middleton Albion of this day.

**Article**, *from the* Middleton Albion, *31 December 1859, the text of a piece given by Bamford at his recent reading in Mills Hill: a comic conversation, partly in dialect, set in a wooded part of Alkrington near Middleton, between an unemployed weaver called "Simpler", a gentleman called "Factfinder", and "Squire Acreland", touching upon the beauties of the woodland, the way to identify a gentleman, and the time and money wasted by unemployed weavers seeking work.*[43]

**Obituary**, *from the* Middleton Albion, *31 December 1859, of James Dyson, one of the "humble great" and a veteran reformer of the period 1817–19.*

So ends 1859.

---

43. The piece is reported to have been taken from Bamford's *Walks*, but does not appear in the 1972 reprint, edited by J.D. Marshall.

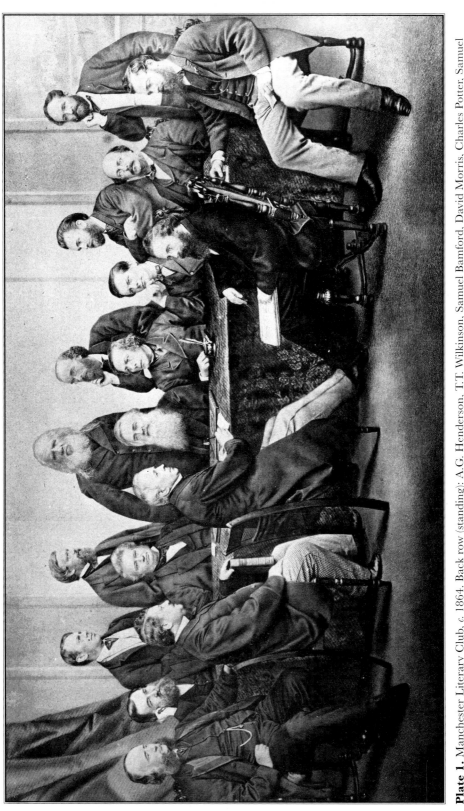

**Plate 1.** Manchester Literary Club, *c.* 1864. Back row (standing): A.G. Henderson, T.T. Wilkinson, Samuel Bamford, David Morris, Charles Potter, Samuel Smith. Middle row (behind table): Joseph Chattwood, Charles Hardwick, John Harland, William(?) Richardson, Ben Brierley, F. Trachsel, Edwin Waugh. Front row (in front of table): John Page, J.P. Stokes, Charles Swain, Anon.

**Plate 2.** Middleton's leading citizens gathered at the annual Agricultural Show in 1864, including 1. Thomas Dickins, with wife and daughter; 2. Henry Whalley; 3. Dr Oswald Dickin; 4. Thomas Mills of the *Middleton Albion*; 5. Edmond Howarth.

**Plate 3.** Samuel Bamford, photographed by Jackson Brothers of Middleton, 1856.

**Plate 4.** Jemima Bamford, photographed by Jackson Brothers of Middleton (entry for 16 September 1858).

**Plate 5.** Samuel Bamford: the "stereoscopic likeness" which he sold to promote himself (entries for 2, 5 and 8 March 1859).

**Plate 6.** Thomas Mills, of the *Middleton Albion*, a supporter and friend of Bamford.

**Plate 7.** Samuel Mellalieu, whom Bamford regarded as an enemy (entry for 15 April 1859).

**Plate 8.** The Old Boar's Head, Middleton, where Bamford did a public reading in July 1859. It still contains a "Sam Bamford room".

# LITERARY EXERCISES.

## SAMUEL BAMFORD

**Respectfully informs the inhabitants of Middleton and the adjacent townships that, on the Evening of**

# WEDNESDAY NEXT,

### At the Assembly Room, Boar's Head Inn, Middleton,

#### HE PURPOSES

# READING AND RECITING

### Extracts from his own works, and those of other Authors.

He will also, if required, enter into statements as to when he ceased being a handloom weaver; what employment he next adopted, when he ceased that employment, why he ceased it. Why he removed to London, the nature of his employment there, why he ceased to be so employed, with correspondence relative to the same. His present engagements, his future prospects, and various other matters.

The Doors will be open at half-past Seven, the Exercises will commence at Eight. TICKETS: Platform One Shilling, Front Seats Sixpence, other seats Threepence. Tickets may be had at the above Inn, of Mr. Wm. Jones, Rhodes, and at the Printer's.

*7th July,* 1859.

T. MILLS, PRINTER AND BOOKBINDER, MIDDLETON.

**Plate 9.** Poster for Bamford's Middleton reading, 7 July 1859.

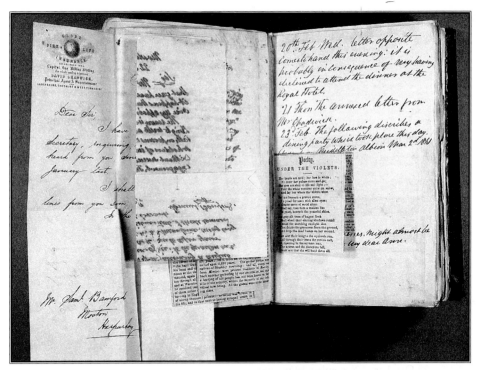

**Plate 10.** A typically crowded page of the diary, with entries, letters in and out, newscutting, and comments by Bamford. (Entries for 20–23 February 1861).

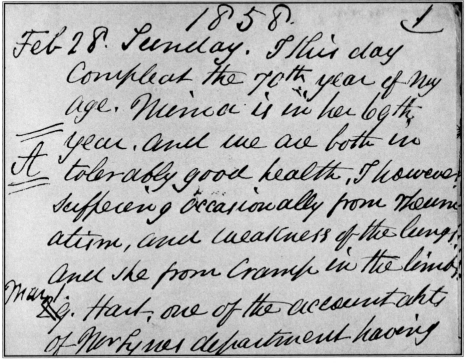

**Plate 11.** The opening of the diary.

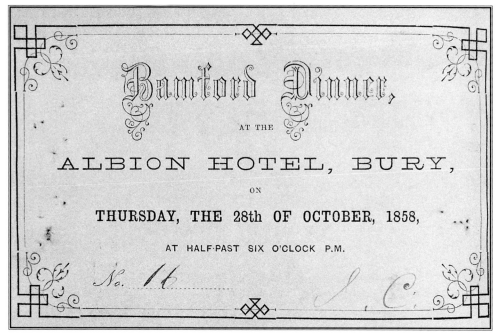

**Plate 12.** A ticket for the dinner in Bury that marked Bamford's return to the reform platform (entries for 28 October–3 November 1858, and Appendix 2).

**Plate 13.** Moston Bottoms, *c.* 1867. Despite its closeness to Manchester, the Moston in which Bamford lived remained semi-rural.

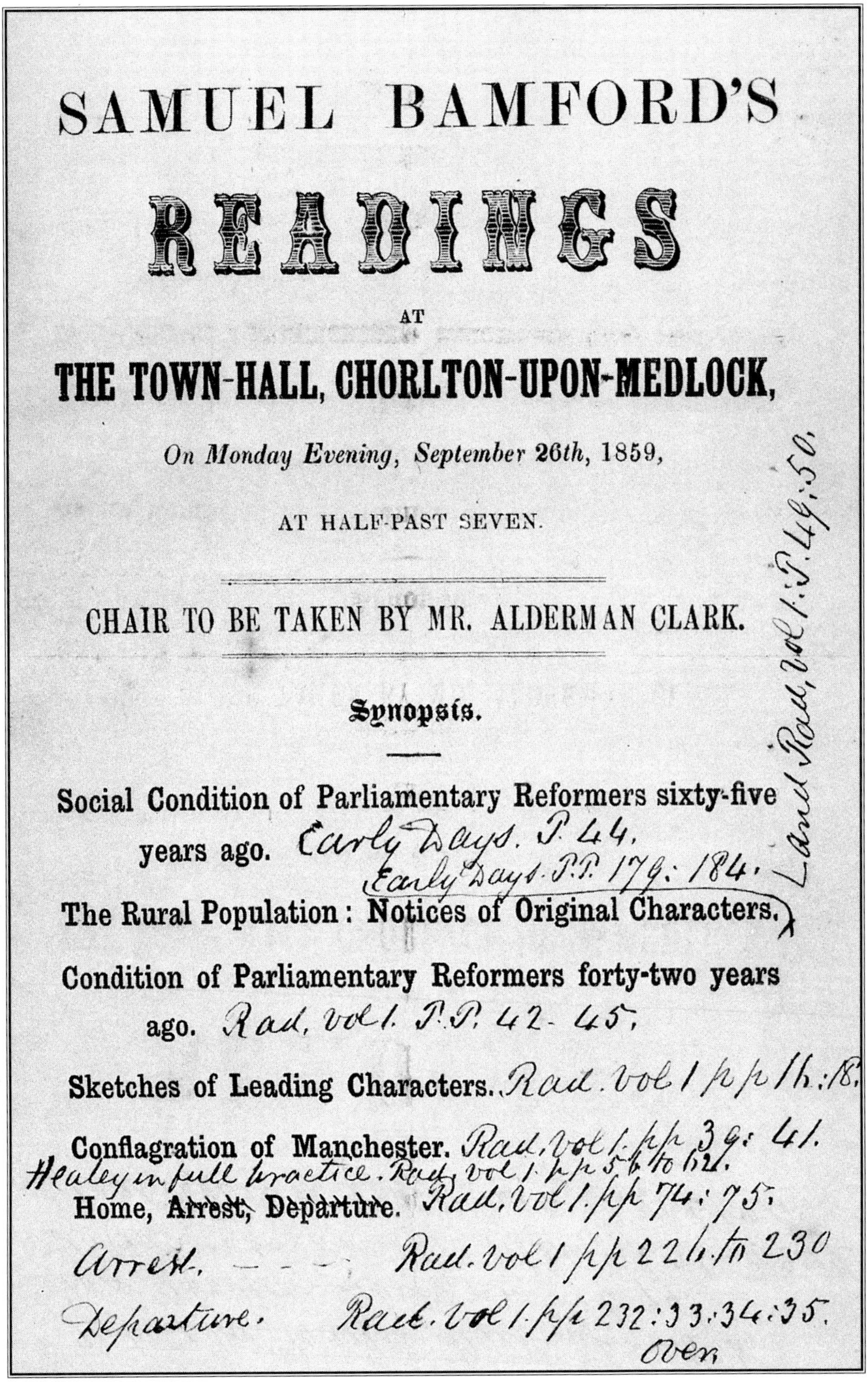

# SAMUEL BAMFORD'S

# READINGS

AT

# THE TOWN-HALL, CHORLTON-UPON-MEDLOCK,

On Monday Evening, September 26th, 1859,

AT HALF-PAST SEVEN.

## CHAIR TO BE TAKEN BY MR. ALDERMAN CLARK.

## Synopsis.

Social Condition of Parliamentary Reformers sixty-five years ago. *Early Days. P. 44.*
*Early Days. P.P. 179: 184.*

The Rural Population : Notices of Original Characters.

Condition of Parliamentary Reformers forty-two years ago. *Rad. vol 1. P.P. 42 - 45.*

Sketches of Leading Characters. *Rad. vol 1 pp 16: 18.*

Conflagration of Manchester. *Rad. vol 1. pp 39: 41.*
*Healey in full practice. Rad. vol 1 pp 56 to 62.*
Home, Arrest, Departure. *Rad. vol 1. pp 74: 75.*

*Arrest. — — —. Rad. vol 1 pp 226 to 230*

*Departure. Rad. vol 1. pp 232: 33. 34: 35.*

*Over.*

*Land Rad. vol 1. P. 49. 50.*

Plate 14. A programme for one of Bamford's readings, with his own annotations; the content was carefully planned (entries for 19–26 September 1859).

# 8

# POVERTY AND PRIDE

*The new year began for the Bamfords with a heartwarming mystery gift, eventually explained three weeks later; a visit from Dronsfield on 22 January, with the new baby named "Bamford", completes a happy episode. Bamford's drive for self-reliance faltered and slid towards a devastating setback. Plans for readings in Manchester and Prestwich came to nothing, while the Reform movement's way nationally appeared to be blocked by the new Palmerston government. Hence, when friends in Burnley arranged for Bamford to visit there, it was for the apolitical occasion of the annual soirée of the Mechanics' Institute, and Bamford's reminiscences of the heroic self-improvers of his youth were, to his disgust, largely ignored in some of the press reports. To make matters worse, Bamford caught a chill after the meeting and for the first two weeks of February he was apparently too ill to write up his diary. The report of his illness in the press, prompted an admirer from Oldham, the journalist R.S. Gowenlock, to make an appeal on the Bamfords' behalf. It is hard to tell who was the more hurt by this encounter: Bamford, in his humiliating sense that Gowenlock's letter had "torn the veil of decent privacy away" and turned an old radical into an object of pity, or Gowenlock, in having an honest attempt to help so publicly thrown back in his face. The whole tragic and painful episode damaged both Bamford's self-image and his credit with his friends and supporters, and speaks volumes about the gulf of understanding between the classes in Victorian England.*

## 1860

**Sunday January 1st.** This morning, when Mima opened the door a man put down a small tea chest, saying the carriage was paid. In reply to her questions he said it came last night by Omnibus, and was going away when she asked him if he would have a glass of ale, which he declined, intimating that he had not time to stop: he seemed wishful to avoid being much noticed, and went down the street without delay or further comment. On my coming down stairs we opened the box and found it prettily ornamented inside with evergreens, rosettes, and an inscription "A Happy new year to you." It was nearly filled with a fillet of a leg of mutton, a good lump of cheese, a mutton pie: sundry cakes, several mince pies, raisins, sweetmeats etc., and two small bottles, one containing a noggin of whiskey, with a written paper pasted on it inscribed "a toothful for the awd veteran Bard! Sam Beamforth," and the other "a drop of spirits of comfort for Little Cherry Bud, Mima" the latter being brandy.

Who this handsome token of remembrance has been sent by, I have not the most remote certain idea. Joseph Ramsbottom called during the forenoon, and we talked about poets and poetry, and at night an old neighbour from Charlestown, and her daughter stepped in and those, with Mrs Hall occasionally calling, were the whole of our visitors on this day.

**Monday 2nd.** Set off to post a letter, and walk as far as Brierleys. Also to make enquiry at the Omnibus office, respecting the box which we had received; and which the man said came by the 'bus on Saturday night: At the office nothing was known of such a thing. Met Brierley who was coming to my house, and having posted my letter we returned and came back together. I told Brierley all about the box, but he seemed not to know anything about it, and after taking one glass in accordance with the custom of the season, he went to see a friend in Hulme, to make enquiries about a suitable room to have a reading in, and also to learn something probably about the Mr Taylor who came to see me on Friday last.

Went in the afternoon to tea, with my wife at the house of our landlord, next door; we were most plenteously entertained. Myself, wife, his brother, brother in law, three sisters in law, Mr and Mrs Hall and their girl Elizabeth: After tea general conversation ensued, and at Mr Halls request, I read Jimmy the Jobber, from Brierleys "A Day Out," this gave great satisfaction, and afterwards I read several extracts from my "Radical" which also seemed to please much! We spent a very cheerful and agreeable evening, and came home about ten o'clock.

**Tuesday 3rd.** Went to Middleton, and very foolishly spent 5/- in Xmasing amongst friends. Mima went to Brierleys, and there got a hint that the box had been sent by Dronsfield, Travis, and a few friends at Hollinwood. I must thank them by brewing a peck and inviting them over.

**Wednesday 4th.** The annexed note from Burnley.

*Letter*, *T.T. Wilkinson*,[1] *2 Cheapside, Burnley, to Bamford, 3 January 1860.*

Dear Sir,
When I met you at Sir James Kay-Shuttleworths, you intimated something respecting lecturing in Burnley but, if I remember rightly we did not think that a proper time for you to do so.

We are now, however, about to hold our Annual Soiree, at the Mechanics Institute on the 2nd of February next, and our Directors would very much wish you to be present. You have many admirers here and your presence would form a good introduction to them.

If you agree to accept our invitation you will not be required to give more than an address of about 20 minutes in length – your expenses will be paid – and you will be well provided for at the expense of the Institution. Sir James is expected to be present, probably as chairman.

Personally, I may state that your being here would give me the greatest pleasure; I should be accounted a flatterer by the multitude were I to state how much your whole character is admired by
                    Yours most faithfully,
                         T.T. Wilkinson.

**Thursday 5th.** I write to say they may expect me.

---

1. T.T. Wilkinson (1815–75), master at Burnley Grammar School, active in the Burnley Mechanics' Institute and the Union of Lancashire and Cheshire Institutes, author and literary figure; *Preston Guardian*, 10 February 1875. (See Plate 1.)

**Friday 6th.** Took a walk through Blakeley, Crumpsall, Cheetham Hill, Smedley and Harperhey, home again. At Crum[p]sall Green, looked for, and found with difficulty, the site of the cottage farm house where my once dear Catherine lived when I kept company with her: every vestige of the building is swept away: what was then a neat garden in front of the house, is now a kind of field-garden, and the ground where the house stood, is an open grass covered plot. Everything seems changed, like myself: an old, dim eyed man: alas poor Catherine. She has been in her grave fifty years, and I am left halting and stumbling amid the ruins of old scenes, how changed!

Miss Taylor called with a small Christmas present of plumb pudding and two mince pies for which we could not do less than thank the kind lady: She sat down and talked with me about my own pursuits and I told her frankly how I sought employment by reading and reciting from my own works and those of other authors, and she approved of my scheme: then we conversed about the book I had sent her – Brierleys "A Day Out": she had been from home eleven weeks, at some place in Wales and had not therefore seen me during the time. I told her all about the book, and that the description of "Miss Jackson," in the book, was taken from herself, with some chronological allowances, and "Bunk Ho" was meant for the residence she, at present occupied. She seemed more surprised and amused by this information, than displeased. And who was the author? And what was he? And was I certain he intended as I had said; all of which interrogatories I answered in the affirmative and gave her reasons for so doing. And thanking her again for her kind remembrances, she went away at near dark to walk home.

**Saturday 7th.** Mima put me out of temper by rambling off to Rochdale Road, to Chorltons and Brierleys, so I took another long walk to Newton Heath, under the railway arch at Lamb Lane, past Andrews dye works, and up through Harperhey, home. Went to the tea party at the Mechanics' Institution at night, recited "God Help the Poor," and brought out Joseph Ramsbottom who, after he had recited two excellent pieces, "The poachers soliloquy," and another, of his own productions, I introduced as "the Harperhey poet," shortly I hoped, to become a national one and a name that would live in the annals of literature. The company, at first, seemed taken by surprise, and then gave him fervent and continued applause, I was glad at having been the means of making the Harperhey people acquainted with one whom I am persuaded is destined to win a name that will be enrolled amongst those of the true poets of nature.

**Sunday 8th.** Ramsbottom and a friend came over and we talked about the publication of his poems. I advised him to date them as they were produced, and to print at his own risk, if necessary, a couple of thousands of a tract containing some three or four of his best poems; they would bring his name out and would be sure to sell. He had best however think about it until next Sunday.

**Monday 9th.** A sale of the effects of the late Robert Consterdine. A very good and pretty cradle of mahogany took my attention, and indeed that of everyone who cast an eye upon it. I asked the old woman in care of the things about it, and she said it was about 51 years since it was first used: it was made for Robert (the deceased). Ah, I said, if his poor mother had known that he would ruin his health, squander the property of the family, and die in a madhouse, she would have felt sad indeed, as she rocked him to sleep.

**Tuesday 10th.** A very misty day. I must stop in doors.

**Wednesday 11th.** Had another long walk thro Blakeley, Crumpsall, and Cheetham Hill, to Smedley and home.

**Thursday 12th.** Had an invitation to the Soiree of the Literary Institute at Middleton on the 23d the Hon Algernon Egerton[2] to preside. See their quarters acc[oun]t on the other side: a rather paltry concern it would seem, and an act of much presumption, their pressing him to come and take the chair. He refused their invitation in the first instance, so I have heard, and only consented when they sent a second pressing invitation. After that they set about getting him a place to sleep at, and applied to Mr Lees of Alkrington Hall, who did not know what to make of the proposal, and on Friday, when I was at Middleton had been making enquiries about the matter, poor man, it would seem the idea of lodging an Hon. Egerton, rather perplexed him: a very assured set, these fellows must be: they should have secured lodgings before they invited him.

**Friday 13th.** At Middleton: sent in a note consenting to attend the Soiree.

*Report, from the* Middleton Albion, *14 January 1860, of the quarterly meeting of Middleton Literary Institute, solvent but at a low level of activity. The Secretary, Ambrose Fawcett, remarked that it had suffered from "false promises" of "succour from other quarters", "and the teaching, with one brilliant exception, was confined to a few members, who had sacrificed much time in teaching others, and consequently neglected themselves". The members were advised in future to rely upon their own endeavours.*

**Saturday 14th.** On seeing the report in the Middleton Albion of the financial matters of the Middleton Literary Institute, I regret having promised to attend the Soiree. I think their business, which is of a paltry nature does not authorize them to press for the attendance of gentlemen of high position: it looks almost like a humbug; a hoax, and I don't like it.

The slip opposite I cut from the Ashton and Stayley Bridge Reporter of this day.

*Letter, from the* Ashton Reporter, *14 January 1860, from "Veritas", accusing the poet John Critchley Prince in detail of "being in the habit of palming upon publishers and editors compositions said to be original, but which are in reality only second hand pieces, having been slightly altered in the wording or measure ... One cannot read with pleasure or profit the compositions of a man who plays*

---

2. Algernon Egerton (1825–91), of Worsley Old Hall, son of the first earl of Ellesmere and Conservative MP for South Lancashire 1859–67; *Manchester Guardian*, 15 July 1891.

*such mean tricks upon his friends, and it is to be sincerely hoped we have seen the last of them". The Editor comments: "We hope the exposure will induce him to set more uprightly in future."*

**Saturday 21st.** Went to Middleton and got 250 amended slips printed.

Whilst at Assheton's Arms, H. Shuttleworth and two others came into the smoking; the facial expression of one being very disagreeable to me. Said he was employed at the Manchester Town Hall; but that, I did not entirely credit. Shutt would treat with a glass and so, mine being out, I accepted one at his expense. When first these <u>two</u> came in, they looked at me and at the room, as if uncertain how to act, and then retired. Shutt however came and sat beside me, and we began talking about the condition of farmers, as compared with what it once was, the employment of machinery in farming, and matters of that sort, when the two, who seemed to be with, or to belong to Shutts company, again entered the room, and took part in the conversation: but they seemed suspicious, and uneasy. Shutt intimated that they were on business (with him) as I understood: and in a few minutes they both left the room, followed shortly afterwards by Shuttleworth. I remained some time conversing with another young man and was preparing to leave when the girl entered and took away Shutts glass only half drunk, saying he was upstairs. So I walked down to Mills's and came home.

***Advertisement*** *from the* Middleton Albion, *21 January 1860, for the second annual soirée of Middleton Literary Institution on Monday January 23rd. The list of gentlemen "invited, and ... expected to take part" is headed by the Hon. Algernon Egerton, MP, and includes Samuel Bamford and Edwin Waugh.*

**Saturday 21st.** The following from Dronsfield at Hollinwood.

***Letter****, James Dronsfield, Hollinwood, to Bamford, 20 January 1860.*

Worthy Friends,
I must confess that myself, Travis, and Mason, are the guilty party, and may never worse guilt burthen our consciences.

We agreed to have a friendly joke to enliven our spirits on entering the "New Year," and I am glad to hear of the welcome reception it met with, for I can assure you that it gave us great pleasure to hit upon so happy an idea to show our loving respect to the "Old Happy Pair." Although it was but an humble gift it was accompanied by the good wishes of the givers.

A real emblem of the Lancashire peasantry – <u>Plain without but possessing rich qualities within</u>, hoping that you may both live to enjoy a many Christmas Boxes, is the sincere wish of your humble servant
                              Jas Dronsfield.

P.S. If it should be a favourable day on Sunday next, I and Mrs Dronsfield and the second volume to old Sam "Young Bamford" intend coming to your house after dinner we shall come through Newton by the omnibus. J.D.

Very strangely I read that <u>Sunday</u> into <u>Monday</u>; and was quite surprised when they came and we were not prepared thinking that on Monday we should have time to make all things convenient.[3]

**Sunday 22nd.** Ramsbottom came in the forenoon and had a chat. My wife got an excellent potato pie for dinner, (nearly all potatoes though) and after we had set it away Waugh made his appearance, so we brought out our pie, warmed it in the oven, and made the best excuses we could for so poor a dinner. We had not expected him to dinner, but according to appointment, that he would come on Sunday morning with Charles Hardwick, and have a ramble out to the neighbourhood. They came not however, and we prepared and took the homely meal I have discribed. As I, and Waugh, after dinner were preparing to go out Dronsfield from Hollinwood and his wife with their little baby, <u>Bamford</u>, in her arms, came to the door; so after sitting down a bit, and explaining (for in this case I had been unaccountably mistaken) firmly persuaded that Dronsfield, in his letter mentioned <u>Monday</u>, as the day of their visit, whereas Sunday was the day, Dronsfield, Waugh and myself, went down to Blakeley and had a glass each at the Golden Lion. After that came up to Barns Green to the New Inn, and had several glasses each there. Then came to my house to tea. Brierley joined us at the New Inn, and at near ten o clock the company left. Dronsfields going to Brierleys house, where they stopped all night, and Waugh home to Strangeways.

**Monday 23rd.** Not well at all; so wrote an excuse for not going to the "Grand Soiree and Concert", at Middleton, took part of a glass of whisky toddy, after tea, and during all night was very much hurried in my water; that whisky had certainly been doctored.

**Tuesday 24th.** Went with Brierley to Manchester, to see about a room in Hulme but did not find on[e]. Waugh and Chas Hardwick who promised to come over on Sunday morn. Percy urgent again, to sit for my likeness in chalk. Promised to see Jacksons and speak to them about it.

**Wednesday 25th.** The annexed letter from Dronsfield. This worthy blacksmith is the only person who has hitherto, McDougal excepted, spoken out honestly and candidly about my affairs. Clowes, Waugh, my Bury friends, and Oldham friends, have all been <u>mum</u> on that head.

***Letter***, *James Dronsfield to Bamford, 24 January 1860.*

Worthy Friend,
We stay'd at Brierleys all night and arrived safe at home on the following morning by the 'Bus.
    I must say that I felt rather melancholy after enjoying such a deluge of excessive mirth the over night. I think the whiskey removed the fulcrum of my tongue to the

---

3. Written by Bamford on the letter.

middle, when one end was up the other was down, but I hope there was no offence given. I wanted to draw Waugh out on the subject of "Compensation" or Pension because I think that there is no individual on earth more worthy or that has a more just claim for remuneration than you have. But let them call it what they will, if you ever get it the country will say that you were deserving of it or you must not have had it.

It is the cry of every one I meet with that you ought to have amends for your past sufferings and not be obliged to go from place to place to give readings, at your age it is a task that has broken down the constitution of younger men than you, to stand before a crowded audience in a steaming hot room, and then to turn out and perhaps to travel miles in the chilly night air. I know that you have suffered from the effects of such journeys this winter and for these reasons you ought to have some provision made, for as the old saying is "It is easier walking when they have an horse by the bridle", but after all I should never knuckle to anyone. I admire your firmness in that respect it gives me pleasure to see your mettle sprung and your old Saxon blood flowing through its temple of firmness.

We join in sending our kind love to you both.

James Dronsfield.

P.S. I have been thinking that this little drama of yours is worth of being sent to one of the local newspapers, viz. "The Christmas Box" but I will not send it without your consent. Drop me a line early.

**Wednesday 25th.** The affair of the Middleton "Grand Soiree and Concert" has turned out worse than I expected. The annexed letter will explain.

**Letter**, *Thomas Mills to Bamford, 24 January 1860.*

My Dear Mr Bamford,

I beg to forward you slips as ordered I trust they will answer your intentions.

I am very sorry you could not make it convenient to come over to the Soiree last night; it seemed that the strangest fatality had thrown itself over the whole concern. Of the invited guests who figured on the placard the following were absent – of course some unavoidably others not so as you will learn hereafter.

Hon (?) Algernon Egerton
Rev. T Clulow
Rev. Marmaduke Miller
Rev. J. Kightley
Jas. Lees Esqe JP
Dr Hudson
Mr Saml Bamford
Mr Edwin Waugh

Of the unavoidable absentees I need say nothing; those who really could not attend by circumstance over which they had no control must be excused, but what can be said of a person who is styled Honorable and who unmistakeably says

I will be with you to preside over your meeting if you fix the day for the 23rd inst., and then at the last moment shabbily sneaks out of his obligation to redeem his word of honor. On Monday morning (Yesterday) the Secretary of the Institution receive a letter as did Mr Dickins informing them that the Hon. A. Egerton had received a letter from some parties acquainting him that the Institute was composed of a body of <u>extreme Radicals Infidels opposed to church and state etc. etc. etc.</u> principles of course quite opposed to those of the honorable gentleman, therefore under these circumstances he is compelled to withdraw himself from his engagement. Mr Dickins and the Secretary have an interview which resulted in Mr D. proceeding to Worsley to see Mr Egerton to disabuse his mind of the false impression which had been conveyed. Well the upshot is the gentleman is sorry to have been so deceived but upon receipt of the dastardly letter he engaged himself with other parties so that he seems to be in a fix, but mind you for private and confidential reasons cannot consent to give up the letter.

I really felt troubled for the young men, there had been no attempt to deceive in the least. Mr Egerton had been fully made acquainted with the state of the institute, and here the poor innocent victims are hoaxed and made a laughing stock of by certain scrubby ill disposed parties – our political adversaries. But the members have been wrongly abused for I have little doubt were they individually canvassed as to their politics I am strongly of opinion that there would be formed a majority in favour of the Honorable gentleman who had so very handsomely set them down as extreme Radicals; would they were Rads. I say what a contrast have we here of the Rads and the Blues; how was it last year under the presidency of John Cheetham Esq his predecessor as Parliamentary representative?
A different state of things was it not. But of course it is just as well as could be expected.

Nothing but disappointment will accrue to the working classes of this country if they hang their faith upon tories.

I must however conclude as time is pressing promising you additional information when I meet with you.

I therefore remain<br>
Yours truly,<br>
T. Mills.

God forgive me if I am wrong, but I cannot help a suspicion that the three men I saw at Middleton on Saturday, had something to do with the concocting of the calumnious letter to Egerton. Shutt. is a decided tory; and the appearance and manner of the other two, excited my strong aversion. Why however, I scarcely know, except that I did not like them. The following from Manchester Examiner and Times Thursday 26 Jan.

**Letter**, *from the* Manchester Examiner, *26 January 1860, from "A RAD", attacking the Hon. Algernon Egerton for pulling out of the Literary Institute soirée.*

**Thursday February 2nd.** Took the 3.40 train at Salford station, for Rose Grove, intending to go to Gauthorpe Hall before Burnley, but we were a long time in going, and near Huncoyt[4] we broke down the end of the cylinder coming out, and letting all the water run upon the line. So turned back to Accrington, and after considerable delay we set forward again, but as I found I should be too late for calling at Gauthorpe, I went on to Burnley, paying the difference in fare 1d. An hour after time when we got to Burnley: felt unwell, as indeed I had done before leaving home, not being quite well during several days. Went into a respectable looking Inn, and got a hot glass of whisky toddy and warmed myself, for I felt cold and chilly. Then went to Mr Wilkinsons 4 Cheapside, took a cup of tea with him, but it was not of my sort, besides I was not in condition for anything. Went with him to the Soiree, the place was a large and handsome room quite filled: Colonel Townley[5] had just taken the chair, with him on the platform were Lord Norreys, Gen. Scarlett,[6] Sir James Kay Shuttleworth, and many gentlemen and manufacturers of the neighbourhood. Gen. Scarlett moved and spoke, as see annexed.[7]

**Report**, *from the* Burnley Advertiser, *4 February 1860, of the annual soirée of Burnley Mechanics' Institute. General Scarlett spoke in favour of the motion "That the education of the artisan and the operative is of great public advantage, inasmuch as it tends to stimulate invention, to promote discovery, and to advance the arts." He warned that "unless education led the intellect to greater probity and right principles it was more of a curse than a benefit", and praised the Volunteer Movement, hoping that many educated at the Institute "might turn their minds to military matters and be of benefit to their country".*

... Whilst I followed by saying the resolution was so self evident it did not admit of disquisition and so in illustration I would give them the history of a poor lad who made his way to fame and fortune by his own unaided talent. I then narrated to them how I met a gentleman at the gates of Cobbett's farm at Barn Elms near London, who, being starved off his loom at Gooden Lane Heywood, enlisted in a Cavalry regiment and went with Wellington through all his campaigns of Portugal, Spain, and France, and at the Battle of Waterloo was a Captain of the 10th hussars. When peace was made in 1815 he came home, and married a lady worth 80 thousand pounds, who brought him one son and died leaving him the interest of her property and his half pay to live upon and to bring his son up which he was doing by educating him as a Barrister. On my expressing an opinion that his advance in life must have been caused by some peculiar trait in his personal character, or by some strange coincidence of events, he s[ai]d he was never drunk in his life; when he first entered the army he did not know a letter in a book, but with his bounty money, he bought elementary books and made himself master of reading, next of writing, and so prepared himself for the duties of a non commissioned

---

4. Huncoat.
5. Colonel John Towneley (1803–76), substantial landowner of pre-Norman Conquest stock, MP for Sligo 1848, 1852–3, one of the principal promoters of the Burnley Mechanics' Institute; *Manchester Guardian*, 6 November 1876.
6. Sir James Yorke Scarlett, GCB (1799–1872), youngest son of the 1st Lord Abinger, distinguished himself in the Crimean War; he resided at Bank Hall, Burnley, and was a prominent local patron; MCL.
7. Perhaps Bamford's response to General Scarlett's speech was provoked in part by his bearing the same name as James Scarlett, the prosecuting counsel at Bamford's trial for treason at York in 1820.

officer. He was always, with his horse and accoutrements ready for service, and if a man was wanted instanter for any duty, they knew where to find him. His regiment was generally with the advanced guard; with General Pictons "fighting brigade", as it was called; they were often in action, and lost many officers and men, and as the former fell, he gradually stepped forward and took their places, until he attained the rank of Captain. On my saying that a life like his, ought to be committed to writing and given to the press, he said he wished to have done so when he retired from the service, but he found he was short of grammar, and did not know whether he was writing sense or nonsense. This stopped him, and he sought the society of literary characters. Cobbett, he knew very well, and had often been in his company. Other men of literary celebrity he had also become acquainted with. At length he bought Cobbetts and Lindley Murrays Grammar, and commenced writing and studying grammar every morning, from five to 8 o'clock, and in a short time he was as good a grammarian as Cobbett himself.

This account I gave the meeting as the best comment which I could make on the resolution. When I entered on the narrative the "gentlemen of the press," as they term themselves, treated it as they would have done a piece of reading out of a book, and like blockheads as they were, they laid down their pencils and shut their books. The Manchester Examiner and Times, dismisses my speech as follows.

**Cutting**, *from the* Manchester Examiner and Times, *4 February 1860.*

---

MR. SAMUEL BAMFORD seconded the resolution, and in doing so contrasted the facilities which existed now for the acquisition of knowledge, in comparison with what existed when he was a boy. At the conclusion of his speech, he recited his "Song of heroes."

---

Whilst the stupid and stultified Guardian merely says, Mr Samuel Bamford gave an address (or speech) replete with personal reminiscences.

**Newspaper cutting**, *unattributed, giving a short summary of Bamford's Burnley speech.*

---

SAMUEL BAMFORD, Esq., in seconding the resolution, said that the honourable and gallant General had so well described the resolution that he need not say one word about it, for to say that the education of the working classes was beneficial was to say that white was white and black was black; however, it was a very pleasant truth, and one they should endeavour to realise. He could recollect the time when there was nothing like that assembly to be seen or heard of in the country. He told how, with great difficulty, in Middleton, a number of young men formed a kind of institution, and purchased a number of books for their instruction, and how, after a time, it fell into the hands of persons who broke it up altogether. He also related a touching anecdote of a weaver, who entered the army, being unable either to read or write, but who, by diligent study and perseverance, won his way by degrees until he was made captain, He concluded by reciting a poem, written by himself, after hearing of the glorious deeds done by our brave army in the Crimea.

---

Sir James Kay Shuttleworth, in seconding a vote of thanks to the Chairman took occasion to pay me a high compliment as one of those by whose exertions the prosperity they at present enjoyed had been realized: it was to such men as I they were indebted for the comforts of their present position: there I sat, a humble individual whom he was proud to call his friend.

From the Soiree I went with Sir James in his pheaton to Gawthorpe Hall, in doing which I think I increased my cold, for I was quite warm at coming out of the room, and the night air was chilly. I spent a very comfortable night in my excellent bed, but at morning felt bowels disturbed, and I was parched with thirst. During a walk after breakfast, Sir James gave me a sovereign, and after questioning me as to my means of living said – so I understood him – that he would see if something could not be done towards permanent, – or a better provision for me – Parted from my kind host, and his kind sister, Miss Kay, and arrived in Manchester in due course.

On the platform at Salford saw Mr Thos Wrigley of Timberhurst Bury, and Mr John Grundy, solicitor of the same town, both of whom having passed me, just turned round and looked, passed on and did take any further notice of me, nor I of them; I despised their money pride, more sincerely I dare assert, than did they my humble poverty. Got home unwell, quite disorganised in health, and so laid, sent for the doctor and took physic. Doctor says I must keep in bed and remain as quiet as I can.

**Letter**, *T.T. Wilkinson, Burnley, to Bamford, 30 January 1860.*

My dear Sir,
It has been arranged this evening that you may <u>second</u> the Report. I send you one enclosed and a programme. The Directors would suggest that you introduce a pleasant anecdote or two respecting your early days, or respecting your efforts at self-instruction in youth, into your address. You will know how best to select from the many incidents in your life.
   Hoping to see you in good time, I remain, Dear Sir,
                Yours very truly
                T.T. Wilkinson.

**Saturday 4th.** The above from the Directors of the Burnley Mechanics Institution, and acting on their suggestion, my address was thrown out by the reporters, as something not worthy of a place in their notes.

**Tuesday 7th.** Received a post office order for two pounds.

**Letter**, *T.T. Wilkinson, Burnley, to Bamford, 6 February 1860.*

My dear Sir,
I enclose you a P[ostal]. Order for £2.0.0 which the Directors wish to transmit to you as a slight remuneration for your attendance at their Soiree. If you consider this allowance too little you may say so <u>to me</u> and I will put the matter before the Board.

Your "Passages" have given me much pleasure. I feel proud of having formed your acquaintance.

Yours very truly

T.T. Wilkinson

**Saturday 18th.**[8] Mima went to Middleton to get the order cashed, and heard there was a newspaper account of my being ill: see annexed.

***Cutting***, *from the* Manchester Examiner and Times, *18 February 1860.*

---

Mr. S. Bamford – We regret to hear that Mr. Samuel Bamford, the well-known Radical writer, was attacked by sudden and severe illness, after returning to Moston, from attending the late *soirée* at the Burnley Mechanics' Institution; but his many friends will be glad to know that he is now recovering, although but slowly. Mr Bamford is in his 74th year.

---

**Sunday 19th.**[9] Received through the hands of Mr McClure, my neighbour, a sovereign enclosed in the annexed note. The hand writing I don't clearly recognise, thought I think it has some resemblance to that of my long lost friend Harland of the Guardian.

***Handwritten note.***

Feby 18 1860. A Friend of Mr Bamford, begs his acceptance of the enclosed.

Wrote to my unknown friend.

To "a friend" with grateful acknowledgement for compensation.

Samuel Bamford.

McClure told my Mrs who took the note that he would deliver it duly the following morning, and would come and see me at night: he added that several of his acquaintance were about doing something for me, which he would further explain when he saw me. Up to this day (27th Feb.) he has neither called nor sent.

Gowenlock and Potter called in the afternoon and sat some time up stairs, but I don't recollect that anything of a particular nature was discussed.

**Tuesday 21st.** Potter again called, and seemed somewhat excited. He said Gowenlock had written a letter to the Examiner and Times about me, which must have a good effect; it was a very excellent and touching letter, he had read it to him

---

8. The dates on this and the following entry have been altered by Bamford from "8th" and "9th" to "18th" and "19th", tallying with the date of the cutting.
9. Date supplied; "20th" written and deleted by Bamford.

(Potter) the night before, and straight sent it off by post. I thanked Potter for calling, and for the interest he took in my welfare, but after he was gone I could not suppress a fear that something would be found in the letter, – if it appeared – that would have been better left out. I had often remarked that these things are generally overdone in some one, or more particular instances.

**Wednesday 22nd.** Here is the letter. I was greatly hurt on reading it. Mima was quite distressed.

*Letter, from the* Manchester Examiner and Times, *22 February 1860.*

---

### MR SAMUEL BAMFORD

*To the Editor of the Examiner and Times.*
Sir, – From your paper of Saturday last, and also from a personal visit in the afternoon of that day, I am sorry to find that the old reformer, Mr. Bamford, is suffering from a severe attack of illness; and, what makes the matter worse, he is struggling with the most absolute poverty. Mr. Bamford has no means of gaining wherewith to support himself and his aged wife, but by giving occasional lectures, readings &c., which I very much fear, if even he could secure the necessary engagements, his health would not enable him to follow successfully; and even if he could, it would only secure him a bare putting on for the day, and would still leave the future dark and uncertain. It has occurred to me that something might be done, with a reasonable expectation of securing to Mr. Bamford and his wife sufficient to keep the wolf from their door. It is unnecessary to refer to the labours and sufferings that Mr. Bamford has gone through in the interests of great measures, the realisation of which the country is now rejoicing in; but if either his political history, or his local literary standing, or his manly English character be considered, I think that a sufficient claim would present itself to justify the grant by government of the usual allowance in such cases, viz. £50 a year. This would be a great thing for Mr. Bamford, as it would place him beyond the reach of absolute want, or the dread of a workhouse board. I should be glad if you would give this a place in your valuable, widely circulated, and influential paper, and still more so if its insertion should lead to what is so desirable. It will never do to allow a person like Mr. Bamford, who has so distinguished himself in the cause of human progress, to wither away in obscurity under the blighting hand of want.
                    Yours,
                            RUPERTINO
    Oldham, February 21, 1860.

---

**Thursday 23rd.** A load of coal, which Geo Nelson sent from Mosston colliery with 200wt of cannel: very acceptable present.

**Friday 24th.** Here is my reply from the Examiner and Times of this day (See annexed).

*Letter*, *from the* Manchester Examiner and Times, *24 February 1860.*

---

### SAMUEL BAMFORD

*To the Editor of the Examiner and Times.*

Sir – I beg to say that I have never authorised either my friend "Rupertino," or anyone else (for he is my friend, though in this instance acting painfully on my feelings) to make such an appeal on my behalf as appeared in your columns of yesterday. I have never complained to anyone of having to "struggle with absolute poverty," and though I, or rather we, have not been able to "keep the wolf from the door," we have been right cheerful-hearted at our frequent achievements in keeping him from entering in. The utmost we have ever hoped or wished for, in the way of public assistance, has been that such encouragement might be awarded to my readings and literary exercise as was commensurate with their merits; or that some potent and influential party amongst your "great men," – great-hearted ones I mean, – might be found to support the claims of a humble individual to reparation for injuries sustained during a great national struggle for legislative amendments. I have a persuasion, founded I trust, on reason and justice, that the nation owes me compensation for wrongs never yet righted; for injuries never yet redressed, which I endured during the ruder times and darker days of my repeated arrests and imprisonments; and I have waited to see whether any of our influential reformers, in a reformed House of Commons or out of it, would take up the cause of one, at least, of the oldest English reformers now living, one who has never been less than steadfastly faithful to "his order and his cause;" but there has not been any active sympathy from that quarter. My first wish has been to win my own daily bread by my own exertions; and that failing, to receive from the nation, or from the government as its organ of management, such compensation for wrongs and injuries as I may be justly entitled to. More than these hopes and wishes we have never indulged. The claim for compensation has not yet been publicly mooted, though soon I hope it will be. My readings, to which in the meantime I look for support, have not been so remunerative as I had reasonably, I trust, expected. Where little, however, has been received, little has been made to suffice; and never forgetting that "noble is the strife of duty," with hopeful hearts we have been content to wait for better times.

　　Other terms and allusions of my friend's letter I pass unnoticed; they jar on chords and feelings which public observation only desecrates. Knowing, however, his kind disposition and goodness of heart, I cannot entertain the slightest idea of his wishing to cause pain; and hoping that neither his communication nor this my reply, will cause me to stand disparaged in public estimation, I am, sir, your obedient servant,

　　　　　　　　　　SAMUEL BAMFORD.

　　Moston, Harpurhey, 22nd February, 1860.

---

Received also the letter on the other leaf from Sir James Kay Shuttleworth, with a cheque for five pounds.

*Letter*, *James Kay-Shuttleworth, Gawthorpe, to Bamford, 23 February 1860.*[10]

---

10. On the envelope, Bamford has written: " Ans^d same day .

My Dear Mr Bamford,

I have been very much concerned to hear of your indisposition since your visit to Burnley.

That only increases the anxiety which I expressed to you, when you were my guest at Gawthorpe, that some provision should be secured for your declining years.

It will give me great pleasure to second any efforts of your more influential friends in Manchester, and to concert with them how, from my solitude and retirement, I can be in anyway useful in promoting some recognition of those claims on public gratitude which you have established, and to which I have always been ready to bear my humble testimony.

Meanwhile, I think your kindness will rightly interpret my sense of what is due to your noble independence of character, if I ask you to gratify my own feelings by allowing me to contribute of my superfluities to your necessities, the enclosed cheque for five pounds.

With sincere respect and every good wish, I am,

Your faithful friend

James P. Kay Shuttleworth.

**Saturday 25th.** The following from the Examiner and Times of this day.

YOUNG REFORM – The tone of Mr Bamford's letter, which we published yesterday, prevents our undertaking to acknowledge small sums received on his behalf. Any donations forwarded on his account shall, however, be duly handed over.

**Sunday 26th.** A foolish letter from Henry Fletcher, Swan Court Market Street, which after perusing I put in the fire.

Ramsbottom in the forenoon who brought a copy of Poems by Edw^d Capern,[11] Rural Postman of Bideford – Bide-ford – very pretty some of them are, chiefly on rural and domestic subjects, such as a government like ours may consistently enough patronise by a pension of £50 a year.

Brierley and Page came in the afternoon, and some talk was had as to what had best be done on my account. Page, seemingly, taking a strong interest in the matter. I told them, my plan at as present sketched out, was to get up a reading or two: and simultaneously to be preparing a memorial to government, – or a petition to the House of Commons for compensation for wrongs and injuries of my former years. Bright was mentioned by Page as a likely one to give it effect, but I did not tell them how coldly he had behaved towards me. Ultimately it was understood, that as soon as I began to go out of doors, I should look out, and determine on a room and give my circular to the papers as an advertisement, and so things stand for the present.

11. Edward Capern (1819–94), the "Bideford Poet". His volume of *Poems* (1856) was much praised and he was awarded a civil list pension of £40 per annum by Palmerston in November 1857; *DNB*.

**Monday 27th.** A bitter cold day. No going out, so wrote up my Diary, and Mima brewed "a peck of malt."

Not one of my Middleton "friends" has been to see me during my illness, nor this weeks end, as I fully expected, thinking the newspaper articles would stir them if nothing else did: not one from Oldham, or Hollinwood, or Manchester, except Page and Brierley. A set of friends somewhat [like] Christs disciples, who all fled – one even cursed him – when the frowns of adversity began to lour.

**Cutting**, *from the* Middleton Albion, *26 February 1860: an exchange of correspondence between Ambrose Fawcett for the Middleton Literary Institute and Algernon Egerton MP. In response to a request from Fawcett for the name of the informant whose allegations against the Institute led Egerton to withdraw from the soirée, Egerton declines.*

**Tuesday 28th.** My birthday: this day compleats my 72$^d$ year: all gone like a dream. A bitter cold day and very stormy; wind N.W., fearful work I am afraid on the English and Irish Western coasts.

Received a letter with P.O. order for 16/- for my books, he does not say which, from my friend G. Smith of the Commercial Inn, Stayley Bridge. He had heard of my being unwell, and I suppose had seen the letters of Rupertino and myself in the Manchester paper.

**Wednesday 29th.** The first day of my 73$^d$ year. The annexed from Rupertino appears in the Examiner and Times of this morning. Sent a reply.

**Letter**, *from the* Manchester Examiner and Times, *29 February 1860.*

---

### MR BAMFORD.

*To the Editor of the Examiner and Times.*

SIR – It appears to me that a word in reply to Mr. Bamford's letter, or rather in explanation of my own in reference to him, is necessary.

Mr. Bamford acknowledges me to be his friend, and acquits me of any intention to wound his mind, whilst he at the same times says that what I intended as an act of friendship acts painfully on his feelings. The acknowledgement and acquittal are just, for long before I had the pleasure of knowing Mr Bamford personally, I esteemed him through his writings, and since it has been my privilege to know him more intimately my esteem has increased, whilst a strong sympathy has been created for him by a belief in a state of things affecting his position to which I cannot now further refer. The painfulness of the action of my letter upon Mr. Bamford's feelings is to me somewhat unaccountable, as I cannot see that is contains anything unwarrantable or calculated to injure him. Since reading his letter, I have submitted the one I wrote to mutual friends, and neither can they perceive in it ought to justify the feeling that he manifests, or the charge that he implicitly brings against me of a want of that delicacy of feeling which ever prevents obtrusiveness.

Perhaps my justification will best appear by a comparison of the substance of my letter with that of Mr. Bamford's reply. I said that Mr. Bamford was not only unwell, but was struggling with absolute poverty; he says that he has not been able to keep the wolf from the door. I said that Mr. Bamford's only mode of gaining a livelihood was by giving lectures, readings, &c., and that this was at the best but temporary and uncertain; he says that his readings, to which he looks for support, have not been so remunerative as he expected. I said that under the circumstances, taking into account the labours and sufferings, the literary standing and the manly character of Mr. Bamford, a sufficient claim could be made out to justify government in granting him an allowance of £50 a year; he says that the nation owes him compensation, and that he has expected from it, or from the government as its organ of management, such compensation for wrongs and injuries as he considers himself justly entitled to. My object was to call the attention of the leading Reformers of this district to Mr. Bamford's claims, with a view to justice being done to him; he says that he had hoped and wished that some potent and influential party amongst our great men might be found to support the claims of an humble individual, but that he has not received from that quarter any active sympathy, altho' he hopes that in some form the question will soon be publicly mooted. Now, looking at my statements, and at the corroboration which Mr. Bamford gives to them, is it less wonderful that he should have deemed it necessary to write on the subject at all, and especially to do so on a tone which could not but give pain to a disposition which he allows to be kind, and wound a hearts he acknowledges to be good? The appeal was not made to charity, but to justice, on the grounds of merits hitherto unrewarded. Yet Mr. Bamford blames me, as one of the public, for asking for him that consideration which he says he has expected, and which he blames the public for not having awarded to him; he blames me for publicly mooting a question which he hopes will soon in some form be publicly mooted. I cannot but think that it would have been much better if Mr. Bamford had maintained silence; and I am not alone in this feeling even among those who are proud to consider themselves Mr. Bamford's friends.

And now, allow me to express my sincere wish that neither my former letter nor this will in the least disparage Mr. Bamford in public estimation; nor will they, I trust, disparage me. My former letter I penned with a wish to serve a friend, quite earnest enough to save me from a blush; this I write with as earnest a regard for my own reputation, not wishing to be regarded as a Paul Pry, void of all sense of those proprieties which ought to be observed in social intercourse; for

The humble records of my life to search,
I have not heeded with mere pagan beats.

Of course, after Mr. Bamford's disclaimer, I cannot venture to move further in the matter. I will not, however, on this account, allow my sympathies to congeal, or icicles to gather around my heart, but shall most heartily rejoice over the success of any movement tending to realise what I still cannot but ardently wish for – the recognition and reward of the services and talents of one "of the oldest English Reformers now living; one who has never been less than steadfastly faithful to 'his order and his cause.'" Let me say, however, that if Mr. Bamford expects to find, on waking from his slumbers one morning, a hand stuck through the clouds, holding a horn labelled "Bamford's compensation," he will most certainly be disappointed. Even what is palpably just is generally only to be secured by effort. This letter will, so far as I am concerned, close the correspondence.– Yours, &c.,

RUPERTINO.
Oldham, Feb. 25th., 1860.

**Thursday 1st March.** Mrs Nelson came, and brought a fowl, a bottle of wine, and a dress for Mima.

**Friday 2nd.** Potter from Oldham called and informed me that Gowenlock wrote a very "gem of a letter" to the Editor of the Examin^r and Times, before the one which appeared signed "Rupertino", in which letter he mentioned by name about half a dozen leading characters in Manchester who ought, or who might take up my business, and act as a committee in the matter: that the Editor sent a private note in reply, declining to drag the names of these gentlemen before the public, but promising if Gowenlock would send a shorter letter, without objectionable notice of individuals, he would publish it, and therefore, the second letter which appeared, and to which I replied was sent. This shows me that my friend Gowenlock had no perception whatever, of propriety in this transaction: to drag the names of gentlemen before the public in the manner he would have done, would have damned at once, both me and my cause. The freedom he took with myself, was but little less rude and ungraceful, but that, the Editor could permit: I was but a poor man.

**Saturday 3rd.** The annexed appears in this days Examiner and Times.

*Letter*, *from the* Manchester Examiner and Times, *3 March 1860.*

---

### RUPERTINO V. SAMUEL BAMFORD.

*To the Editor of the Examiner and Times*
SIR – Will you have the goodness to admit to your columns a few lines in reply to "Rupertino's" letter, which appears in your publication of this day. It is far from my wish to cavil at exceptionable terms in my friend's correspondence; to his goodness of heart and kindly disposition I have already borne testimony, and though he intimates that, in consequence of my observations, he "cannot move further in the matter," and that his letter of to-day "closes the correspondence so far as he is concerned," I hope that I am not to consider that his friendship has taken a final and immovable distance. This is the first day of my seventy-third year, and at my time of life, with all the gloomy anticipations of my friend's letter before me, I can but ill afford to lose a friend. I wish I may not do so in this case; but still I cannot but chafe at the restraint which would impose silence, and apparent acquiescence, in matters which, however well intended, I could not but feel to be unnecessarily explicit. We have never been ashamed of honest poverty, and hope we never shall be; but we have always maintained that self-respect which has exacted the respect of others. Whatever may have been our exigencies and our difficulties, we have never made a talk of them. We have kept them to ourselves, scarcely to a friend so much as distantly alluding to them. In the humblest condition of honest life there is such a thing as becoming pride, and that pride we have constantly endeavoured to be worthy of, and to maintain. "Rupertino's" letter has, however, torn the veil of decent privacy away, and has given everyone a motto on which to found observations. All the good which he purposed might have been obtained, by arrangements of a less obtrusive nature; a dozen steadfast friends might have effected all that is desired, without communicating one word respecting our

household difficulties. "Where there is a will there is a way," it is said, and had the real earnest, thoughtful will to serve us been moved, it would have operated without making the great city of Manchester, with all its attendant towns and boroughs, aware of so small a requirement. In a word, my friend, "Rupertino" has performed a kind action, in a way which has produced to us as much pain as an unkind one would have done. I have ventured to demur to the manner in which the thing has been done, and to intimate that I have experienced pain, mingled with my feelings of gratitude; and for this, it seems, I am to stand condemned, not only by "Rupertino," but "by some who are proud to consider themselves my friends." So it seems, after receiving an act of kindness, I am not to express an opinion as to the manner in which the act has been performed. – I am, sir, your obliged servant,

SAMUEL BAMFORD.
Moston, Harpurhey, Feb. 29, 1860.

---

*Letter, from the* Middleton Albion, *3 March 1860, from "Lover of public justice", criticising Algernon Egerton MP over the Middleton Literary Institute soirée affair.*

Henry Grimshaw from Charles town called and bought a copy of Early Days.

**Sunday 4th.** Ramsbottom was here at night. I agreed to present his "Sons Appeal to a Dissolute Feyther" to someone of the Manchester papers: I had considerable trouble in persuading him to have his foolish spelling corrected, but succeeded in some instances.

**Monday 5th.** An envelope covering 120 postage stamps, from Knott Mill branch office, without one word of explanation.

Mrs Nelson came, and brought me a handsome wrapper for neck, very comfortable.

**Tuesday 6th.** Went to Manchester and got the cheque which Sir James Kay Shuttleworth [sent], also Post Office order sent 16/- by G. Smith from Stayley Bridge.

Saw McClure in Market Street, who told me the Sovereign sent on Sund the 12th ult. was sent by a Mr Allen of the firm of Harrison and Allen brass founders.

Called at Guardian and Exam^r offices and found the Guardian's charge for insertion of my circular as an advertisement would be £2, and the sum for three insertions £5.10: the Exam^r £1-7-0 + £1 each for three insertions. Left Ramsbottoms poetry at the Examiner: saw a proof, and corrected it, with a promise of its appearing tomorrow.[12]

Came home by Bus, somewhat wet and got v[ery] cold. Letter from Mechanics Institution at Preston.

---

12. Sentence added opposite.

**Wednesday 7th.**  Ramsbottoms poetry appears, see annexed.

**Cutting**, *from the* Manchester Examiner and Times, *7 March 1860, Joseph Ramsbottom's poem "Appeal by a son to his dissolute father", the appeal being to stop drinking and look after his destitute family, with manuscript alterations to dialect renderings by Bamford.*

**Thursday 8th.**  At Manchester, by ten oclock bus, when certain snobs are in the habit of going.[13] Aspell of Middleton, Tom Ashworth coal dealer late of Rochdale, now of a house standing out of the highway near the Harperhey toll bar; One Monks an engraver, of Barnes Green, and Holcroft, a silk manufacturer living in the lane below me, were in the bus, together with several respectably dressed females, who no doubt thought themselves no "common stuff." Their presence made not the slightest difference to me, so I took my seat as if not a soul was in the thing but myself; not a word was however vouchsafed to me, nor so much as a recognition, whilst I seemed to be unaware of any other bodily presence save my own, and so went on to the Wellington. Got shaved, and went to the Mechanics Institute in Major Street, and found the charge for the lecture hall there would be two pounds: the Athenaeum I found, on enquiry, would be the same; the town Hall eight pounds and the long room at the exchange eight pounds.

Henry Boddington, brewer, touched me on the shoulder at the corner of Princess St, and I must go with him: so went to the Slip in Blue Boar Court, a house with which he is beginning to so business with: We had a glass of ale each, he getting change for a sovereign, the silver he put in his pocket, and the half sovereign he slipped into my hand in a very kind manner, saying it was to buy a cap for my Mrs. The bar keeper entered, and they began talking on business matters, so I left them.

Got 13 <u>Early Days</u> of John Heywoods in Deansgate: went to Abel Heywoods and bought two copies Life of a Radical, for which I paid: took parcel containing one Early Days and 1 Radical, to the Bank Top Railway for Geo. Smith, Commercial Inn, Stayley Bridge: then came back through the Manor Market and found the 1/2 past 2 bus, Harperhey Omnibus: the one I had come by in the morning just passing up the street (Shudehill) as I got there. I beckoned the conductor to stop, a policeman did the same, as well as a man who stood upon a cart, but he stood on the step behind looking at us and did not pull the bell: he would not stop: that was evident: This is another indication of the altered position which the letters of my friend Rupertino have forced me into. I am not, it would seem, any longer sufficiently respectable to sit in omnibus company, nor to be taken up by an omnibus guard.

Went down to the Swan wishing to sit down and rest a little, for I was quite tired and exhausted for breath. Edm[d] Howarth from Middleton was there,[14] and would have paid for a hot glass of toddy for me, but I declined it, feeling that the twopenny worth of gin whith which I had already been served would be quite as much as I could take.

---

13. At this period, senior white-collar staff would not start work until 10 a.m., later than their staff.

14. Edmund Howarth (dates not known), Middleton cotton master, poor law guardian, civic improver and Liberal; see entries for 16 and 19 May 1860. (See Plate 2.)

We came together by the three o'clock Middleton Omnibus, to Barns Green, he insisting on paying <u>both</u> fares, and when I got out under pretence of shaking hands, he put half a crown into mine, desiring me to give his respects to my old woman. So I took the money towards my "national compensation."

**Friday 9th.** Mrs Dickin, the wife of my old friend Oswald Dickin of Middleton made her appearance at my house. I was surprised to know whatever business could have caused her to visit us here, after our being here a year and 8 months without either herself or her husband calling to see us. As an excuse for this she said Mr. D never came to Manchester by this road, but always drove through Cheetham Hill, which indeed is likely enough. At length it came out that Mr D had had some talk with McDougal of Chadderton, respecting me, and that betwixt them – as I understood – something was to be done for me. I asked her "in what way?" and she said, "by way of a subscription as she understood." Mr Dickin had also met with a Mr Dearden[15] an attorney, when he was over at Southport, who enquired about me: he was a very rich man she said, and a bachelor. Mrs Dickin had on Tuesday, the 6th, received a letter from Mr Dearden, which she presented to me (see the letter annexed). That morning the 8th he had received another, wishing me to call upon him, and that had caused her to come over. She stopped to tea, made various enquiries, and seemed to take much notice of our place, so that I thought her main object in paying this personal visit, was to make out a report of the actual state in which she found matters: if so she would probably report us as being in good condition for we did not make any show of penury, or scant. We gave her a glass of our little ale, which she drank with a relish, and my wife made her a very good tea, which she seemed to enjoy heartily; some newly baked bread which had but just come out of the oven pleased her very much. She said she had called at Mrs Halsalls to enquire us out, and one of their girls came to show her our door, and she was to call at Halsalls again in returning. Consequently there will probably be some considerable talk betwixt the two, about us, our habits, modes of living, character amongst our neighbours, and other matters, and as we have never made any extraordinary exertions either to offend or to conciliate our neighbours – who are all Church or Chapel goers, which we are neither – I dont suppose the budget made up by the two gossips would be an over favourable one.

On reviewing in my own mind, this transaction, there appears to be a degree of mystery about it which renders it, on the whole, repugnant to my feelings. In the first place Dearden writes to Dickin wishing to know where I live. Dickin, no doubt answered that on the day he got it, the 7th stating where I lived, Mosston, Nr Manchester, and thereupon Dearden, instead of writing direct to me, writes again to Dickin; and the invitation to call upon Dearden is communicated to me by Dickins wife, who makes a journey for the purpose. This is so unacceptably roundabout, and ambiguous that I dont like it. I suspect there is something connected with it, which means no good to me.

---

15. Josiah Heaton Dearden (1808–64), solicitor, member of John Shaw's Club, see F.S. Stancliffe, *John Shaw's 1738–1938* (1938).

Is Dearden employed by someone else to gain information, of any sort, or all sorts about me? It would almost justify a conclusion to that effect, since he would never take this method of ascertaining my whereabouts on his own account. I will try to know more on Monday. I have experienced so much hypocrisy [and] double dealing that I have become almost distrustful of everyone, and every transaction. God help me! Am I losing my senses?

**Letter**, *from J. Heaton Dearden, 34 Cooper Street, Manchester, to Oswald Dicken Esq., Middleton, 6 March 1860.*

My Dear Sir,
Can you tell me where I can find Old Bamford. I have a notion whether correct or not I am not certain that he either does or did retire some where about Chadderton.

You did not make your appearance at Altcar. I hope nothing "Contra temps" prevented you.

I am faithfully yrs<br/>J. Heaton Dearden.

**Poem**, *from the* Oldham Standard, *10 March 1860.*

---

### TO SAMUEL BAMFORD
### ON THE SEVENTY-SECOND ANNIVERSARY OF HIS BIRTHDAY
### FEBRUARY 29, 1860.[16]

All Hail, old bard! this day we come
With greetings warm and new,
And round thy humble cottage-home
Our friendly offerings strew.
Though changeful time does pass away,
Like dreams of joys and tears,
And skies, which smile upon to-day,
May frown on coming years.
A friendship founded on esteem
Does no mutations know,
But whether storms their furies teem
Or gentlest zephyrs blow,
It stands erect, like forest-king,
Which revels in the blast,
Or in the sweetest tones does sing
To sunlight round it cast.

---

16. The poem is long and repetitive, apparently written without time for revision; only the first and last stanzas are given here. Compare the very different "Lines to Mr Samuel Bamford on his seventy-sixth birthday, February 28th 1864", by "R.R.B." of Old Hall, Stand, *Homely Rhymes*, 64.

And thus, old bard, to thee we come,
   With greetings warm and new,
And round thy humble cottage-home
   This day our offerings strew.
          ...
The future is a cloud-wrapped scene,
   Where human thought but gropes;
Nay, where man's thought has never been,
   Except in faith and hopes.
Well, we will hope and we will pray
   That, unto thee and thine,
Through life, on each succeeding day,
   A brighter sun may shine.
Beyond we know all will be well,
   For God His word has given
That all the pure in heart shall dwell
   Close to his throne in heaven.

RUPERTINO
Oldham, March 5, 1860.

---

**Sunday 11th.** Miss Taylor sent a fine rabbit, which on being cooked was found to be gross, and out of season.

Dronsfield, Travis and Mason from Hollinwood called in the afternoon, took tea, and after they were gone 2/6 were found in my wifes tobacco box, which more than paid for their entertainment.

# 9
# ROYAL BOUNTY

*On 13 March great news arrived: Lord Palmerston, the prime minister, had agreed to grant Bamford £50 from the Royal Bounty fund – the well-known fund used by the queen to reward her deserving subjects. Bamford's delight was soon succeeded, however, by anxiety over whether a one-off gift (which is soon absorbed by creditors and necessary expenditure) could be converted to a pension. Nonetheless, a much more relaxed spring and summer followed, with no major public appearances but with long nostalgic walks around Middleton (on Good Friday), visits to and from Dronsfield at Blackley Wakes and Oldham Wakes, and a bittersweet return in September to Manchester workhouse, where his mother and half his family had died when he was young – an episode which forever conditioned his view of the great city. Bamford could hardly contain his excitement at the appearance of the Lancashire novel* Scarsdale *in July, when he alone knew the identity of the author of a work that was briefly the talk of Manchester. Bamford went down with flu in April, but more ominous was Mima's illness, which put her out of action for over a month in May and June – a portent of sad times to come.*

**Tuesday 13th.** Went to see Mr Dearden, who only wanted – or pretended he only wanted – to know if I had any knowledge of the family of Dearden. Whence they sprung and where chiefly located? I could not inform him, so our interview was very brief, but before I came away he slipped five shillings into my hand, for my trouble, as he said, in calling upon him. I now believe the whole thing was only an excuse for giving me something.

Went to the Steam Engine brewery at York Street but Clowes was not at home, nor in town: would be away until tomorrow night.

Came by the Middleton Omnibus. Some talk with Edm^d Howarth, and when I rose to come out at Barnes Green he put half a sovereign into my hand unseen by the other passengers and desired me to give his respects to "the old woman."

At night Ramsbottom came and informed us that D. Morris had received a letter from Mr Bazley stating that he had presented a letter or memorial to Lord Palmerston, on my behalf; that his lordship had awarded me £50, and that it would, Morris said be probably continued. This very pleasing news was quite unexpected by us, and caused a state of feeling which I may discribe as one of pleasing pain.

David Morris, it seemed, had written a very urgent letter on my account to Mr Bazley, who immediately sought, and obtained an interview with Lord Palmerston, when what I have noted down took place.

I had not seen, or communicated with Mr Morris since the night of the Soiree at Burnley; so it is likely all that Morris wrote to Bazley was gleaned from my correspondence with Rupertino in the columns of the Examiner and Times.

**Wednesday 14th.** The annexed paragraphs are what the Manchester papers say about the affair.

*Item* *from the* Manchester Examiner and Times, *12 March 1860.*

---

### MR. SAMUEL BAMFORD.

The following letter from Mr.Bazley, M.P., will be read with interest by the numerous friends of Mr. Samuel Bamford. It will gratify them to hear that the grant from the Royal Bounty Fund is to be continued to him in future years:–
London, 12th March, 1860.

"Dear Sir, – After the requisite preliminary arrangements, I was enabled to be favoured with an interview with Lord Palmerston on Saturday last, and then I urged the merits of Mr. Samuel Bamford, as deserving the recognition of his lordship, as the dispenser of the Royal Bounty Fund in aid of unrequited literary and public service. I am glad to inform you that my appeal was most kindly and favourably received, and his lordship said he would place fifty pounds at once at the service of Mr. Bamford; but whether he could be permanently admitted as a yearly recipient would require further consideration, as many applications had at some future day to be decided, and that Mr. Bamford's claim should not be neglected.

I am not acquainted with the forms of procedure in the payments of grants of the Royal Bounty Fund, but I am now sending Mr. Bamford's address, "Moston, Harpurhey, Manchester," to Lord Palmerston's private secretary, who will, I hope, initiate some communication, direct or through me, what course to pursue. If however, you have any suggestion to offer, I shall be glad to receive it.

I assure you that I have had great pleasure in contributing my humble services, in calling Lord Palmerston's attention to the unrewarded labours of Mr. Bamford, who, as a patriot and a friend to constitutional progress, has earned for himself the respect and high estimation of his neighbours and countrymen; but whose faithful advocacy of civil and religious rights has, I regret, been insufficiently appreciated. When you see him, remember me to him. – Believe me to remain, most faithfully yours,
Thos. Bazley.
David Morris, Esq.

---

*Cutting*, *from the* Manchester Guardian, *14 March 1860, a reproduction of the same letter, with a brief editorial note expressing pleasure and supporting Bamford's claim for a pension.*

Went to Middleton, and corrected proof of my amended circular.
   The following from David Morris.

*Letter*, *David Morris, 1 Market Place, Manchester, to Bamford, 13 March 1860, addressed to "Samuel Bamford Esqr, Reformer Poet Laureate".*

My Dear Sir,
After meeting you at the Burnley Soiree, I thought much about you, and as a result wrote to Mr Bazley M.P. a long statement of your case and requested him

to use his powerful influence with Government to obtain a suitable recognition of your long, faithful and successful services in the cause of social and political elevation of the people.

I have now the happiness to inform you that to a certain extent his efforts have been successful. How much further he can succeed I know not yet, but assure you neither he or I will be content untill your last days – which I hope may yet be very many – are made as comfortable as you and I can possibly desire.

I have sent copies of Mr Bazley's letter to the Examiner and the Guardian for which please look tomorrow and take that as if I had sent you a copy.

Hoping what I have done will meet with your approval, I am with the greatest respect and admiration

Yours very truly,<br>David Morris.

**Thursday 15th.** Letter from the Lords of Her Majesty's Treasury with instructions to write to the Paymaster General.[1]

*Copy letter*, *Bamford to the Paymaster General, Whitehall, 15 March 1860.*

Sir,

I am informed by a Communication, from the "Treasury Whitehall" dated 14 March 1860 – the signature not legible – that "on the recommendation of Viscount Palmerston", you have "been authorised by the Lords Commissioners of Her Majesty's Treasury" to pay to me, the sum of £50: and that, "upon application being made to you by letter, you will cause a form of receipt to be furnished to me which can be negotiated through a Banker."

Personal attendance not being convenient, I have therefore to request, that you will forward to me such form of receipt as is herein specified. I am Sir,

Your Obedient Servant<br>Samuel Bamford.

*Copy letter*, *Bamford to Smith P. Robinson, Lancashire Reform Union, Newalls Buildings, Manchester, 15 March 1860.*

Dear Sir,

Understanding that my case has at length attracted the attention of the Lancashire Reformers Union, and that a motion on the subject has been entertained by them, I take the liberty of forwarding a few of my circulars showing the grounds on which I have solicited public attention to my literary exercises, and on which I claim <u>compensation</u> for wrongs and injuries which had not been recognised until yesterday (anniversary of the passing of the reform bill) when a communication was dispatched to me from the Treasury, for the receipt of £50.

---

1. The letter from the Treasury is missing.

As the subject has been, in a greater or less degree mooted in your (our) association, the circulars will tend to a correct understanding of my case as it at present remains. I am Dear Sir

Your Obedient Servant,

Samuel Bamford.

**Friday 16th.** This day 40 years ago, 1820 – commenced the trial at York. The following to T. M. Gibson Esqr MP.[2]

*Copy letter*, Bamford to T.M. Gibson MP, 21 March 1860.

Honoured Sir,

Doctor John Watts, of Manchester, informs me by letter, that you have been the medium, in one instance, for laying my claims to compensation before Viscount Palmerston, one consequence of which is that I have received an order on the Paymaster General for £50.

A very grateful pleasure therefore requires that I should thank you for your kind interference on behalf of one who, being personally unknown to you, could not have presumed to solicit your interference in this matter, but who is not on that account the less sincere in expressions of all respectful and deferential feelings with which your generous aid has inspired him; and who is truly, Honoured Sir,

Your Obliged Servant

Samuel Bamford.

**Saturday 17th.** Letter from the Paymaster General with form of receipt for £50. Letter from Dr Watts.

*Letter*, Dr John Watts to Bamford, 17 March 1860.[3]

My Dear Bamford,

When I heard of your illness [it] seemed to me that so good a public servant ought to be requited out of the national funds; and knowing your independence of spirit I could not humiliate you by asking your consent, so drew up a memorial to the Premier and got it signed and forwarded to Mr Milner Gibson with a request that he would say something in favour of it.

It seems that David Morris had also done something of the kind through Mr Bazley and as Mr Bazley [influenced] the result I should not [write] this note but that Mr Gibson states that your claims [were] taken into consideration [with those] of other candidates and pending settlement of the matter you need not tell

---

2. Entry added on verso, later (21 March?), hence the inconsistency with the date of the letter, which must in fact have been sent at the earliest on the 17th, the date Watts' letter arrived.
3. The letter is damaged; sections in square brackets are conjectural.

any [one else that] I have taken any interest in the matter as I shall be only [happy that] the result tends all to relieve you from anxiety by keeping the [wolf from] the door.

    When sufficiently recovered I shall be glad to see you again.

Yours very truly

John Watts.

**Letter**, *Smith P. Robinson, Lancashire Reformers' Union, Manchester, to Bamford, 16 March 1860.*

Dear Sir,

I have yours of yesterday and am happy to hear that the Treasury has at length been induced to notice your claim to a compensation for the sufferings you endured in the cause of truth and justice forty years ago – I hope that £50 will only be the first annual instalment which you may live many years of good health to enjoy.

Yours very truly

Smith P. Robinson.

**Sunday 18th.**  The following to Viscount Palmerston.[4]

Sent the annexed to Thos Bazley Esq^r. MP.

**Copy letter**, *Bamford to Thomas Bazley MP, Manchester, 17 March 1860.*

Honoured and Esteemed Sir,

For your generous interference with Viscount Palmerston, on my behalf, I would express to you all the grateful sentiments which kindness such as yours ought to inspire. Those sentiments, I beg to assure you I experienced in a degree to which any expression which I have at command is inadequate. Accept therefore, dear Sir, as an acknowledgement of, in full, this feeble effort to thank you.

    On a former occasion you were kind enough to inform me that you would present any petition or memorial which I might prepare, and had not my friend, Mr Morris, promptly and unknown to me taken up the business, it was my intention shortly to have asked your advice as to the best mode of procedure, whether by memorial to Viscount Palmerston, or by petition to the House of Commons. The initiary step has however been taken [and] it has freed me (I may say us) from much anxiety and we are very grateful.

    I am glad to inform you that my business has been promptly attended to by the Treasury. I have already received a form of receipt from the Paymaster Generals Office, which form, on my signature being attached, becomes negociable by any banker.

---

4. The letter to Palmerston is missing.

I take the liberty of inclosing a few of my circulars, which show the grounds on which my claims to compensation are based, and I presume to think that by whomsoever such claims are candidly considered they will be deemed considerable.

I remain Dear Sir,

Your obliged humble servant,

Samuel Bamford.

**Letter**, *Bamford to T.M. Gibson MP, 21 March 1860.*

Honoured Sir,
Doctor John Watts, of Manchester, informs me by letter, that you have been the medium, in one instance, for laying my claims to compensation before Viscount Palmerston, one consequence of which is that I have received an order on the Paymaster-General for £50.

A very grateful pleasure therefore requires that I should thank you for your kind interference on behalf of one who being personally unknown to you, could not have presumed to solicit your interference in this matter, but who is not on that account any the less sincere in expressions of all respectful and deferential feelings with which your generous aid has inspired him, and who is truly, Honoured Sir,

Your obliged servant,

Samuel Bamford.

**Wednesday 21st.**  The following to Sir J.P. Kay Shuttleworth Bart.

**Copy letter**, *Bamford to James Kay Shuttleworth, 21 March 1860.*

Dear Sir James,
You very kindly in your last communication offered to cooperate with my friends at Manchester towards procuring for me, some compensation or other provision for the wants of old age. To me, the present seems a befitting time for your friendly aid: two separate parties entirely without my knowledge, or I believe, that of each other, caused applications to be made to Lord Palmerston on my behalf, and the result has been that I have received an order from the Paymaster General for £50, Lord Palmerston also promising that, on "the approaching settlement of the pension list", my claim to be placed on the list, shall be taken into consideration with that of others, and that "Mr Bamford's claim shall not be neglected."

I presume to inclose a few circulars, showing the grounds on which I think my claim might have been put forward by my friends. I know not in what light it has been exhibited, but to me it seems, they might have pointedly alluded to the fact that 42 years had passed since the wrongs and injuries of which I was the sufferer. That some consideration might be allowed for loss by such lapse of time; that I am now in the 73rd year of my age, my wife being in her 72nd, that we must in the course of nature shortly require some one to live with us and be a keeper in the house, which will impose additional expense; and that whatever was the compensation or allowance awarded, it could not be long wanted by persons of our age. I allude to these matters because it seems as if my friends had acquiesced in or adopted the idea that if the £50 was continued, and that only, all would be done which was desirable or requisite. I am sincerely grateful for what has been done so far as I may judge, but I cannot but feel a further impression on recurring to the facts as to my age and other considerations which I have above enumerated, and I think if these matters could be clearly represented to Lord Palmerston before "the settlement of the pension list," he might probably be induced to recommend such an allowance as would not only place us above exigent independence, and would make us comfortable for the remainder of our days.

I am aware this is a delicate matter to discuss: in your discretion however, I have perfect confidence; if it seem to you rather sordid and ungrateful on my part do not, I beg of you, permit the idea to remain, or you will do me an injustice. I am quite sensible of the difference betwixt £50 and nothing, but I cannot away with the persuasion that, after having laboured long and suffered much, in preparing the harvest of freedom and plenty, the old weather-beaten labourer may modestly ask to sit down, with a few of the comforts, and all the necessaries of which temperate habit requires. If therefore dear Sir James, you have any connections in the great metropolis, or any medium by which you could procure the considerations I have advanced to be presented to the noble Lord who has the direction of these matters you would, I am persuaded, be rendering me such aid as I am sure you would be glad to do by engaging the influence of said connections in furtherance of the wishes I hereby confide to your Honourable, and highly esteemed co-operation: remaining dear Sir James,

your very humble and most grateful Serv<sup>t</sup>,

Samuel Bamford.

**Friday 23rd.** Took my receipt on the Paymaster General to the Manchester and Salford Bank, when I was requested to bring the letter of instructions from the Lords of the Treasury, which was necessary in order to supply certain n[umber]s which were in blank in the last letter. I ventured to express a different opinion, that the filling in of the n[umber]s was not required in that document, and that if they were they would be supplied at the office in London. The gentlemen at the Bank were however of a different opinion, and desired me to bring the other letter which I promised to do.

Mima called at "Our Uncles," and took from under his care certain articles which she had left with him: paying him very liberally for his care-taking, and then setting off home. I intended calling on D. Morris before I left the town, so went down Shude Hill and fell in with Thomas Ashton, late of Middleton who had heard of my "good fortune", and congratulated me. He was one of the 4 youths whom in 1819 I placed at the head of the Middleton procession with branches of laurel in their hands; he reminded me of this; and said, he was the only one living of the four: He has lately removed to Oldham, and keeps a public house at Bottom oth Moor. So here is another place I shall have to call at when I visit that borough. As the day continued wet and the omnibus would start soon I gave up the intention of staying in town, and preferred returning home and getting my damp clothes off, so took the 'bus and got home to a warm fire and comfortable refection.

***Insertion****: a handwritten slip.*

Not Bury Cymbalin but home made Cymbalin
With Miss Taylor's comp^ts to Mr Bamford.
The best I ever tasted. SB[5]

**Saturday 24th.** Took the Lords of the Treasury's document to the bank; they looked at it, and seemed to ponder on it some time, apparently unable to make the two documents fit and dove-tail, as I thought they would be; and then, a clerk was sent to tell me, to come again on Wednesday, and so my business for that day was done.

Called on D. Morris, who had nothing new; took the 'bus and came home.

**Sunday 25th.** Ramsbottom called in the forenoon, Gowenlock and his son after dinner: He informed me, as matter which he knew to be fact, that the whole of the correspondence (newspaper) betwixt himself and me, had been sent to London, meaning, as I supposed – to our friends Bazley and Milner Gibson there; in which case, the correspondence, or part of it might possibly find its way to Lord Palmerston, and if so there was not anything in my letters of which I need be ashamed: Gowenlock also said, that Dr. Watts memorial was not got up, nor forwarded until after the one presented by Mr Bazley had been dispatched. He was of my opinion that more than the £50 per ann. ought to be awarded me: Mrs Rogerson, he said, had recently had that, – her late husbands pension – continued to her; at which I was surprised, never having heard of it; if so it has been managed by her friends here very secretly, and with much dispatch: in a manner vastly different from that in which my "friends" are in the habit of acting: If it is so, and if it has [been] managed this quickly and secretly it has been with a view to forestall any application on my account: however I wish the poor widow well, and next after myself, I certainly should wish she had it: May she make a good use of it, and avoid second marriage.

Gowenlock left after tea, as he wished to shown his son William, his little brothers grave at the cemetery.

Grimshaw and Smithies called on their return from Chapel, and ordered two Radicals and 1 Early Days.

25th Sund.[6] Was informed by a letter that I had been unanimously chosen one of the committee to act on the "the Heywood Testimonial", a proceeding I never authorised; a honour I never desired; and an office I shall never fulfil.

A testimonial, so called, of something which is to be presented to Abel Heywood for his conduct in resisting the intended diversion of Clarks Charity, from the purpose for

---

5. The third line is in Bamford's script.
6. This part of the entry added overleaf.

which it was bestowed to the founding and supporting of a "Ragged School". In resisting this diversion Heywood acted very properly, but he only did his duty, and I don't see any decent pretence for a testimonial. I shall not co-operate with any fag-end of his followers.

**Monday 26th.** Went to Manchester, and brought some writing paper, and two pocket handkerchiefs. Called at Cave and Severs, for Mr Severs book, Cheetham Society's Series of publications – on the Shuttleworths of Gawthorpe.[7]

**Tuesday 27th.** Went to Charlestown and took the books which had been ordered by Grimshaw and Smithies.

**Wednesday 28th.** Went to the bank at Manchester and drew my Royal Bounty £50: deposited £30 of it in the savings bank, that being the largest sum they could receive at once. Gave Mima £1. 8. to redeem a few things from Our Uncles, she coming straight home, and I following in the afternoon. Weather wet and cold which gave me a bad head and a disordered stomach. Mima went to Whittakers and paid off the shop score £1-2-0, so all straight there.

**Sunday 1st April.** Brierley and Ramsbottom both called in the afternoon. Brierley to get me to copy a newspaper paragraph about the yearly meeting of the Hollinwood Discussion Society which took place last night, and Ramsbottom to beg an old newspaper in which appears a letter of his on the extension of the ten hours act to bleach-works.

**Friday 6th.** Good Friday. I have almost entirely kept the house since Sunday, hoping by care and warmth, and low diet to get rid of a cold which has settled on me in the form of that stupid old plague, the influenza. Today it being fine and warm, that is warm sun, but cold air as I found when I had got upon the road – I must need go to Middleton for a walk, so went, and took a stroll round Club Houses, the churchyard, Back oth Brow, and to the Corner Alehouse; Afterwards down to Mills's whence I stepped into the Omnibus and came home by half past one o'clock. In the church yard, found that some person of the name of Hilton at Rhodes had put up a handsome head-stone at a grave, the very next, and close to that of my Ann: too close rather, since in placing side stones the workmen have displaced the fringe of willows on Ann's grave; none of the flowers have however, been disturbed, and the crocuses in many beautiful varieties make a very pretty and [impressive] object, forming a strong and [impressive][8] contrast to the foolish and pretentious looking carved slab which stands on end beside the flowers.

Jenny Pollitt, – that was, as blown as a frog. Betty Collinge, one of my early sweethearts, and Hannah Frankland, my cousin, the two last old, feeble withered women. Oh how changed. Everything at Middleton, and every body seems wo[e]fully

---

7. The Chetham Society published four volumes of household accounts of the Shuttleworths of Gawthorpe at this period (vols 35, 41, 43 and 48), edited by John Harland.
8. In each case, "impressive" deleted by Bamford.

changed; the few that I met, once my companions, all feeble, tottering, pale faced, shrivelled, and seemingly, <u>cold hearted</u> which is the worst of all: Why cannot I be so also. My heart, as compared with those of others, is still young, having a warm living glow of kindly feeling, and pulsing away to all the kindly remembrances of youthful sunny days. I am almost afraid I am too young, and that I shall live until nothing is left for me but misery until

> The world is dark on every side
> A frowning desert wild and wide
> Whence joy hath fled, where hope has died
> And left a voice of wailing.

Went in the afternoon, by invitation to see Miss Taylor's flower garden. A most splendid show of crocus and other early flowers. Afterwards had a long chat with Miss Taylor, in the parlour; she is in a very feeble and delicate state of health, sorry am I to say it: I should think she suffers much in health from quietude, and almost solitary listlessness. Find I have taken cold by my Middleton journey and the two glasses of ale I had. My head is worse than when I set out.

**Saturday 7th.** Brierley called. He was going to Middleton to attend a meeting of Warpers[9] at Harrisons, Masons Arms. He will have a chance of meeting with some of my calumniators, and probably of hearing some of their disparagement, before he comes away: indeed I should not wonder if the meeting has been got up by some of my left handed friends, for that purpose. Elijah Ridings it seems, has sent copies of his rubbishey publication, "The volunteer" to Lord Palmerston, Lord John Russell, and Mr Bazley, doubtless with the view of getting something like myself, from the Royal Bounty.

**Sunday 8th.** Will and Edwin Ridings, brothers of Elijah were here. Sat and talked an hour on various matters, (chiefly on the extension of the suffrage, with Edwin) who on that subject is I am sorry to find, a <u>Norman</u>. They went from here to go down to Collyhurst, – as they said – doubtless to see Elijah.

Literary Institute.
The annexed slip is from the Middleton Albion of Ap[ril] 7th.

***Report***, *from the* Middleton Albion, *7 April 1860, of the quarterly meeting of the Middleton Literary Institute, marked by a lively debate about opening the Institute on Sundays. In favour, it was argued that "it would afford greater facilities to working men" and "would tend to moralize and elevate the working classes". Against, it was argued that Sunday opening "might draw young people from the sabbath school" and risked alienating "the religious party" who had saved the Institute from ruin in the past, following the example of "the institution at Royton ... composed of infidels, whose souls were lost, in the corrupt stuff which they read, from such authors as Tom Paine". The vote was 15–8 in favour of Sunday opening.*

---

9. The workers who prepared the powerlooms for operation.

**Friday 13th.** Saw Mr Morris at Manchester, but nothing new had occurred. Called also at the Mill of Mr Bazley, but he was not within. Saw John Heywood, and left with him My Walks in So[uth] Lancashire and Tim Bobbin, with an appointment to see him again at the expiration of a fortnight.

**Saturday 14th.** Went to the Counting house of Mr Bazley, who narrated to me how he applied for an interview with Lord Palmerston, which was readily granted, his lordship being quite disposed to act favourably in my business, offering at once to place £50 at my disposal, and appearing very willing to continue the grant by placing my name on the list of annual recipients, adding that my claim should not be neglected when the settlement of the pension list [came]. Mr Bazley said that from the very kind manner in which his lordship expressed himself, he (Mr B.) thought I had not any cause to doubt the grant being continued. Called at Belfields: paid him a shilling I had borrowed, got a glass of whisky toddy, and came home: unwell from influenza, – the stupid disorder, neither killing nor curing, and no getting rid of.

**Sunday 15th.** Mimas relations from Bakslate,[10] nothing will satisfy but we must go over, so we will, when fine weather arrives and I am shut of this execrable head plague.

**Sunday 22nd.**[11] Hannah Frankland (cousin) from Middleton here, and I gave her two sovereigns towards three which I owed her as an old debt.

**Friday 27th.** Middleton. Gave cousin H. Frankland another sovereign in full repayment of the debt I owed her.

**Tuesday 1st May.** Called on Dr Watts. He had been at London and had seen Mr M. Gibson, who had not heard anything of my affair, but would bear it in mind.

**Wednesday 2nd.** Letter from Leigh to give a lecture on the "reform Union." There is not such a thing.
    Influenza still very troublesome.

**Friday 4th.** Called on my some what cool friend Clowes, who, as a reason for their not putting forward a second reading in Chorlton on Medlock, stated that much harrass and confusion had been caused by the absconding of an official named Egar, with a considerable sum of towns money. He (Clowes) had himself offered to put down a pound towards the payment for the room, but the thing had not been responded to; and I reminded him, it was now too late in the season. I doubt not however he will do something next back-end if I should find it necessary.

**Thursday 3rd.**[12] Went with Mima to Middleton, and looked at Mr Dickins house which is to let at Simifield. It would do.

---

10. Bagslate, near Rochdale.
11. Entries for 22 April, 27 April and 1 May are on the verso, usually reserved for additions and insertions.
12. Entry placed by Bamford after that for May 4th.

**Sunday 6th.** Brierley, wife and child here to tea.

**Tuesday 8th.** To Middleton.

**Friday 11th.** House new papered, very smart.

**Tuesday 15th.** At Manchester. Called at Newalls Buildings and left a shilling for my years subscription to the Reformers Union, the last, I am of opinion which I shall pay towards the support of the present managers.[13]

A tall young man one of the "men about the place" asked me if the annuity had been granted by government yet? I told him that matter was [not] decided yet, and he was so good as to inform me that I was indebted to Doctor Watts only for the memorial which had been presented by Mr Milner Gibson. So it seems, I have not any cause to thank the Lancashire Reformers Union for anything. I was rather pleased to learn this since it proved to me that my former opinion of their feeling towards [me]. At the door people were crowding around a small table, and signing petitions to the House of Commons, and a memorial to Lord Palmerston in furtherance of the repeal of the paper duty: it was raining at the time, so I did not stop to sign in the street, but attached my name to two blank sheets which lay on the desk of the committee room up stairs.

Met Ballantyne[14] in Market St who took me to his editorial Office No 1 Cromford Court, and got me to promise him a copy of my Radical for a review in his paper, the "Manchester Review", it is a bitter anti Bright and Cobden publication, and on reflection I fear the consequence will be, that if he gives a clever notice (which he promises to do), and which may possibly come under the observation of Lord and Lady Palmerston – he professes having a rather intimate connection with that circle – it will set the whole crew of Newalls buildings against me, they supposing that as a good notice of my book appears in an anti Bright paper, I have become an opponent of that gentleman and his friends, whereas, the fact is I am not changed at all. I certainly don't acquiesce in all that Mr Bright or his party say or do, but in general politics I go with them; whilst on Parliamentary reform Mr Bright has decidedly disappointed my expectations. Ballantyne however, must have his book. I have promised it, and cannot omit performing.

**Wednesday 16th.** Went to a Complimentary dinner to Mr Edmund Haworth late poor law guardian, who had been ousted by Cabal and an actively promoted party feeling. A m.s.[15] testimonial expressed in highly commendatory terms: handsomely bound, and signed by all who had attended the dinner was presented to Mr Haworth. A programme of toasts and resolutions gave opportunity for a profusion of turbid, inflated, and grossly absurd oratory, which, to me was amusing, and would have been

---

13. Bamford's membership card for 1860 is attached.
14. Thomas Ballantyne (1806–71), Scot, weaver, and then journalist, first for the *Manchester Examiner*, and later editor of the *Manchester Review*, *The Statesman* and *St James's Press*; *Manchester City News*, 9 September 1871.
15. That is, manuscript.

really enjoyable for the exquisite simplicity of ignorance which was displayed, had not the cab been waiting for me at the door. The Chairman was tiresomely loquacious, the speaker on "the Constitution of England" spoke on anything, and almost everything except the Constitution, of which he evidently knew very little; one or two addresses were neat and to the point because they were brief: all the rest was such a hodgepodge of words, word, words, as I hope I never again shall demean myself by sitting or standing to hear repeated. Got home a little before two o'clock, no better for my dinner.

The annexed exquisite morsel of <u>poetry</u> is taken from the Middleton Albion of the 12th.

**Poem**, *from the* Middleton Albion, *12 May 1860, "On the death of the Rev. Matthew Lawler", by John Fitton.*[16]

**Thursday 17th.** Mima unwell in her bowels; took her tea, and was better.

**Friday 18th.** Mima unwell all day. Went to Newton Heath to call on Doctor Pegg, but he was at home and I could not find him. Mima so much worse when I got home that I determined to call in Mr Pinder, and [he] came instantly, and found the cause of the pain in bowels to arise from her rupture which was out of place: he easily returned the bowel, made up some medicine, which I fetched, and she passed a tolerable easy night having a good sleep.

**Saturday 19th.** Mima no better. Doctor attends and orders powders to be taken every four hours. I had left word at Newton Heath for Mr Pegg to come in the morn[in]g, but as I had in urgency, called in Mr Pinder, I dispatched a note, by a girl, informing Mr Pegg of the circumstance, and that he need not come. Mr Pegg did not receive my note in time, and whilst Mr Pinder was here he came. The matter, of course was explained, and both parties were satisfied. The powders were continued, with water, tea, and gruel for drink – she being very thirsty, with much pain all day: Passed another uneasy night and was very unwell when the doctor came in the morning.

As a curiosity I preserve a copy from the Middleton Albion of May 19th of Mr Howarths complimentary dinner.

**Report**, *from the* Middleton Albion, *19 May 1860, of a dinner and presentation of an address to Edmund Howarth, cotton spinner, in recognition of his services "in the cause of sanatory reform, gas economy, and poor-law guardianship, etc., etc., in and for the townships of Middleton and Tonge". A toast was proposed from the chair to "The Lords of the Manor of Middleton", Sir Samuel Morton*

---

16. The poem accompanies an obituary of John Fitton of Chapel Street, Middleton, a one-time staunch Chartist and self-taught amateur geologist and chemist, noted for his annual pyrotechnic displays each fifth of November at St Michael's church, Tonge, who had died aged 39 leaving a widow and seven children – "truly one of the humble great", *Middleton Albion*, 12 May 1860.

*Peto, and Edward Ladd Betts, Esq.,*[17] *suggesting that they might be invited by their tenants to come and meet them, after which "there would be a way opened for a Town Hall". The suggestion was favourably received by their local agent.*

---

... Mr. Samuel Bamford, on rising to make a few remarks, was greeted with loud cheers. He directed his observations chiefly to silk weaving, observing that there were as good a set of silk weavers in Middleton as could be found anywhere, and were well qualified to any kind of work that might be brought before them; they deserved good treatment and good work, and he hoped the masters would bear this in mind. They had a character for honesty and regularity of work, and that was one great and important element in trade. He thought the silk trade was only temporarily affected by the French commercial treaty, and that it would last only a very short time. The cotton trade was but of recent introduction, and would have been introduced at an earlier period had it not been for the Suffield family, and Mr. Bamford here cited an instance in which certain gentlemen had come from Manchester to take land for the erection of works in Middleton, but on account of being treated in an ungentlemanly manner by the Suffield family, they returned to Manchester in disgust. Messrs. Peto and Betts would never be guilty of such ungentlemanly behaviour, but were at all times ready to set land for useful purposes.

---

**Sunday 20th.** A day of pain; and much suffering: very uneasy and restless. Vomits all the liquid she takes; better towards evening when doctor comes.

Messrs David Morris, T.T. Wilkinson of Burnley called, and after they were gone Dronsfield, Travis, and two others from Hollinwood called in but Mima being so unwell, they did not stay. Doctor says Mima is better than she was at morning.

**Monday 21st.** Mima continues very unwell.

**Tuesday 22nd.** Mr Pinder approved of my calling in other advice on Mimas case. Went to Manchester and got Doctor Roberton[18] of Chorlton on Medlock to come over: he met Mr Pinder, and the result was that an injection, very strong, with salt, turpentine, and oil, was ordered, and bottle of medicine were ordered, and administered with but little beneficial effect, very ill she remained all day, – all night.

**Wednesday 23rd.** Mima no better: the injection was twice repeated at night and at about five on Thursd morning the bowels were brought to act and a regular evacuation followed.

---

17. Sir Samuel Morton Peto (1809–89), a prominent civil engineer whose company's commissions included numerous railways, docks and public buildings (including Nelson's Column), and a leading Liberal, at that time MP for Finsbury. Edward Ladd Betts (1815–72), partner in the construction firm of Peto and Betts. The two men had bought the Suffield estate in 1845; *DNB*; *Proceedings of the Institution of Civil Engineers* xcix (1896), 400–3.

18. John Roberton (1797–1876), Manchester doctor, specialist in diseases of women and children; Liberal and confidant of Richard Cobden; MCL.

**Thursday 24th.**  Mima better, very much all day.

**Sunday 27th.**  Received the following.

*Circular, from Lancashire Reformers' Union, 26 May, 1860, to notify that a meeting will take place on Tuesday 29 May to discuss the rejection of the Paper Duties Abolition Bill.*

What new fit of attention has seized these gentlemen of Newalls Buildings that they invite me to act on the Council of the Union? Surely something is in the wind which has not yet come to sight.

**Tuesday 29th.**  Went to Manchester, and gave notice at the Savings bank for the withdrawal of ten pounds. This is taking out much too soon, but it must be done in order to meet expenses of wife's illness. We must have hard times of bad living for this: Mima continues to improve.

**Thursday 31st.**  Mima much better, we must get rid of nurse and all attendants this week.

**Sunday 10th June.**  Mima so far recovered that she leaves her bed, takes food in small quantities, and is in all other respects much improved. I have paid the nurse for the last time, and I expect and hope Mima will be able to come down into the house in a day or two. Since the 17th of May she has been unwell, and since the 18th I have had to wait upon her, night and day. Mrs Steel a neighbour helping, as occasional nurse, and to keep things in order in the house. My dear wife has every confidence in me, and is very grateful for my kind attentions, and I am quite satisfied with having done my duty as became a husband to a sick wife. I have expected losing her notwithstanding all my care, and my mind has been so harrassed, and my bodily health so wearied with constant fetching and attendance that I have not had either time or disposition for writing the diary.

**Wednesday 13th.**  Ben Walker of Middleton, is dying from a mortification which commenced in one of his big toes: afterwards affected the whole foot, and has now extended to his hip: he was sensible, and lay propped up by pillows in bed; he knew me. Called me by name, took my hand, and I bade him an eternal farewell.

Called at the Coach Office, and paid for my last cab fare on the night, or rather morning of Mr Howarths complimentary dinner, 7/-. I could have done with the money very well, and the book keeper, after I had paid him, said he understood the fare was to be charged to Mr Walton, the treasurer for the dinner. I however, was satisfied, on the whole that I had paid it, as I don't like to incur too many obligations to my "Middleton Friends".

Whilst taking a glass of punch at the Boarshead, Dr Dickin came in, and we adjourned to the Asshetons Arms, where by Mr Harrisons invitation I took dinner with him, Mr Dickin, and a traveller from Manchester. Came off by the 4 o'clock 'bus.

**Thursday 14th.** Ben Walker died at about 4 this afternoon.

**Monday 18th.** Mima down stairs for the first time this sickness.

**Tuesday 19th.** Manchester. Stopped by a little fellow in High St, whose name I forget: by Kelly in Walker St, and next by Jas Hoyle of Fern Grove, Bury who pressed me to call on him when I went that way: on the other side of the street S.P. Robinson, of Newalls Buildings, who nodded, and I just recognised him. A glass or two of punch at Belfields with Mr Greenwell, and a French cook, an intelligent man, who told us how to make an onion dumpling – an excellent relish. A pair of stockings for myself, 1/9 – pork pie, and oranges for Mima and so home by five o'clock 'bus.

**Thursday 21st.** Mima been down in the house all day.
The annexed from Dronsfield.

*Letter, James Dronsfield to Bamford, 20 June 1860.*

Dear Bamford,
Will you be kind enough to let me know if "Mima" is on her feet again and if you are all right of the influenza. I should have been over on Sunday last but I had an engagement in another quarter. On Wednesday next you will very likely receive a call from my mother and sister and my wife with young Bamford, they are intending having an outing Blackley way but you must not provide anything for I can assure you they will not turn out on a picnic without being well stored with the necessaries of life.
                    I am yours with much esteem
                            Jas Dronsfield.
If they come they will very likely trouble you for a drop of hot water but I hope it wont put you to any inconvenience. J.D.

**Saturday 23rd.** The following from the Manr Guardian of today: they remind me of passages in my Walks in South Lancashire, see pp.219–220, and of My Life of a Radical, see p.54, Vol. 1.

*Two extracts from the novel* Scarsdale, *from the* Manchester Guardian, *23 June 1860, one describing the view from the summit of Hambledon Hill and the other describing Market Street, Manchester, thirty years ago.*[19]

If I am not mistaken in my expectation, I shall find more passages approximating to myself and my books when I come to examine "Scarsdale, or Life on the Lancashire

---

19. The sections of *Walks* and *Passages* mentioned by Bamford also describe the landscape in the region of Hambledon Hill. In the *Scarsdale* extract, Bamford has underlined the phrase "like a great sea of awful waves"; *Passages* includes the phrase "like a region of congealed waves", 54.

and Yorkshire border thirty years ago." I have a suspicion that its author, or one who has had a hand in it resides in the neighbourhood of Burnley.[20]

**Sunday 24th.** Midsummer day. 50 years, I believe since I and Mima were married: what changes and strange events have taken place, and passed like shadows in a phantasmaria: a long troubled dream of darkness, storm and sunshine. Mima cheers me with her company downstairs, and Brierley calls in the afternoon, on his way to Oldham.

**Tuesday 26th.** At Manchester. Called on David Morris, who now informed me that on the previous day he had a long talk with Mr Dunckley,[21] the Editor of the Examiner and Times, about me. (He did not state how the conversation affected me; my friends always take care not to let me know what others say of me behind my back: and especially as I suspect, if something favourable has been said.) Dunckley however, I was given to understand, would write a lengthened notice of my book, towards the years end, when my friends would be turning their attention towards the settlement of my pension – if I am to have one – the newspaper notice can then be printed off on slips, and distributed to such as may be able effectively to aid in the endeavour. I was disappointed and chagrined at hearing this, about "the years end", and I said I understood from a former communication – see Dr Watts; letter of 17th Mar – that at the time Mr Milner Gibson applied to Lord Palmerston the latter said my claim should be "taken into consideration at the approaching settlement of the pensions list" from which I understood, the settlement would occur at some early date. Mr Morris said Mr Bazley would be in town soon, and he (Morris) would then see him, and get to know if he could, when the settlement would take place. Greatly dissatisfied I came away.

**Wednesday 27th.** A day of cold wet weather yet our promised visitors from Hollinwood came in much discomfort: we did our best to make them comfortable, but the whole thing was a failure I am sure, as well it might be, and they returned in a cart, as little at their ease as they came. Sorry were we, and troubled on their account.

**Thursday 28th.** At home depressed in mind. Afternoon severe storms of thunder and rain. What a rage of tumult the late comet has caused in the elements: how far does it extend? when will it cease? not yet I fear. Tis past midsummer, and we have scarcely seen summer; will the season be displaced, distroyed? the crops remain ungrown, and the harvest unreaped? if so, "God help the poor" and guide their rulers aright. Good pilotage will be wanted.

**Saturday 30th.** The following literary notice from the weekly Guardian. The book is, I am of opinion, written by Sir James P. Kay Shuttleworth of Gawthorpe Hall.

---

20. *Scarsdale* was, of course, by James Kay-Shuttleworth.
21. Henry Dunckley (1823–96), editor of the *Manchester Examiner and Times* 1854–89, writer under the pseudonym 'Verax'. He edited an edition of *Passages*, published in 1893; MCL.

*Review* of Scarsdale: or, Life on the Lancashire and Yorkshire border, *from the supplement to the* Manchester Weekly Guardian, *30 June 1860, hailing it as "another rich contribution to the literature of Lancashire fiction" in succession to those of Harrison Ainsworth, Mrs Gaskell and others.*

**Sunday 1st July.** H. Grimshaw, Mary Ann, and the two children called: also Ann Lord.

**Monday 2nd.** Went to Middleton, and looked at Ann's Grave. Called at New Inn.

**Saturday 7th.** Dr. Pinders bill £3. 6. 6.

**Tuesday 10th.** Mrs Nelson informed Mima that Doctor Roberton had been asking about her state of health. So I wrote to him an account of her progress and present condition, intimating also that I should be happy to pay any charge he might be pleased to make. The annexed was his reply.

*Letter, John Roberton, 299 Oxford Street, Manchester, to Bamford, 10 July 1860.*

> My dear Sir,
> It gives me sincere pleasure to hear of the recovery of your excellent wife. Long may she be spared to you in health & comfort. There is no fee for the visit I paid.
>     With my kindest regards to Mrs Bamford, believe me
>                         very Faithfully yours.
>                         John Roberton.

**Wednesday 11th.** Wrote again a suitable and grateful acknowledgement. Not copies of either letter.

**Thursday 12th.** Wrote to Sir J. Kay Shuttleworth Brt. as follows.

*Copy letter, Bamford to James Kay-Shuttleworth, 13 July 1860.*

> Dear Sir James,
> The matter about which you cautioned me for silence, has I see come out. I have heard much about it at Manchester, and have been once or twice rather closely questioned respecting any knowledge or suspicion which I might have of the authorship, but as I promised I have remained "mute as death", excepting that I have said that if I betted on the subject at all it should be that neither Mrs Gaskell nor Miss Martineau were the authoresses of "Scarsdale"; I have seen the volumes, and have read their tables of contents, as well as some extracts and observations on the work in the Manchester papers, one of which I thought it right to forward by this post. Of the working out of the story I cannot as yet form an opinion, nor if I could should I feel at liberty to obtrude it, but I may venture to say that some of the extracts which I have seen are very truthful pen sketches of natural scenes and frequently recurring incidents in "Life on the Lancashire and Yorkshire border."

The booksellers and all the people about them, are sorely puzzled as to who can be
the writer: the book however is to be "a great success," a second Adam Bede.
I have not had the pleasure of <u>one</u> line from you on the subject of my gift from the
Royal Bounty Fund, nor of my almost promised <u>compensation</u> from the pension
list which were the chief subjects of my last communication. I am, Sir James,
                    Your obedient servant,
                    Sam<sup>l</sup> Bamford.

**Friday 13th.** Brierley and his little girl called. Brierley ill.

**Sunday 15th.** Ramsbottom and two of his friends called. In talking of the rifle
volunteer movement, I foolishly, and thoughtlessly said "I was glad to see the rifle corps
established and spreading: how could a country be better defended, or to whose defence
could it be more properly confided, than to those who dwelled in it. Let the people be
once thoroughly armed, and they would soon have the government in their own hands",
or words to such effect. This language, or idea, or both, I thought, seemed to excite the
notice of one of the strangers, and his features assumed a thoughtful expression; probably
he would deem it to be the very extreme of revolutionary radicalism, whereas I only
meant to say that in such case, the people would have a wider basis of Parliamentary
reform, with suffrage coextensive with householdership, and would thereby possess the
power to make their own House of Commons, and their own laws.

**Tuesday 17th.** Received the annexed letter from Sir James Kay Shuttleworth.

***Letter**, James Kay-Shuttleworth, 38 Gloucester Square, Hyde Park, to Bamford, 16 July 1860,
enclosing a separate "private and confidential" letter.*

Dear Mr Bamford,
Your letters in the Manchester Papers, at the period when your friends were
finally exerting themselves on your behalf rendered their exertions fruitless, and
caused them in a short time to desist from efforts which you in particular cases
publicly criticised.
    I myself thought that your feelings were entitled to all the respect you claimed,
but a thorough bred Lancashire man like yourself should at seventy years of age
have learned, that which we can each of us, in Lancashire, claim and expect with
confidence, justice, and even kindness. We should be expecting much more than is
the <u>custom of the county</u>, if that justice and that kindness were always in perfect
harmony with the feelings of the poetic ... race whose chivalrous sense of ... and
also of their own claims on public gratitude are rejected by their ruder Lancashire
neighbours as ... [rom]antic.[22]

---

22. The text is damaged here; underlining in the original. Kay-Shuttleworth seems to be advising Bamford
    to accept that it is in the Lancashire character for his down-to-earth neighbours to be sceptical about
    his perhaps romantic sense of himself.

I have no doubt, bye and bye, that this unfortunate obstacle to the exertions of your friends will have been removed from remembrance, and thus you cannot find among them a truer friend than

J. P. Kay Shuttleworth.

Private and confidential

Dear Mr Bamford,

I also have my suspicions, as you have, as to the authorship of Scarsdale, for I find that some materials which I had collected (through various friends, and among them from you) at the request of a literary ally, connected by family with Lancashire, have certainly been used in "Scarsdale", but whether by my literary friend himself or not I cannot inform you.

As, however, it is clearly the author's design to maintain his incognito I have not made any inquiry, I think that both you and I are under the seal of honour to obliterate all traces which could lead to the detection of the authorship. Say nothing.

My belief is that if Samuel Bamford would as the author of the "Radical Autobiography" apply to the publishers Smith, Elder & Co, Cornhill, and ask for a copy to review it, they would certainly send him one out of compliment to his reputation, and because it would be their interest to enlist his services in the provincial journals.

I am very sorry to say that I have no means of helping you in such a request, but, as the book is by a fellow worker with you in exciting sympathy for the condition of the working classes, I counsel you to ask for it frankly and in a straightforward manner from Smith, Elder & Co, 65 Cornhill EC. Yours ever

J. P. Kay Shuttleworth.

**Thursday 19th.** At Manchester: took five pounds more out of the savings bank: fifteen pounds only, now remain.

Waugh has been saying at Kelly's that "An Irish lady, or one residing in the neighbourhood of Rochdale," had written the new novel "Scarsdale." I said, neither Irish, Scotch or Rochdale lady had written it" but as to who the real author was I did not know nor would I pretend to have an opinion on the subject.

Went to Middleton in the afternoon: took a white rose from Ann's grave, and called for Mima, at Alice Walkers, returned by 'Bus: Brierley came at night and talked with me about going to Staly Bridge, and Hollinwood wakes.

**Friday 20th.** The annexed from Elijah Ridings, and sent the following reply to Mr Thorp.

**Letter**, *Elijah Ridings to Bamford, 20 July 1860.*

D[ea]r Sir,

I am requested to inform you that you are invited very respectfully to dine with Henry Thorp Esq of Oak Bank, Alderley whose place of business is at 25 Piccadilly, Manchester. Mr Thorp sends his compliments to you and very much desires to see you. Should you not be able to come, be so kind as to write to Mr Thorp, stating the fact. I should be very glad to see you at his house. You must be in Manchester, say Merchants dining room, corner of Fountain St. at ½ past one, or at 25 Piccadilly ¼ to 2 o'clock on Saturday afternoon.

Wishing this note may find you and yours in good health.

I remain,

Yours Resp<sup>y</sup>

Elijah Ridings.

N.B. Your expenses will be paid.

**Copy letter**, *Bamford to Henry Thorp, Manchester, 20 July 1860.*

Sir,

I have received from Mr Elijah Ridings an invitiation to visit you on Saturday. Mr Ridings informs me that he should be glad to see me at your house. In reply, I have to say that I am too much engaged to come to Alderly, and that if I were not you surely could not expect me to accept an invitation expressed and coming from an intermediate person.

I am, Sir,

Your obedient servant,

Samuel Bamford.

**Letter**, *Henry Thorp, 25 Piccadilly, Manchester, to Bamford, 21 July 1860.*

Sir,

I should indeed be grieved to think that Mr Ridings letter to you, written on my behalf (I did not see the letter, & therefore know not its contents) had been taken in the light of a slight – Being personally unacquainted, I felt it would be presumptuous in me to address you direct, therefore was glad of the opportunity of availing myself of Mr Ridings services with whom I understood you were acquainted.

Though not to be called a "Literary Man", my tastes are decidedly in the direction of Literature and the great portion of my leisure hours are spent in perusing the works of the living and the dead.

Deriving so much pleasure from the works of others, it forms not an unnatural result that a feeling of sympathy and gratitude should rest in the hearts of those who read towards those who write. Your works hold a prominent place in my Library, & I have perused them with much interest.

Yours very respy

Henry Thorp.

P.S. I propose some Saturday this summer riding or driving round by Harperhey, Middleton and Cheetham Hill. If so, I should like to call on your residence at Mosston, if not considered by you, as too great a freedom.

Paid Mr Pinders bill 3. 6. 6 and wrote to Sir James Kay Shuttleworth as see next page.

**Copy letter**, *Bamford to James Kay-Shuttleworth, 20 July 1860.*[23]

Dear Sir James,
As, in consequence of the wish of the author of Scarsdale to maintain his
incognito you have not made any inquiry, I have pleasure in making known to
you that a new light on that subject has come forth; a light that may [possibly]
settle ... with yourself and ... any person who may have entertained
"suspicions" on that much discussed subject. On Thursday I was at
Manchester, and ... that one of a ... written by either an Irish lady or one
residing in the neighbourhood of Rochdale. I was so bold to say, "It was <u>not</u>
written by an Irish lady, or by a Rochdale lady, or by any lady at all." I still
however have my <u>suspicions</u>, but the author may depend on my <u>immutable</u>
<u>silence</u> with respect to his identity, unless I receive his permission to speak
affirmatively thereupon.
    At present I am engaged on the completion of what I think will be an
important document with reference to myself, and my individual case; which
I regret to find, is not <u>clearly</u> understood even by some friends, in ... of whose
partiality, as well as those of my own feelings, I wrote the letter in the Manchester
Examiner and Times. I could not therefore, even if Smith Elder & Co. [were to
send a copy] "review" it. With respect to your other intimation, about their ... of
my services in the periodical journals, having an idea ... I should be glad to
[oblige] you, were I assured that such words would be acceptable; possibly when
I have finished my personal undertaking I may write down a packet of readable
matter on some of the many strange episodes which come, as it were, like beings
from eternity, when I begin to reflect on things long past.
                    I remain, Dear Sir James,
                        Your faithful humble friend,
                            Samuel Bamford.


**Letter**, *James Kay-Shuttleworth, 38 Gloucester Square, Hyde Park, to Bamford, 23 July 1860.*

My Dear old '<u>Radical</u>' friend,
Your brave characteristic letter deserved an immediate answer, especially as you
take in good part my snubbing about the letters.
    It will not do to grumble too loudly about neglect, or the mistakes which
friends may make in their mode of helping you, – all that discourages friends, and
places obstacles in their path.
    Before I leave town I will make every exertion in my power to revive your
claims for a pension.
    The growing interest in the early history of the cotton trade – and the local and
domestic politics of Lancashire – will help your just claims.

---

23. The letter is damaged and in parts beyond recovery; some readings are conjecture.

When I am at Gawthorpe I hope you will pay me another visit and I will try to persuade someone of your own 'kidney' in politics and relish for genuine Lancashire life to meet you at my home.

Yours sincerely

J.P. Kay Shuttleworth.

**Wednesday 1st August.** Called on Mr Thorpe and he is to come over on Saturd[ay] week.

**Thursday 2nd.** Middleton. They are about forming the new Burial ground. The old wall is down, they are cutting for the foundations of the new one, which it seems to me, will not be either deep enough, or strong enough.

The roses are all gone off Anns grave. The radicals, or that party which calls itself such are becoming despicable in Middleton: the tories are taking fresh heart. A weaver (Joe Heywood) said that Parliamentary reform and free trade had been more hurtful than beneficial to the nation. (Stupid).

2000 silk weavers and hands generally out of work at Middleton. Bad trade arises from the dearness of the raw silk and bad trade in France as well as in England.

**Sunday 5th.** Met Brierley, Leech, Dronsfield, Travis and Fletcher, at the [Miles] Platting Station: took the rail for Ashton 10.30: Met Gowenlock and Crompton at Ashton Station: walked on to Stayley Bridge. Smith of the Commercial Inn, not at home: dirty, ill looking Irish wench, the only living being in the house: bar and liquor locked, and the daughter, the "young miss," at Church: Neither meat, drink nor eatables or drinkables of any kind, to be seen, felt or smelled, nor scarcely any fire to cook with if there had been meat: by friend Smith: fine keeping of a respectable Inn. Stormed out in quest of a dinner, and found one was to be had at the Cross Keys. So the whole party adjourned thither, a very fair dinner at one o'clock. Shoulder of mutton: mutton chops, yorkshire pudding: potatoes, fruit pie cheese and ale. 1s. 4½ᵈ each: had a glass each after dinner and gave the girl a shilling. So came away: up the street to Smiths again: find daughter filling two pennorths over the top of the bar: father gone to Bills o'Jacks in Saddleworth:²⁴ expected him home soon and so we (the party) would take a walk towards the Bushes and call as we returned. Bushes a long way to: so returned and after about a two miles walk called at Smiths again: Smith not come back: and daughter gone out to "take a walk". Sadler the Supt. of police tried to get us a drop of something to drink but could not. Miss had locked all up and taken the keys: fine daughter this of Smiths. We turned out again, for the third time. Sadler got us into a decent little house in the street. Sat and had refreshment: landlord owned me, he having been one of a band that played for the reformers at Peterloo: came off to Ashton, where Gowenlock and Crompton took a omnibus for Oldham. Dronsfield, Travis and Fletcher set off to walk home and Brierley, Leech and myself took rail to Miles Platting, whence walked separately home.

---

24. Bill's o' Jack's, a popular country inn.

I was in very poor condition for enjoyment all day: a dull spiritly party on the whole: Damn all such pleasure trips, say I. But I am no longer young: and the young only should associate with the young. I was therefore out of place, and am afraid I was a drag on the spirits of my younger friends.

**Monday 6th.** A letter and inclosures of memorials from Sadler, our friend of yesterday, requesting my influence in his behalf, with either Mr Bazley, MP or Mr Milner Gibson: with neither of whom do I know that I have any influence.

**Thursday 16th.** At Manchester. At Cheetham College library, looking for that part of the Cheetham Societies work which has been prepared by Mr Thomas Heywood, and treats of the Lancashire dialect. The work is not out yet, and consequently is not in the hands of the librarian.[25] Learned that the Mr Thomas Heywood is, in some way, connected with Heywoods bank at Manchester, and consequently with the same Heywoods. In my "Walks in South Lancashire," is a note from a S. Heywood, of Welshaw[26] near Bury (extracted from the Manchester Guardian) impugning a statement of mine respecting "Radcliffe Old Hall," to which note I replied satisfactorily I think.[27] These Heywoods it would seem, have now, and have had during some years, a grudge against me: hence we have this S. Heywood attacking my statement in 1844, and latterly, (in the Cheetham Society's work not yet out,) a Thomas Heywood, as I learned from a glimpse of the sheet that was shown to me at Gawthorpe Hall) nibbling at my Lancashire dialect: there is, or has been, a cause for all things comprehensible; and there must be one for this coincidence of the Heywoods showing a non favourable spirit towards me. And the only circumstance which I can recollect as being in the least calculated to create such a feeling is the one that when Sir Benjamin Heywood established the Mechanics Institution at Manchester neither I, nor any of my friends at Middleton joined Sir Benjamin's undertaking, but nearly at the same time, or shortly after, we commenced a similar Institution at Middleton, ours I think, being about the second in date, in Lancashire. The Heywoods might possibly feel hurt at our setting up, what they might construe into an opposition; however it is, or has been, I have never found the Heywoods to be friends of mine: When I published my books, I found but little encouragement from that quarter; and I cannot but recollect, that when Lord John Russell[28] visited Manchester (the year I have forgotten) he made his home at Claremont,

---

25. Thomas Heywood (dates not known), antiquarian and author of *On the Dialect of South Lancashire* (1860; reprinted in Chetham Society lxvii, 1862). Heywood argued (as did Bamford) that south Lancashire dialect was close to Anglo-Saxon, but also believed (as Bamford did not) that the pioneering dialect writing of "Tim Bobbin" (John Collier, 1708–86) was close to both. Bamford's 1850 edition of Tim Bobbin's *Lancashire Dialect* had "corrected" it in line with the south Lancashire dialect of his own day. Heywood's only mention of Bamford's work on Bobbin was in a footnote (p.70) to George Richardson's satirical attack on it, *Tim Bobbin's Ghost* (see entry for 3 September 1861). No wonder Bamford was cross.
26. That is, Walshaw.
27. See *Walks in South Lancashire*, 281–8.
28. Lord John Russell (1792–1878), leading Whig politician, prime minister 1846–51 and 1865–6, and at this time Foreign Secretary in Palmerston's government 1859–64; *DNB*.

and returning to London, gave A.A. Watts,[29] who had established a Tory newspaper at Manchester (The Courier) and had always been a Tory and an ...[30] a pension of a hundred a year. When at a later date Lord Palmerston visited Manchester, he also put up at Sir Benjamin's, and returning from thence gave Charles Swain, another Tory, though of a mild stamp, a pension of fifty pounds a year: Last of all, though Sir Benjamin, and his party might be innocent in this matter, he gave Bolton Rogerson a fifty pounds pension, which was better bestowed than either of the other two.

Met Mr Cheetham of Firwood, near the Old Church, and no sooner was he gone, than I fell in with Dr Watts, who reminded me about the date of his last letter which I had promised to furnish him. Bought some meal at bottom of Deansgate and came home.

**Friday 17th.** Sent Dr Watts the promised date with one of my last circulars and "Addenda" dated Aug 7th.

**Sunday 18th.** Middleton Wakes. At Middleton with Dronsfield. A dull concern. Came away by six o'clock bus.

18th Sund.[31] Gowenlock and Potter came to my house, and followed me to Middleton, but missed me.

**Tuesday 20th.** At Manchester, Greenwell and another at Belfields. Kelly showed me a vol. of Scarsdale, just to peep at, but I had not time, coming away at one o'clock. Fell in with Spencer, who had just received half of a ten pound note from his circle at London and would get the other half on writing for it, poor fellow, he has been sadly "put to it." Stopped and shook hands with Councillor Brittain.[32]

**Thursday 22nd.** At Middleton: nothing new except falling in with the little excise man and the sudden death of Jenny Halliwell which took place on Tuesd. evening: all that lot are gone. A good shuttance except Jenny.

**Friday 23rd.** The annexed is my circular up to the present date: copies have been sent to all the names under dates of Aug 17 and 21, but as yet not any notice has been received, either approving or disapproving.

***Insertion***: *a revised version of Bamford's circular "Right against wrong", dated 7 August 1860, with minor amendments and a lengthy set of addenda documenting his political career: see Appendix 1.*

The death of Robert Story was, no doubt accelerated by the 100 bottles of wine which his friend (true friend) the Duke of Northum[berlan]d left him on his (the

---

29. Alaric A. Watts (1797–1864), briefly editor of the *Manchester Courier* before a long career in London journalistic circles; awarded a civil list pension of £100 in 1854; *DNB*.
30. Word illegible.
31. Inserted opposite.
32. Thomas Brittain (b. 1806), founder of the Manchester Microscopical Society and the Manchester Scientific Students Association, occasional scientific lecturer; *MCL*.

Dukes) departure for the continent. The Duke had promised Bobby to do something for him, and doubtless he would have done, if he, Bobby, would have [had] patience and remained at his desk in his hole, at Somerset House, until there was a passable ground for an application to government on his behalf; I advised Robt to get out of the <u>hole</u>, as soon as he could, with due regard to the Duke's views: I also advised him to quit that ugly swampy place, in Battersea, where he had already lost two children, by consumption; he however preferred stopping at the beggarly unmeaning spot and sailing up and down the stinking river twice a day; at night, I know he was in the habit of taking his whisky toddy freely and that and the 100 bottles of wine and his stinking voyages and his low damp dark cellar, that he sat in all day knocked him off. So ends Bobby, who after all was not what we call in Lancashire, "A Jannock Chap."[33] Witness his wishing to introduce me on my first going to London, to "a detective" (Inspector Dodd), then his opening of my letter from Dixon (of the City), and lastly his shabby return (shabby, very shabby, and inhospitable, or that of his wifes) for our kind and most welcome entertainment of himself and family at New Street Portland town.

**Saturday 25th.** The annexed letter from Dronsfield; and the printed matter from the Middleton Albion of this day.

*Letter*, *James Dronsfield to Bamford, 24 August 1860.*

Dear Bamford,
I felt rather disappointed that you did not come on Thursday afternoon, with the weather so favourable, but it would not have been so pleasant if you had gone home the same evening; but however I shall expect you both on Sunday next without fail, you can walk to the train, at Dean Lane Station, it leaves Victoria at ½ past 9 a.m. book to Werneth and I will wait your arrival, it will be an easy walk down hill from Oldham and should it be a fine morning you will have a beautiful landscape view of the fine open country laying westward. I shall do my best to make you both comfortable. I have arranged with my Mother to provide you a comfortable bed for we are determined that you shall both spend a night with us, and we can get a select knot of friends together to enjoy a social glass, with our worthy host Mr John Pollitt [at] Philo. It being Oldham Wakes there will be no working on Monday so that we shall be able to spend a few pleasurable moments the morning following, and you can return at leisure. There is an Omnibus leaves Manchester at 10 am, but it will perhaps be crowded with people going to Oldham Wakes so that I should prefer the Railway, and for another reason, Mrs Bamford I believe never was in Oldham so that she will visit both places with one journey so I hope that you will favour her for once it is not very often you do take her out and I am sure my mother and Mrs Dronsfield will be delighted to have a

---

33. Jannock was bread made from oat meal and sour milk, traditional to south-east Lancashire. To be "jannock" meant to be earnest, faithful to one's purpose.

chat and a cup together. So remember Sunday next, 35 past 9 train, Newton Station, book to Werneth. There is no other train until 1pm and that will be too late you must be in time for dinner, no afternoon coming we shall expect you, <u>do come</u>.

I am yours,<br>
With much esteem,<br>
James Dronsfield.

P.S. I should think that we shall not always have the weather wet at least I am in hopes that it will be fine on Sunday next, but you will not be much exposed should it be any ways unfavourable except the short walk from your house to Newton, we can have a Cab from the Station to Hollinwood and also when you return. J.D.

**Poem**, *from the* Middleton Albion, *25 August 1860: "Lines on 'The Floral Grave,' the grave of Samuel Bamford's daughter, in Middleton churchyard; from 'Literary Reminiscences and Gleanings,' by Richard Wright Proctor."*

**Sunday 26th.** Miss Taylor sent peas. Mima and I met Dronsfield at the Werneth Station: dined at his house at Hollinwood: after dinner went with him to Oldham. Gowenlocks, Potters, his new picture, copy from Rosa Bonheure:[34] whilst he was at Paris. Councillor Taylor who owns the picture came: would not take fifty pounds for it. Gowenlock, Potter, Brierley and self went down to Hollinwood to tea at Dronsfields. Afterwards to Pollitts at Philo, where I recited some of my old poetical pieces, then to Old Mrs Dronsfields, where we had a nice snack and Mima and I remained all night: very good accommodation; breakfast in the morning and so came away by Omnibus.

Notice the annexed charge of the Judge at South Lancashire Assizes.

**Newspaper cutting**, *source not given. The opening charge of the judge at South Lancashire Assizes, Baron Martin, stating that, with seven cases of murder, eleven of manslaughter and seventeen of burglary, "he had never seen such a calendar in the whole course of his experience".*

**Tuesday 28th.** Went to Proctors in Long Mill Gate, who told me Robt Story died of Bronchitis. Called at the Registrars Office. Mr Gardiner not in. Stepped inside the lodge at the Workhouse: entered name in a book and looked inside the yard. Very great changes: must go again some day, with regular order for admission. Came home by bus.

**Sunday 2nd September.** Miss Taylor again sent a present of garden stuff, gooseberries, and cauliflowers. Forwarded by the messenger, a very grateful acknowledgement and one of my circulars with the addenda: this is "Casting my bread upon the waters," as it were. She will probably show the documents to some one or more of her friends.

---

34. Rosa Bonheur (1822–99), celebrated French painter of animal subjects who achieved international fame with an exhibition in 1855.

Mima and I invited to attend the funeral of her cousin Ann Crooks. Brierley came in the afternoon, and <u>Gabriel Tinto</u>,[35] with his son, at evening.

**Tuesday 4th.** At Manchester. Dr Watts had not received answer from Mr Milner Gibson: he had sent my circular with an "Addenda" to Lord Palmerston, but had not received any reply: Will see Mr Bazley this week, and I am to call again on Friday and get a list of the names attached to the memorial which the Dr sent. Fell in with a Mr Slater from Hedge Lane; and returned by Omnibus at one o'clock.

4th Tuesd. A man who said his name was Moors from Tonge lane called to me in the market and showed an order for 61 pounds received from a relation at the Cape of Good Hope. The order was payable 31 days after sight and I advised him to present it at one of the Banks and they would instruct him how to proceed, but was going to some brewery in Salford and preferred taking advice there respecting the payment: So I cautioned him to be very careful about his money when he got it, and left him.

**Wednesday 5th.** A shocking accident on the East Lanr rails at Elmshore.[36] 10 killed outright and 56 lamed, or otherways injured.

A Spy. See below, the slip taken from the Examr and Times of this day.

---

DELICATE and Private Inquiries and Commissions to Execute in any part of England. Secrecy strictly observed. – Address H., Post-office, Fenton, Stoke-on-Trent.

---

**Thursday 6th.** Ann Crooks of Middleton buried.

**Sunday 9th.** Ramsbottom called.

**Tuesday 11th.** Manchester. Saw Mr Bazley who had not heard anything further from Lord Palmerston: said as I had received one fifty pounds, we must wait for the expiration of the year, and then if a further remittance does not take place his lordship must again be reminded of my case.

Did not say anything as to <u>how</u> I was to <u>live</u> in the mean time.

Mr David Chadwick came in whilst was at Mr Bazley's and afterwards walked with me up the street. Said as my case was in the hands of Dr Watts and David Morris, it could not be better: They would doubtless do their best to get me [a] pension; and they would be justified in applying for one of the lowest grade, £50 for instance, which ought to be granted. My patience was sorely tried: Why should these men who call themselves my <u>friends</u> be continually harping on £50 as if an old patriot was never deserving of more under[37] any circumstances than [this]; why Alaric Watts, has his

---

35. A puzzle. "Gabriel Tinto" is traditionally identified as the pseudonym of George W. Anthony (1810–59), drawing master and art critic, but he had died the previous year.
36. That is, Helmshore.
37. Volume 3 ends here, volume 4 begins.

100; Swain and the Bideford postman have their 50, and surely an old patriot, who has suffered for having served his country, is deserving of a more respectful consideration than any mere poet or rhymester of these. Besides I have been upwards of forty years uncompensated, and ought to have an extra consideration for that. But I never shall have justice: I see and feel that those who are deemed my friends, are not to be depended upon.

**Thursday 13th.**  Miss Taylor sent a couple of very nice cauliflowers.

Went to Manchester Workhouse, where Mr Rickards[38] Chairman of the Guardians, and Mr Crewdson, another Guardian, met me and introduced me to the Matron. Was shown through the house and recognized many of the old rooms and passages. The room in which my mother died was nearly in the same state as when she lay there, and I in a bed beside her: it is now the Governors bedroom. When entering this room I reverently took off my hat, which I had kept on in consequence of the cold draughts in the lobby, covered my face, and gave my thoughts to a brief, but solemn retrospection of the death scene of my beloved, and affectionate parent. Had she lived, my course of life would probably have been far different from the one I have passed through. The room in which my little sister Hannah, and my brother James lay in their coffins, all disfigured by the frightful smallpox is the same. My Uncle Thomas's bedroom, in which he died is now the governesses sleeping apartment.

I took a lunch of bread and cheese, and a couple of glasses of ale, with the governor and governess, in the room of the former, and thanking them for their hospitality, I came away.

**Friday 14th.**  Miss Taylor sent two very nice cauliflowers, the kind good lady.

**Sunday 16th.**  Should have gone with a party on a trip to Woodhead, but I disengaged from it, and am glad I did so: a cold gloomy, wet day.

During the night I was rather alarmed on finding I could not make water. I rubbed the part, and in a short time the obstruction ceased. Is this attack the fore runner of disease that shall take me hence? God forbid 'tis a sore affliction.

**Tuesday 18th.**  Thought it best to write to Mr Binney, who after a silence of almost three years, had been enquiring about me.

*Copy letter*, Bamford to Edward Binney, Manchester, 18 September 1860.

My once kind and dear friend,
A gentleman whom I met a day or two since at Manchester, informed me that Elijah Ridings had stated to him, that in a conversation which he had recently held with you, you had expressed surprise at my not publishing a new edition of

---

38.  Charles H. Rickards (1812–86), wholesale paper merchant, magistrate and chairman of the Manchester Board of Guardians, 1855–69; MCL.

my book (Life of a Radical, I understand). It is so long since I had either the pleasure of your conversation, or the benefit of your advice, though I have never known <u>why</u> our friendship was interrupted, that I knew not what to say, when the gentleman urged me to call upon you: that you had not entirely forgotten me; and that you still occasionally at least bestow a thought on my proceedings, was evident: I felt therefore, that duty to myself, as well as the regard which for "auld lang syne" I still cherished toward you, required that I should thank you for your unexpected reminiscence of a humble friend; one who never yet "turned a cold shoulder" on any acquaintance, without letting him know <u>why</u> I did so. I could not, therefore, do less than write to you since a personal visit would not have been becoming on my part, and might have been disagreeable; or an inopportune trespass on your time and attention.

My last communication was addressed to you in the early part of Aug<sup>t</sup> 1857: to that note, I did not receive any reply: you ceased to correspond without <u>assigning any motive</u>, and humble though I was, and am, I could not think of <u>begging</u> a continuance of friendly intercourse, and hence I suppose, its cess[at]ion.

As I have yours in hand, I think I ought to inform you that the occasion of my not republishing the Radical is the fact of the Copyright of 1000 of it were sold to Abel Heywood in 1858. I have not exchanged probably more than ten words with him since, and I suppose he expects the sale of the edition to last until I am out of the way; and in truth I begin to think his expectations will not be disappointed.

To John Heywood I have sold an edition of 1000 copies of "Early Days". I am thus precluded from any movement with respect to these two works: and a <u>continuation</u> of the Radical, which I could wish to live to see published, I am prevented from embarking upon by the want of a responsible undertaker.

I enclose you a circular which I have been distributing to a few friends and old acquaintance[s]; and an address of the same, wherein readers may see my course, whether in <u>prison, on trial; in government employ</u> or dependent upon their commendation and <u>good wishes,</u>

I remain, dear Sir,
yours truly,
Sam<sup>l</sup> Bamford.

**Wednesday 19th.** Received the following reply from Mr Binney.

*Letter*, *Edward Binney, 40 Cross Street, Manchester, to Bamford, 19 September 1860.*

My dear Sir,

I beg to acknowledge the receipt of your letter of the 26<sup>th</sup> [sic.] instant.

It is quite true that I did not reply to your letter of the 26<sup>th</sup> July 1857 – If you see it you will find that it needs no reply – after receiving it you came down to Manchester and did not call on me. (1)[39] I afterwards met you in the yard in

---

39. Bamford's footnotes: see below.

Somerset House, (2) and you appeared quite friendly with me therefore when I saw you in Greenwood's omnibus going to the inauguration of the Brotherton's statue and you turned your back to me when I said "How are you Mr Bamford" (3) I did think it strange. I have not quarrelled with you. I should like to see something done for you and your good wife and altho' my engagements will not permit me to take any active part in any such scheme I will do what I can to assist. I remain

Yours truly<br>Edw<sup>d</sup> Binney.

1) I did not call on him when I came to Manchester, because he had not replied to my letter.

2) This meeting in the yard was on another occasion, and long anterior to the time he mentions.

3) When he came into Greenwoods omnibus, he slightly spoke to me, and I as slightly returned the compliment, and there the affair ended.

He will be "willing to assist," will he? Well, if I am very hard put to it, I may possibly ask his assistance, not else.

**Thursday 20th.** Paul Halliwell, once an intimate acquaintance of mine, afterwards a friend of "Jonny Judas's"; latterly a pauper on the Middleton Union, and now the pet underling of Edmund Howarth, slunk out of my sight today; the fellow, no doubt has been playing the traitor and calumniator, and cannot face me up.

**Friday 21st.** At Fern Hill with Mima to dinner. Came away early, and got home to tea.

# 10

# JUST COMPENSATION?

*The autumn of 1860 began badly for Bamford: anxious inquiries via Kay-Shuttleworth about his pension quickly brought the bad news that the pension fund could not be used to reward political services or compensate for political wrongs. Bamford was enraged, and embarked on a vociferous campaign to gain "just compensation". He was fired up by reports of speeches from both the prime minister, Lord Palmerston, and the leader of the reform movement, John Bright, in which they attributed the prosperity of the present to the reforms of the past. Emboldened by the success of a reading at Lees in November, Bamford embarked on what was for him a brave and risky undertaking: a reading, arranged by himself, at Manchester's prestigious Athenaeum. Would Manchester follow Palmerston and Bright in embracing its debt to the radicals of the past, or would he suffer another humiliating rejection? The result was a qualified success, and Bamford could face the end of the year with some relief.*

**Monday 1st October.** Wrote to Sir. J.Kay Shuttleworth; see opposite.

***Copy letter***, *Bamford to James Kay-Shuttleworth, Gawthorpe, 1 October 1860.*

Dear and Honoured Friend,
The terms of your last communication did not strike me as requiring any immediate reply, and I laid it aside until something turned up which might give me a reasonable claim to your brief attention. First however, let me recur to your letter.

I should be sorry if you incurred any harassing or troublesome exertion on my behalf, and more especially so, should such endeavours prove of no avail: In your last you say you will try to revive my "claim to a pension": did my letters then, in the newspapers, <u>damage</u> that claim? or cause it to be lost sight of? if so I was certainly, very much misunderstood, for I only intended to assert my right to that decent, honest pride and that immunity from painful attention, however well meant, to which any working man, who respects himself may with becoming reserve lay claim: to that decent, honest pride, in fact, which if properly understood, and rightly estimated, would lead all who honour me with their friendship, to be proud of their humble friend, whose self respect was such as was worthy of their approval.

I am very grateful for your kind intentions, and for whatever inconveniences you may have encountered on my behalf; though, not having heard from you, I do not suppose that you have been successful. My thanks are not however, the less sincere and fervent on that account.

I shall be curious to know what sort of a gentleman who is, "one of my own kidney in politics" and "a relish for real Lancashire life", whom you will try "to persuade to meet me, at your house". To you I would only say, don't vouchsafe too much persuasion since he might after all esteem me but, "a dull fellow". I have become of late so accustomed to stern and ...[1] reality, that I have almost forgotten the beguilement of imagination.

---

1. Word illegible.

Scarsdale continues to be talked about: and what do you think they say? I was dining a few days ago at the house of a respectable tradesman, several ladies being present, and not much time had elapsed ere "the new book, Scarsdale", became the subject of conversation, intentionally so, it seemed to me, and "Sir James Kay Shuttleworth", was mentioned as the supposed, and very probably, real author. They were sure I "knew something", about the author; and I was earnestly and repeatedly pressed on the subject, until at length I felt called upon to say that I knew not anything more of the authorship than they knew themselves; that I certainly had my suspicions, that as they were only suspicions, I did not feel at liberty to say more. I think something has oozed out from your visit to John Heywood's book shop at Manchester: for one or two of the ladies intimated that I had, in some way, interfered in the matter of the book; and finding suspicion was taking that social course I declared at once, that they were greatly mistaken, that I had not any certain knowledge more than themselves who was the author; that I had not read the book, save extracts in the papers and that with the production I had not had any share, either by word, or writing. The second vol was brought into the room, and they [asked] me if my name was not in the book? I replied that I did not know; I had not read the book, nor had I any idea that my name was connected with it, and at last I think I gave them a quietus.

I may inform you before I close, that my Manchester friends do not appear to have made any decided hit in the matter of my pension. Mr Bazley has not heard anything further from Vic$^t$. Palmerston and Mr Milner Gibson does not seem to hear more about it. A strange indifference appears to have succeeded their impulsive, and indiscreet zeal on my behalf. I shall not urge them to urge Lord Palmerston on the subject, so I suppose the business will dose until next session of Parliament when I shall, I suppose, apply at the bar of the Commons for my rights; for Compensation; and if I get that, I will endeavour to live, happily if I can, without the receipt of anything in the way of a boon, or pension. I am Sir James,

yours with true respect,
Samuel Bamford.

The annexed slip is from the Middleton Albion of the 29th (Sat).

**Cutting**, *from the* Middleton Albion, *29 September 1860, a summary of the addenda to Bamford's revised circular, "Right Against Wrong"*.

**Wednesday 3rd.** Mr Coulborn called and left me a ticket for the Agricultural Dinner, Middleton: also pressed on me, very kindly, the acceptance of half a sov[ereign], to pay cab hire home. So very handsomely, and kindly done, that I did not feel authorized in not accepting frankly.

**Thursday 4th.** Went, and though a rather good dinner, I did not enjoy it at the late hour of five p.m. About 200 sat down: some fine horses, cattle and hogs at the show; the rector in the Chair, and the toasting of the Clergy, with the responses of three or four parsons and their toadies was sickening. I got in with some difficulty, to make a short address, not mentioned in the Manchester papers, and murdered in the Middleton one.[2]

4th Oct. Thursd. Sent copies of my circular with the addenda to the Guardian and the Exam[r] & Times.

**Sunday 7th.** The annexed from Sir J.P. Kay Shuttleworth, ending my doubts as to any compensation from Government.

*Letter*, *James Kay-Shuttleworth, Gawthorpe, to Bamford, 6 October 1860.*

*Confidential.*

> Dear Friend,
> I made cautious but careful inquiries in London, why a grant had been made to you from the Royal Bounty fund only.
> The explanations given to me from well informed sources were – (a) that the pension fund is not applicable to the compensation of any form of political service or for injuries ... sustained in that class of public efforts. (b) That claims on <u>other</u> grounds had been pressed, reviewed, and set aside.
> It was irksome to me to relate this to you.
> I hoped to do so personally some day when you and John Spencer, and some other of my friends among the peerage of virtue were visiting me here.
> I received your note at Brougham, and but for the allusion in it to other worthies, I would have shewn it to Lord Brougham.
> Could you write me a letter very simply and without complaint stating what you have down for public freedom: and how you have of late years supported yourself by your own pen?
> I think that I shall have an opportunity of using such a letter before the close of this month.
> > I am yours truly
> > J.P. Kay Shuttleworth.

They have funds, it seems, to give away to venal authors, toadies, and the spawn of lickspittles, but not one doit have they to do justice: to pay just debts, or make compensation to those they have robbed of their rights, imprisoned wrongfully, and otherwise injured: a superb government truly!

**Tuesday 9th.** Sent the annexed in reply to Sir James.

*Copy letter*, *Bamford to James Kay-Shuttleworth, 9 October 1860.*

---

2. The *Middleton Albion* report, 6 October 1860, reads: "Mr. Samuel Bamford then addressed the company, and showed how the objects of the society, in a social point of view, would be materially aided, if the society awarded prizes for good workmanship in the department of silk weaving, &c." See entry for 10 October.

Dear Sir James,

In narrating what I have done for public freedom, I don't see how I can properly omit what I have suffered in its promotion, not as a subject of complaint, but as matter of fact only. Active exertions being one part, or stage of acting or doing; and passive endurance being another phase of the same action; and both requiring wear and tear of life in proportion to their intensity, I will therefore note down, so far as I recollect, what I have done and <u>suffered</u>, in promoting and supporting public measures, which I believed would, and which I certainly intended to produce public benefit if carried into effect.

In 1816, I was the chief founder, the chief leader, the chief secretary, and, in fact the chief for thought and action, of the Middleton Hampden club the object of which was to obtain a reform of the Commons House, and a repeal of the Corn Laws.

In 1817, I attended a meeting of delegates at London, and won over the powerful advocacy of Mr Cobbett to suffrage at 21 years of age, he having previously pleaded for household suffrage only. In the same year I was the means of protecting the members of our society, and the public of our district generally, from the instigations of spies, and the unlawful proponents of incendiary agents. Oliver[3] and Mitchell[4] being at that time moving about the County amongst the people, the former unknown to me, and the latter not, as yet, suspected. Machinations however emanating from them, the origin not as yet known: I frequently became cognisant of, combated and frustrated. About this time, I was arrested on suspicion of High Treason, by virtue of a warrant by Lord Sidmouth. I was chained, and escorted by dragoons and police, was consigned to the New Bailey prison at Salford, from whence, heavily chained, and mixed up with others who had been arrested at a private meeting – of which however, Mitchell, if not Oliver had a knowledge. I was conveyed to London, was chained to the bedstead at Bow Street; taken before the Privy Council, committed to Cold Bathfields prison, and after five examinations before the Council, was discharged and returned home. During my absence, Oliver and Mitchell, had free range through the country, and then it was that a series of <u>private</u> delegate meetings was mounted and carried into effect, ending [in] Derby and Chesterfield, at which the [action of] Brandreth and his fellow delegates was arranged and determined upon. During my absence in prison the two incendiaries, the spy and his coadjutor, made their head quarters near Middleton, which they surely would [not] have dared to do had I been in the neighbourhood: it would almost seem as if my arrest, and conveyance away were intended to have the country clear for

3. W.J. Richards (dates not known), known as "Oliver the spy", government *agent provocateur* inside the radical movement in the spring of 1817, subsequently exposed. Bamford had encountered and resisted him, see *Passages*, chapters 12 and 26; E.P. Thompson, *The Making of the English Working Class* (1963), 711–34.

4. Joseph Mitchell (dates not known), Lancashire radical and political missionary in the Peterloo period, associate of Bamford, and the contact through whom Oliver the spy infiltrated the radical movement. He was accused and cleared of being a spy of himself, and Bamford had earlier regarded him as "an egregious dupe ... not a spy"; *Passages*, chapters 12 and 26, Thompson, *Making of the English Working Class*, 713–18.

their operations: however intended, such was its effect; I was kept in ignorance of the [activities] of those two wicked men until it was too late, and mischief was unavoidable. Thomas Bacon one of the sufferers came to me on a secret mission, (after my return from London) he wished to find out a certain person, whom I knew well enough, but did not know that he was engaged in anything secret. Bacon had made me aware that something was going on, but what, I could not fathom. I therefore denied knowing such a man, gave Bacon good advice for which he scarcely thanked me, and sent him away the way he had come. In a few weeks afterwards he was tried at Derby, and with fourteen others was transported for life: a dread looking young man who was with him, being hung and beheaded with Brandreth and Ludlam.[5]

On the 16 of August 1819, I, accompanied by many thousands of my neighbours, attended a meeting at Manchester, the object of which was to petition for an extension of Parliamentary franchise, and a repeal of the Corn Laws: About two oclock on the morning of the 26th August I was again arrested on a charge of high treason, and again, guarded by soldiers, horse and foot ... in the New Baily. I was kept ... 22 days: Examined and committed to Lancaster Castle, charged with misdemeanours, was bailed out; at [the succeeding] March assize had a trial of 16 days, [and] defended myself in a manner and with [testimony], which brought credit to myself and the Cause I represented. I earned a compliment from the opposite leading Counsel and a pointedly favourable summing up from the venerable judge: was found guilty. I was sent to London: was nearly on the point of sleeping in the street from want of money. [I] was relieved the morning following by a kind friend, and on the last day of Easter term 1820 was sentenced in the court of Kings Bench, to twelve months imprisonment in Lincoln Castle: taken from the court to the Kings Bench prison, where I was detained several days, then manacled, conducted to [Newark] and from thence to Lincoln Castle where I remained during the time for which I was sentenced.

In 1826, when the starving hand-loom weavers of Burnley, Padiham, Blackburn, and their neighbourhoods were destroying machinery, they were invited by parties wishing for an opportunity to plunder, to repeat their distinctive outrages at Heywood, Middleton and Oldham; truthful information of this was communicated to me; also that the invitation had been accepted and the Monday following was the day appointed for commencing operations. I determined to see these deluded men, and to stop their proceedings if possible; and accordingly I went [on my own] responsibility, and at my own efforts, on the hills above Haslingden, and met a number of the leaders near Hambledon to whom, after being introduced by a person who was in their confidence I addressed such facts and arguments as very much altered their view of the undertaking; and when the main body assembled in

---

5. This was William Turner. He and Bacon had visited Bamford in Middleton in May 1817 in preparation for the abortive Pentridge rising, which led to the executions of Jeremiah Brandreth and others, an operation in which Oliver the spy had been closely involved. See E.P. Thompson, *The Making of the English Working Class* (Penguin edn, 1968), 711–34.

the morning following and heard what their leaders had to say respecting my visit, there was such a divided opinion amongst them, that the intention was abandoned, and they separated without proceeding to action; and thus possibly great devastation of a very populous district, or districts was prevented.

In 1832 I was compelled to take the office of Constable; and in 1841, the year of Feargus O'Connors, "plug-drawing holiday", I was a leader of Special Constables at Middleton, the town and immediate neighbourhood remaining free from the visits of disturbers.

Such are the chief incidents of my exertions for public good as I recollect them off hand; and of ... exercises arising from the same source; the consideration of all being respectfully submitted by,

your obliged and humble servant,<br>Samuel Bamford.

P.S. I may add that in 1826 I became a correspondent of a London daily newspaper; in 1829 I wrote for several of the Manchester weekly papers; afterwards for the Guardian, and the Chronicle, and occasionally for The Times, until 1839, when I commenced publishing my "Passages in the Life of a Radical", and from thence ceased newspaper correspondence, as a means of subsistence. I afterwards published in succession, "Poems", in one vol; "Early Days", one vol; and "Lancashire Dialect", one vol. The writing and publishing these works occupied me from 1839 to about 1848. In 1851 my friend the late Mr John Wood offered me employment at Somerset House, and to my subsequent great regret and discomfort, I moved to London. During the long protracted, "Preston turn out", I wrote several articles for Cassells Weekly Newspaper, which I intended to be corrective of the pernicious writings which Mr Dickens was issuing at that time.[6] Political party considerations – as I believe – stopped the continuance of my articles – and since then I have not followed writing as a means for subsistence but I have derived some help from the sale of copyright. In 1857 Mr Wood died and in 1858 I left Somerset House; came down to Lancashire and settled near my present residence, at Mosston, Harperhey, Manchester, where hoping the best, and fearing not the worst, I steadfastly, and with good heart await, whatever measure of weal or woe, may be allotted to me.
S. B.

I should like very much to know if, the knowledge could possibly be obtained, what these claims on other grounds were, "which had been pressed on Lord Palmerstons notice", by whom they were pressed, and why withdrawn? This information would give me some idea as to my real position; without it I am lost in a mist; a void which I cannot pierce or comprehend.

---

6. *Cassell's Illustrated Family Paper*, 28 January, 11 February and 25 March 1854, three fictionalised didactic sketches about the great Preston cotton strike (or, rather, lockout) of 1853–4. Bamford portrays the workers debating the issues and eventually proposing a reconciliation, whereas Dickens' sketch in *Household Words* on 11 February emphasised conflict and demagoguery. (*Hard Times*, based in part on the lockout, did not appear until afterwards.)

Did I get the <u>whole</u> of your letter? There are remarks referring, as I suppose, to other slips, or other matter, (a), and afterwards (b).

Your faithful, humble

S. B.

Before you say anything to Lord Brougham about me [let me] refer you to page 28 of my Life of a Radical (chap. 5).[7]

**Wednesday 10th.**  The following to Middleton Albion.

***Copy letter***, *Bamford to the* Middleton Albion, *10 October 1860.*[8]

SIR, – Permit me to correct one small part of your generally clever report of the above proceeding. I am represented in your report as having said, "The objects of the society would be materially aided, if the society awarded prizes for good workmanship in the department of silk weaving." There is an evident inconsistency here; how could I expect an agricultural association to award prizes to silk weaving? What I did say was somewhat to this effect: That I had been much pleased with the exhibition of agricultural produce set forth that day; the fine beasts and products of the farm shewed the advance which had taken place in the breeding and cultivation of things necessary to the sustenance of man. This kind of thing; these exhibitions, would not however stop with mere agricultural shows; there would be exhibitions for the improvement of God's farming stock: for the material improvement of man; it was impossible that improvement should stand still. We were on the verge of an eternity of improvement, and why should we not go forward boldly, and realize all the advantages we could. We had what were called societies of "Free Gardeners," why should they not in reality become gardeners, each cultivating his own garden, with prizes once a year for the best arranged and most productive garden; this would be better, more civilizing than their quaint old rush-carting; better than their running in mobs to Belle Vue. Exhibitions of improvements would progress, or I was greatly mistaken; they would I hoped be found ere long, operating on domestic matters. Why could not the working classes of Middleton, for instance, get up an exhibition once a year with prizes, or honourable distinctions, for the cleanest and the neatest cottage; for the cleanest and the neatest beds and bedrooms; for the best ordered loom shops; for the best loom; and why, above all, should not the weavers of Middleton have an exhibition once or twice a year for the production of the best pieces of

---

7. Chapter 5 of *Passages* concludes with Bamford's assessment of Henry Brougham, whom he had heard speak in the Commons in 1817. Bamford criticises Brougham for at times "bowing to his own image, and sacrificing reason and principle to caprice or offended self-love", but sets against these his work for the abolition of slavery and for popular education: "These are indeed blessings beyond price – rays of unfading glory.– They are lord Brougham's; and will illumine his tomb when his errors and imperfections are forgotten".

8. The event referred to is the annual dinner of Middleton Agricultural Society at the Old Boar's Head Inn.

cloth, silk or other fabrics? Why, in fact, should there not be endeavours at improvement in all other things as well as agricultural produce?

The above, though perhaps not all that I said, will give a tolerably fair idea of the purpose and intention of my brief address.

I remain, Sir, yours truly,

SAMUEL BAMFORD.

**10th Wed.**  The annexed from office of Manchester Exam^r & Times.

**Letter**, *A. Ireland*, Manchester Examiner and Times, *to Bamford, 9 October 1860.*

Dear Sir,

Mr Dunckly will be glad to see you any day (except tomorrow) about 1/2 past one o'clock, on the subject of your letter.

Yours very truly,

A. Ireland.

**Thursday 11th.**  Went to see Mr Dunckley at the Office of the Exam^r & Times: found him a frank and pleasant person of rather low stature, with a remarkably fine head, and a look of ready, and sound intelligence. We talked about my communication (the circular, and addenda) and about my case generally, and the conclusion was, that he would give the two documents in the paper of Tuesday next. He intimated that he would after a short delay, write an article himself on the subject, advocating my claims: he wished however to put it on a different footing from the one I had chosen. On the footing of <u>literary merits</u>, and he thought if properly pleaded on that ground the claim could not be refused. I said that would bring me on the <u>pension list</u>; a thing I had not asked for, nor ever would. I had not any wish to see my name on the list which read like a beggarly roll of paupers receiving their pay. I never should ask for anything but "just compensation", and if I got that I should not want, nor would I accept either pension from government, or any other gift, dole, or gratuity, which they could bestow. What I asked was in fact, "pay me, what you owe me; what you wrongfully deprived me of 40 years ago": "make good the damage you then committed, and keep your favours until I ask you for them." A claim on the pension list for literary services would in reality be a claim for an indulgence, for a favour, and that was what I hoped never to submit to. Finally it was agreed that Mr D. might urge my case on any grounds he chose, only letting it be clearly understood that <u>I</u> asked for <u>just compensation</u> only.

**Friday 12th.**  Middleton. Isabel Hudday here to tea: went with her to Omnibus at 1/2 past 7.

**Sunday 14th.**  Brierley and Ramsbottom both called before dinner: the former showed a photographic vignette for this forth coming work "Bunk Ho", done from a sketch by Potter, who is still at London painting. The 14th No. London Review commences an account of the "Shakespeare Acland forgeries," opening a strange view of human motives and actions.

**Tuesday 16th.** My addenda appears in the Manchester Examiner & Times.[9]

***Cutting***, *from the* Middleton Albion, *13 October 1860: Bamford's letter of 10 October, headed "dinner at the agricultural show", printed exactly as written.*

***Cutting***, *from the* Middleton Albion, *13 October 1860: addenda to Samuel Bamford's circular, continued from 29 September.*

Went to Manchester: to Ardwick Green looking for a room to read in. Called at Clowes's in York Street. Clowes not at home.

**Wednesday 17th.** Sent annexed to Exam[r] & Times.

> Dear Sir,
> You will probably receive some communications having reference to your brief account of my career in your paper of yesterday. That which you publish, I shall most likely have opportunities for perusing in print; and it strikes me, that I should, of right have the option of reading the whole, and of copying such as I may deem worth the trouble, as well as of replying to any which I may choose to notice in that way. This appears to me, a matter of simple justice to myself, and hoping you will have the same view, I remain
> Yours respectfully<br>Samuel Bamford.
> An intimation to <u>B.M.</u> in your "notices to correspondents," will suffice.

**Friday 19th.** Middleton. Hannah Frankland, Mrs Kenyons, Walkers, Young Greenwood, Ald. Hickup. Home at five p.m.

Messenger with two hares sent by T.B. Potter, Esq, returned many thanks: and gave one hare to Ann, who is ill, next door.

**Saturday 20th.** The annexed from The Manchester Weekly Guardian & Express of this day.

***Cutting***, *from the* Manchester Weekly Guardian and Express, *20 October 1860: an unsigned comment.*

---

I regret to hear that it has been necessary to make an appeal to the public on behalf of Mr. Samuel Bamford. His "Passages in the Life of a Radical" made some sensation, a few years ago, in literary and political circles. Mr. Thomas Carlyle was, I remember, much struck with it, and praised it so highly to Lord Derby that his Lordship borrowed it of the author of "Sartor Resartus," and admitted that he was much interested in the book and its author. That Mr. Bamford bore a firm,

---

9. This appears to be an error for *Middleton Albion*.

temperate, and honourable part in the great Reform agitation, in days when it required both moral and physical courage to be a Reformer, is, if I remember aright, borne out by his book. No one need be ashamed to avow that he had read with profit what Carlyle has praised and Derby admired; and Mr. Bamford's friends will, I trust, be enabled to put the veteran Reformer upon some method of providing for his own maintenance, so that he may be able to pass the evening of his days in comfort and tranquillity.

---

**Sunday 21st.** Dronsfield and Travis here to tea. Ramsbottom called forenoon.

**Friday 26th.** At Manchester. Called on David Morris, and afterwards on Dr. Watts, who had not yet heard from Mr Milner Gibson relative to my affair. Dr. W. spoke discouragingly of my views with respect to Parliamentary interference. Barbers case was mentioned, and I reminded him that Barber was wrongfully transported on the supposition that he had broken the law, whilst I was put in prison, in defiance of law (under the habius corpus suspension act), and afterwards, in 1820, though the judge declared I had "recommended peace and order." Still he seemed to have but a poor opinion of the business.

**Sunday 28th.** Received the annexed from my friend T.B. Potter. A most satisfactory epistle – it must be – in reply to my very grateful letter of thanks, my circular, and my addenda.

*Letter*, *Thomas B. Potter, Pitnacree, Dunkeld, to Bamford, 26 October 1860.*

My dear Sir,
I am glad that you were pleased with the trifling present of game I sent you. Yr letter has been forwarded to me here in Scotland where I have been staying with my family the last four months.
It must be an immense satisfaction to you to see the changes since you were in Lincoln. Much yet has to be done, however, both in England and on the continent. I for one am proud to call myself still a 'Radical Reformer'.
Ever Respectfully,<br>Thomas B. Potter.

**Thursday 1st November.** At Middleton. Heard that a memorial on my behalf, had been got up – could [not] learn by whom – and handed round by Dr. Dickin, and very generally signed by respectable inhabitants. Could not learn to whom the document was addressed, but the rector, Mr Thomas Ashton and Mr Dickins, magistrates, had signed it; in fact it had been backed by everyone to whom it had been presented, except <u>one</u>, and he was Mr E.K. Brown, the Manager of Stone and Kemps silk manufactory at Middleton. This news of the memorial quite surprised me, as I had not previously any idea of the kind; it was however to be kept quite secret from me. I was not to know anything at all about it.
Lord Palmerston's recantation and confession at Leeds – see annexed.

***Newspaper cutting***, *source not stated, reporting a presentation to Lord Palmerston by Leeds Corporation. Sections of Palmerston's acceptance speech about the benefits of reform and progress, and the political labours which brought them about, are underlined by Bamford, and quoted in the draft piece of writing which follows.*

***Draft*** *of a letter or speech by Bamford, 1 November 1860.*

### Lord Palmerston at Leeds.

In a circular which Samuel Bamford occasionally distributes to friends, and to intelligent persons of all classes, he says, "If Parliamentary reforms and Free trade, have been conducive of good to the people of Britain, those who have laboured long and suffered much in the obtainment of these measures, have a just claim to the grateful attention of their fellow subject." Lord Palmerston, in his reply to an address from the Corporation of Leeds, on the 26th of October declared that Free trade, and Parliamentary reform have been conducive of good to the people of Britain: he says "we have seen the Corn laws abolished, a change which has produced contentment and prosperity to a great portion of the community, for whereas, when the seasons were adverse, and the price of food was raised, it was natural for men to think that the high price of provisions was created by the sordid avarice of a portion of the community, now, every man must feel that if his food is dear it is the result of the inclemencies of the season, and not the consequence of any misgovernment of man." He further is reported to have said, "and we have since then all seen the great improvement in the political organization of the Country, which was effected by the Parliamentary Reform of 1832. Well gentlemen, these changes were the result of long discussion and conflict of opinion and of interests; and if they had been accomplished by a stroke of the pen, they would not have accomplished that good which they have effected being the result of discussion, and coming upon a country prepared to receive them, and sensible of the advantages which they brought with them". Such is Lord Palmerstons opinion of these two great measures, now that they are embodied in the laws of the land, and are working well for the country, a very sensible and cordial concession it is. Samuel Bamford, and thousands of his working and starving fellow countrymen were advocates of these measures forty years ago. They felt, by dire hunger, and want in all its forms, that if the high price of provisions was not "created", it was increased by "the sordid avarice of a portion of the community," who being unjustly constituted law makers, enacted unjust laws; hence Bamford and his class became Parliamentary reformers; their long and frequent "discussions, and conflicts of opinion", produced public meetings, and partitions for redress, in reply to which the Habeus Corpus act was suspended; new and restrictive laws were enacted, Bamford "was twice arrested on charges of high treason: he was five times in custody before the Privy Council; he was on nine different occasions conducted in chains to various and distant parts of the county; he stood a trial of ten days, and conducted his own defence, in a manner, and with a testimony which brought credit to himself and the cause he represented; and for promoting generally, by argument and "discussion" good measures in the worst of times, he was confined in a greater number of prisons, than, on like charges, has any other Englishman alive; Lord Palmerston's recantation of former error, and his cordial avowal of his present opinions are creditable alike to his head and his heart ... out that compensation which has been long delayed, to that old Bard and ... to be honest, in the worst of times,[10]

> When wrong was right, on Georges side;
> And truth, and justice, were denied.

**Monday 5th.** Went to Middleton and then heard that the memorial on my behalf was sent to Lord Palmerston, and advocated either a yearly continuation of the fifty pounds grant, or a single repetition of the same: that Mr Oswald Dickin had originated it: that Mr Bazley MP was to present it, or to forward it: and that Mr Wrigley, Keeper of the Manchester Exchange had temporary care of it until he could place it in Mr Bazley's hands. Dickin himself refused to give me any information whatsoever about it, but desired me to keep quiet, until he could ride over to my house some of these mornings, and communicate all the news.

**Wednesday 7th.** Went to Hollinwood and borrowed 30/- from W. Travis, the last half crown of the fifty pound from the Royal bounty fund being all I had left, and several matters being very pressing.

**Saturday 10th.**[11] Received the annexed from Mr W. Halliwell of Lees.

***Letter**, W. Halliwell, Springhead, Lees, near Manchester, to Bamford, 9 November 1860.*

Dear Sir,
I have arranged with a few friends to support me in the effort to get an audience.
   Monday the 19th Nov. is the day we have fixed upon, I want you to meet me in the Manchester Exchange on Tuesday next and bring a copy of the placard to be issued and also if you have any tickets of admission bring them.
   You will be my guest on the occasion and I assure you if a large audience can be got I shall be glad.
                    Yours truly,
                    Wm Halliwell.
I shall be found at pillar E near the stairs say at a quarter past ten on the Exchange.

**Sunday 11th.**[12] Mima was sick and vomited at breakfast time: she was very unwell in other respects, and complained of pain in her bowels.
   Ann Hall her niece from Bakslate came to visit us on Friday afternoon and on Saturday night. Wm Hall, her husband came, taking their departure on Sund[ay] after dinner.

---

10. Manuscript damaged.
11. Entered after 12 November.
12. Entry added opposite.

**Monday 12th.**[13] Saw Mr Wrigley at the Exchange, Man<sup>r</sup>, and asked him about a memorial relative to me, which I understood he had some connexion with. He desired me not to question him too much, but informed me that the memorial was for a yearly allowance to myself, donation from the Royal Bounty Fund. He said it was such as would do me good: advised me to not take any notice of it, and if anything occurred which required my attention, he would write to me.

**Tuesday 13th.** Saw Mr Halliwell and gave him some tickets, and made arrangements for going to Lees on Monday afternoon. To be at Halliwells to tea, at latest, and then to the Peoples Hall at Lees: to remain at Halliwells all night, and return on Tuesday morning. Mr. H. said the spirit of the old reformers had died out, and was quite forgotton. Lees, was in the reform days, one of the most public spirited villages in England, and now not half a dozen persons could be found who took any interest at all in the cause. "Church and King", and the parsons had everything their own way: the parsons had all influence amongst the people; they went amongst them from house to house, and whilst infusing "religion" they depressed every sentiment of political patriotism. Under the circumstances an audience worth speaking to of the working classes, could not have been formed at Lees, and himself and a few friends in the neighbourhood had agreed to contribute a few pounds to pay me, and discharge expenses, and the tickets would nearly all be given away: a couple of pounds would at any rate be secured for my trouble in going over. I assented to this, under the discouraging circumstances which he had mentioned, and so we parted. Though a couple of pounds will certainly be a smaller remuneration than I had calculated upon, under my present circumstances it will be acceptable: will be "a put on", and by the time it is gone, something else may perhaps turn up.

**Wednesday 14th.**[14] Mr Eaton druggist of Harper Hey made up a bottle for Mima, for which he refused to take payment: it was certainly a good medicine and rendered service, though it did not much relieve the pain in bowels, or rather in the internal "linings" (membranes of the belly).

**Thursday 15th.** Mrs Nelson came over. Mima ill in bed. Mrs N brought some apples, "bitter sweets", not good, and a bottle of sherry wine. She also asked how our coals were, and said she would mention it to Mr N. when he returned from Northumberland, and we must have a load sent. I said we should be glad to pay him for the coal, and would be satisfied if he gave us the carting of them, as we should then be sure of having the right <u>quantity</u> and <u>quality</u> which were matters of some consideration in the article of coal. Mrs N. said however, we must have a load without any payment whatever, which set our minds at rest with respect to firing for Xmas.

**Friday 16th.** Mima much better; and downstairs all day. Called in Mr Pinder yesterday who made up some medicine which has done her much good.

Our neighbour Kays house is to let, and I have spoken for it – taken it in fact – for one week in order to secure it for my poetical friend Joseph Ramsbottom.

---

13. Bamford has written "Tues" in error.
14. Entry added opposite.

**Monday 19th.** At Lees. A very good attendance at the Peoples Hall, my friend, Mr Wm Halliwell taking the chair. I read first my circular, "Right against Wrong," then gave an extempore discription of the conditions which reformers were subjected in 1817 and 1819 then read the discription of my domicile at Middleton and of my wife and child: of my arrest, conversation with Nadin and occurrences at Sam. Ogdens, new Bailey etc. interrupted by frequent and loud expressions of applause. The Dying Dragoon followed and Awd Crooklegs closed the performance. Stopped at Mr Halliwells all night and the following morning walked back through Austerlands to Oldham, coming home by 11 o'clock train. £3-0-0, a very seasonable supply.

**Tuesday 20th.** A load of coal lying at the door when I got home. Mr Nelson.

**Saturday 24th.** The following report appears in the Oldham Standard of this day.

**Report**, *from the* Oldham Standard, *24 November 1860.*

---

## MR. SAMUEL BAMFORD'S READINGS

On Monday evening last, Mr. Samuel Bamford, the well-known and venerable Parliamentary Reformer, entertained the inhabitants of this place to readings and recitation from his own works and other authors, at the People's Hall. The body of the hall was well filled, and on the platform were several gentlemen and a few ladies. When Mr. Bamford made his appearance on the platform, he was cheered most heartily. William Halliwell, Esq., of Springhead, who was appointed chairman, said that Mr. Bamford had exercised in days gone by an important influence; but unfortunately, like many others, he had not been well paid for his patriotism. He (Mr. B.) would appear before them as an historian and a poet, as well as a patriot. When he (the chairman) was travelling a few years ago on the continent of Europe, he visited the plains of Waterloo, and as the associations connected with the great battle came rushing back to his memory, he thought of the poem by his friend, entitled "The Dying Dragoon." That composition was alike creditable to his head and his heart, and he should be glad if Mr. Bamford would recite it for them. The chairman then introduced Mr. Bamford to the meeting. He said he thought he should do well to confine his efforts to two objects; he would endeavour to interest their feelings and improve their understandings. He thought it was well that the present generation should be informed of what their fathers and grandfathers had done, and the sufferings and persecutions they had endured in order to procure the blessings of freedom which we now enjoy. Our forefathers had sowed the seed of civil and religious liberty, and we were now reaping the harvest. He had never in his life seen the working classes enjoying as many comforts as they did now. But he would remind them that the sun of prosperity would not always shed its halo around them. Everything in this world was given to change; it was sunshine to-day and darkness to-morrow. He would counsel them, therefore, to provide for the dark night of adversity that must, sooner or later, fall upon them. He then read an extract from a pamphlet entitled "Right against Wrong;" after which he read extracts from his own works relating to events in which he had taken part. In 1817 he was deputed from Middleton to attend a reform meeting at London. The deputies were called upon to give their opinion as to the extent of the suffrage. He (Mr. Bamford) was in favour of universal suffrage; Mr. Cobbett was for manhood suffrage of 21 years of age. While in London he was arrested on suspicion of high treason, was taken six times before the Privy council, but nothing could be proved against him. Here followed an account of his arrest in the dead of night, and a very graphic description of his happy home. The allusion to his wife sitting by the fire late at night, with his young daughter reading to her from the good old Book, and anxiously awaiting his return was touching and pathetic. His altercation with the soldiers demanding admittance into his house brought out into bold relief not only his brave and courageous heart, but also his rich and keen wit. With his hands and arms chained, he was conducted into the street. In passing along he cried out "Hunt and Liberty." His affectionate but indignant wife repeated the cry. One of the officers threatened to blow out her brains if she was not silent. "Blow away," said she; "Hunt and Liberty for ever." The scene at Samuel Ogden's – the public house where they halted on their way to Manchester – was equally good. Repeated bursts of applause came from the audience while reading these incidents. At the request of his friend Mr. Halliwell, Mr. Bamford then recited the "Dying Dragoon." He had now, he said, given them a faint picture of the social condition which their forefathers occupied. He did not come there merely to amuse them, and to raise a laugh; he wished to benefit them. Mirth was a good thing, however, and in its proper place he would rather promote than restrain it. He would, therefore, now give them something of a more lively and facetious character. Mr. Bamford then gave "Jemmy the Jobber," in a manner which proved that he was perfect master of the Lancashire dialect. After a piece entitled, "A Good Appetite," he concluded by thanking the audience for the attention they had given him; and he hoped that what he had said might awaken serious and profitable reflections. – A vote of thanks was then given to Mr. Bamford for his reading, &c. In reply Mr. Bamford said that we seemed to be standing on the verge of an eternity of improvement. Great and important changes were taking place, but he might not live to see the good that would result from them. He hoped, however, that the rising generation, with the flood of knowledge that was being poured on them, would avail themselves of the opportunities provided for improving their minds. He hoped especially, that they would seek to become good fathers, good sons, good brothers, and good citizens. On taking his seat the old patriot was loudly cheered. – Mr. Jeremiah Walker, on proposing a vote of thanks to the chairman, said that he well remembered the events of which Mr. Bamford had been speaking. Reformers in those days had to creep into any hole or hide in any corner. They could not give their opinion as they could now. In 1819 times were very bad – the harvest in many places had not been reaped. He recollected taking round a petition for parliamentary reform, and that, he believed, was the first petition that had ever been sent to the legislature from the parish of Ashton. It was impossible, he said, for him to describe the stirring events of those times. His friend Bamford had been an unflinching advocate for parliamentary reform and a repeal of the Corn laws, and he had justly said that our forefathers fought and suffered for what we now enjoyed. – Mr. Bamford seconded the motion, and said that he had known Mr. Halliwell in days gone by. He was then an influential reformer, and was ever ready to give his earnest support to all measures that were calculated to ameliorate the social condition of the people. – The motion was carried with acclamation, and the proceedings terminated.

**Sunday 25th.**  The following letter from Mr Halliwell brings agreeable news.

**Letter**, *William Halliwell, Springhead, to Bamford, 24 November 1860.*

> Dear Sir,
> I wish to make a further payment to you on account of your lecture please meet
> me on the Exchange on Tuesday next about 12 o'clock.
>                                Yours truly
>                                Wm Halliwell.

**Cuttings**, *from the* Manchester Examiner, *21 November 1860, extracted by Bamford from a speech by John Bright MP at the annual soirée of Wakefield Mechanics' Institution, 19 November 1860, referring to the benefits of the repeal of the corn laws and the common interest of all classes in progress and prosperity.*

**Tuesday 27th.**  Went to the Exchange at Manchester, and saw Dr. Watts near the door, who told me he had spoken with Mr Milner Gibson; and in allusion to my affair of the compensation matter he had said Mr Watts had best induce, if necessary, Mr Bazley to again bring the subject under the consideration of Lord Palmerston, when he (Mr Gibson) would support the application. This appeared to have been all that Mr Gibson had said.

Saw Mr Halliwell inside the Exchange who informed me that in company with friends who were to have been parties to my reading at Lees, he had moved that though they did not attend, they ought to consider themselves responsible, and that, consequently he had received several sums on my behalf: He paid me £1-15-0.

Bought the new magazine "Temple Bar", at Kellys. Kelly said he was of opinion Sir James Kay Shuttleworth was the author of "Scarsdale".

**Wednesday 28th.**  Wrote as annexed to the Editor, Oldham Standard.

**Copy letter**, *Bamford to the Editor of the* Oldham Standard, *28 November 1860. The letter is badly damaged. Bamford writes to correct a statement in the "generally very fair report of my readings at Lees" that Cobbett had been in favour of manhood suffrage in 1817. What Bamford had said was that "Mr Cobbett was in favour of household suffrage only" until convinced "of the practicability of manhood suffrage by me".*[15]

**Saturday 15th December.**[16] Allen Mellor sends the annexed, with 20 shillings worth of postage stamps; forgetting to send or to <u>mention</u> the balance of – shillings which he kept in hand, arising from what was given to him, on my acc[oun]t after my last reading at Mills Hill Chapel. His conduct, in this matter has not been correct: See his letter of that date.

**Letter**, *Allen Mellor, Chadderton, to Bamford, 12 December 1860.*

---

15.  This refers to the famous Crown and Anchor meeting of January 1817, described in *Passages* I, ch. 4.
16.  There is a 17-day gap in the diary at this point; nothing appears to be missing.

My Dear Sir,

I beg to enclose you 20/- which your friend the Dr. [h]as obtained from Mr
Cheetham as a donation for you. I believe you are to be on the civil list for next
year, and I can truly say that no one will rejoice more than I shall in all that brings
you comfort and happiness for the remainder of your days. I am, my dear Bamford,
Truly yours,
Allen Mellor.

Sent the annexed to Messrs Cheetham and Dickin.

**Copy letter**, *Bamford to James Cheetham, 15 December 1860.*

Dear Sir,

Mr Allen Mellor writes to me, inclosing twenty shillings worth of Postage stamps,
which he says my "friend the Dr has obtained;" I assume he means "obtained
from you as a donation." I am truly obliged to Mr Dicken for his thoughtful
attention; and to yourself for your kind appreciation of my position and of my
humble deserts; and if you will allow me to place your donation to the list of
"contributions to my compensation fund", neither your generosity nor my
gratitude will be thereby diminished.

I have many previous acts of kindness to thank you for and I now do so with
kind respect, remaining Dear Sir,
Your obliged servant,
Samuel Bamford.

**Copy letter**, *Bamford to Thomas Dickin, 15 December 1860.*

Dear Sir,

Mr Allen Mellor writes to me, inclosing postage stamps to the amount of one
pound, which he says have "been obtained by you from Mr Cheetham", of
Firwood Mills "as a donation". I accept the pound, as coming through you; and
as being accompanied, – which I am sure it would be – by Mr Cheethams kindly
welcome. Mr Mellor calls it a donation; but I shall do both Mr Cheetham and
myself the credit of entering it in the list of contributions to my Compensation
fund", illustrious names will be found there; names that will be saluted and
remembered when you, and I, and Mr Cheetham are no more.
Yours truly,
Samuel Bamford.

I now determine on a reading at Manchester,[17] and after viewing the rooms at the
Mechanics Institute, The Athenaeum, and the Exchange, select the latter; Mr Wrigley, the

---

17. Bamford, unusually, seems to have written this whole Manchester episode up in retrospect, disguised by
use of the present tense (see, for example, the inclusion of a cutting from 2 January in the entry for
29 December). Perhaps Mima was ill again, or perhaps the Manchester reading, which was of great
symbolic significance for Bamford, occupied all his energies.

"Master" of the latter concern directing his porter to shew "this person," the room "No 1": this seemed a somewhat strange expression, after the interest he had professed to feel on my behalf in the Memorial business: the room was at present occupied as a show place for pictures, but was expected to be at liberty in a day or two, and I could then have it. When however I went again it was "engaged for a month," and on my mentioning the room in Ducie Place, that also "was engaged". I must own, that these announcements took me by surprise, and caused a suspicion that they were mere shuffles, evasions, equivocations to get rid of me, in fact; an idea which aroused in my heart scorn and indignation: So I went and engaged at once, the library hall at the Athenaeum, at a charge of 2 guineas, for the 27th Dec[r]. Brierley undertaking to assist by reading a passage or two from his "Bunk Ho" and "A Day Out." I next advertised, and got tickets printed, and in order to raise the money for the room I turned out, though sorely against my will, to sell tickets. Sir James Watts[18] took ten shillings worth; Messrs Potter & Morris took 20 shillings worth; Mr Brooks of Butterworth & Brooks 10 shillings worth; these are all "great houses." Eccles Shorrock & Sons six shillings: John Waterhouse, 2/6. Dr Watts, sold ten shillings worth for me. Mr Belfield of the Golden Lion, Danesgate[19] sold 10 shillings worth. Mr David Chadwick took five shillings worth, E.W. Binney five shillings worth – Dearden Solicitor Cooper Street, 2/- Ralph Mellor, of the Weight and Measures Office 2/- worth: The Mayor of Manchester 2/- worth (and told me of another Memorial now being signed on my behalf, himself having signed it only a day or two before) John Heywood bookseller, 2/- worth. Edwin Slater 5/- worth: David Kelly 2/- worth: the Secretary at the Athenaeum, handed over to me 17/- for tickets sold. B. Brierley 8/-, and my neighbour R McClure £1-11-0 and A.W. Gilbody of Bridge street 2/-. Whilst about        was drawn at the door on the night of performance, so that my receipts would amount to      and my expenditure to      leaving me a gainer by about        .[20]

### Account slip.

My Reading at the Athenaeum, Manchester, 27th Decr 1860.

| Tickets sold | |
| --- | --- |
| Sir James Watts | 0-10-0 |
| Messrs Potter & Norris | 1- 0-0 |
| Gilbody, Bridge St | 2-0 |
| Mr Brooks, Butterworth and Brooks | 10-0 |
| Mr Eccles Shorrock | 6-0 |
| Mr John Waterhouse | 2-6 |
| Mr Dearden Sol[icito]r | 2-0 |
| Dr. Watts | 10-0 |

18. Sir James Watts (1804–78), of Abney Hall, highly successful merchant (of S. and J. Watts and Co.); prominent Manchester Liberal, and mayor 1855–7; MCL.
19. Bamford's version of Deansgate.
20. The sums are left blank.

| | |
|---|---:|
| Mr Belfield | 10-0 |
| Athenaeum | 17-0 |
| John Heywood Books[elle]r | 3-0 |
| Edwin Slater | 5-0 |
| D. Kelly | 2-0 |
| R. McClure | 1-11-0 |
| R. Mellor | 2-0 |
| D. Chadwick | 5-0 |
| – Page | 4-0 |
| Brierley | <u>8-0</u> |
| | 6- 9-6 |
| Brought over | |
| E.W. Binney | 0- 5-0 |
| The Mayor of Manchester | 2-0 |
| | |
| Expenditure | |
| Advertising in the Guardian: | 15-6 |
| In the Examiner: | - - - |
| Printing of tickets | - - - |
| To two servants of the Athenaeum | |
| on the night of Performance | - - - |

The two paragraphs on the opposite leaf appeared in the Examiner and in the Guardian before the performance, and no doubt rendered good service:

**Announcement**, *from the* Manchester Guardian, *no date.*

---

MR. BAMFORD'S READINGS. – We perceive that Samuel Bamford is about to give, this evening, at the *Athenaeum*, a series of readings, in which he is to be assisted by Mr. Ben Brierley, the author of "A Day Out," and one or two other small works. We have known Mr. Bamford extremely well for more than forty years, and have always had cause to admire his great natural abilities and his manly independence of character. Though we never shared in his extreme opinions on politics, we could not help approving the moderation which he displayed in advocating those opinions, and the manner in which he exercised a not inconsiderable personal influence amongst the working classes in his neighbourhood, in discouraging that resort to force and violence which was so frequently suggested by Mr. Fergus O'Connor and other dangerous demagogues. We shall, therefore, be very glad to learn that his readings have proved successful.

---

**Cutting**, *from the* Manchester Examiner and Times, *26 December 1860. A longer preview of Bamford's Athenaeum reading, giving a brief history of Bamford's early struggles, reviewing some of his works, querying the failure to grant him a literary pension, and appealing for the public to support the event.*

The two following paragraphs appeared on the day after the performance; That in the Guardian being first and appropriate, and that in the Examiner being neither the one nor the other, but slighty and disrespectful to the readers, and discreditable to the reporters, or to the sub-editor, under whose eye it doubtless passed.

**Report**, *from the* Manchester Guardian, *28 December 1860.*

---

READINGS BY MR. SAMUEL BAMFORD. – Last evening, Mr. Samuel Bamford (the well-known veteran author of the "Life of a Radical," and various other works, assisted by Mr. B. Brierley, also a Lancashire author) gave a series of readings at the Athenaeum. Mr. Bamford commenced by reading some passages from his early publications, accompanying the reading with extemporaneous reminiscences of scenes in which he had been an actor. On a recent occasion, he said, Lord Palmerston, at Leeds, referring to the great changes which had been effected in the shape of Parliamentary and municipal reform, said that those changes were the result of long discussion and conflict of opinion. He, (Mr. Bamford) did not think it would be going away from the course of regular discussion, if he endeavoured to show what sort of discussions these were to which His Lordship had so frankly and candidly referred, and to which he attributed the great advantages enjoyed in the present day. Mr. Bamford then referred to the condition of the people of Lancashire in 1817, and to the struggle made for reform. He gave a graphic sketch of his own apprehension on the charge of high treason, minutely describing the elaborate preparations taken by the military and police to secure their prisoner, and the strong body guard which accompanied him to the New Bailey. Mr. Bamford afterwards read several of his own poems, all of which, particularly the "Pass of Death," written by him on the occasion of the death of Canning, were highly appreciated by the audience. Mr. Brierley's contributions to the evening's entertainment, which consisted of extracts, of both a grave and gay character from his own works, written in the broadest Lancashire dialect, very agreeably varied the proceeding. The attendance was not as large as could have been desired, whether we consider the chief giver of the entertainment or its high general character.

---

**Report**, *from the* Manchester Examiner and Times, *no date, of Bamford's Athenaeum reading: Bamford recited "with much feeling" and "the entertainment generally was well received".*

**Saturday 29th.** Belfield paid me 10/- for tickets he had sold.

A resident of Stretford or Urmston was in the bar parlour and in conversation with him was one Hulbert, a resident of Middleton, who is a warper at <u>Stone and Kemps</u> Mill, at the latter place: a circumstance, as I think, of no very friendly import to myself.

The general taste of the Manchester people will be understood by contrasting my humble performances; their slight attendance, and their very brief and grudging notices by the newspapers, with the following report, taken from the Examiner of 2d Jan. 1861 of a performance by two musical celebreties.

***Report***, *from the* Manchester Examiner and Times, *2 January 1861, of a performance in the Free Trade Hall of a "musical, comic, and fanciful" repertoire, enjoyed by an audience of some 3,000. A further 3 concerts are to be held in the Assembly Rooms, Free Trade Hall, and one more in the Great Hall.*

When I called on Mr David Chadwick, who is Principal agent here for the Globe Fire Insurance Company, he offered to make me a local agent, and to place every advantage at my service. I shall certainly try my luck in this line, being already somewhat disgusted with the humiliating circumstances attending the sale of tickets by personal application. Sir James Watts, looked at me; turned from me, and again entered into conversation with a person who stood beside him. But who can wonder: he lives in an ancient hall; the Prince Consort was his guest during one night, he has a fire-grate which cost a thousand guineas, and the Queen knighted him. So Sir James Watts may perhaps deem himself privileged to put a slight on one who came to ask a favour. And yet, I dont see how a performance by such a person as myself could be made to pay even the expenses without these personal exertions in the sale of tickets, and that, I certainly cannot long put up with.

It appears that my friend Mr Bazley, in that business of mine relative to an application to have my name placed on the list of Government annuities, has had the "go by", very adroitly played upon him: a letter – of which the annexed is a copy – was placed in my hand by Dr. Dickin of Middleton.

***Transcript*** *of a letter from Evelyn Ashley, 10 Downing Street, to Thomas Bazley MP, 8 December 1860.*

> Sir,
> In acknowledging the receipt of your communication of the 29th Nov. I am
> desired by Lord Palmerston to inform you that the claims of Mr Samuel Bamford
> will be considered in connection with those of other candidates for Civil List
> pensions when the List for 1861–2 comes up for settlement, that for 1860–61
> being already full,
> > I am Sir,
> > > Your obed Serv$^t$
> > > Evelyn Ashley.

My claims to be "considered along with those of others"; why my claims have been in existence 40 years and more: I am in my 73rd year, a time when according to the course of nature I ought to have been dead: and may reasonably be expected to die any day: and yet my claims await <u>"consideration"</u>: the put off; the shuffle is shameful; it is dishonest.

# ILLNESS AND INSURANCE

*In the early weeks of 1861 Bamford took up David Chadwick's offer of an agency for the Globe Fire and Insurance Company; but he was not a successful insurance salesman, and after a series of rebuffs and temporising responses, his efforts in this direction soon waned; his optimistic report of potential future business to the company's Secretary at the end of February was virtually the last mention of the matter in the diaries. There was still the occasional reading, and still correspondence about his pension claim to be written, but the reform movement had almost completely stalled, and the diary gives almost no attention to political affairs. Indeed, as his curmudgeonly response to an invitation to a testimonial dinner to Hutchings, the secretary of the Manchester Mechanics' Institute, shows, Bamford was becoming increasingly cantankerous. Perhaps this reflected renewed concerns about health. Mima started the year with a fit, and suffered others later in January. Bamford himself was unwell on and off until on 16 March he clearly suffered a slight stroke, an event which he took as a warning, redoubling his efforts to pursue a pension.*

The year begins ominously for us: this morning (1 Jan. 1861) at three o'clock, Mima had [a] fit of the old epileptic sort: not a violent one, but sufficiently so to make me come down stairs with a weary heart. I know she had latterly not had her wonted discharge from the nose; and though grieved I was not greatly surprised.

**Tuesday 1st January.** Brierley came up, and paid me the balance of money drawn for the sale of tickets by him: it was 8/-.

Went with him to the New Inn and we were taking a glass of toddy when Mr Chatwood of Bury, Mr Parks, and two others entered: they ordered something to eat, and me, of course must stop and dine with them: I could not for the life of me account for their appearance at that time and place: but as Chatwood and Parks were active parties at my last reading at Bury, I suspected they were about some business of the like nature. We talked about railways, on which subject Chatwood and I did not agree: he had seen Charles Swain lately, and said I should go and visit him: I remarked that Swain had never called on me, or written to me though I had been down here in Lancashire two years and a half; that he had not called on me, or sent for me when he was in London, and that I did not see why I should run after him now. I said, above all things, I prized <u>earnestness</u> and <u>sincerity</u> in my friends. I was both earnest and sincere, but Charles Swain was neither the one nor the other; of course, on this subject Chatwood and I held different opinions: Chatwood is one of the Swain clique, I should have recollected; and has a bust of him in his study at Bury; then we talked about the poetry of Festus,[1] which I "phophoo'd," in comparison with "the Song of the Shirt" and "the

---

1. A reference to Philip James Bailey (1816–1902), editor of the *Notts Mercury*; briefly resident in Manchester in the late 1830s, at which time he published his epic 800-page poem "Festus", which Bamford praised in *Passages*.

bridge of Sighs" by Hood:[2] of "Paradise Lost", which I also scouted, as far inferior to some of Miltons miscellaneous poems; in short, on very few subjects could Chatwood and I agree, for I saw he was determined to please himself by assuming a vast amount of positive information on almost every subject (this in fact is his distinguishing annoyance) and I was equally bent on maintaining my own honest convictions: so we drank toddy, poor stuff it was, and smoked bad cigars, and the afternoon wore on heavily with me, and I felt relieved when they departed. Chatwood has a precise, circumstantial, and presuming way of dogmatizing on whatever subject is discussed; his manner is tiresome and repugnant to my feelings, and I am impatient during its exhibition.

I am persuaded they came on some business relative to myself, perhaps something about a reading to come off at Bury, or something of the sort, but as I did not succumb to their "great little man": the subject was given up. One of the party frequently left the room and was absent some time; at last he brought with him a man named Royson of Blakeley, who seemed to know me very well, and was profusely civil, but of whom I knew not anything, save that his mother was well acquainted with my parents, and his father used to supply me with newspapers once a week.

On my return home I found that Ophelia, Dronsfields little girl had come from Hollinwood, bringing a new years gift of spiced bread: lump of cheese, ditto of bacon, a pot of preserves, and various other good things, with her father and mothers best wishes, a happy new year &c. The dear kind people. It was nearly dark when she came, so Joseph Hall took her, in the Omnibus, to her grandmothers at Manchester, and there she would remain until morning; the annexed letter also came.

**Letter**, *James Dronsfield, William Travis and Harry Mason, Hollinwood, to Bamford, 1 January 1861.*

Worthy Friends,
We send you this small present as an acknowledgement that we still retain you in our memories you must not look upon the intrinsic value of the articles, the Basket contains but receive them as an emblem of the sincere respects of those by whom you will ever be remembered with warm hearted affection.
  And I am sure that it will be a pleasurable consolation to you both to know that they are accompanied by the kindest wishes for your future welfare.
                    We remain,
                      Yours truly,
                        James Dronsfield
                        Wm Travis
                        Henry Mason.

**Christmas card** *with holly and ivy, bearing a printed greeting:* Wishing you the Compliments of the Season.

**Wednesday 2nd.** Wrote and sent off, the adjoining.

---

2. Thomas Hood (1799–1845), poet, most famously of the "Song of the Shirt"; *DNB*.

**Copy letter**, *Bamford to James Dronsfield, 2 January 1861.*

Dear Dronsfield,

I regretted much not being at home when Ophelia came yesterday. I and Brierley had gone up to the New Inn at Barns Green, and were having a glass of toddy, when some acquaintances of mine, from Bury, made their appearance, and we had to sit down and take more toddy and what would be charged as a dinner – though I did not eat many mouthfuls – an afternoon spent rather dully – for the toddy was poor stuff, entirely non-effective on me – and enduring the pressing dogmatism of one of the party, made me glad when they departed.

I found your very kind and thoughtfully provided new year's gift carefully arranged in the kitchen when I got home. Mima was deeply touched by your testimonial of remembrance, she had been crying, and I must confess, old and rugged, and somewhat blunted in feeling as I am, that I deeply felt the genuine sympathy and respect which yourself and friends had thus evinced towards two old – poor I may also add – honestly poor, – proudly poor folks, who have suffered for the good of their Country. How different your conduct and feelings from those exhibited by the great, proud, and rich City of Manchester – the richest City for its extent, of the greatest nation known to man, which great rich city pours out its thousands to concerts, balls, and other amusements, and could not afford to me, an old Belisarius[3] in the cause of freedom, an attendance on my late reading, sufficient scarcely to clear expenses. Time however will avenge and rectify all this; and the day will come when this circumstances will be remembered to the shame of the great, proud city;- as surely as Dumfries is now, and for ever must be, ashamed of the <u>death of Burns</u>.*

Brierley had given me a copy of your new journal, The "Oldham Times" in which I soon detected a nook occupied by intelligence from "Hollinwood", that I suppose was some of <u>your</u> "handy work", and, I must say, it made a very respectable appearance. Your correspondence will, I should think, be useful to the paper: I must have a talk with you about this new line of business, when I see you. Meantime I trust you will [be] able to render service to the new publication, without becoming inattentive to your honest work by the hammer and anvil.

I and Mima are at present in tolerably good health: we salute yourself, family, and friends with the best wishes of the season: same also, to your good old mother and your sister: and I remain,

Yours truly,

Samuel and Jemima Bamford.

* This private and not by any means to be published.

**Thursday 3rd.** Went to Middleton, but did not make arrangements for a reading, as I had intended doing, the time, Christmas being, as was said, against it.

---

3. Belisarius: a Roman general blinded as a punishment for conspiring against the Emperor Justinian and reduced to begging for a living.

**Saturday 5th.** Went to Manchester early, and called at Mr Bazley's Mill, but he was not in; would be at 1/4 past 11, so went to John Atkinsons, where I found a good fire, and sat down to a glass of good hot toddy, which Rudkin, who was there before me, paid for and would do. Called at John Heywoods and showed him the shameful omission of the word <u>more</u> at p.131 of his edition of my "Early Days", where it says, "we want less Priestianity, and Jesus Christ Christianity," instead of <u>more</u> Jesus Christ Christianity. He gave me a sovereign, which said two "old Rads" had left for me. Went at 1/4 past 11 and <u>saw</u> Mr Bazley, who said he would go to Parliament early in February, and would then see Lord Palmerston personally, and urge my claim to a pension, on his attention. I remarked that Lord Palmerston seemed not to bear in mind that my claims had been hanging over during upwards of forty years, and consequently ought to take precedence of any others, especially when my age was remembered, which rendered my life less certain than that of younger persons, and my tenure of any allowance which I might receive much shorter than that of a younger person. Mr Bazley repeated that he would do his best in the business; he would be urgent and would have the co-operation of Mr Milner Gibson, and perhaps of other members.

He said I might take a copy of the letter of Lord Palmerston's private secretary (8th Dec[r]) and show it to any friend, making use of it with discretion.

I also mentioned to him about Mr David Chadwick having offered me an agency in the Globe Fire Insurance establishment, and showed him how the agency of his insurance, and of half a score others would benefit me, if I could get them, without the least additional charge to the parties insured, and he said I should be doing what was quite right in endeavouring to obtain any advantage irrespective of whatever might be derived from the government: he would look over his insurances, and see what could be done and would write to me.

Got up to the Omnibus with some difficulty, my breathing being bad: Came home coughing all the way, and sat a long time before I could take my tea.

**Sunday 6th.** Mills from Middleton, four children, and two friends called, bringing some New Years gifts: so stopped[4] their bottle of Cowslip wine – very good – and Mima gave the young ones some spiced loaf, and after sitting talking during half an hour, the whole went back.

**Copy letter**, *Bamford to John Heywood, Manchester, 6 January 1861.*

Dear Sir,
On my arrival at home yesterday, I found your note, which had been delivered during my absence.

Pray inform the two "Old Rads", who sent me the sovereign that I have entered it on the list of "Contributions to my <u>compensation fund</u>," where it will in after days be found greatly to their credit.

---

4. That is, unstoppered.

I wonder their <u>names</u> should have been withheld; they surely cannot be ashamed, or afraid to contribute to the liquidation of a just claim, made by the oldest of the old ones.

Yours truly

Samuel Bamford

**Monday 7th.** Wrote as see annexed to J.P. Kay Shuttleworth.

***Copy letter***, *Bamford to James Kay-Shuttleworth, 7 January 1861.*

Dear Sir James,
In your last letter you stated that some well informed sources you had ascertained that the pension fund is not applied to the compensation of any political services; or for injuries or loss sustained in that class of public efforts, and that claims on other grounds had been pressed, reviewed, and set aside. I wished in reply if I recall it aright, to be informed, were it compatible with your engagements, what the other claims were which had pressed and reviewed, and set aside, and why they had been so disposed of? My reply is dated these three months since, and I have not yet heard from you. I am naturally desirous to hear something further about these proceedings. My friends in other parts have kindly taken up the matter, and have memorialized Lord Palmerston, the reply of whose secretary, here before me states that "the claims of Mr Samuel Bamford will be considered in connection with those of other candidates for civil list pensions when the list for 1861–62 comes up for settlement." In March last Lord Palmerston promised that my claims should be taken into consideration; it appears they have been so, and have been "set aside": now a hope, a futile one, I am inclined to think, is set up, and I am referred to the coming settlement of 1861–62. I hope you will be able to afford me the information I desire. Don't hesitate from a wish to avoid causing me disappointment or upset: I am so used to these things that I seldom expect any thing else, and [am] prepared for them. Dear Sir James,

Your obed$^t$ and obliged humble servant,

Samuel Bamford.

Your letter is marked <u>Confidential</u> and the confidence has not been violated. Might I <u>now</u> have your permission to make use of your information, without saying from whom, or under what circumstances it was received? SB.

**Wednesday 9th.** Received the annexed from Sir J.P. Kay Shuttleworth, with its inclosure. Went to Hollinwood and paid of[f] Travis's debt of 30/- to which he had made me most welcome. Spent an hour with him and Dronsfield and returned by the three o'clock bus, found letter from Sir James.

***Letter***, *James Kay-Shuttleworth, Hyde Park, to Bamford, 9 January 1861.*

My Dear Mr Bamford,

I was about to write to you to offer you all the best wishes of the season, and in order to gratify my own feelings in not making this an empty compliment to request that you would pardon my asking you to honour me by accepting the enclosed cheque for Five Pounds as a proof of my sincere sympathy and constant good will grounded on the respect due to your character, patriotic efforts and the firmness with which you have borne your lot in life.

I will avail myself of the information conveyed in your note to ascertain whether there is any sufficient ground for a further expectation than that which I conveyed to you.

If there be I will let you know.

No good would arise (even if I were at liberty to disclose the sources of my previous information) from my writing anything more definite than I then did.

[Be] full well assured that you have a sincere friend and well-wisher in
yours sincerely
J.P. Kay Shuttleworth.

Present this cheque personally and endorse it in the Branch. One line only in reply to assure me of its safe arrival.

**Thursday 10th.** Wrote to Sir James and sent it off see overleaf.

*Copy letter*, Bamford to James Kay-Shuttleworth, 9 January 1861.

My very Kind and Generous Friend,

Your letter, with its inclosure of a cheque for five pounds came to hand this morning during my absence from home. I have only common forms of expression wherein to set forth my fervent and grateful emotions: I thank you most sincerely.

The interference of other friends, to which I alluded, took the form of a memorial from Middleton, my native town; it was originated and carried out, before I was aware that anything of the kind had been contemplated, and it was signed – so I have been informed, for I have never seen it – by the rector, two magistrates, and as many of the respectable inhabitants as were deemed necessary; addressed to Lord Palmerston, and asking that an allowance of some sort from Government, might be assigned to me. It was afterwards backed by the Mayor and a number of the leading characters of Manchester, and it was this memorial to which I alluded as having elicited the reply that it would be taken into consideration "when the list of claimants 1861–2 came up for settlement: that for 1861 having been already full." I have not breathed one word of what you communicated in your note of October 9th or I could have informed them that claims on my half had been "pressed, reviewed, and set aside"; that I should have done, had I had your permission, and without such permission it will never be made known by me.

I remain, Dear Sir James,
Your obliged Humble Servᵗ·
Samuel Bamford.

I shall look with impatience for the announcement of "Whalley Nab" by the author of Scarsdale.

10th Thur.[5] At Manchester all day. Got cash for the cheque and an order from Mr Langton for my photograph and stereoscopic portrait. Bought two rabbits, one for self, and other for our neighbour, and returned by 'bus.
10 Thur. This evening as I sat by the fire, Mima fell twice at length on the hearth: her old disorder of fits having it appears, returned again.

Ah well aday! as if I had not trouble of mind enough already.

**Friday 11th.** Manchester: took the photographs, stereoscopic, portraits, Mr Langton[6] taking two slides, and two others, one Booth Hall, and the other Wood End, top of Boggart Ho Cloof.

**Saturday 12th.** At home. Potter called in the afternoon. He had been with B. Brierley who had given up his situation as a warper at Brennan and Sons. I am afraid he is getting into a loose way, and is acting wildly. Potter had had some conversation with Mr Councillor Taylor, of Oldham about me. Mr Taylor wished something of permanent benefit to be done for me, and he would put down twenty pounds if nine other gentlemen would subscribe a like sum each, towards purchasing an annuity for me. I informed Potter of the proposed plan of providing for me by getting a sufficient number of Insurance policies, whereby a sufficiency would be received without the least charge to my friends: We agreed that this idea might be pursued, and meantime Mr Taylors proposal should be left at rest. On Monday morning he said he should depart again for London. Address 1, Oxford Street.

John Lord came and has his Kesmus pot and we sat talking a long time about his mother, his hens, and Grimshaws.

Went over (date forgotten) to Mr Halliwells Mill at Spring Head, Lees. Mr H. was absent from home, but saw his son James, and dined with him: He said they did Insurance business with his brother in law, but he would mention my visit and its object to his father when he returned from Liverpool. I dined at Mr Halliwell Jun[rs], and come away weary and breathing difficulty to the station at Oldham; thence to Middleton, and so home by 'bus.

**Tuesday 15th.** Saw Mr Halliwell on the Exchange, and he said all their insurable property was at present covered by policies in different offices, but if anything new was put up he would bear me in mind.

**Sunday 20th.** Brierley came, and gave me a sovereign which he had received from a Mr J.H. Mellor of King St., Oldham, as a present to myself.

---

5. Entry added opposite.
6. Probably Robert Langton (*c*. 1825–1900), wood engraver and book illustrator, who came to Manchester about 1850; prominent in the Manchester Literary Club and the Lancashire and Cheshire Antiquarian Society; MCL.

**Tuesday 22nd.** Saw Dr. Dickin and Mr John Clarke, agent at Middleton, to Sir S.M. Peto who said I might examine, at any time, certain old documents and papers which he had, and which formerly belonged to the Assheton family at Middleton. Dickin could not inform me where the rough draft of the memorial was to be found, but he would enquire about it.

**Wednesday 23rd.** Edm^d Howarth, at the Asshetons Arms, gave me to understand that at one of the Reform meetings held at Middleton, about the 16th May 1859, a person named Sam^l Mellalieu had spoken disparagingly of me in reference to an affair betwixt myself and one Tho^s Dane whom about the year 1838, I had summoned for indecent exposure of his person in a garden opposite the window of my residence at Middleton: This, Howarth said, he had controverted at the time, and had since proved Mellalieus representations to be entirely contrary to the truth, as set forth by Dane himself. I told Howarth how it was, and expressed my astonishment and regret that with so many "friends", who heard what Mellalieu said, I had not been made acquainted with the circumstances until now – Howarth seemed to think he had done his duty to me by controverting the report at the time. This took place probably at the Demonstration noticed under the date of 23rd May, 1859 (No 66)[7] and the Mellalieu who spoke it was the chief promoter of the regulation, carried at a Committee meeting, from which I was absent, to exclude non electors from attendance at the dinner. Having secured my absence, the calumniator could safely, as he thought, give expression to his calumnious falsehoods. What his actual expressions were, I have yet to learn, and I will do that as soon as possible.

**Thursday 24th.** Mrs Nelson, who had totally forgotten to notice us during the Xmas holidays, wrote to enquire about our health and I replied as follows.

***Copy letter****, Bamford to Mrs Nelson, Fern Hill, Pendleton, 27 January 1861.*

> Dear Niece,
> In reply to your kind enquiry, I have to inform you that we have both been ill. Mima has had three fits; and I have been almost killed by difficulty of breathing.
> We are now much better: and, if the weather remains favourable we hope to remain so. With kind respects to all your family,
> > Yours truly,
> > Samuel Bamford.

***Advertisement****, from the* Middleton Albion, *26 January 1861, for Bamford and Brierley's forthcoming reading at the Boar's Head, Middleton ("Front seats 1s.; second seats 6d.; other seats 2d. Tickets available from the Albion Office"), together with a supportive editorial comment, rehearsing Bamford's claims to recognition.*

---

7. That is, notebook 66 in Bamford's numbering.

**Saturday 26th.** Went to Clowes's at the brewery who was rather cool I thought, but talked about getting up a reading for me at the town hall. I said it must not be like the last which was lost by not being noticed in the newspapers.

Called on Harland in Repton Street and told him about the old papers I was at liberty to inspect at Middleton, at which he seemed much pleased.

**Monday 28th.** Mary Ann, the eldest daughter of my late sister's daughter came and brought us, O wonderful! a bottle of <u>gin</u>, for two old people. I said I never drank gin: at which she seemed surprised. I however took it, and Mima not being at home, I prepared a cup of good tea, with bread and butter, of which she partook heartily. Mima came afterwards.

At 1/2 p[ast] 9 a.m. I went to Middleton by the bus, and thence walked to Royle in Thornham to see some old writings which Mr Clarke had. He was at Middleton, so I came back, and again missed him. So gave up for that day and returned.

Dronsfield gave me the annexed printed fragment which he had picked up on my daughters grave when he last visited Middleton.[8]

> 5. But I am jealous of my heart
>    Lest it should once from thee depart;
>    Then let thy name be well impress'd,
>    As a fair signet on my breast.
>
> 6. Come, my Beloved, haste away,
>    Cut short the hours of my delay:
>    Fly like a youthful hart or roe,
>    Over the hills where spices grow.

**Tuesday 29th.** Received a circular from the Ballot Society, and sent the annexed reply.

***Copy letter***, *Bamford to Edwin H. King, Newall's Buildings, Manchester, 29 January 1861. The letter is damaged and partly illegible, but Bamford writes briefly in support of the secret ballot "such as is carried on in the United States of America". An extension of suffrage without the ballot would be unwise, and the efforts of reformers "ought to be directed to securing the ballot before any other move".*

**Wednesday 30th.** Reading with Brierley at the Boarhead, Middleton. Received One pound and two pence gross receipts, and expended 12/-. The annexed notice in the Albion of Feb. 2nd which was written by myself, is quite within the truth.

***Report***, *from the* Middleton Albion, *2 February 1861.*

---

8. The lines, in very small print, are taken from a book or newspaper.

MESSRS BAMFORD AND BRIERLEY'S READINGS: – On Wednesday night, the readings by Messrs. Samuel Bamford and Benjamin Brierley took place at the Boar's Head Assembly Rooms. Mr. Bamford, after some appropriate introductory remarks, quoted as indisputable dicta, passages from Lord Palmerston's reply to an address from the Leeds Corporation, in October last, wherein his lordship admitted that the Parliamentary Reform Act of 1832, and the repeal of the corn laws, though obtained after "much discussion"; and "conflict of opinions and interests," had proved highly beneficial to the country. Mr. Bamford then showed by his readings, and occasional remarks, how, in his locality, and amongst his own class, those discussions originated in the distress of the working people, and were carried on by reading Cobbett's Tracts, and by proceedings at public meetings. "The conflicts of interests" he illustrated by describing the rude force to which he was subjected at the time of his last arrest on a charge of high treason; the comfortable assurance by Nadin, that he was "making his last journey," and the description of the soldiers and himself "having bait" at Owd Sam's, at Harpurhey, were graphically given; and, together with his "God Help the Poor," and some stanzas from a wild poem of later date, were received with frequent applause. Mr Brierley read in a very effective manner, extracts from his two publications – "A Day Out," and "Bunk Ho':" a piece from the latter descriptive of a night alarm, and sudden dispersion of a carousing party, during the "Peterloo times," caused hearty laughter; the making up of a dummy "to liken Owd Crootlegs," the hanging of him "i'th Ho' Cloof," his concealment in a stable, his discovery by "Owd Ned," who, when "deawn cruttlt th' carcuss oppo th' floor," fled in a panic "deawn th' keaw lane, and never stopt, till he fund hissel i' th' middle o' Owd Betty Allen's duck hole, three feelts off;" the discovery of the dummy hanging the morning following; the running of men, wimmin, and chilther, with "Lung Jammy, " who left his doytchin, but "turnt back lest he should dhream abeawt it;" the appearance of Jonathan, the constable, who, speaking to Jerry Lane, gives him sixpence, and orders him to be, "at th'inquest:" who promises Little Robin, a quart of ale to cut Croot Legs deawn, "i'th name o'th' king:" and his sad blank when, discovering the figure was only rags and old hay, Little Robin "axt him heaw soon he thought th' crooner ud goo oer him", caused successive bursts of laughter. The "Hazle cloof boggart" followed with like success; and the company separated with a vote of thanks to the readers.

**Friday 1st February.** A load of coal from Mr Nelson which I acknowledged as follows.

*Copy letter*, *Bamford to Mrs Nelson, 1 February 1861.*

Dear Niece,
I have to thank Mr Nelson for another load of coal, and I desire you will express to him my sincere thanks to the same. They arrived on Thursday, just in time; for we were nearly out, and had ordered a small bag to carry on for the present. We experienced very much the benefits of your last load, which carried us

through the sharp colds and storm of the late severe weather; and which we sat, with warm toes, at least, – a great comfort to old ...,[9] – we were not unmindful of the source whence the comfort was derived.

Yours truly,

Samuel Bamford.

To Mr Bazley, as see the adjoining.[10]

**Copy letter**, *Bamford to Thomas Bazley, 1 February 1861.*

Dear Sir,

Supposing that you will on an early day, depart for London, I take the liberty, now, at the last opportunity, to remind you of our last conversation, when you kindly intimated your intention to look up your insurances with a view to effecting some of them; through my agency, with the Globe office. I should be most happy to receive your commands with reference thereto, and await respectfully, your decision on the subject.

You will, of course, see Lord Palmerston respecting the memorial lately transmitted on my behalf; and I shall be duly informed, through the medium of some of my friends, whether or not your kind endeavours have been successful.

I remain, Dear Sir,

Your obliged humble servant

Samuel Bamford.

**Saturday 2nd.** The following is from the Manchester Weekly Express & Guardian of this day.

**Cutting**, *from the* Manchester Weekly Express & Guardian, *2 February 1860: a satirical comment on a proposal by* The Times *that a subscription should be started for Richard Cobden in his time of hardship.*

"To him that hath shall be given, but to him that hath not, shall be taken away, even that which he hath."

**Sunday 3rd.** Received the annexed from Mr Bazley.

**Letter**, *Thomas Bazley, New Bridge Mills, Manchester, to Bamford, 2 February 1861.*

Dear Sir,

My Insurances chiefly expire at Midsummer and I cannot tell till then whether it will be possible for me to make a change as indeed I am more likely to reduce them than to increase them, but of course I will see what I can do.

---

9. Word illegible.
10. Dated in error by Bamford "2nd Feb Frid."

I shall take care to wait in person upon Lord Palmerston as soon as possible and will faithfully urge your claims upon him, but fearing an inconvenient delay to yourself I have desired my Cashier to pay you, whenever you call here, the sum of five pounds which I wish you to accept as a donation from myself.

Mo[st] faithfully,

Tho[s]. Bazley.

**Monday 4th.** Wrote to Mr Bazley as follows.[11]

*Letter*, *Bamford to Thomas Bazley, 5 February 1861.*[12]

Dear Sir,

I have this day received at your counting house, five pounds, for which I tender most sincere and respectful thanks: it will help me materially in any delay which may ensue. Meantime I shall prepare a further and a stronger statement of my case, to be brought before Parliament, if necessary, than any which has yet appeared.

Dear Sir,

Your Obliged Humble Servant

Samuel Bamford.

**Friday 7th.** Received the annexed; and on the 11th sent the annexed reply.

*Circular*, *from Robert Rumney, H.D. Pochin and David Chadwick, 5 February 1861, inviting Bamford to a farewell dinner for Mr Hutchings, late secretary of the Mechanics' Institute before he leaves the country for Brazil.*

*Draft letter*, *Bamford to David Chadwick, 11 February 1861.*

Dear Sir & Friend.

You surely cannot be in earnest, about my attending this dinner at the Royal Hotel. Looking at the affair as it is presented to my mind[13] I cannot but feel that I should be entirely out of place in such a company[14] on such an occasion. You will therefore pardon my non attendance.

To Mr Hutchings I am indebted for kind offices on several occasions. I respect him much: I wish he may be entirely prosperous in his new undertaking; and that both he and his family, may enjoy as much happiness as is allotted to the conditions of human existence.[15]

Yours truly,

Samuel Bamford.

---

11. This is not a copy letter, but transcribed into the diary.
12. Bamford wrote "Jan." in error.
13. Altered by Bamford from "as it must be".
14. Altered by Bamford from "I should be isolated, unfitted and beyond all propriety at such a place".
15. Altered by Bamford from "as the conditions of human life admit".

**Wednesday 13th.** At Middleton, looking over old writings at Mr Clarks office; found some very old, which I could not decypher. Very cold, got warm with sitting with W.C. Ridings, at Corner house.

**Sunday 17th.** The adjoining comes to hand, and is on the 19th replied to.

**Letter**, *David Chadwick to Bamford, 16 February 1861.*

Dear Sir,
I was under the impression that you were an old and intimate friend of Mr Hutchings, and had arranged to <u>present</u> you a ticket for the dinner.
   If you can, and feel inclined, to attend, we shall be very glad to see you, and you will please to take this note as the Invitation.
                         Yours very truly,
                              D. Chadwick.

**Copy letter**, *Bamford to David Chadwick, 19 February 1861.*

Dear Sir,
After your very kind and repeated invitations to the dinner, which yourself and friends purpose giving to Mr Hutchings, I should certainly have felt bound to attend, and should have attended, could I for one moment have realized the persuasion that in doing so I should be acting with propriety. But the more I have thought of it, the more have I become convinced of the entire unsuitableness, under present circumstances, of my appearance in such a company on such an occasion. I must therefore entreat that you will dismiss from your mind all idea of my being one of the party, which however I wish may share the enjoyment of a very happy evening.
                    Your obliged Serv$^t$,
                         Samuel Bamford.

Why should I be seen at any such stirs? A poor devil, who can't tell whence the next sixpence must come from. I should have to sit as mute and humble "as if my soul were not my own"; obligated to every one around me for a glass of wine: looked upon as one merely tolerated; taken in and allowed to sit at table from pity; a plate is perhaps handed round for a contribution, and what should I have to give in any such account? I should be taken there to be merely a witness of the triumph of one who has made friends by being the pliant servitor of a <u>clique</u>, a <u>party</u>, which I have not been, never would be! As good as saying, "Look Bamford, you can see what you have missed." I am quite certain I am far best by keeping clear of all such entanglements. I have been in Manchester now, nearly three years since my coming from London, and this party have never before noticed me, and why should I dance at their feasts?

**Wednesday 20th.** The letter on the other leaf is an invitation to a feast of quite a different discription: it is given by a worthy and honest young fellow; the keeper of a beer house, at Crab Lane head, to a number of the oldest people in the district; the dinner will I suppose, and hope, chiefly consist of a good hot potato pie, with some pudding, perhaps and a good brown home brewed ale. I must by all means attend this homely refection and I promise I will attend unless the weather be severe indeed.

### Invitation card:

Mr Samuel Bamford
You are requested to attend a Dinner, given by Mr Chadwick, Paul Pry, Crab Lane, 23rd February, 1861.
  Dinner on the table at 5 P.M.

*Letter*, *James Dronsfield to Bamford, 17 February 1861.*

Worthy Friend,
It was the intention of Travis and myself to have come to see you, but we took into consideration the propriety of seeing a few friends at John Pollitts in order to form a working committee to get up a benefit for you. We intend to hold a meeting on Wednesday night, and we will afterwards report to you the proceedings. You must in the meanwhile look up your tickets and we shall very probably call for them on Sunday next if we dont see you before.
  My Mrs will perhaps give you a call tomorrow, Monday in the forenoon so that you can send over the tickets if you have them at hand, together with a "Radical" for Travis and an "Early Days" for me. You must select such of your own compositions for your portion of the evenings entertainment as will have a tendency to prevent the audience from growing prosy. We have met with good encouragement so far. You shall not have any risk in the matter at all events.
                  I am yours truly
                  Jas. Dronsfield.

Called at Brooks's office in Severn Court to ask about the rough notes of the memorial from Middleton, but nothing could be heard of it; the whole lot at Middleton are a lot of the most unsatisfactory "friends", which a man was ever mystified by.
  Binney wanted the rough draft, whereas if he was very earnest, why could he not draw up another; the facts are known to him as well as to Whalley at Middleton.
  I am extreamly dissatisfied with the whole affair. I have even some premonitions that this Middleton affair has been an emanation and scheme of deep perfidy; but more anon.

**Wednesday 20th.** Letter opposite comes to hand this evening: it is probably in consequence of my having declined to attend the dinner at the Royal Hotel.

**Thursday 21st.** The annexed letter from Mr Chadwick.[16]

---

16. This and the previous appear to be two references to the same letter.

**Letter**, *David Chadwick, Manchester, regional agent for the Globe Fire and Life Insurance Company, to Bamford, 20 February 1861.*

Dear Sir,
I have a note this morning from the Secretary, enquiring how it happens that he has not heard from you, since your appointment on the 14th January last.
    I shall be glad to receive a call, or a few lines from you soon as convenient.
    In the meantime,
                    I am, dear Sir,
                            Yours truly,
                                    D. Chadwick.

**Copy letter**, *Bamford to M. Newmarch Esq., Secretary to the Globe Fire and Life Insurance Company, 22 February 1861.*

Sir,
Mr David Chadwick writes saying that you have written to him enquiring how it happens that you have not heard from me since my appointment as agent in January.
    The reason is I have not, in reality, had anything to write about. I have made various calls on persons whom I knew were users or holders of insurance on property, but hitherto without succeeding in effecting any direct engagements.
    From one I have received promises: from others encouraging replies as to future operations: and the information I have received [leads me to believe] that but little business will be done by me, until present engagements with business affairs draw towards a close.
    I purposed sending in an account at the quarters end: and by that time I hoped to exhibit a statement which would justify reasonable hopes of my becoming a useful ancillary to your office; to the quarters end, I must therefore ask you to defer your expectations, and in the meantime, using every exertion as a decisive trial, I shall remain,
                    your obedient servant,
                            Samuel Bamford.

**Saturday 23rd.** The following discribes a dining party which took place this day. (Taken from Middleton Albion, Mar 2nd 1861).

**Report**, *from the* Middleton Albion, *2 March 1861.*

---

### BLACKLEY.
### REMARKABLE ASSEMBLY OF AGED MEN.

On the afternoon of Saturday last, the 23rd of February a dinner was provided for a select party of aged men, who met at the house of Mr. Samuel Chadwick, beer retailer, Crab-lane Head, Blackley. Thirty-six took their seats at the tables, and a number of dinners were sent out to persons who from age, or infirmity could not attend. The feast was in the right old English style, and well befitting the venerable guests who partook of it. Excellent roast beef, boiled mutton, and ham, with beautiful potatoes boiled in the "gradely Lancashire way," with plenty of genuine home brewed ale, formed the first course; this was followed by a couple of rich "hunters' puddings" in a blue flame of brandy, and to these succeeded apple pie and capital cheese; the tables having been cleared, ale, pipes and tobacco were produced, and the hoary visitors commenced the enjoyment of smoking and conversation; old friends and neighbours were greeted in kindly tone; acquaintances of early youth were recognised and reminded of days and scenes long past; the friendly hand, though tremulous with age, was offered and pressed, and pleasurable emotion somewhat saddened by the reflection that, after this, they would never more all meet again, might be supposed to give the expression of several countenances which were noticed. A chairman, however, was appointed, music was called for, and one with a good heart, but rather wavering voice, sung about "Nelson and Collingwood, and the brave British Tars," another gave a ditty on "Fair London Town," whither he went "all for to seek his fortune," and engaged in the service of "a fine young lady, which proved his overthrow," for on his preferring to marry "pretty Polly, the chamber maid," she brought a charge of robbery against him, and he concluded "Now for I must die." Another described the career of a poor lad, a fustian weaver, who, in "the hard times," known as "the barley times," left his loom and enlisted into a cavalry regiment; came home at the short peace, and when war again commenced, again joined the army, going with Wellington through all the campaigns of Portugal and Spain, and at Waterloo being a captain in the 10th Hussars, he received twelve wounds in the service, but none of them either disfigured or disabled him, and on returning to England he married a lady with a fortune of ninety thousand pounds; he never was drunk in his life, and to that next to having escaped death in the field, might be attributed his great success in life.[17] The venerable company continued thus enjoying rational and harmless pleasure until half-past nine o'clock, and departed well pleased and very thankful, having duly acknowledged their obligations by a vote of thanks to their worthy entertainer and his kind and obliging wife, three times three cheers accompanying the fervent acclaim. The names of the guests, their residences, and their ages were committed to writing, and the following is a summary of their ages in six lots of six persons each:– Lot 1, six persons from 84 to 79, 484 years; lot 2, from 77 to 75, 458 years; lot 3, from 74 to 73, 142 years; lot 4, from 72 to 71, 429 years; lot 5, from 71 to 69, 420 years; lot 6, from 68 to 64, 404 years. – Total united ages, 2633 years. The greater portion were natives of Blackley township; and all, except one from Moston, were present residents of Blackley. Such another gathering by one entertainer, and such a feasting of old people has not been known on that side of the country, within the memory of any individual now living. All the guests were of the labouring class.

---

17. This was a favourite story of Bamford's: see entry for 2 Feb. 1860, describing his reading at Burnley.

***Newspaper cutting***, *source not stated: a poem, "Under the violets" by Oliver Wendell Holmes,*[18] *including the verses:*

> Her hands are cold; her face is white;
> No more her pulses come and go;
> Her eyes are shut to life and light;-
> Fold the white vestures snow on snow,
> And lay her where the violets blow.
>
> ......
>
> If any, born the kindlier blood,
> Should ask, What maiden lies below?
> Say only this; a tender bud,
> That tried to blossom in the snow,
> Lies withered where the violets blow.

The beautiful verses, might almost be supposed to refer to my dear Ann.[19]

**Thursday 28th.** My 73rd birthday.

**Saturday 2nd March.** Literary and musical entertainment at Hollinwood. Strangely wet and stormy; and, considering the weather, a very respectable attendance. Stopped all night very comfortably at Mrs Dronsfields, and returned home Sunday at noon.

***Letter***, *John Harland, 7 Repton Street, Upper Brook Street, Manchester, to Bamford, 1 March 1861.*

My Dear Mr Bamford,
I wrote to Sir Morton Peto, and I have this morning received from Mr John Clark, of Middleton, a note stating that "Sir Morton Peto sees no objection to complying with the request." As I cannot get to Middleton myself, I have therefore to ask you to continue your kind examinations of the deeds, and to bring me half a dozen at a time, signing a receipt for them when borrowed, on my behalf, and when I return one batch, picking out for me another half dozen, till we have sifted the oldest of them pretty well.
   In choosing 6 old parchments please take the following rules for your guidance.
   1. Take the very smallest parchments you can find.
   2. They must have small writing. (The tall writing you spoke of will be fines and recoveries, which are not very interesting. I want the original grants of lands, etc.)
   3. If any seals to the deeds, please choose those with white seals first: and next, those with dark green wax.

---

18. Oliver Wendell Holmes (1809–94), American writer, who had recently come to prominence as a result of his volume *The Autocrat of the Breakfast Table* (1857–8); see *Dictionary of American Biography*.
19. Bamford would refer to his daughter Ann, who had died aged 25, as their "tender bud".

I shall be in this house till the 20th instant; and after that at "Moorfield Cottage, Old Lane, Swinton." Mrs Harland joins me in kind remembrances to Mrs Bamford and yourself.

Yours ever truly,

J. Harland.

**Monday 4th.** Went to Middleton and looked out seven old documents for my poor lame friend John Harland at Manchester, which I delivered to him at his house on the 7th, same month.

### Receipt.

Seven documents: received from Mr John Clarke of Middleton; marked from 1 to 7. by Samuel Bamford, 4th March, 1861 and by him delivered to Mr John Harland, 7th of same Month.

**Letter**, *David Chadwick to Bamford, 4 March 1861.*

Dear Sir,
Mr Hutchings, late of the Manchester Mechanics Institution having had a testimonial presented to him consisting of an address which has been signed by a many gentlemen of influence in Manchester. He has expressed a desire that your signature should be added thereto.

   If convenient to call here tomorrow for the purpose of reading it and complying with his wishes I shall be glad.

I am yours truly,

For D. Chadwick

W. Robins.

**Friday 8th.** Brierley came, and I gave him two pounds of the money which Mrs Dronsfield brought yesterday (£8-0-0) He was not for having anything: he seemed not to expect it, but I said he must recollect he had a family to provide for, and he had been out of work. So he took the two sovs wrapped in a bit of paper. I almost regret I did not give him three pounds; but I must make it up some other time.

**Report**, *from the* Oldham Times, *9 March 1861.*

---

#### MESSRS BAMFORD AND BRIERLEY'S READINGS.

On Saturday evening last a literary and musical entertainment took place in the Hollinwood National School, in honour of Samuel Bamford, the popular author; Mr. Alderman Radcliffe in the chair. The chairman, in opening the proceedings, regretted that the night was so unfavourable, as it no doubt would prevent many from attending who would have been happy to have patronised a worthy veteran like Mr. Bamford. A company of glee singers, under the direction of Robert Dransfield, contributed greatly to the evening's entertainment. Mr. Bamford was well at home in describing the interior of his humble cottage at Middleton some forty years ago, and how he was looked upon as a dangerous character, and led manacled to prison, because he advocated at that time the same views on political Reform as are now entertained and acknowledged by eminent statesmen to be, if carried out, great benefits to the people of England. Mr. Bamford also read several of his poems in a manner which was truly appropriate to his homely style of composition. Mr. Benjamin Brierley, author of "A Day Out," "Bunk Ho'," "Sweepings from Traddlepin Fold," &c., read two or three extracts from his own works, and kept the audience in a succession of titterings, with now and then a convulsive broadside, as he described passages in the matrimonial career of the immortal Linderinbant. He also read an interesting story from "Bunk Ho," entitled "Hazel Clough Boggart," in a masterly style; and we may infer from the versatile manner in which each character was delineated, that the author had paid no little attention to the personation of his originals.

---

**Letter**, *William Waterhouse, Victoria Mill, Hollinwood, to Bamford, 9 March 1861.*

Dear Sir,
Enclosed you will please receive Balance sheet for last Saturday Nights <u>reading</u> which I trust you will find satisfactory – we were all of us very sorry for the unfavourable weather which we had, as we felt confident that we should have had a crowded house had it been fine, thereby realising a handsome sum for yourself – however small the balance I am sure it will have been thankfully accepted – I have no means of sending you the tickets but will leave them with Mr James Dronsfield so that you will be able to get them the first time you are over. Hoping Mrs B and yourself are well

I remain yours,<br>respectfully,<br>William Waterhouse.

P.S. I may also say that the entertainment itself was considered a perfect success by the parties attending it, a many of them having spoken highly of it.
W.W.

1861. Dr William Waterhouse in a/ct with Mr Samuel Bamford Esq.

March 2nd

| | | | |
|---|---|---|---|
| Mr Alderman Radcliffe's donation | 5 | – | – |
| Councillor Buckley's donation | 1 | – | – |
| Joseph Dyson's donation | | 7 | 6 |
| receipts from the sale of programmes | – | 2 | 2 |
| 41 tickets sold @ 1/- each | 2 | 1 | – |
| 34 tickets @ 6d | | 17 | – |
| Subscribed by the Committee | | 3 | – |
| | 9 | 10 | 8 |

| | | |
|---|---|---|
| Feby 24 & March 2nd two advertisements | 4 | – |
| in the Standard paper | | |
| " two advertisements in the Times | 5 | – |
| " 50 large bills for windows | 7 | – |
| " 100 programmes | 5 | – |
| postage stamps | | 10 |
| paper & envelopes | | 4 |
| Brierley & Clarke's expenses | 5 | – |
| Gas in school room | 1 | – |
| Mr Samuel Bamford | 8 | – – |
| provisions etc. for singers | | 2 6 |
| | 9 | 10 8 |

Wm Waterhouse Secretary

**Copy letter**, *Bamford to Councillor W. Buckley Esq., 9 March 1861.*

Worthy and Respected Sir.
The Dr. and Cr.[20] account of the Secretary to the late "Literary and Musical Entertainment" at Hollinwood, has come to my hand this day; and in the account your name stands before a contribution to the disbursements of one pound. As the principal recipient I feel much pleasure in discharging the duty of thanking you for your kind assistance on the occasion. There is scarcely reason to doubt, that had not the weather been very unpropitious, the attendance would have been numerous: and notwithstanding the remarkable storms of that evening and night, the audience was greater than I had anticipated, and appeared both discriminating and well pleased. The Committee, the vocalists, and the Secretary, all gave their services gratuitously; they are each worthy of great commendation; whilst the receipts owing to the timely aid of the <u>honoured</u> <u>chairman</u>, yourself and <u>other</u> <u>friends</u>, were amply abundant for the occasion, and leave me conscious of a deep obligation to remain, your obedient servant,
                              Samuel Bamford.

**Copy letter**, *Bamford to James Radcliffe Esq., J.P., Oak Cottage, Hollinwood, 9 March 1861. The letter is badly damaged. Bamford thanks Radcliffe at length for his donation at the Hollinwood reading, and states that "so long as mental health continues … recollections of pleasant incidents which occurred on that night, will be cherished by me".*

**Sunday 10th.**[21] Miss Taylor brought two pieces of very rich Cimblin,[22] one from Bury, and the other home made. Her nephew and another gentleman were with her. This is the second or third Simblin Sunday on which this good Lady has remembered us in a similar way. Her home made cimblins are certainly the best.

---

20. Debit and credit.
21. Mid-Lent Sunday; in Bury, styled Cymbalin Sunday (and familiar elsewhere as Simnel Sunday).
22. Cymbalin.

***Insertion****: a paper slip.*

Home made
Bury Cymbalin.

**Wednesday 13th.** At Middleton: A person who gave his address as Abraham Smith of Levenshulme called during my absence wishing to see me: he bought a copy of Early Days for which my wife thinking perhaps, to be on the safe side, charged him 4/-. He gave her 5 and refused the change: he looked at my portrait and said he had never seen that person before.

**Friday 15th.** Wrote Mr Smith as follows.

***Copy letter****, Bamford to Abraham Smith, 15 March 1861.*

> Sir,
> When you called at my residence the other day you left 5/- as payment for one of my books, (Early Days). My wife, in mistake, told you the price was 4/- when the selling retail price is 2/6 and I have never charged it more. I would have inclosed for you thirty postage stamps, but being doubtful whether or not this address will find you, I request you to inform me where I can see you in Manchester, or at what place there I could leave the money – 2/6 – for you.
> >                 I am Sir,
> >                         Your obedient serv^t,
> >                                 Samuel Bamford.

**Saturday 16th.** Went to Middleton, and returned by 'bus: as coming down Mosston Lane, the feeling and use of my right foot almost left me. I continued however to walk, though lamely like one who is paralysed, as indeed I was: by the time I arrived at my own door the sensation, or rather want of sensation had left me, except that a slight numbness, weakness, and giddiness remained. This was paralysis. A kind of intimation to warn me of failing health: and to prepare for what must follow in the course of nature. Well, my Father died, I believe in his 72nd year, my brother in his 74th, my sister in her 73rd. I am now in my 74th year, and my turn – which I neither fear nor regret, is drawing towards me.

**Sunday 17th.** After a night of very good rest I got up and rubbed myself all over with a towel dipped and wrung out of cold water; this during many years has been my custom every 2d or 3d morning, but during the last three weeks Mima having been unwell, it has been discontinued, and the omission has, in my opinion, been the chief cause of this attack.

**Monday 18th.** Again well rubbed with the cold wet towel, and then with a dry rough one; my lameness is better, but feel a little weak and numb on the right side during the walk which I took to Middleton. Got a glass of hot toddy at the Boarshead, did a little business with Mills the printer and returned by 'bus.

**Wednesday 20th.** The following from John Harland.

*Letter*, *John Harland, 7 Repton Street, Manchester, to Bamford, 19 March 1861.*
My Dear Sir,
I write a line to prevent your coming by mistake to this house, which I leave
tomorrow (Wed) for "Moorfield Cottage, Old Lane, Swinton," – my future home.
The 7 deeds etc., have been ready the last 10 days, and any day you feel inclined
and at leisure, I shall be glad to see you at Swinton. The Swinton 'bus starts from
the corner of Cross St, Market St at 9 and at 11 a.m.; and at 1.30 4 and 5 p.m.
You get down at the Swinton toll-bar and then take the left road, which leads to
Worsley. The second lane to your right is Old Lane, and the first house in that
lane on your right, is my cottage, where I shall always be glad to welcome an old
friend.
    Do you think Mr Clark would allow you to kill 2 birds with one stone? I mean –
to bring with you 6 deeds and take back the 7, at once, so as to save the double
journey.
    If he wishes, I will send him each time a Receipt for the deeds lent, – by post.
    A friend of mine and yours called on you the other day, but you were out. He
says you have got a very pretty little place.
    Mrs Harland joins me in kind regards to Mrs Bamford and yourself, and I am
ever.
                    Faithfully yours,
                    J. Harland.


20 Wed. To Middleton again by bus, thinking to go thence to Oldham by train, but the
weather becoming stormy, wet and cold, I only went to Mr Clarks office, and not
finding him there, I called at the printing office, took a glass of hot toddy at the
Roundabout, and came back by bus.
    Pickstone, and a little man called. What for I don't know.

# 12

# PALMERSTON AND THE PENSIONS

*The spring of 1861 was rather miserable for Bamford. Having finally got sight of the mysterious Middleton memorial, and spurred on by his poor health, he made a further effort to have his Royal Bounty grant converted to a pension. He was to be bitterly disappointed, not merely because the announcement of the Pension List in late April did not contain his name, but because the grant of a £50 pension to John Close, a working-class poet from Westmorland whose poetry was ridiculed in the London papers, brought the whole system into contempt, and damaged his own despairing efforts to sway Palmerston in his favour. By mid-May his finances were again parlous, and he was forced back to the pawnshop, and into selling books and other small valuable items. Perhaps understandably in the circumstances, Bamford's peevishness and sense of isolation became increasingly marked. The haughty and ungrateful tone of his letters of late April and early May in response to the call for a subscription for John Critchley Prince did not help his public profile. His failure to attend the funeral of the baby Dronsfield had named after him – one of his least appealing social failures – must have hurt his loyal friend deeply.*

**Thursday 21st.** The following from Mills of Middleton.

**Letter**, *Thomas Mills to Bamford, 20 March 1861.*

My Dear Mr Bamford,
Agreeably to my promise I have now the pleasure of enclosing you a copy or
I presume so much as can be remembered of the Memorial sent to L^d Palmerston
on your behalf, and trust the same will be satisfactory to you so far as it goes.
　　I have not time just now time to express an opinion upon it. It seems to
embrace a wider ground than I anticipated and to be couched in very fair and
becoming language.
　　Your "Right and Wrong" and "Memorial" are ready and will be sent on per
10 o/c Bus tomorrow Morng.
　　　　　　　　In g^t haste,
　　　　　　　　　　Most truly yrs,
　　　　　　　　　　　　Tho^s Mills.

Copy of Middleton Memorial
(Damning with faint praise as usual)

(copy, but only from memory)[1]
To the Right Honourable Lord Viscount Palmerston, First Lord of the Treasury,
Prime Minister of Great Britain etc, the Memorial of the undersigned, chiefly
inhabitant of Middleton, in the county of Lancaster,

---

1. This comment in the same hand as the memorial. See entry for 6 September 1861.

Humbly sheweth,

That 12 months ago they learnt with great pride and satisfaction that your
Lordship had been pleased to grant a donation of 50l, to Samuel Bamford, of
Moston, Nr Manchester and native of Middleton, and commonly known as the
Lancashire Bard: and that the donation was greatly heightened by the manner in
which it was given.

That Samuel Bamford is now in his 73rd year, and his only source of livelihood the
uncertain one of giving public readings from his own and other authors' works:
and that these readings are necessarily attended with great expense.

That Samuel Bamford has been a great political sufferer, having, in ruder times,
often and for years, been chained, tried, confined and abused; – all for the
advocacy of principles in full operation in our own happier times.

That Samuel Bamford for many years performed great public services, as chief and,
almost, only country correspondent to the London Press: that he is also the author
of many works of a highly useful and moral character, both in poetry and prose.

That under these circumstances; – his years and increasing infirmities; his
precarious livelihood; his trials, losses and incarcerations; and the pacific tendency
of his numerous writings; – your memorialists would fain hope that your Lordship
would perceive, in this, a proper case for the recommendation of some annuity for
his few remaining years.

**Note**, *in Bamford's handwriting, on the reverse of the Memorial.*

Not the least allusion, in this precious specimen of cant and twaddle, to what Scarlett
said in my favour at York, nor to the remarkable summing up of the Judge with
reference to me; nor to my interference with the starving hand loom weavers in 1826,
which probably prevented a great distruction of property, and the loss of some lives at
Heywood, Middleton, and Rochdale. Nor to the injurious reflections and reproaches
to which I was subjected in consequence of my interference with the weavers and my
subsequent employment as a correspondent of the London Daily press: nor to my
truthful, trustful integrity in general matters; nor to my faithful services during seven
years under the Board of Inland Revenue, nor the handsome testimonial which
I received from the Accountant General, on my leaving that employment: all these
points of striking and important interest are herein ignored by my very sincere and
generous friend (Henry Whalley, as I understand) who drew up this concoction of
damming, "faint praise", though another "friend", whom I look upon as, "a loose
screw", had I think something I to do with the very qualifying phraseology of the
document. I have indeed cause to say, "deliver me from certain of my friends".

21 Thur. At Middleton and saw Mr Clarke who ordered the carpenter to open all the
boxes for my inspection. He did so, and I looked over most of their contents, which
were chiefly rent books; books of account, and a great number of miscellaneous
documents, chiefly respecting roads, coal mines, and other matters connected with the
Middleton and Thornham property, all of comparatively modern date.

Brought four papers away and intend showing to Mr Harland on Tuesday.

**Saturday 23rd.** Went to Hollinwood to W^m Travis's (walked it across the fields) expecting to find a pair of new shoes there, which he had promised to have ready but, we are always subject to vicissitude, and poor Travis had not made the shoes; his children had been ill of the measles all week, and his wife was now almost hourly expecting to want the midwife; so I rested and took a draught of home brewed ale, and came back by bus to Newton Heath; getting home tired, I, who used to never know what "being tired" was.

**Sunday 24th.** Cut the opposite slip from the Manchester paper. I call it the formal open[ing] of the war, or campaign, betwixt the employers and the employed; if this continual strife betwixt the two classes does not ere long lead to dreadful scenes in old England, I am much mistaken; in this instance, the employers constantly refuse to lessen the <u>time</u> of working but they <u>reduce</u> the amount of wages, a proceeding which clearly points to their wish to cut short the supplies which the operatives are very judiciously and very becomingly applies to the formation, and progress of Cooperative stores and Manufactures; the employers are trying to stop that; the workers will persevere, and now will come the struggle for "the plank which is to save the drowning man"; the workers have not any other means for self preservation, and the employers seem determined they shall not retain it. May God defend the right for now begins "the tug of war".

***Newspaper cutting***, *23 March 1861, source not stated, reporting various industrial disputes, mostly over wages, in the north-west, Coventry and London.*

**Tuesday 26th.** A dull, cold dolourous day. Went to Harlands at Swinton, along a dull, black dolourous looking road, to a plain dull looking cottage, a farm house, made into one. Very unwell of myself: Came back; a cold damp air, and reached home quite knocked up.

**Wednesday 3rd April.** Sent the annexed to Mr Bazley.

***Copy letter***, *Bamford to Thomas Bazley, 4 April 1861.*

Honourable Sir, Kind Friend.
I herewith inclose for your perusal and consideration a copy of a petition to the House of Commons which I have thought might be suitable for presentation should the late memorial to Lord Palmerston not prove effective. I very much wished to have seen you, and probably should have visited upon you before this, had not the state of my health, from a slight attack of paralysis, and other ailments following it, prevented me from leaving the house; cold and unsettled weather also preventing my doing so. I will however, if possible, get down to your counting house, some fine morning, should such occur before your return to London. The Session of Parliament will speed on fast, and it will be necessary to be on the alert if anything effective must be done in my case; as soon therefore, as you can ascertain whether or not it will be necessary to petition House of

Commons; by communicating the simple fact to me here, you would confer a
great additional obligation. The petition I hope you will feel to be such as might
be presented, with credit to the applicant, in any Court; Would you Sir, may I ask,
undertake to present such a petition? And, would you move "that it be printed":
on that would depend a deal, since if it got into the hands of very many members
a sensation would be felt, and possibly expressed.

I remain Honourable and kind Sir, your obliged and grateful servant
Samuel Bamford.

**Friday 4th.** Posted the next to Smith at Rochdale; a pretty plain document I think.

***Copy letter***, *Bamford to James Smith, Rochdale, 4 April 1861*.[2]

Mr Smith,
Near this time two years since when I had a public reading at Rochdale
(29th May 1859) I should have addressed you as, "my very good Friend": now,
with sorrow I say it, I cannot so accost you. Since that time, I have not either seen
you, received a message from you, or a note, or any indication whatever, that you
or your family are either living or dead, or that you cared one straw, whether I or
my wife were either in this world, or had removed to the next. Now this has
seemed very strange to me: so sudden, so to me, unaccountable a change, has not
happened without causing great pain and surprise both to myself and my old
partner. The friendship betwixt you and I, was based on so truthful, honest, and
manly a foundation, that the idea had never occurred to me, of its becoming
dissevered except by death. I had, in my course through life, been acquainted with
so many light, ever changing characters, that I had learned to value the common
run of friends, or rather professing friends, at their true worth, and the more to
estimate rational ..., and the grounds of it, Christian rectitude, as the great
treasures of humble mans life, to which, for active use and solace might be added
the social conversation and esteem, of a few faithful and chosen friends of the very
few, who in 1859, I still saw in that light, you were one: nearly all my old friends
have disappeared in the shades of that land whither we are all hastening, you still
remaining like a lonely comrade, after a long battle, and we hailed your
appearance as we should that of a lost brother; how bitter must have been our
surprise, our disappointment, and our poignant Regret, when we ... give a Cold
shoulder on our anxious, ... intended solicitude. But, dwelling on these things too
long, I shall forget the purpose and intent of my writing, which is, to ask you, as a
<u>honest</u> <u>man</u> what is the <u>cause</u> of this <u>change</u> in your <u>conduct</u>? it must certainly
have been caused either by something which I have done or said, or by something
which some other person has done, or ...[3] to me, as I trust you have been, you will
let me know at once, what it is which I have done, or what it is which some other

---

2. The letter is damaged.
3. One line obliterated.

person has said or done to my prejudice. I am particular on this point, because I know that I am beset: by <u>secret enemies</u> beset, and ever have been, since I offended some of the "great ones of the land" by my honest, upright, adherence to the cause of the people, which is that of truth and right. It is now nearly three years since I returned from London, and in this time I have appeared often in public, hoping, by that means to obtain a clue of some sort, to the nest of reptile calumniators which have defiled my path. Will you, my once friend, be again a friend, and denounce the slander who has been whispering in your ear and poisoning your mind.

Your truthful well wisher

Samuel Bamford.

**Letter**, *Thomas Bazley to Bamford, 5 April 1861.*

Dear Sir,

I really shall be glad to assist to the utmost of my power in procuring for you the aid from the Royal Bounty Fund to which I think you fairly entitled. Perhaps a year has not passed since the last grant and I wish you to inform me, addressed 3A King Street, St James' Square, London, when you received it. Very soon I will see Lord Palmerston in person upon the subject. In case of need I will of course present your petition to the House

Mo[st] truly yrs,

Thos Bazley,

**Sunday 7th.** Jas Smiths reply.

**Letter**, *James Smith, Rochdale, to Bamford, 7 April 1861.*

Dear <u>Friend</u> Bamford,

I have received your letter and I am rather surprised at what it contains it is true there has no correspondence passed between us for the length of time you state but I can assure you that not one single word ever escaped my lips which was detrimental to your character in any shape. I know the History of your public character as well as most men and I am sure I need not tell you here how I have admired it and do so now as much as ever I did in my life you may blame me for neglecting to write to you but that is the utmost extent of what you can censure me for with Justice for I can assure you that not a single individual ever came out with an expression to me that would hurt your feeling, if you had heard every word since I last saw you in Rochdale therefore I hope you will discard those thoughts for they are wrong for it is not possible for any man to poison my mind against you nor would I allow you to be maligned and your character vilified in my presence without resenting the affront but it is never attempted in my house by any one whatever is said when your name comes in question it is quite the reverse of that. I think I have said enough on this subject to convince you that you cannot charge me with anything only neglect no man in England was gladder than I was when Lord Palmerston made you that small present if I did not write to you I had a knowledge of what was going on and if you ever meet with Mr Edwin Waugh he will be able to state to you what took place betwixt him and me on the subject previous, and it is my wish and nothing would be more pleasing to me than to hear that something was done for you so that you and your good Wife could live comfortable together the remainder of your Days, without having any labour to perform has you have done enough and suffered more than enough in your Days to be allowed the indulgence of living with comfort both in Body and Mind. I here conclude with my very best respects to you and your good Wife and I hope this will find you both in the best of health as I am glad to say that this leaves me and my good Wife as well has we can expect.

I Remain yours truly<br>James Smith.

Ramsbottom and Brierley called; the latter offered me what he called a commission of twenty per cent on the sale of his last 6d book: I thought it rather strange that he should wish me to negociate the sale of one of his pamphlets to the booksellers, but at length, and to oblige him, as I thought, I assented. Still I don't like the job, on second thoughts and I don't think I shall go on with it.

**Monday 8th.**  Wrote Mr Bazley as the annexed.

***Copy letter***, *Bamford to Thomas Bazley, 8 April 1861.*

Honourable and kind Sir.
With many thanks for your ready attention to my note of the 4th instant. I have to inform you that the Paymaster Generals cheque for £50 issued on the recommendation of Viscount Palmerston on my behalf, was dated 17th March 1860. I have not a distinct idea as to what will be the nature of your next application to his lordship: I remark however that you generally refer to "the Royal Bounty fund", which is for the payment of incidental donations only, such as my last was; and not to "the Royal Pension list", which is continuous, and which, as I understand my friends the memorialists at Middleton had in view.

I remain<br>Honourable and kind Sir,<br>Your obliged Humble Servant<br>Samuel Bamford.

**Tuesday 9th.**  The annexed from Gowenlock with answer.

***Letter***, *R.S. Gowenlock, Oldham, to Bamford, 6 April 1861.*[4]

---

4. Written on the blank fold of the Bazley to Gowenlock letter next printed.

Dear Sir,

At the suggestion of Mr J,. Dronsfield I wrote Mr Bazley on the subject of permanent grant to you and on the other side you have his reply. I intended to ask Mr Councillor Taylor to write also but from the tone of Mr Bazley's reply I should hardly think it necessary showing as it does thorough heartiness in the matter. I think that you could not consider that I have over-stepped the line especially in the part I have again taken; if you should unfortunately, for me ... again my apology.[5]

I was very sorry to hear from Dronsfield of your illness, but think that you are again recovering.

> My dear sir,
> with great esteem,
> Yours,
> R. Scott Gowenlock.

**Letter**, *Thomas Bazley to Gowenlock, 5 April 1861.*

Dear Sir,

I am favoured with your letter of yesterday. Be assured that it will afford me sincere pleasure and satisfaction to accomplish the object, which we have in common, of preserving a permanent aid from the Royal Bounty Fund for Mr Saml Bamford. At the earliest convenient moment I shall see Lord Palmerston upon the subject.

> Mo[st] truly yrs
> Thos Bazley.

**Copy letter**, *Bamford to R.S. Gowenlock, 9 April 1861.*[6]

My Dear Sir,

I am greatly obliged by your kind interference with Mr Bazley relative to my business with Lord Palmerston in ...[7] office. My claims seem to have lost their place, and been "put off" for another year: a few more such "puttings off", and should my name then be ...[8] way just now: [I] have had an attack of paralysis; and though the lameness has left me, my whole system, or machinery of health, has received a benumbing shock, which intimates to me, a beginning of an end, which I can contemplate without either fear or regret. I have never had a doubt that Mr Bazley would do all that he could on my behalf, but a gentle nudge in a friendly way may not, at times, be quite useless. I have sent to him a slip or two similar to the inclosed, and he writes in between saying that he will see Lord Palmerston himself, and if so, and he finds the case against me, he will, with the copy of my petition in his pocket, be able to let the noble viscount see that I am

---

5. The letter, hastily scribbled, is indecipherable at this point.
6. The letter is damaged.
7. Word obliterated.
8. One line obliterated.

purposed to bring my case before the House of Commons, for Mr Bazley has undertaken to present my petition, should such a proceeding be necessary: for the present however, not a word of this to the newspapers or indeed to the public generally. I should like to have your opinion on this petition. I think, – but you will perhaps smile at a parents partiality, – it is about the most fully founded, the most logically set forth, and the most coherently expressed petition of any ever presented to the English Parliament: and if its prayer is not granted either by the Treasury or Parliament an indelible disgrace will attend to the English nation of this day. But more of this when I see you, which I hope to do soon, either here or at Oldham.

If you see Potter tell him I have been talking and thinking about him these last two or three days.

Yours truly,<br>Samuel Bamford.

**Letter**, *R.S. Gowenlock to Bamford, 12 April 1861.*

Dear Sir,

I received yours with form of petition which I sincerely trust will not require to be presented. The petition I entirely approve of if that course has to be resorted to, and I think also that should you be driven to the necessity of having it presented your friends should pour in petitions by dozens upon my Lord Palmerston upon the subject and if that will not do that as a last resort the matter should be fully sifted through the metropolitan and provincial press, contrasting the claims neglected with those recognised by the prime minister. I should be sorry indeed if this should be found to be necessary, but still if nothing be done in the proper course my feeling is entirely that injustice in this instance should no longer be allowed to lurk behind the Treasury Bench. You know my views; on your literary merits alone the allowance ought to be granted; but if refused on both literary and political grounds the public should at least be acquainted with the exertion of the wrong. We have of course all been charmed with the writing of ...[9] and we have also been delighted by those of Samuel Bamford: whilst the former has provided food for the imagination, the latter has taken care that imagination on descending from its lofty flights should find a broad spread, with ... rather than imaginary food, and the public I think would hardly concur with the opinion of his Lordship that the ... descendant of the fiction writer is more deserving of a crumb than he who has not only furnished intellectual but phisical bread to the millions of the trading classes of this large industrial district and the Country at large. Excuse this hasty scribble which I fear you will hardly be able to decipher and believe me,

Yours truly<br>R.S. Gowenlock.

P.S. I should be pleased to see you in Oldham if you are not able to come soon, I shall take an opportunity of seeing you at your own house.

---

9. Name illegible; presumably a reference to a recipient of a literary pension.

**Sunday 14th.**[10] Travis came and brought me the best pair of shoes I ever had on my feet.

**Thursday 18th.** Five days been looking over, and burning old and useless letters and papers of various sorts; very unwell all the time, but now am better. Mima went to Manchester this day, and got 10/- at "Our Uncles"; a dark look out: Nothing heard from Mr Bazley. Lord Palmerston is unwell at home.

**Saturday 20th.** The annexed appears in the Manchester paper of this day. So much for Samuel Bamford's compensation, or remuneration.

*Newspaper cutting, 20 April 1861, setting out the Civil List pension grants for the year June 1860–June 1861. There are two annual pensions: "£50 per annum on Miss Barbara Bell, in consideration of the eminence of her late father, professor of law in the University of Edinburgh, as a jurist and of her straitened circumstances; £75 per annum on Mr. John Burnett, on account of the services rendered by him to art as a line engraver and author, and his advanced age". Seventeen lump sums of £25–£100 are also listed, including "£50 on Miss Jerrold, in consideration of the literary merits of her father, the late Mr. Douglas Jerrold", and £75 to the daughter of the late Leigh Hunt.*

**Monday 22nd.** Went to Newton Station, though very shaky and unsteady in the morning. Potter went with me to Mr Yates's in Church Lane. Mr Y. unwell, but glad to see me: a right hearty Lancashire welcome; told him of my recent ailment. Mrs Yates glad to see me, both the old folks very agreeable. Yates will try to do something in the insurance way at Midsummer.

Went with Potter to the Angel, and he went to look after Gowenlock, who had not been at the office that day: Potter also called to see Brierley at the office of the Oldham Times, which I had asked him to do. I wished to see Potter and Gowenlock alone when I would lay before them some of my plans for a bettering of my case, and a clearing up of all old ambiguities. Potter brought with him back a Mr G of Manchester, whom I did not desire to see: he being one of those whom I don't exactly understand. Another person, a Mr B. followed who boasted of having been trained by old John Knight;[11] a third person also joined us who said he had frequently been in my company at some place which I did not recollect having ever visited. Thus private and useful conversation betwixt Potter and myself was prevented by the obtrusion, of persons whom I either knew not at all or but slightly knew.

Potter would have me to dinner at his house, but the cookery was not of my sort, and I ate only a few mouthfuls.

Went down to Gowenlock's house; he was at home unwell: we must however sit down, and after a time whisky was brought out. Now I thought I should have a good opportunity for introducing some serious talk about my affairs, and just as I was about beginning the subject, Brierley arrived. Potter had quite unnecessarily given him the

---

10. Entry inserted later.
11. John Knight (1763–1838), leading Manchester radical of the Napoleonic era; MCL.

cue and he had followed down here. So now I had nothing for it but to join in the broken and idle chat which took place. After sitting a tiresome while, they went with me down to Stock brook where I wished to so some insurance business with Mr Smethurst, but he was at Southport, so we came away to the public house at the Middleton Junction where we sat down and had each a glass, Gowenlock paying for mine. When the Oldham train was due, Potter left us saying he had a person to meet in Oldham: Gowenlock and Brierley then began talking about their road home, and it appearing that Brierley would go to his lodgings at Hollinwood, Gowenlock said it was of no use him stopping and he would also take the Oldham train, which had not yet moved from the station, being waiting probably for some Rochdale or Yorkshire train coming in. Gowenlock accordingly left, and shortly after, Brierley recollected, or pretended to recollect that he had a bundle to take from Oldham to Hollinwood, so he also got up and bade my good bye, thus they mizzled away, one after another; a very unkind departure, as I felt it to be. I got on the 6.30 train from Oldham, and the particulars of my journey home will probably appear in a letter which I have sent to the Manchester Guardian of this day.

**Letter**, *Bamford to the Editor of the* Manchester Guardian, *no date.*[12]

### (Exaction by Railway Officials)[13]

Sir,

On Monday evening last, I was a passenger by the 6.30 train from Oldham, my intended destination being Newton Heath. On arriving at the latter place, the carriage from which I should have emerged, was a long way from the platform: we were over a hollow place, and thinking that surely the carriages would be moved so that we could step upon the platform, I hesitated to take the ugly leap below me; sixty years before I should not have hesitated, but now I am 73 years of age, and being almost certain it could not be intended that we should jump or drop into the ditch over which the footboards hung, I asked one of the two porters if we should not be moved forwards? He said something, merely motioned with his hand, shut the door and turned the handle, and the train began to move. Now, I thought, all will be right, we shall stop at the platform, but the speed was increased, the train passed the station, and I found that instead of being landed at the next place to my home, I was being conveyed to a greater distance from home. I suspected also, that for this act of provoking abduction the officials at Miles Platting would modestly demand extra fare, and so they did: on presenting my ticket, the porter said, "another penny Sir."
"I shan't pay it," was the reply: the door of egress was then closed, and I had to appear before two officials who gave me the choice of paying the penny, or waiting for the next train back to Oldham, by which they would put me down at Newton Heath. I declined paying, said I felt wronged in being brought from

---

12. The letter is Bamford's original, returned to him by the paper.
13. Originally headed "Insult and Exaction by Railway Officials". The brackets are Bamford's.

Newton Heath at all, and gave them to understand that I would bring the matter before a magistrate, but reflecting that an inconvenient time might elapse before the train came, and that then it would merely replace me at Newton Heath, I deemed it best to pay the penny, and be making the best of my way home; for I was very tired having had a long walk, darkness was setting in, and I should be in the night air, which, in consequence of recent sickness I wished to avoid. I therefore paid the penny, and then was suffered to leave the place of detention. I should certainly, from a sense of duty to others, have made this complaint before a magistrate – I had three witnesses, fellow passengers, who would have corroborated what I have stated respecting the Newton Heath Station. I happen however to be in circumstances which forbid risk of expenditure in law, and hence I, though a Citizen of the freest nation in the world, am compelled to submit to what I feel to be a wrong, committed by the might of wealth against the right of defenceless justice.

I am Sir, Yours respectfully,<br>Protestant.

24th April 1861.

Sent to the Guardian with my card enclosed and its receipt was acknowledged, but it was ultimately left out, and I got it back from the office this day, May 2nd. Such is the attention shown to the complaint of "a poor man"; to a gentleman, and especially to one "well known on change", how different; this is the most despicable form of snobbery. SB.[14]

**Wednesday 24th.** Replied to that passage in the annexed letter, which intimates that I have experienced the same public watchfulness and care which was bestowed on Swain and Rogerson.

**Letter**, *from the* Manchester Examiner and Times, *11 April 1861, from James Travis about John Critchley Prince, reed maker and poet, who has fallen on hard times. The letter proposes a public subscription for Prince, extending to him "the same public watchfulness and care" which has already been extended to Swain, Rogerson and Bamford.*

**Saturday 27th.** The letter headed "John Critchley Prince", appears in the Manchester Examiner and Times.

**Letter**, *from the* Manchester Examiner and Times, *27 April 1861.*

---

### JOHN CRITCHLEY PRINCE.

Sir, – I observe that your correspondent, Mr. Travis, in Tuesday's paper, in reference to Mr. Prince, writes under a mistake in supposing that the same

---

14. Bamford's note added on letter.

"watchful care" which was most worthily bestowed on Swain and Rogerson was extended to Samuel Bamford. This idea probably originated in an expression which appeared in your paper of March 14, 1860, wherein it was said the friends of Mr. Bamford would be glad to learn that the £50, which at the instance of Messrs. Bazley and Gibson had been awarded him, "would be continued." Doubtless many of your readers and the public generally are of the same opinion; but, I regret to say, they are greatly mistaken. Mr. Bamford has written and published various works in prose and poetry, which have been much commended; he was also a leader of the pioneers who 45 years ago broke up the sodden ground of public feeling and opinion in England, prepared it, and threw in the good seed which brought forth parliamentary reform and free trade – those great national "changes and improvements," which, as Lord Palmerston said at Leeds in October, 1860, had "brought contentment and prosperity to a great portion of the community." Mr. Bamford has been a public benefactor, and he has done more for the country than the country has done for him; as yet, however, his public services have not met with that "watchful care," which in many other instances has been so "worthily bestowed." Let it therefore be understood that Mr. Bamford has not been provided for; that remuneration for services rendered forty years ago has not been awarded; and now, in the 74th year of his age, as I am well informed, the old veteran, instead of being led to the harvest-feast and bid to repose in[15] the evening of his day, is looking out for any honest employment suited to his capacity.     J.R.
March 24, 1861.[16]

---

**Monday 29th.** Sent the following to Mr Bazley, and by the same post a memorial to Lord Palmerston, copy of which on the other side.

*Copy letter*, *Bamford to Thomas Bazley, 29 April 1861.*

Honble and Kind Sir,
Under the impression that a memorial from myself would not be in the least improper, whilst it might be more effective than one from other person or persons, I have this day compiled one partly from the petition, a copy of which I forwarded to you. I know not whether I have addressed his lordship in strictly court terms or not, but perhaps you will have the kindness to look the memorial over, and if there be any great, or insufferable departure from the due form, you will please to let me know; and I will write out another Memorial. I have not used the common phrases of a petition, because it is not one: but simply a memorial of the grounds on which my case is founded, leaving the whole for Lord Palmerstons consideration.

I see by the newspapers, that the Civil List pensions to the 1st of June are granted: my name as before, not included; if the next list does not appear before

---

15. Corrected by Bamford from "bed to repose on".
16. J.R. is Samuel Bamford, and the date should be 24 April; see entry for 24 April.

the 1st Jan. we must perish, unless meanwhile the Royal Bounty Fund could be moved to aid. Honble and kind Sir,

Your obliged Servant,

Samuel Bamford.

**Draft of a memorial** to the Prime Minister, Lord Palmerston, 29 April 1861, constructed mainly of pasted sections of Bamford's circular, lighty adapted, with two significant additions:
(1) A reference to Palmerston's speech at Leeds, attributing current prosperity to the Reform Act and the repeal of the corn laws, "for striving to introduce which he [Bamford] underwent grievous punishment". (See entry for 1 November 1860).
(2) A reference to Bamford's literary achievements:

Your Memorialist asks also to state that he is the author of various literary productions: namely, "Passages in the Life of a Radical"; "Early Days"; "Walks amongst the Workers"; "Dialect of South Lancashire", and Poems, all of which have been highly commended by the public press; your Memorialist has also written and published Tracts and many fragmentary, and incidental papers, the general motive and tendency of which have been the support of right against wrong; the conservation of peace, and the protection of life and property.

**Tuesday 30th.** The following appears in the Examiner and Times of this day.

**Letter**, from the Manchester Examiner and Times, 30 April 1861.

---

### SAMUEL BAMFORD.

*To the Editor of the Examiner and Times.*
Sir, – Allow me to inform your correspondent "J. R." that some ten years ago a public subscription was raised for Samuel Bamford in this city, in recognition of his political services and literary merits. The late Mr. Joseph Brotherton was chairman of the committee, and to the best of my belief between £400 and £500 was raised, at all events such an amount as induced the committee to consider the expediency of investing it in an annuity, contingent on the lives of Mr. Bamford and his wife. Mr. Bamford dissented from such an appropriation of the fund, and elected to receive the entire sum in cash, and shortly afterwards accepted a government appointment in Somerset House. Of his conduct towards his committee, and the whole body of the subscribers during the canvass on his behalf, the less said the better, as a recapitulation of his procedure might deter any effort which such friends that he has acquired since that period might endeavour to originate in his favour. I fear few of those who were associated with the first public subscription would be disposed again to risk an outrage upon their feelings, amongst whom is your obedient servant,
A MEMBER OF THE BAMFORD TESTIMONIAL AND THE ROGERSON TESTIMONIAL COMMITTEES.

---

30. Write with a heavy heart as follows.

**Copy letter**, *Bamford to Allen Mellor, Firwood Mill, Chadderton, 30 April 1861.*

> Friend Mellor,
> I shall be in your neighbourhood on Wednesday, and propose seeing you either at the Mill or at your house. I regret exceedingly having to intimate that the small balance you hold in my favour, would be very acceptable just now: I had intended <u>never</u> to have mentioned it – as indeed I have not done to any one – but <u>necessity</u> compels me now to remind you of it: and I hope the payment wont materially inconvenience you. It appears very strange, but <u>you</u> like too many of my friends, seem to have deserted me: whatever can have been the cause? surely not this trifle of moneys? you should have let me know.
> Yours truly<br>Samuel Bamford.

Don't mention this to Whalley: not a soul knows.[17]

**Wednesday 1st May.** Comes to hand from Allen Mellor: the following: a shabby excuse.

**Letter**, *Allen Mellor to Bamford, 30 April 1861.*

> My dear Bamford,
> I am in receipt of your letter and beg to say that the matter to which you allude had intirely escaped me, indeed I did not know that I held a balance in your favour until reminded of it by yours of this days date – this sum is if I mistake not 5/-. I know that 3 1/- tickets were never paid for, or the balance would have been 8/-.
> I shall be glad to save you the trouble of coming for it, and I will enclose it tomorrow in stamps, I would do so at once but I cannot get them tonight.
> I beg to say that I am sorry this matter has been allowed to slip, but as my motives were perfectly pure I fear no man knowing, much less my esteemed friend Whalley.
> I wish seriously to say that I entertain the highest respect for you, as I think my past conduct proves.
> Yours truly,<br>Allen Mellor.

**Letter**, *Thomas Bazley MP, 3ᴬ King Street, St James's Square, SW, to Bamford, 30 April 1861.*

> Dear Sir,
> I am favoured with your letter, and Memorial to Lord Palmerston, of yesterday. More than a week ago I wrote a strong note on your behalf to Lord Palmerston but to which I have not yet obtained a reply, and I am now waiting to hear from him. I told

---

17. Written upside-down on the top of the letter.

Mr Milner Gibson that I had written to his <u>Chief</u> and asked him to speak in support of my application which he promised to do. The course I will pursue shall be this. I will tonight confer with Mr Gibson and induce him to join me in a personal application, and if I obtain no satisfactory result before Saturday next, I will then take your memorial to Lord Palmerston's residence to present it to him in person.

You know that his Lordship has been ill, and has been much harassed in public affairs, hence the delay which has arisen.

Dear Sir, Mo[st] faithfully yrs<br>
Tho<sup>s</sup> Bazley.

1 May Wed. Went to Salford, and dined with Mr and Mrs Clowes: sold them a copy of Early Days, 2/6.

Mima went again to "Uncles" and left her ring, 3/0: Left my letter to the Ex member of "Bamford and Rogerson Testimonial Committees." Left it a[t] Examiner and Times office.

Binney not in his office. Gone to London this morning.

Three years this day since I left Somerset House.

**Thursday 2nd.** At Manchester. Could not find Mrs R. Called at late N. Lloyds and sold his brother a shillings worth of postage stamps: Sold Mr Greenwell half a crowns worth.

A person had been at Belfields vilifying me, but Belfield silenced him by telling him the truth, and he went away in a different humour.

The rich bit of critical exposure on the annexed leaf is from the Guardian of this day: originally from the Critic.

**Cutting**, *from the* Manchester Guardian, *2 May 1861, about John Close,*[18] *"the Kirkby Stephen Poet", recently granted a civil list pension.*

---

### A PENSIONED "POET," & HIS "LITERARY MERIT."

In the Civil List Pension List, published a week or two ago, appeared the name of Mr. J. Close, to whom £50 a year has been awarded "on account of his literary merit and the distressed circumstances in which he is placed." As, in all probability, few of our readers know anything of Mr. J. Close, and his "literary merit," the following extracts from an article in the Critic may prove interesting:–

... Another benefactor who comes in for a slice of "the Poet's" praise is "John Whitewell, Esq. of Kendal," in whose honour, "on reading in the papers that he had gone to France to meet Cobden, with patterns of his carpets," Mr. Close composed the following:–

Well may Kendal in him glory,<br>
Well may nations chant his name;

---

18. John Close (1816–91), printer and "the Kirkby Stephen poet"; Boase.

When they gaze upon his carpets,
Which from Whitwell's warehouse came.

First at London's Exhibition,
Now to France he hastes away;
There to meet great Cobden musing,
On the Treaty – papers say.

See the man! His fine eye beaming,
Full of kindness – love to all;
Oft he smiles on sons of poesy,
Listens kindly when they call.

... Intrinsically he is, of course, contemptible; the only interest we can attach to him is the example which he affords of the manner in which the civil list pension for literary merit are distributed. Low as the royal favour to literary men may have fallen, it has never stooped as low as this. We have had the Queen's governesses palmed off upon the nation as persons of literary merit; we have had the distant relatives of naval and military men receiving the rewards justly due to those who have added to the stock of human knowledge; but never before (so far as we are aware) has the absurdity of the whole institution been so shamelessly and manifestly demonstrated as by this grant of a pension to the privileged idiot of a county. Is this an intentional insult to literature, or is it a blunder? Has Lord Palmerston been taken in by the petition of the five hundred gentlemen of Westmoreland, or has he designedly bestowed the nations guerdon upon "the Poet of Kirkby Stephen," in order to signify his contempt for the whole order of men of letters? It matters little which explanation be the true one. Either way, the granting of these pensions has now been reduced to the *ne plus ultres* of absurdity, and for the credit of the nation we demand either that they be discontinued, or that the grant should be entrusted to persons really able to weigh the merits of the claimants.

The following in the House of Commons May 2nd.

**Cutting**, *from the* Manchester Guardian, *2 May 1861, giving an account of a parliamentary question to Lord Palmerston about the poet Close's pension. Palmerston affirmed that it was in response to a petition signed by the earls of Carlisle and Lonsdale amongst many others, and stated:*

... Mr. Close was one of those men, of whom several had appeared lately, who being in a very humble station, and with little education, had with the force of genius distinguished themselves by their efforts. They were not equal to Burns, but still they deserved, by their character, to be placed in the same category.

**Friday 3rd.** Sent by post to Mr Bazley, notices by the public press of "Life of a Radical," "Early Days" and "Poems".

**Copy letter**, *Bamford to Thomas Bazley, 3 May 1861.*

Honble and Kind Sir,
I presume to think you scarcely need be ashamed if you permit the inclosed
notices of some of my literary productions to come under the observation of Lord
Palmerston. I have only just found them, whilst looking over arranging old
papers; and as you expect seeing his Lordship tomorrow these inclosures will be
available if you deem it proper to make use of them on that occasion: The Honble
Mr M Gibson may also please to usefully appropriate one or two of them. With
grateful respect I remain, Honble Sir,
Your obedient Servant<br>Samuel Bamford.

3. Heard that Bamford the young son of James Dronsfield of Hollinwood was dead of
measles.

**Saturday 4th.** See my reply to Ex-member, adjoining leaf.

**Letter**, *from the Manchester Examiner and Times, 4 May 1861.*

---

### THE EX-MEMBER OF THE BAMFORD AND ROGERSON TESTIMONIAL COMMITTEES.

*To the Editor of the Examiner and Times.*
Sir – I beg to inform the above correspondent, whose letter appears in your
Tuesday's publication, and who seems to have a motive – a not very pure one – in
coupling the reminiscence of my testimonial of 1847 with some more recent
benefactions in favour of the unfortunate Rogerson, deceased, that I don't regret
the appearance of the member's letter, since it is open speaking, and gives me (by
your courtesy) a chance of reply, which shall be brief, and to the point. "F. R."[19]
states that I was one of those "who, 45 years ago, broke up the sodden ground of
public feeling" on the subject of parliamentary reform (sodden then, as it is now,
though from a different cause). Does the "Ex-member" deny that I was such?
"F. R." says I have been "a public benefactor;" and if parliamentary reform and
free trade have been great national changes and improvements – and Lord
Palmerston himself asserts they have – then have I been a public benefactor, and
no one can disprove it. But "F. R." says – and herein seems to lie the galling rub, –
that I "have done more for the country than the country has done for me." And,
in reply, "the Ex-member" sets forth what the country, or rather Lancashire, did for
me 40 years ago, when both parliamentary reform (of a sort) and the abolition of
the corn-laws had been accomplished. A committee, of which the "Ex-member"
was, it seems, then a member, raised for me, in the form of a testimonial,

---

19. Bamford means to refer to "J.R.", the form in which the letter he cites was actually signed.

"between £400 and £500," which sum he says "I received in cash." I have to say that I never received either one sum or the other. And – oh, shocking! – shortly afterwards I "accepted a Government appointment at Somerset House." Should I have asked the permission of the "Ex-member" before I accepted the appointment? Next, my conduct towards "the committee and the whole body of subscribers" is misrepresented. I never was at issue with the committee collectively: with some two or three of that body I neither did nor could agree. I could not comprehend the position they seemingly wished to impose upon me, of humble acquiescence in all their proceedings. Was I, who had stood up and pleaded for the right fearlessly before the magnates of the land, to stand in silence while a clique of questionable friends at Manchester tried to humiliate me? I did not. I spoke freely and truthfully, as I would at this day – as an Englishman ought to speak at any time; and amongst those who felt offended was, it seems, the "Ex-member." He writes also as if the whole body of subscribers was dissatisfied. How did he learn that? Did the "whole body of subscribers" go to "Ex-member" in a body, and complain of my behaviour? If so, this is the first time I have heard of their dissatisfaction. On the contrary, I received at the time many expressions of approval; and not more than half a dozen, exclusive of the clique in the committee and their friends, who disapproved. But how stands the question? If I had been benefactor to the country, the country has repaid me; I suppose that is what "Ex-member" means when he mentions the "four or five hundred pounds." Well, suppose there were four hundred pounds – though I never received that sum, or, according to my recollection, any sum very near it; but suppose there were four hundred, it would probably not be more than a pound a mile for all the miles I have been dragged across the country in chains of fetters, saying nothing of my being twice arrested on charges of high treason, of my being once thrust into a felon's stone cell, and on the second occasion into a felon's lockup, at the New Bailey; of my being five times taken into custody before the privy council; of my being chained to the bedpost at Bow-street; of my being on five different occasions conducted in chains to various and distant parts of the country; of my having stood a trial of ten days at York, where I conducted my own defence in a manner and with a testimony which brought credit to myself and the cause I represented; of my – not withstanding the pointed compliment of the counsel for the prosecution, and the remarkably favourable summing up of the Judge – having been found guilty; of my foot journey to London, to submit to judgement, and of my destitute condition when I arrived in the metropolis; on my being sentenced to 12 months' imprisonment in Lincoln Castle; of my detention in the King's Bench Prison; of my imprisonment at Lincoln; of my return journey with my wife, and of our passage of torment over the burning, blistering causeway on the other side of Stockport; and lastly, of our arrival at home, saddened by the discovery that our dear child had taken a disorder which seldom leaves its victims till death, and which finally brought her to the grave. All this, saying nothing of the sorrows of home, of the wife weeping in silence, of the child wailing at the door, of the dreary disorder in a place ransacked by myrmidons of a Manchester police and majestry, of the cession of all comforts and the disruption of all peace and order, and, not the least of these troubles, of the bereaved hearth and the desolate void, which is felt as well as seen, in the place whence a beloved one has departed. Had such outrages and trials been forced upon "a gentleman" or a lady, all England would have echoed, and very properly, with indignant execration; but their object having been "only a poor man," the equivalent, now raked up by this "Ex-member," is pitifully cast in the sufferer's teeth after a lapse of fourteen years.- I am, sir, yours obediently,

SAMUEL BAMFORD.

Moston, Harpurhey, May 1st, 1861.

---

Went over to Allen Mellor's at Lower Roofs, Chadderton, and got the five shillings I was so much in need of: a farm of eight acres, very prettily situated.

Saw Mr Cheetham at the Middleton Junction who professed a wish to serve me, but could not do anything in the way of Insurance he being already engaged with the Lancashire Insurance concern.

Mr Smethurst of Stock Brook was similarly engaged with other concerns, so I took not anything by my journey, in the way of insurance.

Came back through Middleton.

**Sunday 5th.**  Received the annexed from Mr Bazley.

**Letter**, *Thomas Bazley to Bamford, 4 May 1861.*

Dear Sir,

Mr Gibson could not accompany me to see Lord Palmerston and I have therefore seen him myself. After waiting an hour I could only obtain a very short conversation with him, because he was most pressingly engaged, and I was not fortunate in procuring a definite reply to my repeated application, but foreseeing that he might not be able to afford me his personal attention, I took with me another strong appeal in a note which I wrote for the purpose and left it with him, and he promised me his early consideration. I deeply regret this delay, but I will be prepared to attack him again in a few days, and to be accompanied, if possible, by Mr Gibson. I assure you that I feel very anxious about the result of my applications on your behalf and you may rely upon my continuing them till we know the result.

Most faithfully yours
Thos Bazley.

Your favour of yesterday duly received.

Dronsfield down this morning giving particulars of his boy's death, and inviting us to the funeral on Tuesday.

Mr Bazley is acting faithfully in my cause.

Brierley came in the afternoon and gave me to understand that he intended writing an article respecting me (and my claims I suppose) for the Oldham Times. I think he could not select a more apt subject, especially after the exposure of humbug Close "The Kirby Stephen Poet." We laughed heartily at the affair. Travis's brother and wife called in as they went past.

**Monday 6th.** Went to Manchester, and saw Mr Binney, whom, after many painful struggles, I asked to lend me a sovereign, which he did, without hesitation. We had much talk about my affairs and he seemed to have but slight hopes of any success by bringing my case before the H of Commons; he however expressed much interest in my proceedings and I and my wife are to go to his house to tea tomorrow afternoon, when I shall have an opportunity of showing him copies of all my papers; and whether he approves of them or not, he will, I expect be useful in my coming struggles to obtain my rights.

Wrote to Dronsfield as annexed.

*Copy letter*, Bamford to James Dronsfield, Hollinwood, 6 May 1861.

Dear Dronsfield
I beg yourself and Mrs Dronsfield's leave if we should not come to the funeral of Dear Bamford tomorrow. I have been at Manchester today, and am expected to meet a gentleman tomorrow, whom if I disappoint, I may very likely lose many good turns in my present struggles to obtain what I have a right to. I want to show him my papers, and to advise with him as to some future proceedings; and if I miss the present opportunity, I may probably not have another so fitting. Our absence cannot make any difference to the dear deceased; whilst it may make a great one in my future affairs; you will therefore I know ... for our sakes excuse our absence on this occasion.
Yours truly,<br>Samuel Bamford.

Mr Cobden having been mentioned as one likely to be of service in my cause should it come before the H of Commons, Mr Binney said when he was applied to in the case of Mr Sturgeon,[20] he (Mr C.) said he never did, and he never would use his influence towards enabling any person, not even his most intimate friend, obtain a grant of public money.

How did this principle square with Cobdens acceptance and appropriation of 80 thousand pounds of public money, as much "public money" as if it had come out of the taxes: so much for consistency.

**Tuesday 7th.** Self and Mima went to Mr Binneys at Cheetham Hill. Strangely, as it seemed to us, Mrs Binney was not at home. Mr Binney had given me the invitation on Monday, and consequently we expected a comfortable house and a kindly reception. The servant [said] Mrs would probably return shortly, so we were shown into a room where the least glimmer of fire only was visible. The day was gloomy and very cold, as cold as mid-winter; in that room we sat about an hour, and then, after asking for, and obtaining a glass of water, which my wife wanted, she being faint as well as starved

---

20. William Sturgeon (1783–1850), pioneering electromagnetist and itinerant lecturer; in receipt of a government pension in the later 1840s; MCL.

after her walk, we took our departure, and had got nearly into the high-road when a boy told us, a lady wanted us: it was Mrs Binney whom we had met but a few minutes before, seemingly in haste; she was coming from the Manchester road. whilst we were going the contrary way: she hastened to us, and begged us to return, apologising for her absence from home, the cause of which I did not distinctly understand, though I could not entirely resist a secret misgiving that her absence had been intentional. I however, must say, that I am become almost suspicious of every person, and every transaction, which appears in the least dubious – and God forgive me, if I wronged Mrs Binney on this occasion. We went back of course. I informed Mrs Binney that my wife was unwell having been overheated by the walk, and then become chilled by sitting in the room. Tea was therefore speedily on the table, and a decanter with brandy added warmth to the very welcome beverage. We had just commenced the repast when Mr Binney came home, and we all sat down to a regular tea bagging. A fine little boy named "Willie" played about the room; my wife's indisposition, both of health and temper, for she, like myself had been much disturbed by the strange absence of Mrs B. – disappeared under the influence of the genial, warming refection, and we and we stopped chatting comfortably until about half past seven. Mr Binney coming with us to show a better way than the one [we] had come.

**Wednesday 8th.** To Middleton: taking with me the old documents I brought away from Mr Clarkes on the 7th March. Mr Clarke not at the office, he being unwell at home, left the old writings with the woman at the place, who put them in the box, and I looked all the leaves and other papers and parchments over, and brought away five separate papers one I think of the 3rd Ed. 3rd and the other of Hen. 5th.

Sold a copy of Early Days as I came back in the omnibus.

**Thursday 9th.** A very fine morning. Went to Mr Harlands at Swinton, who rather surprised me by saying he had sent the writings I had brought last time back, to Mr Clarke by post, the understanding being that he should keep them until my coming again. He was perhaps dissatisfied at my long absence and silence, caused by my being unwell after the paryletic attack, though he did not say anything on that head. Stopped [to] dinner, and after that had conversation, of no particular moment, until about five o'clock when I came away and walked to Pendleton, where I took Omnibus and so home. Mr Harland put into my hand two shillings towards my trouble and expenses. I would not have accepted anything had [we] not been almost at extremity in ways and means for carrying on.

9th. Saw Dr Watts in St Anns Square who said he had seen my letter in the Examiner and Times, in reply to Ex-member, and approved of it: He had also written, he said strongly, to Mr Bazley and Milner Gibson, and the latter had replied saying he would accompany Mr B. to Lord Palmerston and support the application on my behalf.

9th cut the annexed from one of the Manchester newspapers.

***Newspaper cutting***, *source not stated, reporting on the Poet Close's reaction to the news of his pension, and to the controversy it has caused locally and nationally.*

**Monday 13th.** Went to Manchester and bought two copies of Radical at A. Heywoods: Called at Brierleys and saw in his "Oldham Times" an announcement that Mr E Watkin[21] of Manchester, was to give a lecture on Parliamentary Reform in the Town Hall of Oldham. I did not make any observation on this to Brierleys wife, though I was certainly much hurt to see that a young man, a young Parliamentary reformer, should be preferred to give a lecture on that subject whilst an old veteran like myself, who must have large knowledge of the subject from experience; and who was on the verge of the distress from want of due encouragement in the way of lecturing, should be passed by.

**Tuesday 14th.** Sent a parcel to Potter at Oldham, including the two vols. of Radical, and one vol. Early Days, with a note to the following purport. "Esteemed Friend. Herewith you will receive the books which were ordered, at the Angel, the last time I was up at Oldham, and I regret having to say – necessity compels me – that is you could let me have the money (11/6) on any day between now and Friday, you would materially oblige yours truly Samuel Bamford.

The Early Days was a copy I had long had in the house, paid for, and the immediate profits on the Rads would be 2/3: early Days 2/6: to total immediate increase of my state of cash 4/9, which to me at present was worth trouble to realize. So I made up the parcel and dispatched it to Potter, with the note inclosed, by railway from Newton Heath Station, and came home satisfied with having done well.

**Wednesday 15th.** Potter from Oldham called and paid me for the books. Making my stock of cash into the respectable sum of 14/-. I opened my mind to him pretty freely respecting the calling in of Mr E.W. Watkin to lecture on Parliamentary Reform, whilst I was standing aside, as it were, ready for an engagement, and on the verge of distress. I did not blame himself for I knew him to [be] one of the kindest of my friends. But I could not but feel it to be very unkind, and disrespectful that I should be passed by, whilst a young man, who comparatively could know but little of reform, was called upon to lecture. I asked who was at the getting up of the affair, and Potter said he knew very little about it but Mr John Taylor (Councillor Taylor) would, he supposed, be the chairman. I said Mr Taylor was not a friend of mine; when I last read at Hollinwood, he sent back his couple of tickets, <u>unpaid</u> for. I said if such a thing as this affair of Watkins had occurred to a friend of mine, and I had been able to command a pen, it should not have passed without a severe castigation in some newspaper or other. I begged Potter to understand that I did not blame him in the least: I knew he was incapable of such unworthy conduct: I blamed others however severely, and the time was not far distant when they would be ashamed of the course they had taken. I was sorry I said to have given him the trouble to have come down with the money. I understood that Brierley came home on Wednesday nights, and

---

21. Edward W. Watkin (1819–1901), railway manager and promoter, son of a local liberal, MP for Yarmouth 1857 (unseated on petition) and Stockport 1864–8; at this time also a member of the Manchester City Council; *DNB*.

expected he would have called with the change as he went past. Brierley, he said would not come home that night – which was the one on which the lecture was to be given, and he assigned as a reason, that he would have to be at the lecture, and to write out a report of it for the paper (Oldham Times). The Editor, he said, had left the office, and Brierley would, this week, have to write the leader; probably his report of the lecture would be made to suffice for one. I desired Potter to send me a Oldham Times, and he promised that I should have one by Sunday morning.

I asked Potter if he knew any one who was disposed to purchase books, or odd articles of furniture, as I would not run into debt if I could avoid it but would sell of my books, and superfluous household furniture. Potter seemed hurt at this, and desired me not to sell my things.

**Thursday 16th.** Went to Manchester and bought a small lot of beef and some tea; my expenses 4d and my exchequer at night containing 8/6 out of the 14/- of yesterday.

**Saturday 18th.** After providing shop stuff for the weeks end, have only 3/6, whilst 1/1ᵈ is owing for washing, and on Monday 2/6 will be wanted for rent: so that I am a penny worse than nothing: An effort must be made, but in what direction, I know not.

**Sunday 19th.** I have indulged a hope that the intimation which I gave Potter the other day, would have been made known by him to some of my Oldham friends, and that I should have seen one or two of them down here today, but I am disappointed. Brierley I suppose is so engaged with his literary productions for the Oldham Times, that he has not leisure to think of us, or to come up, and Gowenlock, I have often thought, has been more distant since the evening of last Wakes Sunday, when I recited verses from my "Homely Rhymes on Bad Times" at Pollits, which to him would probably seem very irreverent.

> "In Lancashire the cotton trade
> was presently thrown all aback
> and some who mighty sums had made
> Began to feel their credit slack
> And then there came a thundering crack
> Which made our men of straw to stare
> Whilst Church and King look'd densely black
> Saint Chapel man betook for prayer
> Though sometimes he would turn and swear."[22]

I did not know then, that he was of a separatist class of Methodists.

---

22. A stanza of Bamford's poem "Homely rhymes on bad times", first published, with minor differences, in *Homely Rhymes*, 33.

19th 8 p.m. Brierley has just been and I have shown him my small telescope which I purpose to sell, and intimating that he may enquire if any Oldham friends are desirous to possess such an article. I tell him I am in difficulties from want of a little money to carry on with until I hear from London. I have also books to dispose of, and deem it only honest and honourable to convert superfluous articles into cash if I can, rather than trouble friends for assistance. Brierley says he will mention the circumstance tomorrow to friends at Oldham.

**Monday 20th.** Went to Manchester and called on Dr Watts, who said he had seen Mr Bazley in London, the week preceding; that Mr Bazley had seen Lord Palmerston on my account, and would shortly call upon him again to obtain a decisive answer respecting my case. The Dr. also said that Mr B suspected some one had been earwigging his lordship in a manner inimical to my interests. I said the same thing had, I believed, been going on amongst my friends at Manchester, not one of whom, however, had ever denounced to me, either the calumny or the calumniator: I had tried in vain to get a tangible hold of the latter, and the fact disclosed a fearful state of social morality. I showed Dr Watts some books which I wished to sell. I told him I was now so circumstanced, that I must sell, and convert into money superfluous articles of books or furniture: that I deemed it not a degradation to do so, but a honest means of putting on for a time, and therefore honourable. Dr W. said I ought not to sell my library: I should not part with my friends (the books) but I said I was compelled to part with them: I had not any other resource left: he however declined to sell for me any of my library books, but would try to dispose of some of my current publications, if I would bring them to him. I said they were in the hands of Abel Heywood, and his brother John, but I would try to get some of them. I did not tell him, as I might have done, that Abel Heywood had had the Radical in his hands nearly three years: and that during that time, I had never condescended to ask him to give me credit for a single copy, and did not like to ask him now; and that I had not money to pay for any books I might want.

I left Dr Watts scarcely knowing what to do.

Called on Ralph Mellor at the Weights and Measures Office, and st[at]ed my case to him, when he immediately gave me five shillings, he would not advance it as a loan, – but freely gave it me: he also took me to the Star Inn to see Mr Stelfox, with a view to induce him to purchase one of my books – I had with me "Ellis's Metrical Romances", "The Half Century", by Washington Weeks; and "Chartism", by Thomas Carlyle, – Mr Stelfox was not in, and I was to see Mr Mellor when I again went to Manchester.

Called at John Heywoods bookshop, but neither he, nor the son were in – they were gone to dinner, so left a note requesting that a dozen (13) Early Days might be made up and sent as a parcel for me, to the station in Shudehill, to come by the Harperhey Omnibus.

**Tuesday 21st.** Wrote to Mr Bazley, as see annexed.

**Copy letter**, *Bamford to Thomas Bazley, 21 May 1861.*

Honble and Kind Sir,

Doctor Watts informed me yesterday, that [he] had seen you in London: that you had seen Lord Palmerston once, on my account, and that you intended seeing him again very shortly, and obtaining a decisive understanding relative to my claim for "wrongs endured," or "remuneration for services rendered": Doctor Watts also added that, "you suspected some one had been earwigging his lordship with matter adverse to my interest", and that, "I should not be deemed a proper object for a Civil List pension." Should such have been the case, and should his lordship have thereupon formed his determination without letting me know what has been said against me, and hearing my reply, which I can scarcely believe, it would indeed, be an Irish instance of compensation for injuries, by adding one greater than all the rest. I may however say to you Sir, that I have during some considerable time, suspected this kind of detractive earwigging, was going on here in Manchester; and that even friends, persons who otherwise are well disposed towards me, have submitted to become the recipients of injurious statements or insinuations, without, in any one instance, denouncing either the calumny or the calumniator, to me, the injured person. This is not English! it is indeed sad work! Cruel friendship! and I hope that Lord Palmerston will set an example of a higher spirit, of a more manly discrimination by declining to pass judgement on one of the Queens humblest subjects, until he has been audibly charged, and heard in his own defence.

Humble and kind Sir,

Your obedient servant,

Samuel Bamford.

**Wednesday 22nd.** Walked to Middleton, taking with me an article headed "Middleton", intending to show it to Mr John Clarke, the agent to Sir S.M. Peto and Mr Betts; and to get it inserted in the Middleton Albion of next Saturday. Saw Mr Clarke at the office and undertook to dine with him at Walkers. Strolled up to the new burial ground, and found field daiseys and a few primroses in bloom on Anns grave. Blue bells and lilies were coming on, but the roses appeared to have been sadly cut down by the late severe weather.

When dinner was finished at Walkers, I read the article I had brought, to Mr Clarke. W.C. Ridings came into the room and I afterwards went with him to Mills's of the newspaper office. The article was at Mills's suggestion, slightly altered and I left it for insertion in the Albion.

Walked home across the fields, and Boggart Ho Clough, and came in very much tired.

Brierley was to have called on me this evening but he has not appeared.

**Thursday 23rd.** At Manchester, saw Mr Greenwell and borrowed half a sov. from him. Got a lunch of excellent roast beef at Belfields. Home by 'bus, and sold a copy of Early Days to Mr Wilkinson. My parcel of <u>books</u> from John Heywood had been lying there since Monday.

**Friday 24th.** The letter opposite from Mr Bazley.

*Letter*, *Thomas Bazley, London, to Bamford, 23 May 1861.*

Dear Sir,
I really cannot understand the course taken by Lord Palmerston in reference to
my applications on your behalf. First I presented the Memorial – second, I spoke
to him, and that he might not forget at the same time handed him a written
request – third, an urgent appeal <u>both</u> in <u>person</u> and by <u>note</u> – and fourth,
I handed to him your own memorial with my further written appeal. This week
he has been away. On Tuesday next I expect to be able to pronounce either a yes
or a no.
                                     Mo[st] faithfully,
                                             Thos Bazley

Walked to Middleton to correct the proof of my article on the town; got bread and
cheese, and a glass of ale at Walkers, and trudged back.
      24th. Mrs Nelson was here during my absence at Manchester and pressed Mima
very much to go up on Monday and take me. Her daughter Fanny, Mrs Hamilton was
over from Lincolnshire and she wanted to see us <u>very much</u>. So Mima undertook that
we must go.

**Sunday 26th.** Received the annexed from Mr Bazley; it being the second barefaced
shuffle which Lord Palmerston has acted respecting my application for compensation,
or remuneration for injuries received, or services rendered.

*Letter*, *Thomas Bazley, London, to Bamford, 25 May 1861.*

Dear Sir,
After my <u>six</u> applications on your behalf, you will see by the enclosed note from
the private Secretary of Lord Palmerston that two of them are acknowledged with
an unsatisfactory reply. In another year it is possible that renewed efforts may be
successful, and in the mean time I hope your friends will contribute that assistance
for you, which we have been unable to procure from Government. By this Post
I am writing to Mr Alexr Ireland and to Dr Watts, requesting them to promote an
arrangement which I have suggested to them, and which I shall cheerfully support
by my own aid. You may if you please consult them.
                                     Most faithfully yours
                                             Thos Bazley.

*Enclosure*: *letter from Evelyn Ashley, 10 Downing Street, to Bazley, 24 May 1861.*

Sir,
I am desired by Lord Palmerston to acknowledge the receipt of your applications
of the 4th and 14th ult. in favour of Mr Samuel Bamford – and to inform you that

this case and claims shall be considered in connection with that of others when the proper time arrives for settling the Pension List for 1861–62.

I am Sir

Your most obedient

Evelyn Ashley.

The following appears in the Middleton Albion of yesterday.

**Cutting**, *from the* Middleton Albion, *25 May 1861.*[23]

---

MIDDLETON.

The present advantages and great capacity of improvements which the town of Middleton, and adjacent districts, possess, are not known, nor, of course, rightly appreciated by that class of monied men who are generally on the look out for improvable and paying speculations; but as no very tangible reason has been assigned why the place should not be estimated at a value approximating its real worth, a brief notice of some of the principal advantages adherent to the town and manor, may not be either useless or devoid of interest.

The town of Middleton is situated at a distance of five miles from the city of Manchester, five from Rochdale, three from Oldham, and six from Bury: at which places there are good turnpike roads, from Manchester through Middleton, and to Rochdale, being about one of the best ten-mile roads in England; whilst by rail thirteen trains arrive from Stockport to the surrounding towns and boroughs every working day of the week. The surface of the ground, presents a pleasant undulation of hill and dale, offering great facilities for drainage; the subsoil in the valleys and on the levels is a rich loam and on the hills a light soil, or sand and gravel. Water is plentifull and coal from the surrounding townships is abundant and cheap; the air is bracing and salubrious, the duration of life being, in many instances, greatly prolonged. The number of inhabitants, according to the census of 1861, was 9,874, of whom, probably 1,800 are engaged at the silk loom in the township, exclusive of assistants, and of those persons who know them, and know the manufacture, few there are who will not allow that a better lot of silk weavers is not to be found in a like population in England; probably also, no equal number of working people, in their branch, have been more regularly entrusted with a like amount of valuable material, and have returned it in fuller quantity, and more completely manufactured than have the Middleton weavers: and as a consequence, known good workmen from that place are employed when others from different localities are but partially engaged; it may also be said, that in all England, out of a like number of weavers located in one spot, not so great a number can be found sitting under their own roof-tree, and working on their own premises; nor probably not in any town or district of a like number of inhabitants, can be found so many benefit societies, known as sick list, sick club, burial

---

23. Written by Bamford: see entry for 22 May, and compare his earlier description of Middleton from *c.* 1842, *Walks in South Lancashire*, 228–33.

societies, money clubs, and lodges of Free Gardeners, Foresters, odd Fellows and Masonic associations, all well established, and with amply realized funds, as in the town and district of Middleton. Besides silk weaving, the principal manufactories are cotton weaving, cotton spinning calico and silk printing, and the common employments of English Country towns are in operation here: an excellent mechanician and workman makes repairs, or alters machines adapted to all kinds of manufacture, whilst equally good crafts-men with the hammer and the anvil, with the plummet and the trowel, in brick work, stone, or common wood work, are at hand when required. The church is situated on a pleasant elevation; it is a venerable and picturesque structure, said to have existed before 1291 and to have been partly rebuilt in 1524. The new burial ground recently inclosed, and laid out with walks and terraces surmounted by a group of tall trees, is singularly well adapted for interments, being, so far as hitherto discovered, one huge bank of sand. The living is a rectory, value about £1200 per annum; and in a valley below the church on the eastern side, is a grammar school, built and endowed by Doctor Alexander Nowell, in 1572. There are in the town several day and Sunday schools, which are very well attended; whilst religious bodies, dissenting from the church, own eight paces of worship. There are also a Free Library, a Botanical Association, and a body of Vocal and Instrumental Musicians, such as are not often found in a country place, and Annual prize exhibitions of floral and Horticultural products; with an extensive, and well organised Agricultural Association, with its prize exhibitions of horses, cattle, swine, poultry, farming implements and apparatus, and horticultural products, gives an interesting finish to the annual fetes of the district. The earnest teacher of religion would here find an ample field for the exercise of his zeal; for the moral philanthropist, abundant material is at hand; for the social improver, matter for profound reflection and active endeavour is offered; and to the political reformer, the history of the place will say, "Pull off thy shoes from thy feet, for thou standest upon the graves of men whose voices were heard, and whose influence was felt for reform, when the House of Commons was but the nominee of the Lords, and the rental of the proudly mean Norman sprout was upheld by a sordid tax on the poor man's loaf."

---

**Monday 27th.** The following relative to the poor fellow "Poet Close" who though a fool, has I think been rather hardly used, is taken from the Guardian of this day.

***Cutting***, *from the* Manchester Guardian, *27 May 1861: a further piece taken from* The Critic *attacking the poet Close. Many local people had contacted the magazine denouncing the pension petition as "a fraud ... perpetrated on Lord Palmerston". Close himself had issued a placard comparing himself to the neglected Burns and claiming not charity but the "Englishman's right – Bread of his Country".*

27th Mond. Mima and I went to Mr Nelsons at Fern Hill Pendleton. We walked to Manchester – money being too scant for Omnibus. All the town crowded with country people come a sight seeing, their Whitsuntide money not being all spent during the previous week: At dinner, a knife that was not clean, to begin with; dry hard bread on the table, evidently some that had been left from the previous day; potatoes nearly cold: bitter beer, which I cant endure, or porter which I don't like: So I took water, and after that wine. Sherry from a driblet that was brought in a decanter. Mrs Nelson, Miss Nelson, Mima and myself the only persons at table, Mrs Hamilton[24] on whose account real or pretended – we had been invited had not made her appearance, so her <u>name</u> was not mentioned by the two guests. After dinner Master Nelson arrived from London: and <u>then</u> two <u>full</u> decanters were brought upon the table. Saw how the <u>thing</u> was being carried on, but took not any outward notice. I was tired, and wanted to be going, and so an early cup of tea was produced. Miss Nelson had disappeared as this was being got ready, and when we had finished our cups and were about rising to come away, Mrs Hamilton made her appearance, with parasol in hand, as if she had just come into the house; my impression was that she had been in some neighbours house, or in some room up stairs, remaining out of ken until notified to come – she had been detained "at the dentists", having something done to her teeth, and had only got away just in time etc, etc, etc, – Her mother had been just before expressing regret at Fanny's being away "at the dentists," when I settled the matter by saying in my blunt way, "Oh, it doesn't matter". We had only a few minutes of Fanny's company, and then came away. Met Mr Nelson on the way to Pendleton, and after customary salutations and enquiries walked down Pendleton and to the Omnibus in Shude Hill, so came home much fatigued. Got a cup of our own homely tea, very good. I thought the whole of this Fanny-visiting, and dining affair, was as compact a piece of acting as I had ever noticed. They have had the chance this time, and they have used it; but if they ever catch me again I'll forgive them.

---

24. Bamford's great-niece, married to the Revd James Hamilton of Halliwell, near Bolton; see entry for 21 June 1859.

# 13

# SUBSCRIPTION

*Despite the final dashing of Bamford's hopes of a pension, in early June his circumstances suddenly improved as a result of Thomas Bazley's decision to try to secure a private subscription for him from which a regular income could be derived. Initially, to Bamford's frustration, things appeared to move very slowly, but Bazley's letter of the 21st July which provided him with £1 a month put Bamford in a better frame of mind. Part of the problem lay in uncertainties as to the precise intentions of those involved in the subscription, including Dr John Watts, who had become Bamford's chief contact with them, and who was apparently toying with the idea of a reprint of all Bamford's works, a scheme complicated by the portions of the editions of* Passages *and* Early Days *that Bamford had sold in 1858 and 1859 which were still in the hands of the publishers.*

**Monday 27th May.**[1] Before I went to Nelsons I called on Dr Watts – having sent Mima on by the 'bus: the Dr read to me a letter which he had received from Mr Bazley relative to his frequent applications on my behalf and the postponement of my claims. I asked had not Mr. B. proposed an arrangement of some sort on my behalf and the Dr. said he had proposed that a subscription should be raised: the Dr did not say whether or not the proposal would be acted upon, nor did I utter one word for or against it. I felt that was a matter on which I could not, with propriety make use of any expression, and therefore I was expressively silent.

Called at Mr Irelands office, but he was in London: expected home that evening.

**Tuesday 28th.** Took six copies of my "Early Days" to Dr Watts who paid me for them 15/- Saw Ralph Mellor at the Weights and Measures Office, who put into my hand 5/- which he had got from Mr Stelfox of the Star Inn. I felt this was coming "too low." However went with Mellor into the Bar, and took a glass of porter – only this and bitter beer here – Stelfox came and conversed with us and as we sat Mellor narrated some curious traits of conduct in the late Sir John Potter, and D. Maude[2] the Magistrate who after lying under the table all night would get up, wash himself, go upon the bench, and play the d—l with poor rimy smutty drunkards. I never had a high opinion of D.M. either as a man or a magistrate; the way in which he met, and dealt with the Chartist plug-drawers was disgracefully pusillanimous.

**Wednesday 29th.** Not very well this day. I stopped at home and wrote to Mr Bazley as annexed.

***Copy letter**, Bamford to Thomas Bazley, 29 May 1861.*

---

1. An addition to the entry for 27 May which concludes chapter 10.
2. Daniel Maude (dates not known), stipendiary magistrate in Manchester 1838–60, later residing in Marylebone; MCL.

Honble and Kind Sir,

I wished to see Mr Ireland before I wrote to you, and have called twice at the office but on both occasions he was in London. I cannot therefore, longer delay tendering my respectful, and most earnest thanks for your consistent advocacy of my claims to compensation or remuneration from Government. And I cannot but indulge a hope, that if my case is again, at the proper time, brought under the notice of Lord Palmerston, the application will be successful at the next settlement of the Pension list, which I venture to surmise will be in July. Dr Watts gave me to understand that meantime, and for present use, you had suggested a subscription on my behalf: this is doubly kind and thoughtful of you; and though I would certainly drag on without such help if I could, my position, sorry am I to say it, leaves me without alternative: I am entirely in the hands of those who have the means and the will to render aid. I may observe, that on the 8th of Dec^r 1860, a reply in nearly the same words as your last, was sent to you from Downing Street; since then there must have been a "settlement of the Pension List", and my claims, if "taken into consideration", must have been passed over. I venture therefore to suggest, that in the meantime, whether friends at Manchester choose to act as you propose or not, I have fair grounds for an application of the Royal Bounty Fund, as a means of timely aid, and of some recompense for long waiting, and hope deferred. As a resource against present daily exigencies, I am selling a few books and trying to dispose of my small library; I know not that I have any cause for shame in making this known, it is a honest and creditable course, anything rather [than] incurring hopeless debt, or becoming burdensome to friends. Your generous offer, in furtherance of a subscription I deeply appreciate, and if by any honest means I can be ensured of necessaries until I have finished a book which I have in hand, I hope thereafter to be able to clear my own way, Honble and kind Sir.

Your very grateful Serv^t

Sam^l Bamford.

**Thursday 30th.** Mima fell beside the drawers and cut her head.

**Friday 31st.** Called twice at the Examiner and Times Office to see Mr Ireland, but on both occasions he was engaged. On my stepping up stairs a third time, he was not so, and the boy took in my name, and coming out said, "in a moment"; at that instant another person entered the outer office where I stood, and a minute after, a young fellow, came out of the inner office where Mr Ireland was, and told the last comer to walk in, which he did to the strong discomposure of my feelings. I took it as an intentional snub put on me, and was tempted to walk right away, and leave my <u>friend</u> Ireland to find out that I knew when I was unworthily treated. I reflected however that the offence might possibly not be intentional, but a mistake of the young fellow and quite unknown to Mr Ireland. So I remained waiting about ten minutes and then was called by Mr Ireland, who received me quite cordially. I said I understood he had received a communication from Mr Bazley relative to some business of mine: he said the communication he understood, was for Doctor Watts:

yes, and himself also, Mr Bazley had made known to me. Mr Ireland then accepted that view of the thing, and produced a letter from Mr Bazley, which he read, but which I did not distinctly understand, in consequence of my deafness; it was in substance similar the one I had received. Mr Ireland further said, that Mr Bazley recommended the setting up of a subscription on my behalf, to support me until another year, when probably an allowance would be made to me by government: he himself, would be[3] five pounds, and if ten or twenty gentlemen could be found who subscribe[d] each the like sum I should be comfortably provided for until something further took place in my favour. I did not question him as to the manner in which Mr Bazley's proposal had been received, but he proceeded to inform me that they (meaning as I understood himself and Doctor Watts) had agreed to send out circulars to such gentlemen as they thought were likely to promote the subscription, and so to raise a fund which would be deemed sufficient for the occasion. Messrs David Chadwick, and David Morris, were also mentioned, incidentally, as likely to act in the business: I expressed my sincere thanks to Mr Bazley, to themselves, and to any gentleman who gave assistance; and said I would send by post copies of my circulars, which would lay before Mr Ireland the whole of my case as it stood. Mr Ireland said I was many times more deserving of a pension than any in the last years list, and alluded to the case of John Close, whom I said I thought had been on the whole hardly dealt by; he was a fool no doubt, but he should not, on that account, for he could not help it, be abused. Leigh Hunt,[4] he said got two hundreds a year; and Lord John Russell wrote him, at the time, a highly flattering and complimentary letter, saying what pleasure it afforded him to make some compensation, for the losses he had sustained, and hardships he had undergone during previous administrations. (This was news to me, since Sir James Kay Shuttleworth had informed me, in a letter which appears in this Diary, see     [5] that it was a settled point at the Home Office, <u>that there was not any fund, for compensation of losses sustained, or injuries received, in consequence of government proceedings</u>).

I left Mr Ireland in a more comfortable frame of mind, than I had found him; but how we must subsist until the circulars are sent out, and gentlemen respond to them, – if ever they do – I am at a loss to determine. I don't perceive any way except trespassing on friends, by borrowing money, or selling books; the latter I must again try, unless I speedily receive an invitation to call on Watts or Ireland.

31st. The above from the Manchester Guardian (London Correspondent) of this day.

**Report**, *from the* Manchester Guardian, *31 May 1861, that the warrant for the poet Close's pension has been cancelled by Palmerston. The writer calls for a refereeing system to prevent such episodes in future.*

---

3. That is, give.
4. James Henry Leigh Hunt (1784–1859), most famous of the early nineteenth-century essayists and critics; also a Romantic poet and a prominent London literary figure; *DNB*.
5. Reference never inserted. See entry for 7 October 1860.

**Monday 3rd June.** The poor unfortunate John Close is disposed of as above, Examiner and Times of this day.

*Report*, *from the* Manchester Examiner and Times, *3 June 1861, confirming the cancellation of the poet Close's pension.*

*Letter*, *John Watts, branch office of The European Assurance Society, King Street, Manchester, to Bamford, 4 June 1861, requesting him to call on Thursday.*

**Tuesday 4th June.** Wrote as annexed to R. Cobden Esq. M.P. inclosing Right against Wrong; Addenda; and Petition to Commons.

*Copy letter*, *Bamford to Richard Cobden, 4 June 1861.*

> Honble Sir,
> Herewith I take the liberty of inclosing for your inspection and consideration, a copy of a petition which I have prepared for presentation to the House of Commons, should it be ultimately deemed expedient to come before the House with such petition: the accompanying documents explain, if not the whole of my case, sufficient of it for present purposes: and I do not suppose that, from a person in my position, and the course of life which has been marked out – thrust upon me, I may say – a stronger claim for compensation could be well made out. My case has been, on several occasions, brought under the notice of Lord Palmerston, and in March 1860, I being confined by sickness, he, at the instance of Mr Bazley, sent me fifty pounds from the Royal Bounty Fund; and promised at the same time, that when the Civil List pensions were settled, my claims should be taken into consideration; but from that time to the present, although there must have been <u>one</u> if not <u>two</u>, settlements of the Pension list, my claims have not been acceded to: and I have come to the conclusion, that an application of a more impressive influence than that of individual members of Parliament will be necessary to obtain for me that "compensation for wrongs and injuries sustained", or that "remunerations for services rendered", a persistance in the withholding of which would be a lasting reproach to this rich, and powerful nation; and a flagrant injustice to myself. Mr Bazley has promised to present the petition, should I conclude on bringing it forward: and may I ask you Sir, if, on such occasion you would give it your cordial and powerful support.
> > I am Honble Sir,
> > > Your Obdt Servt
> > > > Samuel Bamford.

**Thursday 6th.** Received the following.

*Letter*, *Richard Cobden, London, to Bamford, 5 June 1861.*

Private.

Dear Sir,

I have this morning received your note of yesterday and lose no time in saying
that as a general rule, petitions to Parliament on questions of an individual or
private character, are not very successful. Such matters are left to the
responsibility of the Executive. Let me advise you therefore to withhold your
petition until other modes of bringing the government to a favourable
consideration of your case have been exhausted. I wish to take an opportunity of
conferring with Mr Bazley on the subject, and I shall be happy to do any thing in
my power to promote the object you have in view, and I remain

Very truly yours

R. Cobden

6 Thur. Replied as annexed.

**Copy letter**, *Bamford to Richard Cobden, 6 June 1861.*

Honble Sir,

I shall certainly now, as you so advise, withhold my petition for the present: Such
friends as I have consulted here, are of the same opinion; and under all
circumstances it agrees with my own. Your note of yesterday also adds to my
satisfaction by your implied approval of my claims, and your kind promise of
support at such time and in such manner as may be most expedient. Your
proposed conference with Mr Bazley will, I trust lead to a confirmation of your
good intentions; and meantime I shall be happy to answer any further enquiries
that may be deemed necessary.

I remain, Honble Sir,

Your obliged serv[t]

Sam[l] Bamford.

Went to Manchester and called on Dr Watts who gave me four pounds out of money
collected towards my compensation. Intimated that himself, Mr Ireland, David
Chadwick, and David Morris had the business in hand. I asked him when I was to call
again? and he said any time I chose; when I was in town, from which I understood
I was to call for more money when I wanted it: he said, he did not know whether or
not he ought to give me the names of the gentlemen who had subscribed. I said there
were reasons both for and against that, but I did not press it at present. I asked if,
during the collection he had met with any unpleasantness, and he said he had not in
any instance. I assured him I would use the money very economically; and he replied,
he did not doubt it.

At the top of Market Street I was stopped by a person whom I recognised as a
nephew of the late Robert Story,[6] the Gargrave poet: at the Rainbow tavern we had

---

6. See entry for 7 August 1858.

some talk together, and he said his uncle spent his annual holiday (the month of September) in a trip to Scotland, Ayr, Dumfries and what is called the land of Burns: his uncle had composed a poem on Burns, for the celebration of the Centenary of his birth; the best poem, the nephew said which Story had ever written: he found many friends in Scotland; and consequently had to take a great deal of whisky, but somehow or other he got starved (probably in coming home) and became unwell: and not paying attention to the state of his health, the cold settled upon his chest, and ultimately became <u>bronchitis</u>, which killed him. He was buried at Battersea, and his widow he – the nephew supposed – would be provided for by the Duke of Northumberland.

When I gave up employment at Somerset House, I left Story in the situation of an extra clerk in the Audit-office, his place of business was down in one of the low gloomy cellars on the left hand from the entrance out of the Strand: a place, the being constantly confined to which, was enough to distract the nerves of any man and drive him mad. I used to talk to him, and advise with, both about his affairs and my own, for I was always more frank with him than he was with me. I counselled him to get out of that dolourous looking den as soon as he could, and at last he informed me that he had made known to his friend the Duke of Northumberland, his wish to be released from his present situation and placed in some other, and that the Duke had advised him to remain as he was for the present, and in due time, if something better was not offered him, he himself – the Duke – would see that he was made comfortable: That, I said, was like a true nobleman, and the Duke, I had not any doubt, would prove a true friend to the last. But his good health, I remarked, was not likely to be very continuous; the old dog kennel in which he worked – poring over figures and adding up and proving sums from morning to night, was against it; then his residence was at Battersea, a low, foggy, humid piece of ground, with a thick, stagnant atmosphere; in which he had already lost two daughters and was certainly not the most suitable for the two who remained. His mornings walk to his employment was in the range of the fetid river fogs, through Chelsea and Pimlico, about two or three miles of the worst air to be met with in the neighbourhood of London. Whilst his return in the evening was still worse if possible, it being a threepenny paddle by steamboat which was more like a paddle in a gutter rather than any thing else, or a churning of all the abominable excretions which animal and vegetable life produces and casts away. I warned him to be aware of these things to leave the cold humid air of Battersea, and get upon higher and drier ground, such as Clapham, or Wandsworth Common, or Islington, or Hampstead, but whatever I said did not seem to make much impression. Nor did I consider that the gift of a hundred bottles of Sherry, which the generous Duke ordered to be delivered [to] him, when he – the Duke went abroad, would tend much to his well-being; wine was a liquor which Story was not in the habit of taking: his now frequent use of it would cause a change, perhaps a not very healthful on[e] in the receptive organs and bodily fluids, and diseased action of the liver and heart might be the consequence. Story listened to me; but I never, from his manner could perceive that he adopted my advice. So I left him. When I came away from Somerset House: he remained in his old den, earning I suppose, his 8/- a day, and I turned out, to seek such fortune as a cold world could not for shame withhold: He is dead, and I am here yet: the dead more happy than the survivor.

**Saturday 8th.** At Manchester. Called on Mr Greenwell and tendered him the ten shillings which I had borrowed, adding to them many sincere thanks, but Mr G. declined taking them; saying I was quite welcome to them; and he intended at the time to make a gift of them. I replied that I was not in a position which authorized me to refuse favour of that kind: but his lending me the money when I wanted it, was I thought, quite sufficient obligation, and I should be well pleased to discharge it. Mr G. however, begged my acceptance of the loan: and I thanking him again returned the four half crowns into my pocket. Without calling at any other place I came up to Shudehill, and took the Omnibus, for Barns green.

**Monday 10th.** Three years this day since we commenced house keeping in Mosston: How we have been preserved from starvation seems to me a wonder.

**Sunday 16th.** The annexed notice of George Poulton, an occasional extra clerk at Somerset House, is cut from the Middleton Albion of yesterday.

***Advertisement*** *from the* Middleton Albion, *15 June 1861.*

---

MIDDLETON AND TONGE
PUBLIC BATHS

---

The Directors of this Company beg to announce
that they have engaged
PROFESSOR POULTON
The "CELEBRATED AMPHIBIOUS MAN," and
"CHAMPION SCIENTIFIC SWIMMER OF
ENGLAND",
to go through his Wonderful Evolutions in Water,
on MONDAY EVENING,
the 24th instant.
Further particulars in next week's publication.

---

George – now become "Professor Poulton" – is the son of a Mr Poulton who had during many years been employed about Somerset House in a very subordinate capacity; he lived in the suburbs of London some where in the neighbourhood of Kingsland, and kept a book shop and a circulating library, which was attended by his two daughters, who were discribed to me as being rather attractive in person. Mr Lyne, our Accountant General was said to patronize the shop. Whilst I was in the voucher office in Arundel Street, the elder Poulton took a situation at one of the desks, and soon afterwards his son George took another place, and when we afterwards removed to Somerset Place, both Poultons went with us in the Accountant Generals department. The elder Poulton was a regular clerk on the establishment, and the son, for some reason or other was favoured by being taken into employment each autumn and continued so employed during each winter, and until the summer months, when being an adept at swimming, he left the desk and took his summer tour to the bathing places on the coast, or to whatever inland town he deemed best for payment. In this way "Professor Poulton" could do a convenient stroke of business both for himself and his employers at London, and I have not a doubt, that if a letter of <u>enquiry</u> on <u>any subject, or</u> relative to <u>any</u> person were forwarded for the "Professor", he would do his best to return such an answer as would please the powers that be. Since I left London George has been down at Manchester every summer: on one occasion when I came down on a visit, B—h another clerk in the Accountant Generals Department followed me, and when I, to my great surprise met him face to face in Salford, I was not much puzzled to account for his being there; the truth flashed upon me, that go wherever I would, a spy would in some character or other be dodging my steps: This fellows appearance at Middleton is the result of a continuance of the system; which has not, I believe, been relaxed since I first went to Somerset House.

Our old neighbours Chorlton and his wife came in the afternoon, and stopped [to] tea: and before they were gone, three others from Middleton dropped in; this was really inconvenient to us, as we had to put on the kettle afresh and make tea for them: we could not do less, though our stock of bread, butter, and groceries for the week were nearly all consumed: After these three were gone Brierley made his appearance, bringing me an Oldham Times, newspaper, and a copy of "Sweepings of Treaddle-pen Court" which he expected me to sell for him to some of the Manchester booksellers, I [to] have a commission of twenty per cent. I declined undertaking the sale, alledging, as an excuse, that I did not wish at present, to call upon either of the Heywoods: on the 5th of next month three years would have expired since I sold a thousand copies of my Life of a Radical to Abel Heywood, and I would rather not have any communication with him until the expiration of that time: with John Heywood, I was similarly circumstanced, his three years would be compleated on the 8th of next December.

Whilst I and Brierley sat talking, only a short time before dark Travis and Dronsfield from Hollinwood arrived: I was certainly chagrined at their coming creeping, as it were, just when night was setting in, especially as Dronsfield had given me to understand by letter, that he and his wife would come, and I had asked them not [to] omit so doing. Consequently I expected them to an early tea. The three talked on various matters; but one of my deaf bouts was upon me, and as they conversed in the ordinary conversational tone, I did not understand one half of what they said. The chief subject appeared to be Brierley, the Oldham Times, and Brierleys concerns, and it was not until they had risen to their feet and were about to depart, that any question was put as to <u>my</u> affairs. I felt this want of attention very much, and had Brierley not been present I should have obviated it at once by introducing the subject of my London affairs, and perhaps, by letting them know how I stood with Manchester friends; as it was, they went away without any very clear knowledge as to my actual position.

We had not any refreshment to offer these latter friends, so I sent Mima out for a quart of ale, but Travis put down a shilling insisting on her taking it and refused to receive change from it (Generous man).

**Saturday 29th.**[7] Received the annexed.

*Letter*, *Henry Thorp, 25 Piccadilly, Manchester, to Bamford, 28 June 1861.*

Dear Sir,
Mr Edwin Waugh and another gentleman a friend of his are coming up to drink tea with me at my lodgings Suttons Farm, Alms Hill, Cheetham Hill on Tuesday evening next at 1/2 past 5.

As the days are now warm and long I thought I would take the liberty of asking you if you favour me with your company – I should be much pleased to see you as I am sure Mr Waugh and his friend will be –

In order that you may not be discouraged by the distance, if you will give us the pleasure of your company, I will order a coach to be at your door say @ 5 o'clock on Tuesday and the same shall take you home on the ev\g. I am dear Sir,
Your most true friend,
Henry Thorp.

**Sunday 30th.** Sent the annexed reply.

*Copy letter*, *Bamford to Henry Thorp, Manchester, 30 June 1861.*

Kind Sir,
I cannot think of again disappointing you, and must therefore avail myself of your conveyance on Tuesday afternoon, and take a cup of tea with you and Mr Waugh and friend.

My health however, I must inform you, is, though at present tolerable, – of precarious continuance; and I shall therefore desire to make an <u>early</u> departure. Paralysis, deafness, and fast decreasing sight, are but poor assurances of a cheerful visitant; and from all those I suffer, or have suffered during the last half year: the paralysis, fortunately, has not, as yet, lamed me; at times however I am "as deaf as a post," and my sight has suddenly, of late, begun to darken, and grow indistinct: A good cup of tea however – not too strong – will, – though it cannot make me as sprightly as younger friends, enable me to spend a couple of hours cheerfully with them. Dear Sir,
Yours truly
Samuel Bamford.

*Newspaper cutting*, *source not stated, reporting that, following an appeal to Lord Palmerston and the Earl of Carlisle, the Poet Close has been awarded a £100 payment from the Royal Bounty fund in recompense for the liabilities he incurred between the announcement of his pension and its withdrawal.*

---

7. Bamford wrote "Sat. 28th".

**Friday 5th July.** Sent the following to Abel Heywood.

***Copy letter***, *Bamford to Abel Heywood, 5 July 1861.*

> Sir,
> It is three years this day since you purchased from me, the right and authority
> to print and publish a thousand copies of my Passages in the Life of a Radical.
> I think it is time I should know something about them, and I will thank you to
> inform me, by post, what number you have on hand.
> Your Obd<sup>t</sup> Serv<sup>t</sup>
> Samuel Bamford

***Letter***, *Abel Heywood to Bamford, 5 July 1861.*[8]

> Sir,
> Without knowing the quantity which are in the hands of Simpkin & Co. I think
> the quantity yet in hand is 500 copies. The bound will be about 50 unsold – The
> sale has been slower than I had anticipated.
> Yours truly,
> Abel Heywood.

5th July. Frid. The annexed from Mr Harland.
Replied by return of post.[9]

***Letter***, *John Harland, Moorfield Cottage, Swinton, to Bamford, 4 July 1861.*

> Dear Bamford,
> I am wondering how it is I have not seen you for some time. I only hope that it is
> because you are better imployed; and not because of any ailment. I have been
> several times laid up for a few days in bed; but I am soon up and about again.
>     Now that the wretched business of "poet Close" is over, do you think there
> would be any service to you in a letter to the <u>Guardian</u>, showing your claims, but
> not offering you the insult of comparison with him? I should like to talk it over
> with you. I would write it, and would base your claims, not on 300 or 3000 names
> signed to a document, but on 3 grounds – 1st what you have <u>done</u> for your
> country and your fellow men; 2nd what you have <u>suffered wrongfully</u> and 3d, for
> your literary merits as poet and prose writer and for your age, at which a man
> who has done his best for others, no less than himself, has a right to expect rest
> and comfort in his declining years. In support of these claims I would make such
> short quotations from your works, as would show even the blindest of prime
> ministers that your claims are well founded and well grounded.

---

8. A hastily scrawled note.
9. Bamford's reply is missing.

I am giving myself the treat of reading your books a <u>third</u> time; and I will ask you, while I think of it, if you ever finished the story of "The Traveller" of which only 6 chapters are printed in your "Walks in South Lancashire" (1844) If there was ever a 2nd vol. of the "Walks" I never saw it, and must have it, if buyable. If you have any such, please bring it with you, the first day of settled weather, when health, leisure and inclination conspire to bring you hither, an ever welcome guest. Mrs Harland joins me in kind regards to Mrs Bamford, who we should be glad to see with you here, whenever practicable. Hoping soon to see you I am Dear Bamford
Heartily yours,<br>J. Harland.

I returned the last papers to Wm Clark of Middleton some time ago, with a letter of thanks.

4th and 5th. Mima had several snatches of fits. Eating too many new potatoes.

5th. Geo Ward killed.

**Monday 8th.**  Saw D. Chadwick, and explained all to him about my Insurance business. 8 Mon.[10] Mr Chadwick informed me that the subscription would realize, or was intended to realize fifty pounds a year for me during life, or until government made a provision for me. Circulars had been sent by himself, Dr Watts and David Morris, to gentlemen in Manchester, and the subscriptions were in response to such circulars; he asked the age of my wife, and on being informed 72 he said the allowance, whatever it amounted to, had best be for both our lives. Desired me to call on him next week and he would go with me to Dr Watts, with a view to some arrangement.

**Wednesday 10th.**  Inquest at Blue Bell on Hughs the Collier.

**Friday 12th.**  From R. Mellor, Manchester.

***Letter***, *Richard Mellor, Office of Weights and Measures, City of Manchester, to Bamford, 11 July 1861.*

Dear Bamford,
I have seen our mutual friend Mr Stelfox, at the Star and he has said on two occasions he wishes to see you.
    Pray call at your first convenience.
I am, Dear Sir,<br>With kind regards,<br>Yours very truly,<br>Rd. Mellor.

---

10. Inserted opposite.

Called with Mellor on Stelfox – and he explained that he wished me to take dinner with Mellor, himself, and Waugh and E. Ridings, so I called afterwards to make arrangement and he was not then in.[11]

12th July. Frid. Went to see Mr Harland at Swinton, and we talked over his intention to write to the Guardian on my claims to government compensation. I gave him copies of all my printed slips and circulars, as well as slips of the reviews which have at various times appeared respecting my prose and poetic compositions, so that, with those, and my books, of which he has a compleat copy, he had matter enough to write upon. He said he should write the letter the day following (Saturday) and after taking tea – not very sweet (I wonder the ladies have not the good old way of letting strangers sweeten for themselves) I came away. Harland slipping something into my hand as we parted (five shillings I afterwards found, and was almost sorry he had done so) I was just two minutes too late for the Omnibus, and so walked to Pendleton, and thence by 'bus to Manchester, and so home.

**Thursday 18th.** Called on D. Chadwick at Manchester. I had arranged with him on the 8th to call this week, when he would go with me to Dr Watts, and make some arrangement about the payment of my Manchester share of the National Contribution towards compensation – I know not what other name to give it – Mr Chadwick now seemed to understand for the first time, that I had already received four pounds, and five pounds from Dr Watts. I said I had; and Mr Chadwick would have heard me say the same earlier, had he questioned me on that point, but he had not so questioned me, and I supposing that all three (Watts, Chadwick and Morris) were equally informed of all transactions, had not mentioned the circumstance of the two payments to Mr Chadwick. He seemed satisfied however on finding now, that it was so: Formerly he had said these payment[s] would be continued during my life, or until I was otherwise provided for; now however, he said I was certain to have it "during a year, at least", I might make myself easy for that time; this I felt to be a difference, and I could not readily account for it.

　　[In] the Guardian of this morning however appears Harlands letter on my behalf, and I have since cogitated whether this letter, coming forth as it does, in the columns of a print which, to say the least, is not friendly to the party with which Dr Watts, Ireland, and my other two known friends act, may not have caused an alteration, or a variation on the purpose with which this friendly interference was begun. May not they, seeing that a party adverse to their own, was taking me by the hand, have become suspicious of my integrity, and consequently cool on my behalf? I do not like to attach undeserved suspicions to my friends, but human nature is human nature throughout the whole breed, and the idea struck me as not impossible. Mr Chadwick came into the office whilst I was there; I attended in consequence of an engagement to call upon him. When he would go with me to Dr Watts (though what for I did not exactly know) and he now said he had seen Dr Watts – probably only just left him – and therefore he

---

11. Written by Bamford on the back of Mellor's letter.

had no occasion to see him again, nor had I either, until I went at the time of payment, in a fortnight: if there is to be anything like vacillation or party feeling in this business I shall not like it; and at present it seems to me that my present friends (Watts, Chadwick, and Morris) had seen the article in the Guardian and thence judged that I was going over to another party, and they consequently changed their tune from that of a provision during my life, or until provided for by government, to a certitude of provision "during <u>one</u> year," at least. These surmises will however be set at rest when next I see Dr Watts on the 1st August.

*Letter, from the* Manchester Guardian, *18 July 1861, signed "Palmam Qui Meriut Ferat" (John Harland), extolling Bamford's virtues as a writer and peaceful reformer, paraphrasing Bamford's circular, concluding: "Is not this a fitting case for a pension?" A note by Bamford identifies the person who "pronounced him the raciest writer of Saxon English since Cobbett" as Isaac Disraeli.*

18th Thursd. Mr Allen of the Guardians office lent me his file of the Guardian for 1830, very kind: he sent a messenger to his house at Prestwich for it.

**Friday 19th.** Received the annexed from Mr Harland and acted on his suggestion by sending off copies of the Guardian to Mr Cobden and Mr Bazley, but in haste forgetting to attach postage stamps. I had to write to each of them, including two stamps in each letter: supposing they would pay the extra charge, which I afterwards learned they would not. Very much annoyed: The fact is I am becoming exceedingly dull and short of memory, as well as dim-sighted: sure signs of the end approaching. Still, I look well folks say, and I eat well, and keep well but my intellects have undergone a great alteration, and I cannot expect, nor indeed wish to be a burden on my friends long.

*Letter, John Harland to Bamford, 18 July 1861.*

My Dear Bamford
My letter is in to-day's <u>Guardian,</u> (Thursday) 4th page, top of 5th Col; and I write to suggest that you should get a few copies of the paper, and mark the letter, not with the pen, but with scissors, (cutting the title a little and turning it down so as to direct attention to it immediately on opening and spreading the paper). Then send it by post, putting a postage stamp on each, to such men as Bazley, Cobden, Bright, Massey, Disraeli, and any other influential friends. I shall be glad to hear if any good effects result.

Have you given my note to Mr. Taylor? Have you got a Volume of the <u>Guardian</u> at home in consequence?

If you have seen Abel Heywood and made any bargain to buy back your own books from him, I shall be glad to hear the result.

I am again laid up in bed with a very painful gathering abcess.

Mrs H, and my daughters join me in kind regards to Mrs Bamford and yourself.
                    Yours ever truly,
                            J. Harland.

**Sunday 21st.** Received the annexed from Mr Bazley: This is doing business as it should be done: A dozen such contributions would make me indifferent to any Government provision; indeed, I had rather not have any dealings with Government people at all; the Country, the people of Lancashire especially, are the parties who have benefited by my exertions and sufferings, and they are the parties who ought to make immediate Compensation; besides, after living free, as it were all my days, I don't like the idea of dying with a Government collar round my neck: it would not be the sort of death which an old patriot ought to submit to.

**Newspaper cutting**, *20 July 1861, reporting grants of civil list pensions made on 18 April 1861 for the period 20 June 1860 to 20 June 1861. Bamford's name is not amongst them.*

**Letter**, *Thomas Bazley to Bamford, 21 July 1861.*

Dear Sir,
I am sorry that you have taken the trouble of sending me a couple of postage stamps. The letter in the Guardian Paper is excellent and establishes by just reasoning your claims to public compensation, but as of old, the race is not to the swift nor the battle to the strong. Some aristocratic influence might obtain from Lord Palmerston a pension with your acceptance, but I feel that a cotton spinner, the representative of his neighbours industry, has no power to procure a reward for public services, talents, and patriotism. The annexed will I hope be welcome to you.
              Dear Sir, Faithfully Yrs,
                    Thos Bazley.

The annexed was as follows.[12]

**Note** *from Thomas Bazley, London, to Mr J. Cooke, New Bridge Mills, Water Street, Manchester, 20 July 1861.*

Pay Mr Saml Bamford on the first of August and on every succeeding Month, as long as may be required. One pound.

The annexed from Dronsfield at Hollinwood. I wish him success, but I cant attend the Wakes: the afternoon also is showery. Betty Collinge from Rochdale, and her sister Mary were here in the afternoon.

**Letter**, *James Dronsfield to Bamford, 20 July 1861.*

Dear Bamford,
You must excuse my seeming negligence in not coming to see you according to promise. I have been busily employed in looking up my friends to obtain a situation in the Gas and Water Department at Oldham. The election takes place

---

12. Written by Bamford on the back of Bazley's letter.

on Wednesday next. I don't expect that I shall succeed in getting it as there are so very many applicants. The salary is £125 per annum.

It is our Wakes tomorrow, Sunday, if it is fine I shall expect to see you over, to dinner and spend an afternoon with a few select friends in some cosy corner. My wife and my Mother have not been able to fix on a day when to come to your house to spend an afternoon with Mrs Bamford, they will come the first opportunity no doubt, we don't forget you, but we have been so busily employed whitewashing and cleaning out for the wakes.

I am yours<br>James Dronsfield.

**Monday 22nd.** A lady called and rather pressingly invited myself and wife to a prayer meeting, at my neighbours, Mr John Pickstone. I told her my prayer was work, and got rid of her as quietly as I could.

This day I begin to copy from the Manchester Guardian, the report about the "Infernal Machine," at Hurst, near Ashton under line; in Guardian of July 12th being the first.

**Tuesday 23rd.** By the Examiner and Times of this day it appears that another great scoundrel, and one of the most bitter of my enemies – what for, I never knew – has passed from this life into hell, if there be such a place: his virulent endeavours to detach friends from me, and to increase my enemies, have been of long continuance, and unceasing: his abusive letter to Tait for his kindly notice of my poems; and his subsequent epistle, inclosing one from Mitchell, to Howitt, when he edited the Peoples Journal were expressions of a malignity seldom evinced except by beings allied to the Infernal. Nightingale also, another of the same batch – the contemptible Elijah Dixon set, died on the same day: a worthy couple, entering the sulphurous regions hand in hand. My enemies, and false friends are slipping away before me, very fast. Amos Ogden, James Dyson, for he, though one of the better sort, was never truly honest, – Johnny Judas, the Fiend, Paul Halliwell, a hypocrite, (like his mother old Ann) and a turn coat. Joe Mitchell, the Friend and Coadjutor of Oliver the spy; who was the real spy, I have reasons for believing, Oliver, being his instrument only. Old Prentice,[13] the Scotch mendicant, who pilfered from my book, and sponged on every one he could get alongside of: and little skinny ignorant, and impudent Jimmy Wroe[14] who, by a set of blockheads, was made editor of a newspaper, and was about as fit for the business as a pig on a midden. All are gone. I had hoped many a time to have a grand set to with them, either separately or collectively, but they have given me the slip, and I have only now to do justice to their memories, by discribing their actions, and that will be condemnation enough. See the slip on the other leaf: one of the crew.

---

13. Archibald Prentice (1792–1857), Scot, editor of *Manchester Times* 1828–47, an important figure in Manchester radicalism, and author of *Historical Sketches and Personal Recollections of Manchester* (1851), which Bamford thought had borrowed too freely from his own works; see Turner, *Reform and Respectability*, 7–13.
14. James Wroe (1789–1844), editor of the radical *Manchester Observer*, 1819–21.

*Obituary*, *from the* Manchester Examiner and Times, *23 July 1861, of William Willis, one of the old "Manchester Radicals", a bookseller and a friend of Cobbett, Cartwright, Hunt and Detrosier, who died on 16 July aged 54. Chronic debt and bankruptcy blighted his bookselling business; against the information that he borrowed £10 from his father to set up in the trade, Bamford has written: "many a time". The obituary concludes: "his simplicity, trustworthiness and other genial qualities, will live long in the reminiscences of his many sorrowing friends".*

**Sunday 28th.** Dronsfield and Travis here; stopped [for] tea.

**Thursday 1st August.** Jim Harrison of Middleton died, this day, as I am informed: no great loss to his neighbours, or fellow subjects generally.

1 August. Went to Mr Bazley's Counting House, and presented his order for one pound, to be paid "on the 1st of every month, so long as it may be required." The little man, the Cashier met me at the Counting house door, saying, "Mr Bazley is not here: he will be down next week." "Oh," I replied, I think I can do business with you, and so I opened my old pocket book, and took from it a paper (the order) and presented it to the gentleman. Another had entered by a door opposite, and went into the back counting House, and my little man, after looking carefully at the paper I had given him, and pausing, shortly, took it into the back room, where he remained, half a minute, and then returning, he counted out twenty shillings from a cash box, and gave them to me. I counted them after him, and found them all right. "You will be coming again," said the little man. "Yes I suppose I shall," I replied. "Come or send." "Either will do perhaps." "Yes, either come or send," said the little man. "Good bye." "Good bye."

David Morris gave me to understand that the present motion in my favour. was originated by himself, Dr Watts, and David Chadwick, entirely from a sense of public justice to my case, as presenting strong claims to public compensation. They agreed that something should be done, and sent out circulars to parties whom they thought most likely to aid in contributing to a fund which should relieve me from exigency, and make myself and wife comfortable during the remainder of our days. Mr Morris seemed to think that "fifty pounds a year," or a pound a week, was about the thing desired: and said they had already got what would be about 48 pounds, – whether continuously or for the present only, he did not say, – I was sorry to hear, that amongst other persons, he had sent a circular to <u>Field</u>, Secretary, – so he stiles himself – to "the Oldham Analytical Literary Institute" – a pretentious piece of humbug – Mr T.T. Wilkinson of Burnley, had, I understood, been written to, and agreed with the justice of the object: but thought "I had better not come so prominently before the public, lashing my opponents in the newspapers," but should let "some one else do it": Yes, but some one else does <u>not</u> do it; so I do it myself, besides, Doctor Franklin observes, "Is there anything thou wishest to be done? do it thyself." Sir James Kay Shuttleworth, had been, it seemed written to, on my business, but had not replied.

What can be amiss with Sir James? is he too, turning the cold shoulder? Mr Morris said if there had been a public appeal, and a notice that subscriptions would be received by himself, Dr Watts and Mr Chadwick, any required amount would have been raised off hand; but Dr Watts said that would be putting back any thing which might be forthcoming from government, and he therefore was decidedly against it. I said, if the choice was left with me I should prefer a public subscription, to anything which government might grant: I had been all my life striving for national freedom and I should like to die entirely free of all government shackles and obligations. I thought, a public recognition of my claims, would be more creditable to the public and to myself, than a government pension: a miserable and degraded set were already on the pension list: I would rather not appear amongst them, but if it came to the question whether I should go to Downing Street or a board of guardians, I should prefer the former.

Mr Morris said something about diffusing the subscriptions by making them of small amount. I thought that an erroneous idea. In Milner Gibson's case, the money was not sought after, or cared for, in my case a competency first of all was desired, and that could not be secured without a certain amount of money.

So it is, with these men, good and true, in their way: they get a certain set of ideas, and carry them into all the operations of life: Mr Morris would have the subscriptions of small amount, and proportionately diffused; if a dozen gentlemen were to come forward like Mr Bazley, he would probably almost recoil from the prompt accomplishment of his own proposal.

At Dr Watts office I had to wait some time, a gentleman being with him on business; he came into the outer office, and put down 4-10-0, which, in the miserable light of that dolorous place I could not see, but put it in my pocket, to be counted after, and scrawled something as like my name as I could guess, and came away, promising, at the Drs request to call again soon, as he wanted to see me.

**Saturday 3rd.**  Should have gone to Man[chester] but it was a wet, stormy forenoon, so remained at home all day.

**Sunday 4th.**  Blakely Wakes.

Once more came that forward, and obtrusive young woman from Manchester, whom we have several times tried to get rid of, but it seems, as yet, without avail. She is the daughter of parents who were neighbours, – disagreeably familiar ones – when we resided at Charlestown. She has, of course, known us ever since, and appears determined to continue to know us: her father is one of that loose, idle, disreputable class, who will undertake any kind of momentary job, sooner than stick to his work (house painting). When I was at Somerset House, he annoyed me twice by calling at my place: once he had a fellow from Manchester with him, who was over liquored, and I got rid of the couple as soon as possible. They had come to London, on this as well as the former occasion, on some business connected with a new sick and burial society, which this impudent fellow had got up: and the funds of which were, I suppose, spent in these kind of journeys; at any rate the society, soon afterwards disappeared, and is now, not to be heard of. Soon after my return to Lancashire, he had the assurance to call at my house, in company with one Clarke Cropper and one Finlan (James), two of the broken down Chartist Association of London, who had come to Lancashire, on a speculative tour, spying the land. Finlan was the chief agent for an Assurance Company, whose head office was at London. Clark Cropper was made agent for the same concern at Oldham, and our friend(?) Bethel was dubbed to the same rank at Bolton; others of the squad being located as agents, at different places in the neighbourhood of Manchester. Finlan lived in high style in a very expensively furnished house, until he was found out, cheating the society, and forging documents. When he, having run his course, disappeared, Bethel at Bolton, this young miss informs me, gave up his agency, because he would [not] have recourse to the same dishonest means which Finlan and others had: Their plan was, she says, to send up names to the head office at London, as those of members who had paid up their insurances; they themselves (the fraudulent agents at Manchester) having paid, for them; then, at the expiration of a quarter, or half a year, the suppositious person was returned as dead; and the insurance money whatever it might be, was by the aid of forged certificates, drawn by the fraudulent agent here. Finlan had been practising this trick as the only means for making the agency pay, and meet expenses; it was a common thing, she intimated, amongst the agents, and as her father (honest man) could not act as others did; he could not live on the profits of his trade, and gave it up. I must cut this young hussy's acquaintance as well as that of her father, and I shall do it roughly if she comes again; it is one of those unfortunate acquaintances which are easier formed than got rid of: rid however, I will be.

**Thursday 8th.** Dr Watts desired me to get from A Ireland and Co, an estimate of what would be their charges from printing the whole of my works. This with a view, as I understood, to some ulterior plan for their reproduction, and my permanent benefit: so I called at Irelands, but as I had not the books with me I must call again.

**Monday 12th.** Saw Mr Ireland, and he gave me the annexed estimate of the charge for reprinting and binding my publications. This estimate I showed to Dr Watts, and gave him a copy of it. When he calculated the cost of the whole at about four hundred pounds; and said for the present week he should be engaged on the election, and after that he would consult some parties – he did not say whom – on the subject. So the thing stands over during this week, and I left him.

I know not what Dr Watts ulterior views are, but I shall be very unwilling to enter into engagements which may involve me in responsibilities for printers bills. I have had enough of that difficulty: and will not renew it.

**Estimate** *for printing from the Manchester Examiner and Times office, 9 August 1861, with calculations by Bamford for the cost of printing and binding 1,000 copies each of* Passages *(c.£134),* Early Days, Poems, Walks *(£79 each) and* Dialect *(£66), or some £435 the lot.*

**Two newspaper cuttings**, *source not stated, reporting the swearing in of the jury at South Lancashire Assizes and the high number of serious indictments.*

12 Mon. My neighbour Phillips called as he returned from Rochdale, and said I might expect a letter this week from my friend James Smith. He had seen Smith, he said, and the latter was for writing to me.

What this can mean; or why Smith is for writing to me, I cannot divine. A message coming through Phillips does not augur much good for me? such is my opinion of my plausible neighbour.

# 14

# HIS LAST CAMPAIGN

*The subscription saga continued on into late summer, with Watts only finally abandoning his ideas of a standard set of Bamford's works at the end of October. Bamford's own lack of enthusiasm for the scheme, or any variant of it which would have enabled him to publish further instalments of his autobiography, and his conscious decision not to return to platform performances as the winter season opened, once again reflect the dimming of his former energies. Ominously, Mima continued to ail, suffering another slight stroke on 23 September and a fall on 4 December. Compensation came in the form of a stream of obituaries of old enemies, culminating satisfactorily in that of "Joe Fielding, the lying newspaper reporter of Middleton" in December. Bamford also took grim satisfaction in unravelling the unhappy and disreputable private life of his rival poet Edwin Waugh. Amidst all this, he was pleased to act as the patron of the new Lancashire poet Joseph Ramsbottom in October, and although he does not record his feelings at reading the fictional account of him in William Howitt's* A Man of the People *on 9 November, he must have been profoundly satisfied to find his role in history so sympathetically dramatised. The close of the year brought gifts and good wishes from several sources. The diary ends abruptly on 26 December with the essentials of his final security in place, and his robust pride and fragile faith in his friends intact.*

**Wednesday 14th.** Mima and I went to Middleton, and I trimmed about Anns grave probably for the last time. Walked home through the fields, and across the clough. A rough road, but, as I think, shorter. Mima sadly tired.

**Friday 16th.** The Anniversary of our great meeting on St Peters field; 45 years have passed since that terrible and distressing scene; how soon gone! and become part of the past eternity. Nearly all my Middleton friends of that day are dead; (traitors many of them became). I and Mima still remain, true to the old cause, but living amongst people whom we don't understand.

**Monday 19th.** The annexed from Brierley. The verses appearing on the 17th.

**Poem**, *from the* Oldham Times, *17 August 1861, Bamford's "Lines written on the anniversary of his daughter's decease", with ms corrections.*[1]

**Letter**, *Ben Brierley, Oldham, to Bamford, 19 August 1861.*

Dear Bamford,
I hope you will excuse the liberty I have taken in making use of one of your poems for the Oldham Times: but the fact is, when I heard it read by Mr. Gowenlock,

---

1. *Homely Rhymes*, 96–7, where it is explained as: "Written Oct. 15, 1836, being the anniversary of my daughter's decease, and two years after that event". In dating the cutting, Bamford has written "1831" in error. Bamford has corrected "dawn-born" to "down-borne".

I could not resist the temptation offered of securing an insertion of what I consider to be a <u>Grand poem</u>. I send you half a dozen slips, and will send you a paper when I can lay hold of one. I know that I ought to have asked your permission, but presuming on your good nature, I did it without. I however consulted our friends Gowenlock and Potter, and they said – put it in.

I am almost afraid to ask how you are getting on, as I have not been to see you for so long a time, and as I don't hear of your getting your pension. Having so many difficulties to contend against myself, it grieves me that I cannot assist others only in good wishes, which won't fill the pantry. Hoping the morning may soon dawn upon you brighter than you depict it in your poem, allow me to be,

Yours sincerely,

B. Brierley.

**Report**, *from the* Manchester Guardian, *23 August 1861.*

---

DEATH OF MR RICHARD OASTLER. – This gentleman died, yesterday, at Harrogate, in the 73d year of his age. He was well known in Yorkshire and Lancashire as the "Factory King." He was a man of a large and benevolent heart, and of generous, though violent and erratic impulses. Many years ago, as will be remembered, he was actively and very prominently associated in the efforts to ameliorate the condition of the factory population, by the reduction by legislative enactment of their hours of labour.

---

The above a gracious account of a bad man; his instructions to the factory hands how to damage, and stop machinery by inserting knitting needles or other small bits of metal betwixt the wheels; his advice to the operatives, to draw their money from banks and sick funds, and purchase weapons, also to practice military drilling with a view to resist the constituted authorities when the time for action arrived, ought not, in summing up his character, to have been forgotten. This "King," as the silly fellow loved to be styled, made use of his employers property; was sent to prison, refused to take the benefit of the insolvent act, because he would either have to confess to dishonesty, or incur the risk of a prosecution for perjury, and so was liberated at last as a matter of favour from his employer.

**Sunday 25th.** Middleton Wakes.

John Coates, and others from Royton called; as going away Coates put a two shilling piece into my hand, and would do. So I have entered it as so much towards my compensation fund.

**Thursday 29th.** This day being the completion of the monthly (4 weeks) appointment for my Manchester contribution payment, I called on Dr Watts, and found the place occupied by Sam¹ Ingham, a licensed victualler, and Chairman of the licensed victuallers association, who, instead of withdrawing as he ought in decency to have done, invited me to "come forward," and then remained on the spot, as if he were privileged to take part in my business, an act of impudence at which I felt indignant. Dr Watts cordially took my hand, and said he had not been able to compleat what he had intended on my account: he had been looking after a certain person, and expected to see him in a few days, when something definitive would be arranged on the point he was alluding to. (I understood him to allude to the publication of my works, or some part of them). From this passage of conversation, Mr Impudent Ingham, who remained close present, could not make any definite meaning, and I was glad of that: I then, seeing Dr Watts did not say anything about the money, (monthly payment) asked what I was to understand "about that other business," and Dr Watts said he was not quite prepared, but probably would be by the 1st of next month (Sept). As Ingham kept his impudent face thick to the matter, I saw the propriety of Dr Watts cautious and ambiguous replies, and bidding him "good bye", I came away. I felt however, that there was an impropriety in Dr Watts speaking to me at all, on that business, in the presence of any third person, and especially in that of the very presuming individual then obtruding.

Before I left town, I learned that Edwin Waugh, quitted his lodgings in Strange ways, on the night of Monday preceding (the 26th) his "trunk and his carpet bag," were at a certain place, on that evening, and he was leaving his lodgings, but where he was going, was not known by my informant. He seems especially careful to obliterate all trace of his whereabouts, like the red Indians, who are said to cover their retreating footsteps with leaves: let us take up a few leaves, and try if we cannot find a trace.

A few weeks ago, a Mrs Merril, a neighbour of mine living in the row of houses, leading to Barnes Green showed me a paper with the name of Edwin Waugh written upon it. She said it was left by a man who seeing a notice of "Apartments to Let" in her window, had called to inquire about them; he had taken the rooms, and approved of them, and had agreed to take them; he told her that I and Mrs McClunan knew him, and she now wished me to tell her something about him. Was he a married man she asked (she is a widow, with three children: she is 30 or 35 years of age, and rather hand-some looking. One daughter aged about fifteen, lives with her parents at Middleton; another child, younger, a boy, and her eldest daughter aged about seventeen, live with her.) I said he was certainly married; and his wife and three children live at Rochdale; he had discribed himself as "a writer", and I said "I understood he did write occasionally," but she had better enquire further. I could not inform her where he lived, nor whence his place of business was, nor anything further than he sometimes wrote for the newspapers. She said she had a friend, "an elderly gentleman," who would find him out, and give her the information, and so I left her. On the morning of Tuesday the 27th – the morning after his leaving his lodgings in Strangeways, Mrs Merril was in the garden plot at her front door, as I went down the lane. She caught a glance of me, and then stooping disappeared below the fence, and when I came up she was not to be seen. She had undoubtedly stooped, crept in at the door, and closed it, plainly speaking, as an act could speak, "I don't want to talk with you:" it immediately struck me, she was afraid of being questioned about Waugh, and that idea led to the supposition that she had accepted him as a lodger, and had a not very creditable or pure connection with him. My wife had, I learned put her on her guard with respect to his character; told her about his wife and three children being on the parish at Rochdale; about his having been living with a woman in Strangeways, who was supposed to have kept him, or nearly so, and about his general habits of profligacy and faithlessness in his arrangements, so Mrs Merril knew enough to warn her of any connection, and the consciousness of her having acted imprudently, to say the least of it, (so it appeared to us) made her unwilling to be questioned about the matter.[2]

**Friday 30th.** As Mima and I were returning from Blakeley, Mrs Merril was again at her front door. We were almost-close opposite to her before she was aware, and then she suddenly turned round, and pretended to be dusting something from the door, as if wishful not to look us in the face, instead of coming forward, and frankly accosting us, which she might have done and probably would have done had she not had something on her mind which she could not face out: we however did not put her to any severe trial, but walked past, merely saying "a fine day." This was another leaf lifted from the foot prints, and convinced us, that this poor silly woman had committed herself to something which she was anxious to conceal. She was fairly cautioned for her own good; now probably we shall have her for a backbiting enemy until Waugh has cleared her out and then too late, she will find her mistake.

**Sunday 1st September.** Went into the Clough, and from thence strolled by Slack Houses (poor Alice O'nadin) and old Corkers, to Crab Lane head. Sam Chadwick gave me the roll of names of old men whom he feasted on the 23d of last February and I fastened to it with gum, the newspaper report of the 2d March.

**Monday 2nd.** At Manchester, received one pound at the Counting House of Mr Bazley, and five pounds from Dr Watts who, in reference to the publication of my works suggested the employment of a suitable person to canvass for subscriptions (four would be required, at one guinea each). Edwin Waugh he mentioned as one likely for the business. I, at once set Waugh aside as unsuitable in every respect, and the determination was deferred until next week.

**Tuesday 3rd.** Went to see Mr Harland at Swinton: had much conversation with him, and came back by the five o'clock 'bus. With respect to the publication of my works he advised what entirely agreed with my previous idea, (that I should, first of all get to know what Abel Heywood would take for the 500 copies of the Radical, which he says he has on hand; then determine about republishing, and to engage a canvasser if such be deemed necessary: but not by any means, have anything to do with Waugh: in this also I cordially agree with Mr Harland. He thought also, that I should get to see a form of the Circular, which my friends at Manchester are issuing on my behalf, a thing I had previously considered as only proper, and waited for an opportunity to make enquiries on that point: Mr Harland thought, Mr Binney would be a likely person to aid me in such enquiry. On my coming away he slipped a paper containing five shillings into my hand. I told him I would rather not; I did not want it. I was

---

2. Waugh, whose marriage was an unhappy failure, had begun living with a well-to-do Irish widow, Mrs Moorhouse, in Strangeways in the late 1850s: M. Vicinus, *Edwin Waugh* (Littleborough, 1984), 13.

already provided for (I had previously made known to him what Messrs Chadwick, Morris, and Watts had done on my account) but he persisted in pressing his gift, and so I told him I must enter it in my book, as so much contributed towards my "National indemnification fund."

The annexed was cut from a catalogue published by John Gray Bell, a bookseller of Oxford Road Manchester. "Etymology of Names of the towns, villages, hamlets, and other places in the County of Lancaster," was doubtless compiled by R.J. Richardson, and is now thus presented in his MS. "Lonkyshur Laygens, – The Incantation of Spirits, wi' Sam Bamforth in Boggart Hoyle Cloof, original unpublished MS. and other similar matters", may have been written (copied) by the late Mr Richardson, but probably (judging by the style and animus) of the thing, from a MS. by Judd o'Ikes (George of Isaacs) George Richardson, one of the carrion grubs, of our lowest literary putrescence: of whom more will be found, in my continued memoires.[3]

**Insertion:** *extract from a catalogue published by John Gray, Bookseller, Oxford Road, Manchester, giving details of the Richardson manuscript mentioned above.*

**Tuesday 10th.** Mr Pickstone my neighbour living at the great house here, (old mad house) called and asked me if I should like to be introduced to Mr Earnest Jones?[4] who, as he said, had come to live near at hand? I said I had not any wish to be introduced to Mr Jones at all: Oh then, getting up, he said, "I must tell him": "No, no, I said, don't tell him anything." "Don't use my name in any way," and so he went out, not exactly pleased, as I thought.

**Thursday 12th.** The annexed lines have appeared a second time, in one of our local newspapers, and in an imperfect state as may be seen.

**Poem**, *from the* Middleton Albion, *31 August 1861, Bamford's "Lines written on the Anniversary of His Daughter's Decease", as published in the* Oldham Times *on 17 August, with similar corrections to those on 17 August.*

Inquest on the body of — Greaves, of Fields farm, Chadderton, near Hollinwood; killed by the wheel of his cart going over his head, near the coalpits. Inquest at the Blue Bell, verdict "accidental," 24 years of age, married four months; wife in a state of distraction: poor thing!

**Friday 13th.** Wrote to Abel Heywood as annexed.

---

3. George Richardson (1804–86), Manchester writer, poet, calico printer and a founder of Manchester Literary Club. His anonymous satirical poem *Tim Bobbin's Ghost* (Manchester, 1850) ridiculed Bamford's *Dialect of South Lancashire* (1850), a revised edition of Tim Bobbin's *View of the Lancashire Dialect* (1746); see entry for 31 October 1861.

4. Ernest Jones (1819–69), barrister, poet, leader of Chartism in the 1850s, and editor of the Chartist *People's Paper* 1852–8. Lived and worked in Manchester during the 1860s; *DNB*.

***Copy letter****, Bamford to Abel Heywood, 13 September 1861.*

Sir,
Would you please to let me know, at your earliest convenience, what would be your <u>lowest charge</u> – cash – for 150 copies of my "Passages in the Life of a Radical," sheets?

***Letter****, Abel Heywood to Bamford, 13 September 1861.*

Sir,
The price of 150 copies, would be 2/3 per copy in sheets.
                    Abel Heywood.

**Saturday 14th.**  See his reply          £10  0  0
                                             5  0  0
                                             3  7  6
                                            18  7  6[5]

**Tuesday 17th.** Dr Watts still adheres to the idea of a canvasser for my proposed publication. I reminded him of the fact that Abel Heywood had, as he alleges, 500 copies of my Radical in sheets, for which he would probably demand 2/3 a copy – cash – and that it would be necessary, in the first place, to get these copies out of his hands, or, at least out of his control: that John Heywood had probably, as great a number of Early Days on hand; and that they also should be redeemed before any new publication was undertaken, or even the intention of such a thing announced. Still he clung to the idea of a canvasser; and we parted with the understanding that the matter should stand over for a week; he meantime talking it over with Mr Ireland, and the other gentlemen. "I should not mind riling you a little," he said, "for your own benefit," from which I gathered, that he would not hesitate at applying the money in any way he might deem most beneficial to me: a course in which I should probably acquiesce provided I deemed his application of it most to my benefit. At present I did not make any noticeable remark to his rather significant avowal.

Mr David Chadwick, to whom I mentioned Dr Watts's plan was of opinion that the money would be easily gotten by canvassing for 500 donations of one pound each, as by canvassing for 500 subscriptions to my proposed book: in which opinion I coincided. He thought I should succeed best if I was to turn out myself, and canvass for the book, and I told him I could not undertake that; he seemed to expect that A Ireland and Co, might be induced to take the business efficiently in hand; but I could not adopt his view of the matter, and thus the business remains till my next call.

**Thursday 19th.** Mima and I, took a walk across Mosston to Newton. We found the brow on the other side of Jack-bridge-clough a rather tough one to climb, and I had,

---

5. This is a calculation for the cost of 150 copies @ 2s. 3d. Binding would be 4d–5d per copy (see 12 Aug.), leaving little room for profit.

with some difficulty to pull Mima up. Just the reverse, as I said, of "John Anderson My Joe", who, with his old wife "went toddling down." Ours was a "toddling up," and a hard pull we found it. At a public house at Miles Platting, I treated her with three penorth[6] of spirits, and myself with a glass of ale, in celebration of our brave walk, tough struggle with the road, and triumph over it. Bought some very good coffee and chicory at a new shop in the street which was once Lamb Lane: Came along the new road platting across Dene Clough, and so to the turnpike road, Harperhey, and home.

**Saturday 21st.** Went to Manchester, and found Mr D. Morris at Grants "Temperance" up a[n] entry from Smithy Door: a dark place called the "Smoke Room," but there I could not find Mr Morris. At a small room which serves as a bar, the young woman informed me Mr Morris was in the smoke-room, and leading the way back again, she pointed Mr Morris out to me in a dark corner. He now rose and came to me, taking my hand. I told him about not speaking to me when I could not see him, and he said he was reading at the time. We sat down at a table apart from [the] others, and he now informed me, in answer to questions that he wrote the circular which was sent out, on my account, and that his son copied it. About forty copies were written; he had not a copy remaining on hand; possibly his son might have one: he did not seem to be in a communicative mood on this point: Mr T.T. Wilkinson of Burnley had written to Sir J. Kay Shuttleworth, and had since seen him, and Sir James said, in reference to my affair, "he" (Bamford) "shall not want": he had not himself (Morris) had any conversation with either Dr Watts or Mr Chadwick relative to my business, since I last saw him (Morris).

In conversing with Dr Watts I elicited from him that he had not any funds on hand; that he collected, once a month, from the gentlemen who stood pledged, what money was wanted: that in case a canvasser was engaged he contemplated the canvasser being paid from a seperate fund, and the money pledged to me, not to be touched for any other purpose: he should think a good canvasser would obtain 400 guinea subscribers, in three months! Canvasser to have ten per cent; he assented to my suggestion that himself, Chadwick, Ireland, and Morris should meet, and that I also being present the whole business should be discussed: and so it remains at present time.

**Sunday 22nd.** Dronsfield and his little girl Ophelia called: he was agreeable that he Travis and myself should have a[n] "out" some Sunday, through Royton: there inspect the "Self Improvement" school, thence through Thorpe; to Auzlewood[7]: find out the old road Wall-gate, thence to Wall-bank and Hanging Chadder, finding out some clue, if such exists to the origin of the very significant name of that place: thence to Slattocks, and so to Middleton, they would return through Tonge, and I should come home by 'bus.

Mima was very low spirited, and it was also agreed that she should go to his mothers at Hollinwood for a day or two: when fine weather could be some what depended upon.

---

6. I.e. three pennyworth.
7. That is, Ouslewood or Oozewood.

**Monday 23rd.** Mima this morning, was considerably changed in her look and way: I thought she seemed slightly affected by paralysis, and I got up early and prepared her some arrowroot, with just the least of wine in it. She was dull and heavy, and one side of her face seemed a little larger than the other.

**Tuesday 24th.** Mima about same as yesterday: it is evidently a slight paralytic stroke which she has had.

**Wednesday 25th.** Mima not much better, I have applied a blister behind the left ear, and keep her in bed as much as possible.

An envelope with wedding cards of Mr and Mrs Poynting, late Miss Mary M. Harland, of Moorfield Cottage, Swinton, daughter of my friend John Harland. May they live long and be very happy.[8]

***Cutting**, from the* Manchester Examiner and Times, *24 September 1861, headed "Mr Frederick Wilde – Lancaster insolvent court". Wilde, a bookbinder, late of Corporation Street, Manchester, applied for discharge of his insolvency, opposed by "Mr Ernest Jones on behalf of Mr Hugh Kerrish", a printer and publisher. Abel Heywood, who had helped Wilde discharge his debts, provided a character reference, stating that Wilde was "the best bookbinder in Manchester" and that "an honester man there is not in Manchester" (Bamford's emphasis). Wilde was discharged.*

Alderman Heywood and his testimony. A greater scoundrel there is not in Manchester, or the next town to it, according to his opportunity: Heywood, in real honesty, and very truth, I don't think much better than Wilde: one plausible rogue, white washing another. –

    Abel Heywood
    Abel Anything,

**Thursday 26th.** Mima no better: the blister behind her ear not having produced a decided improvement in her health, another was placed on the left side of her neck, and some gentle medicine was given.

**Friday 27th.** The blister has risen well and I think she is better, more rational, and of a better tone of mind: her left leg and foot were cold, and I rubbed them with a brush and with my hand, and afterwards they were quite warm.

27th Frid. Potter from Oldham called.[9]

**Saturday 28th.** Mima better again this day: the annexed letter from Clowes of Chorlton-Medlock, lies over for my consideration, for, as I can now live without public performances I feel not much inclined to undertake them; but I will consider.

---

8. Wedding cards not included.
9. Added opposite.

*Letter*, *T. Clowes, Steam Brewery, York Street, Chorlton-upon-Medlock, to Bamford, 26 September 1861.*

Dear Sir,
A few friends and myself think we can get you up another reading in our Town Hall, about the middle of November if you are willing, and able to do your part. If so let me know and I will do my best to forward such a movement and Mr Priestley, myself and another would like to select the passages to be read, which we are, I may tell you, all of the opinion should be from your own prose works, with kind regards,
      I am respectfully,
        Tho$^s$. Clowes.

**Sunday 29th.** Mima: came down stairs and remained below several hours.

**Monday 30th.** Mima down stairs nearly all day, doing odd jobs.

**Tuesday 1st October.** When I went to Mr Bazleys this afternoon, for my monthly allowance of £1; the cashier seemed scarcely prepared to pay me. He went down some steps and into another room where he stayed about half a minute, and then came back and took a sovereign from a box or drawer, and placed it before me with the remark "a fine day". I thanked him, asked, "is Mr Bazley quite well", very well, was the reply and so I came away.

Dr. Watts had seen and spoken to David Morris, who did not at all coincide with his view of raising 400 subscribers at a guinea each, and the D$^r$ seemed now a little at fault as to how we should move in the matter of publication. I said the first thing to be done, as it appeared to me, was to get the publications as they at present stood, out of the booksellers hands: to do that would probably cost £100, and if they were once clear of the booksellers. I thought a plan could be struck out whereby an arrangement could be made with Alex[ande]r Ireland and Co., for the publication of the whole of my books simultaneously, and at a low price, which would however secure to me a profit or royalty sufficient for my subsistence during life. He seemed to approve of the idea and would in the mean time get to know what would the cost of redeeming the two works Early Days and Life of a Radical from the booksellers hands. So the business remain, till next time I go. Received £4-10-0.

Lost my good alpaca umbrella, which a respectable looking person, who was however, a thief, took from the bar of the New Inn at Barnes Green, leaving me a shabby dirty rag of a calico one in place. Had he not been a thief he would have returned it, or written to the landlady, but he has gotten a better by the exchange, and every time he sees his prize his conscience will tell him he is <u>a thief</u>.

Mima keeps gradually though slowly improving in health.

My sight is fast leaving me I find.

**Friday 4th.** Middleton. Mills not at home. Paid Mrs Mills 11/- for printing.

So Henry Shuttleworth it seems who is Treasurer to the Middleton Agricultural Association, won a prize for cheese, which cheese he had purchased from Cliffe (one of the judges for cheese) and Cliffs wife delivered it at Shuttleworths on the morning of the exhibition.[10]

Had a long chat with Oswald Dickin at "the Corner House," and came off by omnibus.

Mrs N came in the forenoon and brought a present of tea, and a bunch of flowers. Bindloss, it seems is off with his engagement to Emily (daughter) and Jame[s] Wanklyn a parson is on with one to Mary Ann. At night: a boy brought a hamper and when we opened it the following morning it contained <u>six</u> pint bottles of porter. <u>Six</u> pint bottles: not quite three quarts – magnificent donation!!

**Saturday 5th.** At home.

**Sunday 6th.** Mills's three children came and brought a note from their father. Also one from Oswald Dickin and a draft, rather "the draft" of the Memorial sent from Middleton, to Lord Palmerston on my behalf: A <u>pretty mess</u> of documents are those on the opposite page marked (29) the memorial quite as good as could be expected from Whalley.[11]

6th Sund. Our neighbours informed us on Monday morning that a person was at our door last night after we had gone to bed, and on

**Monday 7th.** The annexed letter from Whalley[12] explains, so far as it explains anything, the circumstance: What a precious ass this Whalley must be: his letter, like his Middleton Memorial explains not anything; it has neither beginning, middle, nor end of it. To whom was Mr Schwabes communication addressed: and what was the purport of it? Nothing said.

**Wednesday 9th.** Miss Taylor called and left a bottle of ginger wine. Sage gruel in a pitcher; sago in a parcel, cinnamon and biscuits, very good lady.

9th. A load of coal from Mr Nelson which 10/- I enter as so much to the "Contribution."

**Thursday 10th.** Poor Ann who is dying at next door had some of the gruel and a biscuit, and she shall also partake of the wine.

**Friday 11th.** A man from the warehouse of Mr T.B. Potter at Manchester brought a hare as a present; another person accompanied the messenger, who said Mr Potter was in Scotland. I skinned the hare, cut it up, and put it in the stew pot, the same evening.

**Saturday 12th.** Middleton. Saw Mills, Dickin and Clarke, bought tea from Thos. Ball. Whalleys "small communication," was a sovereign, inclosed in a letter cover, from

---

10. Henry Shuttleworth (d.1880), farmer, landlord of the Old Boar's Head in Middleton, a Conservative, and a founder of the Middleton Agricultural Society; *Middleton Albion*, 2 October 1880.
11. No documents are inserted, but see entry for 21 March 1861.
12. No letter survives.

Mr Edmund Schwabe son of the late Salis Schwabe:[13] he had lately read my book, and was much pleased with it. I accept his present, as a contribution towards my National Compensation fund and have inserted it in the list accordingly.

**Sunday 13th.** Ramsbottom recited to me a startling poem which he has recently "touched up," and in a way finished. I advised him [to] give it to the press, and I am to have a copy for that purpose. I read to him also, an uncommon poem, in the Weekly Express and Guardian called "The Deserted", which he also spoke highly of. Mrs Ramsbottom and Alice Walker from Tonge, with each a young one were here to tea in the afternoon.

Mima not so well today.

**Tuesday 15th.** Went to Clowes's brewery. Clowes not at home: Saw Mrs Clowes and her mother. Called at the office of Dr Watts, but he was not within: Went to John Heywoods and paid him £1- 1- 0 for last lot of Early Days.

Mima keeps improving slowly.

**Thursday 17th.** Mima complaining of a giddiness: at night she is again blistered.

Mrs Binney, her two very fine children, and servant called. Mr Binney in Scotland.

**Friday 18th.** Took Mrs Binneys parasol, which she had left yesterday, to Cheetham Hill. Called at old friend Prescotts: a nice freshening walk, and a rare trip of discovery for Greaves's dog Lady. Bought a loaf, and part of a leg of mutton at Needhams, Harperhey: the mutton dry and tough, as I afterwards discover.

Mimas head much better.

*Letter*, *Jenny Prescott, Cheetham Hill, to Bamford, 18 October 1861.*

My dear Friends,

I was little aware when I was told of an enquiry after the health of Mr Thos Prescott and myself; from whom that enquiry proceeded. It has indeed been a source of pleasure to find we are still remembered by those we thought had entirely forgotten us. Twice I have written without receiving an answer and feeling you wished to cease all intercourse I wrote no more. I now hope you will soon call again, both if equal to it; for greatly should we enjoy seeing you guests once more at our table.

I am sorry to hear you have both been invalids. I am on the list and have suffered much.

Accept our kindest regards, and believe me,
very sincerely yours,
Jenny Prescott.

---

13. Salis Schwabe (1800–53), of Westphalian Jewish descent, came to the Middleton area in 1832 to found the massive cotton print and dyeworks at Rhodes. Member of the Anti-Corn Law League, friend of Cobden and Mrs Gaskell; see *Manchester Guardian*, 30 July 1853.

**Sunday 20th.** Ramsbottom here in the forenoon; said the worst week for trade he had ever known. Recited one of his poetical pieces. a very good one; only a little too Byronic, in the too frequent repetition of "Fare thee well." After noon, John Mellor and friends took tea, and received my present of books for the Royton Literary Institution.

The noted J.B. Horsefall,[14] late Editor of the Factory Operatives guide (to ruin) as I afterward added, they told me was in America, and doing well, in a money sense; he abandoned his wife and children soon after their arrival, and had now a family by another woman. His wife and children were also doing well, being settled at Buffalo.

**Monday 21st.** Travis from Hollinwood was here: not in good health: he took tea, and his visit gave us much pleasure.

Mima slowly recovering.

**Tuesday 22nd.** Called on Dr Watts at Manchester; he had consulted with David Chadwick, and Morris, and they both were of opinion that to attempt a subscription for the publication of my books, would, under the present condition of trade, and of the country generally, be futile. He was strengthened in this opinion by the reception which the subscription to Milner Gibson's testimonial was responded to: persons who were accounted rich, and were known to be friends to popular instruction failed in promoting the acknowledgement to Mr Gibson, in a manner which their known predilections justified an expectation of: So Dr Watts, who is a strong party man, of the Milner Gibson, and so called "Manchester School" argued that because Milner Gibson's testimonial did not proceed as it should have done; a subscription for the republication of Samuel Bamford's books would, in Manchester, fall to the ground. I reminded Dr Watts that I had never been very expectant on the subject of my subscription, and he was now satisfied but remarked that persons who were realising great sums of <u>money</u> by the repeal of the paper duty, refused, or neglected, to subscribe to Mr Gibson's testimonial.

The idea of canvassing for the publication of my works had been, therefore abandoned by these friends of mine: such having been determined on Dr Watts had not quested either of the Heywoods as to what they would charge for the whole lot of vols which they separately held in their stocks.

Dr Watts had seen and conversed with Mr Bazley a few days ago, and he was of opinion that nothing would be done by Palmerston, in the way of pension for me: in that case I said, I must appeal to the House of Commons, but the usual time of publication in the newspapers had not yet expired. Dr Watts thought that appeal to the

---

14. J.B. Horsfall (dates not known), Royton weaver, Chartist and trade unionist, and a long-standing opponent of Bamford's. The two engaged in an extended newspaper dispute in the *Manchester Examiner and Times* from February to May 1852, in which Horsfall questioned Bamford's accounts of his early radical activity. The *Factory Operatives Guide and Labourers Advocate* was a short-lived newspaper published at the time of the 1853 Preston strike, in which Horsfall took a leading part. In the later 1850s he emigrated to the America, but he returned in 1866.

Commons would be of no effect, if I petitioned for money. I should not get it: Whether I got it or not, I would, if need were, try it. I would endeavour to clear my way, and know, either that the Government would be just and grant me compensation, or that they would not, and in the latter case I would strive to know <u>why</u> they would not. I would not continue to live in a state of mystification. Dr Watts said the proper course would be to petition for a Committee to enquire into my case: and I said I would do so.

Called at David Morris's, but he was not within; at Grants temperance place they said he was not there; and the room was so dim with smoke that I could not see whether he was or not.

Came home by 'bus, and brought a quart of paraffin oil from Heatons.

**Thursday 24th.** The annexed came to hand.[15]

***Letter***, *Robert Kershaw, Royton, to Bamford, 23 October 1861.*

Sir,

I enclose a resolution passed at a Meeting convened for transacting the business of our Institution, and hope you will accept the same with our best wishes for your future welfare.

On behalf of the members of the Royton Literary Institution, I am,
Yours truly,
Robert Kershaw
Secretary.

***Resolution slip.***

Royton Literary Institute, October 21st 1861.
Resolved that the best thanks of the members of the Institution be tendered to Mr Samuel Bamford for his liberal gift of the Books which he has thought proper to bestow on this Institution; and that our Secretary be requested to send a copy of the resolution to him and enter the same in our Minute Book.
President
James Pickup.

Census of 1851, Population, Educational. Religious. Trade and Professions, Criminal. With various tables and accounts of great use.[16]

Found Ramsbottom['s] fine poem "The Destitute" thrust under the door when I came downstairs this morning.

---

15. A note by Bamford is added on lined exercise book paper: "Royton Literary Institution. Vote of thanks for books."
16. Bamford's note; purpose unclear.

George Nelson, who married my sisters daughter called at the close of eve: he was going to tea at the residence of one McKenna (Booth Cottage.) This was the first time that G.N. has darkened my door since I came to live in Mosston: he might as well never come; for he has never yet been the man who has asked about our welfare, or mooted any subject or matter relative to our condition in life.

**Saturday 26th.** Went to Cheetham Hill and found my esteemed friend Mrs Prescott in excellent health and spirits, though as she informed me, much reduced in means of living, they having lost by some misfortune, which she did not explain, nor did I ask, as much as 400 pounds a year of the income they once had.

Went into the Chapel yard and looked for dear lost Catharines grave but did not find it. Nor could the Sexton direct me to it.

Returned home by the field road, by Crumsall[17] hall, and near the place where once stood the farm house (Crumsall Green) where Catharine once dwelt, and where I went to see her: the site of the house, the farm stead, and yard now all cleared and swept away. Catharine too disappeared and I too shall soon do the same.

**Sunday 27th.** Ramsbottom came in good time, and I read over his poem "The Destitute", and offered some suggestions for improvements: but he is tenacious of his own original conceptions, and I found much difficulty in moving him to my views. Lindley Murray was appealed to.[18] Ramsbottom adhered to what I knew to be erroneous conclusions. I advised him to send his poem, which is, on the whole, an excellent one, to some of the London publications, but he seemed chary on that point.

**Monday 28th.** At Middleton, learned on conversation with Old Liddle, that Jimmy Harrison, (Sharp Jimmy) died from an operation on a strangulated hernia: the operation performed by Oswald Dickin, and a Mr Kershaw of Royton: he survived two days only.

**Thursday 31st.** Ramsbottom was here as soon as I came down stairs this morning. He had seen a copy of a spiteful doggrel piece called "Tim Bobbins Ghost" and asked me about the author of it, and what could have given him occasion to pen such a thing. So I told him a truthful, but certainly damaging story about George Richardson and how in revenge for my not[19] having exposed his dishonesty in the Testimonial Collecting affair, he thought fit to attack me in doggrel rhyme.

Ramsbottom afterwards recited to me a very striking poem, which he had thrown together on Sunday afternoon, called "Out of Work". I advised him to let it go to the press; it would attract attention and do good to the operatives whether employed or non employed: So I am to have a copy to give to the newspapers.

---

17. Crumpsall.
18. Lindley Murray's *An English Grammar*.
19. The 'not" is clearly an error by Bamford.

***Manuscript*** *of Ramsbottom's poem. The first and last verses run as follows.*

### Eawt o'work[20]

Aw'va a little sad tale folks, to tell,
Its bin towd you by plenty afore:
Un plenty ull know it full weel
Before this next winther is o'er
Eawr mesther has lockt up his mill,
Un beawt wark, you known weel ther's no bráss
Un beawt brass ther's no meight un theerfore
Eawr case is a hard un, by th' Máss,

... To th'poor Box aw went yesterday[21]
Un to get summat eawt hard aw thried
Bo th'big wigs they o'shook ther yeds
Un sed aw'd best goo "i'th'inside":
So to th'Bastile aw'm beawn uppo th'broo
Un theer aw'st ha't wear eawt my time
Its mooar like a prison nor a whoam
Un poverty's threated like crime.

Nov. 1861 Harperheigh.

Mrs Binney, her sister, and young heir, came this afternoon. They are, it seems, from the County of Salop: but the sister has some expectations of being married and settling in this neighbourhood.

**Friday 1st November.** Went to Manchester but neither Dr Watts nor Mr Cooke were at their respective offices, so took a glass of hot whisky toddy at the Star Inn and came home.

**Saturday 2nd.** Dr Watts gave me five pounds, and the clerk at Mr Bazley's, one pound.

**Sunday 3rd.** Morn. Ramsbottom brought me a copy of his poem The Destitute. Grimshaw and Mary Ann here at night.

---

20. Written in a hand other than Bamfords, presumably Ramsbottom's, and inserted several leaves later. A revised version was published in Ramsbottom's *Phases of Distress: Lancashire Rhymes* (Manchester, 1864), 15–22.
21. The previous first line, unfinished and deleted, runs: "to th'Bastile aw'm beawn" ...

**Tuesday 5th.** A book called The man of the people, is lent me: the first time I had heard of it; written by William Howitt, and published by Hurst and Blackett. 1860. 3 vols.[22]

The annexed slip, taken from the book, (the Editors introductory remarks and concluding paragraph excepted) appears in the Middleton Albion of Saturday the 9th.

*Cutting, from the* Middleton Albion, *9 November 1861.*

---

### LEADERS OF WORKING MEN FORTY-FIVE YEARS AGO

In a work recently published in London, entitled "the Man of the People," our Middleton political leader, whom we are always proud to own, is described along with Philip Stanton and Adam Criche, – two other zealous advocates of peaceful reform. The last two named are on a tour amongst the distressed operatives of the northern districts, who had been almost goaded to outrage by the incendiary harangues of men of the class of Oliver, the spy, and his co-operators.

"... And especially was Philip pleased with a silk weaver, who invited him to his humble tenement, and introduced him, with much pride, to his neat, comely wife and blooming little daughter. This young man, named Samuel Bamford, who has since become widely known for his poetry, and his "Life of a Radical," was then unknown except to his own neighbourhood, but was equally a poet, and a sagacious politician. Bamford was a rather muscularly-built man, of intelligent countenance and lively grey eyes. There was the self possession of a man, conscious of superior ability in his air, – though his dress was like that of his class – a brown, somewhat coarse, and thread-bare coat, light waistcoat, and Kerseymere smalls, worsted stockings, and strong hob-nailed shoes. Yet under that guise, Philips saw a man of singularly shrewd sense, and a knowledge beyond his station. He had a strong feeling of his own clear headedness, and exercised as strong an influence over his fellow-workmen. These men had engaged an unused Methodist Chapel for their meetings, and there, Philip not only addressed them himself, but heard Bamford and others deliver speeches that did them the greatest honour. Bamford was as energetic as Philip himself in advocating peaceable agitation, and pointed out the certain mischief of any attempt at physical force.

"It was a cordial to Philip to find such men as these sprinkled amongst these teeming hoards of humanity. But it was when on a Sunday afternoon he made a long walk with Adam and Bamford through the neighbouring copses and over the grey craggy moors, that he saw all the soul of poetry which lived in the souls of such men, and coursed along like the clear sparkling waters down their moor land channels. There Bamford repeated his "Hours in the Bowers," and exclaimed 'and what want we here but food to eat and raiment to put on? Give us but the

---

22. A fictional sketch of Bamford appears in volume iii of Howitt's *A Man of the People*, pp. 54–7 and 95–8; the essential section is here extracted. There are minor divergences from the original text, significant perhaps only at the start of the paragraph, which in the book reads: "Equally was he pleased with a silk-weaver at Middleton ...". Later (pp. 95–8) Criche encounters Bamford again, this time withdrawing to the hills with Dr Healy after news of an imminent attempted rising, "the wisest and soundest-headed of the artisan reformers thus fleeing from the impending evil".

simplest requirements of life, and liberty to boot, and the Lancashire mechanic, with his home and family, his book, his paper, and his moorland walks, will not envy the lord in his hall, or the king on his throne."

If our veteran patriots are thus celebrated during life, what may not be said of them when death has silenced alike friend and foe: when justice shall make known the whole truth of their lives: and when their calumniators and abettors of calumny shall receive the full measure of their infamy.

---

**Sunday 10th.** Mills sends me three copies of the Albion – very good.

The following notice of the death of a bad malicious man is from the Albion of the 10th.[23]

*Notice, from the* Middleton Albion, *9 November 1861, of the death of Thomas Smithies of Wood Street, Middleton, a former deputy constable of the town.*

**Friday 15th.** Walked to Middleton, thence to the Railway Inn Tonge, where I got a good Welch Rabbit and then started home, walking the whole way, but felt rather too much worked up.

**Saturday 16th.** Cassells, I see is quoting freely from My Life of a Radical, in his cheap History of England. These quotations, in which my book is honestly acknowledged as an authority, should be the means of selling a large number of copies; half of the edition I should think, yet I scarcely expect that "Abel Anything," the honourable Alderman will acknowledge to having sold a dozen extra copies; we shall see how he moves.

**Sunday 17th.** Ramsbottom was here, and agreed to let me give his poem "Eawt O Work" to the Manchester papers.

**Friday 22nd.**[24] Got my five pound note, which I wished to have stored till the 1st December, changed, and took Ramsbottoms poem to the Examiner and Times Office; to call on Tuesday for a proof. Saw Mr Greenwell at Belfields: Belfield is leaving his house on Tuesday.

**Sunday 24th.** Ramsbottom came expecting to see a proof of his poem: he will come again on Tuesday evening.

Dronsfield and wife were here to tea. Dronsfield urged me to place my literary property, both books and MS. in the care of trustees, so that if I should die suddenly. or become incapacitated, they might be applied in accordance with my directions, previously made known. A very good suggestion and one I should carry into effect, if

---

23. Actually the 9th.
24. Dated "23 Fri" in error.

I only knew, who to select as trustees. I must think about the matter, as indeed I have often done already. Dronsfield, at going away left, and would leave half a crown on my wife's lap. She would have returned it, we felt it was too much from a poor working black smith.

**Tuesday 26th.** Saw Mr Dunckley, the Editor, at the Examiner Office, and he said himself and Mr Peacock had read Ramsbottoms poem "Eawt O'work," and duly considering all parts, they were of opinion that it was too much in arrear of public opinion and sentiment for admission to their columns. I said I thought it was in advance of public sentiment: but they, of course, were the judges of its fitness for their paper. It was concluded that the copy should be returned to me, by post.

**Wednesday 27th.** The copy of Ramsbottoms poem did not come by post this morning, and I went to the Examiner Office where I saw Mr Ireland, who made a note of mem[orandum] for Mr Peacock, to send me the poem by the post that evening.

**Thursday 28th.** Ramsbottoms poem comes to hand this morning inclosing the annexed note.

*Letter*, *H.B. Peacock, Daily Examiner and Times Office, 1 Pall Mall Court, Manchester, to Bamford, 27 November 1861.*

> My dear M^r Bamford,
> Mr Dunckley and myself have read the inclosed and considered the propriety of its insertion. There is, in my humble opinion, excellent lines in it, but it also contains what we can scarcely accept, if we are to act consistently with the general views of the journal.
>     I regret this very much, as it would have given all of us who are workers here, much pleasure to find your pen at work in our columns.
>                     Always faithfully,
>                     H.B. Peacock.

I had intended to have given the poem to the Guardian, but on second thoughts, I concluded to place it in my Diary, as a sample of thoughts and language which our liberal newspaper editors are afraid to lay before their readers. Our boasted "Free press", after all is a cowardly press, and shrinks from giving free and honest expression to the popular sentiment on matters connected with what is called religion, and religious teachers.

**Sunday 1st December.** Potter and Brierley were both here in the evening, and we had much conversation about literary matters, both agreeing with me, that ample material for a very interesting work might be found in the anecdotes and traditions of the reform days of 1815 to 1819; and Brierley said, chiefly in reference to what had appeared in the "Man of the People," and was now currently put forth in Cassells Cheap History of England, that it was probable some of the London litteratuers, would be down here before long, lodging, or rather becoming the guests of the big moneyed snobs at Manchester, and picking up from them and their visitors, materials for a work on that interesting period.

I rather think Brierley had seen the Article about Phillip Stanton, Adam Criche, and myself in the Middleton Albion.

Brierley is sick of Oldham: his wife declares she wont stop there; and Potter would like very much to live in this neighbourhood: he little knows what a miserable set of Church going, and Chapel going, narrow minded, ignorant, and prejudiced beings they are.

**Monday 2nd.** Went to Manchester to draw my monthly dole. Watts had not the whole sum which he wished me to receive, so I was to call again either in two hours, or tomorrow. I chose the latter, and after receiving my one pound from Mr Bazley's cashier, I purchased a rabbit and came home.

**Tuesday 3rd.**[25] Dr Watts was not in the office when I called; his young man said he was gone round the corner to a Mr Megsons and would return in a minute. He soon came and gave me five sovereigns and a receipt as follows, which I signed.

"2d Dec^r 1861
Received from John Watts, five pounds on Account of Mr Bamford's subscription."

In conversation afterwards, he took occasion to inform me that he had not seen Mr Bazley since a few evenings past, when he came [to] a meeting in the Mayors Carriage, with the Mayor and Mr Bazley: he also said he was going to Liverpool the day following to serve on the jury; but would speak to the judge, and try to get exempted.

**Wednesday 4th.**[26] Mima much better, going about and doing odd jobs in the house, but in the afternoon she fell down one or two steps of the stairs and hurt her head, and sprained her left ancle. She was so helpless I feared she had suffered another parylatic stroke, but it proved not so bad; though she was and still continues lame, with much pain[27] of the injured part.

**Thursday 5th.**[28] Mima still lame and complaining grievously. I have bathed the ancle in hot water and rubbed it with a bottle I got from Mrs Greaves, and it is better.

**Saturday 7th.** Mrs Binney and her son "little Willie" called in the afternoon and brought a present of a pork pie and a nice piece of spare rib; very kind. Mima still lame, but mending.

**Sunday 8th.** Ramsbottom here in the morning: seemingly concerned about his little girl, who is ill of the scarlet fever; Jane Grimshaw calls at night.

---

25. Bamford has written "2nd" in error.
26. Bamford has written "3d" in error.
27. Bamford has written "paint".
28. Bamford has written "4th" in error.

**Wednesday 11th.** Dr Pegge called and saw Mimas ancle; said it was neither bone broken nor disjointed, but a tendon was lacerated: to bathe with warm water, and bind it with a broad roller, not too tightly; he will call again when coming this way.

**Thursday 12th.** Did as ordered; the swelling and inflammation are much abated, and the pain gone, except when she presses on the left foot.

**Friday 13th.** Mimas foot still better, but she is very low spirited, pitiably distressed about imaginary wants, and intimates – as she often has done – a wish for self destruction. I try to cheer and comfort her, and find a cup of good tea does her good.

**Sunday 15th.** Dronsfield, Travis and Lees, from Hollinwood spent a few hours very agreeably.

**Monday 16th.** Prince Albert died on the 14th; a good man; a great loss to his family and the nation.

**Tuesday 17th.** Joe Fielding, the lying newspaper reporter of Middleton (Tonge) died at three o'clock this morning. A bad-hearted malicious person was he.

**Letter**, *Thomas Mills, Middleton, to Bamford, 18 December 1861.*[29]

My dear Mr Bamford,
We are just at this moment surrounded and enveloped with subjects of a most sorrowful and pitiable nature. I have scarcely time to detail to you everything in connection therewith, but if you have time to stop over I should be glad to see you.
　　Mr Howarth is at Liverpool assizes seeking redress from the man who is charged with seducing his daughter whilst on the other hand the man so charged has entered a cross action against Mr Howarth for libel. The former it is said claims damages £2000 and the latter £3000.
　　We have several very sudden deaths awfully so in one or two cases. A man named Solomon Pownall was found dead in bed a day or two ago. Thos Blomeley of High Barn farmer died on Sunday morning but the most awful is the case of Joseph Fielding the Reporter and Schoolmaster he died this morning about 3 o'clock. Last night he went to a meeting at the primitive methodist school to take notes of the proceedings which were respecting the abatement of silk weavers wages by Harrop, Taylor & Co.
　　I am extremely sorry to say that Fielding took occasion to enlist the contempt of the crowded meeting against ourselves. You will perhaps have noticed re this the par[agraph] in the Albion of last Saturday on trade in which it says that the silk winders at Kemps were earning on an average 17/- per week &c. &c. Fielding took advantage of the opportunity to hold this up to the opprobrium of those

---

29. The letter dated 18th, but the envelope postmarked 17th.

present at the meeting and whilst in the act of doing so or on sitting down he was cut down by an apoplectic stroke. He was conveyed quickly from the meeting got home as soon as possible where he lingered till the time mentioned.

I am most truly sorry for the circumstance the solemnity and dreadful nature of the event restrain my worse feelings and cannot although an ill was intended to me yet for the sake of those near and dear to him I say I am sorry for him.

Excuse more till I see you

Yours most truly

Tho$^s$ Mills.

**Wednesday 18th.** Mima better today.

**Thursday 19th.** Walked to Middleton and back, cut a willow from Anns grave on the 21st, stuck it down in Mr Greaves's garden.

**25, Xmas Day:** Miss Taylor brought us some Xmas greenery, and two very nice and good mince patties; the good lady.

**Thursday 26th.** A letter arrives from Sir James Kay Shuttleworth, containing an order on the Manchester and Salford Bank for five pounds. I thought Sir James had forgotten me, as many of my "friends" have done, but I am

*End of diary.*

# APPENDIX 1

# SAMUEL BAMFORD:
# RIGHT AGAINST WRONG

*Bamford's diaries contain four versions of his circular: 28 March 1859, 27 June 1859, 15 November 1859, and 7 August 1860. The following version is based upon the first one, dated 28 March 1859 and printed in the* Middleton Albion *for 2 April. The footnotes indicate variations in later versions, and substantial additions are given as appendices. Unless stated, these alterations and additions are retained in later versions. Minor changes of grammar and phrasing are ignored. Taken together, the alterations show a change from the earlier versions, headed "Samuel Bamford", designed to advertise Bamford's return to the area and his services as a public reader, to the later versions headed "Right Against Wrong" and focused on winning support for his claim to compensation.*

SAMUEL BAMFORD, the Lancashire Bard and Old Druid, for such he has been aptly termed, and the earliest English political sufferer now living, was one of a small band of parliamentary reformers who, in 1816, founded an association at Middleton, called the Hampden Club. In 1817 he was deputed to attend a meeting at the Crown and Anchor Tavern, London, when he attracted attention by demonstrating the practicability of universal suffrage, and thereby engaging Mr. Cobbett's powerful influence in the support of that principle of parliamentary reform. When, in the same year, the *Habeus Corpus* act was suspended, he was arrested, by virtue of a secretary of state's warrant, on suspicion of high treason; was chained and conveyed, under an escort of dragoons and constables, through the townships of Tonge, Chadderton, Oldham, Failsworth, Newton, and Manchester, to the New Bailey prison at the latter place; and was, on the following morning, with seven others, heavily chained, and, guarded by king's messengers and police officers, sent off to London. On their arrival at the police office in Bow-st, their chains were removed, but the prisoners remained strictly guarded, and were at night chained to their bed-posts. On the following day he was, with the others, taken before the privy council, and remanded to Coldbath Fields prison. He was afterwards produced at five different times before the privy council, when no charge having been substantiated against him, he was liberated and sent home. In 1819 he was again one of the leaders of a vast movement in favour of parliamentary reform and free trade, and headed a procession from Middleton and Rochdale of ten thousand sober, respectable, working people, besides a great multitude who accompanied them, to the meeting on St. Peter's Field, at Manchester. He remained on the field until the meeting was attacked and broken up by the military, when he narrowly escaped the sabres of the yeomanry. Ten days afterwards he was again arrested on a charge of high treason, was again chained and guarded by a military force, both of horse and foot, in addition to a body of police constables; was a second time conducted to the New Bailey at Manchester, and the charge of high treason having been abandoned, he was charged with sedition and conspiracy, and was, with other prisoners, conveyed in chains to Lancaster Castle, whence, after several days detention, he was liberated on bail. At the March assizes following, at York, he conducted his own defence with an ability, a manner, and a testimony, which elicited for him a most favourable summing up by the judge, and the direct commendation of the prosecuting counsel. He was, however, one of five who were convicted of having attended an illegal meeting, and consequently, though with very limited resources, he had to travel to London in fulfilment of his bail, and making his appearance before the judges in the Court of King's Bench, he was sentenced to twelve months' imprisonment in Lincoln Castle. From the presence of the judges he was taken to the King's Bench prison, where after the lapse of a few days, he was once more confined by chains and conveyed to Newark, where the chains having been removed for a temporary purpose, he refused again to submit to them, and the remainder of the journey was performed without manacles. On the expiration of his sentence of imprisonment he left the castle at Lincoln, with the good opinion and commendation of the authorities of the place, and, taking his wife's arm; they walked home together.[1]

Thus, for honestly, consistently, and constitutionally promoting parliamentary reform and free trade, both of which measures have since been sanctioned by law, have been approved of by some of those who punished him for seeking their introduction, and which measures are now subjects of gratulation to great statesmen and the whole country,[2] he was twice arrested on charges of high treason; he was five times taken before the privy council;[3] he was on five different occasions conducted in chains to distant parts[4] of the country; he stood a trial of ten days, defending himself with a manner and a testimony which brought credit on himself and the cause he represented; and, as will be seen, for advocating a good measure[5] in the worst of times, he has been confined in a greater number of prisons (seven times[6] in six different ones) than, on like charges, any other Englishman has been.[7]

Such is a summary of the political life of Samuel Bamford, the last survivor of those reformers who, both in 1817 and 1819, were the victims of contumely, outrage, and unjust condemnation. The wrongs of those days have not been righted, – the injuries he suffered in mind, body, and estate, have not been redressed; instead of that, others have been added; and because he has been too independent, too incorruptible for mere party; because he would pursue the even tenor of a manly and upright course,

---

1. In June 1859, this entire first paragraph is replaced by addition A below. In November 1859, this in turn is replaced by addition B. Some of the material on Bamford's political career cut from the first version is covered in the addenda to the final version (addition E).
2. November 1859: "both of which ... whole country" omitted, the sense being covered by addition D below.
3. November 1859: "taken in custody before the Privy Council".
4. June 1859: "various and distant parts".
5. June 1859: "advocating good measures".
6. November 1859: "nine times".
7. In November 1859, a new paragraph is inserted, addition D below.

despising flattery and subserviency on the one hand, and the brawling of faction[8] on
the other, for adhering to measures rather than men, he has incurred the unfriendly
reserve of many whose party views he would not adopt.[9] Still he has not complained;
[he] has awaited his opportunity,[10] and now, with honest pride, he beholds Lancashire,
in common with the whole nation, enjoying benefits resulting from his endurance forty
years ago.[11] The great mass of the people, as well as many of their rulers and
legislators, are now felicitating themselves on the changes which he laboured to
introduce, and for striving to introduce which, some who are now honoured and
powerful in the land joined in denouncing and punishing him. Political martyrs, come
from whencesoever they may, are now welcomed, sheltered, and sustained by the
generous reformed people of England, and if "a still small voice" be heard, intimating
that one of *their own community* "remains unrequited," shall it be deemed an
unseasonable observation?[12]

Thus, Samuel Bamford, in the 72nd year of his age, and after forty years delay,
remains unrequited; and now, when the country is resounding with orations is favour
of reform; when the people are impatient for their rights, and will assuredly obtain a
portion of them; and when political suffering is a sure passport to kindest national
attention, he thinks he may, with honest confidence and becoming self-respect, remind
his countrymen that he also has been a sufferer, and that he awaits such compensation
for past endurance as the nation may award.[13] Meantime, as a mode for honest
subsistence he is ready to enter into engagements for readings and recitations from his
own works, and those of other authors; for readings from the works of the Lancashire

---

8. June 1859: "mere faction".
9. June 1859: "he incurred the detractive envy of the mean and base, and the unkind reserve of that class
   of friends who always ignore the unfortunate, or those they deem to be such". In November 1859 the
   whole section "instead of that ... deem to be such" is omitted.
10. June 1859, this phrase replaced by: "he would not stoop to that; he has awaited the progress of events,".
    In November 1859 this is expanded to: "he would not stoop to that; complaint is for those only whom it
    may compensate, and he is not of that class. He has awaited the development of his own life, and the
    course of public events, until the harvest which, 'in ruder times and darker days' he helped to prepare, is
    being gathered in. There is a holiday of freedom and plenty in the land,". In August 1860, it is again
    expanded to: "... he is not of that class; but with steadfast purpose, and perfect certitude of ultimate
    right, he has awaited ...".
11. November 1859: "resulting from the endurance and labours of himself and his fellow patriots forty years
    ago".
12. In November 1859 this last sentence is omitted and a fresh paragraph begun, with a first sentence
    added: "Long may this jubilee continue, (alas that hovering around should be other possibilities) and
    long may the people of England, knowing thus the value of free institutions, promote that sound
    knowledge which leads to their wise extension".
13. In June 1859, this sentence is re-arranged to fit at the end of the previous paragraph, and the final
    phrase after "sufferer" is omitted. This is followed by addition C, advertising Bamford's literary works.
    In November 1859 it is revised again to read: "SAMUEL BAMFORD meanwhile, in the seventy second
    year of his age, and after forty years delay of just compensation, conforming to the social rule that for a
    honest subsistence, honest exertion of some sort shall be applied, adopts a vocation for which his years
    and capacity qualify him".

poets, and prose writers generally; from the dialect of Tim Bobbin, with observations and strictures on the same; he would also hold meetings, to be carried on by interrogation and reply, under proper regulations; would state his views on youthful training, which, if properly carried out, would leave workhouses and prisons uninhabited; he would speak on parliamentary reform, which is not yet understood; and lastly, he would read in its true sense – the Gospel of Jesus Christ, which contains the essential of all improvement in morals, politics, and religion. If the public only encourage such performances, and bestow on them a moderate portion of that attention which has been lavishly bestowed on others, the required compensation will be secured, and justice will be satisfied.[14]

Mosston, Harpurhey, 28th March, 1859.[15]

*Additions*

*A. (June 1859): revised introduction.*

The story of SAMUEL BAMFORD, the Lancashire Bard and Old Druid, as he has been, and may be, aptly termed, forms a remarkable chapter in the romance of real human life. He is the oldest poet in the county, if not in England; is the oldest known parliamentary reformer, and is certainly the oldest English political sufferer now living.

---

14. In June 1859, the final two sentences are replaced by the following short paragraph: "For the present, as a means for earning an honest and respectable sustenance, he purposes readings and recitations from the above works, and those of other authors; from the works of the Lancashire poets and prose writers generally; from the dialect of Tim Bobbin, with observations on the same; he would on these occasions encourage interrogation by questions previously submitted in writing; would state his opinions on youthful training, which if properly carried out would leave workhouses and prisons uninhabited; and if questioned, would speak on parliamentary reform, which is not yet either fully understood, or justly appreciated." Ms. alterations on a copy inserted in the diary in early August 1859 change "an honest" to "a honest" (a dialect amendment) and delete the phrase "by questions previously submitted in writing". Only the first of these ms. alterations is carried through to the November 1859 version.

15. The four versions each end differently. In June 1859 an additional last section reads:
"Orders for books or engagements for literary exercises, may be addressed, Samuel Bamford, Mosston, Harperhey, Manchester.
A Photographic Likeness, or Stereoscopic Slide, with autograph, One Shilling each.
June 27th 1859."
In November 1859, this is replaced with:
"These exercises and conversation will afford to those who are disposed to support right against wrong, opportunities for evincing their approval of the course which Mr Bamford has pursued, and the means he is exercising for the sustainment of a useful and talented profession.
*Mosston, Harperhey, Manchester, 15th Novr., 1859."*
In August 1860, "for the sustainment of" becomes "for sustainment by", and the final sentence is altered to read: "opportunities for evincing their just and honourable preference, by countenancing Mr. Bamford's endeavours to dispense useful and interesting information". A four-page "Addenda" follows, addition E below.

*B. (November 1859): further revised introduction, with new title.*

RIGHT AGAINST WRONG

------OO------

To whomsoever may feel interested in the support of Right against Wrong.

If Parliamentary Reform and Free Trade have been conducive of good to the people of Britain, those amongst them who laboured long and suffered much in the obtainment of such measures have a just claim to the grateful attention of their fellow-subjects.

Of the few who so laboured and suffered, and who still survive, SAMUEL BAMFORD stands the most prominent. He is the oldest poet in the county, if not in England; he is the oldest historically known radical reformer; and he is certainly the oldest English political sufferer now living.

*C. (June 1859 only): literary announcements.*

His literary productions have been extensively read, and uniformly quoted with commendation. "Bamford has much of the rich old well of English undefiled in his poetry," said the *Manchester Guardian*. "What poet might not have been proud to have written the poem on the death of Canning?" said *Tait's Magazine*. "Hath the spirit of the classic Grey descended on a Lancashire weaver, or did he of the 'Ode to the Passions' meet him at the handloom, and throw his inspiring mantle over him?" *Ibid*. "We incline to an opinion, that his 'God help the poor' is a poem of the highest order of poetical ability." *Spectator*. "Few, we are persuaded, can read Bamford's poems without sympathizing warmly with his kindly and affectionate breathings and feelings, and their hearts beating in unison with his patriotic lays." *Manchester Advertiser*.

Of his *Life of a Radical*, the following favourable opinions, among many others, have been given:–

"It throws new light on a very important period of our history; it explains events which can never lose their interest in a commercial community. – *Athenaeum*.

"He has been confined in more prisons for the cause of freedom than any Englishman living. Some of his best poetry was written in these prisons." – *Tait's Magazine*.

"Instead, however, of being the production of a soured or disappointed politician, it is the work of an imaginative, and even poetic mind; we have rarely met with a more agreeable writer." – *Anti Corn Law Circular*.

"His arrest, and that of his comrade – their journey, and examination before the Privy Council, are told with an effect which gives to their narrative far more interest than would be felt in reading the most amusing work of mere fiction." – *Bolton Free Press*.

"We want more men like this Lancashire Radical; – devotees of principle rather than those who merely profess it. We have had too much of man-worship, and it bitter fruits, already. And oh! how its nature and its bitter fruits are shown in the volume before us." – *Sheffield Iris*.

His Published Works are – **Early Days**, 1 vol. 2s. 6d.; **Passages in the Life of a Radical**, 2 volumes in one, 4s. 6d.; **Lancashire Dialect**, Corrected, 1 vol. **Poems**, 1 vol.; and **Walks in South Lancashire**, 1 vol. The three first works being in print, Mr. Bamford will be able to supply copies to order; and for the two last, he will be happy to receive orders with a view to a corrected and enlarged publication. Poems 1s. 6d., and Walks in South Lancashire, 3s. 6d.

*D. (November 1859). Additional paragraph.*

With pride and satisfaction he repeats this statement, that on nine separate occasions, and within the precincts of six different places of confinement, was he yielded up the victim of unjust laws, despotically administered. Never before was an Englishman, and never again will an Englishman be so immolated for such a cause. Parliamentary Reform has been wrested from the usurpers; the starvation corn laws have been erased from the statute books; the curtain has fallen on that act of the drama, and another is in progress.

*E. (August 1860). Addenda.*

## ADDENDA.

SAMUEL BAMFORD promoted parliamentary reform and free trade by becoming in 1816 the chief founder, the chief reader, and the chief secretary of the Middleton Hampden Club, the object of which was to obtain a reform of the Commons House, and a repeal of the taxes on food.

In 1817 he attended as a delegate, a meeting at the Crown and Anchor Tavern, London, and attracted notice by demonstrating the practicability of carrying into effect a suffrage extended to every male of 21 years of age, whereby he won over the powerful advocacy of Mr. Cobbett, who had previously supported household suffrage only; and secured the passing of a motion by the meeting for the more extended franchise. In Cobbett's Weekly Political Pamphlet of February 22nd. 1817, in "a letter to Earl Grosvenor," the occurrence is stated as follows:–

"Some persons in the meeting agreed with me, but the majority were clearly on the other side, though my objections had, as I thought, not been removed. At last, a very sensible and modest man, whose name I am sorry I have forgotten, and who came from *Middleton* in Lancashire, got up, and gave an answer to my objections in somewhat theses words:– 'Sir, I cannot see all, or any of the difficulties which Mr. Cobbett believes to exist in the way of taking an election upon the principles of universal suffrage. I have seen with how much exactness the lists of all male inhabitants in every parish, *inmates* as well as *householders*, have been made out under the *Militia Laws*, and I see no reason why regulations, which have been put in force universally for calling us forth to bear arms in defence of the country, and of the estates, and property of the country, should not be put in force again, and by the very same officers, for calling us forth to exercise our right of suffrage at elections.' This was enough says Cobbett, for me. The thing had never struck me before."

Soon after this meeting, in 1817, he was by authority of a warrant from the Secretary of State, arrested on suspicion of high treason, and was five times taken in custody before the privy council, when nothing being found against him, he was discharged.

On his last appearance he pleaded his own cause and that of the poor as follows:–
"My Lord, if you think proper to wait for information that will establish a charge of high treason against me, your lordship may wait for ever, as I am certain that no such truthful information will ever arrive. He also stated that his conduct had been the opposite of treasonable; though he had done all that lay in his power to forward the cause of reform, he had always done it openly; that he did not think His Majesty's ministers were properly acquainted with the situation of the country; that he did not see how they could be, considering the partial channels through which, it appeared to him, they derived their information; that the gentry, or what were called 'the higher classes,' were too proud, or too indifferent to examine minutely into the abodes of poverty and distress, and that many of them were interested in returning false or partial statements of things; that the poor would be content if they could procure, by hard labour, the necessities of life, but that they could not do, even by their utmost exertions; that if His Majesty's ministers were thoroughly acquainted with the state of the country, they would be surprised that it was not a scene of confusion and bloodshed. He said far more than this, but as he had not the means of committing the particulars to writing, he gave a few of the heads which he remembered."

On the 4th day of his trial at York, 20th March, 1820, Bamford addressed the court. His speech, though brief, was deeply impressive, and when on the ninth day Mr. Scarlett made his reply to the whole evidence for the defendants, in commenting on that of Bamford, he said:– "When he mentioned the name of that defendant, he could not but express his regret at the situation in which he saw him now placed; he (Mr. Scarlett) admired his talents, and the respectful manner in which he had conducted himself in the course of his defence; and probably others also, as well as himself, were sorry that he was not found in better company." Such was the testimony voluntarily rendered by the leading adverse counsel. The venerable judge also, in his charge on the tenth day, spoke as follows:–

"The next evidence was that relating to Bamford, and it only showed that he recommended peace and order; still he was identified with the placards (inscriptions on the banners) if they (the jury) thought the illegal. If a meeting for considering a reform in parliament be illegal, he is an offender; but it was his lordship's duty to tell them it was not. There was no illegality in carrying sticks, unless they were for an unlawful purpose; nor banners, unless their tenor was such as to excite suspicion of the objects of those who carried them, or concurred in bringing them with an evil intention. As to numbers, they alone did not make a meeting illegal, unless attended with such circumstances as did actually excite terror. Such circumstances were forbidden by the law."

.    .    .    .    .

"With respect to Bamford, all that had been proved in his speech was a recommendation to peace and order. There were no sticks in his groups, save a few common walking sticks carried by old men; there were women and girls in the throng, and it was for the jury to consider whether Bamford and these people, carrying their wives and daughters to such a crowd, meant to create, on that day, riot, tumult, and disorder. With such an intention, nothing was less likely than that they would carry to the scene those who were the dearest objects of their affection. According to the evidence for Bamford, the people in his party, so far from being tumultuous, were peaceable and joyful; and the drilling, as it was called, so far from being illegal and nocturnal, was open and innocent, the only object being merely to enable the people to attend the meeting as conveniently for each other and the public as was possible."

The learned judge then enumerated the names of witnesses who swore that the parties spoken to on the 16th of August went to the meeting in the utmost peace, and conducted themselves while there with equal tranquillity. "There was no act of violence, according to these witnesses, committed by them; no violation of peace which would bring them under the reprehension of the law. *So far in favour of Bamford.*" Notwithstanding all that Mr. Scarlett and the venerable judge had said in Bamford's favour, the stupid and unrighteous jury returned his name amongst those of the guilty, and he was sent to prison.

In 1826, when the starving hand-loom weavers of Burnley, Padiham, Blackburn, and their neighbourhoods, were destroying machinery, delegates were sent by parties wishing for an opportunity to plunder, inviting them to do the same at Heywood, Rochdale, and Middleton. Bamford, having been certified of this, went at his own expense, and on his own responsibility, and meeting a number of the leaders on the hills near Hambledon, he laid such facts and arguments before them as caused them to pause and reflect, and when the main body met the morning following, to begin their enterprise, they could not agree, and the undertaking was abandoned. For doing this, Bamford was denounced as a traitor to the cause of the working men. In the same year also, he became a correspondent of a London daily paper, and his new avocation requiring that he should attend public meetings, courts of justice, and places generally of public resort, it was necessary that he should be more exact in appearance than whilst he was at home at his loom. A couple of clean shirts a week, coat carefully brushed, clean shoes every morning, and a neat neck tie, were changes that could not escape the observation of neighbours, some of whom charitably concluded that he had really now "become a government spy." Inexpressive scorn was his only answer: and, except the approbation of his own conscience, and the contentment of an honest heart, such injurious reflections were the only returns he got for having thus endeavoured to serve others. During thirteen years in which he remained a correspondent of the public press, he never omitted, on all fitting occasions, to plead for the right against the wrong; for the weak against the strong, and for the poor working man especially, whenever with truth and justice he could do so; yet, because he had ceased to be "a weaver," and could earn an honest subsistence without being subject to the dictation and abatements of " a putter out," or of an employer, the working weavers never heartily forgave him; he was not longer "one of them," and being so alienated, the bonds of friendship gradually became relaxed, until on their part coldness supervened, and detraction, the cowardly weapon of the ineffably base, was, by a certain clique, made use of. Thus it is that *miserable envy*, the bane and the canker-rust of the working classes, separates from them the very men whom of all others are the most desirous and the most able to serve them. Such persons would often continue on friendly terms with their former comrades, but they are in very many cases repelled by ungrateful and offensive language and conduct, and thenceforth stand apart.

In 1832 he was compelled to take the office of constable; and in the year of Feargus O'Connor's "plug-drawing holiday," he was a leader of special constables.

In 1851, his friend the late Mr. Wood, chairman of the Board of Inland Revenue, offered him employment at Somerset House, and he, to his great subsequent discomfort and regret, removed to London. In 1857 Mr. Wood died, and in 1858 the following correspondence closed Bamford's connection with government business.

*(The circular reproduces the correspondence between Bamford and L. S. Lyne on 24 April 1858, as set out in the diary.)*

Thus he hopes it will be remembered that he was an early prompter of reform and free trade, which measures have led to the present free and prosperous state of the country; that in striving to introduce those beneficial measures he suffered various and repeated arrests, public exposures, and imprisonments; that a nation is responsible for the acts of its servants or accredited agents, and the nation of this day, or the government on its behalf, is in barest justice bound to rectify and atone for, so far as they can, the errors and crimes of preceeding governments; that the wrongs of his political life have not been righted, nor have the injuries he, and those near and dear to him, suffered, been redressed; and that now, in the 73rd year of his age, after forty years delay, and under the pressure of circumstances which at the present time ought not to have been found existing, he asks for JUST COMPENSATION for his unmerited punishments. The arrear of his grievances has, he feels, stood over too long; and he trusts that the GREATEST, the RICHEST, and the most POWERFUL NATION known to man, will not suffer the just claims of one of the humblest of its citizens to remain unrequited.

*Mosston, Harperhey, 7th August, 1860.*
*T. Mills, Printer and Stationer, Middleton.*[16]

---

16. A ms. note by Bamford on the bottom of the circular reads: The above documents, or extracts from them, are proposed as the grounds of a memorial to the Secretary of State, for Compensation to Mr. Bamford.

# APPENDIX 2

# PARLIAMENTARY REFORM, BY AN OLD RADICAL

*From the* Middleton Albion, *6 November 1858, taken in turn from the* Manchester Examiner and Times, *3 November 1858.*

On Thursday, the 28th ultimo, about forty of the admirers and friends of Mr. Samuel Bamford author of "Passages in the Life of a Radical," and other works, dined together at the Albion Hotel, Bury, T. Grundy. Esq., of Bankfield House, presiding. In responding to the toast of his health, Mr. Bamford gave a sketch of the progress and present position of Parliamentary Reform, as follows:–

"When I first commenced the public advocacy of parliamentary form, and that is upwards of forty years ago, annual parliaments, universal suffrage, and abolition of the corn laws, were the only things asked for. That was in 1816, when Major Cartwright, Wm. Cobbett, and Henry Hunt, were the men who directed the attention of the working classes to the real cause of the many and grievous work and food privations which they endured. Then Hampden Clubs, with their committees, were formed; public meetings were held, the atrociously bad government, corrupt parliament, and oppressive laws were denounced in public speeches, resolutions, and petitions, which, being expressed in unmistakable English, left not any pretence for doubting or misconstruing their meaning. The whole manufacturing, mining, and other operative population of England, Wales, and Scotland, was agitated by its newly-acquired knowledge. The demand reform was loud, unanimous, and astounding to the boroughmongers. The *habeas corpus* act was suspended. Many were arrested, and sent to prison without knowing who their accusers were, or whether any distinct charge was made against them. Then Oliver the spy, with his friend and coadjutor Mitchell, appeared amongst the working men of Lancashire and Yorkshire, and from these two persons, aided by a subordinate residing near Middleton, emanated the secret delegate and plot meetings in Lancashire and Yorkshire, which caused many to be arrested, and ended in the tragedy of Brandreth and his companions at Derby, where three were hung and beheaded, and about a score were transported for life.

"After this came the great meeting on St. Peter's Field, at Manchester, where from nine to thirteen persons were killed, or received their death-wounds; many received wounds and hurts of which they never were cured, and some hundreds were injured by sabre cuts, bludgeoning, and being trampled upon. At this meeting banners were displayed, emblazoned with the words, 'Parliaments annual,' 'Suffrage universal,' 'Vote by ballot,' "No corn laws'. The ballot had become a condition of parliamentary reform, and the corn laws, being a consequence of parliamentary corruption, their repeal would, of course, result from its purification, and henceforth the demand was for annual parliaments, universal suffrage, vote by ballot, and no corn laws.

"I will not remark at length on what took place after the meeting, but many were arrested, tried, and imprisoned on various charges. The grand jury at Lancaster found true bills against parties who had attended the meeting, whilst bills of indictment containing true charges against the real law breakers and aggressors were thrown out of court, rejected. History contains the indelible records of those dark transactions and troublous times,

> When plots were based on cruel fraud,
> And outrage walked at noon abroad,
> And guilt was honoured and rewarded,
> Whilst innocence to jail was guarded;
> And wrong was right, on George's side;
> And truth and justice were denied.

"History being now within the reach of every working man in England who can read, these things will eventually be talked about and understood on every cottage hearth in the land.

"The chartist scheme of reform was sanctioned by Daniel O'Connell, Dr. Bowring, Sir W. Molesworth, J. A. Roebuck, Feargus O'Connor and other political and influential characters, who added three conditions to the old or Cartwright scheme, the said conditions being 'qualifications to sit as member irrespective of property,' 'electoral districts,' 'and 'payment of members.' Thus was produced what they called the charter, there not being, in fact, any charter at all, but only six proposals for a new law. I will, however, for brevitys' sake, call it the chartist plan, and will consider the six points as they stand in the scheme.

"I may observe that latterly a proposal has been made to vary this plan by introducing triennial parliaments for annual ones, and manhood suffrage instead of universal; the term manhood suffrage being certainly more definite than the former one, whilst triennial parliaments would be so slight a variance in principle, that it appears to me more like an evasion than a remedy. Let that pass, however, it is not a matter we shall differ about, since neither annual nor triennial election would, in my opinion, improve the composition or amend the proceedings of the House to make voting by ballot compulsory at all elections for members of parliament.

"We all know or at least we have been told often enough, that, 'for a nation to be free it is sufficient that she wills it.' Now, the first thing in this chartist scheme of reform is, 'annual parliaments,' and as we don't find annual elections taking place, we may conclude the nation does not want them; and sorry should I be, radical as I am, if she did want them. General elections, let them occur whenever they may, are national inflictions, permitted and continued because they are part of what we call our 'glorious old constitution,' and because, old though it be, and some what imperfect mayhap, we can't do without it until another as good or better is found. But though we may object to the frequent recurrence of general elections, it does not follow that we should decline any benefits resulting from elections when they do occur. Short reckonings, we know, tend to lengthened agreements, and frequent agreements between members and their constituents would tend to continued confidence and respect; and, as there appears not to be any demand for annual parliaments, let us try to obtain all the good they would yield, without incurring the pains and penalties which their annual disruption, tumult, and asperity would produce.

"'Where there is a will there is a way,' as we all know, most certainly when Englishmen are concerned for if they once get a notion that a thing should be done, and especially that 'it would pay,' they are sure to do it. Now, for annual parliaments, the electors of Oldham have shown us both the will and the way. Their members are pledged to render account of their stewardship at the end of every session, and I believe they are also pledged to resign should their conduct in parliament not have been satisfactory to the voters. Here, then, is annual accountability for their actions, with annual liability to be displaced; and, consequently all the good that would result from annual elections, without their disadvantages. Short reckonings tend to lengthen friendships, and the member who has only one session to account for will be far more likely to show a satisfactory balance than he who has seven, or even three, to tot up. But to the electors of Oldham, what matters it whether parliaments be of three, seven, or ten years' duration, so long as they and their representatives come together every Michaelmas, and either agree to go on as before or to dissolve the connection? This is something like a straightforward and common sense way of doing business, and if the elections of Oldham can work on this plan – and they can, they are working on it – why cannot those of any other borough, or all the constituencies of this county, or of the nation, do the same.

'The next thing on the list is universal, or manhood suffrage, and that I consider to be already disposed of. When the qualification to sit as members irrespective of property, was granted, manhood suffrage, also, was conceded in principle. Shall John the blacksmith sit in parliament, making laws, whilst Will the bricksetter is not allowed to vote? Nay, shall the blacksmith himself, worthy enough, and wise enough to be a legislator, not be deemed fitting to be a voter? Can so monstrous an absurdity be continued as that the same man shall be qualified to make laws and not qualified to vote at the election of those who make them? When our sapient and thoughtful senators took off the property qualification, they did that which they could not see the end of, they did not perceive that the principle might be applied more ways than one. We have got the concession, however, and let us use it for further national advantage, and so have done with the suffrage question.

"Annual parliaments and universal suffrage thus disposed of, let us pass the vote by ballot, and that, I hope, will be earnestly and unceasingly required until it is gained. On this point all the strength and weight of popular influence should be concentrated, and he who shrinks from his share of the common endeavour, or who shuffles and parleys, when he should be acting, should be deemed unworthy as one who showed defection in the presence of a common enemy. In every constituency committees should be formed whose business it should be to urge this question on public attention, and to keep it constantly before the public, as a matter of vital importance to the purity of our electoral system. Such committees ought also to promote, by every legal means, a law.

"The next condition of chartist reform, 'qualification to sit as a member irrespective of property,' having been conceded, may now be acted upon at any election which occurs, and it probably will be acted upon at the next general election.

"Electoral districts should not be lost sight of, but the condition not being of such immediate urgency as the ballot, it may be left aside until more important measures are secured.

"Nor is 'payment of members' a question of present urgency; if any constituency sends a member who requires payment, they have the option of making temporary payment, and may raise the necessary funds by voluntary subscription.

"So now, of the chartist scheme, annual parliaments, or all the good they would confer, may be obtained at the next general election, or at any intermediate election which occurs, if the consistency so will it; at the ensuing one for Manchester, for instance, where I hope the necessary pledges will be distinctly required and given. Committees should be established in every constituency for the promotion of this thing; reform committees should be found everywhere, and especially in the manufacturing, mining, and general handicraft populations. Let this be done, and we shall have something a great deal better than triennial, or even annual, elections, and that, too, without waiting whilst the Lords and Commons pass a law.

"In these days, such scenes as those at Manchester can never occur. Representative government, making laws, supporting laws, and itself controlled by the laws, is now the birthright and inheritance of every English child born. The old oppressors – with their savagery, their dungeons, chains, gallows, and beheading blocks; with their decoy agents, sham-patriots, and incendiary spies; with their obsequious magistracy, irresponsible police, and drunken yeomanry, have passed away for ever. The sufferers, also, are nearly all gone; and I, the last of the prisoners of 1817 and 1819, consecutively, in my own name and those of my departed friends, thank you for recognition of the cause for which we struggled, – that of parliamentary reform and untaxed food."

# SELECT BIBLIOGRAPHY

**Works by Bamford**

*An Account of the Arrest and Imprisonment of Samuel Bamford of Middleton on suspicion of High Treason. Written by himself* (Manchester: George Cave, 1817)

*The Weaver Boy; or, Miscellaneous Poetry* (Manchester: Observer Office, 1819)

*Miscellaneous Poetry* (London: Thomas Dolby, 1821)

*Hours in the Bowers. Poems, etc.* (Manchester: The Author, 1834)

*La Lyonnaise* by Charles Berenger (Manchester: The Author, 1839), rendered into verse by Bamford and later included in *Homely Rhymes* (1864)

*Passages in the Life of a Radical* (published in parts 1839–41)

*Poems* (Manchester: The Author, 1843)

*Passages in the Life of a Radical*, two volumes (Manchester and London: 1844)

*Walks in South Lancashire and on its borders: with letters, descriptions, narratives and observations, current and incidental* (Blackley: The Author, 1844)

*Early Days* (London: Simpkin, Marshall and Co; Manchester, 1849)

*Dialect of South Lancashire, or Tim Bobbin's Tummus and Meary, revised and corrected, with his rhymes, and an enlarged and amended glossary of words and phrases ... By Samuel Bamford* (Manchester, 1850)

*Some Account of the Late Amos Ogden of Middleton* (Manchester, 1853)

*Dialect of South Lancashire*, second edition (London: J.R. Smith, 1854)

*Passages in the Life of a Radical*, one volume (London: Simpkin, Marshall & Co.; Manchester: Abel Heywood, [1858])

*Early Days* (Manchester: John Heywood; London: Simpkin, Marshall & Co., 1859)

*Homely Rhymes, Poems, and Reminiscences ... Revised and enlarged edition* (Manchester: Alexander Ireland and Co.; London: Simpkin, Marshall & Co., 1864)

*Bamford's Passages in the Life of a Radical, and Early Days ... Edited with an introduction by H. Dunckley*, two volumes (London: T. Fisher Unwin, 1893)

*Passages in the life of a radical, etc.* [abridged]. (London: MacGibbon & Kee, 1967)

*The Autobiography of Samuel Bamford. Vol. I: Early Days, with An Account of the Arrest etc.; Vol. 2: Passages in the Life of a Radical.* Edited and with an introduction by W.H. Chaloner (London: Frank Cass & Co., 1967)

*Walks in South Lancashire and on its borders, etc.*, edited with an introduction by J.D. Marshall (Brighton: Harvester Press, 1972)

*Passages in the life of a radical*, ed. Tim Hilton (Oxford: Oxford University Press, 1984)

**Studies of Bamford**

W.H. Chaloner, "Introduction", to volume 1 of his edition of *The Autobiography*

James Dronsfield, *Incidents and Anecdotes of the Late Samuel Bamford* (1872)

Morris Garratt, *Samuel Bamford: Portrait of a Radical* (George Kelsall, 1992). (With a further bibliography)

Catherine Hall, "The Tale of Samuel and Jemima: Gender and Working-class Culture in Nineteenth-century England", in H.J. Kaye and Keith McClelland, eds, *E.P. Thompson: Critical Perspectives* (1990)

Martin Hewitt, "Radicalism and the Victorian Working Class: the Case of Samuel Bamford", *Historical Journal*, 34.4 (1991), 873–92

Martin Hewitt and Robert Poole, "Samuel Bamford and Northern Identity", in *Northern Identities*, edited by Neville Kirk (Ashgate, 2000)

Terence Anthony Lockett, *Three lives: Samuel Bamford, Alfred Darbyshire, Ellen Wilkinson.* (London: University of London Press, [1968])

Joe Pimlott, *The Life and Times of Sam Bamford* (Manchester, Neil Richardson, 1991)

Robert Poole, "Samuel Bamford and Middleton Rushbearing", *Manchester Region History Review* viii (1994), 14–20

# INDEX

Underlined entries indicate biographical footnotes.

Albert, Prince, 356

Allen, Mr, 211

Anthony, George W. (Gabriel Tinto), _243_

Anti-Corn Law League, xv, 93

Armitage, E., _23_

Ashmore, Mr, 20

Ashton, John, _16_

Ashton, Thomas, 222, 256

Ashton-under-Lyne, 37, 61, 90–2, 104–5, 110, 119, 123, 127, 155, 168, 238–9, 261

Ashworth, George, 100, 105, 108, 111

Ashworth, Henry, _88_

Ashworth, Tom, 212

Aspell, Mr, 212

Atkinson, John, 271

Audenshaw, 120–1, 135

Bacon, Thomas, 251

Bailey, Philip James, _268_

Ball, Thomas, 346

Ballantyne, Thomas, _227_

Bamford, Ann, x, 14, 169, 178, 254, 284
  death of, xi
  grave of, 18, 72, 77, 224, 233, 235, 238, 242, 314, 337, 357
  poem about, 337–41

Bamford, Daniel, 93, 288

Bamford, Hannah, 244

Bamford, James, 244

Bamford, Jemima ("Mima"), x, xxi, xxvi, 5, 46–7, 58, 79, 83, 104, 123, 135, 136, 141, 193, 195, 197–8, 204, 208, 222, 226, 228–30, 232, 241–3, 246, 258, 268–71, 276, 319, 320, 326, 329, 339–40, 342–5, 347–8, 354–7

Bamford, Mary, xix

Bamford, Samuel
  **Life to 1858**

early life (to 1815), x, 61–2, 66, 72, 125, 128–9, 133, 149–50, 163, 178–9, 244

radical period (1816–21), x–xi, 14, 21, 37–8, 42–3, 64, 84, 90, 104, 115–16, 117–18, 127–8, 139–40, 163, 181, 222, 250–3, 256, 257–8, 260, 277, 307, 352–3, 358–66, 367–70

middle life (1821–39), xi–xii, 14, 25, 30, 84–7, 115–16, 133, 160, 179–83, 239, 251–2, 291, 335, 365–6

literary period (1839–51), xii–xiii, 133, 252, 302, 306–8, 335, 350, 362–3

London period (1851–8), xii, xvi, xxv, 1–10, 14–15, 19, 23, 46–7, 68, 82–3, 106, 122, 133, 157, 245–6, 252, 268, 291, 323–6, 335, 366

**public appearances, readings, speeches etc.**, xxv–xxvi, 24

Ashton-under-Lyne, 90, 168

Audenshaw, 121–3, 126–7, 135–6, 138–9

Blackley, 11–12, 27–8, 40–1, 282–3

Burnley, 194, 201–4

Bury, 31–6, 38, 183–92, 268–9

Chadderton, 169–77, 182, 184–5, 192, 308

Chorlton-upon-Medlock, 54, 52, 94, 138, 151, 158–64, 189, 226, 344–5

Harpurhey, 24, 26, 63

Hollinwood, 40–1, 285–7, 311

Hulme, 190–1, 198

Lees, 259–62

Manchester, 54–8, 79–80, 263–7

Middleton, 45, 49, 52, 59–62, 128, 131–4, 182, 249, 253–5, 275–7

Oldham, 63, 107, 117, 135–6, 139, 142–52

Rochdale, 63, 83, 96–7, 104–8, 110–11, 114, 293–5

Salford, 57–9

Stalybridge, 64, 97, 103–5, 109, 114–19

Stock Brook, 123, 125–6, 128–9

**writings**

*Passages in the Life of a Radical*, xi–xii, xvii,
    xxix, 21, 29, 30, 57, 70, 74–5, 81, 86, 88,
    91, 96–7, 99, 102–3, 194, 212, 231, 245,
    252, 253, 255–6, 260, 305, 326, 328,
    336, 340–2, 353, 362–3

*Early Days*, xi–xii, xix, xxix, 58, 63, 65, 70,
    73, 76, 83, 91, 95, 98–9, 106, 212, 245,
    252, 305, 336, 347, 363

*Walks in South Lancashire*, xii, 91–2, 226, 231,
    239, 329, 336, 363

*Dialect of South Lancashire*, xi, 226, 252, 336,
    363

*Account of Amos Ogden*, 13, 181

journalism, xi, xiii, 30, 44, 53–4, 77–8,
    84–7, 156–7, 252, 316–17, 365

planned writings, xxiv–v, 9, 99, 156–7, 336

poetry, xiv, 55–7, 62, 64, 93, 98–9, 104,
    106, 117–18, 242, 252, 305, 312, 336–7

**Miscellaneous**

Civil List pension, 290–8, 301–9, 313–17,
    319–23, 320–2

Insurance agency, 267, 271, 274, 278, 282,
    329–33

Royal Bounty Fund, 216–24, 258–9, 294–8

Subscription/compensation funds, xxvii,
    99, 110, 112–16, 124–5, 139–41, 143,
    204, 205–11, 213, 243–4, 247–52, 254,
    257–8, 263, 267, 271–4, 279, 298,
    300–2, 306–8, 320–1, 323, 328–51,
    355–7

Bamford, Thomas, 244

Bamford, William, 71, 74, 79–80

Barber, Mr, 140–1, 143, 256

Barlow, George, 144

Barlow, Jonny, 19

Barlow, Samuel, 60, 106

Barlow, Tom, 19

Barns Green, 19, 20, 40, 161

Batsford, Mr, 320–2

Bayley, William, _103_, 108

Bazley, Thomas, _13_, 24, 35, 37, 39, 59, 92, 95,
    120, 141, 145, 216, 220, 223, 225–6, 232,
    239, 243, 248, 258, 262, 267, 271, 278–9,
    292, 294–8, 301, 303–10, 313, 315,
    319–23, 331–5, 340, 345, 348, 351, 355

Belfield, Mr, 42, 44, 52, 54–7, 83, 92, 98, 106,
    122, 123, 161, 190, 226, 231, 240, 264,
    304, 314, 353

Bell, John Gray, 341

Bethel, Mr, 11, 22–3, 335–6

Betts, Edward Ladd, _229_, 314

Bewick, Thomas, _30_

Bindloss, Mr, 346

Binney, Edward W., _12_, 19, 68, 244–6, 281,
    304, 309–10, 340

Binney, Mrs, 347, 351, 355

Blackley, xxiv, xxvi, 11–12, 24, 27–8, 29, 40,
    67, 123, 190, 282–3
    wakes, xxiv, 11–12
    Mechanics' Institution, 40, 67–8, 77–9,
    123, 190

Blomeley, Thomas, 356

Bobbin, Tim, see John Collier

Boddington, Henry, _212_

Boggart Hole Clough, _16_

Bolton, 80, 335–6

Bonheur, Rosa, _242_

Booth, G., 186

Booth, Mr, 114

botanists and horticulture, 18, 253–4,
    316–17

Bowlee, 21, 30

Brandreth, Jeremiah, 250–1, 367

Bridge Hall Mills, 29, 33

Brierley, Ben, xxv, _14_–15, 21, 23–4, 26, 32, 36,
    40–2, 49–50, 56, 63–4, 84–6, 107–9,
    111, 114, 117, 120, 139, 148–52, 155,
    165, 169, 185, 193–5, 198, 207–8,
    224–7, 232–5, 238, 242–5, 264–70,
    274–7, 285–7, 295, 298–9, 308, 311–14,
    326, 337–8, 354–5

Briggs, Jonny, 21, 30

Bright, Jacob, _95_–6, 100, 105–7, 111

Bright, John, xiv, xviii, xxviii, _15_, 34–5, 38, 42,
    46, 50, 63, 66, 78, 88, 95–6, 100, 104,
    117, 124, 146, 150, 158, 163, 178–9,
    193, 207, 215, 227, 247, 262, 331, 338

Brindley, James, _103_

British Museum, xxix, 9, 157

Brittain, Thomas, _240_

Brooks, John, 59

Brotherton, Joseph, _12_, 246, 302

Brougham, Lord Henry, 133, _161_, 181, 249, 253

Brown, E.K., 256

Brundrick, John, 95

Buckley, Edmund, _56_, 90–1, 127

Buckley, George, 90–1, 137–8

Buckley, John, 90–1, 137–8

Buckley, Lieutenant, 97

Buckley, W., 97, 286–7

Buckston, "Old", 142

Burnley, 201–4

Burns, Robert, 24–6, 47, 55, 61–4, 69–70, 118, 125, 149, 270, 305, 317, 324
  poetry of, 24, 40, 62, 84, 173

Bury, 183–90

Butterworth, Edwin, _77_, 78, 84–5, 107, 112
  Butterworth Memorial, 81, 84–90, 107, 112, 114, 120, 180

Butterworth, Hiram, 120

Butterworth, James, _78_

Capern, Edward, _207_, 244

Carlisle, Earl of, 31–2, 305, 327

Carlyle, Thomas, _56_, 68–9, 255–6, 313

Cartledge, Mr, 138

Cartwright, Major John, 138–9, 334, 367–8

Cassells _History of England_, 353–5

Catherine, 20–1, 195, 350

Chadderton, 169–77, 308

Chadderton & Tonge Mutual Improvement Society, 169–77

Chadwick, David, _57_, 59, 111, 243, 264–71, 279–85, 321, 323, 329–31, 334, 341–3, 348

Chadwick, Samuel, 281–3, 340

Charlestown, 18, 22, 224, 193, 335

Chartism and Chartists, xiv–xvi, xxix, 22–3, 55, 74–5, 89, 139–40, 178, 182–3, 252, 335–6, 366, 368–70

Chatterton, Thomas, 149–50

Chattwood, Joseph, _31_–3, 183, 186, 188, 191, 268–9

Cheetham Hill, 20, 195–6, 213, 236, 309, 327, 347, 350

Cheetham, James, 175–6, 182, 240, 263, 308

Cheetham, John, _60_, 64, 94, 100, 108, 114, 200

Chetham Society, 224, 239

Chorlton-upon-Medlock, 13, 54, 67, 71, 94, 138, 151, 158–9,162–4, 170, 184, 226

Christianity, 122, 165–6, 259, 271, 361

Clarke, John, 275–6, 280, 284–5, 289, 291, 310, 314, 329, 346

Clarke, Walter, _54_, 162–3

Cleave, John, _94_

Clegg, Mr, 98–100, 106

Cliff, Mr, 345–6

Close, John, 290, _304_–10, 317, 321–2, 327–8, 339

Clowes, Thomas, 52, 54, 57, 67, 71, 94, 123, 138–9, 146, 150–1, 158–65, 171, 184, 198, 216, 226, 255, 276, 304, 344–7

Clulow, Revd T., 199

Coates, John, 150, 338

Cobbett, John M., _90_

Cobbett, William, x, xxix, 62, 64, 139, 163, 201–2, 250, 261–2, 277, 331, 334, 358, 363, 367
  _Cobbett's Weekly Register_, 62, 149

Cobden, Richard, 15, 50, 51, _124_

Collier, John ("Tim Bobbin"), 61, 133, 161, 226, 239, 350, 361

Collinge, William and Betty, 52, 122, 224, 332

Collins, Samuel, 36, 40, 69, _73_, 117, 134

Colne, 143, 152, 155

comet (1858), 28

Consterdine, Robert, 160, 195

Cooper, Thomas, _89_, 94

Corn Laws, x, 257

Coulborn, Thomas, 124, 137, 149–51, 248

Coupe, Joseph, 150

Cowen, Joseph, _163_

Crab Lane Head, 280–3, 340

"Cranberry", 17–18

Crapper, Old Dame, 20

Crewdson, Isaac, 244

Crompton, Samuel, 80

Crompton, Tom, 32, 183, 186, 238

Crooks, Ann, 243

Cropper, E. Clark, _22_, 281, 335

Crosby, James, 127, 135, 137, 150

Crossland, Mr, 183

Crumpsall, 195, 350

Dane, Thomas, 275

De Quincy, Thomas, 185–6

Dearden, Josiah Heaton, 213–16, 264

Delaunay, Charles H., 12, 16, 18–19, 24–5,
    30, 32, 35, 40, 51, 72, 77, 79, 94, 123,
    161, 190

Dennison, Archdeacon, 19

Derby, Earl of, xvii

Dewhirst, John, 106

Dewsbury, Tom, 161

dialect, 44, 53–4, 117, 148, 188, 192, 211–12,
    239

Dickens, Charles, 57, 159

Dickin, Mrs Oswald, 213

Dickin, Oswald, 22, 52, 58, 83, 93, 117, 180,
    182, 213–14, 230, 256, 258, 267, 275,
    346, 350

Dickins, Thomas, 17, 60, 66, 163, 177, 256,
    263

Disraeli, Benjamin, xvii–xviii

Dixon, Elijah, 90, 333

Dixon, William Hepworth, 68, 241

Doherty, Mr, 73, 160

Dransfield, Robert, 285

Dronsfield, Bamford, 126, 134–5, 197–8, 231,
    306, 308–9

Dronsfield, James (and wife), iii, xxvi–xxvii,
    11, 23, 26, 32, 38–40, 55–6, 92, 114,
    117, 126, 134, 139, 165, 178, 193–4,
    197–9, 215–16, 229, 231, 238, 240–2,
    256, 269–70, 272, 276, 281, 284–6,
    290, 296, 306, 308–9, 326, 332–4,
    353–6

Dronsfield, Ophelia, 126, 269–70, 343

druids, 104, 190, 358, 361

Dunckley, Henry, 232, 254, 354

Dyson, James, 17, 95, 189, 191, 332

Dyson, Joseph, 18, 286


Earnshaw, Mrs, 143, 155

East Brent, 19

Eaton, Mr, 259

Edwards, Edward, 19

Egar, Mr, 226

Egerton, Algernon, 196–200, 208,
    211

Epstein, James, xxix

Fairbairn, Thomas, 13

Fairbairn, William, 190

Fallows, Edmund, 102, 110

Fawcett, Ambrose, 196, 208

Field, Charles, 63, 77–8, 83, 180

Fielding, Joseph, 85, 105, 169, 177, 337,
    355–6

Finlen, James, 22, 23, 355–6

Fitton, John, 238

Fitton, Robert, 30

Fletcher, Henry, 168, 207

Fletcher, W.H., 36, 77, 238

Folds, Mr, 20

Ford, Ann, 22, 89

Ford, John, 18, 122, 128

Fox, William J., 141, 143

Frankland, Hannah, 224, 226, 255

French, Gilbert, 75–6, 80


Gardiner, Ner, 242

Garnett, Mr, 34

Gaskell, Elizabeth, 60, 93, 103, 233

Gaskell, Revd William, 103

Gawthorpe Hall, 143, 201, 203, 239

Gibson, Henry, 24, 28, 30, 72

Gibson, Thomas Milner, xvi, xviii, 42, 50, 91,
    155, 219, 221, 223, 226–7, 232, 239,
    243, 256, 262, 271, 301, 304, 306, 308,
    310, 348

Goadsby, Thomas, 59, 90

Gordon, Alexander Duff, 9

Gowenlock, R. Scott, 71–2, 81, 86, 90, 107,
    114–17, 120, 123, 126, 135–6, 139,
    144, 146, 157, 162, 168, 193, 204–15,
    223, 238, 240, 242, 295–9, 312,
    337–8

Grant, P., 44, 77

Greaves, James, 36, 41, 83, 347

Greaves, Mr and Mrs, 341, 355, 357

Greenwell, Mr, 353

Greenwood, Edwin, 88

Greg, R.H., 15

Grimshaw, Henry, 44–5, 89, 122, 124, 128,
    211, 223–4, 233, 274, 351

Grimshaw, Jane, 45, 122, 155, 355

Grimshaw, Mary Ann, 11, 275, 345, 350

Grundy, Edmund, 29

Grundy, John, 90–1, 203, 367
Grundy, T., 367

Hall, James, 16
Hall, Joseph, 84, 269
Hall, William and Ann, 71, 193–4, 258
Halliwell, Ann, 333
Halliwell, Jenny, 240
Halliwell, Paul, 246, 333
Halliwell, Wm, 258–62, 274
Halsall, Mrs, 213
Hamilton, Revd James Milne and Mrs Fanny, 136, 315, 318
Hammersley, J.A., 80
Hampden Clubs, x
Hardwick, Charles, 33, 34, 198
Hargreaves, Miss, 19, 149
Harland, John, 34, 51–2, 68, 204, 276, 284–5, 289, 291–2, 310, 328–31, 340, 344
Harpurhey, ix, 24, 26, 63, 112, 124, 277
Harrison, David, 109
Harrison, Jim, 333, 349
Harrison, John, 16, 18, 230
Harrison, Joseph, 87, 117–18
Harrop, James, 43
harvest homes, 19
Harvey, William, 119
Healey, Dr Joseph, 21, 162
Heap, Mr, 106, 188, 191
Heron, Joseph, 39
Hetherington, Henry, 94
Heywood, 29, 183, 201, 251, 291, 365
Heywood, Abel, xvi, 11, 14–15, 20, 28–9, 48, 50, 70–1, 73, 92–4, 97, 99, 118, 137, 212, 223–4, 245, 311, 313, 326, 328, 331, 340–4, 348
Heywood, Benjamin, 16, 72, 239
Heywood, John, xxii, 63, 65, 67, 70, 73, 76–7, 91, 93, 95, 98–100, 106, 123, 132, 134, 136, 138, 151, 160, 170, 190, 212, 226, 245, 248, 264–5, 271, 313–14, 326, 342, 347–8
Heywood, S., 239
Heywood, Thomas, 239
Hibbert, John T., 175
Higginbottom, George, 127

Higginson, Mr, 32
Hilton, Mr, 224
Hirst, E., 143, 152, 155
Hobson, Samuel T., 98–9
Holcroft, Mr, 212
Holden, William, 179–83
Holgate, Mr, 106
Hollinwood, 23–4, 36, 38, 40–1, 84, 117, 134–5, 242, 284–7, 291, 311
    Discussion Society, 224
    Filho, 40, 117, 134
    wakes, 135, 235
Holmes, Oliver Wendell, 284
Holt, John, 21
Hood, Thomas, 269
Hooson, Edward, xvi
Hopwood, Mrs, 19, 20
Hopwood, Robert, 105, 108–9
Horsfall, J.B., 348
Howarth, Edmund, 107, 131, 133, 212, 216, 228, 230, 246, 275, 356
Howitt, William, 138, 333, 337, 352
    Man of the People, 252–3, 354–5
Hoyle, James, 231
Hudson, J.W., 51, 199
Hulbert, Mr, 266
Hulme, 191, 194, 198
Hulme, George, 184
Hunt, Henry, xxix, 74, 94, 138–9, 334, 367
Hunt, James, 182
Hurst, Ambrose, 84, 120, 139, 333
Hutchings, E., 13, 16, 19, 28–9, 54, 57–8, 268, 279–80, 285

Ingham, Samuel, 14, 338–9
Inland Revenue, xii, 1–13
    See also Somerset House
Institutional Association of Lancashire and Cheshire, 51, 62–3, 74, 79, 98, 176
Ireland, Alexander, 89, 254, 315, 319–23, 330, 336, 342–3, 345, 354
Ireland, Alexander & Co., 89–90, 336

Jackson, Jonty, 21
Jacksons the photographers, 16, 22, 28–9, 72–3, 77, 79, 110, 176, 185, 198
Jaques, Betty, 157

Jerrold, Douglas, <u>57</u>, 68, 298
Jewsbury, Geraldine, <u>68</u>
Jone o'Grinfilt, 150
Jones, Ernest, xvi, xxix, 22, 48, <u>341</u>, 344
Jones, William, 22
Joyce, Patrick, xxiv
Jumbo (Middleton Junction), 16, 22, 28–9, 72, 83

Kay, John, 186–9
Kay Shuttleworth, James, x, xxviii–xxix, <u>132</u>–57, 194, 201, 203, 206–7, 211, 221, 224, 232–8, 247–9, 262, 272–3, 321, 334, 343–6, 357
  *Scarsdale*, 231–7, 240, 248, 262
Kay, Tom, 88, 92
Kelly, David, <u>152</u>, 231, 235, 240, 262, 264–5
Kelsall, H., 104
Kelsall, W., 145
Kent, James, 42, 52, 73, 102, 175
Kenyon, John, 61
Kenyon, Mr, 22
Kershaw, Robert, 349–50
Kightly, Revd J., 174, 198
King, Edwin H., 276
Knight, John, <u>298</u>
Knowles, Richard, xix

Lamb, Joseph, 136
Lancashire Reformers' Union, xvi, xviii, 64, 65, 67, 73, 78–9, 81, 84, 87–8, 95, 120–1, 139, 158, 170–1, 218, 227, 230
Langton, Robert, <u>274</u>
Lawler, Matthew, <u>17</u>, 227
Leech, Mr, 20, 238
Lees, 259–62
Lees, J., 176–7
Lees, James, 17, 195
Lees, Joseph, 150
Leigh Hunt, James Henry, 298, 321
Liddle, Dr, 29
Liddle, "Old", 350
Literary Institutions,
  Middleton, 36, 49–50, 60–2, 196–200, 208, 211, 225
  Oldham, 63–4, 83, 84–6, 178
  Royton, 172–3, 348–9

Liverpool, 124
Livesey, Thomas, 24, 32, <u>81</u>, 83, 88–9, 96, 100, 104–6, 111, 124, 183, 186, 188
Livsey, (James), 24, 28–9
Lloyd, Mr, 19, 98, 304
Lord, Mr, 104
Luddism, see machine breaking
Ludlam, Isaac, 251
Lyon, Richard, 161, 165

McClure, R., 204, 211, 264–5
MacDougall, Alexander, 169, 174–7, 184–5, 198, 213
McKenna, Mr, 350
Mackie, Ivie, <u>23</u>
McWhinnie, Mr, 108
machine breaking, 145, 147, 156–7, 178–9, 251–2, 291, 365
Manchester, ix–xi, xiv, xvi–xix, xxiv–xxv, 13, 19, 28, 29, 42, 48, 51, 55–8, 62, 72, 79–80, 84, 87–8, 95, 98, 106, 121, 122, 138, 158, 161, 170–1, 180, 211, 212–13, 224, 231, 232, 239, 243–4, 248, 256, 263–7, 270, 271, 285, 311, 313, 314, 319, 323–5, 334–5, 348–9, 355
  Athenaeum, 51, 76, 212, 263–6
  Chetham's Library, 239
  Free Trade Hall, xviii, 90
  Grammar School, 61
  Library, xix, xxiii, 19, 151
  Manhood Suffrage Association, xvi, 43–4, 48, 50–1
  Mechanics' Institute, 13, 19, 28, 29, 51, 55–8, 212, 239, 285
  People's Institute, 48
  Town Hall, 212
  Workhouse, 244
Marsland, John, 105
Martin, Baron, 242
Martin, Mr, 15, 49, 56
Martineau, Harriet, 233
Mason, Harry, 196, 214, 268
Mason, Hugh, <u>90</u>, 91, 155, 168
Mason, Thomas, <u>91</u>, 168
Maude, Daniel, <u>319</u>
Mechanics' Institutes, 31, 172–3, 179

Blackley, xxiv, 11–12, 24, 27–8, 29, 40, 67, 123, 190
Bolton, 80
Burnley, 201–4
Harpurhey, 24, 26, 63
Institutional Association of Lancashire and Cheshire, 51, 62–3, 74, 79, 98
Manchester, xxvi, 13, 19, 28, 29, 51, 55–8, 212, 239, 285
Middleton, xiii, 25–6, 179–82, 239
Oldham, 178
Preston, 211
Salford, 57–9, 119
Megson, Mr, 355
Mellalieu, Samuel, 102–3, 110, 275
Mellor, Allan, 32, 36, 40, 42, 45, 81, 102, 106, 118, 123, 125, 175–6, 178, 181, 183, 185, 262–6, 275, 304, 309, 314, 320, 330–1, 349
Mellor, J.H., 274
Mellor, John, 348
Mellor, Ralph, 264–5, 313, 319, 329–30
Merril, Mrs, 339–40
Methodism, 125, 128–9
Middleton, xi–xiii, xvii, xx, xxvii, xxxi, 14–15, 17, 18, 21–2, 25–6, 28–9, 55–6, 72, 77, 93, 102–3, 175–7, 183, 194, 197, 224–5, 238, 239, 250–2, 256, 289, 291, 314, 316–17, 337, 353, 357
  Agricultural Society, 253–4
  Hampden Club, 250, 358, 363, 367
  horticultural and agricultural shows, 18, 248–9, 253–5, 346–7
  library, xxiii, 179–83
  Literary Institute, 36, 49–50, 60–2, 196–200, 208, 211, 225
  machine breaking and Luddism, 178–9, 251–2, 291, 365
  Mechanics' Institute, 25–6, 179–82, 239
  Methodism, 128–9
  Old Hall, xv, 9
  Reform Association, xxv, 52, 55, 60, 65, 67, 73, 78
  Reform movement, 51, 59–60, 65–7, 73, 78–9, 81, 99–103, 106–7, 275
  Sunday School, 128–9
  Wakes, xx, 16, 18, 150, 240

Middleton Junction, see Jumbo
Miles Platting, 342–3
Miller, Revd Marmaduke, 199
Mills, Thomas, 15–18, 20, 32, 35, 39, 42, 45–6, 48–9, 52, 54, 55, 58, 67, 71, 73, 78, 83, 89, 90, 93, 96, 98–112, 118, 123, 127, 136–7, 152, 165–6, 168–9, 174–5, 178, 180, 182, 197, 199–200, 224, 271, 288, 290, 314, 345–6, 353, 356–7, 366
Milnes, R. Monckton, 141
Milton, John, poetry of, 28, 62, 74, 269
Mitchell, Joseph, 250, 333, 367
Monks, Mr, 212
Montgomery, Walter, 94, 117
Moore, Abraham, 96
Moors, Mr, 243
Morris, David, 51, 62–3, 71, 74, 82–3, 143–4, 216–26, 229, 232, 243, 256, 264, 321, 323, 329–35, 341, 343–9
Moston, ix, xiii, 71, 82, 325
mutual Improvement Societies, xxix, 169–77

Nadin, Joseph, 260, 277
Needham, Mrs, 128, 347
Nelson, George and Elizabeth, 36, 68, 80, 104, 136, 139, 166, 169, 206, 211–12, 234, 247, 260–1, 276, 278, 316–20, 347, 351
Newall's Building, 64, 78, 84, 87–8, 94–5, 107–8, 170–1, 227
Newmarch, M., 282
newspapers and journals
  *Ashton Reporter*, 110, 196–7
  *Ashton Standard*, 116–17
  *British Volunteer*, 43
  *Bury Times*, 184, 187–92
  *Cassell's Illustrated Family Paper*, 252
  *London Review*, 254
  *Manchester Courier*, 240
  *Manchester Examiner & Times*, 34–5, 57, 129–30, 169, 202, 207, 210, 254, 266, 320–1, 353–4
  *Manchester Guardian*, 34–5, 43, 51–2, 156–7, 190, 202, 252, 266, 328–31
  *Manchester Mercury*, 43
  *Manchester Observer*, 77–8, 87
  *Manchester Review*, 227

*Middleton Albion*, 17, 44, 49, 55, 122, 125
*Morning Chronicle*, xiii, 252
*Morning Herald*, xi
*Oldham Advertiser*, 86, 90
*Oldham Chronicle*, 90
*Oldham Times*, 252
*Protector* (Ashton), 90, 105, 110, 114
*Rochdale Observer*, 104, 111
*The Times*, 252
Normans, 176, 225
Norreys, Lord, 201
Northumberland, Duke of, 15, 240–1, 323
Nuneaton railway accident, 10, 98
Oastler, Richard, xi, 338
O'Connor, Feargus, xii, xvi, xix, 75, 178–9,
    252, 265, 366, 368
Ogden, Amos, <u>13</u>, 21, 160, 169, 181–2, 333
Oldham, 42, 63–4, 77–8, 81, 83–7, 96–7, 117,
    120, 123, 144–51, 168, 176, 178, 180,
    241–2, 298–9, 312
Oliver the spy, <u>250</u>–1, 333, 352, 367
Ormrod, Oliver, <u>104</u>, 111

Page, John, <u>118</u>, 136–7, 207–8, 265
Paine, Thomas, <u>119</u>, 225
Palmerston, Lord, xvi, 34, <u>56</u>, 93, 193,
    216–27, 232, 240, 243, 247–8, 252,
    256–8, 262, 266–7, 271–3, 277–9, 290,
    292, 294, 295–8, 301–8, 310, 313–17,
    320–2, 327, 332, 346, 348
Parliament, xv–xviii, 144, 206, 207, 227, 234,
    292–3, 296–7, 305, 322–3, 348–9,
    367–70
Peacock, Henry B., <u>33</u>–4, 36, 79, 84, 151,
    190, 354
Pearson, John and Robert, 23
Peat, Robert, 29, 98
Pegg, Dr, 110, 228, 356
Pendleton, 165–8, 317–18
Percy, William, <u>89</u>, 95, 198
Peterloo, xii, xvi, xx, xxvii, xxix–xxxi, 15,
    36–7, 50, 60, 64, 139, 181, 222, 238,
    277, 337, 367
Peto, Samuel Morton, <u>229</u>, 275, 284, 314
Phillips, Mr, 92, 336
Pickstone, John, 289, 333, 341
Pickup, James, 349

Pinder, Dr, 228–9, 233, 236, 259
Plant, John, <u>156</u>
Platt, John, 120, 142, 146, 148
Platt, Robert, <u>103</u>
Pochin, H.D., 279
Pollitt, Jenny, 224
Pollitt, John, 134, 240–1, 280
Potter, Charles, <u>68</u>–9, 71, 77, 79, 83, 90, 96,
    97, 99, 103, 107, 117, 120, 123, 135,
    139, 142, 146, 148–9, 168–9, 176, 185,
    204–5, 210, 240, 242, 254, 274, 297–9,
    311–12, 338, 344, 354–5
Potter, Edmund, <u>43</u>, 45
Potter, John, xvi, <u>23</u>, 319
Potter, Thomas, 168
Potter, Thomas Bayley, <u>108</u>, 168, 255–6,
    346
Poulton, George, 122, 325–6
Pownall, Solomon, 356
Poynting, Mary, 344
Prentice, Archibald, <u>333</u>
Prescott, Thomas and Jenny, 347, 350
Preston, 211
Priestley, Joseph, 151, 158–63, 171, 345
Prince, John Critchley, <u>23</u>, 36, 97, 196, 290,
    300
    poetry of, 56, 116, 118
Procter, R.W., 242
Pubs, inns and beerhouses
    Albion Hotel, Bury, 32, 183–6, 367
    Angel Inn, Oldham, 96, 135, 298
    Assheton Arms, Middleton, 16, 18, 28, 45,
        59–60, 83, 186, 196, 230, 275
    at Middleton Junction, 83
    Bill's o' Jack's, Saddleworth, 238
    Blue Bell, Manchester, 21, 74, 341
    Board's Head, Middleton, 230, 277, 288
    Brunswick Hotel, Rochdale, 100
    Burns's Cottage, Hollinwood, 117
    Cemetery Inn, Harpurhey, 20, 48–50
    Cloggers Arms, Hollinwood, 23
    Commercial Inn, Stalybridge, 97, 103–5,
        109, 114, 238–9
    Corner House, Middleton, 224, 346
    Cross Keys, Rochdale, 83, 88, 96, 100
    Cross Keys, Stalybridge, 238
    Crown and Anchor, London, 163

Filho/Philo Inn, Hollinwood, 40, 117, 134, 241

Golden Ball, Rochdale, 88–9

Golden Lion, Blackley, 198

Golden Lion, Deansgate, Manchester, 264 (See also Belfield.)

King, Manchester, 84

Kings Arms, Oldham, 83, 96, 146, 148

Masons Arms, Middleton, 93, 225

Medlock Inn, Chorlton, 67

Moulders Arms, 14

Mrs Dronsfields's, 134

New Inn, Barnes Green, 15, 19, 20, 23, 29, 39, 84, 161–2, 198, 233, 268, 345

Old Boar's Head, Ashton, 119

Paul Pry, Crab Lane Head, 280–3, 340

Red Lion, Oldham, 83

Roe Buck Inn, Middleton, 107

Royal Oak, 21

Samuel Chadwick's, Blackley, 282–3

Samuel Ogden's, Harpurhey, 260–1, 277

Star Inn, Manchester, 319, 351

Suffield Arms, Middleton, 182

Swan, Manchester, 212

Radcliffe, James, 285–7

Radcliffe Old Hall, 9, 239

Ramsbottom, Joseph, _185_, 193, 195, 198, 207, 211–12, 216, 223–4, 234, 243, 254, 256, 259, 295, 337, 347–55

Rayner, Mr, 168

Reach, Angus, xiii

Reform Bill of 1832, xv, xvii, xxix

Reform movement, xii–xviii, xxv–xxix, 34–40, 45, 50–2, 54, 90, 99–103, 106–8, 119–21, 135, 139–40, 143, 226, 259, 275, 311

Bamford's views on, xiv–xv, 37–8, 42–4, 45, 50–2, 54, 59–60, 66–7, 78–9, 90, 99–103, 106–8, 135, 139–40, 170–1, 226, 234, 238, 276, 311, 367–70

See also Lancashire Reformers' Union; Manhood Suffrage Association; Middleton

republicanism, 55

Reubens, Sir Peter Paul, _77_

"Review Society", 94–5

Rhodes, xv, 22, 181

Richards, W.J., see Oliver the spy

Richardson, G.B., 120–1, 123, 126, 150

Richardson, George, 30, _342_, 351

Richardson, R.J., _183_, 186, 191, 342

Rickards, C.H., _244_

Ridings, Elijah, _24_, 32, 36, 48, 50, 52, 138, 225, 235–6, 244, 330

Ridings, William C., 40, 48, 52, 104, 225, 280, 314

Roberton, Dr John, _229_, 233

Roberts, W., 106

Roberts, W.P., _48_, 163–4

Robertson, James, 43–4, 48–9

Robinson, Smith P., _64_, 78, 84, 87, 108, 171–2, 218, 220, 231

Rochdale, 83, 88–9, 96–8, 100, 104–8, 110–11

Roebuck, John Arthur, _35_, 369

Rogerson, John Bolton, _14_, 16, 36, 40, 44–5, 48, 56–7, 63, 76, 83, 108–9, 118, 136, 180, 182, 190, 240, 300–4, 306

Rogerson, Mrs, 185, 190, 223

Royson, Mr, 269

Royton, 137–8, 172–4

Rudkin, Mr, 271

Rumney, Robert, 279

Russell, Lord John, xviii, 225, _239_, 321

Rutter, W.S., _17_–8

Saddleworth, 120

Sadler, Mr, 97, 238–9

Salford, xi, 174

Peel Park library, 119, 151–2, 156–7, 169, 190

Saxons, 9, 199

Scarlett, James, 201, 291, 364–5

Scarlett, Sir James Yorke, _201_

Scholes, Mr, 14

Schwabe, Edmund, 347

Schwabe, Salis, xiii, _346_–7

Scott, Walter, _Ivanhoe_, 9

Sever, Charles, 163, 165, 171

Seville, Peter, 60–1, 81, 84, 174

Shakespeare, William, 115, 254

plays of, 129

readings from, 95

Shiel, Mrs, 46, 81–3
Shuttleworth, Henry, 197, 209, 345–6
Shuttleworth, John, 13, 163
Shuttleworth, William, 163, 170
Sidmouth, Lord, 250–1
Simms, Aunt, xix
Slater, Edwin, 95, 98, 264–5
Smethurst, Mr, 35, 125–6, 299
Smith, Abraham, 288
Smith, George, 97, 98, 100, 103–5, 109–11,
    114, 116, 118, 121, 208, 211–12,
    238
Smith, James, 83, 88, 96, 105–6, 108, 111,
    293–4, 336
Smith, John, 67–8
Smithies, Thomas, 223–4, 353
Somerset House, ix, xiii, xx, xxv, xxix–xxx,
    1–10, 19, 70, 106, 114, 122, 133, 145,
    152, 241, 246, 252, 302, 304, 307,
    324–6, 335, 366
    See also Inland Revenue
spies, ix, xxx, 19–20, 127–8, 190–1, 214, 243,
    250–1, 294, 326, 365
Stalybridge, 97, 103–5, 108–9, 114, 116,
    118–20, 238–9
Stanley, Lord Edward, xviii, 177
Stavacre, Mr, 17–18
Stelfox, Mr, 313, 329–30
Stephens, J.R., 116, 118
Stewart, Andrew, 63, 81, 88–9, 100
Stores Smith, J., 15
Story, Robert, 14–15, 240–2, 323–4
Stubbs, Mr, 17–18
Sturgeon, William, 309
Suffield, Lord, 13, 21, 25, 158, 179–82, 229
Summerskill, Bill, 22
Swain, Charles, 29, 240, 244, 268, 300–1
Swallow, S., 119–22
Swift, George, 75
Swinton, 292
Syne, L.T., 1–14, 131

Tait, William, 138, 333
    Tait's Magazine, 362
Taylor, James, 190–1, 194
Taylor, John, 96, 148, 242, 274, 296, 311, 331
Taylor, Joseph, 56, 71, 76, 122

Taylor, Miss, 136, 165, 195, 215, 223, 225,
    242, 244, 287, 346, 357
Taylor, Robert Heape, 100
Taylor, Thomas, 180–1
Tennyson, Alfred Lord, 12, 26, 28–9, 32, 41,
    56, 147
Thorp, Henry, 235–6, 238, 327
Tomlinson, Richard, see Montgomery Walter
"Tommy the Baker", 36–7
Tonge, xiii, 17, 22, 28, 158, 163, 343, 347,
    353, 356, 358
Tootal, Edward and Margaret, 166–7
Tootal, Sally, 167
Tories/Conservatives, xvi–xvii, 17–18, 127,
    170, 200, 238, 240
Towneley, John, 201
trades unions, 143, 145, 147, 178–9, 292,
    356–7
Travis, James, 300
Travis, William, 38, 42, 114, 117, 194, 197,
    215, 229, 238, 256, 258, 269, 272, 281,
    292, 298, 308, 326, 334, 343, 348, 356
Turner, John Aspinall, xvi, 92, 95, 144
Turner, Jonny, 14, 79
Turner, William, 251
Tweddell, George, 186–92

Urquhart, John, 57, 59

Varley, Mr, 155
Volunteer movement, 201–3, 234

wakes and rushbearings, 253
    Blackley, xx, xxiv, 11–12, 15, 335–6
    Hollinwood, 135, 235
    Middleton, xx, 16, 18, 150, 240
    Oldham, 241–2, 312
Walker, Alice, 18, 235, 347
Walker, Ben, 83, 230–1
Walker, Jeremiah, 201
Walker, Mr, 89, 255
Walker, Robert and William, 181
Wanklyn, James, 346
Warburton, William, 95
Ward, George, 329
Waterhouse, William, 286–7
Waterloo, 201, 283

Watkin, E.W., 311
Watts, Alaric, 240
Watts, Sir James, 267
Watts, John, 39–40, 42, 44, 48, 219–21, 223, 226–7, 232, 240, 243, 256, 262, 264, 267, 310, 313–15, 319–23, 329–31, 334–7, 339–51, 355
Waugh, Edwin, xii, xxiv, xxvii, 23, 32–4, 36, 48–50, 60, 62, 84, 89, 95, 98, 136, 148, 152, 155, 197–9, 235, 295, 327, 330, 337, 339–40
weavers and weaving, 84–5, 133, 145, 147, 149, 201, 229, 238, 251–2, 253–4, 316–17, 356–7, 365
Weeks, Washington, 313
Weller, Sam, 95
Whalley, Henry, 78, 106–7, 110, 125, 180, 281, 291, 303, 346
Wheeler, Thomas M., 163–4
Whigs/Liberals, xvi–xviii, 99–103, 106–7
Whitworth, Mr, 95
Widdup, John, xxx, 74–5
Wilde, Frederick, 344

Wilde, Mr, 184
Wilkinson, T.T., 194, 201, 203–4, 229, 314, 334, 343
Williams, Mr, 104, 119–20
Williamson, Mrs, 83
Willis, William, 138, 335
Wilmot, Mr, 48, 50
Wilson, George, 52, 94, 108, 162–5, 171, 189
Wilton, Earl of, 9
Wolstoncraft, Joseph, 78–9
Wolstoncroft, Samuel, 16, 19, 77
Wood, Colonel, 119
Wood, John, xii, 8, 68, 70, 131, 133, 252, 274, 366
Wood, Mr, 127
Worthington, Walter Law, xix
Wrigley, Edwin, 33
Wrigley (of Manchester Exchange), 258–9, 263
Wrigley, Thomas, 29, 33–4, 191, 203
Wroe, James, 333

Yates, Mr, 141, 148, 298